DEDICATION

In Memory of

John Edward Donovan
Ruth Christine Walker Donovan

SOCIOLOGY
THE BASICS

MARJORIE E. DONOVAN

Pittsburg State University, Kansas

Kendall Hunt
publishing company

Cover image © Shutterstock.com

Kendall Hunt
publishing company

www.kendallhunt.com
Send all inquiries to:
4050 Westmark Drive
Dubuque, IA 52004-1840

ISBN 9781524938130

Published in the United States of America

BRIEF CONTENTS

CONTENTS

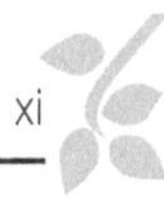

PREFACE

One of the primary objectives of this book is to provide a sociological background for understanding society, day-to-day life, social structure, and contemporary social issues in the twenty-first century. The hope is that with exposure to basic sociological perspectives and tools for understanding social life that people will arrive at and embrace a new level of understanding and cooperation.

While the genesis of this book is the sociological tradition and sociological theory and methodology are its foundation, its scope is firmly embedded in a strong interdisciplinary approach that is gender inclusive. As such, the author's survey of human society has a strong historical comparative perspective that helps us better to understand the globalized world in which we participate.

In *Sociology: The Basics* the reader will find up-to-date Box Readings, tables, graphs, research, and recommended readings--to make the book as up-to-date as possible. In the Student Guide and Activity Book that accompanies this textbook, students and instructors will find Fill-in-the-Blanks Exercises, Key Concepts, a variety of Learning Exercises, and Multiple-Choice and True-False Questions for each chapter. Additionally, we have developed, field-tested, and provide you with Consortium for Uniform Educational Standards (CUES) Checklists of essential knowledge elements (EKEs) contained in each chapter. These CUES checklists are included as the last two pages of each chapter of the Student Guide and Activity Book. The author's intent is to create a textbook offering a comprehensive and current discussion of introduction to sociology that can meet the needs of anyone teaching or taking a course in introduction to sociology.

The Student Guide and Activity Book is meant to be used in conjunction with the textbook, *Sociology: The Basics*. The chapter headings in the Student Guide and Activity Book correspond to the chapters of this textbook. Each Student Guide and Activity Book chapter is divided into four sections. The first section includes fill-in-the-blanks exercises, which are useful for students to gain mastery of key concepts covered in the book's chapters. The second section is a Word Bank of key concepts that are covered in the chapter. The Word Bank also contains the concepts that the student will need successfully to complete the "fill-in-the-blanks" exercises. The Third Section consists of learning opportunities based on the materials covered in this textbook. These learning opportunities are designed to enhance the learning experience and engage the critical-thinking skills of persons with diverse learning styles. The fourth section of the Student Guide and Activity Book includes CUES Checklists for essential knowledge elements contained in each chapter of the textbook.

The CUES method of instructional delivery and assessment represents the application of epistecybernetics, a new science of knowledge stewardship that has been utilized in a wide variety of learning contexts. For instance, the U.S. Air Force has used it for evaluating and enhancing the efficacy of its pilot training curriculum (Ergish, 1997). Within the past several years, scholar teachers have successfully applied and field tested the CUES model within the context of instructional delivery and assessment in both large and small sections of introduction to sociology courses, within the context of other courses, and within the context of sociology program assessment. In an era that stresses the importance of outcomes-based assessment, CUES check sheets provide instructors with a simple tool for measuring the level of self-reported student efficacy with regard to the essential knowledge elements that comprise the course.

One of the primary objectives of this book is to model valuable sociological perspectives for understanding the social relationships, history, and cultures that constitute everyday social life. Every chapter of this textbook demonstrates the links between theory and research. Students are presented with sociological concepts that they see in their daily lives and in scholarly research. Each chapter is multicultural and gender inclusive. The author uses both the most current research and classical studies to illuminate the ongoing processes of sociology as these are manifest in the daily lives of all collectivities in the United States today.

It is the author's hope that students and instructors will appreciate the clear writing style of the book and the systematic presentation of material within each chapter. Each chapter presents a wealth of demographic and economic data to help students understand the past and plan for the future in a complex and globalized world. Tables, figures, and graphs are used extensively throughout the textbook.

Instructors, whether on the quarter or semester systems, will find the interdisciplinary approach of this book refreshing. Instructors will find the bibliographic references and the suggested readings in each chapter of the textbook particularly useful, as these can serve as a working bibliography for student papers and research projects. The list of key terms and important names will assist students to focus on the important concepts and ideas presented in each chapter. In addition, the fill-in-the-blank, multiple-choice, and true-false questions found in each chapter of the Student Guide and Activity Book provide students with yet another way of learning and mastering the material. In field testing this book, we have found that when we use these very same questions as exam questions, there is still a considerable distribution of scores, and students experience a significant reduction in evaluation apprehension.

Students and instructors will find the Learning Exercises in each chapter of the Student Guide and Activity Book useful and refreshing. The learning exercises can be assigned as in-class or as out-of-class learning opportunities. Students perceive that answering these Learning Exercises helps them to process the material and retain it. Instructors perceive that having students answer these questions in a non-threatening format--e.g., as a "take-home" opportunity wherein students can re-write their answers as many times as they want within a specified time frame--enhances their critical reasoning abilities.

Marjorie E. Donovan
May, 2017

ACKNOWLEDGMENTS

I thank my parents, John Edward Donovan and Ruth Christine Walker Donovan, without whose love, encouragement, and sacrifice this work would not have been possible. I thank Buddy, Sheba, Lucia, Francesca, and Bella for their loyal and true companionship. I thank Alexander for his devotion to Lucia and Francesca. I owe a special debt of gratitude to Olivia Logue. I thank my many instructors and students. I want to thank Michael A. Kelley for sharing with me bodies of scholarship, for his encouragement throughout this project, and for modeling best practices in teaching. I would like to thank Barbara Bonnekessen for her leadership and encouragement. I would like to acknowledge the contribution of Gary D. Wilson for his authorship of the Sex and Gender, Race and Ethnicity, and Religion chapters throughout the first edition of this textbook. I would like to acknowledge the contribution of Bradley P. Cameron for his authorship of a Box Reading on Therapeutic Jurisprudence and the Municipal Court for the Crime and Deviance chapter.

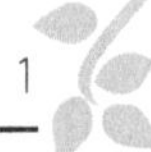

CHAPTER 1

Perceiving and Understanding Social Life Sociologically: Theory and Methods

SOCIOLOGY AS THE STUDY OF SOCIAL STRUCTURE

Sociology is the scientific study of society, its origins, organization, institutions, development, and change. We want you to develop a sociological understanding of society and contemporary social issues. In this textbook you will learn various sociological paradigms to help you understand social life and analyze social issues.

A **theory** is a set of interrelated principles and definitions that conceptually organizes selected aspects of the empirical world in a systematic fashion. A theory has several useful purposes. It helps us to understand social life and it helps us to make predictions about social life. When we conduct research, theory guides us in formulating research questions and it helps us to make sense out of the data that we collect. A concept that is closely related to theory is "paradigm." A **paradigm** is a fundamental framework for making sense out of (and for attributing meaning to) happenings, events, and objects in the social world. Major paradigms in sociology include **conflict theory,** consensus theory (sometimes called **structural functionalism** or social order theory,) and **symbolic interactionism**. You will learn about these paradigms throughout this textbook. Perhaps an analogy might be useful to help you understand the role of theory in the practice of sociological inquiry. In sociology, theory is an engine that pulls both the research train and the train of understanding. We will explore the nature and practice of conducing sociological research later in this chapter.

Sociology uses the term social organization or **social structure** to refer to stable and recurring patterns of social relations. People live in networks of social structure and in networks of groups. It is through these networks that people cope, organize, and reorganize their lives (e.g., Viterna, 2006). Sociologists are interested in social structure--how groups are put together--because it influences our behaviors and perceptions.

This was demonstrated, for instance, in the path-breaking research on bystander intervention conducted by sociologist Bibb Latané and his colleagues (Latané and Darley, 1968; Latané and Nida, 1981). This research demonstrated that for intervention to occur in an emergency situation, three factors must be present. If even one factor is missing, intervention does not occur.

What are the three factors of Latané and Darley's "decision tree"? First, the potential intervener must perceive the event. Sounds simple and easy, doesn't it? It's actually more complicated than it might at first glance appear. Many people fail to notice many things, for many reasons, just one of which is that we have limited attentional resources (See, for instance, Myers, 2008; Keirsey & Bates, 1984; Squire, 1987; Minsky, 1986).

Second, the potential intervener must define the situation as an emergency. The process whereby one examines and evaluates a situation before arriving at a decision regarding the meaning and nature of a situation and before deciding which actions and behaviors are appropriate is referred to by sociologists as the **definition of the situation**. The term was first used by Chicago School sociologists W.I. Thomas and Florian Znaniecki (1918) in *The Polish Peasant in Europe and America* (Theodorson and Theodorson, 1969: 105).

The social and psychological response to help victims requires that the potential intervener define the situation as an emergency. It could be many other things. For instance, some years ago, the author of this textbook was walking in a somewhat "seedy" part of the state capital of one the most populous states in this nation with a fellow sociologist, when she noticed two men assisting a third who was prostrate on the ground. "Look," she said, "There are two men assisting an injured person in need!" Her more street-wise companion responded, "They're 'rolling' [robbing] a drunk!" In other words, her definition of the situation was inaccurate. If a person defines a situation as other than an emergency, that person tends not to intervene.

Third, the potential intervener must decide if she/he has the responsibility to intervene. In the example above, both the author and her companion, who were strangers to the person who was getting mugged, decided that a near-by police officer was the more appropriate person to lend assistance. So, even though they both noticed the event and eventually defined it as an emergency, neither of them intervened to help a stranger in need. Each decided that the responsibility for intervention belonged to someone else.

Latané and Nida's (1981) research also demonstrates that a stranger is most likely to accept responsibility for intervention in a situation defined by the stranger as an emergency when no one else is around. Latané and his colleagues have conducted four dozen experiments that compared help given to bystanders who perceived themselves to be either alone or with others. In about 90 percent of these comparisons, involving almost 6,000 people, lone bystanders were more likely to respond help (Myers, 2008: 446; Latané and Nida, 1981). In internet communication, too, a person is more likely to respond helpfully to a request (e.g., someone asking for the link to the campus library) if the person thinks she/he alone (and not several others as well) has received it (Blair et. al, 2005). In short, a person is *most likely to intervene* in an emergency situation if there are no other bystanders present. If others whom one does *not* know (strangers) are present with the bystander in the emergency situation, there is a shifting of responsibility, which Latané and Darley term a "diffusion of responsibility" (1968). In public places, large numbers of strangers impede others from helping strangers in agony. If others who are friends, colleagues, and acquaintances of the bystander are present in the emergency situation, intervention is more likely to occur than if they were strangers to one another. In other words, a bystander helping a stranger in need is understandable, sociologically, *not* as a "random act of kindness" but as due to the definition of the situation and social structure i.e., the way the

group is put together. Thus, a sociological understanding of social life is constructed, at least in part, by looking for, locating, and interpreting stable and recurring patterns of social relations. In these patterns of social relations small differences make big differences.

SOME FUNDAMENTAL PARTS OF SOCIAL STRUCTURE

John Steinbeck, the famous American novelist, understood social structure. In *The Grapes of Wrath* (1939: 213), John Steinbeck observes that "In the evening, sitting about the fires, the twenty were one. They grew to be units of the camps...Every night relationships that make a world, established; and every morning the world torn down like a circus." What Steinbeck is referring to is the growth of social structure in the night-time camps that migrant laborers formed each night on their way to California or while traveling around California during the dust bowl years of the 1930s.

That quote is part of a larger passage wherein Steinbeck perceptively describes what is involved in making a social world. Steinbeck describes how collections of people who previously had not known each other would, in the particular context of traveling as a migrant, recognize that they in fact had a lot in common, and would form, on the spur of the moment as it were, small societies, with everything that the term "society" implies. Steinbeck describes the emergence and growth within the camps of fellow feeling (**solidary order**); the emergence of leadership (**imperative order);** the growth of rules and their sanctions (**normative order**); and the growth of you-do-this-for-me-and-I'll-do-such-and-such-for-you relationships (**exchange order**). Steinbeck describes, in other words, all the relationships that make a world.

We may conceptualize societies and social life as consisting of normative order, solidary order, imperative order, and exchange order. These are some of the parts of social structure that we find in all societies, past and present.

Ritual also is a part of social structure that we find in all societies. The terms **ritual** and *rite* often are used interchangeably by sociologists. A ritual refers to a "culturally standardized set of actions with symbolic significance performed on occasions [and by persons] prescribed by tradition. The acts and words that comprise a ritual are precisely defined and vary ... little if at all from one occasion to another" (Theodorson and Theodorson, 1969: 351).

Rituals are found in all human societies because they serve important functions (Theodorson and Theodorson, 1969: 351). First, according to Durkheim rituals are important in the creation and maintenance of social solidarity (Kertzer, 1988; Edelman, 1988; Berezin, 1994). Second, rituals are believed, by the participants and by the persons conducting them, to have the power in themselves to produce certain results. For instance, this is the case with certain religious rituals and quite generally with rituals associated with **exuvial magic**. A belief in exuvial magic is found in many hunting and gathering societies. *Exuvia* is the plural form of a Latin noun that literally translates into English as the cast-off skins or coverings of various animals, including snakes. More generally, the term refers to any part of an animal—a cast-off scab, eyelash, strand of hair, piece of a hoof, or an entire organ—such as the heart, liver, brain, liver, etc. In exuvial magic, if a priest or shaman has even a part of a person (her or his *exuviae*), the shaman is believed to be able to control the entire person by performing certain rituals.

Third, rituals are a means of relieving feelings of anxiety in times of crisis. Fourth, rituals are important as symbols. Thus, the lowering of the nation's flag to half mast for a full month was a way for the nation to pay its deep respect to the late President Ronald Reagan.

Sociologists have studied these parts of society, these categories of experience, ever since the very birth of sociology, because by doing so sociologists arrive at a sociological understanding of social life. A lot of human conduct may be understood in terms of these categories of experience; in terms of playing roles in these categories of experience; in terms of humans trying to construct, to affirm, to reinforce, to de-construct, and even to replace these systems.

Sociology identifies, describes, and analyzes the components or parts of social structure, that is, the basic categories of experience that make a world. This analysis is accomplished at one or more levels of analysis—at the **micro** or small-scale level, at the **macro** or large-scale level, and at the **meso** or in-between level.

The sense of the "we" is one of the kinds of relationships that makes a world. It's one of the things in the camps that Steinbeck describes that make him feel it would not be an exaggeration to say that in the evening, sitting around the campfire, the twenty were one, because this sense of identity, of solidarity, of loyalty, of "we-ness" developed. The concept of solidarity is illustrated throughout the text. We belong to groups like our families, to whom we are loyal and in interaction with whom we initially construct our identity, our sense of "who we are."

Sociology also focuses on another thing that Steinbeck says makes a world—- quid pro quo relationships. "Quid pro quo" are three Latin words that mean "this for that" in English. Sometimes in our daily lives we call use the colloquial term "tit-for-tat" relationships to refer to the exchange order in social life. We will study the exchange order in this textbook. See Table 1.1 on Exchange Principles in the theory of sociologist Georg Simmel. If a student says to you that she/he will help you study for a test in introduction to sociology if you help her/him study for the test in chemistry, that's the exchange order at the micro level in social life. When the Obama administration used back-channel diplomacy with Russian President Dmitry Medvedev in February 2009, signaling that the United States might forgo installing and maintaining an anti-missile system in Poland and the Czech Republic (tit) if Russia uses its clout with Iran to dissuade Iran from developing and testing nuclear weapons and the long-range missiles to deliver them (tat), that was the exchange order in action at the macro level (Hurst, 2009).

TABLE 1.1 EXCHANGE PRINCIPLES IN THE THEORY OF GEORG SIMMEL

1. **Attraction** The more social actors perceive one another's respective resources as valuable, the more likely an exchange relationship is to develop among them.
2. **Value** The greater a social actor's need for a resource of a given type, and the greater the scarcity of that resource, the greater the value placed on that resource by the social actor.
3. **Power** (3a) The more valuable a social actor perceives the resources of another social actor, the greater is the power of the latter over the former; (3b) the more a social actor's resources can be used in many types of exchanges (e.g., beauty, writing ability, money), the greater are that actor's options and power in social exchanges.
4. **Tension** Many social exchanges involve attempts to conceal both (4a) the intensity of a social actor's need for a resource of a given type and (4b) the availability of a resource of a given type. A lot flows from this, including a fundamental tension that can erupt into other social forms, including conflict.

Source: Adapted from Jonathan H. Turner, *The Structure of Sociological Theory* Fifth Edition (Belmont, CA: Wadsworth, 1991), Table 14-1, p. 301.

Sociology also focuses on another thing that Steinbeck says makes a world--rules, norms, and sanctions. **Norms** are rules of behavior that are backed by negative and positive sanctions. A **negative sanction** is a punishment and a **positive sanction** is a reward. Sociologists use the term **normative order** to refer to the various forms of norms (such as folkways and mores) and the behaviors related to them. **Folkways** are norms that have relatively mild sanctions attached to them, such as norms of etiquette that say that one should avoid touching or otherwise drawing attention to certain body parts (genitals, anus) in polite company. Folkways are very important in social life.

Mores (sounds like MOW-rays) are norms that have strong sanctions attached to them, such as the death penalty or many years of imprisonment for attempting to overthrow the government of the United States through the force of arms. Another example of a more is provided by the prohibition of the practice of **suttee** by British authorities in India during the nineteenth century. Among high caste Hindus the cultural practice was for a widow to throw herself alive upon the funeral pyre of her deceased husband. If she did not do so, family members would do it for her. This cultural practice is known as suttee or sati.

British authorities prohibited this particular cultural practice and imposed the death penalty on those who compelled reluctant wives. This conflict of normative orders is encapsulated in the following story taken from the life of General Sir Charles James Napier, the British Army's Commander-in-Chief in India in the mid-1840s. In response to the complaints of Hindu priests who wanted to continue the practice, the General replied as follows: You say that it is your custom to burn widows. Very well. We also have a custom. When men burn wives alive, we hang them and confiscate all their property. Build your funeral pyre. Next to it my carpenters will construct a gallows. You may follow your custom. Then we will follow ours (Steyn, 2006: 193).

Technically, a **mos** is one more. More is the plural form of mos. However, given the widespread state of sociological illiteracy, many people use these terms sloppily and incorrectly. For instance, many people use the term "more" as the singular form and "mores" as the plural form. Whichever terms you use, folkways and mores are important parts of social structure in all known human societies. Much human behavior is to be understood as attempts to establish, to re-enforce, to resist, to de-construct and to re-construct the rules (norms) by which we legitimately conduct ourselves. Hence, we study normative order throughout this textbook.

From its earliest days, sociology has focused on another thing that Steinbeck says helped to make these migrant camps worlds or societies--leadership. Leadership emerges in the nighttime camps, and it is a form of what the German sociologist Max Weber (sounds like mAHHx VAburr) calls **domination**, the right-to-command-and-the-duty-to-obey relationships. The German word "Herrschaft" is frequently translated into English as "domination" or authority. **Authority** (domination) is a term sociologists use to refer to legitimate power. For example, a police officer has the authority to direct traffic to drive through a red traffic light; and we, as drivers, have the obligation to obey. It is an authority relationship, a relationship of the-right-to-command and the-duty-to-obey.

Power, as defined by Max Weber, refers to the ability to get one's way in the face of opposition. Power may be either legitimate or illegitimate. If a person comes up to the driver's side window of my car while I am stopped at a red light and points a loaded gun at my head and tells me to get out of my car or I'll get a bullet through my head, and then that person steals my car, that person had power over me. That person got her/his way in the face of my opposition. It is an example of the illegitimate use of power, but it is power nonetheless.

Sociologist Robert Bierstedt makes a distinction between power, which he sees as coercive, and **influence**, which he sees as persuasive. Influence is the ability to effect a voluntary change in a social actor's behavior, opinions, or attitudes through persuasive action (Theodorson and Theordorson, 1969: 202). Power, authority, leadership, and coercion are part of what sociologists term imperative order.

Imperative order refers to the various forms of domination and the behaviors related thereto. Imperative order is one of the relationships that makes a world, and we study imperative order throughout this textbook. Many of the major transformations and conflicts that we are witnessing in the world today are analyzed throughout this text in terms of the relations among the processes of solidary order, normative order, imperative order, and exchange order. These transformations include those occurring in the countries of the Middle East, Middle Europe, Africa, Latin America, and the Far East. A basic understanding of relationships that make a world helps make intelligible transformations in social worlds at the macro, micro and meso levels. Sociologists study social structure to arrive at an understanding of social life.

SOCIOLOGY AS THE STUDY OF GROUPS AND COLLECTIVITIES

Sociology is the scientific study of group behavior. As used by sociologists, a **group** is a collection of two or more persons characterized by shared goals, solidarity, and sustained interaction. In a group, the members share one or more goals, such as baking a cake, building a bomb, earning three credit hours in an academic course, or winning a war. Members of a group also have a sense that those who belong it are different, for better or worse, than persons who are not members of the group. And lastly, members of a group interact over a sustained period of time Even in a college club that meets once a week for forty-five minutes, its members, over a period of time, will have had sustained interaction. In contrast, sustained interaction does not characterize persons who do not know each other but who simply happen to be crossing the street at the same time.

If two or more persons do not share sustained interaction, one or more common goals, and solidarity, they are not a group. There are several collectivities of two or more persons that are not groups. For instance, a **social category** is a plurality of persons who do not form a group but who have at least one similar social characteristic or status in common, e.g., occupation, or age, gender, social class, ethnicity, and so forth. In her Presidential Address to the American Sociological Association, Sociologist Cynthia Fuchs Epstein noted that gender is "the most basic and prevalent category in social life throughout the world" (2007: 2).

THE CLASSIC SOCIOLOGICAL TRADITION

Sociology as a disciplined scientific study is of relatively recent origin. Sociology was born in the tumultuous nineteenth-century in Western Europe, a time and place of political, economic, and social upheaval. Old ways of life were under, and it was not clear what would emerge when the dust settled. Crisis frequently provides opportunity for innovation, including in the realm of ideas. Many social theorists in Europe endeavored to understand what was happening and what would emerge from the turmoil. Some of these thinkers were the founders of sociology. We now briefly introduce you to the ideas of some of the key founders of European Sociology and then introduce you to the development of Sociology in the United States, finishing up with a look at sociology today.

Auguste Comte and the Positivist Tradition in Sociology

By the early eighteenth century in Western Europe, religion was a major paradigm for understanding social life. However, religion as a way of knowing came under attack in eighteenth-century Western Europe and for many persons was displaced by other idea systems--first by rationalism and then by positivism. **Rationalism** is the philosophical position that valid knowledge has reason and logical thinking as its source. From the point of view of rationalism, if I wanted to arrive at the best answer to any question, I could simply use reason and think logically. In other words, rationalism rejects religion, empiricism (empirical investigation) and experience as sources of valid knowledge. In contrast to rationalism, **positivism** is the philosophic position that valid knowledge has as its source direct observations perceived by the senses. The aim of the positivist is to formulate general laws or theories that express relationships between phenomena. The researcher first collects empirical data and then uses empirical observation and experiments to demonstrate that a particular social phenomenon does or does not fit a specific theory.

Auguste Comte (1798-1857) coined term sociology and he is regarded as the founder or "father" of sociology. Auguste Comte is a French philosopher who had an abiding interest in **epistemology**, which is the study or theory of knowledge, its origins, nature and limits. Comte placed sociology, this new science that he had created, at the top of the structure of human knowledge. Auguste Comte maintained that sociology could and should be scientific, by which he meant that sociology should deal only with propositions (hypotheses) that are empirically testable. The positivist tradition in modern sociology stems from Comte's formulations.

Emile Durkheim

Emile Durkheim (1858-1917) is another French positivist who, like Auguste Comte, advocates the adoption in sociology of the scientific method, the formulation of theories about the causal relationships between social phenomena, and a focus on social structure as an independent variable. Durkheim argues that the way a group is put together--its social structure--has important social and psychological effects.

According to Durkheim, the subject matter of sociology should be based on the accumulation of social facts. Durkheim defines a **social fact** as a social phenomenon that is distinct from individual, biological, and psychological phenomena. Durkheim makes the following three points about social facts: Social facts are (1) external to the individual; (2) objective, in the sense that they are not simply a product of subjective definitions; and (3) social facts are coercive, in that they constrain the individual's behavior.

Durkheim's interests and focus, like those of Marx and Weber, are historical and comparative. You may well ask, "Why have a comparative historical focus if one wants to understand social life?" The reason is simple yet multifaceted and resides in three assumptions made by Durkheim, Weber, and Marx. First, is the assumption that in order to understand any society, we need to comprehend its history. Second, is the assumption that comparison is necessary for understanding: we understand something, at least in part, only insofar as we understand how it is similar to, as well as different than, something else. Third, these theorists appreciated that if we want to understand any society, we must first discern the processes (parts) of which it is composed.

A fundamental concern with social solidarity (sometimes termed cohesiveness) and social change informs Durkheim's scholarship. Durkheim studied the implications of the presence, absence, and strength of social bonds between the individual and the collectivity.

THE SOCIOLOGICAL STUDY OF SUICIDE

The single most stressful event in the lives of many human beings is the loss of a loved one, especially a family member, through death. The sense of loss frequently is profound for individuals, families, and their communities. In the United States, if the cause of death is suicide, those immediately and even indirectly affected invariably ask "Why?" Of course, at other times and in other places, such as in feudal Japan and in ancient Rome, suicide was defined as an honorable and/or redemptive ritual. In the contemporary United States and in a large portion of the modern Western world, when suicide occurs, those affected tend to ask "Why?"

A *common-sense* answer is that the person who committed suicide was deeply distressed. Through a reconstruction of the personal tragedy, people guess at what led to this sad event. After close examination, many people eventually rationalize the other person's behavior. In the United States, some may even conclude that, as an adult of sound mind, one has a personal right freely to choose to end one's own life.

From a *psychological and/or psychiatric perspective*, the causes of suicide are often linked to clinical depression and personal crisis. From a *medical perspective*, suicide may be viewed as caused by a chemical imbalance in the brain that, in turn, causes clinical depression and/or flaws in cognition.

Sociologists, on the other hand, view suicide and its causes differently. As scientists, we make markedly different assumptions and use different methods to investigate the causes of suicide. For example if we look at suicide rates and categorize them, we observe a *pattern*. Please see Table 1.2. In 2007, the most recent year for which statistics are available, the rate of suicide for single white Protestant middle- and upper-middle-class males (21.9) is more than 3.8 times as great as that of their female counterparts (5.7) and 2.5 times as large as that for lower-class African-American males (8.8). The lowest rate of suicide is for African-American females (1.7), whose rate is less than one-third of the rate for white females (5.7).

TABLE 1.2 SUICIDE RATES PER 100,000 POPULATION IN THE UNITED STATES, BY RACE AND SEX, 2007

Race and Sex	Suicide Rate
Total Population	11.5
Non-Hispanic White Males	21.9
Non-Hispanic White Females	5.7
Black Males	8.8
Black Females	1.7

Source: Adapted from U.S. Census Bureau, *Statistical Abstract of the United States: 2012* (131st Edition) (Washington, D.C.: U.S. Government Printing Office, 2011), Table 128, p. 95.

As human beings, in our lives we all suffer tragedies, smaller ones and significantly larger ones. What accounts for the high suicide rate among those who are financially well off and who, in terms of life satisfaction (Please see Chapter 7, Social Stratification), are the happiest, or at least supposedly the most satisfied, members of society (Argyle, 2002, 1994, 1992, 1991)? Why should they take their own lives at a much higher rate than those nearer the bottom of the stratified order? What explains this apparent anomaly?

French sociologist Emile Durkheim developed a sociological explanation of suicide that makes the apparent anomaly understandable in terms of social cohesion and the normative order in a social setting. Durkheim's explanation of suicide consists of four main points. First, Durkheim argues that society is a complex entity of social structures. Some of these social structures, including the family, religion, work, school, and friendship systems, provide individuals with social support. He terms these **supportive social systems**. These social networks positively integrate individuals into communities and into their society. In other words, individuals become bonded with society through these social systems of support. A recent study of supportive social systems in rural China, documents that these networks offer harbor from harassment, facilitate conflict avoidance, sheltered social actors from the sorts of trouble afflicting many villagers, and also facilitated privileged access to law when conflict was unavoidable (Michelson, 2007: 481).

Second, there are different patterns of solidarity in different social settings. Forms and patterns of solidarity can vary both across societies and within them. Third, the behavior of individuals is influenced and constrained by their social environments.

Fourth, suicide rates are a function of the strength of the normative order and of the solidary ties between the individual and the conventional social order (solidary order). When these ties are strong, suicide is deflected. For instance, what occurs to individuals when personal tragedy happens in agricultural societies? In agricultural societies, Durkheim argued, the moral norms of the community are in place for providing both social and spiritual support. Hence, the individual is supported and protected by a system of kinship assistance. In this setting, a personal loss or tragedy may be experienced by, and receive support from, the whole kinship. Many small traditional farming communities in American society are still organized this way.

However, if the ties between the individual and the supportive social systems are either too strong or too weak, the individual is at increased risk of suicide. These dynamics, according to Durkheim, explain why suicide is more likely to occur among Protestants than Catholics or Jews, why single men have higher suicide rates than married men, and why suicide rates are higher in modern societies than in more traditional ones.

If the solidary ties between an individual and the collectivity are extremely strong, the individual will sacrifice her or his own life for the collectivity. Durkheim terms this action **altruistic suicide**. Suicide bombers, people who are patriots to a cause and who either strap explosives to themselves or who sit in a vehicle containing explosives, and who blow themselves up, are an example. *Kamikaze* pilots during World War II are another example. These young men were the *divine wind*, from the Japanese words "kami," meaning "god" and "kaze," meaning "wind." They piloted aircraft loaded with explosives and crashed them into Allied warships. Altruistic suicide is motivated by a desire to serve the perceived needs of the group, and it is found in societies that tend to de-emphasize the importance of the individual.

According to Durkheim, suicide rates in the latter half of the nineteenth century in various countries were highest among Protestants, lowest among Jews, and Catholics were in-between. In contrast to Catholicism or Jewry, Protestantism emphasizes an individualistic ethos in which individuals are viewed as responsible for their own salvation. Durkheim terms this a "cult of egoism." It places a heavy (overwhelming) burden on the individual, and the group itself is not strong enough to provide the individual with adequate emotional and spiritual support outside of her/himself. In other words, the group is not sufficiently *integrated* (cohesive) to be able communally to mitigate the individual's sense of personal responsibility and guilt for perceived moral weakness and failure (sin). As a result, the individual's sense of personal responsibility and guilt become overpowering and the individual seeks refuge in suicide. **Egoistic suicide**, then, is due to a strong value system, weak group integration, and to an overwhelming sense of personal responsibility. While Catholicism and Jewry have strong value systems, they also have a less individualistic ethos, more integrated communities, and cohesive social systems of support that prove highly valuable when their members experience personal troubles.

Durkheim's argument also extends to marital status. Married men are more integrated into society than are single men. Single men commit more suicide because they lack a feeling of belonging. *Think of social situations in which a single male would feel as if he were "a third wheel"* (less than welcome) *in a social setting. Have you, or anyone you know, ever experienced anything like this?* Indeed, studies of males in prison in the United States, Finland, and France indicate that suicide rates are far higher among the divorced prisoners than among those who are married (Tartaro and Lester, 2005; Lester, 1999; Lester, 1994).

Durkheim argued that in modern industrial societies, traditional curbs on individual behavior had declined, a condition he referred to as anomie. Durkheim's concept of **anomie**, sometimes translated from French into English as "normlessness," actually refers to norms being in flux, the guidelines for acceptable behavior no longer being clear. The term anomie does not necessarily imply a collapse or absence of imperative order or of political authority. Such a situation would be called **anarchy**. In anomie, one or more norms that previously had regulated human behavior effectively either have become irrelevant and/or no longer applicable; they are in flux or weakened.

Durkheim's empirically based argument is that, due to lack of effective restraints, many appetites become insatiable. Guidelines (norms) regarding "how much is enough," no longer are clear. One's level of frustration at not being able to satiate one's (economic, social, sexual, etc.) appetites can lead or drive one to suicide, which he termed **anomic suicide.**

Durkheim's insights thus explain high rates of suicide among persons who, in an objective sense, may be viewed by others as economically (or socially, occupationally, etc.) successful. Because standards of behavior no longer are clear (anomie), and because so many appetites are perceived as insatiable, how does one actually know that one *is* successful? How does one gauge *how successful* one has become? Is one as successful as one's neighbor or best friends? The rapid rise of an individual's expectations in defining what constitutes success, coupled with the continuing elevation of those expectations, make it difficult to come to a lasting assessment of whether one actually *is* successful and what level of success one has achieved. Doubts may surface. Is one merely a *has been* or even on the brink of being on the way *down* the ladder of success? Why doesn't "success" *feel* like one thought it would? These and related anxieties, while appearing merely existential to some, may actually lead people to take their own lives. *Do you know anyone whose suicide may be considered anomic? Everybody has a story. Tell us his or her story.*

Durkheim's analysis would explain the lower suicide rate in the United States of African-American females (in comparison to white females) as due to their higher integration into kinship, family, and community social relations. Carol Stack's study, ***All My Kin*** (1997) demonstrates that in urban areas African-American women form pseudo-kinship social relations as social systems of support.

Karl Marx

Karl Marx (1818-1883), a German social theorist, was profoundly influenced by the ideas of the German philosopher Friedrich Hegel (1770-1831). For Karl Marx, the economy is the most important part of society. Marx refers to the economy as society's **substructure** or foundation. All other parts of society—the family, religion, education, politics, ideas, gender relations, and so forth—he terms the **superstructure.** The

superstructure is viewed as determined (or at least as heavily influenced) by the economy. Thus, for Marx, power is viewed as derived from the substructure. Those who own the **economic means of production,** the property necessary for economic production, have power; those who sell their labor lack power. Marx also believed that in a capitalist society, political and economic decisions are made within the context of unequal exchange relationships between those who have power and those who lack power.

Marx appreciated that people have social relations not only with other people but also with institutions (complexes or bundles of norms). Marx perceived that a person may have one of two objective relationships to the economic means of production: one either owns or does not own them. Marx defines objective class position in terms of a person's objective relationship to the economic means of production. If one owns the economic means of production, one belongs to the class known as the **bourgeoisie.** If one sells one's labor to those who own the economic means of production, one belongs to the class known as the **proletariat**.

For Marx, the economic and political interests of the social classes are antagonistic and different. For instance, the proletariat wants greater control over the relations of production (e.g., the establishment of air-quality standards in the sanding room of the airplane-manufacturing plant), and the bourgeoisie does not want to grant it to them. The proletariat wants a larger share of the fruits of their labor and the bourgeoisie does not want to give it to them.

Marx uses the term **alienation** to refer to the powerlessness of the proletariat. Alienation conveys the meaning that the proletariat feel disassociated from the results or fruits of their labor, and, by extension, from society.

For Marx, social change and history are dialectical processes. The concept of **dialectic** refers to the clash of contradictions. Karl Marx, drawing on the ideas of Friedrich Hegel, views dialectics as consisting of three phases or stages—which he terms **thesis** (the way things are), **antithesis** (the clash of contradictions), and **synthesis** (the emergence of something new). With the passage of time, what once was new becomes merely the way things are, the status quo. The dialectical process thus is a continuing process.

According to Marx, in capitalist society, class conflict reaches its high point, and ultimately a class struggle would ensue. A victorious proletariat would usher in a classless society.

Max Weber –Turning Marx on his Head

The ideas of German sociologist Max Weber (1864-1920) have profoundly influenced sociology. An understanding of some basic sociological concepts aid us in understanding Weber's sociology. In sociology, a **role** is an expectation of behavior. In the logic of sociology as a way of understanding, roles attach to statuses. The concept of status has several meanings in sociology, one of which is that a **status** is a position in a group. An **institution**, also known as a social institution, is an interrelated system of roles and norms organized around the satisfaction of an important social need or function. The "Big 5" social institutions that we find in one form or another in all human societies are the family, the economy, politics, education, and religion.

Weber reminds us that institutions are important. Weber's sociology demonstrates that *the way institutions are structured, the way institutions are put together, matters.* To illustrate this point, the twentieth century ran a series of natural experiments, imposing quite different institutions on two sets of Chinese (the People's Republic and Taiwan), two sets of Koreans (North and South), and two sets of Germans (East and West). The results were striking, almost immediate, and the lesson crystal clear. If you take the same people who have more or less the same culture and impose communist institutions on one group and capitalist institutions on the other, "almost immediately there will be a divergence in the way they behave" (Ferguson, 2011: 11). Social structure matters. Institutions matter.

Weber disagrees with Marx with regard to "what" the engine of social change is. Marx takes the position that the economy—what goes on in the economy, how the economy is structured (e.g., capitalism, the relations of people with regard to the economic means of production)—shapes or drives social change. For Marx, the economy is the engine that drives the train of social change. For Weber, what drives social change is an empirical question that can and must be answered empirically. For Weber, there is no "pat answer" to the question as to what drives social change, no simple looking in one place only (the economy) for the answer. For Weber, the sources of social change may be located in what, for Marx, would be the superstructure. Thus, in Weberian sociology, ideas can be powerful engines of social change. To illustrate this point, in ***The Protestant Ethic and the Spirit of Capitalism*** (1904/1905) Weber locates the cause of the rise of capitalism in *ideas*—religious ideas of a specific type of ascetic Protestantism that is known as Calvinistic Protestantism that arose in western Europe in the sixteen century. So, for Weber, ideas can drive social change.

So, Weber wrote, at least in part, in reaction to what he perceived as Karl Marx's economic determinism. In ***The Protestant Ethic and the Spirit of Capitalism*** (1904/1905), Weber details how rationalization was born and first became embodied in a system of religious ideas known as Calvinistic Protestantism in sixteenth century Western Europe. In this path-breaking book, Weber analyzes how systems of religious ideas were a spearhead of social and economic change.

Weber thus rejects what many scholars perceive as the economic determinism of Karl Marx. In contrast to Marx, Weber perceives that there are three scarce-yet-widely-valued resources that social actors might attach to positions as rewards. Weber terms these resources **class** (people who share roughly similar life chances), **status** (deference, esteem, honor), and **power** (the ability to get one's way in the face of opposition). According to Weber, the relationship among class, status, and power is both variable and an empirical question. Any one of these may also be a spearhead of social change.

The concept of **rationalization** also is a key to understanding Weber's analyses of the modern world. In the Weberian sense, rationalization is an institution. Rationalization refers to the substitution of formal, written rules and procedures for earlier spontaneous, arbitrary, capricious approaches. Rationalization, in other words, refers to the development of greater standardization, coordination, and consistency in organizational structure, which Weber sees as a hallmark of the modern age. In the political order, rationalization may manifest itself in the decline of **patrimonial rule** (arbitrary, capricious, erratic, idiosyncratic decisions of rulers) and its replacement by a standardized system of consistent rule (e.g., parliamentary democracy). In the realm of technology, rationalization may manifest itself in DVDs that work reliably in a variety of DVD players. In the realm of social organization, bureaucracy is an example of rationalization. We will study bureaucracy as a form of as a form of social organization later in this textbook.

Weber also debates or disagrees with both Marx and Durkheim regarding methodology, the proper way to engage in social research. Weber argues that a comprehensive understanding of society must take into account both the objective aspects of social organization as well as the subjective motivations of actors. He refers to subjective understanding with the German verb **verstehen,** which translates into English as "to understand," and which in this context means subjective or empathetic understanding. Weber takes the position that empathetic understanding is necessary if we are to understand social life (Goode, 1997). The paradigms of symbolic interactionism, feminist theory, and post-modernism all embrace verstehen as an approach to understanding social life. These paradigms assume that in order to understand social life,

the objective facts, including economic facts (i.e., objective understanding) are not enough. In order to understand social life, we must view social life through the eyes or perceptions of those who are living it.

THE DEVELOPMENT OF AMERICAN SOCIOLOGY

The theoretical legacies of Marx, Durkheim, and Weber served as a springboard for the development of sociology in the United States. However, American sociology was influenced by two factors that did not have a big impact on the development of sociology in Europe: individualism and pragmatism. As a concept, **individualism** gives priority and legitimacy to one's own wants, desires and goals over those of the collectivity. Individualism also gives priority and legitimacy to defining the self in terms of personal attributes (Myers, 2008). **Pragmatism** is a philosophical view which stresses that concepts and actions should be evaluated and analyzed in terms of their practical consequences. In this view, actions designed to accomplish a desired goal are appropriate by reason of the goal they are designed to accomplish and need no theoretical rationale. Even if there were one or more theories in terms of which the proposed actions logically could be expected to produce the desired results, these *theories are unnecessary* according to pragmatism.

American sociology is far more pragmatic and individualistic than European sociology. Due in large part to the dual emphases of pragmatism and individualism, much American sociology has little impact on European sociology, and many European sociologists simply dismiss much American sociology as consisting of "jargonized trivialities (Ian Robertson, as quoted in Lachmann, 1991: 285).

The first department of sociology in the United States was established at the University of Chicago in 1892. Within two decades, the American Sociological Association was established.

At the University of Chicago early sociologists like Robert E. Park (1864-1944), Ernest W. Burgess (1886-1966), Louis Wirth (1897-1952), and W.I. Thomas (1863-1947) researched juvenile delinquency, urban gangs, the ecology of urban social life, and the cultural adaptations of immigrants (Wirth, 1938; Thrasher, 1936; Thomas and Znaniecki, 1918). Their distinctive approach, known as **the Chicago school**, still exists today. Chicago sociology is called "a school" because its research has several common characteristics. First, this scholarship is heavily influenced by the theories of German sociologists Ferdinand Toennies (1855-1936) and Georg Simmel (1858-1918). Second, this research is concerned with the challenges of community and of urbanization. Third, this research utilizes field research as method of data collection. This approach to data collection relies heavily on detailed personal observations of the daily lives of the people being studied. Fourth, this research tends to embody or belong to the symbolic-interactionist paradigm.

Symbolic Interactionism

Two founders of symbolic interactionism are George Herbert Mead (1863-1931) of the University of Chicago and Charles Horton Cooley (1864-1929) of the University of Michigan. After Mead's death, Mead's students published a compilation of Mead's university lectures as the book, *Mind, Self, and Society* (1934) and they also coined the term **symbolic interactionism** to describe Charles Horton Cooley and Mead's approach to understanding the social world. Both Mead and Cooley emphasize that human nature is socially constructed and, that the individual's sense of "self" is socially constructed (Allahyari, 2000). Symbolic interactionism stresses the importance of language, gestural communication, and role taking in the formation of the mind, the self, and society. This approach provides the theoretical basis of labeling theory and it is a critique of positivism. As a way of knowing, symbolic interactionism stresses that the subjective or inner life of the individual is an important source of social behavior and of social action.

Charles Horton Cooley uses the concept of **looking-glass self** (1902) to refer to the process whereby an individual develops an identity or self concept (self). According to this view we come to know or to define ourselves through the process of internalizing our perceptions of the responses of others to us. Just as we know what our physical self looks like by gazing into a mirror, so too, we know what our "self" is like by using the responses of others to us as a guide.

A familiarity with the meaning of several concepts makes it easier for us to understand symbolic interactionism. As used by Mead, a **gesture** is any physical movement or vocalization that conveys meaning and that also evokes a response in one or more persons. A **symbol** is a sign that evokes a uniform social response from one or more audiences. A flag, Hanukkah, an engagement ring, and Cinco de Mayo are examples of symbols. **Role taking** refers to taking the point of view, attitudes, or behaviors of another person by imaginatively perceiving oneself as the other person, in order to be able to anticipate that person's actual or likely behavior.

Mead emphasizes that "the self" (our answers to the question, "Who Am I?") emerges through the process of social interaction with others. Mead stresses that language, gestural communication, and role-taking are important bases of social life.

Structural Functionalism

American sociologist Talcott Parsons introduced American sociology to structural functionalism in the late 1930s, and that paradigm dominated American sociology for over a generation. Synonyms for structural functionalism are consensus theory, social order theory, structuralism, and functionalism.

What does it mean to take a **structural view** of society? It means two things. First, society is viewed as consisting of parts. Some of these parts, for instance, are roles—expectations of behavior; statuses, positions in a group; norms, and institutions (bundles or complexes of norms). A **total institution** is a place of confinement or partial confinement where persons of a specified type live, have limited contact with the rest of society, and follow a formalized life routine under the direction and control of a bureaucratic staff. Characteristics of total institutions include the following: All aspects of live are conducted in the company of others who are in the same circumstances. All aspects of life are conducted in the same place and are under the control of the same authority. All activities are scheduled by the authorities without consultation with the participants. All scheduled activities are designed to meet the same goal—i.e., to fulfill the purpose of the organization. And, lastly, at least some of the scheduled activities are designed to facilitate the depersonalization that lies at the heart of the re-socialization process. Examples of total institutions include military boot camp, secure mental hospitals, maximum security prisons, seminaries, and convents.

Second, when one takes a structural view, one also views the parts of society as interconnected; this interconnectedness of the parts is called interdependence. Hence, if one part of society changes, it has repercussions on other parts and hence on society as a whole. **Interdependence**—viewing the parts of society as interrelated, so that a change in one part is viewed as having an impact on other part(s) and hence on society as a whole—is central to a sociological way of knowing. Interdependence is central to a sociological way of perceiving the world.

Structural functionalism is a macro structural view that focuses on large-scale structures. Functionalists believe that in terms of understanding human social behavior it makes sense to speak in terms of "society as a whole" or of "the community as a whole." Hence, if a functionalist wants to understand a particular social behavior or institution, the question that tends to be asked is: How does this practice help the society as a whole to persist across time?

A familiarity with the meaning of several concepts makes it easier for us to understand structural functionalism. Robert K. Merton, in his book *Social Theory and Social Structure* (1968: 105), asserts that an important aspect of the sociological way of knowing is an ability to perceive the difference between two types of functions. **Manifest functions** are the purposive and intended outcomes of a social institution. **Latent functions** are the often-time hidden, unrecognized, and unintended consequences of a social institution. For example, a manifest function of work is to give you an income (and, perhaps, some type of meaning in your life). An unintended outcome of work is that work also becomes a place where you develop networks of colleagues and meet people who become life-long best friends. A possible unintended consequence of work is that you become so exhausted through work that you have little energy remaining to share with your family members.

Functionalism uses the term **function** to refer to those instances wherein one or more parts of society operate in such a way that they contribute to the survival and stability of the system. For instance, one of the functions of gift-giving is to re-enforce the solidary order (Hagstrom, 1966). Functional relationships are those that contribute to the well being of society. On the other hand functionalism uses the term **dysfunction** to refer to those instances wherein one or more parts of society operate in such a way that they disturb, hinder, or threaten the integration, adjustment, or stability of the system. Thus, incest is a dysfunction. It threatens the authority and solidary structures of the family.

Social Conflict Theory

Social conflict refers to conscious struggle between groups over resources. The resource may be any number of things: a goal, value, meaning, money, status, power, property, and so forth. Social conflict occurs within, between, and among collectivities. The collectivities engaged in social conflict may be of any size.

In the United States in the mid to late 1960s, social conflict theory was viewed as an alternative to functionalism as a way of understanding human social behavior. Much of this theory drew on the insights of Karl Marx, and hence is termed Marxian or neo-Marxian. "Neo" means "new."

Neo-Marxian theory in the United States developed during the turbulent days of the Civil Rights Movement, the Viet Nam war, urban riots, and concern about poverty in the cities and in the countryside. Neo-Marxian theory posed a theoretical and political challenge to structural functionalism. Once again, social, intellectual, political, and cultural turmoil manifested itself in the emergence of a perceived need freshly to understand the things that make a world. Once again, it was time to toss out old ways of knowing in favor of new ones. Rapid social change and social movements concerning gender inequality, military conflict, racism, and poverty called for new ways of looking at, and of understanding, the world.

Feminist Theory

Feminism has its own versions of social conflict theory, which collectively are called feminist theory (e.g., de Beauvoir, 1949; Millett, 1969; Greer, 1970; Gilligan, 1982; Daly and Chesney-Lind, 1988; Wharton, 1991; Anderson, 1993; Hippensteele and Chesney-Lind, 1995, Almeling, 2007). Feminist theories also ask the question, "Who benefits?" Their answer, "Males; males benefit at the expense of females." **Patriarchy** is a term that refers to male supraordination. If Marxists want to overthrow capitalism, it is patriarchy that feminists want overthrown (e.g., Epstein, 2007; Firestone, 1970).

According to feminist theory, patriarchy must be swept aside and gender-equal relations established in all spheres of social life and of social action. In other words, from a feminist theoretical perspective it would be possible, theoretically, to put the means of production in the hands of the proletariat and yet very little would change for women. Why? Because the means of production actually would be in the hands of male proletarians, not in the hands of female proletarians, and not equally in the hands of either sexes or genders.

Post-Modernism

During the last two decades of the twentieth century, a cluster of anti-rationalist and anti-scientific-method ideas became increasingly prevalent among academic sociologists in the United States, France, and Great Britain. These ideas were variously known as deconstructionism, social constructivism or constructivism, or Science and Technology Studies. An umbrella term for these movements is post-modernism. In American sociology, post-modernism has the objective of dogmatically asserting that the results of scientific findings do not represent any underlying reality, but are purely the ideology of dominant groups within society. An **ideology** is an idea or system of ideas that supports the status quo, the way things are.

The various forms of post-modernism view science as a social practice that produces "narrations" and "myths" that have no more validity than the myths of any pre-scientific peoples. Post-modernism rejects the view that science is a search for truths or approximate truths about the social world. According to post-modernism, science is merely a social practice that encodes a bourgeois and Euro-centric and/or masculinist world-view. Hence, women and various ethnic groups need to develop their own forms of inquiry which need not be as intellectually demanding as the Western male bourgeois variety.

Sociology Today

Sociology is a multi-paradigmatic way of knowing that reflects the cultural diversity of its proponents. Within the past thirty years, sociology as a profession has become more diverse in terms of the gender, race, ethnicity, sexual-orientation, physical-disability, and other attributes of its practitioners. These attributes influence the lives these practitioners live, their perceptions of human social action, the research questions they ask, and the research methods and theories they employ (Bonilla-Silva, 1997, Bonilla-Silva and Lewis, 1997). There are numerous schools of sociological thought and not one of them is dominant in American sociology at the present time.

The various ways of knowing in sociology are not mutually exclusive. Some sociologists use a variety of perspectives, while others subscribe only to one. The perspective of the authors of this textbook is that one should guard against assuming that one way of knowing is right while another is wrong. Each way

of knowing has strengths and weaknesses, advantages and disadvantages. Each is "right" according to its own domain assumptions. A particular theory and a particular method are tools that allow us to focus on particular aspects of social reality to the exclusion of others.

As the author of this textbook, I am not here to advocate any particular sociological way of knowing as the truth. If you are looking for magic bullets or instant answers, this textbook will disappoint you, because this textbook contains no magic bullets or easy answers. My position is that the various ways of sociological knowing, together, allow us to perceive and to understand the multi-dimensional nature of the social world.

There are imperative forces to maintain social order (functionalist perspective), and there are social forces that undermine and cause society to change (conflict perspective, neo-Marxist perspective) (Faludi, 1999). In seeking to understand social behavior and social action, we need to understand how people attribute meaning (symbolic interactionism), and what the meanings are that they attribute. Furthermore, the social order is made up, at least in part, of exchange relations; and both personal and political power are socially organized (imperative order). Social order also is made up, at least in part, of solidary order (e.g., a perceived need to belong) and of rules (norms) of various sorts (normative order).

There are many relationships that make a world. Different theories and different methods are tools that sociologists use in our attempt to understand the fundamentals of social life in the twenty-first century.

POSITIVISTIC RESEARCH METHODS IN SOCIOLOGY

In *Rules of the Sociological Method*, Emile Durkheim tells us how to go about it if we want to understand the social world sociologically (Durkheim, 1938 [1895]). First, Durkheim says that if we want to understand social life, we must rely solely on social variables—not on biological, psychological, or theological variables, for instance. Many social scientists are in apparent agreement with at least part of Durkheim's approach. **The Seville Statement on Violence** is a case in point. In the mid-1980s, the Spanish National Commission for UNESCO convened an international meeting of scientists in Seville, Spain, at which a dogmatic statement, known as The Seville Statement on Violence, was adopted. UNESCO, the United Nations' educational, scientific, and cultural organization adopted it in 1989. The Seville Statement on Violence says that science shall not look to biology for answers regarding why people engage in violence and war. This document dogmatically asserts that "It is scientifically incorrect" to say any of the following five things: that humans have a violent brain, that war is caused by instinct or any single motivation, that humans have inherited a tendency to make war from our animal ancestors, that war or any other violent behavior is genetically programmed into human nature, and that in the course of human evolution there has been a selection for aggressive behavior more than for other kinds of behavior. It is important to recognize that this document has nothing to do with the findings of science but much to do with a significant attempt by an important stakeholder to legitimize a particular point of view to the total exclusion of alternative points of view, regardless of the results of empirical inquiry. Even scientists can act unscientifically. The Seville Statement on Violence has received endorsement by the American Sociological Association, the American Psychological Association, and the American Anthropological Association. Even professional associations can act unscientifically.

The second thing Durkheim says that we need to do in order to understand social life sociologically is that we must use the scientific method as our way of knowing. Durkheim was after all, a positivist and he was endeavoring to establish sociology as a positivist social science.

What is the scientific method as a way of knowing? As a way of knowing, **science** is a logical system that bases knowledge on direct systematic observation. Science is an empirical endeavor. Science as a way of knowing utilizes direct systematic observations derived from the senses (sight, hearing, smell, taste, touch) to develop general principles about a delimited range of phenomena. Science states these general principles in such a way that any competent person may test them, and, on the basis of the results, arrive at a decision whether to accept or to reject them. In other words, you do not have to be a rocket scientist in order to "do science." Any competent person can do science.

Concepts, Variables, Measurement, and Hypotheses

Science has its own language. Let us look at some of the basic language of science.

A basic building block of science is a concept. In science, concepts are "abstract elements representing classes of phenomena within the field of study" (Babbie, 1998: 52). In sociology, "social class" is a concept, as are "norm," "value," and "culture." A variable is a special kind of concept. A **variable** is a characteristic that is common to a number of individuals, objects, groups, or events, and that has either different degrees of magnitude or different categories (for example, eye color: blue, brown, green, hazel, "other") so that individual cases differ in the extent to which they possess the characteristic (expressed in numerical values) or in the category of the characteristic into which they fall. If a variable is considered to be a cause, it is an **independent variable**. In the statement, "Carelessness causes forest fires," carelessness is the independent variable. If a variable is considered the effect, the result, it is termed a **dependent variable.** In the statement, "Carelessness causes forest fires," forest fires is the dependent variable.

A hypothesis is a basic statement that is tested in research. A **hypothesis** is a tentative, testable statement about the relationship between two or more variables; the statement is intended to be tested empirically and either verified or rejected. A scientific hypothesis may be derived from a theoretical system, from the results of prior research, or from your observations of the empirical world.

The use of variables in science depends on **measurement**, a procedure for determining the value of a variable in a specific case. See Table 1.3 on levels of measurement. The assignment of symbols, usually numbers, to the properties of objects or events is called measurement. **Quantitative data** are data in numerical form. They are gathered through measurement and enumeration. Quantitative analysis--also termed quantitative research or quantitative methodology--refers to analysis, research, or methodology that is based on precise measurement and enumeration.

TABLE 1.3 **LEVELS OF MEASUREMENT**

Name	Characteristics of the Attributes of the Variable
Nominal	• Mutual exclusiveness • Exhaustiveness
Ordinal	• Mutual exclusiveness • Exhaustiveness • Logical rank ordering (from greater to lesser, older to younger, etc.)
Interval	• Mutual exclusiveness • Exhaustiveness • Logical rank ordering • Equal distance between the attributes • No true/absolute zero
Ratio	• Mutual exclusiveness • Exhaustiveness • Logical rank ordering • Equal distance between the attributes • True/absolute zero

Some variables are easy to measure, such as when you step on the bathroom scale to ascertain your weight or when you use a thermometer to find out if you have a fever. Sociological variables can be more challenging to measure. For instance, how would you measure a person's social class? If you were a Marxist conflict theorist, you might ask about the person's relation to the economic means of production. Do they own the economic means of production (bourgeoisie)? Do they sell their labor to those who own the economic means of production (proletariat)? Or if you were a structural functionalist, you might ask about a person's income, occupation, and education. Because there are many ways to measure complex variables such as social class, researchers need to make decisions about how to operationalize a variable. **Operationalization** is a process or procedure by which a variable is quantified or stated in numerical form. Operationalization is a set of precise, explicit, detailed instructions for how a researcher measures concepts and variables. This allows researchers to measure any changes that occur in the variable. The researcher must operationalize each of the variables that are used in her or his research. Also, the researcher needs to address both the validity and the reliability of the measures chosen.

Our appreciation of research methods is enhanced by understanding the concepts of validity and reliability. **Validity** refers to the correspondence between what a measuring instrument is supposed to measure and what it actually measures. To the extent that a measuring instrument measures what it is supposed to measure, to that extent it has validity. See Box 1.1 on some types of validity.

In contrast, **reliability** refers to the extent to which the same or similar results are obtained when a researcher uses the same measurement instrument on the same or a similar sample or population of subjects. For instance, when I step on my bathroom scale, the scale says that I weigh 120 pounds. When I step on the same scale the next morning, it says that I weigh 120 pounds. When I step on the same scale a week later, it says that I weigh 120 pounds. This particular measuring instrument (the bathroom scale) is characterized by high reliability. See Box 1.2 on types of validity.

BOX 1.1

SOME VARIETIES OF VALIDITY

Because a measure may be valid by one standard and invalid by another, it can be misleading to speak of validity without specifying the criterion by means of which validity is being assessed. The implication is that a researcher needs to specify the types of validity a measurement instrument possesses or that it lacks. It is not sufficient merely to say, "It lacks validity." The researcher needs to be specific in her or his assessment by noting, for instance, "While it lacks construct validity, content validity, and criterion-related validity, it has face validity."

CONSTRUCT VALIDITY

The extent to which a measure relates to other variables as predicted by theory is termed *construct validity*. Operationalizing the concept "delinquency" as someone below the age of majority who uses illegitimate means to attain a legitimate goal has construct validity from the point of view of Robert K. Merton's theory of anomie. It has construct validity.

CONTENT VALIDITY

The extent to which a measure covers the range of meanings included in a concept is termed *content validity*. The greater the extent to which a measure covers the range of meanings conveyed by a concept, the greater its content validity. Operationalizing the concept "delinquent" as a person below the age of majority who commits a behavior that would not be criminal if that person were an adult lacks content validity. It fails adequately to cover the range of meanings included within the concept. Thus, in addition to the particular meaning indicated in the proposed operational definition, the concept also commonly refers to persons below the age of majority who are deemed by the juvenile court (1) to be in need of care, (2) to have been neglected, or (3)to have committed acts that would be criminal if the perpetrator were an adult.

CRITERION-RELATED VALIDITY

The extent to which a measure is correlated with an external criterion is its criterion-related validity. The greater the extent to which a measure relates to an external criterion, the greater its criterion-related validity. The validity of the Graduate Record Exam and of the Scholastic Aptitude Test is demonstrated by the4 ability of the test to predict college success of students.

FACE VALIDITY

If a measure makes sense as an indicator of a concept, it has face validity. Using income as an indicator of social class seems to make sense "on the face of it" without a great deal of explanation. It has face validity.

INTERNAL VALIDITY

This type of validity refers to the extent to which the results of a study accurately depict whether one variable is or is not a cause of another (Babbie, 1995; Rubin and Babbie, 1993). The level of

internal validity of a study depends on how well the methodology of the study has controlled for threats to internal validity.

EXTERNAL VALIDITY

This refers to the extent to which the findings depicted in a sample or study may legitimately be generalized to settings, populations, and conditions beyond the study conditions. As a general rule, studies based on probability sampling techniques tend to have far higher external validity than those that utilize nonprobability sampling techniques.

BOX 1.2

SOME TYPES OF RELIABILITY

Inter-rater reliability (also known as inter-judge reliability or inter-observer reliability) This type of reliability addresses how *stable* a measure is over several (more than one) raters or judges. If the measurement is not stable over several judges or raters, then changes that you observe in your study may have less to do with real changes in the phenomenon being observed than with the *unreliability of the measuring instrument.* In this type of reliability, the researcher looks at the extent to which the raters agree on their ratings. Inter-rater reliability may be measured in several ways, including the percentage of agreement among the judges.

Test-retest reliability This type of reliability addresses how *stable* a measure is over time. A reliable instrument is stable over repeated administrations. If the measurement is not stable over time, then changes that you observe in your study may have less to do with real changes in the phenomenon being observed than with the *unreliability of the measuring instrument.*

Parallel-forms reliability In this type of reliability, the researcher develops more than one version of the measuring instrument. "Forms" refers to alternate versions of the same measuring instrument. "Parallel" forms are measuring instruments that really do measure the same thing—that is to say, they really are equivalent to each other.

Parallel forms are developed so that they may be used when the researcher wants to obtain essentially the same information from the same people at several different but close-together times and the researcher does not want exposure to the test at one time to affect the respondents' answers at other times. Parallel forms reliability is measured using a correlation coefficient between or among the forms. The correlations among the forms represent the extent of parallel forms reliability.

Split-half reliability Sometimes it is impractical or undesirable to assess reliability with more than one instrument or to have multiple instrument administrations. For instance, the researcher may be under tight time or monetary constraints or the research subjects would not be available for multiple administrations of the instrument.

In split-half reliability, a measuring instrument is developed. It is administered. The test is divided into halves before it is scored. The halves are scored separately. Then the score of one half of the test is compared to the score of the other half of the test.

The most commonly used way to do this is to assign odd numbered items to one-half of the test and the even numbered items to the other half. The researcher computes the correlation of scores between the two halves by using a correlation coefficient. The correlation between the two halves of the test represents the extent of split-half reliability.

Logical Models of Theory Construction

The foundation of theory is a set of assumptions and axioms. An **axiom** is a statement whose truth is so well established that it is unquestioned and virtually accepted universally in a scientific community, or it is self-evident. Of course, what is self-evident today may not be tomorrow and what is accepted unquestioningly at one point in time (e.g., Newtonian physics) may not be at another point in time. If the foundations of a theory are rejected according to the steps of the scientific method, the validity of that theory collapses. In other words, the axioms and assumptions that underlie a scientific theory are important. Discredit them effectively and you discredit the theory. At least in part, perhaps this is the reason that people who adhere to a particular theory seem to become uneasy when a scientist questions the assumptions and axioms on which their pet theory rests.

There are two logical models by means of which theory is constructed, induction and deduction. In research methods, **deduction** is the logical model in which specific hypotheses are developed on the basis of general principles. This is the traditional logical model of science. Sometimes deduction is described as reasoning from the general (e.g., theory) to the particular (e.g., hypothesis) or as applying a theory to a particular case.

In research methods, **induction** is a logical model in which general principles are developed from specific observations. Sometimes induction is described as reasoning from particular instances to the general, or as arguing from facts to theory. In this model, one starts from observed data and develops a generalization (e.g., a theory) which explains the relationship between the objects observed. Sherlock Holmes uses this method. For instance, he might notice that a man who has come to Holmes's office for advice has a Chinese coin as a decoration on a pocket-watch chain, that his right hand is a half-size larger than the left, that he has a tattoo of a certain shape and color, that his tie has a gravy stain on it, that his shoes are scuffed and that his hat has a dent in it. From this he inducts that the man had been a manual laborer at some point (one hand is larger than the other), had been to China (the coin and the tattoo), and that he had fired his maid within the past week (gravy stain on the tie, scuffed shoes, dent in the hat). Within sociology, grounded theory, sometimes used in field work, uses this method (Glaser and Straus, 1967). Grounded theory is addressed below, in our exploration of field research.

Some researchers prefer one of these models to the other. It is important to appreciate, however, that these logical models are not mutually exclusive and one model is not "better" than the other. Many researchers move from induction to deduction and back to induction, and so forth, over the course of a research project.

Purposes of Sociological Research

The scientific method as a way of knowing has prediction as its ultimate goal. Sociological research often serves additional purposes as well. Three of the most common purposes of research are exploration, description, and explanation (Rubin and Babbie, 1993). A research project may, and usually does, have more than one purpose.

EXPLORATION: EXPLORATORY RESEARCH

Sometimes you are interested in a topic about which you and everyone else know practically nothing. You decide to engage in research to provide a beginning familiarity with the topic. Such research is termed *exploratory.*

Sociologist Laud Humphreys (1970) was interested in the phenomenon of impersonal sex in public restrooms, which is known as tearoom trade, and he conducted exploratory research to gain a beginning familiarity with the topic. He did this by going to public bathrooms located in public parks in a large city and he volunteered at each place to be a "watch queen"—somebody who keeps an eye out for the police. If he noticed the approach of a police officer, he warned the people inside who were engaging in quick, anonymous, same-sex sexual encounters so that they could stop doing whatever it was that they were doing.

Humphreys noticed that many of the men who came to the public toilet drove there in cars. He jotted down the license plate numbers of each of those cars. He then got the home addresses and name of the person to whom the automobile was registered, after which he would gather basic demographic information on that household—occupational/income level, marital status, number of children, and so on. He did not reveal the true purpose of being there; instead, he gave a bogus reason.

Through the use of such ruses, sociologist Laud Humphreys discovered that those who engage in impersonal sex in public bathrooms frequently are married, middle-class males who have children, a spouse, a nice job, and are well-respected members of their communities.

Every form and method of research has advantages and disadvantages. An advantage of exploratory research is that it gives us a beginning familiarity with a topic about which there previously had been no scientific information. The major limitation of exploratory research is a product of its very nature: lack of generalizability of research results. Thus, we cannot generalize the findings of Laud Humphreys' study to tearoom trade in other cities or to other countries. In other words, Laud Humphreys study of tearoom trade study tells us something, but what it tells us is quite limited.

DESCRIPTION: DESCRIPTIVE RESEARCH

In *descriptive research*, a researcher observes deliberately and carefully and then describes what is observed. Field research and survey research are descriptive methods appropriate for many research problems.

A Gallup Poll on the attitudes of the American population is an example of descriptive research. If a survey is properly constructed and implemented, and if its results are properly analyzed, a survey can describe a population while making appropriate allowances for the degree of error that exists. Descriptive research is useful for answering the "What" variety of questions: What is the leading cause of death among people aged 13-26 in the United States? What are the voting intentions of the electorate in the upcoming presidential election?

EXPLANATION: EXPLANATORY RESEARCH

Reporting the number of gangs in a city at a given point in time is descriptive research. Reporting *why* some cities have more gangs and more violent gang activity than others, and reporting *why* some cities have more violent gang activity at one point in time than at another are matters of *explanatory research.* A researcher has an explanatory purpose, for example, if she or he wants to explain why someone who is battered remains with the battering spouse.

When one answers "why" questions, one is, in essence, arguing cause and effect. One is making an argument that variable X causes variable Y. What do you need to do in order to prove cause and effect to a scientific audience? Essentially, you need to do three things. You need to demonstrate (1) temporal order, (2) correlation, and (3) check for spuriousness. Let us now look at each of these tasks.

Proving Cause and Effect Relationships

1. Temporal Order

The first requirement in demonstrating cause and effect is to demonstrate that the cause precedes the effect in time. This sometimes is referred to as temporal order: the independent variable must precede the dependent variable in time. While this sounds simple and straightforward, it often causes problems. With an unclear time order, one cannot convincingly make a causal argument. **Causal reasoning** is reasoning about cause and effect.

Suppose, for example, that research reveals, as in fact it does in the United States, that poor people are more likely than affluent people to suffer from schizophrenia. The research question is--which comes first, the mental illness or class position? Does mental illness cause lowered class position? Or is it the other way around--the stresses of being poor actually bring on, or cause, mental illness?

2. Correlations

The second requirement for a causal relationship is that there is a correlation between the independent and dependent variables. With regard to quantitative variables, sociologists use the terms relationship, correlation, and association interchangeably. A correlation between two (or more) quantitative variables refers to a relationship wherein an increase or decrease in the magnitude of one variable is associated with the magnitude of the other(s). When two variables are highly correlated, it is possible to predict the magnitude of one variable from knowledge of the magnitude of the other.

Relationships between variables also may be described as positive or negative. A correlation is termed **direct** (or **positive**) if as one variable increases in size or magnitude the other increases in size or magnitude; as one variable decreases in size or magnitude, the other decreases in size or magnitude. For instance, there is a direct (also known as a positive) relationship between education and income in the United States: as education increases, income increases; as education decreases, income decreases.

Relationships may be described as **negative** (or **inverse**): as one variable decreases in size or magnitude, the other increases in size or magnitude; as one variable increases in size or magnitude, the other decreases. For example, there is an inverse relationship in the United States today between social class and cigarette

smoking: as social class increases, the percent of people who smoke decreases; as social class decreases, the percent of people who smoke increases. There also is an inverse relationship in the United States today between social class and obesity: the higher the social class, the lower the percent of persons who are obese; the lower the social class, the higher the percent of persons who are obese.

Relationships may be described as *linear*, which is the simplest form of relationship, or as *curvilinear*. Positive and negative relationships are examples of linear relationships. In a curvilinear relationship, as variable X increases in size or magnitude, variable Y increases (or decreases) in size or magnitude up to a certain point, and then as X continues to increase in size or magnitude, Y decreases (or increases) in size or magnitude. If drawn on a graph, this curve would be an upside down "U." Another example of a curvilinear correlation is the relationship between family form and type of society (Goode, 1963).

3. Checking for Spuriousness

The third requirement for a causal relationship is that the relationship between two variables cannot be explained away as being due to the influence of a third variable that is the cause of them both. This is sometimes referred to as the issue of spuriousness.

A relationship between two variables is considered as *spurious* when it is actually accounted for by the relationship of the two variables to a third variable. For example, a relationship is observed between the size of a person's social-support network and health status: People with larger social-support networks tend to be healthier than persons with smaller (or no) social-support networks. It is possible that a third variable, such as age, accounts for both variables. And as people age, their friends and family members die; this can shrink the size of social-support networks. As people age, their bodies fall apart--even if they jog, even if they eat their vegetables and fruits. This manifests itself in increased **morbidity**, which is illness. In other words, age may account both for size of social-support network and health status. This is an empirical question, and it can be answered empirically. Were it the case that age accounts both for size of social-support network and for health status, we would say that the original relationship between size of social-support group and health status is spurious.

The insightful reader may have gleaned from the above discussion the important observation that *correlation is not causation*. Correlation is necessary for causation, but it is not sufficient. "X" (the independent variable) may occur in time prior to "Y" (the dependent variable). "X" and "Y" may also be correlated. Yet, it is still possible that "X" is not the cause of "Y." It is possible that some third variable is the cause of both "X" and "Y," in which case we would say that the original relationship between "X" and "Y" is spurious.

To review, most sociologists consider two variables as causally related when it has been demonstrated that (1) the cause precedes the effect in time, (2) there is an association between the two variables, and (3) no likely third variable is the cause of both of them.

Ethics of Research with Human Subjects

Sociologists not only do science, we aim to do science without harming those who are studied. In other words, as sociologists, we do science within the parameters of ethical guidelines whose purpose is the protection of human subjects from harm. Conducting research without regard to ethical principles that protect human subjects can lead to harming people.

An **ethic** is a principle of right or of good conduct. *Ethics* refers to the study of the general nature of morals and of concrete moral choices. Whenever sociologists study, or engage in research involving, human subjects, it is necessary that we follow the ethical guidelines that prevail in sociology (American Sociological Association, 2008) and in allied fields of inquiry. These ethical guidelines include the following eight:

1. ***Voluntary participation***. The research subjects need to be informed that their participation in the study is strictly voluntary and that they may withdraw without penalty at any time they choose and that they may expect no rewards for participation (e.g., early release from prison, custody of their children).

2. ***Informed consent.*** Before they are included in a study, all subjects must be fully informed about the consequences of participation--psychological, emotional, economic, physical, and so forth. In participating, subjects sometimes are asked to confront aspects of themselves or of their lives that may be particularly painful. Subjects need to be informed of this ahead of time. Please see anonymity and confidentiality below.

3. ***Do no harm.*** Just as physicians take an oath to do no harm, so, too, social researchers must do no harm to the subjects in a research project. As researchers, we must not embarrass them, degrade them, endanger their friendships or relationships with family members or with employers, lower their self-esteem, and so forth.

   For instance, if we are conducting research in a small community, and if we include direct quotations from respondents, it is possible that respondents or other members of the community may be able to recognize a response as having been made by a particular individual. That may cause a person embarrassment or even more severe harm. Similarly, research subjects might request a copy of the research report, and the research report may be published as a popular book. Research subjects may be able to identify themselves in various tables in the report and might find themselves characterized as highly authoritarian, homophobic, racist, and anti-democratic. Some of the characterizations are likely to threaten their sense of self worth. Thus, while doing no harm to subjects is easy to accept in the abstract, it is sometimes difficult to execute in particular situations.

4. ***Anonymity***. The researcher protects the identity of all research subjects. By doing this, the researcher helps to protect them from harm. When a researcher promises **anonymity** [An-non-NIM-i-tee], the researcher is unable to identify a particular response with a particular respondent.

5. ***Confidentiality***. When a researcher promises **confidentiality**, the researcher *is* able to identify a particular response with a particular respondent but promises not to do so publicly. If a subject's

participation is confidential but not anonymous, the researcher has an ethical obligation to make this known to the subject as part of informed consent.

6. ***No deception.*** It is unethical to deceive research subjects. Deception, if used in sociological or social-science research, needs to be justified and outweighed by compelling scientific or administrative concerns. Even then, the ethics remain arguable, questionable.

7. ***Truthfulness in Analysis.*** As a researcher, you have ethical obligations to your colleagues in the scientific community. You have the ethical obligation to be straightforward and honest about the findings, shortcomings, and failures of your study. Avoid the temptation to make findings sound like the result of a well-planned study when they are not. Many findings in science are serendipitous.

8. ***Reporting.*** If there are findings that undermine the point you are making, you have the ethical obligation to report them and to discuss their implications for the findings of your study. If you have findings that are surprising or anomalous, you have the ethical obligation to report them as such. Also, there is an ethical obligation to share your research with others. This is how the scientific knowledge base of a field of study grows. There are many venues for sharing research. For instance, a scientist may share her/his research at a symposium, conference, or workshop, or by other means of publication, such as submitting the research for publication in a scholarly journal.

Following these ethical guidelines for conducting research with human subjects enables sociologists to study human subjects without harming people. Many universities have standing committees, known as Institutional Review Boards (I.R.B.), for the protection of human subjects. Faculty (and students) who wish to engage in research with human subjects must first submit their research proposals to the I.R.B. and have their proposals assessed by the I.R.B. as acceptable, before they are permitted to conduct their research.

PROCEDURES OF EMPIRICAL INVESTIGATION: DATA GATHERING TECHNIQUES

Qualitative Methodology: Field Research

Qualitative methodology refers to analysis or methodology that is not based on precise measurement and quantitative claims or statements. For instance, if our goal is to acquire a subjective understanding of a particular group of people, we might make observations of their daily lives without counting instances of particular behaviors. Such research could be described as qualitative.

Field research refers to a way of knowing "that results from deep involvement in, or intimate familiarity with, the settings, activities, and persons studied" (Holstein and Gubrium, 1992: 711). Field research examines people as they go about their everyday lives. Any and all research that has this characteristic--that takes place "in the field"--may be referred to as field research. Field researchers avoid as much as possible any alterations of or artificial interference with the settings and persons studied. They conduct formal and informal interviews. They make observations of activities, interactions, events, and settings. They interact with and talk with people in naturalistic settings. They inspect formal documents (an organization's mission statement, grant proposals) and informal documents (e.g., unpublished diaries, letters).

The ultimate goal of field research is the development of theoretical insights about social life. A more immediate goal is to produce an **ethnography** [eth-NOG-graf-ee], an empirically based analytical description of social life. There are many approaches to the analysis of field data. Many have in common the goal of producing theoretical generalizations based on field observations. An example of this inductive approach is Barney Glaser and Anselm Strauss's **grounded theory** (1967). Glaser and Strauss coined the term grounded theory to refer to the inductive method of observing social life and then developing theory through observation.

In **participant observation** the researcher joins and participates in a group, culture, or subculture, and over time investigates, in great detail, the group's attitudes, values, norms, and views of the world from that group's perspective. This method is commonly used by sociologists and anthropologists to investigate a particular group, culture, or subculture. In this approach researchers must decide the roles they will occupy in the setting--complete observer, participant as observer, observer as participant, or complete participant, among others. The ethics of covert field research are debated by sociologists and by other field researchers (Denzin, 1989). In participant observation the researcher exists in two worlds--the one of the investigator and the other of the participant.

With this approach one is able to discover the myths, norms, symbols, nonverbal communications, leadership structures, cliques, hierarchy, rituals, and kinship patterns of the group. Good examples of research utilizing participant observation as a data-gathering methodology include Elliot Liebow's *Tally's Corner* (1967), William Foote Whyte's *Street Corner Society* (1955), James Spradely and Brenda Mann's *The Cocktail Waitress* (1974), Napoleon Chagnon's *The Yanomamo* (1983), Kai T. Erikson's *All in Its Path* (1976), and Howard Becker's *Boys in White* (1961) and *The Outsiders* (1963).

Quantitative Methodology: Survey Research

One variety of quantitative analysis is survey research. **Survey research** refers to the systematic gathering of data about individuals and collectivities through use of the interview or questionnaire, analyzing the resulting data through statistical analyses, and interpreting the results. Survey research is widely cited as the data-gathering technique most frequently used by sociologists.

The purpose of survey research may be descriptive, exploratory, or even causal. Descriptive research relies heavily on descriptive statistics. Descriptive surveys mainly analyze the data in percentage frequency counts and report the data in tabular form. For instance, in a general election in the U.S. the percent of women, African-Americans, and Hispanics who vote for a particular presidential candidate may be compared with comparable results from previous years.

SAMPLING

In statistics, a distinction is made between a sample and a population. A **population** is the total number of cases with a given characteristic or characteristics, or all members of a given class or set. Thus, we may speak of the population of females in the United States or the population of Hispanic males in Kansas. A **sample** is part of a population.

Probability Sampling

To people unfamiliar with both the theory of probability and the theory of sampling, it seems mysterious that a sample of 1500 persons could represent the voting intentions of people aged 21 years or older in the United States. It also seems bewildering that those 1500 persons can be used to estimate, within known degrees of error, the extent to which values calculated from it (say, the percent who say they would vote for a particular candidate for President) are likely to deviate from the values that would have been obtained had the entire population of persons aged 21 or older been surveyed. The estimate of that error is known as *sampling error*.

Estimates of the amount of sampling error can only be made legitimately if one is using probability sampling. A sample is a **probability sample** if it has been drawn in accord with *probability* theory. Probability theory is part of mathematics and it is heavily relied upon by social scientists. In probability sampling some mechanism of random sampling is used to select respondents. A **random sample** is one in which every case in the population has an equal probability of being selected. For instance, in a random sample of adults aged 21 years or older in the United States, every person aged 21 or older in the U.S. would have the same chance of being selected. In a random sample of households, each household has the same chance of being selected. When we use probability-sampling techniques, we may legitimately generalize the results from our sample to a larger population.

Non-Probability Sampling

A sample is a **non-probability sample** if it is not possible to determine the probability—the statistical chance—that each case in the population has of being included in the sample. The proverbial "person on the street" interview is an example of a non-probability sample. Examples of non-probability samples include samples of convenience (sometimes called accidental sampling), purposive sampling (sometimes called judgmental sampling), snowball sampling, and quota sampling.

QUESTIONING AND QUESTIONNAIRES

Asking people questions as a way of gathering information for analysis and interpretation is often used in survey research, in field work, and even in experiments. There are various modes of question administration.

An interviewer in an interview may ask the questions. The interview may take place face-to-face or over the telephone. The questions may be written down. If written down, a researcher might give or mail the questions to the respondents who are asked to complete them. This procedure is termed *self-administration*. Whatever the mode of administration, we may refer to the sets of questions as *questionnaires*. When an interviewer asks the questions, we may refer to the questionnaire as an *interview schedule*. When the questions are written down and given or mailed to respondents to complete, we may refer to the questionnaires as self-administered questionnaires (Rubin and Babbie, 1993).

Types of Questions

OPEN-ENDED QUESTIONS

In designing questions, a researcher must decide whether to ask open-ended or closed-ended questions. In *open-ended questions*, the respondents provide answers of their own design. For instance, community members might be asked, "What do you feel is the most important problem facing your community today with regard to which the police could be of service?" An interviewer could write down the exact response of the respondent, or a space could be provided for the respondent to write her or his response.

CLOSED-ENDED QUESTIONS

In contrast, in *closed-ended questions*, the respondent is asked to select an answer from a menu of possible responses provided by the researcher. For instance, respondents might be provided with the following statement: "Illegal drugs are the biggest problem faced by our community today" and be asked if they "Strongly Agree," "Agree," have "No Opinion," "Disagree," or "Strongly Disagree." This procedure, named after Rensis Likert who developed it, is known as a Likert scale. Likert-scale questions can be used profitably in questionnaires.

THE ANALYSIS OF RESEARCH DATA

Data Coding and Data Entry

After data are gathered, they normally are entered into a computer file for statistical analysis. This process is called data entry. Data usually are coded in numerical form. Thus, the gender of the respondents might be coded as 1 = Female, 2 = Male, 9 = No Response. If open-ended questions are used, an intermediate step is necessary. For the answers to each question, the researcher first must devise mutually exclusive and all-inclusive categories and then must code the answers of each respondent.

Descriptive Statistics: Measures of Central Tendency

After data have been entered into a computer file for statistical analysis, the researcher may want to describe the data set. Useful descriptive statistics include **measures of central** tendency. Central tendency refers to the grouping of data around the center or middle of a distribution or array of data and, hence, to what is "typical" or "average" in a data array. There are several measures of the average. Three types of "averages," which in statistics are called "measures of central tendency," are the mean, the median, and the mode. Each measure of central tendency has its advantages and disadvantages.

- MEAN: The mean is the most commonly used measure of central tendency, because it is so easy to calculate. The mean of a data set is simply the sum of the measures in the data set divided by the number of measures in the data set. Data must be measured at the interval-level or higher in order to calculate the mean. Note well: The mean is a misleading as a summary measure of a data set if the data are not normally distributed, i.e., if the data set is skewed. If a data set departs significantly from that of a normal distribution, it is skewed. It is conventional practice to represent the mean of a sample by the figure $\overline{x}$ (which is pronounced as X-bar).

Example: Here is a data set: 1, 6, 7, 8, 11, 80. Calculate the mean.

Solution:

1+6+7+8+11+80 = 113

113/6 = 18.9 or 19 is the mean.

- **MEDIAN:** The median is the middle value in a set of numbers that has been arranged from lowest to highest. **Note well**: The median is a good measure of central tendency to use when the data set is skewed. It may be calculated on ordinal-level and interval-level data.

How to calculate the median:

(1) ***In a data set that has an odd number of items:***

Solution:

Rank order the items from lowest to highest

Position of median = (N+1)/2, where N = the number of items in the data set.

Example: Here is a data set: 25, 11, 13, 12, 16, 17, 20. Calculate the median.

Solution:

Rank order the items from lowest to highest

raw number:	11	12	13	**16**	17	20	25
rank order:	1	2	3	4	5	6	7

Apply the Formula

Formula: (7 + 1) / 2 = 8 / 2 = 4

Thus, the position of the median is in the fourth slot according to rank order. Thus, the median is 16.

(2) ***In a data set that has an even number of items:*** **The median is the mean of the middle two ranks.**

Example: Here is a data set: 26 11 25 12 13 21 17 16. Calculate the median.

Solution:

Rank order the items from lowest to highest

Compute the mean of the middle two ranks

Raw number:	11	12	13	**16**	**17**	21	25	26
Rank order:	1	2	3	**4**	**5**	6	7	8

Mean of the middle two ranks = (16+17) / 2 = 33 / 2 = **16.5**

Thus, the value of the Median is **16.5**

- **MODE:** The mode is the most frequent value in a distribution. Some distributions have no mode, because all values appear with equal frequency. Some distributions have more than one mode. For instance, in the following data distribution: 11, 14, 17, 17, 18, 18, 20, 25, 29, 37--there are two modes (17, 18). Each of these values appears twice and no value appears more than twice. Appropriate levels of measurement include nominal, ordinal, and interval. The word "mode" is a noun. The word "modal" is the adjectival form of the noun, mode.

Making Sense of the Data

Data are analyzed in terms of sociological theory, logical analysis, sociological analysis, tabular presentation, and statistical measures. Altogether, these tools assist the researcher in constructing meaning out of mountains of data and thereby provide a basis for a final report.

The general principle, which is contrary to common sense, is that the answers people give to questions do not speak for themselves. This is the case even with closed-ended questions, and even if the questions are both well-constructed and based on a national probability sample of adequate size. Answers acquire meaning when they are compared to something. The comparison may be across time. For instance, you compare the answers of a probability sample to a particular question this year with the answers to the same question from a comparable probability sample of the same population four years ago. Comparisons may be across social categories (e.g., age, gender, race, ethnicity, years of education, marital status, religious affiliation, and so forth) or across other classifications (e.g., geographical region, rural-urban, city size).

Unobtrusive Research Methods

Unobtrusive methods are those methods that do not intrude on the phenomena being studied. For example, a sociologist may rummage systematically through the garbage beyond the curtilage of a dwelling in order to gather information about diet, social structure, and daily life in a community.

Experimental Research Methods

An **experiment** is an investigation in which there is controlled manipulation of the independent variable by the investigator and precise observation and measurement both of the variables and of the results. An experiment is a research method well suited to investigating relationships of cause and effect.

The term **mundane realism** refers to the extent to which an experiment is similar to everyday situations. When asked why they don't more frequently use the experimental method in gathering data, many sociologists reply that many experiments lack mundane realism. The implication is that if the experiment is not highly similar to real-life situations, it cannot tell us much that is enlightening. In contrast, **experimental realism** refers to the extent to which an experiment absorbs and involves the participants. When asked why they so frequently use the experimental method in their research, many social psychologists reply that experiments tend to be high in experimental realism. That is, the experiments tend to absorb the attentional and emotional resources of the research subjects.

As you know, science has its own language. A clear understanding of the concept of "random assignment" aids our understanding of the logic of the classical experimental design as a type of research. In the language of science, the term "random" means the opposite of what the word means in everyday conversation. (This is an example of the principle that the meaning of concepts is paradigm specific.) In everyday language, if we say that something is random—as in a random shooting—we mean to convey that we don't know the likelihood of its occurrence, that we have no way of knowing the likelihood of its occurrence This is one of the reasons why "random shootings" are so scary for so many people.

In the language of science, "random" means the opposite. Thus, when a researcher uses **random assignment** as the mechanism for allocating research subjects either to the experimental or the control

group, each person has a *known* (1 in 2) and the *same* (1 in 2) probability or chance of being assigned to one group as to the other. In an experiment, research subjects are assigned randomly to one of two experimental conditions: to the experimental group, where they are exposed to the independent variable, or to the control group, where they are not exposed to the independent variable. Each research subject has the same chance of being assigned to one group as to the other. This is the principle of random assignment, also known as randomization.

There are many types of experiments. The **classical experimental design** is characterized by **random assignment** of research subjects to one of two experimental conditions. Research subjects randomly assigned to the **experimental group** are exposed to the independent variable by the researcher. Research subjects randomly assigned to the **control group** are not exposed to the independent variable by the researcher.

Random assignment is a critical element in the classical experimental design. Why? Random assignment is viewed as making the research subjects virtually equivalent, except for exposure by the researcher to the independent variable. In other words, if random assignment is utilized, the young, the skinny, the old, the tall, the short, the rich, and the poor are equally likely to be assigned to the experimental and control groups. The only way the research subjects in the two groups differ significantly is in exposure by the experimenter to the independent variable.

If an element of the classical experimental design is absent, the experimental design is termed quasi-experimental, pseudo-experimental, or semi-experimental. If random assignment is not used to assign subjects to one of two experimental conditions, the term **comparison group** is used to designate those subjects not exposed to the experimental stimulus. There are many types of quasi-experimental designs. Social scientists refer to quasi-, pseudo-, semi-, and classical-experimental designs collectively as **experimental methods**.

Field experiments are prominent in program evaluation research, especially in applied areas. Applied areas are many and include education, public health, and proposed social-policy initiatives such as guaranteed minimum-income proposals (e.g., Rosenthal and Jacobson, 1968; Slavin and Karweit, 1985; Rowe, 1974a, 1974b; Jones, 1981; Hannan, Tuma, and Groeneveld, 1977). Also, there are field experiments in the areas of juvenile and criminal justice (e.g., McCord and McCord, 1959a, 1959b; Rossi, Berk, and Lenihan, 1980; Zeisel, 1982).

Quasi-experimental research designs are especially relevant for sociologists in clinical practice and for social-service workers whose practice includes intervention programs for dysfunctional families, for juvenile-delinquency prevention and treatment, for living-skills programs for foster children, for parenting-skills programs for parents at risk of losing custody of their children, and so on.

Regardless of the area of your interests or career or vocational choice, understanding, comprehending, and mastering the tools of research can enhance your success. Either as consumers of research or as producers of it, you will be required to make judgments about a body of information or knowledge.

SUMMARY OF THE SCIENTIFIC METHOD

In this chapter you have studied various aspects of the scientific method as a way of perceiving and studying social life sociologically. Perhaps it would be useful at this point to summarize for you the steps of the scientific method. The scientific method consists of the following steps:

- Problem definition—Identify and define the problem.
- Statement of the research problem. State the research problem in terms of a particular theoretical framework and relate the research problem to findings of previous research, if any has been done.
- Statement of research problem as a hypothesis or hypotheses.
- Select an appropriate methodology or methodologies. Identify and define your independent and dependent variables. Operationalize all variables, justifying your measurement choices in terms of reliability and validity.
- Data collection. Collect the data.
- Data analysis. Analyze the data you have collected. Draw conclusion(s) from the data regarding the hypothesis or hypotheses, and relate the conclusion(s) to the original body of theory with which the study began. Suggest lines of future research.

Everything has advantages (strengths) and disadvantages (weaknesses), including the various methods of data collection. See Graphic 1.1 on the advantages and disadvantages of survey research, field research, and the experiment as methods of data collection.

GRAPHIC 1.1 STRENGTHS AND WEAKNESSES OF VARIOUS METHODS OF DATA COLLECTION

METHOD	STRENGTHS	WEAKNESSES
Survey Research	• Ability to describe large populations, using probability sampling techniques • Ability to establish causality	• Expensive • Time Consuming • May not be able to provide an insider's view (subjective understanding)
Field Research	• Opportunity to study insider's view • Inexpensive	• Cannot generalize beyond one case (lack of external validity) • Difficult to establish causal relationship • Lack of accurate measures • Non-probability sample • Data qualitative—difficult to quantify reliably and validly without sufficient knowledge of research methods
Experimental Methods	• Ability to isolate variables • Replication of study possible • Ability to establish causality	• Lack of mundane realism • External validity (may not be generalizable to research subjects not in the particular study) • Difficulty in obtaining volunteers

READING AND CONSTRUCTING TABLES

Sometimes a picture is worth a thousand words. Tables are visual devices (pictures) for presenting data to audiences. A well-constructed table is helpful to audiences while a poorly and inappropriately constructed one is not.

Let us now review the importance of tables in the research process and what the conventional guidelines are both for constructing and for reading tables. Scientists and other salient audiences who read the reports that you write assume that you are conversant with these guidelines. So, if you want your report to be intelligible to employers, to grant-proposal review boards, and to other consumers of research, you need to follow these guidelines when you write your report.

Tables do not mean much in the explanatory process unless they compare the target group with something. For instance, a table may compare the target group with the control group or with a comparison group, or the table may focus on within-group differences.

Constructing and reading tables requires *attention to detail.* If attention to detail does not come readily to you, please remember that practice can strengthen your abilities in this domain. Practice makes progress.

TABLE 1.4 CROSSTABULATION OF HYPOTHETICAL DATA ON CITY SIZE AND EDITORIAL POLICY REGARDING LEGALIZATION OF MARIJUANA, 2014

	CITY SIZE			
EDITORIAL POLICY	Cities Under 100,000 Population	Cities Over 100,000 Population	Total	
Favorable	**14** 11%	**140** 32%	**154** 27%	Row Marginals (row totals)
Unfavorable	**37** 29%	**175** 40%	**212** 38%	
Neutral	**76** 60%	**123** 28%	**199** 35%	
Total	**127** 22.5%	**438** 77.5%	**565** 100%	Total Sample Size

Source: Hypothetical data

Column Marginals (column totals)

REVIEW OF BASIC CONCEPTS

Statistical tables may be described as consisting, at least in part, of cells, rows, and columns. Table 1.4 presents hypothetical data on variations in editorial content (dependent variable) by city size (the independent variable). In a statistical table, a **cell** is the place for each entry of data. The cells provide for all possible combinations of the rows (horizontal) and columns (vertical) of the table. In a statistical table, a **row** refers to the horizontal listing of data in a series of categories, all of which have a common classification. In Table 1.4,

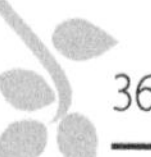

the categories "Favorable," "Unfavorable," and "Neutral" have in common that they are the categories of the variable Editorial Policy. A **row caption** or **row heading** is a title that describes the common classification of the data listed in the rows. In Table 1.4, the row caption is "Editorial Policy."

In a statistical table, a **column** refers to the vertical listing of data in a series of categories, all of which have a common classification. In Table 1.4, the categories "Cities Under 100,000 Population" and "Cities Over 100,000 Population" have in common that they are the categories of the variable, City Size. A **column heading** or **column caption** is a title that describes the common classification of the data listed in the columns. In Table 1.4, the column heading is "City Size."

It is customary to use the columns of a statistical table for the categories of the ***independent variable*** (cause) and the rows for those of the ***dependent variable*** (effect). In Table 1.4, the categories of the independent variable (city size) are located in the columns and those of the dependent variable (editorial content) are located in the rows.

This convention is helpful to someone who reads a table. For instance, let us say that you are reading a table and that you are temporarily confused: you can't tell what the independent variable is and what the dependent variable is. A partial solution presents itself as you remember that you can get a hint by looking at the table. *The physical location of variables on a table tells you something*: the independent variable is located in the columns and the dependent variable is located in the rows. In Table 1.4, city size is the independent variable and its categories are located in the columns. City size is broken down into two categories: cities under 100,000 population and cities of more than 100,000 population. The dependent variable, editorial policy regarding the legalization of marijuana, is located in the rows. The dependent variable is broken down into three categories: favorable, unfavorable, and neutral.

The term **frequency** refers to the number of occurrences of a particular value or category of a variable in a data set. A **frequency distribution** is a classification of data showing the raw or absolute number of occurrences of each subdivision, category, attribute, or value of a variable. A frequency distribution provides a basic ordering of the data in a data set. It is frequently the first step in statistical analysis. A frequency distribution may be displayed in a number of ways: in a table, a pie chart, or a bar chart, for instance. For example, in Table 1.4, in cities under 100,000 population, 11 % of the newspaper editorials favor the legalization of marijuana, 29% are unfavorable, and 60% are neutral. In contrast, in cities of more than 100,000 population, virtually *one-third* of the editorials favor the legalization of marijuana. The larger the city size, the greater the support for legalization of marijuana.

A score is termed raw and is called a **raw score,** or **absolute score**, if it reveals how much of the characteristic of interest is possessed by an individual (or by an event, object, and so forth). A raw score (raw number, absolute number) refers to any datum that provides an absolute, not relative, assessment of one's position on a quantitative variable. Raw scores provide a more precise form of measurement than do ranks. Whereas ranks are data that indicate relative position, raw scores indicate absolute position and provide information absolute comparisons. To say that Tony earned 93 points out of 100 possible on an exam, while Alfred earned 72 points on it is to make an absolute comparison. To say that Tony earned the second highest score while Alfred earned the second lowest score is to make a relative comparison.

A table may present data on just one variable, in which case it is referred to as a *univariate distribution*. A table displaying data on three or more variables is a *multivariate distribution*. A table presenting data on two variables is a *bivariate distribution*. More precisely, a bivariate frequency distribution refers to the joint presentation of the frequency distribution of two variables, both for the same sample or population of subjects. In a bivariate distribution, each category of one variable is combined with each possible category

of the other variable, and the raw number and percent of cases in each possible combination of categories is displayed.

Table 1.4 is a bivariate table or a bivariate distribution. In a bivariate frequency distribution, the cases are analyzed according to the attributes of the independent variable (city size), to discover differences on the dimensions of the dependent variable (editorial policy or stance regarding legalization of marijuana). In Table 1.4, in cities over 100,000 population, 32% of editorials favor the legalization of marijuana, 40% are unfavorable, and 28% are neutral.

A bivariate table sometimes is referred to as a **contingency table** or as a **cross-tabulation table** (or **cross-tab** for short). A contingency table or cross-tabulation table is a method of ordering and of displaying data so that a cross-classification of two or more variables is presented. The table presents the raw number of cases and the percent of cases falling in each combination of categories of the two or more variables.

The raw and percent frequency distributions of each variable, separately, can be found along the edges or margins of the table. Their physical locations are indicated in their names: **row marginals** and **column marginals**. These totals are called **marginal distributions**. In Table 1.4, the right margin provides a raw frequency and a percent distribution for editorial policies. Of the 565 editorials in this study, 154 (or 27%) are favorable to the legalization of marijuana, 212 (38%) are unfavorable, and 199 (35%) are neutral. Similarly, the marginal distribution of city size is found in the bottom margin of the cross-tab. These raw frequencies and percents for cities under 100,000 population and for cities over 100,000 population are the column totals, since city size is the variable heading the columns. Let us call cities under 100,000 population "small cities" and cities over 100,000 population "large cities." Thus, of the 565 editorials in the study, 127 (or 22.5%) came from small cities, and 438 (77.5%) are from large cities. The percentages in the marginals sometimes are called **total percents** because they are derived by dividing each frequency by the total sample size and multiplying the result by 100.

Contingency or cross-tabulation tables are the "bread and butter" of social research. You find them everywhere--in newspapers, in marketing research, in journal articles, in the Uniform Crime Reports, in the National Crime Victimization Surveys, and so on. With a little practice, cross-tabulations or contingency tables are easy to construct, to read, and to understand. We now look at the conventional guidelines for constructing and for presenting data in the form of contingency tables (cross-tabulation tables). Each time you construct a table, you should follow each of these guidelines.

PRINCIPLES OF TABLE CONSTRUCTION

1. ***All tables should be numbered***.

2. **All *tables should have a title*** that indicates what variables are contained in the table.

3. ***All tables should include column headings and row headings***.

4. ***The original raw data*** (sometimes called "hard" or "absolute" data) of the variables ***should be present in the table***. Traditionally the letter n or N is used to refer to the number of cases in a cell. In a cross-tab, present the raw number and percent of cases for each cell and for the row and column marginals.

Please note: If one is analyzing the responses to a question in a questionnaire or survey, it is crucial that you always present the exact wording of the original question or item being examined. Place this material either below the title of the table or below the table number.

5. ***Use no abbreviations*** in the table. Thus, if you are using states, spell out the name of each state. Write California instead of CA; write total percents, ***not*** total %.

6. ***Report all missing data*** in the table.

7. ***Easy to read and interpret***. Tables are presented for the reporting or analysis of information. They should be designed so that they are easy to read and uncomplicated to interpret.

8. ***Cite your sources fully***. Beneath each table, give full bibliographic information regarding the source of the data in the table.

CONCLUSION

All research is in some way connected to real-life events. If concepts are not clearly and precisely defined and measured, the results lack validity. Mastering the fundamentals of sociological inquiry is both exciting in itself and intrinsically worthwhile and it is also important in any career or endeavor. Many careers, including those in business, communications, human resource management, social services, journalism, law enforcement, corrections, and social policy analysis utilize and analyze social-science research. Employers are looking for these critical-thinking skills. In your job or career, you may be asked to conduct surveys, program evaluations, assessments, and interventions. Even as consumers, we need to know how to evaluate data and how to read tables if we want to understand and to contribute to the rapidly changing world of today and tomorrow. Mastering the skills of sociological inquiry directly benefits you both personally and professionally.

SUGGESTED READINGS

Babbie, Earl R., Basics of Social Research Sixth Edition (Belmont, CA: Cengage Wadsworth, 2014).

Babbie, Earl R., The Practice of Social Research 13th Edition (Belmont, CA: Wadsworth Cengage Learning, 2013).

Creswell, John W., Research Design: Qualitative, Quantitative, and Mixed Methods Approaches (Thousand Oaks, CA: SAGE Publications, 2014).

D'Souza, Dinesh, Obama's America: Unmaking the American Dream (Washington, D.C.: Regnery Publishing, Inc., 2012).

Garner, Roberta, Doing Qualitative Research: Designs, Methods, and Techniques (Upper Saddle River, NJ: Pearson Education, 2013).

Kagan, Robert, The World America Made (New York: Alfred A. Knopf, 2012).

Klass, Gary M., Just Plain Data Analysis: Finding, Presenting, and Interpreting Social Science Data Second Edition (Lanham, MD: Rowman & Littlefield, 2012).

Maxfield, Michael G., and Babbie, Earl R., Basics of Research Methods for Criminal Justice and Criminology Third Edition (Belmont, CA: Wadsworth Cengage Learning, 2012).

Ritzer, George, Contemporary Sociological Theory and Its Classical Roots: The Basics (New York: McGraw Hill, 2013).

Rubin, Allen, Essential Research Methods for Social Work Third Edition (Belmont, CA: Brooks/Cole Cengage Learning, 2013).

Sowell, Thomas A Conflict of Visions: Ideological Origins of Political Struggles (New York: Basic Books, 2007).

Sowell, Thomas, Intellectuals and Society Revised and Enlarged Edition (New York: Basic Books, 2011).

Turner, Jonathan H., Contemporary Sociological Theory (Thousand Oaks, CA: SAGE Publications, 2013).

Watson, George, The Lost Literature of Socialism Second Edition (Cambridge, England: Lutterworth Press, 2010).

BIBLIOGRAPHY

Allahyari, Rebecca Anne, Visions of Charity: Morality and the Politics of Homelessness (Berkeley, CA: University of California Press, 2000).

Almeling, Rene, "Selling Genes, Selling Gender: Egg Agencies, Sperm Banks, and the Medical Market in Genetic Material," American Sociological Review, Vol. 72. No. 3, (June) 2007: 319-340.

American Sociological Association, American Sociological Association Code of Ethics, 2008. As of November 2, 2012, available online at http://www.asanet.org/about/ethics.cfm

Andersen, Margaret, Thinking About Women: Sociological Perspectives on Sex and Gender (New York: McMillan Publishing Co., 1993).

Argyle, Michael, Cooperation: the Basis of Sociability (New York: Routledge, 1991).

Argyle, Michael, The Psychology of Happiness (New York: Routledge, 2002)

Argyle, Michael, The Psychology of Social Class (London: Routledge, 1994).

Argyle, Michael, The Social Psychology of Everyday Life (London: Routledge, 1992).

Babbie, Earl, The Practice of Social Research (Belmont, CA: Wadsworth Publishing Company, 1998).

BBC, "Speaking Out Over Jordan 'Honour Killings,'" February 27, 2003. As of October 28, 2012, available online at http://news.bbc.co.uk/2/hi/middle_east/2802305.stm

Becker, Howard S., Boys in White: Student Culture in Medical School (Chicago: University of Chicago Press, 1961).

Becker, Howard S., The Outsiders: Studies in the Sociology of Deviance (New York: The Free Press, 1963).

Berezin, Mabel, "Cultural Form and Political Meaning: State Subsidized Theater, Ideology, and Language of Style in Fascist Italy," American Journal of Sociology, Vol. 99, 1994: 1237-1286.

Bilefsky, Dan, "How to Avoid Honor Killing in Turkey? Honor Suicide," New York Times July 16, 2006, Section 1, p. 3.

Blair, C.A.; Thompson, L.F., and Wuensch, K.L., "Electronic Helping Behavior: The Virtual Presence of Others Makes a Difference," Basic and Applied Social Psychology, Vol. 27, 2005: 171-178.

Bonilla-Silva, Eduardo and Lewis, Amanda, "The 'New Racism': Toward An Analysis of the U.S. Racial Structure, 1960s-1990s," 1997, Department of Sociology, University of Michigan, Ann Arbor, MI. Unpublished manuscript.

Bonilla-Silva, Eduardo, "Rethinking Racism: Toward a Structural Interpretation," American Sociological *Review*, Vol. 62 (June) 1997: 465-480.

Chagnon, Napoleon A., The Yanamamo Third Edition (New York: Holt, Rinehart, and Winston, 1983).

Cooley, Charles Horton, Human Nature and the Social Order (New York: Schocken, 1964). (Originally published, 1902).

Daly, Kathleen, and Chesney-Lind, Meda, "Feminism and Criminology," Justice Quarterly, Vol. 5, 1988: 497-538.

De Beauvoir, Simon, The Second Sex (London: Jonathan Cape, 1949).

Denzin, Norman K., The Research Act Third Edition (Englewood Cliffs, NJ: Prentice Hall, 1989).

Douglas, Mary, Purity and Danger: An Analysis of Concepts of Pollution and Taboo (London, England: Routledge and Kegan Paul, 1966).

Durkheim, Emile, Rules of the Sociological Method Eighth Edition (Chicago: University of Chicago Press, 1938). Originally published 1895.

Epstein, Cynthia Fuchs, "2006 American Sociological Association Presidential Address—Great Divides: The Cultural, Cognitive, and Social Bases of the Global Subordination of Women," American Sociological Review, Vol. 72, No. 1, (February) 2007: 1-22.

Erikson, Kai, All in Its Path: Destruction of a Community in Buffalo Creek Flood (New York: Simon and Schuster, 1976).

Faludi, Susan, Backlash (New York: Anchor Books, 1992).

Ferguson, Niall, Civilization: The West and the Rest (New York: The Penguin Press, 2011).

Firestone, S., The Dialectics of Sex: The Case for a Feminist Revolution (New York: Morrow, 1970).

Gilligan, Carol, In a Different Voice (Cambridge, MA: Harvard University Press, 1982).

Glaser, Barney G., and Strauss, Anselm, The Discovery of Grounded Theory (Chicago, IL: Aldine, 1967).

Goode, Erich, Deviant Behavior (Fifth Edition) (Upper Saddle River, NJ: Prentice Hall, 1997).

Goode, William J., World Revolution and Family Patterns (New York: The Free Press, 1963).

Greer, G., The Female Eunuch (London: Verso, 1970).

Hannan, Michael, Tuma, Nancy Brandan, and Groeneveld, Lyle, "Income and Marital Events: Evidence from an Income Maintenance Experiment," American Journal of Sociology, Vol. 82, 1977: 1186-1211.

Hippensteele, Susan K., and Chesney-Lind, Meda, "Race and Sex Discrimination in the Academy," *Thought and Action*, Vol. 11, (Fall) 1995: 43-66.

Holstein, James A., and Gubrium, Jaber F., "Field Research Methods," in Edgar F. Borgatta and Marie L. Borgatta (Eds.), Encyclopedia of Sociology (New York: Macmillan Publishing Company, 1992), 711-716.

Humphreys, Laud, Tearoom Trade: Impersonal Sex in Public Places (Chicago: Aldine, 1970).

Hurst, Steven R., "Analysis: Obama's Big Stride on Moscow 'Reboot'", Associated Press, March 4, 2009. As of October 28, 2012, available online at http://www.dailytidings.com/apps/pbcs.dll/article?AID=/20090303/NEWS/903030325&cid=sitesearch

Jones, James, Bad Blood (New York: Free Press, 1981).

Kertzer, David, Ritual, Politics, and Power (New Haven, CT: Yale University Press,

Kiersey, David, and Bates, Marilyn, Please Understand Me: Character & Temperament Types (DelMar, CA: Prometheus Nemesis Book Company, 1984).

Lachmann, Richard, The Encyclopedic Dictionary of Sociology Fourth Edition (Guilford, CT: The Dushkin Publishing Group, 1991).

Latané, Bibb, and Darley, John M., "Bystander Intervention in Emergency Situations: Diffusion of Responsibility," Journal of Personality and Social Psychology, Vol. 8, No. 4, 1968: 377-383.

Latané, Bibb, and Nida, Steve, "Ten Years of Research on Group Size and Helping," Psychological Bulletin, Vol. 89, 1981: 308-321.

Lester, David, "Suicide in Prison: A Study of France from 1852 to 1913," European Archives of Psychiatry & Clinical Neuroscience, Vol. 244, 1994: 99-100.

Lester, David, "The Suicide Rate in Finnish Prisons," Psychiatria Fennica, Vol. 30, 1999: 93-96.

Liebow, Elliott, Tally's corner: A Study of Negro Streetcorner Men (Boston: Little Brown and Company, 1967).

McCord, Joan and McCord, William, Origins of Crime: A New Evaluation of the Cambridge-Sommerville Youth Study (New York: Columbia University Press, 1959a).

McCord, Joan, and McCord, William, "A Follow-up Report on the Cambridge-Sommerville Youth Study," Annals, Vol. 322, 1959b: 89-98.

Mead, George Herbert, Mind, Self, and Society (Chicago, Illinois: University of Chicago Press, 1934).

Merton, Robert K., Social Theory and Social Structure (New York: Free Press, 1968).

Michelson, Ethan, "Climbing the Dispute Pagoda: Grievances and Appeals to the Official Justice System in Rural China," American Sociological Review, Vol. 72, No. 3 (June) 2007: 459-485.

Millett, Kate, Sexual Politics (London: Virago, 1969).

Minsky, Marvin, The Society of Mind (New York: Simon and Schuster, 1986).

Myers, David, G., Social Psychology (Ninth Edition) (Boston: McGraw Hill, 2008).

Rosenthal, Robert, and Jacobson, Lenore, Pygmalion in th4 Classroom: Teacher Expectations and Pupils' Intellectual Development (New York: Holt, Rinehart, and Winston, 1968).

Rossi, Peter H.; Berk, Richard A.; and Lenihan, Kenneth, J., Money, Work, and Crime: Experimental Evidence (New York: Academic, 1980).

Rowe, Mary Budd, "Pausing Phenomena: Influence on the Quality of Instruction," Journal of Psycholinguistic Research, Vol. 3, 1974a: 203-224.

Rowe, Mary Budd, "Wait-Time and Rewards as Instructional Variables, Their Influence on Language, Logic, and Fate Control, Part One—Wait Time," Journal of Research in Science Teaching, Vol. 11, 1974b: 81-94.

Rubin, Allen, and Babbie, Earl, Research Methods for Social Work Second Edition (Pacific Grove, CA: Brooks/Cole Publishing Company, 1993).

Slavin, Robert E., and Karweit, Nancy C., "Effects of Whole Class, Ability Grouped and Individual Instruction on Mathematics Achievement," American Educational Review Journal, Vol. 22, 1985: 351-367.

Spradley, James P., and Mann, Brenda, The Cocktail Waitress: Women's Work in a Man's World (New York: John Wiley and Sons, 1974).

Squire, Larry, Memory and Brain (New York: Oxford University Press, 1987).

Stack, Carol, All Our Kin: Strategies for Survival in a Black Community (Boulder, CO: Basic Books, 1997).

Steinbeck, John, The Grapes of Wrath (New York: McGraw Hill, 1939).

Steyn, Mark, America Alone (Washington, D.C.: Regenery Publishing, Inc., 2006).

Tarabay, Jamie, "Activists Seek to Protect Iraqi Women from Honor Killings," National Public Radio Morning Edition, May 18, 2006. As of October 28, 2012, available online at http://www.npr.org/templates/story/story.php?storyId=5414315

Tartaro, Christine, and Lester, David, "An Application of Durkheim's Theory of Suicide to Prison Suicide Rates in the United States," Death Studies, Vol. 29, 2005: 413-422.

Theodorson, George A., and Theodorson, Achilles, G., A Modern Dictionary of Sociology (New York: Barnes & Noble Books, 1969).

Thomas, W. I., and Znaniecki, Florian, The Polish Peasant in Europe and America (Vol. 1) (Chicago, Illinois: University of Chicago Press, 1918).

Thrasher, F.M., The Gang: A Study of 1,1313 Gangs in Chicago (Chicago, Illinois: University of Chicago Press, 1936).

United Nations, United Nations General Assembly, Report of the Secretary-General, Fifty-Seventh Session, "Working Towards the Elimination of Crimes Against Women Committed in the Name of Honour," July 2, 2002. As of October 28, 2012, available online at http://www.unhchr.ch/huridocda/huridoca.nsf/AllSymbols/985168F508EE799FC1256C52002AE5A9/%24File/N0246790.pdf

Viterna, Jocelyn S., "Pulled, Pushed, and Persuaded: Explaining Women's Mobilization in to the Salvadoran Guerilla Army," American Journal of Sociology, Vol. 112, No. 1, July 2006: 1-45.

Weber, Max, The Protestant Ethic and the Spirit of Capitalism (New York: Charles Scribner's and Sons, 1930). (Originally published in German in 1904-1905 and in English in 1930).

Wharton, Amy S., "Structure and Agency in Socialist-Feminist Theory," Gender and Politics, Vol. 5, 1991: 373-389.

Whyte, William Foote, Street Corner Society: the Social Structure of an Italian Slum Second Edition (Chicago: University of Chicago Press, 1955).

Wirth, L., "Urbanism As a Way of Life," in S. F. Fava (Ed.), Urbanism in World Perspective: A Reader (New York: Crowell, 1968). (Originally published in 1938)

Zeisel, Hans, "Disagreement over the Evaluation of a Controlled Experiment," American Journal of Sociology, Vol. 88, 1982: 378-389.

CHAPTER 2

Types of Societies and Social Groups

SOCIOLOGY AND THE STUDY OF SOCIAL CHANGE

From its earliest days, sociology has studied social change. Auguste Comte perceived that the subject matter of sociology is the study of institutions that provide for stability and order in society, which he termed *social statics*, as well as the study of social change, which he termed *social dynamics*.

TABLE 2.1 SOCIOLOGICAL TYPOLOGIES OF TYPES OF SOCIETIES AND SOCIAL CHANGE

Who? Name of Social Theorist	Social Change "Good Old Days"	"Today"
Emile Durkheim	Mechanical	Organic
Ferdinand Toennies	Gemeinschaft	Gesellschaft
Charles Horton Cooley	Primary	Secondary
Robert Redfield	Folk, Urban-Agrarian	Urban Industrial

Sociologists use the term **society** to refer to a group of people with a common culture who occupy a particular territorial area, who have a sense of solidarity ("we-ness"), and who regard themselves as different than non-members. Sociologists have many typologies of types of societies and of social change. See Table 2.1. We now introduce you to some of these typologies of social change that are useful in understanding our social worlds.

Mechanical and Organic (Durkheim)

In *The Division of Labor in Society* (1895), Emile Durkheim distinguishes between society in the past and society today. He perceives these as two fundamentally different types of societies held together by differing types of solidarity or "social glue." He terms these mechanical and organic solidarity. Durkheim views mechanical solidarity as characteristic of what we will come to know as folk societies (Redfield, 1947) and organic solidarity as more prevalent in highly differentiated and heterogeneous social orders.

According to Durkheim, societies characterized by subsistence-level existence, nomadicism, little economic surplus, and considerable homogeneity--including considerable homogeneity on the variables of class, status, and power--tend to be held together by **mechanical solidarity**. It is in these types of societies that humans have spent most of their existence during the past ten thousand or so years. In this type of society, what you believe, I believe, we all believe. While there is a lot of variation across these societies, within each there is considerable homogeneity of beliefs, attitudes, and values. Durkheim phrased this by saying that such societies are characterized by a **common conscience**. In these societies, people are held together by their similarities, by things they have in common.

In contrast, modern industrial societies are characterized by considerable economic surplus and by considerable heterogeneity on the variables of class, status, and power; and by a division of labor based on more than age, sex and ritual. The division of labor is highly developed. Among the constituent groups that comprise such a society, there tends to be considerable variation in language, religion, occupation, values, attitudes, family forms, cultural beliefs, cultural content, and so forth.

Durkheim perceived that as societies move from mechanical to organic, that the norms that guide and that make predictable human behavior may be in flux and unclear. People tend to perceive this lack of clarity as an uncomfortable state of arousal, which Durkheim calls **anomie**.

Durkheim states that modern societies are held together by **organic solidarity**, that is, by the division of labor and the interdependence of their members. The members need each other; they are held together by their interdependencies (their complementary needs and interests).

Durkheim, like Toennies, argues that there has been a long-term trend whereby mechanical solidarity tends to give way to organic solidarity in modern society (Durkheim, 1895). A point that Durkheim was trying to make is not that industrialization and urbanization destroy solidarity but that new forms of solidarity develop.

Primary and Secondary Groups (Cooley)

Charles Horton Cooley makes a somewhat analogous distinction with the concepts primary and secondary groups. According to Charles Horton Cooley (1909/1962) who introduced the term, a **primary group** has common standards of behavior or values and direct, frequent contact among its members (Theodorson and Theodorson, 1969: 178). Relations among members of a primary group are ends in themselves, not means to ends. Members of a primary group are interested in and know about a wide range of aspects of each others' lives and they have a broad range of mutual rights and duties. In other words, the relationship is a diffuse one. The "family and the small, old-fashioned neighborhood" in large cities or in small towns are examples of a primary group (Theodorson and Theodorson, 1969: 178). These groups are considered as primary because they have both the earliest and most profound influence on a person's socialization and development.

Primary groups are important in our daily lives, even in advanced industrial societies. Primary group relationships are an important source of social solidarity and support (e.g., Humphries, Conrad, et. al., 2009).

If a group is not primary, it is a **secondary group**. Secondary group members know each other only in a limited number of roles, and they relate to each other as means to an end outside of the relationship. For example, in a big city, the sales associate at a grocery store has a secondary relationship with the customers who come to the store, and vice versa. The customer wants to be able to walk out of the store with the loaf of bread, say, and the sales associate wants the appropriate amount of money to put in the drawer for the transaction. The interaction between customer and sales associate is a means to an end outside of the relationship; it is a secondary relationship.

Primordial and Nonprimordial Groups (Edward Shils)

American sociologist ***Edward Shils*** makes a distinction between **primordial** and **nonprimordial group**s (1957). Primordial groups are those that come first in our experience. Examples include territorial groups; racial groups, ethnic groups, the community in which we are born; the family into which we are born (which sociologists term the **family of orientation**), and so forth. If a group is not primordial, it is nonprimordial. An example of a nonprimordial group is any class that I teach at the university. For the most part, students enrolled in these courses didn't know each other before they walked into the classes. These classes, then, are nonprimordial groups. Boot camp in the military is another example. People who go through boot camp together do not know each other beforehand. They are strangers before they find themselves together in boot camp. At the beginning of boot camp (as well as at the end of boot campt), they are a nonprimordial group. During the summer of 2013, when Michael Patterson, a 43-year old white husband and father, dove into the water to save from drowning a 4-year old black girl who was a total stranger to him in Georgia, in the United States, it was an act of altruism across primordial lines; and, as such, made the national news (Victorian, 2013; Caulfield, 2013). Even in a core country in the twenty-first century, it is newsworthy when helping behavior occurs across primordial lines, which is testimony both to the enduring power of primoridial ties and to the problematic nature of establishing and maintaining solidarity with non-primordial others.

Sociologists use the term **identification** to refer to the extent that a social actor's sense of self is rooted in group membership. Many social actors in an open modern industrial society have numerous, as well as a wide range of, identities and identifications. Other social actors have few, as well as a narrow or short range of, identities and identifications. To the extent that segments of our identity are rooted in and stem from group membership, we tend to support and to protect those identity groups in order to protect and to enhance our sense of self. The more important a particular identity is to us, and the more strongly attached we feel to an identity group, the more likely we are to sacrifice ourselves and others for that collectivity. Thus, social identities such as American, Muslim, Rwandan, Serb, Croatian, and Slovenian, represent identities for which people are prepared to die (Gourevitch, 1995; Gusfield, 1996). In modern societies many identity groups are nonprimordial groups (Gusfield, 1996).

Creating and sustaining solidarity among non-primordial others is always problematic (Blau, 1987; Popielarz and McPherson, 1995; Holy, 1996). Identification is one source of attachment to nonprimordial groups. **Association**, the reaching beyond primordial ties to establish common cause with others, is another.

A social definition of who we are in terms of the groups in which our identity based--e.g., our race, religion, gender, academic major, occupation, political party affiliation, and so forth--implies a definition of who we are not. The circle that includes "us" excludes "them" (Lindeman, 1997; Gamson, 1995).

In-Group and the Out-Group

Sociologists capture this dimension of social life with the distinction between in-group and out-group. An **in-group** is any group "whose membership has a strong sense of identification and loyalty, and a feeling of exclusiveness toward nonmembers" (Theodorson and Theodorson, 1969: 203). **Loyalty** refers to an attachment to a group as a group (Mayhew, 1971). An **out-group** refers to (1) a group "whose members are considered to be in opposition, or to be in some way alien, to an IN-GROUP" and (2) all nonmembers of an in-group; and to (Theodorson and Theodorson, 1969: 289).

In-group bias refers to the tendency for people who belong to an in-group to favor their own group, to evaluate their group more highly than do people who are not members (Myers, 2002; Gamson, 1995; Roy, 1994; Mullen, Brown, and Smith, 1992). Thus, if you are a member of a particular sorority or fraternity at your university, or if you live in a particular dormitory, you probably hold that group in higher estimation than do those who are not members. In-group bias is found even in socially disparaged or stigmatized groups.

In-group bias also is more likely if the in-group is small relative to the out-group (Mullen, 1991). In comparison with those whose in-group is the majority, to be a female at a conference attended mostly by males, to be a Native-American or African-American student on a campus attended mainly by white students of Anglo-Saxon Protestant descent, or to be a sixty-year old freshman is to feel one's social identity and in-group membership more keenly.

Because part of our sense of self is based on our group memberships, perceiving our own groups as superior or as better aids us in feeling good about ourselves (Turner, 1984). Having a sense of "we-ness" based on group memberships, then, "feels good" (Myers, 2002).

It is noteworthy how little it can take to create in-groups, out-groups, and in-group bias (e.g., Goode, 1963: 203-269; Morris, 1973: 218-248). Thus, Max Weber wrote about the formation of in-groups, out-groups, and in-group bias as resulting simply because people ate together at the same soup kitchen (1958). Once formed, these groups can have profound, if subtle, effects, one of which is the tendency for members to underestimate differences within categories and to overestimate differences between categories (Myers, 2002). The sentiment "Women (or Men, Whites, Gays, African Americans, Muslims, etc.) are all alike" expresses these tendencies. "Boys will be boys, and girls will be girls," also expresses the sentiment or perception that meaningful differences within a group do not exist and neither does any overlap between the categories specified. A tendency in the media to refer to someone as a **prolocutor** (spokesperson) of, say, the Muslim-American community or of women's groups likewise expresses a sentiment that Muslim-Americans (or women) are all alike.

Gemeinschaft and Gesellschaft (Toennies)

German Sociologist Ferdinand Toennies (1855-1936), whose ideas heavily influenced American symbolic interactionism, introduced the term **Gesellschaft** to describe modern societies. He said that Gesellschaft (i.e. modern industrial society) is founded on **artificial will**, which means that human relationships are founded on rational calculation rather than on spontaneous attraction. Other social actors are seen not as ends in themselves, but as means to ends outside the relationship. You say hello to Pat because you want to borrow her textbook. These also are segmental relationships, wherein one relates just to part of a person rather than relating to the entire person.

In contrast, **Gemeinschaft** (e.g., the types of societies that existed in "the good old days," in hunting-and-gathering society, in mechanical society) is founded on what Toennies calls **natural will**, which means that relationships are founded on spontaneous attraction. In Gemeinschaft, relationships are warm, personal, direct, and diffuse (in that they are founded on contact between whole people rather than on contact between just parts of people). That is, in a Gemeinschaft, you know people in all their different roles. In a Gemeinschaft, you also relate to people as ends in themselves, not as means to an end. Thus, you say hello to Pat because you like her, because she is a community member, and because you find such interaction inherently meaningful. The interaction is a positive end or purpose for you. You do not interact with her simply because you want to borrow her textbook, twenty dollars until payday, or a cup of sugar. Gemeinschaft frequently is translated into English as "community."

Toennies goes on to argue that there has been an evolutionary trend, whereby urbanization and industrialization are tearing down the fabric of Gemeinschaft, and are turning the world into an emotionally bleak Gesellschaft. Toennies argues that society is becoming an entity founded on brute force and material interest, whereas in Gemeinschaft, society had been founded on warm personal fellow feeling.

Folk, Urban-Agrarian, and Urban Industrial Society (Redfield)

Robert Redfield (1947) developed the concept of **folk society** as an ideal type to describe the type of societies in which humans have lived for most of their existence on earth. Like Durkheim and Toennies, Redfield perceived that there has been an historical trend whereby urbanization and social change impinge on an earlier type of society and change it into a very different type of society. Redfield perceived that *urban-agrarian society,* also known as feudal society, had fundamentally changed the character of folk society, and that much later on, urban-industrial society changed the character of urban-agrarian society. We now introduce you to folk and urban-agrarian (feudal) societies (Sjoberg, 1947, 1952, 1955, 1960).

FOLK SOCIETY

Folk societies are small, isolated, non-literate, and homogeneous. Each folk society tends to be relatively culturally homogenous--in terms of beliefs and values; in terms of the structure of their major social institutions like the family and religion; in terms of the distribution of class, status, and power. Additionally, a strong sense of solidarity ("we-ness") exists at the community-wide level, and kinship (the family) is the basic category of experience. Behavior is traditional, spontaneous, personal, and relatively uncritical. The sacred prevails over the profane. In terms of technology, tools and weapons are made of wood, stone, bone, and other materials taken directly from nature. Folk societies still exist to this day. Examples include the aborigines of Australia, the pygmies and Bushmen (San) of Africa, and a number of remote Indian tribes in the Amazon basin of South America (Coimbra, 2004;Hill, et. al., 1985; Hurtado, et. al., 1985).

Folk societies are nomadic or semi-nomadic, and their members experience a subsistence-level existence. The reasons for nomadicism are simple. In hunting-and-gathering society (which is another name for folk society), the food gathering techniques normally reduce the supply of edible plants and animals in a given area below the level needed to maintain the human population, and so the group is compelled to move on. A sample of more than 70 hunting and gathering societies from the Human Relations Area Files indicates that about 10 percent were able to maintain a settled, non nomadic life due especially abundant ecological conditions.

Population density is the number of people per unit of an area—for instance, the number of persons per square mile. The average population density in hunting and gathering societies is low, about one person per square mile (Petersen, 1969: 347). It was only after the "invention" of farming and the domestication of animals in early horticultural societies that human population density reached 5.7 people per square mile, which seems to be the minimum population density necessary for the stable transmission of technological innovation to occur (Powell, Shennan, and Thomas, 2009; Jones, 2011; Flinn, 2009; Joyce, 2009).

Population density increases with the level of societal complexity. Sociologists might phrase this by saying that there is a positive relationship between population density and societal complexity. Thus, while the average population density of hunting and gathering societies is 1.0 persons per square mile, the average population density in simple agricultural societies is between 26-64 persons per square mile (Petersen, 1969: 348).

Sociologists use the term **stratification** to refer to the persistent and inheritable unequal access to scarce-yet-widely-valued goods and services. Stratification is found to a greater or lesser extent in all human societies. It is sometimes called structured social inequality. Let us now take a brief look at stratification in folk societies (Nolan and Lenski, 2004; Ackerman, 2003; Lenski, 1984) and, later on in the chapter, we will take a brief look at stratification in urban-agrarian societies,

Stratification in Folk Society

If any single feature of the life of folk societies impresses itself on social scientists, it is the relative equality of folk societies, the relative equality that exists among the members of each folk society. Folk societies are the least stratified societies known to sociologists and anthropologists. The stratification that exists within folk societies is radically different than that which is found in urban-agrarian or in modern urban-industrial societies.

THE ECONOMIC DIMENSION In terms of the economic dimension, there is very little property in a folk society, and there tends to be an ethic of sharing. Food, for example, tends to be shared among the members of the society. There is little or no surplus in folk society, and a nomadic way of life works against the accumulation of material possessions, particularly when everything needs to be carried on one's back. When the frequency of moves is reduced, it is much easier to accumulate possessions of every kind.

There often is some limited inequality in access to economic goods, with certain segments of the population faring a bit better than others. For example, in Andamanese society, the old men enjoy some advantage over the younger. Among the Siriono, the senior wife in a polygynous family and her children are reported to fare somewhat better than the junior wife and her dependent children; and in most folk societies, males fare better than females. These differences, however, represent little more than secondary variations on the basic theme of substantial equality.

POWER As with economic goods, so too with power. The headman's position tends to be part-time. The headman or chief tends to engage in the same daily activities as the other males, since productivity is at the subsistence level and the headman cannot be spared from the routine tasks of production. The limited power a headman has tends to be based on persuasion and consent.

Government by coercion is not an option in traditional folk societies. The leader of the group is not supported by a cadre of specialists trained in the arts of violence who are dependent on his favor and therefore motivated to follow his orders. Rather, all males tend to be trained and equipped for fighting and the same weapons and training are available to all. Dissatisfied followers may always desert their leader and attach themselves to another band.

Government in traditional folk societies is by persuasion. One manifestation of this is the practice of government by general council. Most ethnographic reports from traditional folk societies contain some reference to government by council.

Even in those traditional folk societies that are governed by a headman, his powers are usually quite limited. They seldom extend beyond the bounds of his or her own band. Time and again we read in the scholarly literature that the headman holds her/his place only so long as she/he gives satisfaction. If the people are dissatisfied, the headman is quickly replaced. The upshot is that power is relatively equitably distributed in folk societies.

PRESTIGE In contrast to the economic and status dimensions, prestige tends to be relatively unequally distributed in folk communities, particularly on the bases of age and sex. With regard to age, the old tend to have prestige because they are the receptacles of cultural tradition. With regard to sex, males tend to be more highly honored than females. Other bases of prestige include people viewed as endowed with supernatural powers and people with certain valued personal qualities--like skill in hunting and warfare, generosity and kindness, and freedom from bad temper.

Regarding the interrelationships among class, status, and power in traditional folk societies, it is worth noting that prestige tends to go hand in hand with political influence. Prestige leads to political influence in folk communities.

SOCIAL MOBILITY IN FOLK SOCIETIES We begin our inquiry into the amounts and types of social mobility possible in folk society by looking at case studies of two important positions in folk society generally—that of chief and that of shaman (priest).

Chieftainship One of the best descriptions of the position of a typical chief in folk society has been written by American anthropologist Allan Holmberg (1950: 59-60) over half a century ago when he was describing the Siriono, a South American Indian people living in the dense, tropical forests of eastern Bolivia. Holmberg tells us that presiding over every band of Siriono is a chief (ererékwa), who, nominally, is the highest official of the group. However, the extent of his authority depends almost entirely upon his qualities as a leader. There is no obligation to obey the orders of the chief, no punishment for failing to do so. Unless the chief is a member of one's immediate family, little attention is paid to what is said by a chief. To maintain prestige, a chief "must fulfill, in a superior fashion, those obligations required of everyone else" (Holmberg, 1950: 59-60).

Holmberg reminds us that the prerogatives of chieftainship are few. As a mark of status, a chief always has more than one wife. Additionally, he has the right to occupy, with his immediate family, the center of the house. Other than those prerogatives, the chief has to do all the things that other men of his tribe must do. For instance, he must make his own bows and arrows as well as his other tools; he must hunt, fish, plant gardens, and collect. He makes suggestions as to migrations, hunting trips, and so forth; but his suggestions are not always followed. Holmberg found that in general, chiefs fare better than other members of the band. Why? Because they are the best hunters; they know more about things and are able to do them better than anyone else. From the point of view of exchange theory, then, chiefs are in a better position than most to reciprocate for any favors done them by members of the band.

The foregoing tells us that personal qualities are tremendously important in Siriono society, and the same is true of folk societies generally. If a chief is better than others at important tasks, he/she fares somewhat better than others, but not otherwise.

In some folk communities, the position of chief offers special advantage, though only for a person of special abilities. Spencer and Gillen (1927) report that the position of chief could provide the basis of considerable power among the Arunta of Australia, although they stress that this was true only for an able person. Special advantage, then, was contingent upon performance.

Shaman The position of shaman (priest, healer) tends to be associated with prestige, influence, and special perquisites in folk societies. Among the Northern Maidu Indians of California this office was not inherited, although in other folk societies it sometimes is. However, the point is that, inherited or not, the benefits of the position go only to those who can prove their rights to them. Shamans are constantly on trial, as it were, and those who are unable to demonstrate their competence are not likely to benefit greatly. In addition to the usual tests of their powers in the case of illness, some folk societies provide institutionalized tests that pit shaman against shaman to see whose powers are the greatest. For instance, the Northern Maidu or California held an annual dance to which all shamans were invited. At this dance, each shaman attempted to overcome the others by means of magic. The dance continued until only one shaman was left standing, and that person was declared the foremost shaman of all. Undoubtedly, those who were eliminated early suffered a loss of status, and with it, most of the benefits of their position.

Summary

In folk societies, class, status, and power are largely a function of personal abilities. Inheritance provides opportunity only. To be of value to the individual, confirming actions are required; and where these are lacking, the possession of an office is of little benefit. In other words, there is little transmission of advantage from one generation to the next, and lots of inter-generational social mobility is possible in folk societies.

Folk societies lack certain mechanisms that facilitate the transmission of advantage across generational lines. First, there is little wealth, little surplus, and wealth is one of the best means for passing advantage from one generation to the next. Second, there are no hereditary statuses with established prerogatives that accrue to the incumbent regardless of ability. Third, folk communities do not have class-differentiated subgroups. More highly differentiated societies, including urban-agrarian societies have well defined social classes, but folk societies do not.

Socialization is the process whereby we learn roles and norms, develop the capacity to conform to them, and develop a sense of self. The self consists of our answers to the question, "Who am I?" In folk societies, the opportunities for differential socialization on the basis of class are limited.

The foregoing discussion indicates that the rate of intergenerational mobility is high in folk societies. There is little to prevent the talented child of an untalented parent from rising to a position of influence and leadership. Similarly, there is little to prevent the untalented child of a talented parent from falling from a position of leadership. The rates of intra-generational mobility are also high in folk societies.

For thousands of years people lived in the kinds of communities that we have designated as folk society. We now examine the social forces that led to the demise of folk society and the emergence of a new kind of society.

THE DEATH OF FOLK SOCIETY: THE RISE OF THE CITY

There are folk societies, essentially folk societies that, because of the especially abundant ecological conditions in which they are situated, have surplus; but they do not develop urbanity as a result of that surplus. Rather, they consume the surplus, they use it up. A good example of this are the Indians on a narrow strip of the Pacific coast in the American Northwest, the Kwakiutl. Our knowledge of the Quakiutl is fairly extensive and is largely derived from Ruth Benedict's classic work, *Patterns of Culture* (1934).

The Kwakiutl had a lot of surplus because the Northwest coast was an abundant land, full of fish, acorns, and other good things to eat. Their considerable surplus was expended in a massive system of status rivalry known as **potlatch**. Potlatch is a custom in which a ceremonial feast is held at which people gain prestige by giving away or destroying wealth or property. The more goods a person gave away or destroyed, the greater was her or his prestige. People competed, as it were, to outdo their rivals. At potlatch, one person might say, "I am so rich, I can burn up, right here in front of you, *five* Kwakiutl blankets." And that person would burn them up. Another person would say, "You think *that's* rich? *I* can burn up, right here in front of you, *ten* Kwakiutl blankets." And that person would burn them up. And so it would go. This was conspicuous consumption or "Keeping up with the Joneses" in the most literal sense.

Potlatch is not unique to the Qwakiutl. For instance, I have a Greek American friend who is married to an Italian-American. Each holiday season my friend has the extended family over for what she affectionately terms the family potlatch. Many other Americans, who may not use the term potlatch to describe their behaviors, do likewise on various occasions.

The point here is that among the Kwakiutl, the surplus was not socially mobilized so as to form urban settlement. Instead, it was expended, depleted. The more general point is that it takes social organization, social discipline, to mobilize and to harness the surplus to form urban settlement.

Features of Social Life That Emerge with the City

As a form of human settlement, the city is built on surplus. The city cannot exist without forms of social organization that first create and then harness enough surplus to support a non-agrarian population. Once surplus is achieved, social organization can turn that surplus into civilization, into a city. Standard twentieth-century sociological texts on the city (e.g., Sjoberg, 1960) cite as the characteristics of the city the same set of criteria developed by British archaeologist V. Gordon Childe (1952, 1956, 1957, 1972, 1983; Mayhew, 1970) as a definition of civilization.

The ten features of social life that emerge with the rise of the city, as suggested by V. Gordon Childe are these:

(1) **FULL-TIME SPECIALISTS:** No longer is everybody tied directly to the land. Instead, you get full-time specialists in things other than making a living from agriculture.

(2) **LARGE, DENSE POPULATIONS** Large numbers of persons can live in a small territorial area. By large I mean 5,000 people living on twenty acres. Folk societies could not support 5,000 people living on twenty acres, but pre-industrial cities can.

(3) **ART PRODUCED BY FULL-TIME SPECIALISTS** One of the sorts of full-time specialization that develops are the arts.

(4) **WRITING AND NUMERICAL NOTATION** Writing and numerical notation kept track, for instance, of how much of whose grain was being stored in which priestly granary.

(5) **EXACT AND PREDICTIVE SCIENCES**

(6) **TAXATION** The rise of an urban elite means the rise of taxation, the decline of folk society, the rise of the city. None of this would be possible without taxation.

(7) **FORMATION OF THE STATE** The **state** is a territorial entity controlled by a government and inhabited by a population (Goldstein and Pevehouse, 2010: 10). The state, as Max Weber points out, is a form of political association and a rational institutional order that is the product of social evolution and it monopolizes the legitimate use of violence (Weber, 1968: 904-905). As such. it has certain characteristics, which include the following: the state (a) has a defined, organized government; (b) it has a defined territory—i.e., it has geographical boundaries; (c) it has a more or less permanent population; (d) it possesses **sovereignty**. Sovereignty is a state's right, at least in principle, to do whatever it wants within its own territory. According to the principle of sovereignty, states are separate, autonomous, and answer to no higher authority. The sovereignty principle means that states are not to interfere in the internal affairs of other states. (Goldstein and Pevehouse, 2010: 41). In short, the sovereignty principle means that states are free from external control. Also, (e), states are recognized by other governments.

Max Weber (1968:905) reminds us that the basic functions of the state are the following:

- the enactment of law (legislative function);
- the protection of personal safety and public order (the police function)—the police function is directed against disturbers of internal order;
- the protection of vested rights (the function of the administration of justice);
- the cultivation of hygienic, educational, social-welfare, and other cultural interests (the various branches of governmental administration); and
- organized and armed protection against outside attack (military administration function).

(8) **ERECTION OF MONUMENTAL PUBLIC BUILDINGS**

(9) **RISE OF FOREIGN TRADE**

(10) **EMERGENCE OF A CLASS STRUCTURE**

Those ten things are the characteristics of social life that emerge with the city as a form of human habitation. The thrust of the list is that it is not just technology, it is not just surplus, that makes the city as a form of human habitation possible. The emergence of the city as a form of human settlement is a matter of re-organizing the social life of the community in fundamental ways.

We now look at the development of the earliest cities of which archaeologists have record, the birth of the cities in Mesopotamia and Sumer, in the Fertile Crescent formed by the flood plains of the Tigris and Euphrates rivers, which presently is situated in the state of Iraq.

Rise of the Earliest Sumerian Cities

The earliest cities were built around 3,500 B.C. when people learned the techniques of irrigation, the techniques of plow-based agriculture on irrigated ground. Before the rise of the city along the banks of the Tigris and Euphrates rivers, there were fairly sedentary folk societies located along those same banks, due to the annual floods of the great rivers which carried rich alluvial soil into the mighty valley, with the result that the soil did not wear out, even in the face of digging-stick food-growing technology.

The floods were not an unmixed blessing. Besides depositing the silt into the valley, the floods also deposited a lot of the new silt where residents did not want it—on the tops of their houses, for instance, and killed people and other life forms. After the flood waters abated and the land was dry enough to plow, people would plant their crops; but then, it was not likely to rain anymore, so the crops grow and the sun would continue to shine and a lot of the crops would wither from lack of water.

Realizing the potentialities of the rich alluvial soil, in short, meant *irrigation* and *flood control*. These could not be accomplished on an every-person-for-him/herself basis. Irrigation and flood control meant community tactics—-the investment of a surplus in dams, conduits, ditches, floodgates, and so forth. Irrigation and flood control required a degree of community cooperation, social discipline, and coordination beyond that found in folk society.

The problem in getting community coordination, cooperation, and discipline going was precisely this: the way the average folk-society citizen wanted to utilize surplus time. If the average folk-society citizen living in a fairly abundant floodplain could get a big enough crop by working only, say, six hours a day on the crop, that's all she/he would work. The rest of the time would be spent chatting with neighbors, looking at the sunset. So, getting the irrigation and flood-control systems built and maintained required a fundamental transformation in community organization and this change in community organization was tantamount to the death of folk society.

This transformation of folk society into an urban-agrarian society, this change in community organization, this building of irrigation and flood-control systems, was conducted, as nearly as we can now reconstruct, under priestly aegis, under priestly discipline (Nolan and Lenski, 2004; Gluick, 1986; Childe, 1983; Lenski, 1966). The priests filled the role of social disciplinarians, and the role of social disciplinarian was crucial to the emergence of urban-agrarian society, to the emergence of the city, to the demise of folk society. It was the priests, as the representatives of the gods, who would say, "Hey, you can't just work six hours a day on your crops and then sit around and chat with family and neighbors. No, you need to work those six hours each day on your crops, like you're doing now, and then you must work six hours a day out there digging the ditches, putting up the dams, building the conduits, weeding the conduits, repairing the conduits, and so forth. And remember, this is not my idea; it's the gods' idea." Priests, with priestly authority, first created and then supervised the irrigation system. The earliest Sumerian cities were known as temple communities.

Once the priests had harnessed, had mobilized the surplus into dams, conduits, and flood control, productivity increased tremendously, as did the surplus. It was the priests who creamed the top off of this immensely increased agricultural surplus via taxation. Then the priests in turn used that surplus to support themselves as priests. They used the surplus to support a class of artisans who created luxuries, temples, jewelry and all the other frou-frou for the priestly urban elite. It was the priests who would say, "Hey, you cannot eat up all the grain right now. We must save some of it in the priestly granaries for the people working on the dams." So, a generous portion of agricultural production went into the priestly granary to support the priests; and, as productivity increased, to support a large group of artisans for the priestly household as well as to support a myriad of other specialists, including literary, artistic, military, administrative, and scientific specialists.

This whole complex was supported by religion, by a complex religious belief system. Many religions have explanations of how the world got here and of how human beings got here. While these religious explanations have many names, one secular term for them is **creation myths**.

THE SUMERIAN CREATION MYTH The Sumerian creation myth goes like this (Gluick, 1986): Sumerian theology is built on the premise that human beings were created so that the gods might be relieved of the burden of working for a living. The gods were sitting around one day, working, and one god said to the other gods: "Golly, it's tough to work. I hate to work, in fact. Don't you?" The other gods concurred and said, "Work is burdensome, bad for the digestive system, hard on the back, and generally time consuming." One of the gods had a better idea, a true flash of inspiration: "Hey, I have a better idea, a true flash of inspiration. Let's create people, and people can do the work and we'll just sit here. We'll let some of the people be priests, and the priests will be the intermediaries between the people and us, the gods. The priests will collect all the yummies of life for us, on our behalf." The other gods thought that was a swell idea. So, they made human beings, and they made some of the human beings priests, and then the priests proceed to collect the surplus, not on their own behalf, you see, but on behalf of the gods.

That's one function of religion here, to legitimate the whole structure of social discipline, of social domination, to make this structure meaningful to the dominated. So, if a peasant is out there digging the conduits, weeding the irrigation system, pulling a plow, or paying over the lion's share of their crop as taxes, and asks the question, "Why am I doing this? It's awful. It's burdensome, bad for the digestive system, hard on the back, and generally time consuming. Why am I doing this? Ah, yes! It's my purpose for existence. The gods put me on earth to do this for them. I thank the gods that I can be alive so that I can do this for them."

There is some evidence that religious beliefs serve this function of justifying authority and domination in societies generally and in Ancient Mesopotamia and Sumer specifically, whatever other functions they serve and whatever other meanings they also have for their participants. Marxian conflict theory would identify the justification of domination as one of the manifest functions of religion, and structural functionalism could view this as a latent function.

Later, in Sumer, secular kingship grew up alongside priestly rule. It is very important when that happens, because once secular kingship was created, it was possible for kings to develop sufficient military force to spread their domains outward from the central city—to spread their control and political domination over larger and larger territorial areas. Ecologically inclined sociologists might say, "Hey, that's what in effect has been happening ever since: that cities, once born, have more surplus, more class, more clout, and it

extends its power and influence out over larger and larger territorial areas until there's no long such a thing left as folk society, really." Folk societies, as we have seen, were independent. But the representatives of urban dominance just have to enter a folk community and say, "Welcome to our kingdom. You're working for us now." At that point in time, a folk community is transformed into something different, a peasant society, because they have been transformed into dependent parts of a larger system, and that transforms the character of social life. The character of social life in the peasant village is different in some definable ways.

The foregoing analysis of the rise of the city as a form of human habitation is important because it demonstrates that, from a sociological perspective, the rise of the city is not just a matter of technology, it is not just a matter of "Oh, I know, the plow." It was a matter of transforming independent folk-society citizens into **peasants**, agricultural workers tied to and dominated by an urban elite. The priests were the first urban elites. The emergence of the city was a matter of developing and implementing systems of social discipline, of social control, and of creating a division of labor extending far beyond that based on age, sex, and ritual found in folk societies.

URBAN-AGRARIAN SOCIETY

Urban-agrarian society is not a folk society writ large. A folk society was populated entirely by folk, independent tribespersons, but in urban-agrarian society the folk have been transformed into peasants, agricultural laborers tied to and dominated by an urban elite. A prime difference between folk and urban-agrarian society (feudal society) is that an urban-agrarian society is characterized by the domination of a small urban elite over the peasant rural masses.

Urban-agrarian or feudal society consists of two main parts, the city, in which only a small percent of the total population lives, and the villages in the rural hinterland.

The Peasant Village

The major component of urban-agrarian society, besides the pre-industrial city, is the peasant village. The peasant village has similarities with folk community. First, the villages are small. Second, relations between villagers tend to be face-to-face, very personal, emotional in character, and traditional. Third, kinship is an extremely important organizing principle within the village.

THE DIFFERENCES BETWEEN THE PEASANT VILLAGE AND FOLK SOCIETY The fundamental difference between the peasant village and the folk society is that the peasant village is not isolated. It is not independent; it is not autonomous. When we talking about differences between a peasant village and folk society, we are talking about the ways in which position in a larger network alters the conditions of life for the agricultural worker.

First, production is no longer just for local consumption.

In folk society, production was essentially for local consumption, but in peasant society, representatives of the urban center siphon off a large part of what the peasant agricultural village produces—be these representatives of the church, state, the landlords, the mortgage holders, or a variety of other elements of the larger society. So, that is the first difference—the siphoning off of a part of the product of the group to support urban life and all its paraphernalia. This is associated with the second thing, new attitudes towards work.

Work comes to mean a somewhat different thing to the agricultural laborer dominated by an urban elite than it had meant to the independent folk citizen. Similarities are still there, of course: There is still usually a love of the land. There is still an attitude toward work as worthwhile and as important element of the good life. And hard work is still valued for its own sake. The difference is that there is a rationalization in posture toward work, a rationalization in attitudes toward work. Part and parcel of the fact that you have to get by in face of the constant intrusion upon your world by the forces of the larger society that are coming in to siphon off their shares, is that you want to make sure that "their share" is as little as possible. One way that you can make sure that their share is as little as possible is through careful, precise accounting devices, i.e., through a careful rational calculation of your economic situation. The peasant community goes a long way—to many urban dwellers, a surprisingly long way—towards a rational, utilitarian, and calculating attitude toward work (Friedl, 1962).

A third factor setting off the peasant community from folk society is the limited scope of solidarity. It no longer is society-wide. Relations with the dominant urban center also mean another transformation of rural life, namely the lack of solidarity at the society-wide level. The solidarity of the urban-agrarian society tends to be limited to its subunits—to its constituent castes, guilds, families, occupational groups, ethnic groups, and villages.

The lack of solidarity at the society-wide level is a crucial feature of urban-agrarian society. The solidarity of the small peasant village remains; it has the same sort of solidarity that the folk society has. And the solidarity of the subsectors of the pre-industrial city, to be discusses shortly, remains. The small ethnically homogenous quarters of the city are little microcosms of folk community. But the solidarity of the urban-agrarian society as a whole is lacking. We might express this by saying that a sense of "nationhood" is lacking.

In feudal society, the sense of nationhood does not develop as rapidly as the growth of actual, factual, raw urban domination. In fact, there is more solidarity between the elites of neighboring feudal societies than there is between the peasants and the elites within a particular feudal society.

This is understandable if we keep in mind three things, the first of which is conquest. To a large extent, the boundaries of urban-agrarian society are drawn largely by raw conquest, and conquest, in and of itself, does not automatically create bonds of solidarity between the "conquered" and those who dominate them. Second, the urban center means that new local roles are created in the rural peasant village that did not exist before in the folk society—the tax collector, the local official of the central government, perhaps the traveling merchant or local priest. These functionaries do not usually live in your village; they come occasionally to see how things are going. These functionaries are *in* your community, but not *of* it. They are strangers who relate to the community from the outside. They may be necessary and the peasants may even accept them to a certain extent, but they still are not full-fledged members of the community. They are strangers who have a leg in each world. Thirdly, there is the bandit problem. One of the historic bases of treaties between local villages and the central urban government is that peasants feel that the central government does have a function, and that function is the protection of the village from piracy, protection from bandits. Because another feature of urban-agrarian society is that there is a high level of banditry, a level of banditry that is far higher than that characteristic even of the modern-day United States. The high level of banditry comes about as a consequence of the fact that the central governments in urban-agrarian societies are strong enough to collect the surplus (taxes) from the local villages but not strong enough thoroughly to control with raw power the entire territorial area. Bandits sweep down from the hills into the villages and take a big share of the surplus of the village. Banditry, predation on local villages by bandits, is common. So, an important basis for the loyalty of the village to the central government, then, is the capacity of the central government to protect the village from bandits. When that capacity breaks down, so too does the precarious

loyalty of the village to the urban center. These three considerations are important because they indicate the limited scope of peasant loyalty.

Until quite recently, the average person in the world lived in a peasant village (United Nations, 2004; World Population News Service POPLINE, May-June 2004: 1-2). Quite remarkably, the United Nations' Economic and Social Commission for Asia and the Pacific reports that in 2008, for the first time in human history, more people were living in cities than in rural areas (United Nations, 2004: 31).

In summary, the solidarity of urban-agrarian society tends to be limited to its subsectors—to its constituent castes, guilds, ethnic groups, tribes, and villages.

The Pre-Industrial City

As the attentive reader will recall, urban-agrarian society has two main parts, the pre-industrial city and the rural peasant masses who lived the rural hinterland in villages, and the pre-industrial city that dominated them. **Pre-industrial cities** are all cities existing within a non-industrial social order.

The pre-industrial city never contained more than a small percent of the total population of urban-agrarian society. Gideon Sjoberg (1960) indicates, for example, that in Russia from late seventeenth through the eighteenth century, not more than 3 percent of the population lived in cities; and for all the agrarian societies of the world, Sjoberg's estimates are that the urban sector never constituted more 10 percent of the population, and often it was much less.

WHO LIVED IN THE CITY? A variety of types of persons lived in the city, including the ruler and the ruling or governing class. The ruling or governing class was urban. To be part of the ruling class was to possess the right to share in the economic surplus produced by the peasant masses and urban artisans. The ruling and governing classes often included the upper ranks of the governmental, religious, and educational bureaucracies as well as some merchants and the highest military leaders. The nobility and other privileged classes in the cities often maintained auxiliary homes or estates in the countryside as symbols of high status, to which they repaired periodically, in an attempt to escape an outbreak of disease or, more frequently, for purposes or pleasure or simply to try to escape from the summer heat.

Some merchants also lived in the city, as did some artisans who made accoutrements for the elite, and a fairly large "retainer class"—household servants, a small army of literate clerks, petty officials and tax collectors, and even some professional soldiers who served the ruler and governing class.

Thus, not everyone who lived in the pre-industrial city was of the ruling class. In fact, the ruling class was only about two percent of the total population (Sjoberg, 1960), and they were urban. All those who lived in the city formed, at most, ten percent of the total population. This tiny urban sector, and especially the two percent that was the ruling class, dominated the other 90 percent of the population politically, economically, religiously, and culturally. These are the most highly stratified societies known to social scientists, and this is the case with regard to the dimensions of class, status, and power.

Characteristics that Pre-Industrial Cities Have in Common

The term "pre-industrial city" refers to cities past and present. They exist and have existed in a variety of forms. Not only are there cultural differences, there also are differences in their internal organization and in the functions that pre-industrial cities have. Some were large trading centers, others were largely political centers; some had primarily religious and symbolic functions (e.g. Avignon in the 14th and 15th centuries). When we say "a variety of forms," we also mean that colonialism, industrialization, and all the other effects of the modern world have affected many present-day pre-industrial cities. So, some pre-industrial cities today—perhaps most—are in a process of change to a modern industrial city. So, there is an enormous amount of variation between one pre-industrial city and another, or there can be.

But, despite the differences between trading centers, political capitals, religious centers, and cities in transition, there are certain basic similarities among pre-industrial cities. These similarities are to be understood in opposition to the character of urban life in a modern industrial city. We now turn to a discussion of the characteristics that pre-industrial cities have in common, which also are characteristics that distinguish them from modern industrial cities, and that underscore their traditional or "folk" character of the pre-industrial city. These are basically seven in number.

1. **RIGID SOCIAL SEGREGATION** In the pre-industrial city there is rigid social segregation. The diverse occupational and ethnic groups of the city have relatively little communication with each other. They live in their own separate quarters of the city, often have their own language, marry within their own groups, have their own institutions of education and socialization. There is no such thing, for example, as a national school system in which everybody gets a common education. A person living in a pre-industrial city tends not even to think of him/herself as a citizen of that particular city but rather as a member of an occupational group or ethnic solidary group which simply happens to be located in that urban location.

2. **CASTE** A **caste** is a type of group or collectivity that is defined by means of entrée and egress, by how one gets into the group and out of it. In a caste, one gets into it by being born into it and one gets out of it by death. Caste, then, refers to the tremendous importance of birth and kinship in making a person a member of one or another of the groups of the larger community. Caste is a very prominent feature of the pre-industrial city and of urban-agrarian society.

3. **SMALL LITERATE ELITE** At the top of the caste structure is a very small literate elite. The small literate elite is largely hereditary, and it controls all of the major social institutions in the society. They have their own norms, manners, and customs, and they often speak a different language, a language that is not the indigenous language of the populous. There is little communication between this group and the other sectors of the community.

4. **HANDICRAFT INDUSTRY** Within one's occupational specialization, within one's guild, one learns a craft. One learns to make a whole product from end to end. The name for this is handicraft industry, and it is the economic foundation of the pre-industrial city—apart from its living on the agricultural surplus that is skimmed off the peasants and used by the literate elite.

5. **NORMS ARE TRADITIONAL, CUSTOMARY, SACRED** The norms of the pre-industrial city tend to be traditional, customary, and sacred. Sacred doctrines and traditional codes of behavior define one's place in life; they also legitimize authority. The norms and symbols of legitimacy of authority and power in society are encased in religious and sacred doctrines.

6. **RIGID DIVISION OF LABOR BY AGE, SEX, KINSHIP** There is a rigid division of labor by age, sex, and kinship which continues to be important within the subcommunities of the city. The bonds of kinship continue to be the primary focus of solidarity and loyalty within the subgroups of the city.

7. **RELATIVELY LOW STATUS OF SPECIALIZATION IN TRADE** The seventh feature of the pre-industrial city is the relatively low status of specialization in trade. The merchant's guild is of relatively low status, in comparison with the political and religious elites, and its activities tend to be firmly controlled by the political and economic elites. Traders are not, for the most part, members of the elite even if they are wealthy.

Innovation and the Pre-Industrial City

As mentioned, the pre-industrial city is not a larger folk society. In fact, the pre-industrial city has characteristics in common with the modern industrial city. We now turn to a discussion of four characteristics that pre-industrial cities tend to share with modern industrial cities.

1. **NEW IDEAS** No institutions of insulation—guilds, caste, language barriers—can prevent contact altogether; and from contact comes recognition of diversity and hence new ideas. People become aware that there are different ways of life. And, as we discuss immediately below, these new ideas come to take on a new, a critical, character.

2. **RISE OF CRITICAL THOUGHT** Initially, the role of the literate class was the formalization and elaboration of the sacred traditions, which in folk societies had been oral in character. Initially, the literate class of scribes had no critical function in society. But, once you have a specialized priesthood with generations of hard work at thinking, in a motley array of diverse peoples and groups all living together, one can find the rise of critical thought, and critical thought can produce demands for change. And, in the pre-industrial city there is a social use, a political use for critical philosophy, perhaps for the first time.

3. **STRUCTURED CONFLICT** Regular conflict is old--conflict of one person with another person, conflict of one tribe with another tribe. In "regular conflict" what we have is conflict between similar units over the rights to particular objects. For example, tribes fight with other tribes over which land belongs to whom; clan fights with clan over real or supposed injuries or insults that members of the clan gave to each other; boys fight with boys over who won a game.

   In contrast, structured conflict within a community is new and it comes with the rise of urbanism. In cities, structures conflict, institutions conflict. You also get variable bases of power. Power rests on the control of resources. Once you have differentiated control over different types of resources, you have created different power bases in the society, fundamentally different power bases. So, it is no longer tribe against tribe. It's a new kind of conflict where the two sides are resting their power on fundamentally different resources. Various groups with different bases of power come to fight over where they should fit in the status hierarchy—priestly power conflicts with secular power, the archbishop fights with the king, the emperor fights with the pope, the landed aristocracy fights with the military or with the rising merchant classes. Indeed, the history of urban-agrarian society is largely the history of structured conflict. As the differentiated groups struggle for position, they make alliances with other elements of the population—with the rising merchant guilds, the merchant classes, or with the emerging proletariat, for example. You get a new phenomenon in the world, political history, and that is the next point.

4. **POLITICAL HISTORY** Political history, in the sense of a set of changing alliances between the varying power bases in a society, is born. Hence, with the city also emerges one of the central concerns of sociology, depicting the structure of conflict. It is important to recognize that the urban agrarian social order and the pre-industrial city are not folk societies writ large. It is true that pre-industrial cities have some of the sacredness and some of the traditional characteristics of a folk society, and that in its separate sub-segments a remnant of the folk orientation to the world remains. At the same time it is not like the folk society because of high levels of diversity and heterogeneity in the cities and because of the conflict, both structural and ideological, that arise. It is also not like the folk society because of the distribution of class, status, and power.

Let us now take a brief look at stratification in urban-agrarian societies.

Stratification in Urban-Agrarian Societies

If any single feature of stratification in urban-agrarian impresses itself on social scientists, it is the great inequality that exists among the members of each urban-agrarian society on whatever dimension or aspect of stratification you choose to consider—e.g., stratification on the basis of sex, race, ethnicity, class, power, status, religion, or caste. Urban-agrarian societies are the most highly stratified societies known to sociologists, anthropologists, and archaeologists. They are the most unequal societies known to those who study human societies.

In urban-agrarian societies, ascription becomes an important mechanism for allocating people to social positions. Sociologists say that a position is attained by **ascription** and that a position is **ascribed** to the extent that one gets that position through no efforts of his or her own. Frequent bases of ascription include age, sex, social class, race, and ethnicity, and religious affiliation. See Box 2.1. Ascription is seen in stark form in caste societies, which are nearly purely ascriptive stratification systems.

DHIMMITUDE AND URBAN-AGRARIAN SOCIETY

BOX 2.1

In terms of the distribution of class, status, and power, urban agrarian societies are the most highly stratified societies known to social scientists. This stark and highly structured inequality has many manifestations, just one of which is dhimmitude. Let us briefly introduce several concepts, a basic understanding of which will help to make this exposition on dhimmitude in urban-agrarian society more understandable and will situate it within a larger landscape of intellectual thought and history.

The word dhimmitude comes from "dhimmi," an Arabic word literally meaning "protected." The Arabic noun "*dhimma*" translates into English as a treaty or pact of protection. The followers of Islam are called Muslims and their Prophet is Muhammad, who was born in Mecca in the year 570. Muhammad organized Muslims into a community, and the Muslim community is known as the *umma*. The Muslim holy book is the Qur'an. Islamic law is known as shari'a. The Islamic theological concept of *jihad*, the holy war against non-Muslims, is richly textured and multifaceted, and it establishes a single pattern of relations between Muslims and non-Muslims and is central to their relationship. Furthermore, jihad encapsulates the Islamic worldview of war and peace and is also a specialized domain of Islamic theology and religion.

"People of the book" is a theological term, primarily related to Islam, describing people who, according to the Qur'an, received scriptures revealed to them by God prior to the time of Muhammad. Jews and Christians are referred to as "people of the book." In a state ruled by shari'a, dhimmi was the name applied by the Muslim conquerors to an indigenous non-Muslim (infidel) who was both "people of the book" and who, without fighting, submitted to the Islamic armies via a treaty or pact of protection and who paid the *jizya*, an annual poll tax or tribute. Dhimmis had fewer social and legal rights than Muslims, but more rights than other non-Muslim religious subjects who were treated more harshly (Stillman, 1979; Lewis, 1984).

For over a millennium (638-1683), Islamic conquests expanded over vast territories in Africa, Europe, and Asia. In this process, the Muslim empire incorporated numerous and varied peoples who had their own religion, culture, language and civilization. For centuries, "people of the book" were the great majority of the population in many of these Islamic lands. As such, they were an important source of tax revenue for the umma, as the amount of tax paid by dhimmis in the form of jizya was twice the amount of zakat tax paid by the Muslims (Ye'or, 2002). Although these peoples differed from each other and from their Muslim conquerors in many ways, they were ruled by the same type of laws based on shari'a. This similarity has created a civilization and a type of stratification that was developed and implemented over the centuries among the people of the book who lived in lands vanquished by jihad war and governed by shari'a law. It is this civilization and this system of stratification which is called dhimmitude (Ye'or, 2002b).

Characteristics of Dhimmitude

People of the book who submitted to the Islamic armies without fighting were granted a pledge of security for their life and possessions as well as relative self-autonomous administration and limited religious rights. These rights were subject to two conditions: the annual payment the jizya, a tribute or poll tax paid with humiliation by the dhimmi and submission to the provisions of Islamic law. The jizya is a per capita tax levied on the state's able-bodied non-Muslim males of military age (Kennedy, 2004) who, as people of the book, submitted without fighting in a jihad war. Although the jizya was an annual tax, non-Muslims were allowed to pay it in monthly installments (Hunter and Malik, 2005). Failure to pay the jizya is considered by Islamic jurists to constitute a rupture of the dhimma, which automatically both restores to the dhimmi the status of being an unsubjected infidel and to the umma its initial rights of war—to kill and to dispossess the dhimmi or to expel him (Ye'or, 2002). The pact of protection also is ruptured if the dhimmis rebel against Islamic law, entice a Muslim from his faith, harm a Muslim or his property, give allegiance to a non-Muslim state, or commit blasphemy (Al Mawardi, 2000). Blasphemy, whether by dhimmi or Muslim, was severely punished. In his classic treatise on the principles of Islamic governance, the 10th century Shafi'i scholar Al-Mawardi considered blasphemy a capital crime (Al Mawardi, 2000). The definition of blasphemy included denial of the prophethood of Muhammad, disrespectful references to Islam, and defamation of Muslim holy texts.

The rules governing the pact of protection between the umma and dhimmis were mostly established from the eighth to the ninth centuries by the founders of the four schools of Islamic law and these rules set the pattern of the Muslim community's relations with dhimmis (Ye'or, 2002). We now take a brief look at the political, legal, social, and religious aspects of dhimmitude.

Political Aspects

Dhimmis were prohibited from possessing or bearing weapons, and thereby dhimmis became prey to marauding, pillage, and massacre particularly during periods of insecurity, such as rebellions and invasions. Population transfer was another disability both in times of peace and in times of war. Dhimmi populations were deported for strategic reasons and for economic reasons. Departure had to take place on the same day or on very short notice—two to three days—making it impossible for the deportees to sell their possessions. Furthermore, billeting and provisioning soldiers and their horses and other animals were imposed by law on dhimmis. Soldiers and bests alike had to be lodged in the best houses, or in churches or synagogues.

Legal Aspects

Dhimmis could not give testimony in court against a Muslim. However, Muslims could testify against dhimmis (Friedmann, 2003). This legal asymmetry put dhimmis in a precarious position wherein they could not defend themselves against false accusations leveled by Muslims. Moreover, quite generally, penalties for offenses were unequal between Muslims and non-Muslims. The penalty for murder was even much lighter if the victim was dhimmi. Furthermore, dhimmis were forbidden to defend themselves if attacked physically by a Muslim, or to raise a hand against a Muslim "on pain of having it amputated" (Ye'or, 2002b: 103). If physically assaulted by a Muslim, the dhimmi's only recourse was to beg for mercy. Then, too, dhimmis were forbidden to have authority over Muslims, to possess or to buy land, to marry Muslim women, to have Muslim slaves or servants, or even to use the Arabic alphabet (Ye'or, 2002).

With regard to legal aspects of inheritance, the general principle in Islamic law is that a difference in religion is an obstacle to inheritance (Friedmann, 2003; Lewis, 1984), such that dhimmis cannot inherit from Muslims and Muslims cannot inherit from dhimmis. However, some jurists argue that a dhimmi cannot inherit from a Muslim but that a Muslim can inherit from a dhimmi. Shi'a scholars have successfully argued that if a dhimmi dies and leaves even one Muslim heir, then all of the estate belongs to the Muslim heir at the expense of any dhimmi heirs (Friedmann, 2003; Lewis, 1984).

Social Aspects

A corvée is labor that people in power have the authority to compel their subjects to perform. Dhimmis were subjected to the most degrading corvées. For instance, Jews in North Africa and Yemen were forced to do the job of executioner, gravedigger, cleaner of public latrines, and the like, even on Saturdays and holy days (Ye'or, 2002).

Dhimmis could be visually differentiated from Muslims at first sight. Vestimentary regulations were laid down by the founders of the four juridical schools as early as the eighth century, and they assigned to the dhimmi coarse cloth and specific colors for each religion and special belts and head gear made of particular fabrics and color and in a specified shape. Thus, the shape, color, and texture of their clothing were prescribed from head to foot. Likewise, their houses (by their color and size) and location (separate living quarters in the city).

As to dwelling places, the separation of Muslim and dhimmis was a religious obligation aimed at protecting the faith of the true believers. The different dhimmi groups were confined to districts separate from those of each other and separate from those of Muslims. The houses of the dhimmis had to be smaller, and lower, than those of Muslims. The houses of dhimmis also had to be humble in appearance, often painted in dark colors. Dhimmis were banned from living in certain districts and from living within proximity to venerated mosques (Ye'or, 2002b:101).

As to modes of conveyance, dhimmis were forbidden to ride noble animals, such as a horse or a camel. They were restricted to donkeys or mules, and, at certain periods, were only allowed to ride them once they were outside of town. Dhimmis were forbidden to use iron stirrups and saddle. For dhimmis, the ikaf (pack-saddle) and wooden stirrups would have to suffice, and then only with the dhimmi sitting with both legs on one side, like a woman. The dhimmi had to dismount upon sight of a Muslim.

The law required from dhimmis a humble demeanor. The dhimmi had to hurry through the streets, eyes lowered, always passing to the left (impure) side of a Muslim. The dhimmi had to give way to Muslims on the street. The dhimmi had to remain silent in the presence of a Muslim, only speaking with them when given permission (Ye'or, 2002b: 103). The dhimmi had to accept insults from a Muslim without replying. In the everyday speech and in official communication, dhimmis were frequently referred to by derogatory names, animal names or references being conspicuous (Ye'or, 2002b; Stillman, 1979). In the Ottoman Empire, the official name for dhimmis was "raya," meaning "herd of cattle." In Muslim parlance, "apes" was a standard epithet for the Jews. Christians were frequently called "pigs." In countries where they were admitted to a public bath, male and female dhimmis were forbidden to look upon naked Muslims of their own sex (Ye'or, 200b: 100). If a dhimmi were admitted to a public bath, the dhimmi had to wear bells to signal his presence.

Religious Aspects

Although dhimmis were allowed to perform their religious rituals, they were obliged to do so in a manner not obvious to Muslims (Karsh, 2007). Thus, displaying of religious symbols or icons on clothing or buildings was prohibited. Loud prayers were forbidden, as were the ringing of church bells and the trumpeting of shofars. A shofar is a horn used for Jewish religious purposes. In Jewish religious practice, shofar blowing is incorporated in synagogue services on Yom Kippur and Rosh Hashanah, the Jewish high holy days. Other restrictions included the prohibition on publishing or selling non-Muslim literature. Dhimmis also were not allowed to build new churches or synagogues, or expand or repair existing ones, even if they fell into ruin (Ye'or, 2002). The closing, confiscation, and Islamization of synagogues and churches were common (Ye'or, 2002).

The comprehensive system of dhimmitude permeated Islamic civilizations in urban agrarian societies. It is being revived today through what some term an "Islamic resurgence" and the return to shari'a in some countries. Hence, this pattern is not transient. It is persistent.

CASTE

Caste is an important part of social life in urban agrarian society. About 3,000 years ago, the *Hindu caste system* developed in agrarian India. Society there became divided into *varnas*, which the British later called castes, and which were arranged in a hierarchy. At the top of the Hindu caste system are the *Brahmins* (priests, teachers, physicians). In a descending order are the *Kshatriya* (warriors, rulers, soldiers, civil servants, legislators), the *Vaisyas* (farmers, merchants, and artisans), and *Sudras* (peasants, laborers). A person born in a caste carries the name of the caste as part of his or her surname.

Outside of the caste system are the *Untouchables*, who are viewed as highly polluted and polluting persons by those in castes. Mahatma Gandhi termed the Untouchables ***"Harijan,"*** which translates roughly into English as "Children of God." Today, the term *Dalit* has become synonymous with Untouchable in India. It means "oppressed." Dalits are estimated to number about 250 million people in India, which is about 1/6th (or 17 percent) of the Indian population (Dalit Solidarity, 2013; Antelava, 2012).

The caste system in India regulated social life extensively and minutely. Occupation was allocated on the basis of caste, and marriage occurred within, rather than between, castes. Rituals of purification were prescribed and utilized if one became "polluted" by contact with someone of a lower caste or of "outcaste" status. Even though the caste system was formally abolished in 1949, caste discrimination in India persists to this day.

The most extreme gender stratification is found in agrarian societies. Scholars are in disagreement about *why* gender inequality, as with all forms of inequality, increased so markedly in agrarian societies. Five practices found in agrarian societies illustrate and manifest the highly subordinate status of women and girls in these societies: purdah, footbinding, sati, coverture, and genital mutilation.

PURDAH

In India, the word "purdah," from the Hindi "parda," translates into English as "screen" or "veil." **Purdah** refers to the seclusion of women from public observation, and it is accomplished by wearing concealing clothing from head to toe and by the use of high-walled enclosures, walls, curtains, and screens within the home. The practice of purdah is said to have originated in the Persian culture and to have been acquired in the seventh century by the Muslims during the Arab conquest of what is now Iraq (Ahmed, 1992). In turn, Muslim domination of northern India influenced the practice of Hinduism, which is an example of **cultural diffusion**. Cultural diffusion is the transmission of cultural traits or social practices from one culture or subculture to another through such mechanisms as exploration, military conquest, social interaction, tourism, immigration, the mass media, and so forth. Purdah became widely observed among upper caste Hindus in northern India.

Purdah flourished in ancient Babylon, where no woman could go outside the home unless she was masked and accompanied by a male from her family, and even parts of the household were separated as a practice of segregation. Ancient Assyrian women also practiced purdah. The Prophet Muhammad incorporated the practice of purdah as part of the Islamic tenets of faith. During British hegemony in India, purdah observance was widespread among both the Muslim minority and among upper caste and affluent Hindus. Since then, purdah has become far less widespread among Hindus in India, but the seclusion and veiling of women is still practiced to a greater or lesser degree in many Islamic countries today (Nanji, 1996; Paul, 1992; Mernissi, 1987). The limits imposed by purdah vary according to different countries and class levels.

FOOTBINDING

During a thousand-year period, the institution of footbinding pervaded China. **Footbinding** refers to "the thwarting of the growth of a female's feet" (Kendall, 2005:364). Older women bound the feet of young girls, in a process that took many years and a great deal of pain and suffering. Without meticulous, constant attention, bound feet were malodorous. Women with bound feet were essentially crippled and housebound. Peasant women did not have their feet bound because they had to work in the fields.

The practice appeared in the Sung Dynasty (960-1279). The status of women declined in the Sung: *concubinage*, the acquisition of women without benefit of true marriage, expanded; upper-class dowries increased; and a neo-Confucian ideology with tenets of female seclusion, female chastity, and female subordination emerged and came to reign (Mackie, 1996; Ebrey, 1991). Footbinding was viewed as necessary for a proper marriage to be brokered and for family honor (Ebrey, 1990, 1991), and it continued into the early twentieth century.

SATI

Agrarian societies developed various solutions to "the widow" problem. One such solution is **sati**, also known as suttee, the immolation of a widow on her dead husband's funeral pyre. This custom was more frequent among the priestly and noble families in parts of India, and it persisted into the twentieth century. This practice had the effect of keeping the dead husband's resources in male line (Nielsen, 1990; Goode, 1963; Altekar, 1956).

COVERTURE

Coverture is an English common-law concept. Derived, at least in part, from Roman and feudal Norman custom, it dictated a woman's legal subordination to her husband during marriage (Ferrone, 2003; Bailey, 2002). According to the doctrine of **coverture**, upon marriage the husband and wife become a single legal identity, that of the husband. Prior to marriage, an adult woman (*feme sole*, from the Norman French, meaning "single woman") could freely enter into contracts; she could sell or give away her real estate or personal property as she wished. In contrast, a married woman (*feme covert*), was under the protection or cover of the husband. Her legal existence as an individual was suspended. Coverture renders a married woman unable to own property in her own name, unable to enter into contracts without her husband's consent, unable to obtain a loan without her husband's consent, and she is unable to execute a will without her husband's consent. If she works for income, the income she earns belongs to her husband. Under coverture, marital assets were considered the property of the husband (Cavallo and Warner, 1999).

Even under coverture, however, women had some control over property (Ferrone, 2003). Thus, at the death of her husband, a widow was entitled to one-third of his property as her dower. Because of this entitlement, a husband could not transfer or sell property without his wife's consent. Were he to do so, after his death she could claim that the transfer or sale was illegal and demand return of the property. It is for this reason that wives usually signed their husband's deeds of sale or of transfer, to show their consent. Often a statement that the woman was signing of her own free will and was not being coerced by her husband accompanied her signature.

The doctrine of coverture was imported from England into Colonial America. In the United States, coverture began to be disassembled through legislation at the state level beginning in Mississippi in 1839.

GENITAL MUTILATION

The term female **genital mutilation** (FGM) refers to all procedures involving total or partial removal of the external female genitalia (World Health Organization, 2013; Mackie, 1996). Genital mutilation also is known as female genital cutting (FGC), female circumcision, clitoridectomy, or infibulation. It is an umbrella term that refers to several practices that are deeply embedded in the culture of various groups around the world (e.g., United Nations, UNICEF, 2005; Islam and Uddin, 2001; World Health Organization, 2013; Jones, Diop, Askew, and Kabore, 1999). One practice, common in Egypt, is *sunna circumcision*, after the Arabic word for tradition. In this procedure, the clitoral foreskin (or prepuce) is removed. Sometimes part or the entire clitoris is removed as well. A second practice involves the excision of the clitoris with partial or total excision of the labia minora. A third practice, called *infibulation* (or pharonic circumcision) is more severe. It involves the removal of the clitoris, the labia minora, and most of the labia majora, leaving only an opening large enough for the passage of urine and menses. Infibulation is most common in Africa.

The short-term, immediate health consequences of FGM vary according to the type, severity, and method of the procedure performed. In the short-term, the immediate health consequences include pain, shock, hemorrhage, infection, and death. Long-term consequences include recurring urinary tract infections, difficulties in menstruation, chronic reproductive tract infections, and painful sexual intercourse. The infibulated female must be cut open, so that she can have sexual relations with her husband. She may be sewn up again if he leaves home for an extended period of time, as for a business trip abroad. The infibulated female must be cut open further, if she is to give birth vaginally. Then, following childbirth, she will be again infibulated, only to have to be cut open again, to resume sexual relations with her husband. Over time, these repeated procedures can lead to a buildup of scar tissue, leading to menstrual and urinary-tract complications.

FGM is practiced in 28 African countries as well as in Asia (Indonesia) and the Middle East. It is increasingly common in the USA, Europe, Australia, and Canada, primarily among immigrants from these countries (Amnesty International, 2004). About 140 million girls and women worldwide are living with the consequences of FMG (World Health Organization, 2013). In Africa alone, some 101 million girls age 10 years and older are estimated to have undergone FGM and more than three million girls are estimated to be at risk for FGM annually (World Health Organization, 2013).

The great world conflicts and world transformations that we are seeing today are associated with the impact of urban-industrial society on urban-agrarian society, with the impact of urban-agrarian society on modern industrial states, and with the transformation of urban-agrarian societies into powerful modern industrial states (e.g., Kennedy, 2002; Lin, 2001; Wimmer 2002; Wu and Xie, 2003; Xhou, Zhao Li, and Cai, 2003; Ye'or, 2005).

VIOLENCE IN FOLK, URBAN-AGRARIAN, AND MODERN INDUSTRIAL STATES

Max Weber reminds us that violence is something absolutely primordial: every group, from the household to the largest forms of political association, always has resorted to physical violence when it had to protect the interests of its members and was capable of so doing (Weber, 1968: 904). Since scientists are interested in patterns of behavior, we may well ask whether those who study violence and war in the long sweep of human history and prehistory have discovered or observed a patterning with regard to the prevalence of violence, and, if so, what that pattern is.

Before exploring a large body of research bearing on these matters, let us first review two differing and influential visions of what that patterning might look like. These intellectual traditions or idea systems were given to us in 1754 by Enlightenment philosopher Jean-Jacques Rousseau in his "Discourse on the Origin and Foundations of Inequality Among Men" (Rousseau, 2011, 1754) and by the English philosopher Thomas Hobbes in his book *Leviathan,* which was published in 1651 (Hobbes, 1985, 1651).

A Conflict of Visions: Hobbes (1651) and Rousseau (1754)

The English philosopher Thomas Hobbes (1588-1679) reached his conclusions about the nature of folk or hunting-and-gathering society via a series of logical arguments in his great work, *Leviathan* (1985, 1651). He argues that, in practical terms, all men are equals because no one was so superior in strength or intelligence that he could not be overcome by stealth or the conspiracy of others (Keeley, 1996: 5). Hobbes sees humans as equally endowed with *will* (desires) and *prudence* (the capacity to learn from experience). When two such equals desire what only one could enjoy, one eventually subdued or destroyed the other in pursuit of it. Once this had happened, it was a game changer: the similar desires of others tempted them to engage in the successful approach of the winner. Moreover, their intelligence enticed them to guard themselves against the fate of the loser. In the absence of a power to "overawe" these equals, prudent self-preservation induced every individual to attempt to preserve his *liberty* (the absence of impediments to his will) by endeavoring to subdue others and by resisting their attempts to subdue him. In this way, Hobbes came to envision the original state of human existence (folk or hunting and gathering society) as being "the war of every man against every man." In this kind of society, men lived in "continual feare, and danger of violent death"

(Hobbes, 1985, 1651: 186). In the state of nature, there was no peace anywhere. In short, life was "solitary, poore, nasty, brutish, and short" (Hobbes, 1985, 1651: 186).

Humans escape this state of war only be agreeing to *covenants* in which they surrender much of their liberty and accept rule by a central authority (which, for Hobbes, meant a monarch, a king). For Hobbes, "Covenants without the Sword, are but Words, and of no strength to secure a man at all" (Hobbes, `1985:1651: 223). Therefore, the state (the king) had to be granted monopoly over the legitimate use of force in order to punish criminals and to defend against external enemies; otherwise, anarchy reigns. Civilized countries returned to this condition when central authority was widely defied or deprived of its power, as during rebellions. All civilized "industry," commerce, proliferation of the arts and literature depend on a peace maintained by central government; the "humanity" of humans is thus a product of civilization and of a civilizing process made possible by the state as a form of human organization.

For Hobbes, then, life has its tradeoffs, or, as sociologists might express it, life is an exchange order. One can have a perfectly "free" life—which is nasty, brutish and short; or, one can have life under a state. In this latter condition, one is constrained, some would say "oppressed" but more people live and are alive for more years. It's a tradeoff, an exchange order. For Hobbes, violence and war could be constrained, reigned in, by social innovations, i.e., by what sociologists would call the social institution of the state with its coercive institutions of enforcement.

For the past two centuries the most influential critic of Hobbes's view of folk or hunting-and-gathering society has been Jean-Jacque Rousseau (1712-1778). Rousseau's perspective frames the world of the hunter-gatherers ("primitive man") as innately peaceful and the nature of primitive man as innately good. Our ancestors are seen as living in a peaceful, even idyllic, world where "men were innocent and virtuous" (Rousseau, 2011, 1754, as quoted by Potts and Hayden, 2008: 18). It is corrupt and evil institutions (e.g., monarchy, marriage, monogamy, private property, education, religion) that cause violence and war in human societies, says Rousseau. If we want to do away with violence and war, we must eliminate these corrupt institutions and put others in their place.

Rousseau was no empiricist and he disdained the empiricism of the historian and of the scientist (Keeley, 1996: 6). He paints a portrait of the distant human past (hunter-gatherer or folk society) as one of equality and peace. The original condition of humankind was one of equality where humans were ruled by their passions. These passions could be easily and peaceably satisfied without the "unnatural" institutions of monogamy and private property. Any tendency toward aggression in this "natural condition" (of hunting and gathering or folk society) would be suppressed by humans' innate pity or compassion. This natural compassion was extinguished only when envy was created by the origins of marriage, private property, social inequality, and "civil" society. Rousseau claims that "the savage," *except when hungry*, was the friend of all creation and the enemy of none. Rousseau indeed waxed poetic about "the Noble Savage," which he saw as the condition of human beings living in hunting and gathering societies. In short, the original state of human society is a peaceful combination of free love and communism.

Now that we've become familiar with the ideas of these two different intellectual traditions, let us ask the question as to which position is better supported by the empirical historical evidence. Or, stated somewhat differently, what pattern, if any, is observable in terms of violence and war in the long historical panorama of human existence?

Pattern of Violence Across Types of Societies?

There is an observable, documentable pattern of violence across types of societies, and it is that violence *decreases* from a high point in folk and hunting-and-gathering societies. Let us look at just a few examples.

MURDER RATES Murder rates were very high in hunting-gathering societies. Political scientist Azar Gat (Gat, 2006) and others (e.g., Keeley, 1996; Knauft, 1987; Eibl-Eibesfeldt, 1979: 125-161; Eibl-Eibesfeldt, 1974) document that quarrels were rife among hunter gatherers, resulting in homicide rates that are much higher than in any modern industrial society. For example, the Kung San, also known as "Bushmen" of the Kalahari Desert, had a homicide rate from 1920 to 1955 that was four times that of the United States and twenty to eighty times that of major industrial nations during the 1950s and 1960s (Keeley, 1996: 29). The Copper Eskimo also experienced a high level of feuding and homicide before the Royal Canadian Mounted Police suppressed it (Keeley, 1996: 29). Similarly, the murder rate for the Netsilik Eskimo, *even after the Mounties had suppressed interband feuding,* is four times greater than that of the United States and some fifteen to forty times greater than that of modern European states (Keeley, 1996: 29). With regard to the Gebusi of New Guinea, calculations show that the military of the United States, in addition to its internal homicide rate, would have had to kill practically the *entire* population of South Vietnam during its nine-year involvement there, to equal the homicide rate among the Gebusi (Keeley, 1996: 30; Knauft, 1987:464).

FREQUENCY OF WARFARE As with homicide rates, so, too, with warfare. With regard to frequency of warfare in state and non-state societies, non-state societies are characterized by far greater frequency of warfare (e.g., Gat, 2013; Pinker, 2011; Gat, 2010; Gat, 2006; Keeley, 1999). The high frequencies of warfare in hunting and gathering societies stands in contrast to those of even the most aggressive ancient or modern states. The early Roman Republic (510-121 BC) was attacked or initiated war about once every twenty years (Keeley, 1996: 33). Most inhabitants of the Roman Empire were rarely directly involved in warfare. Most experienced the Pax Romana over many generations.

Historic data on the period from 1800 to 1945 indicate that the average nation-state goes to war about once in a generation (Keeley, 1996: 187-188). Compared that with the figures from an ethnographic sample of non-state societies, where 65 percent were at war *continuously*; 77 percent were at war once every five years, and 55 percent were at war *every year* (Keeley, 1996: 33). The reasonable conclusion is that wars were more frequent in pre-state societies than they are in state societies, particularly modern states.

DEATH RATE DUE TO WARFARE As with frequency of warfare, so, too, with the death rate due to warfare: it *decreases* as societies move from a pre-state (e.g., hunting and gathering) to state societies, just as Hobbes would have predicted. Steven Pinker, in *The Better Angels of Our Nature* (Pinker, 2011: 48-55) documents this long-term historical trend. Among skeletons that had been dug out of archeological sites from Asia, Africa, Europe, and the Americas and that date from 14,000 BC to 1770 AD (Bowles, 2009; Keeley, 1996), the death rate from violence averaged 15 percent (Pinker, 2011: 48). This rate is similar to that derived from eight contemporary or recent societies that also make their living primarily from hunting and gathering (Bowles, 2009). They come from the Philippines and Australia, and their average death rate from warfare is 14 percent (Pinker: 2011: 50). Among pre-state societies that engage in some mixture of hunting, gathering, and horticulture (farming) in New Guinea, the Amazon rain forest, and the Montenegro in Europe, the average rate of death from warfare is 24.5 percent (Pinker, 2011: 50).

Let us compare those rates with rates of death from warfare in state societies. In the cities and empires of pre-Columbian Mexico, 5 percent of the deaths were due to warfare, which is a rate that is a third to a fifth as violent as an average pre-state society. In other words, in an average pre-state society the rate of death due to warfare is three to five times *higher* than in the cities and empires of pre-Columbian Mexico.

The two most violent centuries of the past half millennium of European history have been the 17th with its wars of religion and the 20th with two World Wars. Historian Quincy Wright estimates that the rate of death in the wars of the 17th century at 2 percent and the rate of death in the first half of the 20th century at 3 percent (Pinker, 2011: 50; Harris, 1975). If we add in the remainder of the twentieth century and look at the entire 20th century, the percentage would be even lower (Pinker, 2011: 50). In summary, modern Western countries, even in their more war torn centuries, suffer no more than 25 percent of the average death rate due to war compared with nonstate societies (Pinker, 2011: 52).

SUGGESTED READINGS

Collier, *Wars, Guns, and Votes* (New York: Harper Perennial, 2010).

Gat, Azar, *Nations: The Long History and Deep Roots of Political Ethnicity and Nationalism* (New York: Cambridge University Press, 2013).

Gat, Azar, *Victorious and Vulnerable: Why Democracy Won in the 20th Century and How it is Still Imperiled* (Lanham, MD: Rowman & Littlefield, 2010).

Gat, Azar, *War in Human Civilization* (New York: Oxford University Press, 2006).

Keeley, Lawrence H., *War Before Civilization* (New York: Oxford, 1999).

LeBlanc, Steven A., *Constant Battles: Why We Fight* (New York: St. Martin's Griffin, 2003).

Nolan, Patrick, and Lenski, Gerhard, *Human Societies: An Introduction to Macro-Sociology* Eleventh Edition (Boulder, Colorado: Paradigm Publishers, 2011).

Potts, Malcolm and Hayden, Thomas, *Sex and War* (Dallas TX: BenBella Books, Inc., 2008).

Schneider, Linda and Silverman, Arnold, "The San Peoples of Namibia: Ancient Culture in a New Nation," in Linda Schneider and Arnold Silverman, *Global Sociology: Introducing Five Contemporary Societies* Sixth Edition (New York: McGraw Hill, 2013), pp. 128- 183.

Shlapentokh, Vladimir, *Contemporary Russia as a Feudal Society: A New Perspective on the Post-Soviet Era* in collaboration with Joshua Woods (New York: Palgrave Macmillan, 2008).

Szuchman, Jeffrey (Ed.), *Nomads, Tribes, and the State in the Ancient Near East* (Chicago, Illinois: Oriental Institute of Chicago, 2009).

Workman, James G., *Heart of Dryness: How the Last Bushmen Can Help Us Endure the Coming Age of Permanent Drought* (New York: Walker & Co., 2009).

Ye'or, Bat, *Islam and Dhimmitude: Where Civilizations Collide* Translated from the French by Miriam Kochan and David Littman (Madison, NJ: Fairleigh Dickinson University Press, 2002).

BIBLIOGRAPHY

Ackerman, Lillian A., *A Necessary Balance: Gender and Power Among Indians of the Columbia Plateau* (Norman, OK: University of Oklahoma Press, 2003).

Ahmed, Leila, *Women and Gender in Islam: Historical Roots of a Modern Debate* (New Haven, CT: Yale University Press, 1992).

Al-Mawardi, Ali ibn Muhammad, *The Ordinances of Government* Translated by Professor Wafaa H. Wahba (RFeading: Garnet Publishing, 2000).

Altekar, A.S., *The Position of Women in Hindu Civilization* (Banaras: Motilal Banarsidas, 1956).

Amnesty International, Amnesty International Press Release, "International Zero Tolerance to FGM Day: Effective measures needed to protect girls from female genital mutilation," February 6, 2004, AI Index: ACT 77/018/2004.

Antelava, Natalie, "India's Dalits Still Fighting Untouchability," BBC News India, June 27, 2012, 00:53 ET. As of June 2, 2013, available online at http://www.bbc.co.uk/news/world-asia-india-18394914?print=true

Bailey, Joanne, "Favoured or Oppresses? Married Women, Property, and 'Coverture' in England, 1660-1800," *Continuity and Change*, Vol. 17, No. 3, (December) 2002.

Barnard, Alan J. (Ed.), *Hunter-gatherers in History, Archaeology, and Anthropology* (New York: Berg, 2004).

Barnard, Alan J., *Anthropology and the Bushman* (New York: Berg, 2007).

Blau, Peter Michael, "Micro Processes and Macrostructures," in Karen S. Cook (Ed.), *Social Exchange Theory* (Beverly Hills, CA: Sage Publications, 1987): 83-100.

Philip Caulfield, Philip, "Georgia Dad Paralyzed Trying to Save Drowning 4-year-old Girl Dies in Hospital," New York Daily News, June 28, 2013. As of June 29, 2013, available online at http://www.nydailynews.com/news/national/paralyzed-good-samaritan-dies-hospital-article-1.1385240

Cavallo, Sandra, and Warner, Lyndam (Eds.), *Widowhood in Medieval and Early Modern Europe* (New York, NY: Addison Wesley Longman, 1999).

Childe, V. Gordon, *Dawn of European Civilization* (London: Routledge and Paul, 1957).

Childe, V. Gordon, *Man Makes Himself* (New York: New American Library, 1983).

Childe, V. Gordon, *New Light on the Most Ancient East* revised edition (London: Routledge, 1952).

Childe, V. Gordon, *Piecing Together the Past: The Interpretation of Archaeological Data* (London: Routledge and Paul, 1956).

Childe, V. Gordon, *Prehistoric Communities of the British Isles* (New York: B. Blom, 1972).

Coimbra, Carlos E. A.; Flowers, Nancy M.; Salzano, Francisco M.; and Santos, Ricardo V., *The Xavánte in Transition: Health, Ecology, and Bioanthropology in Central Brazil* (Ann Arbor: University of Michigan Press, 2004).

Cooley, Charles Horton, *Social Organization* (New York: Schocken, 1962) (Originally published, 1909).

Dalit Solidarity, "Advocating the Rights of the Marginalised Dalits: 12 Years of Humanitarian Service (2000-2012)." As of June 2, 2013, available online at http://www.dalitsolidarity.org

Durkheim, Emile, *The Division of Labor in Society* (New York: Free Press, 1964). (Originally published, 1895).

Ebrey, Patricia, "Shifts in Marriage Finance from the Sixth to the Thirteenth Century," in R.S. Watson and P.B. Ebrey, *Marriage and Inequality in Chinese Society* (Berkeley, CA: University of California Press, 1991): 97-132.

Ebrey, Patricia, "Women, Marriage, and Family in Chinese History," in P.S. Ropp, *Heritage of China* (Berkeley, CA: University of California Press, 1990): 197-223.

Eibl-Eibesfeldt, Irenaeus, *Biology of Peace and War: Men, Animals, and Aggression* Translated from the German by Eric Mosbacher (New York: Viking Press, 1979).

Eibl-Eibesfeldt, Irenaeus, "The Myth of the Aggression-Free Hunter and Gatherer Society," pp. 435-457 of Ralph Holloway (Ed.), *Primate Aggression: Territoriality and Xenophobia* (New York: Academic Press, 1974).

Ferrone, Stephen D., "The Evolution of Spousal Rights," *The Estate Analyst*, September 2003: 1-4.

Flinn, Ryan, "Ancient Art, Music Flowered as Communities, Not Brains, Grew," *Bloomberg*, June 4, 2009, 14:00 EDT. As of July 2, 2013, available online at http://tinyurl.com/pje9fq

Friedl, Ernestine, *Vasilika: A Village in Modern Greece* (New York: Holt, Rinehart, and Winston, 1962).

Friedmann, Yohanan, *Tolerance and Coercion in Islam: Interfaith Relations in the Muslim Tradition* (New York: Cambridge University Press, 2003).

Gamson, William, "Hiroshima, the Holocaust, and the Politics of Exclusion," *American Sociological Review*, Vol. 60, 1995: 1-20.

Gat, Azar, *Nations: The Long History and Deep Roots of Political Ethnicity and Nationalism* (New York: Cambridge University Press, 2013).

Gat, Azar, *Victorious and Vulnerable: Why Democracy Won in the 20th Century and How it is Still Imperiled* (Lanham, MD: Rowman & Littlefield, 2010).

Gat, Azar, *War in Human Civilization* (New York: Oxford University Press, 2006).

Gluick, Walter B., "Roots of Technological Responsibility in Religion: The Lesson of Ancient Sumer," in John W. Murphy and John T. Pardeck, *Technology and Human Productivity: Challenges for the Future* (New York: McGraw-Hill Book Company, 1986), pp. 157-168.

Goldstein, Joshua S., and Pevehouse, Jon C., *International Relations* Brief Fifth Edition (New York: Longman, 2010).

Goode, William J., *World Revolution and Family Patterns* (New York, NY: The Free Press, 1963).

Gourevitch, Philip, "Letter from Rwanda: After the Genocide," *The New Yorker* (December 18, 1995: 78-94).

Gusfield, Joseph R., "Primordialism and Nationality," *Transaction*, Vol. 33, No. 2, (January/February) 1996: 53-57.

Hill, Kim; Kaplan, H.; Hawkes, K.; and Hurtado, A.M., "Men's Time Allocation to Subsistence Work among the Ache of Eastern Paraguay," Human Ecology, Vol. 13, No. 1, 1985: 29-47.

Hobbes, Thomas, *Leviathan* (London: Penguin Books, 1985). Originally published 1651.

Hogg, Michael A., and Williams, K.D., "From I to We: Social Identity and the Collective Self," *Group Dynamics*, Vol. 4, 2000: 81-97.

Holmberg, Allen, "Nomads of the Longbow: The Siriono of Eastern Bolivia," Smithsonian Institution, Institute of Social Anthropology, Publication No. 10 (Washington, DC: United States Government Printing Office, 1950). Prepared in Cooperation with the United States Department of State as a Project of the Interdepartmental Committee on Scientific and Cultural Cooperation.

Holy, Ladislav, *The Little Czech and the Great Czech Nation: National Identity and the Post-Communist Transformation of Society* (New York: Cambridge University Press, 1996).

Humphries, Harry L.; Conrad, Browyn K.; Berry, Rimal; Reed, Shelli; and Jennings, Clara Michelle, "Framing the Gift of Life: An Empirical Examination of Altruism, Social Distance, and Material

Incentives in Kidney Donor Motivation," National Kidney Foundation: Spring Clinical Meeting, Nashville, TN, March 25-29, 2009.

Hunter, Shireen and Malik, Huma (Eds.), *Islam and Human Rights: Advancing a U.S.-Muslim Dialogue* (Washington, D.C.: Center for Strategic and International Studies, 2005).

Hurtado, A.; Hawkes, K.; Hill, K.; and Kaplan, H., "Female Subsistence Strategies among Ache Hunter-Gatherers of Eastern Paraguay," *Human Ethnology*, Vol. 13, No. 1, 1985:1-28.

Hutchinson, Sharon E., *Nuer Dilemmas: Coping with Money, War, and the State* (Berkeley: University of California Press, 1996).

Islam, M. Mazharul; and Uddin, M. Mosleh, "Female Circumcision in Sudan: Future Prospects and Strategies for Eradication," *International Family Planning Perspectives*, Vol. 27, No. 2 (June 2001): 71-76.

Jones, Brian, "A Social Network Analysis Approach to Henrich's Model of Biased Skill Transmission: Implications for the MSA (Middle Stone Age)-LSA (Late Stone Age) Transition," Paper presented at the 2011 76th Annual Society for American Archaeology Meetings, Sacramento, CA, March 31, 2011. As of July 2, 2013, available online at http://academia.edu/1318930/A_Social_Network_Analysis_Approach_to_Henrichs_Model_of_Biased_Skill_Transmission_implications_for_the_MSA_-_LSA_transition

Jones, Heidi; Diop, Nafissatou; Askew, Ian; and Kabore, Inoussa, "Female Genital Cutting Practices in Burkina Fasso and Mali and Their Negative Health Outcomes," *Studies in Family Planning*, Vol. 30, No. 3 (September 1999): 219-230.

Joyce, Christopher, "Larger Populations Triggered Stone Age Learning," NPR, June 5, 2009, 12:35 AM. As of July 2, 2013, available online at http://tinyurl.com/pdohgt

Karsh, Ephraim, *Islamic Imperialism: A History* (New Haven, CT: Yale University Press, 2007).

Keeley, Lawrence H., *War Before Civilization: The Myth of the Peaceful Savage* (New York: Oxford University Press, 1996).

Kendall, Diana, *Sociology in Our Times* Fifth Edition (Belmont, CA: Wadsworth/Thompson Learning, 2005).

Kennedy, Hugh N., *The Prophet and the Age of the Caliphates: The Islamic Near East from the Sixth to the Eleventh Century* Second Edition (New York: Longman, 2004).

Kennedy, Michael, *Cultural Formations of Post-Communism: Emancipation, Transition, Nation, and War* (Minneapolis: University of Minnesota Press, 2002).

Knauft, Bruce, "Reconsidering Violence in Simple Societies: Homicide among the Gebusi of New Guinea," *Current Anthropology*, Vol. 28, 1987: 457-500.

Laing, Lloyd, *The Archaeology of Celtic Britain and Ireland, c. AD 400-1200* (New York: Cambridge University Press, 2006).

Lekson, Stephen H., (Ed.), *The Archaeology of Chaco Canyon: An Eleventh-century Pueblo Regional Center* (Santa Fe, N.M.: School of American Research Press, 2006).

Lenski, Gerhard, *Power and Privilege: A Theory of Stratification* (Chapel Hill, NC: University of North Carolina Press, 1984).

Lewis, Bernard, *The Jews of Islam* (Princeton: Princeton University Press, 1984).

Lin, Yi-min, *Between Politics and Markets: Firms, Competition, and Institutional Change in Post-Mao China* (New York: Cambridge University Press, 2001)

Lindeman, M., "In-group Bias, Self Enhancement, and Group Identification," *European Journal of Social Psychology*, Vol. 27, 1997: 337-355.

Mackie, Gerry, "Ending Footbinding and Infibulation: A Convention Account," *American Sociological Review*, Vol. 61, No. 6 (December 1996): 999-1017.

Mayhew, Leon, *Society: Institutions and Activity* (Glenview, Illinois: Scott, Foresman and Company, 1971).

Mernissi, Fatima, *The Veil and the Male Elite* (New York, NY: Addison-Wesley Publishing Company, 1987).

Morris, James, *Heaven's Command: An Imperial Progress* (New York: Brace Jovanovich, 1973).

Mullen, B., "Group Composition, Salience, and Cognitive Representations: The Phenomenology of Being in a Group," *Journal of Experimental Social Psychology*, Vol. 27, 1991: 297 - 323.

Mullen, B., Brown, R., and Smith, C., "In-group Bias as a Function of Salience, Relevance, and Status: An Integration," *European Journal of Social Psychology*, Vol. 22, 1992: 103-122.

Myers, David G., *Social Psychology* Seventh edition (Boston: Mc Graw Hill, 2002).

Nanji, Azim (Ed.), *The Muslim Almanac* (New York, NY: Gale Research, Inc, 1996).

Nielsen, Joyce McCarl, *Sex and Gender in Society: Perspectives on Stratification* Second Edition (Prospects Heights, IL: Waveland, 1990).

Nolan, Patrick, and Lenski, Gerhard, *Human Societies: An Introduction to Macro-Sociology* (Boulder, CO: Paradigm Publishers, 2006).

Paul, B.K., "Female Activity Space in Rural Bangladesh," *Geographical Review*, January 1992: 1-12.

Petersen, William, *Population* Second Edition (New York: The Macmillan Company, 1969).

Pinker, Steven, *The Better Angels of Our Nature: Why Violence Has Declined* (New York: Viking, 2011).

Popielarz, Pamela A., and McPherson, J. Miller, "On the Edge or In Between: Niche Position, Niche Overlap, and the Duration of Voluntary Association Memberships," *American Journal of Sociology*, Vol. 101, 1995: 698-720.

Potts, Malcolm and Hayden, Thomas, *Sex and War* (Dallas TX: BenBella Books, Inc., 2008).

Redfield, Robert, "The Folk Society," *American Journal of Sociology*, Vol. 52, 1947: 293-308.

Rousseau, Jean-Jacques, *Discours sur l'Origine et le Fondement de l'Inégalité parmi les Hommes* (*Discourse on the Origin and Foundation of Inequality Among Men*) Translated and Edited by Helena Rosenblatt (New York: Bedford/St. Martin's, 2011). Originally published in 1754.

Roy, Beth, *Some Trouble with Cows: Making Sense of Social Conflict* (Berkeley, CA: University of California Press, 1994).

Powell, Adam; Shennan, Stephan; and Thomas, Mark, "Late Pleistocene Demography and the Appearance of Modern Human Behavior," *Science*, Vol. 324, No. 5932, June 5, 2009: 1298-1301.

Shils, Edward, "Primordial, Personal, Sacred, and Civil Ties," *British Journal of Sociology*, Vol. 8, 1957: 130-145.

Sjoberg, Gideon, "Folk and 'Feudal' Societies," *American Journal of Sociology*, Vol. LVlll, November 1952: 231-239).

Sjoberg, Gideon, "The Folk Society," *American Journal of Sociology*, Vol. L11, January, 1947: 293-308.

Sjoberg, Gideon, "The Preindustrial City," *American Journal of Sociology*, Vol. LX, March 1955: 438-445).

Sjoberg, Gideon, *The Preindustrial City* (New York: The Free Press, 1960).

Smith, Andrew B., *African Herders: Emergence of Pastoral Traditions* (Walnut Creek, CA: AltaMira Press, 2005).

Spencer, Baldwin, and Gillen, F.J., *The Arunta: A Study of a Stone Age People* (London: Macmillan, 1927).

Stillman, Norman, *The Jews of Arab Lands: A History and Source Book* (Philadelphia: Jewish Publication Society of America, 1979).

Theodorson, George A., and Theodorson, Achilles, G., *A Modern Dictionary of Sociology* (New York: Barnes & Noble Books, 1969).

Turner, John C., "Social Identification and Psychological Group Formation," in H. Tajfel (Ed.), *The Social Dimensions: European Developments in Social Psychology* Vol. 2 (London: Cambridge University Press, 1984).

Turner, John C., "Social Identification and Psychological Group Formation," in H. Tajfel (Ed.), *The Social Dimensions: European Developments in Social Psychology* Vol. 2 (London: Cambridge University Press, 1984).

United Nations, *Female Genital Mutilation/Cutting: A Statistical Exploration 2005* (New York: United Nations, United Nations Children's Fund, 2005). As of June 17, 20078, available on the World Wide Web at URL: http://www.unicef.org/publications/files/FGM-C_final_10_October.pdf

United Nations, *Statistical Yearbook for Asia and the Pacific 2007* (New York: United Nations, 2008).

Victorian, Brande, "Georgia Dad Paralyzed From the Neck Down After Rescuing Drowning 4-Year-Old Girl," *Madame Noire*, June 17, 2013. As of June 29, 2013, available online at http://madamenoire.com/282331/georgia-dad-paralyzed-from-the-neck-down-after-rescuing-drowning-4-year-old-girl/

Waines, David, *An Introduction to Islam* Second Edition (New York: Cambridge University Press, 2003).

Weber, Max, *Economy and Society* Vol. 2 (Edited by Guenther Roth and Claus Wittich) (New York: Bedminster Press, 1968).

Weber, Max, *The Religion of India* (Glencoe, IL: Free Press, 1958).

Wimmer, Andreas, *Nationalist Exclusion and Ethnic Conflict: Shadows of Modernity* (NY: Cambridge University Press, 2002).

World Health Organization, "Female Genital Mutilation," Fact Sheet No. 241, February 2013 (Geneva, Switzerland: World Health Organization, 2013). As of June 2, 2013, available online at http://www.who.int/mediacentre/factsheets/fs241/en/

World Population News Service POPLINE, "Urban Population Will Exceed Rural in 2007," Vol. 26, May-June 2004: 1-2.

Wu, Xiaogang, and Xie, Yu, "Does the Market Pay Off? Earnings Returns to Education in Urban China," *American Sociological Review*, Vo. 68, No. 3, 2003: 425-442.

Xhou, Xueguang; Zhao, Wei; Li, Qiang, Li; and Cai, He, "Embeddedness and Contractual Relationships in China's Transitional Economy," *American Sociological Review*, Vol. 68, No. 1, 2003: 103-127.

Ye'or, Bat, "Dhimmitude: Past and Present: An Invented or Real History," Lecture by Bat Ye'or on Thursday, October 10, 2002, at Brown University as part of the C.V. Starr Foundation Lectureship. Available as of June 22, 2009 at http://www.dhimmitude.org/archive/by_lectureoct2002.htm

Ye'or, Bat, *Eurabia: The Euro-Arab Axis* Fourth Printing (Madison, NJ: Fairleigh Dickinson University Press, 2005).

Ye'or, Bat, *Islam and Dhimmitude: Where Civilizations Collide* Translated from the French by Miriam Kochan and David Littman (Madison, NJ: Fairleigh Dickinson University Press, 2002b).

CHAPTER 3

Culture and Organizations

INTRODUCTION

In this chapter we sociologically explore culture, formal organization and bureaucracy. We also present a brief sociological analysis of Muslim American subcultures so that you may enhance your sociological understanding of this richly textured subculture in the United States. Alexis de Tocqueville then reminds us that a democratic society requires a value system that constrains the power of the state, and de Toqueville views voluntary associations in the United States as an important part of the relationships that make democracy possible for us. Your excursion into sociological ways of knowing enables you to appreciate more fully that participating in voluntary associations satisfies more than just personal needs.

A **formal organization** is a secondary group whose goal is the achievement of explicit objectives or tasks. Formal organizations may be small or large in size and there are many types, including voluntary organizations. Bureaucracy is a particular system of administration of formal organizations. A particular bureaucracy often is described as having its own culture (e.g., Peters and Waterman, 2004; Bellingham, 2001; Vaughan, 1996).

Sociology distinguishes between the concepts of society and culture. **Society** refers to a collectivity of people who occupy a particular territorial area, share a common culture and a sense of unity, and regard themselves as different than nonmembers. While sociology contains no widely agreed-upon definition of **culture** (Gilmore, 1992; Abercrombie, Hill, and Turner, 1994: 98-99), Edward B. Tylor (1871) offered a definition of culture over a century ago that has become a classic definition. Tylor (1871:1) defines culture as "that complex whole which includes knowledge, belief, art, morals, law, custom, and any other capabilities and habits acquired" by humans as members of society.

Since the concept of culture is broad, sociologists break the concept down into smaller parts. **Nonmaterial culture**, sometimes termed **symbolic culture**, refers to all human made *intangibles* that we transmit across generational lines. Examples of nonmaterial cultural attributes or elements include norms, customs, symbols, traditions, attitudes, values, rituals, social structure, ideas, beliefs, language, manners, knowledge, and so forth. In contrast, the term **material culture** refers to all *tangibles*—the kitchen sink, books, fountain pens, the Taj Mahal, soccer balls, underwear, bubble gum, nuclear weapons, and so forth—that humans transmit from one generation to another.

Thus, from a sociological viewpoint culture is a group attribute, something that all human groups possess, and it is a fundamental category of human social experience.

CULTURE

Cultural Elements

Sociologists use the term **cultural element** (or **cultural trait**) to refer to a simple, identifiable, and significant unit of a culture. Attitudes and values, for example, are nonmaterial cultural traits or elements. **Attitudes** are orientations toward certain objects (including persons, whether oneself or others) or situations that are emotionally toned and relatively persistent; and **value**s are generalized standards of behavior that receive expression in more concrete form in other nonmaterial and material cultural elements. A value is a non-material cultural element, an abstract conception of what is desirable, to which members of a group feel a strong, positively toned commitment and that serves as a standard for selecting and evaluating concrete means, goals, rules, and actions (Theodorson and Theordorson, 1969: 455-456).

Sociologists study both *material* and *non-material* cultural elements in order to understand social life. For example, values receive expression in attitudes and norms, which are nonmaterial cultural elements. The value of capitalism finds expression in the economy of the United States, a nonmaterial cultural element. We term "the economy" a non-material cultural element because it is an abstract concept, even though it is at the same time an important social institution. The value of liberty receives expression in the Statue of Liberty, a material cultural element. The value of patriotism receives expression in Mount Rushmore, which is a material cultural element. Values also find expression in institutions. The value of "equality under the law" finds expression, even if imperfectly, in the judicial system of the United States.

Culture Shock

When we find ourselves outside of our familiar culture and in a culture that we perceive as significantly different than our own, we may experience a disorientation known as **culture shock**. When one experiences culture shock, one no longer knows the repertoire of cultural gestures and symbolic cues that make meaningful and accurate communication possible; one no longer knows what to expect or how to make one's needs and wants known to others; one does not understand the gestures and even perhaps the language that other people use.

Social actors do not need to live in another country to experience culture shock. For instance, we may temporarily experience it if we travel to a culturally different part of a city or of a country, if we travel abroad as tourists, or if we move to a different region of our own country.

Also, social actors tend to experience **ethnocentrism**, the perception that the norms, values, institutions, gestures, and other material and nonmaterial components of their own culture are both "right" and preferable to those of other cultures. This tendency is well documented in a global attitudinal survey recently conducted in 21 countries (Pew Research Center, 2013). Over half of Americans (55 percent) in 2007 and 49 percent in Spring 2011 agree with the statement, "Our people are not perfect, but our culture is superior to others," a larger percentage than in Spain, Germany, France, and Britain. But Pakistanis are even more confident than Americans in their cultural pre-eminence: Fully 85 percent of the people in Pakistan, 78 percent of Turks, and 77 percent of a non-national sample of people in Peoples Republic of China believe their culture is superior (computed from data available by Pew Research Center, 2013). Indeed, as is documented by the Pew Global Attitudes Project survey that was conducted in 21 countries in Spring 2011, the belief in a country's cultural superiority is common across *all* regions of the globe (Pew Research Center, 2013).

Subcultures and Countercultures

A **subculture** refers to a culture within a culture. Sociologists use the term subculture to refer to the more or less different folkways, mores, material and nonmaterial cultural traits or cultural elements developed by a group or collectivity within a society. Thus, in the United States, rural youths are more likely to engage in risky behaviors, such as smoking, drinking and driving with an intoxicated driver, than are their urban peers (Heck, Borba, Carlos, et. al., 2004; Holtby, et. al., 2004). Examples of subcultures are the Amish, the Muslims, Sikhs, skin-heads, gays and lesbians, juvenile delinquents, rural dwellers, body builders, motorcyclists, gardening enthusiasts, and so forth.

A **stigma** is an attribution, a social definition that is discrediting for a person, collectivity, or group. There are stigmas of speech (e.g., stuttering, saying "uh" a lot), of the body (blemishes, scars, disfigurement), of character (e.g., untrustworthiness, cowardice, untruthfulness), and of collectivities (what Weber would call **pariah groups**). Some audiences view particular subcultures as pariah groups. A pariah group or collectivity is a group or collectivity that is highly stigmatized (e.g., Sutherland, 2005; Ghose, 2003).

Counterculture is the term that sociologists use to refer to a subculture that rejects key values and norms of the conventional society in which it is situated. In this sense, from the point of view of various indigenous groups, the Europeans who came to North America would have constituted a counterculture. Other examples of countercultures in this country are the Oneida Community of up-state New York (1848-1881) (Kanter, 1972); the old-order Amish; the Bruderhof or Society of Brothers, founded in the United States in 1953; the "flower children" or "hippies" of the 1960s; and present-day white-supremacist militias, such as the Aryan Nations, Christian Identity and others, that view the federal government as an intrusive illegitimate force that they intend to overthrow through violent methods (Flyn and Gerhardt, 1990).

Values

As a nonmaterial cultural element, a **value** is an abstract, generalized conception of what is desirable to which members of a group feel a strong, positively-toned commitment and which serves as a standard for selecting and evaluating concrete means, goals, rules, and actions. In short, a value is a concept of what is desirable and undesirable. Examples of values are justice, freedom, liberty, equality, individualism, and patriotism. The sociological study of values involves the study of attitudes, behaviors, norms, institutions, social interaction, and social structure (Nayak, Byrne, Martin, et. al., 2003; Garcia-Moreno, 2000).

Sociologists use the term **value inconsistency** to refer to the conflict between two or more simultaneously held values. For instance, some core American values may conflict with each other. Thus, sexism and racism conflict with the values of equality, freedom, and democracy (Ferber, 2004; Hallinan, 2001). Efficiency conflicts with the value of democracy, as democracy may be a slow, time-consuming, plodding process.

De-individuation: Getting Lost in the Crowd

In April of 2003, in the wake of American troops entering Iraq's cities, looters, freed from the scrutiny of Saddam Hussein's police, ran rampant. The National Library lost tens of thousands of old manuscripts. Hospitals lost beds. Universities lost computers, chairs, and even light bulbs (Burns, 2003; Lawler, 2003). Over 10,000 objects were stolen from The National Museum in Baghdad (Polk and Schuster, 2005). Such events left people in many other parts of the world wondering how this behavior could have happened.

Sociologists use the term **de-individuation** to refer to a loss of evaluation apprehension and of self-consciousness (Myers, 2008: 272-276; Aronson, Wilson, and Akert, 2005: 559; Lea, Spears, and De Groot, 2001). De-individuation, then, is the opposite of being *self* aware: when we are de-individuated, we lose touch with our "self" (the answers each of us gives to the question, "Who Am I?"). In many parts of the world, soccer fans sometimes attack, bludgeon, and trample each other to death. In the United States, fans at live rock concerts scream deliriously and attack and bludgeon each other in mosh pits; and the United States has a long history of whites, cloaked in the anonymity of Ku Klux Klan long, white, hooded robes, lynching African Americans. In 2005, in the wake of Hurricane Katrina, looters, freed from the scrutiny of neighbors and local police, ran rampant, looting in New Orleans.

The internet offers similar anonymity. Millions of people who were aghast at the looters in New Orleans and in Baghdad were, on those very days, "anonymously pirating music tracks using file-sharing software. With so many doing it, with so little concern about being caught, downloading someone's copyright-protected property and then offloading it to an MP3 player just didn't seem terribly immoral" (Myers, 2008; 273). De-individuation can be elicited or generated in a number of ways, including via communal participation in rituals. Group chanting, singing, clapping, dancing, and the wearing of clothing that masks individuality can all increase solidarity among the participants. These activities also can have the effect of de-individuating those engaging in the activities. Thus, a scholarly cross-cultural study by Robert Watson documents that warriors wearing de-individuating masks or face paint are more brutal to their victims than other warriors (Watson, 1973). Similarly, a study by Andrew Silke (2003) of 500 attacks of communal violence in Northern Ireland, documents that in 206 of the 500 violent attacks, the attackers wore hoods, masks, or other face disguises. Compared to undisguised attackers, the anonymous attackers inflicted more serious injuries, attacked more people, and even committed more vandalism (Myers, 2008: 274).

"Lord of the Flies," a William Golding novel (1954) which has been made into a movie that bears the same title, provides a vivid example of de-individuation. Both the novel and the movie concern young, pre-adolescent boys who are marooned on an island in the South Pacific, with no compos mentis adult present, after their plane crashes. A highly-manipulative youth named Jack, who is a master at leadership, organizes some of the boys into a tightly-knit band of hunters by (1) stripping them of their school uniforms that symbolized loyalty to a different group; (2) painting the lads and himself with the blood from their successful pig hunts, creating on their skins designs that symbolize both ferocity as hunters and loyalty to himself as their leader; and by (3) devising rituals for all the boys of his band to participate in communally.

These rituals involve communal shouting, dancing, singing, chanting, and the use of group slogans (e.g., "The leader has spoken"). These processes de-individualize the boys to such an extent that on one occasion, under the cover of darkness, they communally kill a wise, gentle boy named Simon, mistaking him for a monster.

In an analysis of more than a score of instances in which crowds were present as someone threatened to jump from a building or a bridge, Leon Mann found that when the cover of night or even the size of the crowd gave people the perception of anonymity, the crowd usually baited and jeered the would-be jumper, encouraging her or him to take the fatal leap (Mann, 1981). David Myers (2008: 273) also reports an analysis of 21 instances in which crowds were present as someone threatened to jump from a building or a bridge. When the crowd was either small or exposed by daylight, people usually did not try to bait the person with cries of "Jump!" However, when either the cover of night or a large crowd gave people anonymity, the crowd usually did bait and jeer (Myers, 2008: 273).

De-individuation is especially likely when, after being socially aroused and distracted, social actors experience anonymity while in a large collectivity or wear concealing clothing (Myers, 2008: 300). The result is a diminished sense of self, diminished self-restraint, and an increased "responsiveness to the immediate situation, be it negative or positive" (Myers, 2008: 276).

Cultural Capital

Some social actors, collectivities, and groups are more knowledgeable about, more proficient with, and more adept at the cultural elements of the dominant culture. French sociologist Pierre Bourdieu coined the term **cultural capital**, which others sometimes refer to as social capital, to refer to the extent to which an individual, collectivity, or group is adept with regard to the cultural elements of the dominant culture (e.g., Bourdieu, 2005; Bourdieu, 1992; Bourdieu and Passerson, 1990). Cultural capital thus refers to cultural or social assets of the dominant culture, and these include values, attitudes, beliefs, and competencies in language and culture (Rohlinger, 2007; Eastwood, 2007). For example, in the United States, students who are high in social capital know that they should cover their mouths when they yawn, sneeze, or cough; they know that they should refrain from using their shirt as a handkerchief; and they know that they should not "pick at" their bodies in polite company and that they should blow their noses rather than sniffle. In contrast, students low in social capital not only do not know or practice these cultural competencies, they are also blissfully unaware that their failure to do so is perceived as offensive, rude, and inappropriate by salient social audiences.

The greater the extent to which an individual or group is adept with the dominant culture, the greater the individual or group's cultural capital (Bourdieu and Passerson, 1990). Reading books to their children, teaching children to be polite and to take responsibility for their actions, listening to classical music with their children, taking their children to museums, being concerned with how they dress and comport themselves, making sure their children know and put into practice the difference between outer wear and underwear, affirming the importance of education in numerous ways, encouraging their children to do well in school—-these are some of the ways that parents develop the cultural capital of their children (Alexander, Entwisle, and Olson, 2007; Lee and Burkham, 2002; Bourdieu, 1993). The level of an individual or a group's cultural capital influences its life experiences in important ways (e.g., Aschaffenburg and Maas, 1997; Luttrell, 1997). One of the reasons that a person with a baccalaureate degree is more successful in the economic marketplace is because the social actor has increased her/his level of cultural capital.

Technology and Diversity

Technology is a segment of culture that includes tools and knowledge, and that embraces all forms of productive technique used by humans and by some non-human primates (Goodall, 1968, 1971, 1986) to manipulate the physical environment in order to attain a desired practical result (Lachmann, 1991: 297-298). Sociologists study the relations between technology and other parts of society.

All parts of a culture do not change at the same pace. Sociologist William F. Ogburn (1922) coined the term **cultural lag** to refer to a situation wherein one or more parts of a culture "change at a faster rate than other, related parts, with a resulting disruption of the integration and equilibrium" of the culture (Theodorson and Theodorson, 1969: 99). In other words, cultural lag occurs when the material culture changes at a faster rate than nonmaterial culture. This happens a lot, and it can be disruptive.

Cultures may be large or small. In a society that is diverse in terms of geography, region, climate, age, sex or gender, social class, race, ethnicity, religion, occupation, education, and language, sociologists expect culture to vary across individuals and groups. Below you will find brief sociological analysis of Muslim subcultures in the United States.

Muslim Americans: Largely Middle Class and Mainstream

A DEMOGRAPHIC PORTRAIT

A recent nationwide survey estimates that there are 2.75 million Muslims of all ages in the U.S. population as of 2011 (Pew Research Center for the People and the Press, 2011: 5). The U.S. Census Bureau reports that the size of the U.S., population as of June 15, 2011, was 311,480,826 (U.S. Census Bureau, 2013). Thus, Muslims are 0.9 percent of the U.S. population, which is an increase of 0.3 percent since 2007 when Muslims were 0.6 of the U.S. population (Pew Research Center 2007b).

The Muslim American population is youthful, racially diverse, generally well-educated, and financially about as well off as the rest of the U.S. public. Roughly two-thirds (63 percent) of Muslim Americans were born elsewhere, and 45 percent have come to the United States since 1990. Despite the sizable percentage of immigrants, 81 percent of Muslim Americans are citizens of the United States, including 70 percent of those born outside of the United States. There is a much higher percentage of U.S. citizens among foreign-born Muslims than among the broader immigrant population in the Unites States, where less than half (47 percent) of all foreign-born are U.S. citizens (Pew Research Center for the People and the Press, 2011:5). A relatively large percent of Muslim immigrants are from Arab countries (41 percent) and many also come from Pakistan (14 percent), other South Asian countries (12 percent), and Sub-Saharan Africa (11 percent). Among native-born Muslims, more than half are African American (59 percent), including a sizeable majority (69 percent) who are converts to Islam (Pew Research Center for the People and the Press, 2011: 5).

Although many Muslims are relative newcomers to the United States, they are highly assimilated into American society. With the exception of very recent immigrants, most report that a large proportion of their closest friends are non-Muslims. Muslim Americans also generally mirror the U.S. public in education and income.

Nearly three-quarters (74 percent) of American Muslims endorse the idea that most people can get ahead if they are willing to work hard, which is a higher percentage than among the U.S. public at large (62 percent). U.S. Muslims are about as likely as other Americans to report household incomes of $100,000 or more (14% of Muslims, compared with 16% of all adults), and they express similar levels of satisfaction with their personal financial situation. Overall, 46 percent of American Muslims say they are in excellent or good shape financially, which is more than the 38 percent of the general America public who say this (Pew Research Center for the People and the Press, 2011: 4). Economically, family income among Muslim Americans is roughly comparable with that of the U.S. population as a whole.

The extent to which Muslims are integrated into the economic mainstream of America is in stark contrast to the position of Muslims living in several major Western European nations. Thus, surveys of Muslim populations in Great Britain, France, Germany, and Spain were conducted in 2006 as part of the Pew Global Attitudes Project. These data reveal that Muslims were much less affluent relative to the general populations of those nations (Pew Research Center, 2007b). For example, a majority of Muslims in Germany (53%) reported family incomes of less than 18,000 euros annually compared with 35 percent of Germans overall. A similar gap exists in France. The gap is even larger in Spain where 73 percent of Muslims report incomes of less than 14,500 euros per annum compared with half of the *public nationwide.* In short, in European countries, Muslims are far more *over-represented* in the *lower* income brackets and much more *under-represented* in the *higher* income brackets than is the case in the United States.

THE AMERICAN MUSLIM EXPERIENCE

Nearly half of Muslims in the United States (49 percent) say they think of themselves first as a Muslim rather than as an American (Pew Research Center for the People and the Press, 2011: 4). In this regard, American Muslims are similar to the 46 percent of Christians in the United States who also say they think of themselves first as a Christian first rather than as a citizen of the United States. White evangelicals (70 percent) are much more likely to say they identify first as a Christian (Pew Research Center for the People and the Press, 2011: 4). In contrast, far more Muslims in Great Britain (81 percent), Spain (69 percent), and Germany (66 percent) think of themselves first as Muslims rather than as citizens of their countries (Pew Research Center, 2007b: 3).

Most Muslim Americans (55 percent) say that it has become more difficult in a number of ways to be a Muslim in the United States since the September 11 terrorist attacks. First, more than half of Muslim Americans (52 percent) believe that the government's anti-terrorism efforts single out Muslims for increased surveillance and monitoring (Pew Research Center for the People and the Press, 2011: 2). The percentage of American Muslims who say that they are bothered by a sense that American Muslims are being singled out for more government surveillance is no greater now than in 2007. Today, 38 percent of American Muslims say they are bothered a lot or some by a sense that American Muslims are being singled out by the government for increased surveillance, vs 39 percent in 2007 (Pew Research Center for the People and the Press, 2011: 2). Second, significant numbers of American Muslims report a perception of being looked at with suspicion (28 percent) and being called offensive names (22 percent) (Pew Research Center for the People and the Press, 2011: 1).

To place these findings in context, let us compare them with the experiences of African Americans and, where data are available, with Hispanic Americans. A nation-wide survey conducted in April 2007 asked African Americans to report experiences that occurred "because of your race." Similarly, as part of a comprehensive nationwide survey, Muslim Americans were asked to report experiences that occurred "because you are a Muslim" (Pew Research Center, 2007b: 38). And a 2008 national survey of Latinos in the United States provides some comparative data for Hispanic Americans (Lopez and Minushkin, 2008).

A third of all African Americans and 26 percent of Muslim Americans report that people have acted as if they are suspicious of them in the past year. Roughly the same share of blacks (20 percent) and Muslims

(15 percent) report they have been called offensive names within the past twelve months. Roughly the same share of Latino adults (9 percent) and Muslims (9 percent) report they have been stopped by the police within the past year (Lopez and Minushkin, 2008: 9). African Americans (20 percent) are more than twice as likely as Muslims (9 percent) or Hispanics (9 percent) to say that they have been singled out by the police within the past twelve months. African Americans (10 percent) are also twice as likely as Muslim Americans (4 percent) to say they have been physically threatened or attacked in the past twelve months. Taken together, nearly half (46 percent) of all African Americans report that they have had at least one of these four experiences within the past year, which is 13 percentage points greater than the proportion of Muslims who have personally encountered similar acts of intolerance.

It is worth noting that in this country, African Americans who are Muslim appear to bear a double burden, as they say they face racial (e.g., Nazroo, et. al, 2007) as well as religious intolerance. Overall, half of all Muslims who are African American say they have been the target of bigotry based on their religion in the past twelve months, compared with 28 percent of white Muslims and 23 percent of Asian Muslims (Pew Research Center, 2007b: 38).

Nevertheless, 82 percent of American Muslims are satisfied with the way things are going in their lives and 79 percent rate their communities as excellent or very good as places to live (Pew Research Center for the People and the Press, 2011: 2). About two-thirds (67 percent) of American Muslims say that the quality of life for Muslims in the United States is *better* than in most Muslim countries (Pew Research Center for the People and the Press, 2011: 2). It is worth noting that more Muslim Americans are satisfied with the way things are going in the United States (56 percent) than is the general U.S. public (23 percent) (Pew Research Center for the People and the Press, 2011: 2).

Cultural Universals

Collectivities that persist across time regularly transmit the elements of their culture--signs, symbols, gestures, language, values, technology, and norms, and so forth-—from one generation to another. At least in this limited sense, social scientists concur that **cultural universals**, i.e. cultural elements that are found in virtually all societies, do in fact exist.

Extensive cross-cultural analysis led British anthropologist ***George Murdock*** to conclude that the following are among those cultural elements that are found in virtually all human societies: courtship, marriage, the family, a gendered division of labor, an age-based division of labor, a ritualistically-based division of labor, funereal rites, humor, games, myths, incest taboos, and norms regarding dispute resolution (Murdock, 1945, 1949). Of course, there is immense variation in the expression of cultural universals. Thus, with regard to funereal rites, one culture may specify that the decedent is placed in a certain geographic location so that birds may dispose of the flesh; in another, the decedent's body is wrapped, rituals are performed by functionaries specified in the cultural tradition, and the wrapped body is placed in the ground; in yet another culture, the decedent is burned on a big pyre, and so forth.

Cultural Pluralism

The United States, both historically and today, is a mosaic of cultures. Sociologists use the term **cultural pluralism** to refer to a perspective and an approach to social relations that affirms that cultural heterogeneity

is a goal that should be pursued and attained by society. Cultural pluralism allows for cultural differences so long as these differences do not interfere with the principal values and mores of the dominant society (Gonzales, 1990: 56-57). Those who pursue the vision of cultural relations believe that cultural diversity is good for society, that it should be encouraged, and that it is possible for diverse groups to live in social harmony and to experience mutual understanding and respect. Adherents of social pluralism maintain that these should be the goals of society, not a "blending" or a "melting" of groups, not the domination of one group by the other, and not the independent and isolated existence of each group separate from the others.

In the United States today we see more and more signs of the diffusion and acceptability of cultural pluralism. People from various cultural groups practice many of their cultural traditions.

FORMAL ORGANIZATION

A **formal organization** is a secondary group whose goal is the achievement of explicit objectives or tasks. There are many forms of formal organization. Schools, hospitals, prisons, voluntary associations, corporations, and government agencies are examples of formal organizations. The sociological study of formal organizations usually focuses both on their formal and informal structures.

Voluntary Association

Voluntary association is one variety of formal organization. A **voluntary association** is a formally organized, specialized, secondary group, in which membership is a matter of freely exercised choice and from which members are free to resign. The Girl Scouts of America, The Boy Scouts of America, the Boys and Girls Clubs of America, the Lion's Club, the Kiwanis, the American Rifle Association, the American Sociological Association, and the PTA are all examples of voluntary associations. A voluntary association is a type of formal organization that is formed when people reach beyond primordial ties to establish common cause with others. Hence, voluntary association is a non-primordial form of solidarity in human societies.

The United States continues to lead many other Western countries in volunteer service (Anderson, Curtis, and Grabb, 2006) and for this reason, the United States sometimes is called "a nation of joiners." Americans are more than twice as likely as German and French adults to have contributed time and energy to community service in the past year (Thoits and Hewitt, 2001; Putnam, 2000). Research indicates that countries also vary in the types of associational activity in which their citizens engage (Schofer and Fourcade-Gourinchas, 2001). Membership levels in the United States are particularly high for religious associations and for categories that some analysts refer to as "new" social movements (e.g., environmental, human and women's rights organizations), while associational activity in a country like Germany is far more centered on "old" social movement associations, such as political parties and unions (Shofer and Fourcade-Gourinchas, 2001: 807).

Data from the World Values Surveys document that people in different nations do in fact differ dramatically in their level of involvement in volunteer activities. The percentage of individuals claiming membership in at least one voluntary association ranges from about 70 percent in the United States to less than 30 percent in Japan, France, and Italy (Shofer and Fourcade-Gourinchas, 2001: 807-808). Also, people in the United States tend on average to join a greater number of associations; fully one out of four Americans belongs to four or more voluntary associations (Maurer and Sheets, 1998: vii).

At the turn of the last century, Weber (1911:53) observed that the United States was "the association-land, par excellence," and even earlier, Alexis de Tocqueville (1835) commented on the tendency of Americans to join voluntary associations. In fact, one of the earliest studies of voluntary associations and bureaucracy comes from Alexis de Tocqueville (1805-1859). A French aristocrat, de Tocqueville was commissioned by the French government to investigate the nature of social organization and culture in the United States, and he visited the United States in 1831 to 1832.

Tocqueville published his observations in the book, *Democracy in America* (1835). Tocqueville (1835) and many scholars after him (e.g. Almond and Verba, 1963; Inglehart, 1997) locate the source of greater voluntary association membership in the United States in the different value systems internalized by members of each society. Thus, Tocqueville points out that Americans are leery of, and opposed to, a strong centralized state that could control the lives of the individual (Hamilton, Madison, and Jay, 1787-1788). Tocqueville perceived that these orientations to the world created a very anti-bureaucratic and anti-state culture in the United States.

Tocqueville argues that voluntary associations are schools or training fields for democracy. For instance, in the United States, voluntary associations are organized on the basis of simple democratic principles. Each club has a president, vice president, secretary, and so on. Members vote for candidates for these offices on the basis of one member, one vote, and candidates are elected to office on the basis of a simple majority of votes. Those who "run" for office seek support from other members, to whom they present their views on critical social and political issues. This type of democratic process gives birth to potential local, state, and national leaders. Participation in voluntary associations teaches Americans how to reach, and to govern through, consensus.

Membership in voluntary associations, says de Tocqueville, gives rise to and perpetuates local democracy while fulfilling individual, community, and societal needs. The free association of individuals in voluntary associations reinforces participatory norms, promotes interpersonal trust, and encourages cooperative interaction, all of which are believed to be crucial for achieving effective solutions to many challenges facing the wider community (McFarland and Thomas, 2006; Wuthnow, 1991: 300-302).

Voluntary associations, de Tocqueville stresses, become autonomous powers that compete with, and that limit, the power of, the state. In summary, voluntary associations not only help to meet an individual's needs, they also perform the function of providing both integration and overlapping circles of social support for persons not related by primordial ties. They are important community resources, many of which are independent of state bureaucracy, and they are incubators of democracy.

NETWORKS

A **social network,** or network, is a social actor's total set of relationships. The study of with whom social actors associate and the effects of those choices on social structure and individuals is known as ***social network analysis.*** The units of analysis, or nodes, of a network can be individuals, groups, collectivities, formal organizations, or even nations (Centeno and Hargittai, 2003). Sociologists divide social networks into two categories of intimacy—-strong ties and weak ties (Granovetter, 1973). **Strong ties** are relationships characterized by intimacy, emotional intensity, and sharing. We have strong ties with those people for whom we would make sacrifices and in whom we could confide, and who would reciprocate in kind in these regards. In the United States, women are more likely than men to choose their strong ties from among family members (Moore, 1990; Marsden, 1987).

In contrast, **weak ties** are relationships characterized by low intensity and low intimacy (Granovetter, 1973). Numerous studies indicate that, in the United States, people tend to get jobs more often through their weak ties than through formal job listings, want ads, or employment agencies (Dominguez and Watkins, 2003; Petersen, Saporta, and Seidel, 2000; Montgomery, 1992).

Sociological research indicates that overlapping social circles of networks are vital for the integration of society (Wellman, 1999). Skocpol, Liazos, and Ganz (2006) document the ways in which African American fraternal groups in the United States were important in building, marshalling, and mobilizing the social capital of the African American community for the advocacy of social justice. Networks are also important for the individual (e.g., Kent, 2009; Farkas, 2004). For instance, empirical research documents that people are far more likely to report willingness to donate one of their kidneys to a close family member (95%) or a good friend (86%) than they are to an acquaintance (37%) or a stranger (26%) (Humphries, et. al., 2009). So, people are more willing to donate the gift of life to those who are in their social networks. Similarly, ***Robert B. Cairns and Beverley D. Cairns*** (1994) use longitudinal data to study children and adolescents at risk in the southeastern United States, youth who either engage in or who are victims of aggression and violence; youth who drop out of school, bear children at an early age, run away from home, and so forth. The authors find that friendships with conventional adults are a "life line" that enables many youth to turn their lives around. The youth could turn their lives around "because they did not stand alone...[they experienced] the commitment of a responsible and supportive adult" (Cairns and Cairns, 1994: 237). Furthermore, Hazan and Hutt (1993) also find that youth who had poor relationships with their parents but who managed to construct a warm, supportive relationship during childhood with an adult have more favorable life trajectories than youth utterly bereft of positive affective relationships with adults in the conventional social order. Similarly, in a longitudinal study of an entire **birth cohort** (i.e., all persons born in a given year) in a racially diverse area in the United States, ***Emmy Werner***, of the University of California, Davis, finds that the ability to seek out a helping adult is crucial to being able to thrive despite hardship (Werner, 2001; Werner and Smith, 1992; Werner and Smith, 1989; Werner, 1987). Werner's carefully-crafted study documents that those youth who thrive despite having parents who use drugs, who are convicted felons, and who suffer severe acute and chronic mental disease; who thrive despite being victims of physical abuse, sexual abuse, psychological abuse, and parental neglect were relentless in their efforts to construct, to maintain, and, when necessary, to replace friendships with responsible, caring adults.

Even for those who are not "at risk," network ties provide comfort in times of personal loss (e.g., visiting after the death of a loved one), minor services (e.g., help with the plumbing or with the car when it has broken down), financial support (e.g., a small loan until payday), and information (e.g., about employment opportunities). Integration into social groups also helps us to cope with crisis (Lin and Ensel, 1989; Dean et. al., 1990) and it helps to prevent loneliness and isolation (Stokes and Levin, 1986; Hobfoll, 1988). Social interaction with females is found to do more to relieve loneliness, both for males and for females: both genders perceive interaction with females as more pleasant, more meaningful, and more intimate than those with men (Wheeler, et. al., 1983).

Dense networks of social support have been shown to lead to a lower incidence of cancer and of arthritis and cholesterol issues among workers who have lost their jobs (Argyle, 1992: 237; O'Reilly and Thomas, 1989) and to have positive effects on blood pressure, mental health, pregnancy, and other physical conditions that involve stress (Barnes, et. al., 2008; Sanchez-Martin, et. al., 2001; Johnson, 1992: 1978). In other words, people with more types of relationships and those who spend more time in social activities are at lower risk for disease and mortality than their more isolated counterparts (e.g., Pressman, et. al., 2005; Bisschop, et. al.,

2003; Mendes de Leon, et. al., 2001). Absence of social networks is associated with relatively poor mental health and physical health throughout the life course (Kraus et. al., 1993). When social support is given willingly and with regard for the recipient's perceptions, there is a relationship between social support and reduced morbidity (illness) and mortality (Blazer, 1982; Rook, 1984; Pagel, Erdly, and Becker, 1987).

A famous longitudinal study in California follows 6,900 people in the San Francisco bay area for over nine years (Berkman and Syme, 1979) and finds massive differences in mortality rates among those who, at the beginning of the study, have dense networks versus weak support networks. For males in their fifties, of those with the strongest networks, 9.6 percent had died, compared with 30.8 percent for those with the weakest networks. Many other studies also document this effect, including Schwarzer and Leppin's meta-analysis of 55 studies that involve over 32,000 people (1989).

The sociological study of networks thus illuminates a wide range of social phenomena.

LEADERSHIP

Leadership, in formal organizations and elsewhere, is the function of coordinating group activities toward group goals (Theodorson and Theodorson, 1969: 227).

Formal and Informal Leadership

When a person is the incumbent of a status to which authority is attached in a formal organization, we speak of formal authority and of **formal leadership**. The incumbent of such a position is a formal leader. For example, the President of the United States is a formal leader, as is the Mayor of a city. In contrast, **informal leadership** emerges when individuals are valued by a group because they conform to its norms and contribute to achieving the task of the group. In other words, informal leadership emerges when followers develop social cohesion, and subgroup norms of loyalty, around a particular social actor. In informal leadership, the right to lead stems from one's position in the solidary structure of the group.

Max Weber on Types of Leadership

Max Weber developed a trichotomy of leadership types that corresponds to different forms of authority. The three types of authority or leadership identified by Weber are traditional, rational-legal, and charismatic. The basis of Weber's classification system revolves around the answer to the question, "On what does the legitimacy of the leadership or authority rest?"

Traditional authority is power that is legitimized on the basis of custom. For example, Egyptian pharos and British kings and queens historically traced their right to rule as a mandate and burden that they received either from God or from the gods. This is sometimes known as "the divine right of kings." Traditional leaders base the legitimacy of their rule on custom.

In contrast, an authority system is rational-legal if members accept it because they view its rules as "rational, fair, and impartial" (Abercrombie, Hill, and Turner, 1994: 38). In other words, **rational-legal authority** is based on an organizational structure characterized by clearly defined rules and procedures, a hierarchy of authority (the right to command and the duty to obey), and impersonality. In rational-legal authority, power (the ability to get one's way in the face of opposition) is legitimized by procedures; if leaders obtain their positions through procedurally correct methods, they have the right to act.

In contrast, **charismatic authority** is power that is legitimized on the basis of the exceptional qualities that are attributed to a leader by her or his followers (Andreas, 2007). Joan of Arc, Boadicea, Mohandas Gandhi, Christ, Cesar Chavez, and Martin Luther King, Jr., are examples of charismatic leaders.

Charismatic authority is the most unstable form of authority. Charismatic leadership is inherently unstable, in the sense that it is difficult to transfer it to others. Political authorities in many parts of the modern world realize this. They arrest, imprison, place under prolonged house arrest, exile, kill, or "disappear" the charismatic leaders of social movements that challenge the legitimacy of their rule; that seek political, social, economic, or cultural redress; or that oppose their policies. For example, during the period of apartheid, the white government of South Africa arrested and imprisoned Steven Biko and Nelson Mandela for many years.

If charismatic authority is to outlive the social actor who embodies it, it needs to be transformed into some other form of authority. Max Weber coined the term **routinization of charisma** to refer to the transformation of charismatic authority into traditional or rational-legal authority, or into a combination of rational-legal and traditional authority. The routinization of charisma is always problematic.

Leadership Functions

Sociologists distinguish between instrumental and expressive leadership. ***Instrumental leadership*** is task or goal oriented; it helps the members of the group to complete a task or achieve a goal. Socio-emotional or ***expressive leadership*** provides emotional support for the group members. Research indicates that in many situations--whether in the military, industry, or sports—-effective leaders combine expressive and instrumental styles of behavior. In other words, group cohesion around the leader is an important ingredient of effective leadership (Argyle, 1989). Effective military leaders form primary-group relations with the soldiers in their command *and* they provide clear direction regarding the mission of the group. This combination enables their fighting units to act as an effective group even under conditions of extreme stress and hardship (e.g., Stouffer, 1949; Holmes, 1985).

Leadership Styles

Sociologists have observed three major styles of leadership that tend to be found in groups—-democratic, authoritarian, and laissez-faire. **Democratic leaders** both welcome and solicit input from group members. They use that information in formulating policies and decisions, which the group arrives at through consensus. In contrast, **authoritarian leaders** *impose* policies and activities on the group. Social science research indicates that authoritarian leaders tend to be produced by certain socialization experiences (Argyle, 1994: 53), including physical punishment in conjunction with permissiveness for both aggression and sex. Authoritarian leaders tend to be highly competitive, more aggressive than the average person, and they tend not to be much liked by other members of the group (Argyle, 1994).

"Laissez-faire" is French for "to leave alone." **Laissez-faire leaders** are only minimally involved in the group's decision-making processes. They intervene in the group's decision-making processes only when asked to do so.

BUREAUCRACY

A **bureaucracy** is "an organizational model characterized by a hierarchy of authority, a clear division of labor, explicit rules and procedures, and impersonality in personnel matters" (Kendall, 2005: 193). As a system of administration, bureaucracy is particularly useful when the activities of a large number of people need to be coordinated in order to achieve specific goals. The archaeological record documents the existence of bureaucracies ever since the emergence of the first cities and states in Mesopotamia, Sumer, and ancient Egypt some five thousand years ago.

Characteristics of Bureaucracy

The term bureaucracy is derived from the French word "bureau," which translates into English as desk, table, or office, and from the Greek word "kratos," which means power. As used by sociologists, the term bureaucracy is an **ideal type**, an abstract model that describes the recurring characteristics of some phenomenon. Max Weber analyzed the classic characteristics of bureaucracy (1925/1947), which are the following:

A HIGH DEGREE OF DIVISION OF LABOR AND SPECIALIZATION Bureaucratic organizations are characterized by specialization. Each member of the organization occupies a position (status) to which particular duties are assigned. This division of labor means that specialized experts are responsible for the effective performance of the duties attached to their offices.

HIERARCHY OF AUTHORITY The positions of a bureaucracy are arranged in a hierarchy, a chain of command, so that each position is under the supervision of a higher position. For example, in a university, the faculty in, say, a department of sociology, are under the supervision of their departmental chair; the departmental chair, in turn, is under the supervision of the dean of the college of arts and sciences, and so on. These hierarchies often are visually represented in a formal organizational chart. You can probably find such a chart in the catalogue of your college or university.

EXPLICIT PROCEDURAL RULES All of the formal activities in a bureaucracy are governed by a set of detailed rules and procedures. Weber asserted that the rules and regulations establish authority, legitimate power, in a bureaucracy. These rules and regulations are usually presented, in written format, to employees when they are hired by the organization. Theoretically, these clearly stated rules and regulations cover almost every possible situation that might arise in the organization—hiring, promotion, firing, assessment of performance, salary scales, violence in the workplace, rules for sick pay and other absences, and the everyday operation of the rights, duties, and obligations that constitute the positions in the organization. These rules and procedures, Formal, written rules govern the decisions and actions of the organization.

IMPERSONAL RELATIONSHIPS The social interactions among the members of the organization, and between members of the organization and their clients, are to be guided by instrumental criteria, such as the organization's rules, rather than by socio-emotional criteria based on the officials' personal feelings. The ideal is that the objective application of rules will minimize matters such as personal favoritism or personal animosity.

CAREER LADDERS AND QUALIFICATIONS-BASED RECRUITMENT, EMPLOYMENT, AND PROMOTION In a bureaucracy, functionaries are hired, their performance is assessed, and promotions in rank occur, on the basis of specified criteria or standards (e.g., education, training, technical knowledge, standardized examinations), seniority, or both--so that officials typically anticipate a long-term career in the organization. Favoritism, family connections, and other subjective or ascriptive factors are not appropriate criteria for assessing a person's performance, and they are not relevant factors for hiring, promoting, or firing a person in the organization.

FIXED SALARY The salary of office holders is formally specified by the organization. In other words, the office holder does not charge the clients a fee that the office holder then keeps for his or her own personal gain. There is a separation between private and official income.

RATIONALIZATION For Weber the notion of rationalization in bureaucracy embraces two somewhat different ideas (Abercrombie, Hill, and Turner, 1994: 38). The first of these is efficiency. Ideally, at least, bureaucracy maximizes technical efficiency. Bureaucracies are designed to coordinate the activities of many people in pursuit of organizational goals. Ideally, all activities have been designed to maximize this efficiency. The second idea is that of rational-legal authority. Bureaucracies are run on the basis of rational-legal authority.

Bureaucracy and the Well-Kept Secret

Karl Marx presents a penetrating analysis of bureaucracy (1844). Marx agrees with Weber that bureaucracy has an internal structure based on hierarchy, authority, and power. However, Marx also perceives that a clandestine culture is a universal characteristic of bureaucracy. In striving to attain its goals, bureaucracy develops a clandestine culture, a culture of deception (e.g., Weinstein and Vassiliev, 2000; West, 2001). Within each level of a bureaucracy, all social relations, information, and knowledge become deceptive in character. According to Marx, secrecy, mystification, and deception are universally found within each layer of a bureaucracy, in the relationship of the various levels of the bureaucracy to each other, and in the relationship of the bureaucracy to its various outside publics or audiences. Being open and honest in bureaucratic social relations is perceived as nothing short of betrayal by bureaucratic authority. This is especially true with regard to relations of the bureaucracy with the public. Thus, Marx reminds us that even in a democratic society, bureaucracies are secret societies within a larger society.

Bureaucracy's Other Face—Informal Organization

When we look at an organizational chart, we see the formal, official structure of the organization. In practice, however, there are patterns of interactions that cannot be accounted for by the formal organizational chart. Some of these may actually ignore, bypass, or otherwise not conform to the official rules and procedures of the organization. Over half a century ago, sociologist Charles Page coined the term ***bureaucracy's other face*** to describe this condition, which other social scientists refer to as informal organization or informal structure.

Social-science research documents that **informal organization**—also known as informal relations, informal networking, or informal structure—is important in formal organizations. Informal organization refers to a system of personal reciprocal relationships that spontaneously develops as social actors interact within a formal organization, encounter challenges, and seek to devise solutions to them. An example is the "grapevine," informal communication channels that, with varying degrees of accuracy, spread information within an organization. Informal structure is a way around the official channels of communication which may be slower, less responsive, and which contain their own perspective or "spin."

Informal organization serves to help its members cope with the problems they inevitably encounter in their everyday life in the formal organization, and it can either assist or impede the attainment of formal organizational goals. The informal structure also has been called "work culture" because "it includes the ideology and practices of workers on the job" (Kendall, 2005: 195).

Elton Mayo and his fellow Harvard University researchers first documented the existence and importance of informal structure in ***the Hawthorne studies.*** These studies were conducted from 1924 to 1932 at the Western Electric Company's Hawthorne Works in Chicago, Illinois (Roethlisberger and Dixon, 1939). Management at the Hawthorne works wanted to know how various aspects of the work environment influenced worker productivity. They sent a team of social scientists in to investigate.

The researchers discovered that social factors, including informal structure, are more important than environmental factors as determinants of both worker morale and productivity (Roethlisberger and Dixon, 1939). Thus, workers in one area of the plant, known as the bank wiring room, had established informal norms regarding daily output (group norm), and their idea of a fair day's output was significantly lower than what management wanted. The informal work groups enforced their group norms. If workers failed to meet the informal daily quota, they were ridiculed as "chislers." If workers produced more than the group thought appropriate, they were ridiculed as "rate busters." Besides nasty name calling, another sanction the workers used was "binging," whereby a worker would walk up to a co-worker who was breaking the informal norms of the workgroup and would hit him smartly on the arm. This wouldn't break the offending worker's arm and it wasn't intended to do so. It would hurt. It was supposed to hurt.

In other words, a cohesive work group developed and enforced norms of its own, and it thereby undermined the ability of the larger organization to attain its goal of increased worker productivity. A sociologist might rephrase this by saying that patterns of identification with and loyalty to smaller groups within a large organization affect both the individual members within the small groups and the capacity of the larger organization to meet its goals.

The Hawthorne studies also made researchers aware of ***the Hawthorne effect***: workers improve or modify an aspect of their behavior that is being experimentally measured simply in response to the fact that they know they are being studied (e.g., Franke and Kaul, 1978; McCarney, Warner, Iliffe, et. al., 2007).

Sociology helps us better to understand and to predict the effects of groups on our behaviors, attitudes, opinions, and actions. Have you ever found yourself in a group engaged in a high-risk behavior that you would never have done alone? When you were in mischief as a teen, were you usually part of a group? If so, you were probably experiencing the group polarization effect.

There is a tendency, originally called the "risky shift" (Stoner, 1961) but more widely known as **group polarization** (Ohtsubo et. al., 2002; Rodrigo and Ato, 2002; Brauer et. al, 2001; Muscovici and Zavalloni, 1969), for group participation to accentuate the members' pre-existing tendencies and attitudes (Taylor, Peplau, and Sears, 2003). Does this explain why teenage reckless driving, as measured by death rates, nearly doubles when a 16-or 17-year old driver has two teenage passengers rather than none (Chen et.al, 2000)?

Group polarization occurs in schools, fraternities and sororities, juries, street gangs, voluntary associations, and in committee meetings in formal organizations. For example, compared to members of sororities and fraternities, independents tend to have more liberal political attitudes, a difference that increases with the length of time in college (Pascarella and Terenzini, 1991). On college and university campuses, the clustering of students into mostly White fraternities and sororities and into racial/ethnic minority student organizations tends to strengthen social identities and to increase antagonisms among the social groups (Sidanius et. al., 2004). And, analyses of terrorist organizations around the globe document that terrorism does not erupt suddenly (Moghaddam, 2005; Sageman, 2004). Instead, it arises among people who have been brought together by shared grievances. As they interact among themselves in isolation from a wide variety of potentially moderating influences, their attitudes and positions become increasingly more extreme, resulting in violent actions that the individuals, apart from the group, would not have committed. This may be the case with so-called "suicide cults," where virtually all members collectively commit suicide. An example is the People's Temple. On November 18, 1978, 913 followers of the Reverend Jim Jones committed mass suicide at a site called Jonestown in northern Guyana. Another example is Heavens Gate, a religious cult in southern California, where thirty-nine members committed mass suicide on March 27, 1997, in preparation for ascending into heaven in a space ship.

What causes group polarization? Two explanations have survived scientific scrutiny (Deutsch and Gerard, 1955; Myers, 2008: 282-284)—-informational and normative influence. It is helpful in understanding these explanations to be aware that, as used by sociologists, the term **conformity** refers to a change in attitude, belief, or behavior as a result of real or imagined group pressure.

One cause of group polarization is **informational influence,** which refers to conformity based on accepting as correct evidence about reality that is presented by other people (Deutsch and Gerard, 1955). In other words, a desire to be correct produces informational influence. I wash my hands before a meal because I think you are correct about the germ theory of disease that you discussed with me. You exerted informational influence on me when you told me about germs making people sick.

Another explanation for group polarization is **normative influence**. The term normative influence refers to conformity based on a social actor's desire to be socially accepted by others (Deutsch and Gerard, 1955). In other words, normative influence has its basis in the solidary order. When students tell me that they began to drink alcohol or to smoke tobacco because they wanted their peers to accept them as friends, they are telling me that their peers exerted normative influence in their lives in important ways. A desire to belong to a group, then, can lead social actors to go along with the group's opinions, attitudes, and lines of social action.

Shortcomings of Bureaucracy

Max Weber was ambivalent about bureaucracy. On the one hand, Weber appreciates that bureaucracy is a highly efficient type of secondary group (Brym and Lie, 2005: 155). Thus, bureaucracy is the standard organizational form in the modern world: governments, armies, navies, many churches, colleges and universities, and large economic organizations all operate on the basis of bureaucratic organization. On the other hand, Weber acknowledges, and laments, certain effects of bureaucratic rationality on the individual and on human behavior. Weber and others identify these effects as including ritualism, self-estrangement, oligarchy, bureaucratic inertia, and the perpetuation of structured inequality.

1. RITUALISM Bureaucratic ***ritualism*** refers to a rigid conformity to impersonal rules. Workers follow the rules and regulations regardless of whether the rules and regulations help accomplish the purpose for

which they were designed. Ritualism occurs when the rules and regulations become ends in themselves, rather than means to an end.

2. SELF-ESTRANGEMENT A stress on impersonal rules and procedures can result in the clients or personnel, or both, feeling as though they were replaceable cogs in a huge depersonalized machine. The individual, in other words, becomes psychologically separated from the organization and its goals. This is alienation or self-estrangement, which some analysts also term dehumanization. It can lead to increased worker and client turnover, absenteeism, tardiness, and dissatisfaction with the organization.

3. OLIGARCHY German sociologist Robert Michels (1876-1936) coined the term **oligarchy** to refer to the rule of the many by the few (Michels, 1949). Michels and others argue that there is a tendency in bureaucracy for a small number of people at the top of the bureaucratic structure to make the important decisions. Michels called the tendency for power in a bureaucracy to be concentrated in the hands of a few, "the iron law of oligarchy."

4. BUREAUCRATIC INERTIA The term **bureaucratic inertia** refers to the tendency of large organizations to continue with their policies even when external conditions, including their clients' needs, change (Byrm and Lie, 2005: 157; Reskin, 2000).

5. PERPETUATION OF STRUCTURED INEQUALITIES Some bureaucratic practices have the effect of perpetuating inequalities of gender, race, and ethnicity (Kendall, 2005: 200-201; Bielby, 2000). For instance, in a recent study, sociologists Barbara Reskin of Harvard University and Debra McBrier of University of Miami demonstrate the importance of organizational personnel practices in promoting, or undermining, gender inequality (Reskin and McBrier, 2000). Their analysis shows that the methods formal organizations use to recruit managers strongly affect the sex composition of management.

Until the last third of the 20th century, males had a virtual monopoly of managerial jobs in the United States, with at least 85 percent of managers being male. In fact, women and minorities are still considerably underrepresented in corporate life, particularly in higher-status positions (Green, Tiggers, and Diaz, 1999; Collins-Lowry, 1997).

The sex composition of managers matters. Managers usually earn more than non-managers. They also enjoy greater prestige, authority, and autonomy, and they enjoy greater protection from outside competition (Wright, Baxter, and Birkelund, 1995: 407, 413; Blum, Fields, and Goodman, 1994). The sex composition of managers also affects hiring, compensation, evaluation, and promotion practices (Pfeffer, 1991). For instance, California state agencies headed by women integrated jobs more rapidly than did agencies headed by men (Baron, Mittman, and Newman, 1991), and the more female managers in an organization, the smaller the gender pay gap (Shenhav and Haberfeld, 1992).

Using social networks to identify and select managers is a method that employers tend to favor for its low cost, efficiency, and ability to provide information unavailable though formal sources (Marsden, 1994). However, this method tends to favor in-groups. For this reason, recruiting managers through networks is a barrier to the employment of women and racial and ethnic minorities (Marsden and Gorman, 1999; Braddock and McPartland, 1987). In contrast, posting or advertising managerial jobs, recruiting through employment agencies, and specifying objective selection criteria are open recruitment methods that broaden the applicant pool and that limit ascription.

Research indicates that a diverse workforce, compared to a homogeneous one, is generally beneficial for business. For example, Cedric Herring of the University of Illinois at Chicago, using data from a national sample of for-profit business organizations in the United States, finds that racial diversity is associated with increased sales revenue, more customers, greater market share, and greater relative profits (Herring, 2009). Similarly, gender diversity is associated with increased sales revenue, more customers, and greater relative profits (Herring, 2009).

CHAPTER SUMMARY

In this chapter we present sociological perspectives on culture, formal organization, and bureaucracy. We present a brief sociological analysis of Muslim American subcultures so that you may enhance your sociological understanding of this richly textured subculture in the United States. Alexis de Tocqueville then reminds us that a democratic society requires a value system that constrains the power of the state, and de Toqueville views voluntary associations in the United States as an important part of the relationships that make democracy possible for us. Your excursion into sociological ways of knowing enables you to appreciate more fully that participating in voluntary associations satisfies more than just personal needs. You are now more able than you were a few weeks ago to look for, and to perceive, sociological fundamentals that help you better to understand social life in the twenty-first century.

SUGGESTED READINGS

Bawer, Bruce, *The Victims' Revolution: The Rise of Identity Studies and the Closing of the Liberal Mind* (New York: Broadside Books, 2012).

Black, Edwin, *War Against the Weak: Eugenics and America's Campaign to Create a Master Race* (Washington, D.C.: Dialog Press, 2012)

Ferguson, Niall, *The Great Degeneration: How Institutions Decay and Economies Die* (New York: The Penguin Press, 2013).

Ferreira, Francisco H.G.; Messina, Julian; Rigolini, Jamele; López-Calva, Juis-Felipe; Lugo, Maria Ana; and Vakis, Renos, *Economic Mobility and the Rise of the Latin American Middle Class* (Washington, D.C.: The World Bank, 2013).

Goldberg, Jonah, *Liberal Fascism: The Secret History of the American Left from Mussolini to the Politics of Meaning* (New York, Doubleday, 2007).

Ho, Pin, and Huang, Wenguang, *A Death in the Lucky Holiday Hotel: Murder, Money, and an Epic Power Struggle in China* (New York: Public Affairs, 2013).

Horowitz, David, *Radicals: Portraits of a Destructive Passion* (Washington, D.C.: Regnery Publishing, Inc., 2012).

Malkasian, Carter, *War Comes to Garmser: Thirty Years of Conflict on the Afghan Frontier* (New York: Oxford University Press, 2013).

Mead, Walter Russell, *God and Gold: Britain, America, and the Making of the Modern World* (New York: Alfred A. Knopf, 2008).

Mead, Walter Russell, *Special Providence: American Foreign Policy and How It Changed the World* (New York: Routledge, 2009).

Radosh, Ronald and Radosh, Allis, *Red Star Over Hollywood: The Film Colony's Long Romance with the Left* (New York: Encounter Books, 2006).

Radosh, Ronald, *Commies: A Journey Through the Old Left, the New Left and the Leftover Left* (San Francisco, CA: Encounter Books, 2001).

Tinniswood, Adrian, *Pirates of Barbary: Corsairs, Conquests, and Captivity in th e17th Century Mediterranean* (New York: Riverhead Books, 2010).

BIBLIOGRAPHY

Abercrombie, Nicholas; Hill, Stephen; and Turner, Bryan S., *The Penguin Dictionary of Sociology* Third Edition (London: Penguin Books, 1994).

Alexander, Karl L.; Entwisle, Doris R.; and Olson, Linda Steffel, "Lasting Consequences of the Summer Learning Gap," *American Sociological Review*, Vol. 72, No. 2, (April) 2007: 167-180.

Almond, Gabriel, and Verba, Sidney, *The Civic Culture* (Princeton, NJ: Princeton University Press, 1963).

Anderson, Robert; Curtis, James; and Grabb, Edward, "Trends in Civic Association Activity in Four Democracies: The Special Case of Women in the United States," *American Sociological Review*, Vol. 71, (June) 2006: 376-400.

Andreas, Joel, "The Structure of Charismatic Mobilization: A Case Study of Rebellion During the Chinese Cultural Revolution," *American Sociological Review*, Vol. 72, No. 3, (June) 2007: 434-458.

Argyle, Michael, *The Psychology of Social Class* (London: Routledge, 1994).

Argyle, Michael, *The Social Psychology of Everyday Life* (London: Routledge, 1992).

Argyle, Michael, *The Social Psychology of Work* Second Edition (Harmondsworth, England: Penguin, 1989).

Aronson, Elliot; Wilson, Timothy D.; and Akert, Robin M., *Social Psychology* Fifth Edition (Upper Saddle River, NJ: Pearson Prentice Hall, 2005).

Aschaffengurg, Karen, and Maas, Ineke, "Cultural and Educational Careers: the Dynamics of Social Reproduction," *American Sociological Review*, Vol. 62, 1997 (August) 1997: 573-587.

Barnes, Lisa L.; Cagney, Kathleen A.; and de Leon, Carlos F., "Social Resources and Cognitive Function in Older Persons," in Scott M. Hofer and Duane F. Alwin, *Handbook of Cognitive Aging* (Thousand Oaks, CA: Sage Publications, 2008): 603-610.

Baron, James N.; Mittman, Brian S.; Newman, Andrew E., "Targets of Opportunity: Organizational and Environmental Determinants of Gender Integration within the California Civil Service, 1979-1985," *American Journal of Sociology*, Vol. 96, 1991: 1362-1401.

Bellingham, Richard, *The Manager's Pocket Guide to Corporate Culture Change* (Amherst, MA: HRD Press, 2001).

Berkman, L.F., and Syme, S.L., "Social Networks, Host Resistance, and Mortality: A Nine Year Follow-up Study of Alameda County Residents," *American Journal of Epidemiology*, Vol. 109, 1979: 186-204.

Bielby, William T., "Minimizing Workplace Gender and Racial Bias," *Contemporary Sociology*, Vol. 29, 2000: 120-129.

Bisschop, M. I.; Kriegsman, D.M.; van Tilburg, T.G.; Penninx, B.W.; van Eijk, J.T.; and Deeg, D.J., "The Influence of Differing Social Ties on Decline in Physical Functioning among Older People with

and without Chronic Diseases: The Longitudinal Aging Study Amsterdam," *Aging Clinical and Experimental Research*, Vol. 15, 2003: 164-173.

Blazer, Dan G., "Social Support and Mortality in an Elderly Community Population," *American Journal of Epidemiology*, Vol. 115, 1982: 684-694.

Blum, Terry C.; Fields, Dail L.; and Goodman, Jodi S., "Organizational-Level Determinants of Women in Management," *Academy of Management Journal*, Vol. 37, 1994: 241-268.

Bourdieu, Pierre, "The Political Field, the Social Science Field, and the Journalistic Field," in R. Benson and E. Neveu, *Bourdieu and the Journalistic Field* (Malden, MA: Polity Press, 2005).

Bourdieu, Pierre, and Passerson, Jean-Claude, *Reproduction in Education, Society, and Culture* Second Edition (London: Sage, 1990). Richard Nice, trans.

Bourdieu, Pierre, *Logic of Practice* (Stanford, CA: Stanford University Press, 1992).

Bourdieu, Pierre, *Sociology in Question* (London: Sage, 1993).

Braddock, Jomills Henry, II, and McPartland, James M., "How Minorities Continue to Be Excluded from Equal Employment Opportunities: Research on Labor Market and Institutional Barriers," *Journal of Social Issues*, Vol. 43, 1987: 5-39.

Brauer, Markus; Judd, C.M.; and Jacquelin, V., "The Communication of Social Stereotypes: The Effects of Group Discussion and Information Distribution on Stereotypic Appraisals," *Journal of Personality and Social Psychology*, Vol. 81, 2001: 463-475.

Brym, Robert J., and Lie, John, *Your Compass for a New World* Second Edition (Belmont, CA: Thompson/ Wadsworth, 2005).

Burns, J.F., "Pillagers Strip Iraqi Museum of its Treasures," *New York Times*, April 13, 2003 (www.nytimes.com).

Cairns, Robert B., and Cairns, Beverly D., *Lifelines and Risks: Pathways of Youth in Our Time* (New York: Cambridge University Press, 1994).

Centeno, Miguel Angel, and Hargittai, Eszter, "Defining a Global Geography," *The American Behavioral Scientist*, Vol. 44, No. 10, 2003.

Chen, L.H.; Baker, S.P.; Braver, E.R.; and Li, G., "Carrying Passengers as a Risk Factor for Crashes Fatal to 16- And 17-Year Old Drivers," *Journal of the American Medical Association*, Vol. 383, 2000: 1578-1582.

Collins-Lowry, Sharon M., *Black Corporate Executives: The Making and Breaking of a Black Middle Class* (Philadelphia, PA: Temple University Press, 1997).

Dean, Alfred; Kolody, Bohdan; and Wood, Patricia, "Effects of Social Support from Various Sources on Depression in Elderly Persons," *Journal of Health and Social Behavior*, Vol. 31, 1990: 148-161.

Deutsch, M., and Gerard, H.B., "A Study of Normative and Informational Social Influence Upon Individual Judgment," *Journal of Abnormal and Social Psychology*, Vol. 51, 1955: 629-636.

Dominguez, Silvia and Watkins, Celeste, "Creating Networks for Survival and Mobility: Social Capital Among African-American and Latin-American Low-Income Mothers," *Social Problems*, Vol. 50, No. 1, 2003: 111-135.

Eastwood, Jonathan, "Bourdieu, Flaubert, and the Sociology of Literature," *Sociological Theory*, Vol. 25, No. 2, (June) 2007: 149-169.

Farkas, George, and Beron, Kurt, "The Detailed Age Trajectory of Oral Vocabulary Knowledge: Differences by Class and Race," *Social Science Research*, Vol. 33, 2004: 464-497.

Ferber, Abby L. (Ed.), *Home-Grown Hate: Gender and Organized Racism* (New York: Routledge, 2004).

Franke, Richard Herbert and Kaul, James D., "The Hawthorne Experiments: First Statistical Interpretation," *American Sociological Review*, Vol. 43, No. 5, (October) 1978: 623-643.

Flynn, Kevin, and Gerhardt, Gary, *The Silent Brotherhood: The Chilling Inside Story of America's Violent Anti-Government Militia Movement* (New York: The Free Press, 1990).

Garcia-Moreno, C., "Violence Against Women: International Perspectives," *American Journal of Preventive Medicine*, Vol. 19, 2000: 330-333.

Ghose, Sagarika, "The Dalit in India," *Social Research*, Vol. 70, No. 1, (Spring) 2003.

Gilmore, Samuel, "Culture," in Edgar F. Borgatta and Marie L. Borgatta (Eds.), *Encyclopedia of Sociology* (New York: Macmillan Publishing Company, 1992), Vol. 1, pp. 404-411.

Golding, William, *Lord of the Flies, a Novel* (New York: Coward-McCann, 1954).

Gonzales, Juan L. Jr., "The Settlement of Sikh Farmers in the Sacramento Valley of California," in Mahin Gosine (Ed.), *Dothead Americans: The Silent Minority in the United States* (New York: Windsor Press, 1990), pp. 32-47.

Goodall, Jane van Lawick, *The Behavior of Free-Living Chimpanzees in the Gombe Stream Reserve* (London: Ballière, Tindall, and Cassell, 1968).

Goodall, Jane, *In the Shadow of Man* (Boston: Houghton Mifflin, 1971).

Goodall, Jane, *The Chimpanzees of Gombe: Patterns of Behavior* (Cambridge, MA: Belknap Press of Harvard University Press, 1986).

Granovetter, Mark, "The Strength of Weak Ties," *American Journal of Sociology*, Vol. 78, 1973: 1360-1380.

Green, Gary Paul; Tiggers, Leam M.; and Diaz, Daniel, "Racial and Ethnic Differences in Job Search Strategies in Atlanta, Boston, and Los Angeles," *Social Science Quarterly*, Vol. 80, 1999: 263-290.

Hallinan, Maureen T., "Sociological Perspectives on Black-White Inequalities in American Schooling," *Sociology of Education*, Vol. 74, Extra Issue: Current of Thought: Sociology of Education at the Dawn of the 21st Century (2001): 50-70.

Hamilton, Alexander; Madison, James; and Jay, John, *The Federalist Papers* (New York: Bantam Books, 1982). (Originally published, 1787-1788).

Hazan, C., and Hutt, M.J., "Continuity and Change in Internal Working Models of Attachment" (Ithica, NY: Cornell University, Department of Human Development and Family Studies, 1993).

Heck, Katherine E.; Borba, John A.; Carlos, Ramona; Churches, Ken; Donohue, Susan; and Fuller, A. Hyde, *California's Rural Youth* (Davis, CA: University of California, Davis, 2004). A Report of the 4-H Center for Youth Development, Department of Human and Community Development, University of California, Davis, 2004). Retrieved July 6, 2004, from http://fourhcyd.ucdavis.edu/extending/specialreports.html

Herring, Cedric, "Does Diversity Pay?: Race, Gender, and the Business Case for Diversity," *American Sociological Review*, Vol. 74 (April) 2009: 208-224.

Hobfoll, S.E., *The Ecology of Stress* (New York: Hemisphere, 1988).

Holmes, Richard, *Acts of War: The Behavior of Men in Battle* (New York: The Free Press, 1985).

Holtby, Sue; Zahnd, Elaine; Yen, Wei; Lordi, Nicole; McCain, Christy; and DiSorga, Charles, *Health of California's Adults, Adolescents, and Children: Findings from CHIS 2001* (Los Angeles, CA: UCLA Center for Health Policy Research, 2004).

Humphries, Harry L., et. al, "Framing the Gift of Life: An Empirical Examination of Altruism, Social Distance and Material Incentives in Non-Directed Kidney Donor Motivation," *Journal of Nephrology Social Work*, Vol. 31, (Summer) 2009: 20-27.

Inglehart, Ronald, *Modernization and Post-Modernization: Cultural, Economic, and Political Change in 43 Societies* (Princeton, NJ: Princeton University Press, 1997).

Johnson, J. Randall, "Social Support," in Edgar F. Borgatta and Marie L. Borgatta, *Encyclopedia of Sociology*, Vol. 4 (New York: Macmillan and Company, 1992), pp. 1976-1979.

Kendall, Diana, *Sociology in Our Times* Fifth Edition (Belmont, CA: Thomson Wadsworth, 2005).

Kent, Mary Mederios, "Education, Medical Treatment, and Social Networks Can Promote 'Brain Health' Among U.S. Elderly, Population Reference Bureau, March 2009. As of June 9, 2013, available online at http://www.prb.org/Articles/2009/cognitiveimpairment.aspx?=1

Kraus, Linda A.; Davis, Mark H.; Bazzini, Doris; Church, Mary; and Kirchman, Clare M., "Personal and Social Influences on Loneliness: The Mediating Effect of Social Provisions," *Social Psychology Quarterly*, Vol. 56, 1993: 37-53.

Lachmann, Richard (Ed.), *The Encyclopedic Dictionary of Sociology* Fourth edition (Guilford, CT: The Dushkin Publishing Group, 1991).

Lawler, A., "Iraq's Shattered Universities," *Science*, Vol. 300, 2003: 582-588.

Lea, M.; Spears, R.; and de Groot, D., "Knowing Me, Knowing You: Anonymity Effects on Social Identity Processes Within Groups," *Personality and Social Psychology Bulletin*, Vol. 27, 2001: 525-537.

Lee, Valerie E., and Burkham, David T., *Inequality at the Starting Gate* (Washington, D.C.: Economic Policy Institute, 2002).

Lin, Nan, and Ensel, Walter M., "Life Stresses and Health: Stressors and Resources," *American Sociological Review*, Vol. 54, 1989: 382-399.

Lopez, Mark Hugo, and Minushkin, Susan, *2008 National Survey of Latinos* (Washington, D.C.: Pew Hispanic Center, 2008).

Luttrell, Wendy, *School Smart and Mother-Wise: Working-Class Women's Identity and Schooling* (New York: Routledge, 1997).

Mann, Leon, "The Baiting Crown in Episodes of Threatened Suicide," Journal of Personality and Social Psychology, Vol. 41, 1981: 703-709.

Marsden, Peter V., "Core Discussion Networks of Americans," *American Sociological Review*, Vol. 52, 1987: 122-131.

Marsden, Peter V., "The Hiring Process: Recruitment Methods," *American Behavioral Scientist*, Vol. 37, 1994: 79-91.

Marsden, Peter V., and Gorman, Elizabeth H., "Social Capital in Internal Staffing Practices," in R. Th. A.J. Leenders and S. Gabbay (Eds.), *Corporate Social Capital* (Amsterdam, Netherlands: Kluwer, 1999): 167-183.

Maurer, Christine, and Sheets, Tara (Eds.), *Encyclopedia of Associations: An Association Unlimited Reference* (33rd Edition), Vol. 1, Part 2, *National Organizations of the United States,* Part 2, Sections 7-8, Entries 10229-22761 (Detroit, MI: Gale, 1998).

McCarney, Rob; Warner, James; Iliffe, Steve; van Haselen, Robert; Griffin, Mark; and Fisher, Peter, "The Hawthorne Effect: A Randomized, Controlled Trial," *BMC Medical Research Methodology*, Vol. 7, 2007: 30. As of June 10, 2013, available online at http://www.biomedcentral.com/1471-2288/7/30

McFarland, Daniel A. and Thoman, Reuben J., "Bowling Young: How Youth Voluntary Associations Influence Political Participation," *American Sociological Review*, Vol. 71, (June) 2006: 401-425.

Mendes de Leon, C.F.; Gold, D.T.; Glass, T.A.; Kaplan, L.; and George, L.K., "Disability as a Function of Social Networks and Support in Elderly African Americans and Whites: The Duke EPESE 1986-

1992," *Journals of Gerontology: Series B: Psycholog8icdal Sciences and Social Sciences*, Vol. 56, 2001: S179-S190.

Michels, Robert, *Political Parties: A Sociological Study of the Oligarchical Tendencies of Modern Democracy* (New York: Free Press, 1949). Originally published in 1911.

Moghaddam, F.M., "The Staircase to Terrorism: A Psychological Exploration," *American Psychologist*, Vol. 60 (2005): 161-169.

Montgomery, James D., "Job Search and Network Composition: Implications of the Strength of Work Ties Hypothesis," *American Sociological Review*, Vol. 57 (October) 1992: 586-596.

Moore, Gwen S., "Structural Determinants of Men's and Women's Personal Networks," *American Sociological Review*, Vol. 55, 1990: 726-735.

Murdock, George Peter, "The Common Denominator of Cultures," in Ralph Linton (Ed.), *The Science of Man and the World Crisis* (New York: Columbia University Press, 1945).

Murdock, George Peter, *Social Structure* (Toronto, Canada: The Macmillan Company, 1949).

Muscovici, Serge, and Zavalloni, Marisa, "The Group as a Polarizer of Attitudes," *Journal of Personality and Social Psychology*, Vol. 12, 1969: 124-135.

Myers, David, *Social Psychology* ninth edition (Boston: McGraw Hill, 2008).

Nazroo, James; Jackson, James; Karlsen, Saffron; and Torres, Myriam, "The Black Diaspora and Health Inequalities in the US and England: Does Where You Go and How You Get There Make a Difference?" *Sociology of Health and Illness* (Oxford, UK: Blackwell Publishing, 2007).

Nyak, Madhabika B.; Byrne, Christina A.; Martin, Mutsumi K.; Abraham, Anna George, "Attitudes Towards Violence Against Women: A Cross-Nation Study," *Sex Roles*, Vol. 49, 2003: 333-343.

O'Reilly, P.A., and Thomas, H.E., "Role of Support Networks in Maintenance of Improved Cardiovascular Health Status," *Social Science and Medicine*, Vol. 28, 1989: 249-260.

Ogburn, William F., *Social Change with Respect to Culture and Original Nature* (New York: Dell, 1966). Originally published in 1922.

Ohtsubo, Y.; Masuchi, A.; and Nakanishi, D., "Majority Influence Process in Group Judgment: Test of the Social Judgment Scheme Model in a Group Polarization Context," *Group Processes and Intergroup Relations*, Vol. 5, 2002: 249-261.

Pagel, Mark K.; Erdly, William W.; and Becker, Joseph, "Social Networks: We Get by with (and in Spite of) a Little Help from Our Friends," *Journal of Personality and Social Psychology*, Vol. 46, 1987: 1097-1108.

Pascerella, E.T., and Terenzini, P.T., *How College Effects Students: Findings and Insights From Twenty Years of Research* (San Francisco: Jossey-Bass, 1991).

Peters, Thomas J., and Waterman, Robert H., *In Search of Excellence: Lessons From America's Best-Run Companies* (New York: HarperBusiness Essentials, 2004).

Petersen, Trond; Saporta, Ishak; and Seidel, Mark-David, "Offering a Job: Meritocracy and Social Networks," *American Journal of Sociology*, Vol. 106 (November), 2000: 763-816.

Pew Research Center for the People and the Press, *Muslim Americans: No Signs of Growth in Alienation or Support for Extremism* (Washington, D.C.: Pew Research Center for the People and the Press, August 30, 2011). As of June 8, 2013, available online at http://www.people-press.org/2011/08/30/muslim-americans-no-signs-of-growth-in-alienation-or-support-for-extremism/

Pew Research Center, "After Boston, Little Change in Views of Islam and Violence," May 7, 2013. As of June 6, 2013, available online at http://www.people-press.org/2013/05/07/after-boston-little-change-in-views-of-islam-and-violence/

Pew Research Center, *Muslim Americans: Middle Class and Mostly Mainstream* (Washington, D.C.: Pew Research Center, 2007b).

Pfeffer, Jeffrey, "Organization Theory and Structural Perspectives in Management," *Journal of Management*, Vol. 17, 1991: 789-803.

Polk, Milbry and Schuster, Angela, M.H., *Looting the Iraq Museum: The Lost Legacy of Ancient Mesopotamia* (New York: Harry N. Abrams, Publishers, 2005).

Pressman, Sarah D.; Cohen, Sheldon; Miller, Gregory E., et. al., "Loneliness, Social Network Size, and Immune Response to Influenza Vaccination in College Freshmen," *Health Psychology*, Vol. 24, No. 3, 2005: 297-306.

Putnam, Robert D., *Bowling Alone: The Collapse and Revival of American Community* (New York: Simon and Schuster, 2000).

Reskin, Barbara, "The Proximate Causes of Employment Discrimination," *Contemporary Sociology*, Vol. 71, 2000: 123-143.

Reskin, Barbara, and McBrier, Debra, "Why Not Ascription? Organizations' Employment of Male and Female Managers," *American Sociological Review*, Vol. 65, 2000: 210-233.

Rodrigo, M.F., and Ato, M., "Testing the Group Polarization Hypothesis by Using Logit Models," *European Journal of Social Psychology*, Vol. 32, 2002: 3-18.

Roethlisberger, Fritz, and Dixon, William J., *Management and the Worker* (Cambridge, MA: Harvard University Press, 1939).

Rohlinger, Deana A., "American Media and Deliberative Democratic Processes," *Sociological Theory*, Vol. 25, No. 2 (June) 2007: 122-148.

Rook, Karen, "Negative Side of Social Interaction: Impact on Psychological Well-Being," *Journal of Personality and Social Psychology*, Vol. 46, 1984: 1097-1108.

Sageman, Marc, *Understanding Terror Networks* (Philadelphia: University of Pennsylvania Press, 2004).

Sanchez-Martin, J.R.; Cardas, J.; Ahedo, L; Fano, E.; Echebarria, A., and Azpiroz, A., "Social Behavior, Cortisol, and sIgA Levels in Pre-School Children," *Journal of Psychosomatic Research*, Vol. 50, 2001: 221-227.

Schofer, Evan, and Fourcade-Gourinchas, Marion, "The Structural Contexts of Civic Engagement: Voluntary Association Membership in Comparative Perspective," *American Sociological Review*, Vol. 66 (December 2001): 806-828.

Schwarzer, R., and Leppin, A., "Social Support and Health: A Meta-Analysis," *Psychology and Health*, Vol. 3, 1989: 1-15.

Shenhav, Yehouda and Haberfeld, Yitchak, "Organizational Demography and Inequality," *Social Forces*, Vol. 71, 1992: 123-143.

Sidanius, J.; Van Laar, C.; Levin, S.; and Sinclair, S., "Ethnic Enclaves on the College Campus: The Good, The Bad, and The Ugly," *Journal of Personality and Social Psychology*, Vol. 87, 2004: 96-110.

Silke, Andrew, "De-individuation, Anonymity, and Violence: Findings from Northern Ireland," *Journal of Social Psychology*, Vol. 143, 2003: 493-499.

Skocpol, Theda; Liazos, Ariane, and Ganz, Marshall, *What a Mighty Power We Can Be: African American Fraternal Groups and the Struggle for Racial Equality* (Princeton, NJ: Princeton University Press, 2006).

Stokes, Joseph, and Levin, Ira, "Gender Differences in Predicting Loneliness from Social Network Characteristics," *Journal of Personality and Social Psychology*, Vol. 51, 1986: 1069-1074).

Stoner, James, "A Comparison of Individual and Group Decisions Involving Risk." Unpublished Master's Thesis, Massachusetts Institute of Technology (MIT), 1961.

Stouffer, Samuel, et. al., *The American Soldier: Adjusting During Army Life* (Princeton: Princeton University Press, 1949).

Sutherland, Anne H., "Roma in the United States," in Melvin Ember, Carol R. Ember, and Ian Skoggard (Eds.), *Encyclopedia of Diasporas: Immigrant and Refugee Cultures Around the World* (New York: Springer, 2005), pp. 1068-1074.

Taylor, Shelley E.; Peplau, Letitia A.; and Sears, David O., *Social Psychology* Eleventh Edition (Upper Saddle River, NJ: Prentice Hall, 2003).

Theodorson, George A., and Theodorson, Achilles, G., A Modern Dictionary of Sociology (New York: Barnes & Noble Books, 1969).

Thoits, Peggy A., and Hewitt, Lyndi N., "Voluntary Work and Well-Being," *Journal of Health and Social Behavior*," Vol. 42, No. 2 (June 2001): 115-131.

Toqueville, Alexis de, *Democracy in America* (New York: Vintage Books, [1835] 1990).

Tylor, Edward B., *Primitive Culture: Researches Into the Development of Mythology, Philosophy, Religion, Art, and Custom* 2 Vols. (London: John Murray, 1871). Vol. 1: *Origins of Culture*

U.S. Census Bureau, *U.S. and World Population Clock*. As of June 7, 2013, 18:09 UTC (Eastern-5), available online at www.census.gov/popclock

Vaughan, Diane, *Challenger Launch Decision: Risky Technology, Culture, and Deviance* (Chicago: University of Chicago Press, 1996).

Weber, Max, "Deutscher Sociologentag" (German Sociology Today), *Verhandlungen*, Vol. 1, 1911: 39-62.

Weber, Max, *The Theory of Social and Economic Organization* (New York: Free Press, 1947). Originally published in 1925.

Weinstein, Allen, and Vassiliev, Alexander, *The Haunted Wood: Soviet Espionage in America—the Stalin Era* (New York: Modern Library, 2000).

Wellman, Barry (Ed.), *Networks in the Global Village: Life in Contemporary Communities* (Boulder, CO: Westview, 1999).

Werner, Emmy E., "Vulnerability and Resiliency: A Longitudinal Study of Asian Americans from Birth to Age 30," Invited Address at the IX Biennial Meeting of the International Society for the Study of Behavioral Development, Tokyo, July 15, 1987.

Werner, Emmy E., and Smith, Ruth S., *Overcoming the Odds: High Risk Children from Birth to Adulthood* (New York: Cornell University Press, 1992).

Werner, Emmy E., and Smith, Ruth S., *Vulnerable But Invincible: A Longitudinal Study of Resilient Children and Youth* (New York: Adams, Bannister, Cox, 1989).

Werner, Emmy E., *Journeys from Childhood to Midlife: Risk, Resilience, and Recovery* (New York: Cornell University Press, 2001).

West, Nigel, *VENONA: The Greatest Secret of the Cold War* (London: Trafalgar, 2001).

Wheeler, L.; Reis, H; and Nezlek, J., "Loneliness, Social Interaction, and Social Roles," *Journal of Personality and Social Psychology*, Vol. 45, 1983: 943-953.

Wright, Erik O., Baxter, Janeen; Birkelund, E. G., "The Gender Gap in Workplace Authority: A Cross-National Study," *American Sociological Review*, Vol. 60, 1995: 407-435.

Wuthnow, Robert, "Tocqueville's Question Reconsidered: Volunteerism and Public Discourse in Advanced Industrial Societies," in Robert Wuthnow (Ed.), *Between States and Markets: The Voluntary Sector in Comparative Perspective* (Princeton, NJ: Princeton University Press, 1991: 288-308).

CHAPTER 4

Globalization

INTRODUCTION

For over a century, social scientists have conceptualized the world as a unitary social system, increasingly bound together by overlapping social circles of economic exchange, competition, and cooperation (Erikson, 2006; Fourcade, 2006; Boli and Thomas, 1997:172). This unitary social system sometimes is called world or global culture and the process that created it is called globalization. World or global culture was given a boost after the end of the Second World War, when the United Nations and other bodies (e.g., the World Bank, the International Monetary Fund) established agendas of concern for world society (Goldstein and Pevehouse, 2010). These agendas of concern included a focus on individual rights, human rights, egalitarian justice, and participatory representation; economic development; scientific, medical, and educational development; and environmental reclamation and protection. A wide range of social domains thereby became eligible for international scrutiny, discussion, and social action (Goldstein and Pevehouse, 2010).

There are concepts in sociology that are difficult to define (in the sense that there is little consensus on their definition) and to measure but which nonetheless seem important if we want to understand the worlds in which we live. The concept of ethnicity is one such concept (Weber, 1968: 385-98), and globalization is another. According to Max Weber, an **ethnic group** is a group that entertains a subjective belief in its common descent because of "similarities of physical type or of customs or both, or because of memories of colonization and migration" (Weber, 1968: 389). In short, ethnic groups are based on perceived similarities of culture, descent, or both.

There is no agreed upon definition for **globalization**, which refers to the free flow of commodities, manufactures, transportation, capital, labor, knowledge, culture, and institutions around the world or "the globe." The driving idea behind globalization is free-market capitalism: the more a country opens itself to market forces of supply and demand, the more a country opens its economy to free trade and competition, the more efficient and flourishing that country's economy will be. Globalization thus means the spread of free-market capitalism to virtually every country in the world. Hence, globalization also has its own set of rules that revolve around opening, deregulating, and privatizing the economy in order to make it more competitive and attractive to domestic and foreign investment.

Joseph A. Schumpeter, political scientist and former Austrian Minister of Finance and Harvard Business School professor, expressed the view in his classic work *Capitalism, Socialism and Democracy* (1942) that the essence of capitalism is **creative destruction**, the perennial cycle of destroying the old and less efficient product or service and replacing it with new, more efficient ones. Andrew S. Grove, former Chairman and Chief Executive Officer of Intel Corporation, helped to popularize the view that dramatic, industry-transforming innovations are taking place today at a faster and faster pace (Grove, 1996). Those countries that are most willing to let capitalism destroy inefficient companies, so that money can be freed up and directed to more innovative ones, tend to thrive in globalization. Those countries that rely on their governments to protect them from such creative destruction, in essence are walking away from capitalism, and they tend both to lose their competitive edge and to fall behind. France provides an example. In 1999, French labor laws were changed, *requiring* every employer to implement a four-hour reduction in the legal workweek, from 39 hours to 35 hours, with *no* cut in pay. This change went into effect on January 1, 2000, for business with more than 20 employees, and two years later for businesses with twenty or fewer employees (Triplet & Associés, 2013).

The current globalization system emerged after the end of the Cold War, which happened in 1989, with the fall of the Berlin Wall (Friedman, 2000: xvi). This means that the current globalized world is a recent invention, about twenty-five years old.

Sociological Paradigms and Globalization

However globalization is defined and however globalization is measured, the various sociological paradigms take differing stances towards it. Conflict theorists—whether Marxist, feminist, world-systems, or even post-modernist—are consistently and highly critical of the process of globalization and its alleged effects. Conflict theorists tend to search for, and find, disadvantages inherent in globalization. In contrast, consensus theorists tend to look for, and find, ways that globalization helps societies to exist across time and enhances the quality of life for many people across the spectrum of stratification in these societies. Symbolic interactionists tend to look at the meanings that people develop, use, and implement with regard to the globalization experience.

Sociologists generally have been critical of the effects of economic globalization on the lives of people in developing countries (e.g., Kentor and Boswell, 2003; Dixon and Boswell, 1996). However, in a recent study of globalization and women's employment in Mexico, sociologists Andrés Villarreal and Wei-hsin Yu of University of Texas at Austin find that globalization has beneficial economic effects on Mexican women (2007). Using data from nationally representative surveys of manufacturing firms between 1992 and 2001, Villarreal and Yu find that globalization creates new, and to some extent, better job opportunities for females. Using detailed information from a representative sample of Mexican-owned and foreign-owned export manufacturing firms, the authors find that foreign-owned export-oriented manufacturing firms employ

significantly higher proportions of women at every occupational level than do nationally-owned firms producing goods for sale in the domestic market. The foreign-owned, export-oriented firms pay *higher* wages than do other firms, and they discriminate against women *less* in terms of wages. The gendered wage gap is *lower* in foreign owned export firms compared to nationally-owned firms producing goods for the domestic market (Villarreal and Yu, 2007: 384).

Global Culture

Globalization also has its own dominant culture, which is why globalization is said to be homogenizing to a certain extent. This culture of globalization is called different things, including global or world culture. In previous eras, this sort of homogenization tended to happen on a regional scale—the Romanization of the Mediterranean world and of Western Europe, the Islamification of Central Asia, North Africa, Europe, and the Middle East by the Arabs and later the Ottomans, the Russification of Eastern and Central Europe and parts of Eurasia by the Soviets. With globalization, this sort of homogenization tends to happen on a global scale.

Many of the principles or elements of world culture are contested and generate conflict (e.g., Holohan, 2005). World culture is dynamic, changing, and evolving. The concept of world culture is chuck full of internal contradictions. World culture at the same time increases the bases for solidarity and cohesion, and it also increases the bases for conflict.

Demographic Patterns

Globalization has its own demographic patterns—a rapid acceleration of the movement of people across national borders and from rural areas and agricultural lifestyles to urban areas with urban lifestyles more intimately connected to global fashion, food, markets, entertainment trends, and social movements.

Structure of Power: Three Balances

Today's system globalization has its defining structure of power, which Thomas L. Friedman conceives as consisting of three "balances" that overlap and affect one another (Friedman, 2000: 13-15).

1. **NATION STATES** The first balance is provided by nation states. In the globalization system of today, the United States is still the dominant superpower, and the balance of power among the United States and other states still matters for the stability of the globalization system. This is why you read all the time about meetings among the G-7, G-8, and G-20 states. The states of the world endeavor in a variety of ways and through a variety of venues to cooperate and to enhance the stability of the globalization system.

2. **GLOBAL MARKETS** The second balance in the globalization system is between nation states and global markets (Friedman, 2000: 13). Thomas L. Friedman's name for global markets is "the Electronic Herd," because he conceives of global markets today as consisting of millions of investors moving money around the world with the click of a mouse. In the current era of globalization, the Electronic Herd gathers in

key global financial centers—such as Wall Street, Hong Kong, London, and Frankfurt—which Friedman terms the "Supermarkets" (Friedman, 2000: 13). The definitions and actions of the Electronic Herd and the Supermarkets can have huge impacts on nation states, even to the point of triggering the downfall of governments. Thus, Suharto in Indonesia in 1998 was ousted after the Supermarkets withdrew their support for, and confidence in, the Indonesian economy. The Supermarkets downgraded Indonesian bonds and the Indonesian government toppled (Friedman: 2000).

3. **SUPER-EMPOWERED INDIVIDUALS (ORGANIZATIONS)** A third balance in the globalization system is that between individuals and the nation state. Globalization has brought down many of the walls or barriers that limited the movement and reach of people and at the same time it has wired the world into networks. Thereby, globalization has given more power to individuals not only to act in global markets but to influence both global markets and nation states. Friedman conceives of these latter individuals as "superempowered individuals" and they increasingly can act on the world stage directly, unmediated by a state (Friedman, 2000: 14). Some of these superempowered individuals are angry, others beneficent; but what they have in common is that they can act on the world stage directly.

For example, Osama bin Laden, a Saudi millionaire with his own global network (al-Qaeda) declared war on the United States in the late 1990s (Lewis, 1998) and arranged for the simultaneous bombings of two U.S. embassies in Africa—in Kenya and Tanzania—thereby killing 224 people and wounding thousands of others. In response the U.S. Airforce retaliated with a cruise missile attack on him where he resided in Afghanistan, as though he were a state. The United States fired 75 cruise missiles, at one million dollars apiece, at a person (Gellman and Priest, 1998). That was an action, Friedman maintains, between a super power and a superempowered individual. On May2, 2011, the U.S. killed bin Laden by an attack of Navy SEALS on his compound in Abottabad, Pakistan, where he was then living (Bergen, 2013). The killing of bin Laden is another example of an interaction between a super power and a superempowered individual.

Jody Williams won the Nobel Peace Prize in 1997 for her contribution to helping to build an international coalition to bring about a treaty banning landmines. The treaty is commonly known as the landmine treaty, the Mine Ban Treaty, or the Ottawa Treaty, and it is officially known as the Convention on the Prohibition of the Use, Stockpiling, Production, and Transfer of Anti-Personnel Mines and on their Destruction. Over 150 states have signed and ratified this treaty which went into effect on March 1, 1999. Jody Williams achieved the ban in the face of opposition from all the major powers. As of June, 2013, the United States, Russia., China, India, and South Korea are still among the states that have neither signed nor ratified the Mine Ban Treaty. When asked what her secret weapon was for organizing over 1,000 different human rights and arms control groups on six continents, she said, "E-mail" (Friedman, 2003). Jody Williams is another example of a super-empowered individual.

It should be noted, of course, that what Thomas L. Friedman terms "super-empowered" individuals actually are leaders, and usually the founding leaders, of social organizations—al Qaeda, in the case of Osama bin Laden and the ICBL (International Campaign to Ban Landmines) in the case of Jody Williams. So, as one of the three balances of the current globalization system, what Friedman terms "superempowered individuals" are actually *organizations*, not just persons, no matter how superempowered. Organizations square off with nation states.

Using the lexicon of Thomas L. Friedman, nation-states, the Supermarkets, and super-empowered individuals are the defining structure of power in the current era of globalization. In order to understand the current globalization system or the front page of the morning newspaper, it is important to understand that the current globalization system is a complex interaction among all three of these social actors: states bumping up against states, states bumping up against Supermarkets, and Supermarkets and states bumping up against super-empowered individuals.

INSTITUTIONAL UNDERPINNINGS OF GLOBALIZATION

There is growing recognition of the importance of financial (e.g., money, credit, debt), legal (rule of law), and administrative (governmental) institutions in encouraging the trans-border capital flows that we know as international capitalism. Institutional structures make international capitalism and globalization possible. How did the West European versions of these institutions spread as far and wide as they did?

In a few rare cases—such as Japan—there was a process of conscious, voluntary imitation. More often, however, European institutions were imposed by conquest, which is to say by force, often quite literally at gunpoint. Later in this chapter we will look at the Age of Discovery and even the British Empire as examples.

When the British governed a country, even when they only influenced its government by flexing their considerable military and financial muscles, there were certain distinctive features of their own way of life, of their own culture, that they also tended to disseminate. Some of the more important of these institutional underpinnings of British globalization, as identified by historian Niall Ferguson, include the following (Ferguson, 2002: xxv):

- The English language
- English forms of land tenure (private property)
- Scottish and English banking
- The Common Law
- Protestantism
- Team sports
- The limited state
- Representative assemblies
- The idea of liberty

The last of these is perhaps the most important, because once a colonized society had sufficiently adopted the other institutions the British brought with them, it became difficult for the British to prohibit them that political liberty to which they themselves attached so much significance for themselves (Ferguson, 2002: xxv). Karl Marx might rephrase this by saying that the British system of colonial expansion carried with it the seeds of its own destruction.

According to the work of political sociologists like Seymour Martin Lipset and other social scientists, countries that were former British colonies are far more likely to have achieved enduring democratization after independence than those ruled by other countries (Ferguson, 2001: 9; Barro, 1997; Lipset, 1959, 1994; Lipset, Seong, and Torres, 1993). Indeed, almost every country with a population of at least one million that has emerged from the colonial era without succumbing to dictatorship is a former British colony (Ferguson, 2002: 362). The structure of institutions matters.

An understanding of finance and financial history helps us to acquire a sociological understanding of globalization. We turn now to a brief sociological inquiry into finance in human societies.

FINANCE

Throughout the history of Western civilization there has been a recurrent hostility to finance and those who engage in it, financiers (Ferguson, 2008: 2). This hostility is rooted in the idea that those who make a living from loaning money are somehow parasitical on those who engage in "real" economic activities such as agriculture or manufacturing. According to economic historian Niall Ferguson, there are three causes for this hostility: First, debtors tend to outnumber creditors (i.e., those who loan money), and debtors tend not to feel very well disposed to their creditors. Second, even well before the advent of capitalism, financial crises and scandals have occurred with sufficient frequency to make finance appear to be a cause of both poverty and instability rather than of prosperity and stability. Third, for centuries those who engage in financial services in countries all over the world have tended to derive disproportionately from religious or ethnic minority groups. People from these groups tended to be excluded from land ownership or public office. However, they enjoyed success in finance because of their own tight networks based on kinship and trust (Ferguson, 2008: 2).

Despite deep cultural antipathy to finance and those who engage in it as a living, the ascent of money has been part of the financial evolution of human societies. In hunting and gathering societies (folk societies), there was no money. It is with the rise of the city as a form of human habitation (urban-agrarian society), that the archaeological record first presents us with artifacts which we could term money.

In ancient Mesopotamia, beginning around 5,000 years ago, people used clay tokens to record transactions involving agricultural produce, for instance. A great many of these clay tablets have survived, reminding us that when humans first began to create written records, they did so not to write philosophy, literature, or history, but to do business (Nissen, Damerow, and Englund, 1993; Ferguson, 2008: 27). One such token dates from the reign of King Ammi-ditana (1683-1647 BC) and states that its bearer should receive a specific amount of barley at harvest time (Ferguson, 2008: 27).

The basic concept behind such a token should sound familiar to us because a modern day banknote does something similar. Banknotes, which originated in seventh-century China (Ferguson, 2008: 27), are pieces of paper that have next to no intrinsic worth. They are simply promises to pay (hence their original Western designation as "promissory notes"), just like the clay tablets of ancient Babylon four millennia ago. On the back of the U.S. ten dollar bill it says "In God We Trust." However, the person we really are trusting when we accept one of these as payment is the successor of the person on the front of the ten dollar bill. Alexander Hamilton was the first Secretary of the U.S. Treasury. At the time of this writing, his current successor is Jacob J. Lew. When a person exchanges his or her labor for a fistful of dollars, that person essentially is trusting Jacob J. Lew, and by implication, the Chairman of the Federal Reserve System, Ben Bernake, not to manufacture so many of these things that they end up being worth no more than the paper they are printed on (Ferguson, 2008: 28).

Money is a matter of belief, even faith; belief in the person paying us; belief in the person issuing the money or the institution that honors his or her checks or transfers (Davies, 2002; Williams, Cribb, and Errington, 1997). As Niall Ferguson (2008: 30) phrases it, "Money is not metal. It is trust inscribed." A sociologist might rephrase this by saying that using money is a transaction in the solidary order.

The central relationship that money embodies is that between lender and borrower. Thus, if you look at those ancient Mesopotamian clay tablets, you find that in each case, the transactions recorded on them were payments of commodities that had been loaned. Evidently, the tablets were drawn up and retained by the lender to record the amount due and the date of repayment.

The lending system of ancient Babylon was quite sophisticated (Ferguson, 2008:30). Thus, debts were transferable; hence the inscription to 'pay the bearer' rather than to pay a particularly named person. Clay receipts were issued to those who deposited grain or other commodities at royal palaces, temples, or granaries. Borrowers were expected to pay interest, at rates that often were as high as 20 percent (Van De Mieroop, 1992; Hudson and Van De Mieroop, 2002). Mathematical exercises from the reign of Hammurabi (1792-1750 BC) suggest that something like compound interest could be charged for long-term loans (Ferguson: 2008). Once again, the central relationship that borrowing and lending embodies is trust, i.e., belief in the underlying credibility of a borrower's promise to repay. It is worth noting in this regard that the root of the English word "credit" is *credo*, the Latin word for "I believe."

The long-term trend in ancient Mesopotamia was for private finance to expand. In fact, by the sixth century BC, families like the Baylonian Egibi were powerful landowners and lenders, with commercial interests as far away as Uruk a hundred miles to the south and Persia to the east. The fact that the family thrived for five generations suggests that they generally collected their debts (Fereguson: 2008).

Credit in ancient Mesopotamia was an important beginning. Without the foundation of borrowing and lending, and without the ever-growing network of relationships between creditors and debtors, the economic history of world would scarcely have got off the ground.

Money

The earliest known coins date back as long ago as 600 BC and were found by archaeologists in the Temple of Artemis in what is now modern-day Turkey (Ferguson: 2008, 24). By Roman times, coins were produced in three different metals: gold (the aureus), silver (the denarius), and bronze (the sestertius), ranked in that order due to the relative scarcity of the metals in question (Ferguson: 2008: 24). According to the known archaeological record, coins, while not unique to the ancient Mediterranean, clearly arose there first. Thus, it was not until 221 BC that a standardized bronze coin was introduced to China by Qin Shihuangdi, the first Emperor. In each case, coins made of precious metal were associated with powerful sovereigns who monopolized the minting of money, in part to exploit it as a source of revenue.

The Roman system of coinage outlived the Roman Empire itself (Ferguson, 2008: 24-25). Prices were still being quoted in terms of silver dinarii in the time of Charlemagne, King of the Franks from 768 to 814 AD. By the time Charlemagne was crowned Holy Roman Emperor in 800 AD, there was a chronic shortage of silver in Western Europe. Silver tended to drain away from more backward Europe to the more developed commercial centers of the Islamic Empire that dominated the southern Mediterranean and the Near East.

This shortage of silver was a problem that Europeans sought to overcome in one of two ways. One way was by exchanging commodities, such as timber or slaves, for silver in Baghdad or for African gold, say, in Cairo (Ferguson, 2008:25). Another way was plunder. The plunder solution was embraced effectively by the Spanish monarchy during the Age of Discovery.

GLOBALIZATION I: THE AGE OF DISCOVERY

In discussing the Age of Discovery one of necessity talks about Conquistadors. The root of the English word conquistador is *conquirere*, the Latin word meaning "to search for and subdue" (Morris, 1969: 283). The conquistadors came to the new world from Spain in the fifteenth and sixteenth centuries, expressly to search for and monetize precious metal, both gold and silver (Ferguson: 2008: 19). From 1474 until the 18th century, the country that we today call Spain was technically the union of two kingdoms, Aragon and Castile; but for purposes of simplicity, I will use the term "Spain" (Ferguson: 2008: 20).

Five hundred years ago, in what we today call Mexico the Aztecs were laid low by the Spanish conquistador Hernán Cortés between 1519 and 1521 (Ferguson, 2011: 99) and the Spaniards found vast deposits of silver at Zactecas in Central Mexico (Ferguson, 2011: 99, 101-102). At that time, the most sophisticated society in South America, the Inca Empire, was moneyless. The Incas appreciated the aesthetic qualities of rare metals. Gold was "the sweat of the sun" and silver "the tears of the moon" (Ferguson, 2008: 19). Labor was the unit of value in the Inca Empire, just as it was supposed to be centuries later in Communist society. And, as under Communism centuries later, the economy depended on often harsh central planning and forced labor (Ferguson, 2008: 19; Rummel, 2008; Courtois, Werth, Panné, Paczkowski, Bartošek, and Margolin, 1999; Conquest, 1970; Dikötter, 2010).

In 1532, the Inca Empire was brought low by Francisco Pizarro, the illegitimate son of a Spanish colonel. Pizarro had crossed the Atlantic in 1502 to seek his fortune on behalf of Spain (Meltzer, 2005; Smyth, 1931; Markham, 1970, 1872). The Spanish annihilated the vastly larger army of the Sapa Inca Atahualpa, plundered his kingdom and months later publicly garroted the captured Atahualpa in August of 1533 (Hemming, 1970: 77). The Inca Empire was formally dissolved in 1572 (Ferguson, 2008: 20).

The Age of Discovery: Money Mountain

In what Pizarro's men called Upper Peru but which today is called Bolivia, an Indian in 1545 discovered five great seams of silver in Cerro Rico, a mountain that towers over 15, 000 feet above sea level (Hemming, 1970: 355). Harnessing the riches of that mountain changed the economic history of the world (Ferguson: 2008: 21).

The town of Potosí was founded in 1545 to work the mines. Petosí rapidly became one of the principal cities of the Spanish Empire, with a population at its zenith of between 160,000 to 200,000 people, which was larger than most European cities at the time.

At first, the Spaniards paid the inhabitants of nearby villages to work in the mines of Petosí. But conditions were so harsh and the death-rate so high that from the late 15th century a system of forced labor was introduced and used, whereby males between the ages of 18 and 50 years old in the sixteen highland provinces were conscripted for seventeen weeks each year (Hemming: 1970: 392). Their mortality rate was horrendous, due in part to the hazards of rock falls in the mine shafts and tunnels of Cerro Rico and in part to the exposure of the miners to the mercury fumes generated by the process of refining the silver ore (Bakewell, 2004: 186). As the indigenous workforce was depleted by death, thousands of African slaves were imported to take their places.

A death hole for those compelled to work there, Potosí was where Spain struck it rich (Burkholder and Johnson, 1994). The mines of Potosi filled the coffers of the Spanish treasury for over two hundred years. Thus, between 1556 and 1783, Cerro Rico yielded 45,000 tons of pure silver which were transformed into bars and coins at the mint in Petosí and then shipped to Seville, Spain. There still is a saying in Spanish, "*vale un Potosí*," which means "to be worth a potosí," that is, "to be of great value." Between 1500 and 1800 precious metal worth roughly $175 billion in today's prices was shipped from the New World to Europe or via the Pacific to Asia (Ferguson, 2011: 102; Findlay and O'Rourke, 2007).

The mines of Petosí and other places where conquistadors found plentiful silver appeared to have broken the centuries-old constraint of a shortage of silver in Europe. Convoys of ships transported 170 tons of silver *a year* across the Atlantic (Ferguson: 2008, 25). The Spanish "pieces of eight," made to correspond to the German *thaler* (hence, later, the word "dollar"), became the world's first truly global currency, financing both the protracted wars that Spain fought in Europe and the rapidly expanding trade of Europe with Asia. The Spanish pieces of eight are also known as the Spanish dollar.

For Spain, the silver of the New World turned out to be a **resource curse** (Goldstein and Pevehouse, 2010: 276-277, 357-358; Drelichman and Voth, 2008), like the abundant oil of Saudi Arabia, Russia, and Venezuela in our own time. The concept of resource curse refers to a set of difficulties faced by resource-rich countries. These difficulties include a dependence on one or a few commodities, whose prices fluctuate. This dependence distorts their economies, because other industries often are neglected and wither, putting those countries at a disadvantage relative to other countries. Dependence on one or a few commodities—in the case of Spain, silver—facilitates corruption, increases conflict over the distribution of the valuable resource within the countries themselves, and facilitates the withering of other industries, while at the same time strengthening autocratic elites at the expense of representative forms of governance (Drelichman and Voth, 2008; Ferguson, 2008: 26). In Spanish colonized South America, ultimate power resided with the Spanish Crown and, crucially, the Crown owned all the land (Ferguson, 2011: 102).. The story of property ownership in North America, colonized by Britain, would be very different.

As for Spain, the Spanish appeared to be laying a foundation for a new civilization to be run by a tiny, wealthy Spanish elite from a few splendid cities (Ferguson, 2011: 102). Thus, by 1692, Mexico City had 100,000 inhabitants, at a time when Boston, for example, barely had 6,000 (Ferguson, 2011: 102). The Spanish founded more than twenty universities in the Americas, including the one in Santo Domingo, in what today we call Dominican Republic, that predates Harvard University by almost a century (Lanning, 1971). The sciences of metallurgy and cartography flourished (Barrera-Osorio, 2006; Ferguson, 2011: 102). Spanish missionaries, particularly the Jesuits and Franciscans, flocked by the thousands to Spanish America, to convert what remained of the indigenous population which had been decimated by European diseases the conquistadors had brought with them and with regard to which the indigenous population had no immunity: smallpox, influenza, measles, and typhus (Ferguson: 2011: 99).

The Age of Discovery: Land Allocation

The colonizers of South and North America brought differing institutional blueprints for property allocation and politics (Ferguson, 2011). Most of the colonizers of North America in the seventeenth century were penniless: between 65 and 80 percent of all the Britons who came to the Chesapeake during the seventeenth century did so as indentured servants (Tomlins, 2006). The very price of their passage had been paid, in effect, by a mortgage on their future labor. This was not unusual: fully three-fourths of all European migrants to British America over the *entire* colonial period were likewise indentured servants (Costa and Lamoreaux, 2011; Engerman and Sokoloff, 2011; Ferguson, 2011: 103).

Emigration refers to the departure of individuals or groups from their home country to take up residence in another country (Theodorson and Theodorson, 1969: 129). **Immigration** refers to the entrance into a country of individuals or groups who have left their native country to establish a new place of permanent residence (Theordorson and Theodorson, 1969: 197). **Net emigration** refers to the amount by which the

number of emigrants exceeds the number of immigrants. As early as the 1640s, in England net emigration exceeded 100,000 and it ranged between 30,000 and 70,000 each *decade* until the 1790s (Emmer, 1986).

For many years, Britain's American colonies remained a patchwork of small farms and villages. There were few towns and virtually no true cities. There was no mountain of silver, no Potosí, in the British colonies of North America. There were immigrants who arrived poor and who carried with them templates for property allocation and politics (Ferguson, 2011: 106). The idea of property rights that they carried with them had evolved in the common law courts and the Court of Chancery since the twelfth century (North, 2009). Another idea that they carried with them was that taxation depended for its legitimacy on parliamentary approval: the Crown was granted taxes in return for consenting to the redress of grievances through legislation (Ferguson, 2011: 106).

The property and political institutions of British America were heavily influenced by the ideas of John Locke (1632-1704), a seventeenth and early eighteenth century philosopher whose ideas greatly influenced the founding fathers, the Declaration of Independence, and the Constitution of the United States. In *Two Treatises of Government* (1690), Locke argues that the true state of nature (what sociologists call hunting and gathering or folk societies) is harmonious, a position that Enlightenment philosophers also would champion. People are rational creatures who choose to be governed not purely out of fear but for their mutual good. In a commonwealth or state founded on this basis, Locke suggests, power is delegated by 'Civil Society' to a "Legislative" (e.g., legislature, parliament, Congress), whose majority decisions are based on the implicit consent of all citizens. Locke embraced the idea of a "separation of powers" that would act as checks and balances on each other in the governance of the state. For instance, Locke favored separating the "Executive" from the other branches of government and he saw the Legislative as the dominant institution. According to Locke, the "great and *chief end*...of Men's uniting into Commonwealths...is *the preservation of their Property* (Locke, 1690: Book II, Ch 9). The Legislative may not "take from any Man any part of his *Property without his own consent*", meaning a consent of the majority of the representatives in the Legislative body.

When the first ship of colonials arrived in the Carolinas in the seventeenth century, "The Fundamental Constitutions of Carolina" (Ferguson, 2011: 109-110), which were drawn up in 1669 by none other than John Locke, outlined a scheme where there would be a link between political representation and property ownership. If a man owned 50 acres or more of land within a precinct, he could vote for a member of parliament from that precinct and he could sit on a jury. With 500 acres, you could become a member of the Carolina assembly or a judge (Fertuson, 2011: 112). And, as a voter, you had one, and only one vote—whether you owned 50 acres or a thousand times that amount.

A document, which became known as the Barbados Proclamation, was drawn up to regulate the distribution of land. The important thing is that there was a guaranteed minimum: to every freeman that arrived to plant and inhabit before a certain date in 1672, one hundred acres of land was given to him and his heirs in perpetuity. What if there were insufficient freemen to take advantage of this offer? When the indentured servants had served out the time of their indenture—usually about five or six years—they should be given land.

In England, property rights had been secure, but property was held in the hands of a few (Ferguson: 2011: 111). For instance, in 1436 between 6,000 and 10,000 families of nobles and gentry owned about 45 percent of the land, the Church owned 20 percent, and the Crown 5 percent (Ferguson, 2011: 111). By contrast, in British America, the penniless indentured servant had the chance to get a first foot on the property ladder. This system was introduced not only in Carolina but also in Virginia, Maryland, New Jersey, and Pennsylvania (Ferguson, 2011: 111). This system made perfect sense in colonies where land was plentiful and labor scarce (Engerman and Sokoloff, 2011).

Although the governors were royally appointed, it was assumed that the colonists should have their representative assemblies, which they did in short order. The Virginia assembly met for the first time in 1619. By 1640, eight such assemblies existed in the British colonies, including Massachusetts Bay, Maryland, Connecticut, Plymouth, and New Haven, as well as Barbados (Elliott, 2006). No such institutions existed in Latin America.

While John Locke's ideas about property and politics shaped the institutions of property and governance in the United States (as well as in other parts of the former British Empire, such as Canada, Australia, and New Zealand) in important and enduring ways, it was Thomas Hobbes's ideas that were seminal in the shaping of these institutions in South America (Ferguson, 2011: 106-129). Thomas Hobbes (1588-1679) is an English philosopher of the late sixteenth and early seventeenth centuries. As the attentive reader may recall, we explored some of Hobbes's ideas in Chapter 2, "Types of Societies and Social Groups," of our textbook. For Thomas Hobbes, writing in his book *Leviathan* (Hobbes, 1985, 1651), life before the emergence of the state, when there was no power to keep people in awe, was a war of every man against every man and life was solitary, nasty, brutish, and short. Hobbes argues that men are held to perform their duties only by "fear" and therefore power needs to be delegated to a strong sovereign who is responsible for defence, legislation, justice, and education (Ferguson, 2011: 107-108). The crucial point for Hobbes was that the sovereign needs to be secure against any challenge from below, could not be bound by any "covenant" (constitution), could not be divisible, and could not justly be put to death (Hobbes, 1985, 1651: Part II, ch18, pp. 228-239). Hobbes's sovereign could either be a monarch or a parliament (Hobbes, 1985, 1651: Part II, ch19, pp. 239-250). Hobbes's theory of liberty was that the liberty of a subject consists only in those things that the sovereign has explicitly conceded; in cases of the "the silence of the law," the presumption must be in favor of the sovereign (Ferguson, 2011: 108). Hobbes's arguments are clearly in favor of a strong sovereign.

In the Spanish colonies of South America, land was allocated by the Spanish Crown via the **encomienda** system. The encomienda was a legal system whereby the Spanish Crown owned the land but granted a conquistador, who became known as the encomendero, the labor of a specified number of Indians—who usually numbered in the thousands--who lived on a vast tract of land. The right to exploit the indigenous people was thereby granted to a tiny Spanish elite. Even among the immigrants, the encomenderos were a small minority, perhaps as few as 5 percent of the Hispanic population in Peru (Engerman and Sokoloff, 2011). In Peru, as recently as 1958, 2 percent of landowners controlled 69 percent of all arable land, while 83 percent held just 6 percent which consisted of plots of 12 acres or less (Ferguson, 2011: 125; Brown, 2006).

The Indians were the encomendero's to do with as he pleased, whether to plough the land, plant, and harvest the crops or to dig gold and silver out of the mountains (Elliott, 2006; Himmerich y Valencia, 1991). The encomienda were not granted in perpetuity to a man and his heirs; only slowly did they evolve into hereditary haciendas (Elliott, 2006; Himmerich y Valencia, 1991). The majority of the people were left with only tiny plots of land and their legal title to it was often murky. Thus, in 1910, on the eve of the Mexican Revolution, only 2.4 percent of household heads in rural areas owned any land at all (Engerman and Sokoloff, 2011). In contrast, the rural property ownerhsip rate in the United States in 1900 was just under 75 percent (Engerman and Sokoloff, 2011). Under Spanish rule, there was an absence of the far more widespread upward mobility that characterized British colonial America.

Property Rights and Economic Freedom—for the Sake of the Poor

Peruvian economist Hernando de Soto documents that poor people lose out in the absence of property rights (Norberg, 2003: 90-98; De Soto, 2000). In his book, *The Mystery of Capitalism*, de Soto documents that the problem is *not* that the poor in many Third World countries lack "property" in the sense of the physical assets themselves. People in what we might call Third World or periphery or semi-periphery countries occupy common lands. They build and live in simple houses in shanty towns. They continually improve their simple houses. They establish what we might term small corner shops. What they lack is clear legal title to these physical assets. They lack property rights to the physical assets, not the physical assets themselves.

De Soto estimates that poor people in former communist countries and in the Third World have real estate (buildings and the land that they stand on) worth $9.3 trillion more than is officially registered (Norberg, 2003: 92). That is a huge sum, worth more than the combined value of all the companies listed on the stock exchanges of the twenty most affluent countries (Norberg, 2003: 92). The problem is that governments in countries of the periphery and semi-periphery do not recognize the rights of ownership without an involved, multi-layered bureaucratic process.

De Soto and his colleagues traveled the world trying to register property. What were the results of their research? Obtaining legal title to a house built on public land in Peru took 207 different administrative steps at 52 public offices. Anyone wanting to drive a taxi legally could expect to negotiate 26 months of red tape. In Haiti, people can only settle on common land by leasing it for five years and then buying it. However, simply getting a permit to lease the land involved 65 steps that took more than two years (Norberg, 2003: 92). In the shanty towns of Lima, Peru, getting a legal license for a factory with two sewing machines took 289 six-hour days of traveling to the authorities. Once there, you lined up to see the right people, filled out forms, and then waited for an answer. In addition to the time expended, the process cost a total of $1,231, a sum more than thirty times the minimum monthly wage.

To people without many resources or powerful contacts, these are insuperable barriers. Hence, what many poor people do is to work outside the law, in what euphemistically is often called the informal sector of the economy. In other words, they have no legal protection. They dare not invest for the long term even if they have the cash to do so. Their property is not included in a uniform system of ownership that indicates transactions and who owns what. These are major deficits because without legal clarity with regard to them, it is not clear who is responsible for payments and services to the address. As Norberg indicates, the property thereby remains "dead capital:" properties cannot be mortgaged, depriving the de facto owner of an important source of capital for financing an education or investing in and expanding a business (Norberg, 2003: 93). Also, the property cannot even be sold and the de facto owners cannot expand their businesses by selling shares in them.

De Soto maintains that between 50 and 75 percent of citizens in developing countries work outside the protection of the law and that roughly 80 percent of homes and land are not registered in the names of their present owners (Norberg, 2003: 94). In other words, in countries without a functioning property system, the great majority of citizens is cut off from engaging in modern economic activity and become entrapped in poverty (De Soto, 2003). That is to say, capitalism becomes capitalism for the elite only; it is only the elite who has legal property rights.

This is one of the reasons why Russia's economy took a decade to show any real growth after the fall of communism. It took ten years for the Russian government even to begin introducing a uniform system of private land ownership (Norberg, 2003: 94). Thus, land in Russia is generally considered government property and is just leased or lent to the farmers, making investment pointless and sale or mortgage unthinkable. By the beginning of the twenty-first century, fewer than three percent of a total of some ten million farmers in Russia had anything resembling title to their land (Norberg, 2003: 94). Government ownership of land on this scale sometimes is called "land socialism." Because land often is the basis of borrowing, land socialism impedes the development of a modern credit system. Instead, transactions find their way into the informal market.

The Heritage Foundation and The Wall Street Journal publish an annual Index of Economic Freedom that ranks 177 or more countries of the world in terms of their extent of economic freedom. Economic freedom is an important because it empowers people to work, produce, consume, own, trade, and invest according to their personal choices. According to the *2013 Index of Economic Freedom*, Russia ranks as the 139th freest economy out of the 177 countries of the world that were in the index that year (The Heritage Foundation, 2013). The category of countries of the world into which Russia thereby falls is "mostly unfree." According to the *2013 Index of Economic Freedom*, nations with more trade freedom have stronger economies, less hunger, and better treatment of the environment (Riley and Miller, 2012).

Despite relatively high economic growth achieved mostly through the international sale of oil and gas, Russia's foundations for long-term economic growth remain fragile, in part because Russia lacks an efficiently functioning legal framework. Corruption is endemic throughout the economy, shows no signs of abating, and is a major impediment for investors and businesses. Russia's ranking on the index of economic freedom is *below* the world and regional averages. Russia's legal framework has not been fully modernized, the rule of law is not maintained uniformly across the country, protection of private property rights is weak, and contracts are not always secure (The Heritage Foundation, 2013). Another ranking of countries of the world in terms of economic freedom is provided by the Fraser Institute's *Economic Freedom of the World: 2012 Annual Report* (Gwartney, Lawson, and Hall, 2012). In this ranking system, Russia's rank is 95th out of 144, *after* countries like Iran (83rd) and Rwanda (44th). By means of comparison, the United States is 19th out of 144 (Gwartney, Lawson, and Hall, 2012). The amount of income earned by the poorest 10 percent of the population is much higher in countries with higher economic freedom. Thus, the poorest ten percent of the population in countries that are "least free" in terms of economic freedom have an income per capita of $1,209, while it is $11,382 for their counterparts in the "most free" countries (Gwartney, Lawson, and Hall, 2012: 24). Countries with more economic freedom also have substantially higher per-capita income. For instance, per capita income in countries that are "most free" is $37,691, compared with $5,188 in countries that are "least free" (Gwartney, Lawson, and Hall, 2012: 23).

In terms of the extent of economic freedom, the ranking of Peoples Republic of China is similar to Russia's: The Peoples Republic of China ranks as the 136th freest economy out of the 177 countries of the world ranked in the Heritage Foundation's *2013 Index of Economic Freedom* (The Heritage Foundation, 2013). The category of countries of the world into which China thereby falls is also "mostly unfree." The Communist Party's ultimate authority throughout the economic system undermines the rule of law and respect for contracts. Corruption is widespread. Cronyism is institutionalized and pervasive. All land is state owned in China. Individuals and firms may own and transfer long-term leases that are subject to many restrictions by the state. Intellectual property rights are not protected effectively (e.g., Zibreg, 2013; Hille, 2011; Hille and Menn, 2010). Infringement of copyrights, patents and trademarks is common (The Heritage Foundation, 2013; Partridge, 2012). By means of comparison, the United States ranks as the 10th freest economy in the world and the category of countries into which it falls is "mostly free" (The Heritage Foundation, 2013).

It is worth noting that more than 400 million Chinese were lifted above the international poverty line between 1981 and 2001 (Bardhan, 2006, 2004). For instance, during this time frame, the percentage of rural people living on less than $1 a day decreased from 79 to 27 percent in China (Bardhan, 2006). Yet, as Pranab Bardhan, Professor of Economics at University of California, Berkeley, has argued, no one as yet has convincingly demonstrated that this improvement in their condition is a result of globalization (Bardhan, 2006). As the attentive reader may recall from Chapter 1, "Perceiving and Understanding Social Life Sociologically: Theory and Methods" of our textbook, correlation is not causation. In China, the reduction in poverty instead could be attributed to other factors, such as changes in grain procurement prices, investing heavily in both domestic infrastructure and education, the relaxation of restrictions on rural-to-urban migration, and the massive 1978 land reforms in which the Mao-era communes were disbanded (Bardhan, 2006). In fact, it is for reasons such as these that three-fourths of the Chinese lifted above the poverty line got there *prior to* 1987 and *before* the big strides in opening China up to the world (Bardhan, 2006).

GLOBALIZATION II: MID 1800s–LATE 1920s

From the mid-1800s to the late 1920s, the world experienced an era of globalization, with Great Britain as the dominant global power (e.g., Friedman, 2003: xvi; Ferguson, 2002).

In terms of flows of capital, after the German defeat of France in the war of 1870-1871, Britain forged decisively ahead of France in international flows of capital (Ferguson, 2001: 278; Einaudi, 2001; Feis, 1931). Britain was the world's banker, exporting huge amounts of capital to the rest of the world. This created for Britain a huge accumulation of foreign assets (Ferguson, 2001: 278). No other country came close to Britain's level of foreign investment: the closest, France, had foreign assets worth less than half the British total, Germany had assets worth less than 30 percent of the British total on the eve of the First World War (Ferguson, 2001: 279; Pollard, 1985: 491). This boom in international capital flows coincided with a dramatic expansion of British colonial rule. In 1860, the territorial extent of the British Empire was 9.5 million square miles, compared with 12.7 million square miles in 1909, an increase of exactly one third (Ferguson, 2001: 279). By the eve of the First World War, some 444 million people lived under some form of British rule, one quarter of the world's population (Ferguson, 2001: 279). Only one in ten British subjects lived within the British Isles themselves (Ferguson, 2001: 279).

This era of globalization was dominated by British trade, British culture, British power, the British pound, the British navy, and British military prowess. This era of globalization spread capital, capitalism, markets, population, the English language, British culture, Protestantism, media, and technology around much of the globe. Britain invented and exported railways to other countries and laid the first trans-Atlantic telegraph cables to other countries (Ferguson, 2002: xxiv). The laying of the first undersea telegraph cable between France and England in 1851 changed by a factor of nearly 100 the speed of travel of information (Clark, 2007: 307). No sooner was the transatlantic cable connected in 1866 than banking and financial crises in one part of the globe were quickly transmitted to commercial and political centers continents away (Musson, 1959; Stiles, 2009). By 1870 India was linked to Britain by a telegraph system, partly over land and partly under the sea, which could transmit messages between India and London in twenty-four hours (Clark, 2007: 307). In Thomas L. Friedman's terminology, this era of globalization shrank the world from size "large" to size "medium" (Friedman, 2003: xvii).

By 1910, the world had become economically integrated in a way never seen before (Ferguson, 2011: 218). Railways, steamship lines and telegraphs linked the world together. A person could travel from Versailles to Vladivostok by train. The opening of the Suez Canal in 1869 reduced the length of the journey from London to Bombay by more than 40 percent and that from London to Shanghai by 32 percent, thus bringing the markets of Europe and Asia substantially closer (Ferguson, 2011: 219; Clark, 2007; 309). The opening Panama Canal in 1914 cut the cost of shipping goods from the East to the West coast of the United States by one third (Maurer and Yu, 2011). Sustained improvements in steamships—the screw propeller, iron hulls, compound engines, and surface condensers—made crossing the oceans faster and cheaper than crossing land (Clark, 2007: 308; Stiles, 2009; Dyos and Aldcroft, 1969). Ocean freight costs fell by more than a third from 1870 to 1910. The cost of shipping cloth from, say, England to India, cost less than 1 percent of the cost of the goods (Ferguson, 2011: 219).

Labor flowed across borders as never before. Other than in wartime, countries did not require passports before 1914 (Friedman, 2003: xvii). Between the early 1600s and the 1950s, more than 20 million people left the British Isles to begin new lives across the seas and only a minority ever returned. No other country in the world came close to exporting so many of its inhabitants (Ferguson, 2002: 60). Between 1840 and 1940, 58 million Europeans migrated to the Americas, 51 million Russians to Siberia, Central Asia and Manchuria, and more than 50 million Indians and Chinese to South-east Asia, Australasia or the Indian Ocean rim (McKeowyn, 2004). Up to 2.5 million migrants from South and East Asia migrated to the Americas (Ferguson, 2011: 219). In 1890, 14.8 percent of the population of the United States was foreign born, a record that has yet to be surpassed (U.S. Census Bureau, 2013).

Cultural change flowed across borders as never before. Perhaps the most remarkable expression of this second era of globalization was cultural—more specifically, sartorial—how people dressed and the way they looked. In a short period of time, a mode of dressing that was distinctly Western swept the rest of the world (Ferguson, 2011: 219-224). As with some other transformations in dress (e.g., Aries, 1960), this one, too, first took hold in the aristocracy and upper classes, later spreading down the class ladder. The crucial new garments were, for men, the frock coat, the stiff-collared white shirt, the felt hat, and the leather boot; for women, the corset, the petticoat and the ankle-length dress (Ferguson, 2011: 220).

Japan is a good example of the sartorial transformation during this stage of globalization. The Japanese revolution in dress dates back to the 1870s, although some analysts could argue that it goes back almost two decades prior, to 1853-1854, since that was when gunships under the command of American Commodore Mathew Perry opened Japan to trade with the West (Ferguson, 2011: 221; Wittner, 2005; Kuhn, 1955). In 1870 the Japanese government banned the blackening of teeth and shaving of eyebrows. At around the same time, ministers began to cut their hair in the Western style (Ferguson, 2011: 222). In 1871, an imperial decree ordered high officials to don the European frock coat worn over a high-collared white shirt, and six years later it was standard wear for all public servants in Japan (Hirano, 1993: 124; Ferguson, 2011: 222). In 1884, elite Japanese women started wearing European dress when they were hosting European guests at the newly built Rokumeikan, a building commissioned for the housing of foreign guests of the government, and it became famous for its parties and balls (Ferguson, 2011: 222).

Technology and organizational change flowed across borders as never before. The spread of the new dress code coincided with the rapid growth of the Japanese textile industry. Among the technologies that were instruments of globalization were the railways, steamships, the telegraph, and the mechanized factory. The organizational change was the development of specialized machine-building firms in Britain, and later in the United States, whose business was the export of technology (Clark, 2007: 311-315). For example,

Platt Brothers was a textile machinery maker in England that exported a complete package of services to prospective foreign entrants into the textile industry, including technical information, machinery, construction expertise, managers, and even skilled operators. These firms reduced the risks to foreign entrepreneurs by selling machines on a trial basis and supplying skilled workers to direct operations and to train local labor forces (Clark: 2007: 313; Bruland, 1989: 5, 6, 34). British firms stood ready to export not just cotton but the machinery to manufacture it and the capital necessary to buy it (Ferguson, 2011: 219).

How successful was the British export of textile technology? Japan is a good example. Between 1907 and 1924 the number of cotton mills in Japan doubled from 118 to 232, the number of spindles more than trebled and the number of looms rose sevenfold (Ferguson, 2011: 223). By 1900 textile factories employed 63 percent of all Japan's factory workers (Wall, 1964: 17). A decade later, Japan was Asia's sole net exporter of thread, yarn and cloth. Japan's exports of thread, yarn, and cloth exceeded those of Germany, France, and Italy (Kamisaka, 1910). Japanese textile workers were the most productive in Asia: from 1907 to 1924 the Japanese cotton industry increased output per worker by 80 percent (Kamisaka, `1910: Ferguson, 2011: 224). By 1910, the British textile industry was still the largest in the world (Clark, 2007: 315) and Britain was still the world's largest net exporter of cotton goods (worth $453 million), but Japan was the second-largest exporter of cotton goods at that time (Clark and Feenstra, 2005). Japan had ended the West's monopoly on modern manufacturing.

Similar capital goods exporters developed in the railway sector. British construction crews completed railways in many countries under the captainship of flamboyant entrepreneurs such as Lord Thomas Brassey, who built railways in Argentina, Australia, Austria, Denmark, France, India, Italy, Prussia, Russia, and Spain as well as elsewhere (Helps, 1874; Clark, 2007: 313). India got most of its railway equipment from Britain, and Indian railway mileage by 1910 was significantly greater than that of Britain (Clark, 2007).

Information flowed across borders as never before. The world before 1800 was one in which information and people traveled at astonishingly slow speeds. In the late Roman era, it took 56 days for news to travel from Egypt to Italy, traveling at an effective speed of 1.0 miles per hour (Duncan-Jones, 1990: 7-29; Clark, 2007: 306). By the early nineteenth century information flowed at somewhat faster rates than in the classical and medieval worlds. In 1500 it took 65 days for news to travel from Alexandria, Egypt, to Venice, Italy, traveling at an effective speed of 0.9 miles per hour. In 1857, news of the Indian Mutiny had taken forty-six days to reach London, traveling at an effective speed of 3.8 miles an hour. In 1865, news of Lincoln's assassination had taken 13 days to reach London, traveling at an effective speed of 12 miles per hour (Clark, 2007: 307; Ferguson, 2011: 219). In 1891, news of the Nobi earthquake in Japan--one of the largest earthquakes in earth's history, took 1 day to reach London, traveling at an effective speed of 246 miles an hour (Clark, 2007: 307).

This era of globalization came to an end with World War I. The disruptions of the war itself were followed by six decades of turbulent times in the world economy. In the 1920s monetary problems led to the imposition of tariff controls and limits on capital movement. The Russian revolution isolated the Russia from the world economy. The global Great Depression of the 1930s led to further disintegration of the world economy. Thomas L. Friedman characterizes the roughly 75-year period between the start of World War I to the fall of the Berlin Wall in 1989 as a 75-year lull, hiatus, or time-out between one era of globalization and another. Only in the late 1980s did a new era of globalization, the era we are in now, begin. Let us turn our attention to a few misapprehensions that seem to have crept into the public discussion of the current era of globalization.

GLOBALIZATION III: THE CURRENT ERA OF GLOBALIZATION

Let us take a look at how the United States is doing relative to other advanced and emerging economies in the current era of globalization by focusing on five specific areas: economic growth, unemployment, ease of starting up a new business, competitiveness, and corruption.

Economic Growth

In the current era of globalization, emerging economies sometimes are referred to as the BRICs (i.e., Brazil, Russia, India, and Peoples Republic of China). This grouping acronym was coined by Jim O'Neil to refer to a grouping of countries that are all deemed to be at a similar stage of newly advanced economic development (O'Neill, 2001). This acronym frequently is rendered as "the BRICs" or as "the BRIC countries" or as "the BRIC economies." Another term for the BRICs is "Second World," where the "First World countries" are the most highly economically developed countries, "the Second World" are the economically developing countries, and "the Third World" are the least economically developed countries of the world. In world system theory the most economically developed countries are called countries of "the core," while countries of "the semi-periphery" are countries of a middle level of economic development, and countries of "the periphery" are the least economically developed countries of the world. Different paradigms have differing conceptions of, and names for, countries at various levels of economic development.

In the current era of globalization, BRICs tend to have rates of economic growth that are higher than those of the countries of the core. This phenomenon is called "convergence," and, from the viewpoint of consensus theory, convergence indicates that more of the world's population and more of the world's countries are transforming into healthier and wealthier neighborhoods of the globe.

If we confine our attention to OECD countries (Organization for Economic Cooperation and Development), what do we see? Over the last twenty years, the economy of the United States has enjoyed an average annual real growth rate of 2.5 percent (calculated from data available from The World Bank, 2013). The rate of economic growth in the United States is 67 percent *higher* than the rate of economic growth that the German and French economies mustered.

Unemployment

Unemployment rates are *lower* and have been *lower* in the United States than in many European countries (European Commission, 2013). For instance, the May, 2013, unemployment rate in the United States was 7.6 percent (Carroll, 2013). By contrast, in the European Union, the unemployment rate was *31 percent higher* (at 11.0 percent) in the 27 member states of the European Union and *38 percent higher* (at 12.2 percent) in the Euro area (European Commission, 2013). The Euro area sometimes is referred to as the EU 17 and consists of Belgium, Germany, Estonia, Ireland, Greece, Spain, France, Italy, Cyprus, Luxembourg, Malta, Netherlands, Austria, Portugal, Slovenia, Slovakia, and Finland. In Greece and Spain, in May 2013, the unemployment rate was 26.8 percent (European Commission, 2013).

Youth unemployment rates tend to be higher than the overall unemployment rate. For example, the United States had a youth unemployment rate of 16.4 percent in 2012. A higher percentage of European youth were unemployed. Thus, the youth unemployment rate was fully *38 percent higher* (at 22.6 percent) in the EU 27 and *35 percent higher* (at 22.1 percent) in the EU 17 (OECD, 2012) compared to the United States. Youth unemployment in that year was 28.4 percent in Hungary, 30.3 percent in Ireland, 35.9 percent in Italy, 36.1 percent in Portugal, 51.1 percent in Spain, and 51.2 percent in Greece (OECD, 2012). Sweden's youth unemployment rate stood at 25.2 percent (World Economic Forum, 2012: 57).

To help you put a 38 percentage point difference in perspective, let us do a small thought experiment. Let us assume that Sam earns a score of 94 percent (A) on a test and you earn a score that is just 38 percent lower than his score. What would be your score and the corresponding letter grade on that work item? If your score is 38 percent lower than Sam's, you earned a grade of D on the test (at 68 percent). A thirty-eight percent difference matters. If your score was just 35 percent lower than Sam's score, you still would earn a grade of D (at 69.2 percent). A thirty-five percent difference matters.

In addition, an increasing share of people employed in Europe do not have full-time jobs (OECD, 2013; Gersemann, 2004). For instance, in the United States, part-time employment as a share of total employment was slightly *lower* in 2011 than it had been in 2000 (OECD, 2013) and it was also slightly lower in 2002 than it had been in 1990 (Gersemann, 2004: 24). By contrast, in the OECD countries, part-time employment as a percent of total employment had *increased 39 percent* between 2000 and 2011 (computed from OECD data, OECD, 2013). In Italy part-time employment as a percent of total employment increased 36 percent between 2000 and 2011 and in Germany, the increase was 26 percent (computed from OECD data, OECD, 2013). In 70 percent of the OECD countries for which the *OECD Factbook 2013: Economic, Environmental, and Social Statistics* provide data on the incidence of part-time employment as a percentage of total employment, the incidence of part-time employment had *increased* between 2000 and 2011 (OECD, 2013). This is nothing new: Olaf Gersemann has calculated on the basis of OECD data that between 1990 and 2003, the incidence of part-time employment in Italy rose by 12 percent and in France and Germany by 34 and 40 percent, respectively (Gersemann, 2004: 24). On average, a working-age German works about 2 hours and 35 minutes per calendar day, and for her French and Italian counterparts, the working day is even shorter (Gersemann, 2004: 29).

Ease of Starting Up a New Business

It is much far less burdensome to found a new company the United States than it is in continental Europe (Gersemann, 2004: 59). For instance, one study looked at what government regulations cost an entrepreneur in terms of both time and money to start up a new enterprise (Djankov, La Porta, Lopez-de-Silanes, and Shleifer, 2002). What did their study find? In the United States, an entrepreneur setting up a new business faces a one-time regulatory cost that amounts to 1.7 percent of the U.S. per capita income. In Germany, the corresponding cost is 32.5 percent of the German per capita income. In France and Italy the costs are even higher, at 35.6 percent and 44.8 percent, respectively (Djankov, La Porta, Lopez-de-Silanes, and Shleifer, 2002). Those costs represent significant barriers to establishing new business enterprises.

Competitiveness

The United States is highly competitive in information and communication technologies (IT companies). U.S. companies dominate any ranking of the world's best performing technology companies. For instance, *Business Week* lists the 100 most important IT companies worldwide in "The Tech 100." As of April 2010,

44 of those companies were from the United States. The country with the second highest number of companies listed on that index was Japan, with 11. Taiwan and China were tied for third place, with eight companies each. Brazil and India were tied for fourth place, with six each. Germany had three, France, Italy, and Russia none (Business Week, 2010).

Another measure of U.S. competitiveness is provided by the "Fortune Global 500," an annual ranking of the top 500 corporations worldwide, as measured by revenue. According to the Fortune Global 500 for 2012, the United States dominates the global rankings. For instance, in the 2012 Fortune Global 500 (Fortune, 2012), the United States has the lion's share of Global 500 corporations, with 132 corporations, which is more than 26 percent of the total. The country with the second most was China, with 73. The aggregate revenue of China's global Fortune 500 corporations was *less than half* (47 percent) of that accrued by their counterparts in the United States (computed from Fortune Global 500 data for 2012, Fortune, 2012). In third place in the Fortune Global 500 was Japan with 68 corporations. For fourth place, France and Germany are tied, with 32 corporations each. Great Britain was next, with 26 corporations.

"The World's Most Admired Companies" has been published annually since 1997 by the Hay Group and *Fortune* magazine, and it provides us with another measure of corporate competitiveness. This ranking of companies examines the following nine attributes of corporate reputations:

- Innovation
- People management
- Use of corporate assets
- Social responsibility
- Quality of management
- Financial soundness
- Long-term investment
- Quality of products/services
- Global competitiveness

Where does the United States stand in this particular ranking? Once again, the United States dominates the rankings. For instance, in the 2013 World's Most Admired Companies' ranking, *all* of the top ten are U.S. companies; of the top 50 companies, fully 42 (or 84 percent) are U.S. companies. *None* of the top fifty companies are from China. The only country other than the United States with more than one company that made the top 50 in this ranking is Germany, with two: BMW (at number 14 of the top 50) and Volkswagen (at number 33 of the top 50) (CNNMoney, 2013).

What about manufacturing? The viewpoint that the United States is losing its competitive advantage and that the manufacturing sector of the U.S. economy is in permanent decline or disappearing gained popularity in the 1980s (e.g., Tatom, 2004; Cline, 1986; Marris, 1985; Peterson, 1987). This viewpoint even made its way into popular culture. Thus, in "My Home Town," a hit song from his 1984 album, "Born in the U.S.A.," Bruce Springsteen bemoans the fact that a local textile mill is closing down and that those jobs are gone and are not coming back. After more than a quarter of a century, the sentiment expressed in Springsteen's song remains as strong as ever (e.g., Atkinson, Stewart, Andes, and Ezell, 2012; Scott, 2012; Alliance for American Manufacturing, 2012; Jacoby, 2011; Duesterberg, 2003; National Association of Manufacturers, 2003). Thus, Donald Trump, hotel magnate and TV celebrity, in a recent speech, said that "We don't make anything anymore. We buy from other countries" (Kredo, 2013). Donald Trump's position on this issue is mainstream: a recent Heartland Monitor survey finds that only one in five Americans believes that the United States has the world's strongest economy (Jacoby, 2011). A 2012 survey finds that 55 percent of Americans think that China has the strongest economy in the world, and 82 percent of Americans think that "We don't manufacture anything here in America anymore" (Alliance for American Manufacturing, 2012).

There is one thing wrong with this portrait of the posture of the United States in the arena of global manufacturing: it does not fit the empirical facts. Data support the position that the United States commands a strong manufacturing presence in the global economy. As Mark J. Perry, professor of economics and finance in the School of Management at the Flint campus of the University of Michigan and a scholar at the American Enterprise Institute in Washington, D.C., points out, in 2009, the United States manufactured more goods than the Japanese, Germans, British and Italians, combined (Jacoby, 2011). The amount of manufacturing output in the United States hits a new high almost every year. For instance, between 1980 and 2010, the United States *increased* manufacturing output by 218 percent (Hunter, 2011). The combined sales revenue of the top 500 U.S.-based manufacturing firms in 2012 was $6.01 trillion. This represents a 17.2 percent increase over 2011 sales (Perry, 2013).

Sales revenue is one way to measure the position of a country's manufacturing sector in the world economy. IndustryWeek publishes an annual ranking of the 500 largest publicly held U.S. manufacturing companies based on sales revenue. To put U.S. manufacturing sales revenue into perspective, let us look at U.S. manufacturing sales revenue relative to international gross domestic product (GDP) values (Perry: 2013):

- In 2012, if the top 500 U.S. manufacturing firms were a separate country, they would have been the *third largest economy in the world*, behind No. 1 (the United States) and No. 2 (China) but ahead of No. 4, Japan's, entire GDP of $5.98 trillion (Perry, 2013).
- The sales revenue from the *top ten* manufacturing industries in the United States in 2012 totaled $4.83 trillion in 2012, which was more than Germany's entire gross domestic product of $3.36 trillion (Perry, 2013).
- The single largest manufacturing industry in the United States is petroleum and coal products. The annual sales of that single U.S. industry in 2012 was $1.62 trillion, which was larger than the gross domestic product of Australia (Perry, 2013).
- The second largest manufacturing industry in the United States is computers and other electronic products. In 2012, the annual sales of that single U.S. industry was $814 billion, which was more than the entire gross domestic product of Saudi Arabia (Perry, 2013).
- The *top ten* largest manufacturing companies in the U.S. in 2012 had combined revenues of $1.87 trillion, which is more than Canada's gross domestic product ($1.77 trillion) (Perry, 2013).

The foregoing comparisons help to put the size of the top 500 U.S. manufacturing companies into perspective. They demonstrate that U.S. manufacturing is not withering and disappearing. It is expanding and prospering.

Why do many Americans worry that manufacturing is collapsing, or has collapsed, in the United States? Part of the reason is that fewer Americans work in factories (Levinson, 2013). Then, too, perception fuels the mood of gloom and doom (Jacoby, 2011). Let us look at each of these factors in turn.

FEWER AMERICANS WORK IN FACTORIES Manufacturing employment in the United States peaked in 1979 (Tatom, 2003). Between 1979 and 2012, the number of Americans employed in manufacturing declined 40 percent (Norris, 2012). In 1979, there were 19.6 million workers in manufacturing in this country. Now, the figure is 11.8 million workers (Norris, 2012). In this way, millions of industrial jobs disappeared in the United States and this has meant hardship for many families.

International comparisons of trends in manufacturing employment are hampered by inadequate data, particularly for the emerging economies (Levinson, 2013: 10). Among the top-ranking manufacturing countries, China, Brazil, and India do *not* report complete information on manufacturing employment at the national level and consistent time series data are available for Mexico only since 2009 (Levinson, 2013: 10). What do the best available data show?

Manufacturing employment in the United States fell by 22 percent from 2001 through 2011 (Levinson, 2013). Among the major manufacturing countries for which data are available, Canada, France, and Japan saw declines in manufacturing employment over that period that are similar to what the United States experienced. The decline in the United Kingdom was substantially larger (Levinson, 2013). Over the 21-year period 1990 through 2011, manufacturing employment fell by approximately the same percentage in the United States as in France and Japan, and much less than in the United Kingdom (Levinson, 2013). These figures indicate that the diminished importance of manufacturing as a source of jobs is not limited to the United States.

In the United States, the reduced demand for labor in manufacturing is directly related to dramatic increases in labor productivity (Levinson, 2013: 11). Revolutions in technology enable an American worker to produce far more than his or her counterpart did a generation ago. Even in the shorter term, labor productivity in manufacturing in the United States increased 72 percent between 2001 and 2011, which is a greater increase in labor productivity than that achieved by the United Kingdom and Japan (at 44 percent, each), France (30 percent), Germany (21 percent), Canada (13 percent), and Italy (7 percent) (Levinson, 2013: 11). Average compensation per employee in U.S. manufacturing in 2011 was $35.53 per hour, which is a 41 percent increase since 2001 (Levinson, 2013: 13).

PERCEPTION AND THE AVAILABILITY HEURISTIC A heuristic is a rule of thumb, a mental shortcut, a thinking strategy (Myers, 2010: 90). The **availability heuristic** refers to the tendency for people to judge the likelihood of things in terms of their availability in memory (Tversky and Kahneman, 1973, 1974). If instance of something readily come to mind, people presume that thing is commonplace. Moreover, if instances of something readily come to mind, we tend to perceive that thing as being far more prevalent than it actually is (Klinger, 2010; Lee, O'Brien, and Sivaramakrishnan, 2008; Schwarz, 2008; An, 2008; Keller, Siegrist, and Gutscher, 2006; Klein, 2005). For instance, people typically overestimate the divorce rate if they can quickly find examples of divorced friends (Slovic, Fischoff, and Lichtenstein, 1982). Similarly, after hearing and reading stories of rapes, robberies, and beatings, 9 out of 10 Canadians overestimate—usually by a considerable margin—the percentage of crimes that involves violence (Doob and Roberts, 1988). Because news footage of airplane crashes is a readily available memory for most of us—especially after September 11, 2001—we often suppose that flying in a commercial airplane is dangerous, even more dangerous to life, limb, and property than driving in cars. Actually, travelers in the United States are 230 times more likely to die in a car crash than on a commercial flight covering the same distance (Myers, 2010: 96). For most airplane travelers in the United States, the most dangerous part of the journey is the drive to the airport.

In a story about Americans' anxieties regarding globalization, Ronald Brownstein quotes a Florida teacher who says, "It seems like everything I pick up says 'Made in China' on it" (Brownstein, 2010). To someone shopping for toys, clothes, shoes, or sporting equipment at Walmart, Target, Walgreens, or at other large retailers in the United States, it may seem that way. The Chinese factories that produce the goods that are stocked on the shelves of those stores specialize in low-tech, labor-intensive goods, items that do not require the more advanced and sophisticated capabilities that modern manufacturing plants of the United States possess. U.S. manufacturers make fighter jets, automobiles, pharmaceuticals, air conditioners, semiconductors, and industrial lathes, things that are not on the weekly shopping list of most American consumers. Since many of the things that are on the weekly shopping lists of many American consumers do have "Made in China" on them, using the availability heuristic, it seems to many Americans that "we don't make anything anymore" and that China does. The availability heuristic feeds the perception of a decline in American manufacturing.

Corruption

Since 1995, Transparency International annually publishes the Corruption Perceptions Index (CPI), with corruption defined as the misuse of public power for private benefit. While this particular measure is not without its critics (e.g., Galtung, 2006), it nonetheless is the best known measure of domestic, public sector corruption in the countries of the world. This index scores countries on a scale of zero to 100. A score of 0 indicates high levels of corruption and a score of 100 indicates low levels of corruption. Transparency International also ranks the countries in its index from least corrupt to most corrupt.

The 2012 Corruption Perceptions Index ranks 176 countries of the world in terms of their perceived levels of corruption. Where do *you* think the United States is situated in this ranking? When I ask the students enrolled in my upper- and lower-division courses at a public, regional comprehensive University in the Midwest this question, most students say that the U.S. is among the most corrupt countries in the world. When I ask those students what factors go into that particular assessment, the modal response is "capitalism."

What does the 2012 Corruption Perceptions Index reveal about the perceived state of corruption, or its absence, in the countries of the world? In terms of ranking, the least corrupt country has a rank of 1 and the most corrupt has a rank of 174. Three countries, each with a rank of 1, tied for first place as the least corrupt countries--Denmark, Finland, and New Zealand. The United States, with a rank of 19, is among the *least corrupt* countries of the world, and it has been ever since this index was first published (Transparency International, 2012). The affluent, democratic, capitalist countries of the world are among the *least* corrupt countries on the planet according to this index. Stated somewhat differently, the most economically free countries are the least corrupt (Norberg, 2003: 70). The three countries tied for last place— i.e., as the most corrupt countries on the planet, each with a rank of 174, are Afghanistan, North Korea, and Somalia (Transparency International, 2012). Peoples Republic of China, with a rank of 80, is situated deeply in the corrupt part of the planet, as are Mexico (with a rank of 105) and Russia, (with a rank of 133).

SUGGESTED READINGS

Elliott, David W.P., *Changing Worlds: Vietnam's Transition From Cold War to Globalization* (New York: Oxford University Press, 2012).

Ferguson, Niall, *Civilization: The West and the Rest* (New York: Allen Lane, 2011).

Kacowicz, Arie Marcelo, *Globalization and the Distribution of Wealth: The Latin American Experience: 1982-2008* (Cambridge: Cambridge University Press, 2013).

Kastoryano, Riva, *Turkey Between Nationalism and Globalization* (New York: Routledge, Taylor & Francis Group, 2013).

Kim, Jaesok, *Chinese Labor in a Korean Factory: Class, Ethnicity, and Productivity on the Shop Floor in Globalizing China* (Stanford, CA: Stanford University Press, 2013).

Mann, Charles E., *1493: Uncovering the New World Columbus Created* (New York: Vintage Books, 2012).

Maurer, Noel, *The Empire Trap: the Rise and Fall of U.S. Intervention to Protect American Property Rights, 1893-2012* (Princeton, NJ: Princeton University Press, 2013).

Moghadam, Valentine M., *Globalization and Social Movements: Islamism, Feminism, and the Global Justice Movement* (Lanham, MD: Rowman & Martin, 2013).

Ross, Jeffrey Ian (Ed.), *The Globalization of Supermax Prisons* (New Brunswick, NJ: Rutgers University Press, 2013).

Smith, Keri E. Iyall (Ed.), *Sociology of Globalization: Cultures, Economies, and Politics* (Boulder, CO: Westview Press, 2013).

Sparke, Matthew, *Introducing Globalization: Ties, Tension, and Uneven Integration* (Malden, MA: Wiley-Blackwell, 2013).

Taylor, Jean Gelman, *Global Indonesia* (New York: Routledge, 2013).

Young, Cristobal, "Religion and Economic Growth in Western Europe: 1500-2000," Paper presented at the annual meeting of the American Sociological Association Annual Meeting, Hilton San Francisco, CA, August 8, 2009.

BIBLIOGRAPHY

Alliance for American Manufacturing, *National Poll: Voters See Manufacturing as the "Irreplaceable Core of a Strong Economy"* (Washington, D.C.: Alliance for American Manufacturing, July 16, 2012). As of July 7, 2013, available online at http://www.americanmanufacturing.org/content/new-national-poll-voters-see-manufacturing-irreplaceable-core-strong-economy-0

An, Soontae, "Antidepressant Direct-to-Consumer Advertising and Social Perception of the Prevalence of Depression: Application of the Availability Heuristic," *Health Communication*, Vol. 23, No. 6, 2008: 499-505.

Aries, Phillip, *Centuries of Childhood: A Social History of Family Life* (New York: Random House, 1960).

Atkinson, Robert D.; Stewart, Luke A.; Andes, Scott M.; and Ezell, Stephen J., *Worse Than the Great Depression: What Experts are Missing About American Manufacturing Decline* (Washington, D.C.: The Information Technology & Innovation Foundation, March 2012).

Bakewell, Peter John, *A History of Latin America: 1450 to the Present* (Malden, MA: Blackwell Pub., 2004).

Bardhan, Pranab, "Does Globalization Help or Hurt the World's Poor?" *Scientific American*, Vol. 294, No. 4, April 1, 2006: 84-91.

Bardhan, Pranab, "The Impact of Globalization on the Poor," in pages 271-284 of Susan M. Collins and Carol Graham (Eds.), *Globalization, Poverty, and Inequality* (Washington, D.C.: Brookings Institution Press, 2004).

Barrera-Osorio, Antonio, *Experiencing Nature: The Spanish American Empire and the Early Scientific Revolution* (Austin, TX: University of Texas Press, 2006).

Barro, Robert J., *Determinants of Economic Growth: A Cross-Country Empirical Study* (Cambridge, MA: The MIT Press, 1997).

Bergen, Peter, "Who Really Killed bin Laden?" *CNN World*, March 27, 2013, 6:46 PM EDT. As of June 13, 2013, available online at http://www.washingtonpost.com/wp-srv/inatl/longterm/eafricabombing/stories/strikes082198.htm

Boli, John, and Thomas, George, "World Culture in the World Polity: A Century of International Non-Governmental Organization," *American Sociological Review*, Vol. 62, (April) 1997: 171-190.

Brownstein, Ronald, "Down From the Pedestal: Americans No Longer Think the U.S. Economy is No. 1 a New Allstate/National Journal Heartland Monitor Poll Shows," *National Journal*, December 8, 2010, 6:10 AM. As of July 9, 2013, available online at http://www.nationaljournal.com/magazine/americans-no-longer-think-u-s-economy-is-world-s-strongest-20101209

Bruland, Kristine, *British Technology and European Industrialization: The Norwegian Textile Industry in the Mid-Nineteenth Century* (New York: Cambridge University Press, 1989).

Burkholder, Mark A., and Johnson, Lyman L., *Colonial Latin America* Second Edition (New York: Oxford University Press, 1994).

Business Week, "The Tech 100," for 2010. As of July 7, 2013, available online at http://www.businessweek.com/interactive_reports/it100_2010.html

Carroll, Doug, "May unemployment rates down in 25 states," *USA Today*, June 21, 2013, 11:10 AM EDT. As of July 4, 2013, available online at http://www.usatoday.com/story/money/business/2013/06/21/may-state-unemployment-rates/2445725/

Clark, Gregory, *A Farewell to Alms: A Brief Economic History of the World* (Princeton, NJ: Princeton University Press, 2007).

Clark, Gregory, and Feenstra, Robert C., "Technology in the Great Divergence," pages 277-322 of Michael D. Bordo, Alan M. Taylor, and Jeffrey G. Williamson (Eds.), *Globalization in Historical Perspective* (Chicago: University of Chicago Press, 2005).

Cline, R., "Pressure for Import Protection and U.S. Policy," in United States Trade and Competitiveness, Hearings before the Subcommittee on Banking, Finance, and Urban Affairs, U.S. House of Representatives, Ninety-Ninth Congress, Serial No. 99-46, pp. 454-469.

CNNMoney, "FORTUNE World's Most Admired Companies 2013." As of July 7, 2013, available online at http://money.cnn.com/magazines/fortune/most-admired/2013/list/?iid=wma_sp_full

Conquest, Robert, *The Nation Killers: The Soviet Deportation of Nationalities* (New York: St. Martin's Press, 1970).

Costa, Dora L., in and Lamoreaux, Naomi R., (Eds.), *Understanding Long-Run Economic Growth: Geography, Institutions, and the Knowledge Economy* (Chicago: University of Chicago Press, 2011)

Courtois, Stéphane; Werth, Nicolas; Panné, Jean-Louis; Paczkowski, Andrzej; Bartošek, Karel; and Margolin, Jean-Louis, *The Black Book of Communism: Crimes, Terror, Repression* (Cambridge, MA: Harvard University Press, 1999.

Davies, Glyn, *A History of Money: From Ancient Times to the Present Day* (Cardiff, Wales: University of Wales Press, 2002).

De Soto, Hernando, *The Mystery of Capital: Why Capital Triumphs in the West and Fails Everywhere Else* (New York: Basic Books, 2000).

Dikötter, Frank, *Mao's Great Famine: The History of China's Most Devastating Catastrophe, 1958-1962* (New York: Walker & Co., 2010).

Dixon, W. J., and Boswell, T., "Dependency, Disarticulation, and Denominator Effects: Another Look at Foreign Capital Penetration," *American Journal of Sociology*, Vol. 102, 1996: 543-562.

Djankov, Simoen; La Porta, Rafael; Lopez-de-Silanes, Florencio; and Schleifer, Andrei, "The Regulation of Entry," *Quarterly Journal of Economics*, Vol. 117, No. 1, (February) 2002: 1-37.

Doob, A.N., and Roberts, J., "Public Attitudes Toward Sentencing in Canada," in N. Walker and M. Hough (Eds.), *Sentencing and the Public* (London: Gower, 1988).

Drelichman, Mauricio, and Voth, Hans-Joachim, "Institutions and the Resource Curse in Early Modern Spain," pp. 120-147 of Elhanan Helpman (Ed.), *Institutions and Economic Performance* (Cambridge, MA: Harvard University Press, 2008).

Duesterberg, Thomas J., "U.S. Future Needs Blue-Collar Might; So. Who Cares If Manufacturing Falters or Moves Abroad? Americans Should, Because It Is Imperative for Innovation, National Defense and Jobs," *Chicago Tribune*, August 24, 2003.

Duncan-Jones, Richard, *Structure and Scale in the Roman Economy* (New York: Cambridge University Press, 1990).

Dyos, Harold James, and Aldcroft, Derek Howard, *British Transport: An Economic Survey from the Seventeenth Century to the Twentieth* (Leicester, England: Leicester University Press, 1969).

Einaudi, Luca, *Money and Politics: European Monetary Unification and the International Gold Standard (1860-1873)* (New York: Oxford University Press, 2001).

Elliott, John Huxtable, *Empires of the Atlantic World: Britain and Spain in America, 1492-1830* (New Haven, CT: Yale University Press, 2006).

Emmer, P.C. (Ed.), *Colonialism and Migration: Indentured Labour Before and After Slavery* (Higham, MA: Martinus Nijhoff Publishers, 1986).

Engerman, Stanley L., and Sokoloff, Kenneth L., "Once Upon a Time in the Americas: Land and Immigration Policies in the New World," pp. 13-48 in Dora L. Costa and Naomi R. Lamoreaux (Eds.), *Understanding Long-Run Economic Growth: Geography, Institutions, and the Knowledge Economy* (Chicago: University of Chicago Press, 2011).

Erikson, Emily, "Malfeasance and the Foundations for Global Trade: The Structure of English Trade in the East Indies, 1601-1833," *American Journal of Sociology*, Vol. 112, No. 1, (July) 2006: 195-230.

European Commission, Eurostat *News Release: euroindicators* Revised Version, No. 102/2013, July 2, 2013. As of July 4, 2013, available online at http://epp.eurostat.ec.europa.eu/cache/ITY_PUBLIC/3-01072013-BP/EN/3-01072013-BP-EN.PDF

Feis, Herbert, *Europe, the World's Banker, 1870-1914* (New Haven, CT: Yale University Press, 1931).

Ferguson, Niall, *Empire: The Rise and Demise of the British World Order and the Lessons for Global Power* (London, England: Basic Books, 2002).

Ferguson, Niall, *The Ascent of Money: A Financial History of the World* (New York: The Penguin Press, 2008).

Ferguson, Niall, *The Cash Nexus: Money and Power in the Modern World, 1700-2000* (New York: Basic Books, 2001).

Findlay, Ronald, and O'Rourke, Kevin H., *Power and Plenty: Trade, War, and the World Economy in the Second Millennium* (Princeton, NJ: Princeton University Press, 2007).

Fortune, "The Fortune Global 500," *Fortune*, Vol. 166, No. 2, July 23, 2012. As of July 7, 2013, available online at http://money.cnn.com/magazines/fortune/global500/2012/full_list/

Fourcade, Marion, "The Construction of a Global Profession: the Transnationalization of Economics," *American Journal of Sociology*, Vol. 112. No. 1, (July) 2006: 145-194.

Friedman, Thomas L., *Longitudes and Attitudes: The World in the Age of Terrorism* (New York: Anchor Books, 2003).

Friedman, Thomas L., *The Lexus and the Olive Tree* (New York: Anchor Books, 2000).

Galtung, Frederik, "Measuring the Immeasurable: Boundaries and Functions of (Macro) Corruption Indices," in pages 101-130 of Charles Sampford, Arthur Shacklock, Carmel Connors, and Frederik Galtung (Eds.), *Measuring Corruption* (Burlington, Vermont: Ashgate Publishing, 2006).

Gellman, Barton, and Priest, Dana, "U.S. Strikes Terrorist-Linked Sites in Afghanistan, Factory in Sudan," *Washington Post,* August 21, 1998, page A01. As of June 17, 2013, available online at http://www.washingtonpost.com/wp-srv/inatl/longterm/eafricabombing/stories/strikes082198.htm

Gersemann, Olaf, *Cowboy Capitalism: European Myths, American Reality* (Washington, D.C.: Cato Institute, 2004).

Goldstein, Joshua S., and Pevenhouse, Jon C., *International Relations* Brief Fifth Edition (New York: Longman, 2010).

Grove, Andrew W., *Only the Paranoid Survive: How to Exploit the Crisis Points That Challenge Every Company and Career* (New York: Currency Doubleday, 1996).

Gwartney, James; Lawson, Robert; and Hall, Joshua, *Economic Freedom of the World: 2012 Annual Report* (Vancouver: Fraser Institute, 2012). As of June 26, 2013, available online at http://www.economicfreedom.org/2012/09/18/economic-freedom-of-the-world-2012-annual-report/?gclid=CNzL-N7Ag7gCFVRk7AodNBgAXQ

Helps, Arthur, *Life and Labours of Mr. Brassey, 1805-1870* (Boston: Roberts Brothers, 1874).

Hemming, John, *The Conquest of the Incas* (Orlando, Florida: Harcourt, 1970).

Hille, Kathrin and Menn, Joseph, "Apple Faces Legal Action Over iPad Name," *Financial Times*, October 27, 2010, 8:21 PM. As of July 8, 2013, available online at http://www.ft.com/intl/cms/s/2/4e10735e-e1f3-11df-a064-00144feabdc0.html#axzz1fwD7MtKe

Hille, Kathrin, "Apple Loses iPad Trademark Case in China," *Financial Times*, December 7, 2011, 1:37 PM. As of July 8, 2013, available online at http://www.ft.com/intl/cms/s/2/6bc5ba86-20b7-11e1-8133-00144feabdc0.html#axzz1fwD7MtKe

Himmerich y Valencia, Robert, *The Encomenderos of New Spain, 1521-1555* (Austin, TX: University of Texas Press, 1991).

Hirano, Ken'ichiro, *The State and Cultural Transformation: Perspectives from East Asia* (New York: United Nations University Press, 1993).

Hobbes, Thomas, *Leviathan* (London: Penguin Books, 1985). Originally published 1651.

Holohan, Anne, *Networks of Democracy: Lessons from Kosovo for Afghanistan, Iraq, and Beyond* (Stanford, CA: Stanford University Press, 2005).

Hudson, Michael and Van De Mieroop, Marc (Eds.), *Debt and Economic Renewal in the Ancient Near East* Vol. III (Bethesda, MD: CDL Press, 2002).

Hunter, John, "Top Ten Countries for Manufacturing Production in 2010: China, USA, Japan, Germany…," *Curious Cat Investing and Economics Blog*, December 27, 2011. As of July 7, 2013, available online at http://investing.curiouscatblog.net/2011/12/27/top-10-countries-for-manufacturing-production-in-2010-china-usa-japan-germany/

Jacoby, Jeff, "Made in the U.S.A.," *Boston Globe*, February 6, 2011. As of July 8, 2013, available online at http://www.boston.com/bostonglobe/editorial_opinion/oped/articles/2011/02/06/made_in_the_usa/

Keller, Carmen; Siegrist, Michael; and Gutscher, Heinz, "The Role of the Affect and Availability Heuristics in Risk Communication," *Risk Analysis*, Vol. 26, No. 3, 2006: 631-639.

Kentor, Jeffrey, and Boswell, Terry, "Foreign Capital Dependence and Development: A New Direction," *American Sociological Review*, Vol. 68, 2003: 301-313.

Klein, Jill G., "Five Pitfalls in Decisions About Diagnosis and Prescribing," *British Medical Journal*, Vol. 330, (April) 2005: 781-783.

Klinger, D., and Kudryavster, A., "The Availability Heuristic and Investors' Reactions to Company-Specific Events," *The Journal of Behavioral Finance*, Vol. 11, 2010: 50-65.

Kredo, Adam, "The Donald Goes to CPAC: TV Star and Hotel Magnate Gives His Thoughts on the State of America," *The Washington Free Beacon*, March 15, 2013, 11:54 AM. As of July 8, 2013, available online at http://freebeacon.com/the-donald-goes-to-cpac/

Kuhn, Ferdinand, *Commodore Perry and the Opening of Japan* (New York: Random House, 1955).

Lanning, John Tate, *Academic Culture in the Spanish Colonies* (Port Washington, WA: Kennikat Press, 1971). Originally published 1940.

Lee, B.; O'Brien, J.; and Sivaramakrishnan, K., "An Analysis of Financial Analysts' Optimism in Long-Term Growth Forecasts," *The Journal of Behavioral Finance*, Vol. 9, 2008: 171-184.

Levinson, Marc, "U.S. Manufacturing in International Perspective," Congressional Research Service Report for Congress, 7-5700, R42135. February 11, 2013. As of July 9, 2013, available online at http://www.fas.org/sgp/crs/misc/R42135.pdf

Lewis, Bernard, "License to Kill: Usama bin Laden's Declaration of Jihad," *Foreign Affairs*, Vol. 77, No. 6, (November/December) 1998: 14-19.

Lipset, Seymour Martin, "Social Requirements of Democracy: Economic Development and Political Legitimacy," *American Political Science Review*, Vol. 53, 1959: 69-105.

Lipset, Seymour Martin, "The Social Requisites of Democracy, Revisited," *American Sociological Review*, Vol. 59, 1994: 1-22.

Lipset, Seymour Martin; Seong, K.R.; Torres, J.C., "A Comparative Analysis of the Social Requisites of Democracy," *International Social Science Journal*, Vol. 16, 1993: 155-175.

Locke, John, *Two Treatises of Government: In the former, The false Principles, and Foundation of Sir Robert Filmer, And his Followers, are Detected and Overthrown. The latter is an Essay concerning The True Original, Extent, and the End of Civil Government* (London: A. Churchill, 1690).

Markham, Clements R. (Ed.), *Repots on the Discovery of Peru* Translated and Edited, with Notes and an Introduction (New York: B. Franklin, 1970). Originally published 1872).

Marris, Stephen, "Deficits and the Dollar: The World Economy at Risk," *Policy Analyses in International Economics*, No. 14 (Washington, D.C.: Institute for International Economics, December 1985).

Mauerer, Noel, and Yu, Carlos, *The Big Ditch: How America Took, Built, Ran and Ultimately Gave Away the Panama Canal* (Princeton, NJ: Princeton University Press, 2011).

McKeown, Adam, "Global Migration, 1946-1940," *Journal of World History* Vol. 15, 2004: 185-189.

Meltzer, Milton, *Francisco Pizarro: The Conquest of Peru* (New York: Benchmark Press, 2005).

Morris, William (Ed.), *The American Heritage Dictionary of the English Language* (New York: Houghton Mifflin Company, 1969).

Musson, A.E., "The Great Depression of 1873-1896: A Reappraisal," *Journal of Economic History*, Vol. 19, No. 2, 1959: 199-228.

Myers, David, *Social Psychology* Tenth Edition (New York: McGraw Hill, 2010).

National Association of Manufacturers, "The NAM's Strategy for Growth and Manufacturing Renewal," adopted by the Board of Directors on February 8, 2003, www.nam.org

Nissen, Hans J; Damerow, Peter; and Englund, Robert K., *Archaic Bookkeeping: Early Writing and Techniques of Economic Administration in the Ancient Near East* Translated by Paul Larsen (Chicago, IL: University of Chicago Press, 1993).

Norberg, Johan, *In Defense of Global Capitalism* (Washington, D.C.: Cato Institute, 2003).

Norris, Floyd, "Manufacturing Is Surprising Bright Spot in U.S. Economy," *The New York Times*, January 5, 2012. As of July 8, 2013, available online at http://www.nytimes.com/2012/01/06/business/us-manufacturing-is-a-bright-spot-for-the-economy.html

North, Douglas Cecil, *Violence and Social Orders* (New York: Cambridge University Press, 2009).

O'Neill, Jim, *Building Better Global Economic BRICs* Goldman Sachs. Goldman Sachs Global Economics Paper No. 66. November 30, 2001. As of July 12, 2013, available online at http://www.goldmansachs.com/our-thinking/archive/archive-pdfs/build-better-brics.pdf

OECD, *Newsroom*, "G20 Labour Ministers Must Focus On Young Job Seekers," May 15, 2012. As of July 4, 2013, available online at http://www.oecd.org/newsroom/g20labourministersmustfocusonyoungjobseekers.htm

OECD, *OECD Factbook 2013: Economic, Environmental, and Social Statistics* (Paris, France: Organization for Economic Cooperation and Development, 2013). As of July 6, 2013, available online at http://www.oecd-ilibrary.org/economics/oecd-factbook-2013_factbook-2013-en

Partridge, Mark, "Ten Critical Steps to Protecting Intellectual Property in Global Markets," *IndustryWeek*, May 7, 2012. As of July 8, 2013, available online at http://www.industryweek.com/global-economy/ten-critical-steps-protecting-intellectual-property-global-markets

Perry, Mark J., "If top 500 U.S. Manufacturing Firms Were a Separate Country, They Would Have Been the Third Largest Economy Last Year," *Carpe Diem*, February 9, 2013, 11:50 AM. As of July 8, 2013, available online at http://www.aei-ideas.org/2013/02/if-top-500-us-manufacturing-firms-were-a-separate-country-they-would-have-been-the-third-largest-country-last-year/

Peterson, P.G., "The Morning After," *The Atlantic Monthly*, (October) 1987: 43-69.

Pollard, Sidney, "Capital Exports, 1870-1914: Harmful or Beneficial?," *Economic History Review*, Vol. 38, No. 4, (November) 1985: 489-514.

Riley, Bryan and Miller, Terry, *2013 Index of Economic Freedom: No Boost in Trade Freedom* (Washington, D.C.: The Heritage Foundation, 2012). Special Report #123 on Economic Freedom, October 25, 2012. As of June 27, 2013, available online at http://www.heritage.org/research/reports/2012/10/2013-index-of-economic-freedom-no-boost-in-trade-freedom

Rummel, R.J., *Death by Government* (New Brunswick, NJ: Transaction Publishers, 2008).

Sato, Akio, *Legal Aspects of Landownership in Colonial Spanish America* (Tokyo: Institute of Developing Economies, 1976).

Schumpeter, Joseph A., *Capitalism, Socialism and Democracy* (New York: Harper & Brothers, 1942).

Schwarcz, Steven L., "Protecting Financial Markets: Lessons from the Subprime Mortgage Meltdown," *Minnesota Law Review*, Vol. 93, No. 2, 2008: 373-406.

Scott, Robert E., *The China Toll: Growing U.S. Trade Deficit with China Cost More than 2.7 Million Jobs Between 2001 and 2011, With Job Losses In Every State* (Washington, D.C.: Economic Policy Institute, August 23, 2012).

Slovic, Paul; Fischoff, Baruch; and Lichtenstein, Sarah, "Facts Versus Fears: Understanding Perceived Risk," pages 463-492 of Daniel Kahneman, Paul Slovic, and Amos Tversky (Eds.), *Judgment Uncertainty: Heuristics and Biases* (New York: Cambridge University Press, 1982).

Smyth, Clifford, *Francisco Pizarro and the Conquest of Peru* (New York: Funk & Wagnalls company, 1931).

Stiles, T.J., *The First Tycoon: The Epic Life of Cornelius Vanderbilt* (New York: Alfred A. Knopf, 2009).

Tatom, John A., "Compared to Other Nations, U.S. Manufacturing Job Losses Modest: Most Industrial Nations Have Witnessed Greater Job Losses, " *Tax Foundation*, December 8, 2003. As of July 8, 2013, available online at http://www.mombu.com/culture/cuba/t-compared-to-other-nations-us-manufacturing-job-losses-modest-14765009.html

Tatom, John A., *Manufacturing, Employment, Productivity and the Business Cycle* Background Paper, Number 42. February 2004 (Washington, D.C.: Tax Foundation, 2004). As of July 8, 2013, available online at http://taxfoundation.org/sites/taxfoundation.org/files/docs/6e20a785ad1d03fae4a16dc78 17f8952.pdf

The Heritage Foundation, *2013 Index of Economic Freedom* Edited by Terry Miller, Kim R. Holmes, and Edwin J. Feulner (Washington, D.C.: The Heritage Foundation; New York: The Wall Street Journal. January, 2013). As of June 12, 2013, available online at www.heritage.org/index/ranking

The World Bank, GDP Growth (annual %), 2013. As of July 4, 2013, available online at http://search.worldbank.org/data?qterm=average+annual+real++economic+growth+over+the+last+25+years&language=EN&format=

Theodorson, George A., and Theodorson, Achilles, G., A Modern Dictionary of Sociology (New York: Barnes & Noble Books, 1969).

Tomlins, Christopher, "Indentured Servitude in Perspective: European Migration into North America and the Composition of the Early American Labour Force, 1600-1775," pp. 146-182 of Cathy Matson (Ed.), *The Economy of Early America: Historical Perspectives and New Directions* (Philadelphia, PA: The Pennsylvania State University Press, 2006).

Transparency International, *Corruption Perceptions Index 2012* (Berlin, Germany: Transparency International, December 5, 2012). As of July 9, 2013, available online at http://www.transparency.org/whatwedo/pub/corruption_perceptions_index_2012

Triplet & Associés, Employment Law, "French Law: The Standard French Working Week." As of June 17, 2013, available online at www.triplet.com/50-10_employment/50-20_workingtime.asp

Tversky, Amos, and Kahneman, Daniel, "Availability: A Heuristic for Judging Frequency and Probability," *Cognitive Psychology*, Vol. 5, No. 1, 1973: 207-232.

Tversky, Amos, and Kahneman, Daniel, "Judgment Under Uncertainty: Heuristics and Biases," *Science*, Vol. 185, 1974: 1123-1131.

U.S. Census Bureau, "Long-term Trends: Foreign-Born Population and as Percent of Total Population," 2013. As of June 30, 2013, available online at http://www.census.gov/how/infographics/foreign_born.html

Van De Mieroop, Marc, *Society and Enterprise in Old Babylonian Ur* (Berlin: D. Reimer, 1992).

Villareal, Andres, and Yu, Wei-hsin, "Economic Globalization and Women's Employment: The Case of Manufacturing in Mexico," *American Sociological Review*, Vol. 72, No. 3, (June) 2007: 365-389.

Wall, Rachel, *Japan's Century: An Interpretation of Japan's History Since the Eighteen-Fifties* (London: Historical Association, 1964).

Weber, Max, *Economy and Society* Vol. 1 (Edited by Guenther Roth and Claus Wittich) (New York: Bedminster Press, 1968).

Williams, Jonathan; Cribb, Joe; and Errington, Elizabeth (Eds.), *Money: A History* (New York: St. Martin's Press, 1997).

Wittner, David G., *Commodore Perry and the Perry Expedition to Japan* (New York: Rosen Pub. Group, 2005).

World Economic Forum, *The Global Competitiveness Report 2012-2013* Full Data Edition. Klaus Schwab, Editor (Geneva, Switzerland: World Economic Forum, 2012). As of June 11, 2013, available online at http://www3.weforum.org/docs/WEF_GlobalCompetitivenessReport_2012-13.pdf

Zibreg, Christian, "Apple Loses Three Copyright Infringement Cases in China," *iDownloadBlog*, April 25, 2013. As of July 8, 2013, available online at http://www.idownloadblog.com/2013/04/25/apple-loses-3-copyright-suits-in-china/

CHAPTER 5

Socialization

Socialization is a life-long process in which people learn roles (expectations of behavior) and norms, develop a capacity to conform to them, and develop a concept of self. In this chapter, we take a micro-level look at how people become members of a culture and of a society through the process of socialization. First, we introduce you to some basic sociological and social-science views of socialization. In this context we identify and discuss classic studies of social isolation and the insights they impart regarding basic conditions necessary for successful socialization outcomes. Next, we explain the ideas of seven researchers who have made lasting contributions to our understanding of socialization--Abram Maslow, Sigmund Freud, Erik Erikson, George Herbert Mead, Jean Piaget, Lawrence Kohlberg, and Carol Gilligan. Then, we examine major contexts or agents of socialization—the family, the school, peers, and the media. We conclude the chapter with an excursion into sociological research on the micro-level processes of gender, racial, and ethnic socialization.

BASIC CONCEPTS

Sometimes we learn, or attempt to learn, roles and norms that attach to a position *before* we actually occupy that position, which is known as **anticipatory socialization** For example, when young girls play "house" with dolls, they may be modeling parenting behaviors, and they are doing so years before they actually become parents themselves. Sociologists observing their play would say they are engaging in anticipatory socialization. People may engage in aniticipatory socialization throughout their life course. Likewise, sometimes after we have learned roles and norms, developed a capacity to conform to them, and have developed a sense of self, we find that we need both to *unlearn* those things and to learn new things to put

in their place. This latter process is termed **resocialization.** In other words, resocialization is learning that, from ego's perspective at least, involves both a sharp break with the past and the learning of different norms, values, and behaviors. A "couch potato" endeavoring to transform into a physically-active person is an example of an attempt at resocialization.

There are two major sociological orientations about socialization (Gecas, 1992). The first views socialization primarily as a process whereby culture is transmitted across generational lines. The second views socialization as identity formation, the process whereby we develop a sense of self. Sometimes this second orientation is termed the study of human development.

Sociologists use the term **internalization** to refer to the process whereby norms, values, and statuses become internal to the individual, part of the individual's sense of self. Sociologists also use the term **context** (or agent) **of socialization** to refer to a person, organization, or institution engaging in socialization. A context of socialization may be a person, such as a parent, other relative, a neighbor or a member of your community, and so forth; or an organization, such as a day-care agency or the Boy Scouts or Boys and Girls Clubs of America; or a group, such as a child's play group or a youth gang; or even an institution, such as a school, a juvenile court, a correctional facility, or the media.

Socialization that occurs during the first few years of our lives is termed **primary socialization**, and it is distinguished from that which occurs later in our lives, **secondary socialization**. In our primary socialization, which usually takes place in our families, we learn basic conceptions of self (e.g., "I am female," "I am male") and basic values, norms, beliefs, and motivations. Secondary socialization, which occurs after the first few years of life, may take place within any number of contexts, both familial and extra-familial. Common extra-familial contexts include a school, college, or university; peer group, the mass media, the military, and the work place.

SOCIALIZATION AS HUMAN DEVELOPMENT

Many scholars from varying academic disciplines and frames of reference have endeavored to understand the process of human development. We briefly introduce you to the ideas of Harry Harlow, Abram Maslow, Sigmund Freud, Jean Piaget, George Herbert Mead, Erik Erikson, Lawrence Kohlberg, and Carol Gilligan concerning human development.

Harry Harlow and Isolation: The Study of Monkeys

Research with non-human primates demonstrates the importance for later developmental outcomes of early learning experiences. A series of classic experiments with rhesus monkeys by primatologists Harry Harlow and Margaret Harlow at the University of Wisconsin Primate Laboratory (e.g., Harlow, 1962; Harlow and Harlow, 1962) illuminate the extent to which, among primates, becoming an adequately functioning social actor is dependent upon interaction with others.

The Harlows artificially inseminated female rhesus monkeys and reared the resulting offspring in isolation. In the now famous cloth-mother and wire-mother experiments, isolate-reared rhesus monkey infants had access to soft terry-cloth mothers who gave no milk and to lactating wire-surrogates. The researchers observed that the infant monkeys spent only a few minutes each day nursing from the wire surrogate and virtually the rest of the time clinging ventrally to the cloth surrogate mother. Monkeys need something soft and warm to cling to in order to feel comfortable, reassured, and calm. Correspondingly, basic trust is the first of Erikson's eight human developmental crises (Erikson, 1950), and prolonged ventral clinging to a warm, soft terry-cloth mother instilled a basic sense of security and trust in these infants (Harlow and Zimmerman, 1959).

While the monkeys developed a strong attachment to the cloth mother and little or none to the wire mother, regardless of which one gave milk, in almost all other respects, the monkeys had failed to develop into adequately functioning social actors by the time of adolescence and adulthood. For instance, when the baby female monkeys who had cloth-surrogate mothers grew up, they themselves were artificially inseminated. After giving birth, they did not engage in parenting behaviors with any minimally acceptable amount of competence or diligence. They rejected their young and would not let them nurse. They abused their babies. They would crush their child's face into the floor, chew off its fingers and feet, or even put the infant's head in their mouths and crush it like an eggshell. In primates, then, it appears that adequate parenting behavior has large learned components.

The isolate-reared monkeys of both sexes also failed to learn to copulate. Harlow (1962) reports on his efforts to "re-educate" male and female rhesus monkeys who had grown up in isolation in his laboratory. He paired the isolate-reared mature females with his "most experienced, patient, and gentle males," whom he refers to as *sophisticated males* (1962: 7); and he paired the isolate-reared males with his "most eager, amiable, and successful breeding females," whom he refers to as *sophisticated females* (Harlow, 1962:7). The results were failure for the isolate-reared males and females.

Among primates, then, there are large learned components to behaviors as fundamental as parenting and copulation. While early attachment and trust are important to further development, they do not suffice as a foundation for normal primate development. What else is needed?

Harlow's research documents that peer relations are crucial to the development of the young. If infants with terry-cloth mothers get to play for twenty minutes each day with fellow isolate-reared infants in a playroom supplied with equipment for climbing and swinging, they develop normally in every respect. If deprived of intimate interactions with peers, the young fail to develop normally.

Harlow's research indicates that the effects on monkeys isolated for the first three months of life are reversible. This is equivalent to about the first six months of life for a human infant. However, baby monkeys isolated for the first six months of life are impaired permanently both emotionally and behaviorally.

Studies of Isolated Children

Studies of isolate-reared children show strikingly similar results. From time to time the media and scholarly literature report on children who, in one way or another, have been isolate-reared for years--locked in a closet, garage, or cellar; chained to a bed in a spare room, and so forth (Itard, 1962; Davis, 1940, 1948; Curtiss, 1977; Rymer, 1994). Deprived of all but the most trivial and fleeting human contact, these extremely neglected children have only their genetic resources upon which to draw in order to become human, and they are starkly impaired behaviorally and emotionally as a result. When found, these children lack language ability and merely make grunting-like sounds. They are indifferent to their surroundings. They make no efforts to control bowl and bladder functions. Much like Harlow's isolate-reared monkeys, these children often spend a lot of time rocking rhythmically back and forth on their heels.

These extremely isolated children are sometimes referred to as **feral** even though the term "feral" actually refers to persons who have been reared by animals, apart from humans. The Roman legend of Romulus and Remus is an example of feral children. According to legend, Romulus and Remus are twins who were reared and nursed by a she-wolf. These twins founded the city of Rome which is named after Romulus. The legend of Tarzan provides another example of a feral child.

In a well-known study, René Spitz (1945, 1947) compares 130 infants reared for the first year of life either in a Belgian orphanage or with their mothers in a prison. The prison infants were looked after much of the time by their own mothers. They got lots of hugging and cuddling. The mothers spoke to them a lot. At the end of a year, these infants were robustly healthy, highly curious about their environment, and displayed great motor skills. They vocalized freely, and some actually spoke a word or two. They all understood the significance of simple social gestures. By two years of age, most of these infants could feed themselves with a spoon; they understood commands and obeyed them; they ran playfully around the room; they played lively social games with each other; and they had made substantial progress in toilet training. Over a period of two years, not a single child died.

In the orphanage, the hygienic and medical care were good, as was the food. But, in sharp contrast to their prison counterparts, each of these infants had to share her or his caretaker, a busy nurse, with seven other infants. These infants, as a result, were largely isolated and spent most of their time alone in their cots. The result? From the third month of life onward, these children showed extreme susceptibility to infection and illness. They were sick a lot. Also, their mortality rate was extremely high. A lot of them perished. More than 37% died in a period of two years. Also, their motor skills were severely impaired. Fully 24% were incapable of any locomotion, and only 14% could sit up unassisted. By the age of two, hardly any of them could eat alone, even with a spoon, and hardly any were toilet trained. Very few could dress themselves or say even a couple of words. They were incapable of social play with peers. They displayed bizarre, stereotyped motor patterns. They would grab their heads between their hands and rock rhythmically back and forth, distinctly reminiscent of the isolate-reared monkeys in Harlow's studies and of autistic youth.

What these and similar cases show is that to become an adequately functioning human requires a social process of intensive face-to-face interaction between the developing infant and other people. The evidence supports the position that there may be a critical period during which interaction is essential for subsequent normal development (Emde, 1992). Although humans are resilient (e.g., Werner, 1987; Werner and Smith, 1989), research suggests that there may well be a limit to the length of isolation that a primate, including human primates, can experience in the first years of life without resulting in developmental disturbances that are remarkably resistant to reduction or elimination either by normal measures or known therapeutic techniques.

Let us turn our attention to the understanding of human socialization provided by seven researchers. These seemingly very different idea systems have four things in common. First, each views human development as consisting of a series of stages or steps. Second, the successful completion of one stage is viewed as necessary for the successful completion of the remaining steps. If a person does not successfully complete a stage, that "unfinished business" will impede their successful completion of the remaining stages. Third, one cannot successfully skip a step. And, fourth, in at least some of these views of human development, not very many people actually finish all of the stages.

Abraham Maslow

Abraham Maslow (1908-1970) was born and grew up in Brooklyn, New York. His father hoped he would study law but he went instead to University of Wisconsin to study psychology. There he found his chief mentor in Professor Harry Harlow. He went on to further research at Columbia University where he found another mentor in Alfred Adler, one of Freud's early followers.

Maslow saw human beings' needs arranged in a hierarchy, like a ladder (Maslow, 1943a, 1943b). See Figure 5.1. The most basic needs, at the bottom, are safety needs— such as food, water, air, shelter, sleep. Unless these needs are met, life itself is not possible. These needs must be satisfied in order for us to survive, which is why these sometimes are called survival needs. Then come security needs—the need to feel safe, stable, secure. For example, people feel more comfortable when they believe they live in a predictable world. Another example is the just world phenomenon—people feel more secure when they perceive that people get what they deserve and deserve what they get. After the security needs are satisfied, people can focus on their belonging needs, which sometimes are called the social or love needs—the need for belonging, acceptance, love. The esteem needs come next—the need for self respect as well as the respect of others. For Maslow, the esteem needs also include the desire for competence or mastery of or at something external to the self. Maslow thought that achieving competence or mastery of or at something external to the self is the wellspring that satisfies esteem needs. At the top of the ladder is self-actualization, the need to develop and to actualize one's fullest potentialities and capacities. These are the "be all you can be!" needs. Maslow thought that self-actualized people focus on solving problems external to themselves, have a clear sense of what is true and what is phoney, are creative and spontaneous, are not too tightly bound by social conventions, and are focused on the future and new horizons. Maslow thought that less than one percent of people reach the stage of self-actualization.

FIGURE 5.1 ABRAHAM MASLOW'S HIERARCHY OF NEEDS

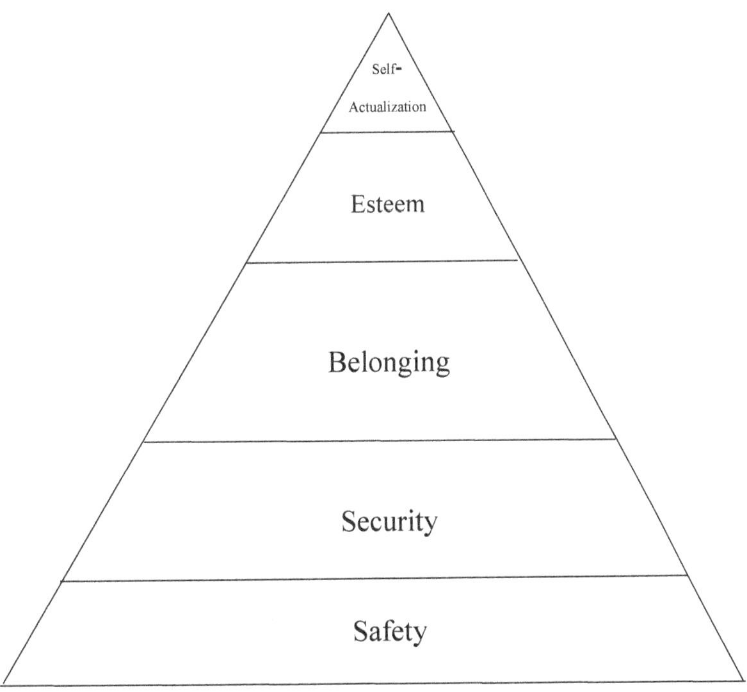

Sigmund Freud

Sigmund Freud (1856-1939), the creator of psychoanalysis, lived in Vienna, Austria, during the same turbulent times as Weber, Durkheim, and Marx. Like other social theorists whose ideas we have examined, Freud's thought was influenced by the currents of social change. He was trained as physician at the University of Vienna. His interests turned to the origins of civilization. Civilization, claims Freud, is made possible by turning our innate sexual and aggressive drives to ends no longer sexual and no longer aggressive, a process he terms **sublimation** (Freud, 1930).

Freud's theory of the relationship among the personality, the individual, and society is the story of socialization. It is a story of contradictions, conflict, and often of pain and suffering. Suffering characterized the bloody First World War where he served as a medical doctor. Freud systematically observed the effects on soldiers of losing fingers, arms, and legs. He observed grown men calling out for their mothers in grueling agony. He observed soldiers imagining that their body parts, which had been blown away or surgically amputated, were intact. Freud observed the psychological effects of prolonged stress and fatigue on soldiers, effects which social scientists today term as delayed stress syndrome.

We can understand how uncontrollable disasters such as earthquakes, hurricanes, floods, and tornadoes wreck our lives. Out of this rubble we start again afresh. But how do we understand envy, jealousy, love, hatred, lack of ability to forgive, guilt, rejection, pity, and acts of kindness and of violence? The Freudian paradigm provides a template for answering these questions.

The force of life for Freud is the **libido**, which is Latin for desire or lust. The aim of libido is the satisfaction of instinctual drives towards survival, pleasure, and pain avoidance. Libido is expressed in the part of our personality known as the **id**. The id is our basic needs, innate sexual and aggressive drives, desires, and pleasures. Id is impulsive, unconscious and covert. Id is petty, selfish, and self-centered. Id in raw form has no rational logic or sense of time. It is the infant's screaming in the middle of church service while the minister calls upon her or his congregation to be saved. Id is a direct cause of caregivers' sleepless nights when newborns cry and demand food and comfort. Id is demonstrated when tots are at peace, calm and smiling, while danger is all around them. A baby's id is satisfied when its need to feel warm and secure is met by the loving arms of babushka. Libido pushes for wish fulfillment, which Freud calls ***the pleasure principle***. Libido is in constant tension or conflict with the part of the personality known as the **ego**. The function of the ego is to regulate our actions in accordance with reason and logic, otherwise known as ***the reality principle***. The reality principle of the ego (e.g., You have a Chemistry 101 exam at 8 AM Monday morning, and you have yet to study and to read three chapters of the textbook) often conflicts with the pleasure principle of the libido (e.g., There is a party you really want to go to on Friday night). The frustration of libidinal energy underlies anxiety.

Ego, a Latin word for "I," is the part of the personality we present to others. Ego is largely conscious, aware of itself. Ego's basic function is appropriately to balance id's demands with the requirements of society, which are expressed in the part of our personality known as the **superego**. Ego is what we put on the line when we request that our needs be fulfilled. Ego is punched, made fun of, pinched, poked, and even battered. Ego protects us and defends us from the unpleasantness of life's disappointments. Ego is largely overt. Ego develops defenses, known as ego defenses, to unpleasant events and thoughts.

Superego is our conscience, the norms, values, notions of right and wrong that we have internalized from significant others who live within a particular historical period and within a specific culture. The activity of the superego is often unconscious. According to psychoanalytic theory, the severity of the superego's pressure reflects the strengths of a person's own aggressive impulses and does not reflect only the actual severity of parents. Superego is the guilt we feel when we eat the last cookie on the plate. Superego urges us to help others in need. Superego respects authority. Superego is the shame we feel when mom disapproves. Superego is society within us.

We may conceive of the id, ego, and superego as representing different drives or desires within us. The id says: "I want it, I want it." The superego says, "You can't have it; it's bad for you." The ego, as mediator or umpire, says, "Well, you can have a little bit of it, later." According to Freud, the battle among ego, id, and superego is ceaseless.

Freud generalizes his concept of libidinal energy in his theory of psycho-sexual development. ***Psycho*** is a root that means breath, life, soul, spirit, and indicates the mind, personality, or mental processes (Morris, 1969: 1055). In Freudian theory, **psycho-sexual development** indicates that the development of mind, personality, and sexuality are inextricably intertwined; one cannot understand the development of the mind and personality without understanding the simultaneous development of sexuality and vice versa. In the normal course of human development, according to Freud, the individual gets instinctual satisfaction from different parts of the body because libidinal energy is associated with different orifices of the body at different age levels. Libidinal satisfaction or frustration at each stage of development is accompanied by particular emotions. Those emotions that are particularly intense or preponderant become consolidated as chronic dispositions, according to Freud. Too much satisfaction or frustration of libido at any stage of development can result in libido becoming fixated at that stage. **Fixation** means that a disproportionate amount of libidinal energy is invested in a particular bodily orifice, personality is dominated by the traits associated with that level of development, and psycho-sexual maturity is not attained.

THE STAGES OF PSYCHO-SEXUAL DEVELOPMENT ACCORDING TO FREUD

According to Freud, there are five stages of psycho-sexual development. Because the content of the first two stages is the same for males and females, it is said that an initial stage of homosexuality underlies all human development in the Freudian paradigm.

1. **ORAL STAGE** In the newborn infant, and until about two years of age, libido is associated with the mouth, and hence this stage is known as the oral stage. The baby's emotional gratification now centers on oral activities, like sucking and swallowing, biting and spitting. Sucking and swallowing are conducive to an attitude of basic trust, and help the infant to develop attitudes of pleasure, acceptance, affection, and security. According to Freud, biting and spitting express rejection, hurtfulness, and destructiveness, which are characteristic of mistrust. The traits viewed by Freud as emerging from oral satisfaction include optimism, tolerance, and generosity. Traits viewed by Freud as emerging from oral frustration include jealousy, hostility, and impatience. Those fixated at the oral stage of psychosexual development are expected later in life to be compulsive talkers, eaters, smokers, and so forth.

2. **ANAL STAGE** From roughly age two to three years of age, libidinal energy is associated with the anal orifice, and hence this stage is known as the anal stage. The baby now derives pleasure from the process and products of its own excretions. These pleasures tend to be opposed by the caretakers who socialize the baby. Hence, this is commonly the age at which toilet training occurs. Those

fixated at this stage of psychosexual development are expected later in life to develop problems with relationships to authority and to lack self-control.

According to Freud, the anal stage is important for ego development and for emotional development. It is with toilet training that the infant is first confronted with libidinal frustration (e.g., refraining from defecating when and where she or he is not supposed to defecate) in exchange for social respectability. Defecation must be confined to certain places and to certain times. This learning of impulse control is important for ego development. The issues confronted by the infant at this time, according to Freud, include giving-withholding, tension reduction-retention release, obstinacy-flexibility, mess-cleanliness, and approval-shame.

3. **PHALLIC STAGE** After the anal stage is the phallic stage, which begins at three to four years of age and which is completed by five or six years of age. This stage sometimes is called the ***Oedipal period*** or ***Oedipal complex*** (***Oedipus complex***), particularly for boys, after a Greek legend in which King Oedipus inadvertently kills his father and marries his mother. For girls, this stage sometimes is called the ***Elektra complex***, after a Greek legend in which Elektra avenges the murder of her father by assisting in the murder of her mother. Libidinal energy now is associated with the penis in boys and with the clitoris in girls. The child shows sexual curiosity and engages in specifically sexual play. The child's attachment to the opposite-sex parent becomes sexualized. Subconsciously the child wishes to possess the opposite-sex parent sexually and sees the same-sex parent as a rival.

The boy fears that his biggest rival, his father, will cut off his penis, which has given the boy much pleasure. This fear is termed ***castration anxiety***, and it is a powerful motivator. The boy who successfully resolves the Oedipal complex deals with this anxiety by "identifying" with his powerful father, internalizing his father's notions of right and wrong, prime among which is that the son give up sexual desires for Mom. At this point, the boy successfully has resolved the phallic stage. In the Freudian paradigm, then, *castration anxiety is the basis for the formation of the boy's* primitive *superego*. Due to castration anxiety, boys develop a robust conscience (superego).

In Freud's paradigm, girls are not as fortunate. According to Freud, from a girl's point of view, the worst already has happened. She has no penis. It must have been cut off and she knows who must have done *that*--the major rival for her father, the mother. The girl who sexually desires her father does not have the powerful force of castration anxiety to motivate her. She already has lost a penis and has only, in the Freudian view, an inferior clitoris. Lack of a penis is a wound to her narcissism; she wants a penis. She has ***penis envy***. Maybe the powerful father will be able to give her one. When it dawns on her that the powerful father can do many things, but, alas, even he cannot give her a penis of her own, she identifies with the mother. She internalizes the mother's notions of right and wrong, prime among which is that daughters gives up sexual desires for Dad. She may not be able to have a penis of her own, now; but ***she can*** eventually ***give birth to one*** (i.e., give birth to a boy child). At this point the young girl, motivated by ***penis envy***, successfully has resolved the phallic stage.

For Freud, the phallic stage is a crucial period of development for both boys and girls and for the men and women they later will become. Many anxieties and conflicts need to be dealt with at this stage, and Freud claims that much of our later personality is determined by the ways in which we resolve this stage of development.

4. **LATENCY** The fourth stage of development is latency, the calm after the storm of the phallic stage. Sexual and aggressive fantasies now are relatively dormant. The latency stage begins after the end of the phallic stage and continues until the onset of puberty, which marks the onset of the final stage of psycho-sexual development, the adult genital stage.

5. **ADULT GENITAL STAGE** This stage is characterized by a move away from a focus on self-pleasure toward a reciprocal pleasure-giving relationship with a person, with reproduction as a goal. Manifestations of the genital stage of psycho-sexual development include social awareness, constructive projects (such as work), and participating in group activities. In short, Freud believes that healthy individuals now put their libidinal energies into family and work, both of which are important for the reproduction of culture and society.

   The first revision of Freud's theory was a result of the currents of social change in which he lived. The major concepts of his system--libido, id, ego, superego, the pleasure principle, and so forth--did not allow him to explain why soldiers who returned from battle in the First World War and who were well removed from combat still experienced recurrent nightmares of the hell of war. In *Beyond the Pleasure Principle*, Freud concludes that there is a compulsion to repeat. This compulsion to repeat is viewed as primordial as the pleasure principle. However, the compulsion to repeat is viewed as in the service of a general destructive force or motive. Freud calls this general destructive force or motive ***Thantos***, the death instinct (Freud, 1920, *Standard Edition*, Vol. 18). A group of constructive motives, which he collectively terms ***Eros***, or the life instinct, contend against *Thantos*.

No doubt some of Freud's positions sound bizarre in the twenty-first century. Indeed, Freud's paradigm has been criticized by many stakeholders on many grounds. These criticisms include the following:

- Adherents and defenders of many religions have been highly critical of Freud's ideas, since he maintained that religion is an illusion that helps the helpless to identify with a powerful male god (Freud, 1927). Freud holds that healthy humans should attempt to live their lives without illusions; people should squarely face their anxieties.
- Feminists claim that Freud's theory is inherently sexist in that it is excessively biological and focuses on the role of father and father-like figures. Some feminists maintain that there are and were female-centered and female-societies.
- Anthropologists criticize Freud's theory as ethnocentric. **Ethnocentrism** refers to the tendency to view the norms, values, and institutions of one's culture as right and as preferable to those of other cultures. Not all societies share Freud's views of socialization and of the role of the father. In some societies, the biological father is pretty much excluded from the family life of the children.
- Methodological criticisms stress the lack of objective, reliable measures of many key concepts, the lack of objectivity in observation, and the difficulty of deriving testable hypotheses from the theory.
- Behaviorists are critical of abstract concepts like id, ego, superego, sublimation, and so forth that cannot directly be observed and measured. They prefer to explain personality development in terms of the rewards and punishments that the individual receives. For behaviorists, behavior is learned, and the mechanisms involved in the process of conditioning suffice to explain differences in competence, motivation, and emotional adjustment. From this point of view, focusing on the past is fruitless. For example, Albert Ellis maintains that thinking is learned, and only by changing

thinking can the individual change the emotional response and thereby move on to appropriate behavior (1973, 1976, 1977).

- Freud's theory also has been criticized as too deterministic and as not giving sufficient weight to social processes in the formation of self. Freud "saw personality as fully developed" or at least as "determined by about the age of four years" (Harré and Lamb, 1986: 247), a position that many social scientists reject. Some social scientists reject Freud's emphasis on sexual drives and pay more attention to social and interpersonal aspects of development. For instance, Erik Erikson, an influential theorist of the psychoanalytic school, stresses interpersonal relationships across the individual's life span as heavily influencing the capacity for development and personal adjustment (Erikson, 1963).

Erik Erikson's Eight Stages of Human Development

Erik Erikson (1863-1931) was a student of Sigmund Freud. Erikson eventually broke with Freud because he thought that Freud's system of thought both underestimated the importance of the social and overestimated the importance of the sexual in human development. Erikson also rejected Freud's view of human development as fixed in the first few years of life (Erikson, 1963). Erikson's ideas, while influenced by the Freudian paradigm, nonetheless stress the importance of *social* relations for human development. Due to this emphasis, Erikson's theory sometimes is called a *psycho-social perspective.* The term "psycho-social" emphasizes that we cannot adequately understand the development of the self (psyche) without understanding the social relations we have with significant others, and vice versa.

Erikson perceives human development as consisting of eight stages. The successful completion of each stage is a foundation for the next stage. Each stage has a particular developmental task, which is conceived of as a polarity and which emerges out of physiological changes and the changing social situation. At each stage, the person is faced with a choice between two ways of coping, an adaptive or a maladaptive way. Only when each stage is successfully resolved, which involves a change in personality, is the person ready to move on to the next stage of development. If a person is unable successfully to resolve a particular stage, she or he will confront and struggle with it later in life (Schultz and Schultz, 1987). We now examine Erikson's eight stages of socialization.

1. **BASIC TRUST VS. MISTRUST** From birth through the first year and a half of life, the major task facing the infant is trust versus mistrust. The infant must establish a first loving, trusting relationship with the primary caregiver, otherwise she/he will develop a sense of mistrust.

   The infant is born helpless and dependent on others for food, warmth, and affection. If caretakers fail to meet her/ his basic needs, the infant will perish. The personality of the infant develops according to the quality of the responses the infant elicits or fails to elicit from the primary caregivers. For instance, when the infant signals through crying and other gestures that she/he is hungry or lonely, do the caregivers respond consistently and promptly by coming to the infant and picking her/him up, cuddling, caressing, reassuring her/him, making her/him comfortable? If so, the infant learns that she/he is capable of getting her/his needs met and that the world is filled with nice people who can be counted on to help. The infant learns that she/he is effective in securing assistance, a gold-medal winner in the Olympics of life, as it were. Such toddlers develop a trusting, hopeful attitude towards others and towards life.

In contrast, when the infant signals that she/he is hungry, uncomfortable, or lonely, if the caregivers are undependable, inconsistent, and rejecting, the infants learns other lessons about the self, life, and the world. The infant learns to respond with anxiety, rage, cautiousness, feelings of inadequacy, despair, and withdrawal. The infant learns that it is a cold world where one has to look out for oneself because others cannot be trusted to help. The youngster learns that she/he is a failure at getting things of importance accomplished.

2. **AUTONOMY VS. SHAME AND DOUBT** Between eighteen months to two or three years of age, the toddler is learning to grasp, to talk, to walk, and to engage in appropriate bladder and bowel continence. The child learns control but may develop shame and doubt if the child's efforts are not handled well.

   The young person's emotions and feelings of personal efficacy and worth develop as a response to the perceived actions of primary caregivers. Are the toddler's efforts at task mastery consistently met with reassurance and encouragement? If so, the toddler is thereby encouraged to develop a sense of efficacy with regard to mastery over self and the environment, and the toddler learns persistence at task. The toddler learns to view herself/himself as a capable person.

   However, if the primary caregivers respond to the toddler's efforts with indifference or with disapproval, the toddler learns shame and feels ridiculed (Goleman, 1997: 195). The toddler learns to doubt her/his ability to influence the world and to accomplish a task.

3. **INITIATIVE VS. GUILT** The next stage, from around two or three to about six years of age, involves the polarity of initiative versus guilt. As children develop their language and motor skills, they become more and more engaged in social interaction with those around them. They need to learn to achieve a balance between a desire for more adventure and more responsibility and learning to control their impulses. In play, children learn to take on the roles of specific others, one specific other at a time, and they develop feelings of efficacy. They learn to view themselves as competent at task mastery. If the primary care givers are encouraging yet consistent in their discipline of the child, the child learns that certain things are not allowed, but at the same time will not feel ashamed when using her/his imagination in playing the role of the other. However, ridicule of the child's attempts at task mastery and disinterest in the child's activities may lead to feelings of guilt, and the child may come to believe that it is wrong to be independent. Encouraging the child in exploration leads to a well-developed sense of personal initiative.

4. **INDUSTRY VS. INFERIORITY** From about age six until the about age 12, the onset of adolescence, the developmental task is industry versus inferiority. The important event at this stage is school attendance, which brings with it a variety of events, including academics, group activities, and friends. Difficulty with any of these may lead to a sense of inferiority. It is important for the child at this stage to perceive pleasure in a need to achieve and in being productive. If the child discovers pleasure in intellectual stimulation, in being productive, in seeking success, she/he develops a sense of competence. The child's relationship with peers and neighborhood become increasingly important. If the child experiences difficulty in moving between the world at home and the world of peers, a feeling of inferiority may develop. A sense of well-being, industry, is attained by striving for and by attaining success in any of a variety of contexts, including mental skills (e.g., winning a

"spelling bee," being good at multiplication tables), physical skills (e.g., jump rope, hockey, baseball), and through producing things.

5. **IDENTITY VS. ROLE CONFUSION** Adolescence, roughly from age twelve to eighteen, is the fifth stage of development. The developmental task at this stage is the construction of a psychosocial "bridge" or arch between where the child has been—- in infancy, toddler-hood, and early childhood—- to where the child is now, to where the child wants to go in adolescence and adulthood. If the child is successful in forging this bridge, the child achieves ego identity. If there are bricks missing in this bridge, the result is role confusion.

6. **INTIMACY VS. ISOLATION** The next developmental stage, from about eighteen or nineteen years of age through age 35, is the first stage of adult development, young adulthood. The developmental task is intimacy versus isolation. ***Intimacy*** refers to one's ability to relate to another human being on a deep, personal level, either in friendship or in marriage.

   For Erikson, the alternative to intimacy is a deep sense of lonely isolation, which may manifest itself in competitiveness and combativeness with others. The competitiveness and combativeness are weapons that one can use to protect a "fearful" self. One pushes others, who could have nurtured the self, away.

7. **GENERATIVITY VS. STAGNATION** From about 35 to 55 years of age, the developmental task is generativity (staying green and growing) versus stagnation. Erikson defines ***generativity*** as an adult's ability to be productive and creative to the benefit of others. Thus, adults make a meaningful potential contribution to future generations when they rear children and when they help rear their grand children. Of course, there are many ways other than through childrearing adults may be productive and creative to the benefit of others. Numerous forms of community service exemplify generativity-- volunteering one's labor in food kitchens and in food pantries for the poor, volunteering on behalf of environmental issues (e.g., recycling, save the whales, etc.), volunteering on behalf of various social-service issues (e.g., working at homeless shelters, working to bring social services to persons afflicted with HIV-AIDS, and so forth (Erikson, 1994:267).

8. **EGO INTEGRITY VS. DESPAIR** The eighth stage of human development begins at about fifty-five years of age, and its developmental task is that of ego integrity versus despair. The developmental issue at this stage is another bridging operation. *When one reflects over one's entire life course, what does one perceive*? If one perceives that, on the whole, one has added more to life than one has taken from it; if one is able to reflect over one's life course in a positive manner; if one perceives that the relationships that one wants to establish and the things that one wants to accomplish no longer can be put off; and if one also is able to come to terms with the transition of death, then one achieves integrity. For Erik Erikson, ***integrity*** involves coming to accept one's whole life, reflecting on that life in a positive manner, and coming to terms with death. An inability to do these things results in a feeling of despair. If the individual views her or his life as a series of bad decisions and opportunities missed, and feels that the time to start afresh is forever gone, the individual will fear death and has opted for ***despair***.

George Herbert Mead's Stages of Human Development

Symbolic interactionist George Herbert Mead (1863-1931) identifies three stages in the process of socialization. The first stage occurs from birth to about three years of age and is termed the ***Imitation Stage***. At this stage of development, baby learns to associate certain sounds that she/he makes with the actions of significant others. For example, baby cries in a particular way and the primary care giver picks up baby, cuddles baby, and feeds baby. Baby cries in a different way and the primary care giver comes to baby, picks up baby, and changes baby's diapers.

Around eighteen months to two years of age, baby develops the cognitive ability to use spoken language. From the Meadian view this is a developmental milestone. Language is a symbolically rich mode of communication and it opens many avenues of socialization.

George Herbert Mead reminds us that play is important. Mead terms the second stage of human development the ***Play Stage***, which lasts roughly from three to five years of age. Part of being able to communicate effectively is an ability to be able imaginatively to construct how ego looks to others. Ego is a Latin word meaning "I" or the self. In the Meadian view, the self—i.e., our answers to the question "Who Am I?"-- emerges in play as a result of learning to imagine how we appear to others who are important or significant to us. More specifically, we develop a self as we perceive ourselves through our perceptions of the responses of others to us.

In the play stage children learn to use language and, in play, to take on the roles of others, one "other" at a time. Imagination leads children to pretend that they are some of the many others they encounter in their lives. A child "plays at" being Mommy. A child may pretend to be "Spider Man," or "Captain America," or "Wonder Woman" or a minister, mullah, or rabbi. An example of the play stage is provided by the game of playing "dress up." In this game, common in the United States, a child puts on, say, Daddy or Mommy's shoes or clothes, which symbolic interactionists term *props*. Props help the child get into the reality of the role they are playing. The child, in play, actually becomes able to see the world, including themselves, from the point of view of, say, Mommy or Daddy. Taking the role of the other is a difficult, sophisticated, elaborate cognitive accomplishment for a young child. The props, talking out loud, and engaging in actions typical of the child's perception of that person are things that assist the child in accomplishing this cognitive feat.

By taking the role of a significant other, the child learns the attitudes, values, and beliefs of that significant other. From play, the child learns that there are rules that she or he is expected to follow in a particular situation ("Wash and dry your face and hands before coming to the dining table;" "Raise your hand and wait to be called on by the teacher before talking in class;" "Cover your mouth with your hand when you cough or sneeze").

When the child gains and develops the cognitive capacity to understand the rules of a game, to play accordingly, and to view his or her position in the game from a number of differing points of view simultaneously, the child enters the third stage of human development, known as the ***Game Stage***.

CHARACTERISTICS OF GAMES In the Meadian view a game is a form of social interaction that requires more cognitive sophistication than does mere play. Games have several characteristics that mere play lacks. First, games tend to be competitive (e.g., a score is kept and there are winners and losers). Second, playing a game (such as baseball, soccer, football, school band, or orchestra) requires that a member cooperates and coordinates her or his efforts with those of team-mates. Third, games are structured according to agreed-upon rules. In engaging in game behavior, a child learns to bring her or his behavior in accord with these agreed upon rules. In short, games require that a child view a common activity from numerous points of view simultaneously, which Mead refers to as the ability to construct a **generalized other**. A generalized other is a composite of all the players in the game and of the rules of the game. It is a normative order. It is a "moral system that the individual internalizes, makes his or her own" (Charon, 2000: 180). It is a set of rules that guides our thinking and behavior: we take others into consideration and actively direct our behavior in relation to the expectations of those others.

Jean Piaget on Cognitive Development

Jean Piaget (1896-1980) is a Swiss-born social psychologist who spent more than thirty years observing and studying the cognitive development of children of varying ages. Piaget wanted to understand human cognitive development. Piaget envisions human development as consisting of four stages.

1. **SENSORIMOTOR STAGE (INFANCY)** The first stage of human development lasts from birth to approximately one and a half to two years of age.. During this stage, a lot of sensory (sight, smell, hearing, taste, touch) and motor development occurs. During the early part of this stage, the infant has no awareness of objects or of people that are not immediately present at a given moment. Piaget called this a lack of "object permanence." *Object permanence* is an awareness that objects and people continue to exist even if they are out of sight. Children acquire object permanence at about 7 months of age. By the end of this stage, children have a clear sense of their own gender permanence (Maccoby and Jacklin, 1987; Cann and Vann, 1995) and they have acquired some language ability.

2. **PRE-OPERATIONAL STAGE (TODDLER AND EARLY CHILDHOOD)** The preoperational stage lasts roughly from age one-and-a-half or two through age six. At the beginning of this period, the child has difficulty in separating self from non-self and in taking the role of the other, whether of a child or of an adult. The most important development at this stage is the maturing of language use. With language development, children become adept at the use of symbols: for instance, they can pretend while driving their toy car across the couch that the couch is actually a bridge. By the end of this period, the child is able, in the Meadian sense, to take the role of the other, one other at a time.

3. **CONCRETE OPERATIONAL STAGE (ELEMENTARY SCHOOL AND EARLY ADOLESCENCE)** This stage lasts from about age seven to age eleven. In this stage, cognitive development is demonstrated through the logical use of symbols related to concrete objects. For instance, children learn to consider viewpoints other than their own, to classify objects, and to understand the concepts of cause and effect. In the Meadian sense, children during this stage acquire the ability to take the role of the generalized other. Children during the beginning of this stage also acquire what Piaget calls the *principle of conservation*—-the conservation of mass and the conservation of measure. The principle of conservation is the knowledge that quantity is unrelated to the arrangement and physical appearance of objects. Children who have not completed this stage do not know that the amount, volume, and length of an object do not change when the shape of the configuration is changed. In other words, if you were to place two identical pieces of, say, play dough in front of a child, one rolled up in the shape of a golf ball, the other rolled into the shape of

a snake, a child who has not completed the beginning of this stage may say the snake piece is bigger because it is rolled out. The beginning of this stage is marked by the mastery of the principle of conservation. Most people successfully complete this stage of development. However, many people do not successfully complete the next stage.

4. **FORMAL OPERATIONAL STAGE (ADOLESCENCE AND ADULTHOOD)** This stage begins around age 12 and continues into adulthood. In this stage, cognitive development is demonstrated through the logical use of symbols related to abstract concepts. During this stage, many people develop their competence in abstract thinking. For instance, people use and develop their capacity to think in terms of abstract concepts (e.g., social class, domination, honor, solidary order), theories (e.g., conflict theory, consensus theory, symbolic interactionism), and general principles (e.g., gravity, equity). People learn to derive testable hypotheses from theory and to collect data with which to test the hypotheses. They learn to test the hypotheses with the data they have collected; and on the basis of probability theory, to come to the correct decisions as to whether to accept or to fail to accept the hypotheses. People learn to construct theory inductively. In short, this stage produces a new kind of thinking that is abstract, formal, and logical.

Lawrence Kohlberg on Moral Development

Lawrence Kohlberg (1927-1987) was a student of Jean Piaget. However, Kohlberg was interested in moral development, and it is through the lens of this interest that he developed his own theory of socialization. Kohlberg views socialization as consisting of three stages. The ***pre-conventional stage*** lasts from birth to about eight or ten years of age. At this stage, most children experience the world in terms of pain and pleasure, and they perceive *what is right as what feels good to me.* "If it feels good, do it," is an apt motto for this stage of development.

Most adolescents and adults successfully complete the next stage of development, the ***conventional stage.*** People who successfully complete this stage of development have internalized, and largely conform to, the social norms of the conventional social order (Figurski, 1992). The individual now defines *what is right* in terms of Mead's generalized other. The individual is capable of bringing her or his behavior into conformity with the norms of the conventional social order.

The ***post-conventional stage*** is reached by few people according to Kohlberg. In this stage, people ponder the legitimacy of the norms of their society. "*This is the norm of my society; but, in terms of a larger ethical system, is it right? Is it moral? Is it just?*" At this stage, people (like Mahatma Gandhi, Rosa Parks, Malcolm X, Cesar Chavez, Martin Luther King, Jr.) ponder the norms and laws of their society. They ponder the meaning of abstract concepts like j, ustice, equality, fairness, freedom, and equal justice before the law. When they perceive that the existing laws are not right, they may work to change them.

Carol Gilligan: Gender and Moral Development

In listening to female's narratives of ethical dilemmas in their lives, Carol Gilligan (1982, 1990, 2011) observes that while Erik Erikson's and Lawrence Kohlberg's stages of human development seem to "fit" the experiences of males in the United States, their explanatory schemes fail to fit females' life experiences very well. Her own research, which relies heavily on data provided by largely white, middle-class children and adults in the United States, forms the basis for her theory of gender and moral development. In essence, Gilligan extends Lawrence Kohloberg's stages of moral development and Erikson's stages of human development by taking gender into consideration. Males and females, Gilligan claims, use different standards of "rightness." Boys use a "justice perspective" that relies on formal rules to define right and wrong. Girls, in contrast, use a "care and responsibility perspective" that assesses or judges a situation with an eye to personal loyalties and personal relationships. For example, boys say stealing is wrong because it breaks the law. Girls are more likely to wonder *why* someone would steal and to feel sympathy for someone who steals to take care of the needs of her family.

CONTEXTS OF SOCIALIZATION

The Family

STYLES OF PARENTAL CONTROL

For almost a century, sociologists have been interested in how parents influence the development of children. *Parental warmth* and *parenting styles* are among the most robust variables in the literature on the family as primary socialization agent (Gecas, 1992). The construct of ***parenting style*** refers to two important elements of normal parenting: (1) parental warmth or supportiveness (also known as parental responsiveness), which refers to the extent that parents are "attuned, supportive, and acquiescent to the children's special needs and demands" (Baumrind, 1991:62); and (2) parental behavioral control of the children (also known as parental demandingness), which refers to "the claims parents make on children to become integrated into the family whole, by their maturity demands, supervision, disciplinary efforts and willingness to confront the child who disobeys" (Baumrind, 1991: 61-62). These two elements sometimes are referred to as "love" and "limits," and they, along with parenting style, are among the most robust variables in the literature on the family as primary socialization agent (Gecas, 1992).

Categorizing child-rearing practices according to whether they are high or low on parental demandingness and parental warmth results in a typology of normal parenting styles: permissive, authoritarian, and authoritative (Maccoby and Martin, 1983). We now examine these parenting styles and their effects on children.

Authoritarian parents are highly directive and demanding, but not responsive. They expect their orders to be obeyed without explanation. These parents provide well-ordered and structured environments with clearly stated rules. This style is more frequent among working-class parents than among the more educated and more affluent. Authoritarian parents are aloof and cold and control their children closely (Kohn, Naoi, Schoenbach, Schooler, & Slomczynski, 1990; Harrison, Wilson, Pine, Chan, and Buriel, 1990; Argyle, 1994). Authoritarian parents compare their children or adolescents' behavior against an absolute set of standards. They emphasize to their children the importance of obedience, conformity, and respect for authority. They use physical punishment and also discourage verbal give-and-take with their children. Children and adolescents from authoritarian families tend to perform moderately well in school and tend to be uninvolved in delinquent behavior. The children and adolescents from authoritarian families tend to react poorly to frustration, with girls particularly likely to give up and boys particularly likely to become

especially hostile. The children and adolescents from authoritarian families also tend to have poor social skills, lower self-esteem, and higher levels of depression (Weiss and Schwarz, 1996; Elder, Nguyen, and Casi, 1985; McLeod, Kruttschnitt, and Dornfeld, 1994; McLeod and Shanahan, 1993; Wilcox, 1998).

Authoritative parents are highly demanding and highly responsive. They base discipline on logical reasoning and explanation, isolation (e.g., sending a child to her or his room as punishment), and appeals involving the threat of loss of love. These parents use far less physical punishment than their authoritarian counterparts. Authoritative parents encourage verbal give-and-take with their children and explain the reasons behind discipline. They want their children to be assertive as well as socially responsible, self-regulated as well as socially cooperative (Alwin, 1990).

The authoritative parenting style, also known as inductive control, is more frequent among intact, middle and professional class families of European descent. Children and adolescents whose parents are authoritative rate themselves, and are rated by objective measures, as more socially and instrumentally competent than those whose parents are nonauthoritative (Baumrind, 1991; Weiss & Schwarz, 1996; Miller et. al., 1993). Children and adolescents whose parents are authoritative tend to have good psycho-social outcomes and far lower levels of problem behaviors in all ethnic groups studied (African-, Asian-, European-, and Hispanic Americans). For example, Clark's classic study of successful parenting practices among poor African-American families produced findings that are consistent with the findings regarding authoritative parenting. In the family experience of successful poor African-American children, Clark found more frequent dialogues between children and parents, clear and consistent limits for children's behavior, parental encouragement of academic pursuits, consistent monitoring of how children spend their time, and warm and nurturing interactions with parents (Clark, 1983; Dornbusch, 1989).

Parental use of authoritative parenting techniques and avoidance of harsh parenting behaviors contribute to adolescents' high scores on self-efficacy: the adolescents view themselves as competent persons whose decisions today influence their lives tomorrow (Whitbeck, Simons, Conger, Wickmara, Ackley, and Elder, 1997). The children and adolescents tend to be self-confident about their ability to master tasks, have well-developed emotional regulation, and are less rigid about gender-typed traits (Amato and Booth, 1997; Thompson, Hanson, and McLanahan, 1994; Wilcox, 1998). The benefits of authoritative parenting are evident as early as the preschool years and continue throughout adolescence and into early adulthood.

Permissive parents are high on love and low on limits. They are more nurturing than they are demanding. The parents are accepting and affirmative towards the children's impulses, desires, and actions. The parents make few demands for household responsibility and orderly behavior. The parents allow the children to regulate their own activities as much as possible, avoid the exercise of control, and do not encourage the children to obey externally defined standards. These children tend to lack self-control, and they tend to have poor emotion regulation, in that their emotions are under-regulated. Children and adolescents from permissive homes also tend to be rebellious and defiant when their desires are challenged, to display low persistence at challenging tasks, and to be more likely to be involved in problem behavior and to perform less well in school.

STYLES OF ATTACHMENT

Attraction refers to positive affective attachment to another person (Stimson, 1992). This concept is straight forward, and it refers, for instance, to the ideal relationship in the United States between husband and wife, or to the relationship between best friends, siblings, girlfriend-boyfriend, mother-child, and father-child. We now turn our attention to scientific research findings regarding the importance for a child's behavior and orientation to the world of attraction, which in some research traditions is referred to as ***attachment***.

Dr. ***Mary Ainsworth*** observes three styles of attachment in her laboratory studies of babies between the ages of one and two (1982). She finds that the styles of attachment are a product of the way the caregivers had treated the infants in the preceding months. When caregivers respond promptly and warmly to their infants' entreaties for contact and comfort, the infants tend to form secure attachments. ***Securely-attached*** babies use their mothers as a secure pad or base from which to explore their environment and from which to operate when playing. When mother leaves the room, these babies show distress; but when she returns, they are reassured, after which they again explore their environment and play. In Ainsworth's view, these infants had learned that they could count on their caregivers to be responsive, which "gave them the confidence they needed for exploration" of unfamiliar territory (Hazan, 1995: 42). These toddlers, when older, have fewer disciplinary problems than those who had been either insecurely or avoidantly attached.

Some caregivers are not as responsive. Some caregivers are inconsistent in responding to their infants. Sometimes they are warmly responsive; at other times, they are variously neglectful or intrusive. Their infants tend to form insecure attachments. ***Insecurely-attached*** babies appear extremely distressed when their mothers leave the room. When she returns, the infants seek contact during the reunion, but also appear angry and have difficulty settling. Later, they tend to stay close to the mother rather than venturing off to play. When they do play, they seem too anxious to enjoy the toys, even when the mother is present. Ainsworth views this behavior as a way of coping with inconsistent caregivers. Their caregivers' unpredictability left them feeling insecure and made them angry.

A third type of attachment Ainsworth notes is avoidant. This form of attachment is associated with fairly consistent rejection on the part of the caregivers. Instead of responding warmly or inconsistently to their infants' bids for contact, these caregivers regularly rebuff the infants. The caregivers seem to avoid close contact with their own infants. In the play situation, the ***avoidantly-attached*** babies seem to focus on the toys and to avoid their mothers when the mothers are in the room, and they display no interest in her comings or goings. Ainsworth views this behavior as indicating that the infants had learned that it is futile to seek comfort from the caregivers and adapt by keeping their distance.

Longitudinal studies on attachment indicate that one of the long-term results of failure to form a secure attachment between the main nurturing figure and infant is an inability to establish intimate ties with another person even as an adult. Researchers have studied the relationship between attachment to a nurturing figure at a young age and its effects on other behaviors (Argyle, 1994; Ainsworth, 1989; Sroufe, 1984; Erikson, Sroufe, and Egeland, 1985; Schneider-Rosen et. al., 1985; Miyake, Chen, and Campos, 1985; Haigler, Day, and Marshall, 1995). Those securely attached to their mothers at age six months or younger are more likely to do the following:

- **AT TWO YEARS OF AGE:** seek their mothers' help when performing difficult tasks. The ability to seek help from a competent source is a valuable asset, a trait or orientation to the world that significantly increases the probability that one will persist at a difficult task instead of giving up and going on to something else instead. Persistence at a task, in turn, is positively correlated with successful completion of a difficult task. *Have you, or anyone you know, ever tried to accomplish a task--to ride a bike, to learn to use a computer for data analysis or for word processing, to learn a foreign language, to learn to water ski or to cross-country or down-hill ski, to sew, to repair your car, for instance--and, had you not asked for assistance, would have given up? Tell us about it.*
- **AT FIVE YEARS OF AGE:** are more resourceful in adapting to changing circumstances and more persistent in coping with tasks (Wilson and Herrnstein, 1985; Bowlby, 1982; Bersheid, 1985; Lewis

> et. al., 1984). In contrast, those who had been insecurely or avoidantly-attached at age six months or earlier, at age five fall apart--become angry, distressed, contrary--when faced with a difficult task.

Weak attachment, these researchers conclude, does not so much lead to a particular form of misconduct—nose picking, or being a bully, or being insolent, or being lazy--as it does to misconduct quite generally. Thus, one child, whom we'll call Jack, was liked by his teachers because he so obviously craved attention. The other children avoided him because he was highly manipulative, uncooperative, and could not tolerate the slightest frustration. Another boy, whom we'll call Denzel, was hostile, devious, manipulative, and sadistic. His teachers didn't like the boy, but several of Denzel's classmates, noting his superb skill in controlling others, were drawn to him.

Similarly, Emmy Werner's longitudinal study finds that secure attachment to the main nurturing figure by age one is strongly related to being slow to anger and to tolerating frustration well in a disorderly household at two years of age; to being cheerful and enthusiastic, seeking help from adults effectively, and being flexible and persistent at age 3; to being able to distance oneself from emotional turmoil, to seeking out and finding adults for guidance and help when parents falter in childhood; and to planning rather than acting on impulse as a teen (Werner, 1987; Werner and Smith, 1989).

GENDER SOCIALIZATION

Socialization to gender begins at birth if not before. One of the first questions friends and relatives ask new parents concerns the baby's gender (Intons-Peterson and Reddel, 1984). Even the newborn's reception varies by its gender. In traditional Hindu India, communities welcome the news of the birth of a male child with rituals of joy and celebration. Village women slam the wooden bolts of their doors back and forth and grind coconut shells in a mortar, all to express joy and praise. This hullabaloo is absent upon the birth of a female child, whose family members are said to look as if in mourning. In the United States, congratulations cards sent to parents typically are gender coded, with different colors, messages, and activities conveyed on the basis of the newborn's gender (Bridges, 1993). Parents frequently provide the infant with bedroom decor, toys (Pomerleau, Bolduc, Malcuit, and Cossette, 1990), and clothes that reliably convey the infant's gender to others (Shakin et. al., 1985).

In the United States, parents perceive their newborns in ways that have more to do with the gender-stereotypes held by the parents than with the physical characteristics of the newborns. Both mothers and fathers perceive their newborn females as "finer featured," as "more delicate," and as "less strong" than newborn boys (Karraker, Vogel, and Lake, 1995). Parents also engage in more rough and tumble play with boys. They lift boys high into the air and swirl them around. They bounce boy infants vigorously on their knees. Parents are more gentle with girls (Eccles, Jacobs, and Harold, 1990). Parents give girls lots of hugs and kisses, a form of interaction not showered upon males. Mothers talk to and touch their daughters more than their sons, and they keep their daughters closer to them (Goldberg and Lewis, 1969).

By the time they are thirteen months old, girls stay closer to their mothers while playing, and return to them sooner, than do boys (Goldberg and Lewis, 1969). Preschool boys are allowed to roam further away from home than are females (Munroe and Munroe, 1971; Nerlove et. al., 1971) and they engage in more unsupervised play (Edwards, 1991).

From preschool age through early adolescence, children play largely in sex-segregated groups and have different play and game experiences (e.g., Bloch, 1989; Carpenter, Houston, and Serpa, 1989). Their reading materials also convey different visions of the good life. In Caldecott Award children's books during the last half century, boys are five times more often shown using production tools (e.g., pitchfork, plow), and girls are four times more often shown using domestic implements such as pots and pans, a broom, and a sewing needle (Crabb and Bielawski, 1994). A study of thirty Caldecott Medal and "honors" books for the period 1984-1994 reveals that a greater number of males than females are depicted both in titles and pictures and that males are described as more potent and active (Turner-Bowker, 1996). The result? The social reproduction of traditional gender roles. Women are the primary providers of socio-emotional support in the home (Rossi and Rossi, 1991). The United Nations reports that ubiquitously cooking and washing dishes are the least shared household tasks (1991).

When mothers play with their daughters, they display a wider range of emotions. When conversing with their children, parents' references to emotion are more frequent and varied, and they mention sadness and dislike more often, with daughters than with sons (Adams, Kuebli, Boyle, and Fivush, 1995). Parents also discuss emotions, except for anger, more with daughters. When mothers talk to daughters about feelings, they discuss in more detail the emotional state itself than is the case with sons (Brody and Hall, 1993). Even when parents make-up stories to tell their preschool children, the stories told to girls contain more emotion words than the stories told to boys. Not too surprisingly, by age two, girls converse more about their feelings than do similarly aged boys (Dunn, 1987, 1988), and they continue to do so as they mature (Adams, Kuebli, Boyle, and Fivush, 1995). Young girls even express more affection in their letters to Santa Clause than do boys (Otnes, Kim, and Kin, 1994), and as adolescents they are more likely than males to express both responsibility and concern for the well-being of others (Beutel and Marini, 1995).

One result of maturation and of socialization is the emergence of **gender identity**, a fundamental sense of self as "I am male" or "I am female." Gender identity emerges and then becomes permanently established between 3 to 6 years of age (Lachmann, 1991: 122). There is some controversy regarding the forces that shape gender identity, and different theoretical positions proffer different explanations regarding the forces that influence its emergence and permanence. John Money and associates at Johns Hopkins University have found, among the children in their professional practice, that gender identity is firmly established by age three (Money and Wiedeking, 1980).

SOME OTHER EFFECTS OF GENDER SOCIALIZATION

Gendered socialization fosters the development of different social skills and orientations to social life (Range and Stringer, 1996). In other words, **gender role** socialization is a basic part of the socialization process. Gender roles, also known as sex roles, refer to expectations of behavior (roles) that are attached to one's perceived sexual status of male or female.

Friendship Groups.

From roughly age two until age eleven, boys and girls play mainly in gender homogeneous groups. Boys' playgroups are larger and more hierarchical than are girls' groups (Knight and Chao, 1989; Grotpeter and Crick, 1996). From a young age, females become more attuned to interpersonal connections, and boys to formal rules; girls become more attuned to noticing, deciphering, and responding in a sensitive way to someone else's subjective feelings as revealed in facial expression, tone of voice, and other nonverbal cues (Brody and Hall, 1993). Not too surprisingly, males value friendships that focus on shared interests and activities (e.g., hunting, football, karate), whereas females place greater value on trust and self-disclosure (Richey and Richey, 1980; Davis, Franzoi, and Wellinger, 1985).

Loneliness.

Male and females also tend to experience **loneliness**, a painful perception that our relationships with others are less meaningful or numerous than we desire, under different circumstances (Myers, 2008: 520; Boivin and Hymel, 1997). Males experience loneliness when deprived of *group contact* that focuses on shared activities, and females experience loneliness when deprived of *close one-on-one relationships that focus on understanding and emotional support* (Douvan and Adelson, 1966; Stokes and Levin, 1986).

Adolescent and adult males who are both less attuned to and less adept at reading emotional content, are (1) less likely than females to define a cross-sexual dyadic encounter as violent in nature (Browning and Dutton, 1986; Demaris, Pugh, and Harman, 1992); and (2) more likely than females to construe friendliness on the part of a person of the opposite sex as sexual interest (Abbey, 1987, 1991a, 1991b; Kowalski, 1993).

Definition of Encounters as Violent.

Research using couple-level data consistently reveals considerable discrepancies when both members of a dating or marital couple are questioned about the incidence of physical violence in their relationship. The general pattern that emerges is that females are far more likely than their male partners to report violent acts, whether perpetrated by themselves or by their partners, in their relationship (Jouriles and O'Leary, 1985; Edelson and Brygger, 1986; De Maris, Pugh, and Harman, 1992; Szinovacz and Egly, 1995; Anderson, 1997). Males fail to define encounters as violent in nature that are perceived as violent by their female partners.

Misreading of Emotional Warmth as Sexual Interest.

Antonia Abbey (1998, 1991b, 1987) and her colleagues have repeatedly found that males are more likely than females to attribute a female's friendliness to mild sexual interest. Misreading emotional warmth as sexual interest can contribute to behavior that females perceive as sexual harassment (Pryor et. al., 1997; Johnson, Stockdale, and Saal, 1991; Saal, Johnson, and Weber, 1989). It may also help explain why eight times as many American females say they have been forced into unwanted sexual behavior than the 3 percent of American males who admit that they ever have forced a female into a sexual encounter (Myers, 2008: 100; Laumann et. al., 1994). Social scientists are not the only ones to notice these differences in perception. Sexual fantasies also express this difference in orientation. Humorist Dave Barry makes the following observation:

> Women can be fascinated by a four-hour movie with subtitles wherein the entire plot consists of a man and a woman yearning to have, but never actually having a relationship... Men HATE that. Men can take maybe 45 seconds of yearning, and they want everybody to get naked. Followed by a car chase. (Barry, 1995, as cited in Myers, 2008: 170).

The School

The school is a major context of socialization, particularly of secondary socialization, which occurs after the first few years of life. In this section, we first briefly examine the school as an arena in which empathy may be learned, and then we examine "the jigsaw classroom" as a context for learning in a multi-cultural context.

Sociologists use the term "taking the role of the other" to refer to taking the point of view, attitudes, or behaviors of another person as one's own by imaginatively constructing oneself *as* the other person, in order to be able to anticipate that person's real or likely behavior. People who are not sociologists tend to use the term "empathy" to refer to what sociologists term role playing or taking the role of the other.

Norma Feshbach (Aronson, Wilson, and Akert, 2005: 423) has pioneered the teaching of empathy in elementary schools. In a thirty-hour program for elementary school children in Los Angeles, youngsters grapple with role-playing exercises that expand their abilities to putting themselves into the position of the other, one significant other at a time. For instance, they might be asked to think about answers to the question, "What birthday present would make each member of your family happiest?" The children also listen to a story and then re-tell the story from the point of view of each of its characters. They also play the role of each of the characters in the story. At the end of the program, the children had increased empathy, higher self esteem, and they displayed less aggressiveness than students who had not participated in the program. In another study, students who had been trained in role playing were less likely to display aggressive behavior and more likely to display generosity than students who had not received the training (Richardson, Hammock, Smith, and Gardner, 1994).

THE JIGSAW CLASSROOM

Jigsaw is the name for a classroom setting designed to increase cooperation across racial and ethnic groups by placing pupils in multi-ethnic, multi-racial small groups and making each child dependent on the other children in the group to learn and master the course material (Aronson, Wilson, and Akert, 2005: 469-472; Aronson, 1990; Aronson and Gonzales, 1988; Aronson and Platnoe, 1997). Elliot Aronson and colleagues at University of Texas designed the jigsaw classroom to enhance cooperation among Anglo, Mexican-American, and African-American pupils after racial and ethnic violence broke out in the Austin, Texas, public schools in 1971.

The jigsaw classroom works in the following way: Pupils are placed in multi-ethnic, multi-racial six-person learning groups. The day's lesson is divided into six parts, and each student is given one of those parts. For example, if students are to learn the life of Cesar Chavez, his biography is divided into six parts. Each of the students has possession of a unique and vital part of the information. The information, like the pieces of a jigsaw puzzle, must be put together before anyone in the group can view the entire picture. Each pupil needs to learn her or his part and teach it to the other members of the group who do not have any other access to that material. Therefore, if Pat wants to do well on the exam about the life of Cesar Chavez, he needs to pay attention to Sean (who is reciting on Cesar's childhood), to Maria (who is reciting about the formation of the Farm Workers Union), and so on.

Through the jigsaw-classroom process, children learn to pay more attention to each other, to encourage each other, to show respect for each other. The formal data from the jigsaw-classroom experiments are clear and striking: Compared with students in traditional classrooms, students in jigsaw groups not only perform better on objective exams than children in traditional classrooms, they show a greater liking for school and for their classmates, a decrease in racial and ethnic prejudice, and an increase in liking for their groupmates, both within and across ethnic groups. Moreover, when children are observed playing at recess in the school yard, the jigsaw-group students are far more likely to engage in intergroup mingling and intergroup play than are children on the school grounds of schools that use more traditional classroom techniques.

The jigsaw approach was first devised and tested in 1971 in the recently desegregated schools of Austin, Texas. Since then, the striking results that Aronson and his colleagues obtained have been successfully replicated in hundreds of classrooms in all regions of the United States and abroad (e.g., Sharan, 1980; Slavin and Cooper, 1999; Juergen-Lohmann, Borsch, and Green, 2001).

Peers

A **peer group** is a primary group whose members are of roughly equal status. The peer group is an important context or agent of secondary socialization of children, especially during adolescence (e.g., Crosnoe and Needham, 2004; Crosnoe, 2002; Crosnoe, Erikson, and Dornbusch, 2002; Johnson, Crosnoe, and Elder, Jr., 2001; Gecas, 1992). Children's peer groups in the United States and England tend to be gender homogeneous and racially/ethnically homogeneous (Crosnoe, 2000; Hartup and Stevens, 1997; Boulton, 1996; Thorne, 1993). These characteristics are observable as early as during the preschool stage of development, and they tend to persist until early adolescence (Finkelstein and Haskins, 1983).

Where young people live and attend school influences peer group formation through two important mechanisms, ***propinquity*** and ***homophily***. Propinquity refers to closeness in physical space. Young people are more likely to befriend those whom they most often see. Homophily refers to liking those who are similar to oneself. Children and adolescents seem to be attracted to those who share their own characteristics, behaviors, and attitudes (Baron and Byrne, 1994). The processes of propinquity and homophily tend to intersect because of the racial segregation characteristic of neighborhoods and schools in the United States (Zhou, 1997). Thus, friendships are far from random; instead, they tend to be socially structured. Integrated neighborhoods, collaborative classrooms, and athletics tend to promote interracial friendships by increasing interaction and opportunities for teamwork among status equals (Aronson and Patnoe, 1997; Schofield, 1993; DuBois and Hirsch, 1990).

Gender is an important organizing principle in peer relations. From a very early age, peer relations tend to be gender homogeneous. That is, very young children tend to segregate activities by gender and to punish attempts at cross-gender activity (Maccoby, 1998). *Can you recall instances from your own life of being negatively sanctioned by peers for associating with cross-gendered persons? Please tell us about it.*

Gender also influences the nature of peer relations (Colarossi, 2001; Crosnoe, 2000; Dornbusch, 1989; Hinde, 1984). Girls' peer groups tend to be smaller and more exclusive than those of boys. Within groups, females give priority to closeness and disclosure, while males typically emphasize shared activities and status (Colarossi, 2001; Frey and Rothlisberger, 1996; Caldwell and Peplau, 1982). Partly due to these differences, girls view their friendships as more intense than do boys (Kuttler, La Greca, and Prinstein, 1999). Specifically, girls mention intimate sharing of thoughts, feelings, and problems and engaging in mutual support more often than boys (Berndt, 1982). Boys are more likely than girls to share *activities* and interests in their friendships. Males also are more likely to spend time with *groups* of males, while females are more likely to interact with a single other female. Additionally, girls' friendship groups to be more exclusive than those of boys, in that girls seem less willing to include a non-friend in an ongoing conversation than boys; and if girls have a stable, reciprocal friendship, they are less willing to make new friends than are boys (Colarossi, 2001).

The Media

Sociologists use the term **mass media** to refer to the organized transmission of a message to a vast audience. Examples of mass media include smart phones, cell phones, iPods, Kindle, the internet, television (TV) programming, advertising and commercials, video games, magazines, websites, songs, newspapers, books, movies, and music. Mass media are an important context or agent of socialization. This is illustrated, for instance, by the fact that people aged 8-to-18-years old in the United States spend 7 ½ hours a day, seven days a week, with media. This is more time than they spend in any other activity, except maybe sleeping (Rideout, Foehr, and Roberts, 2011: 1).

In this section we first review salient patterns of media consumption among 8-to-18-year-olds in the United States. Then we examine songs with violent lyrics before turning our attention to violence on television.

Young media consumers frequently use multiple media simultaneously, which is termed ***media multitasking***. A Kaiser Family Foundation Study finds that more than a quarter of the time (29%) young people use media, they use two or more media concurrently (Rideout, Foehr, and Roberts, 2011). For instance, while watching TV, they flip through a magazine, or listen to music and surf the web at the same. Multi-tasking is widespread. A little over half (58%) of 7th-12th graders say they multitask "most" of the time. Nearly one in three (31%) 8-to-18-year-olds say that "most" of the time they are doing homework they are also using one medium or another—watching TV, texting, listening to music, and so forth (Rideout, Foehr, and Roberts, 2011: 34). Girls in 7th -12th grades are more likely to multitask than similarly aged boys. While 17 percent of girls are high multitaskers, the comparable figure for boys is 11 percent; while 20 percent of boys are low multitaskers, the comparable figure for girls is 13 percent (Rideout, Foehr, and Roberts, 2011: 33). Youth who live in a highly media-saturated home environment are more likely to be media multitaskers. For example, those with a TV or computer in their bedroom, who own a cell phone, or have wireless internet access are more likely to measure as high in media multitasking (Rideout, Foehr, and Roberts, 2011: 33).

As with most behaviors, the amount of time youth spend with media, including watching television, texting, and so forth, varies robustly by age, sex, social class, and race or ethnicity (e.g., Rideout, Foehr, and Roberts, 2010). The amount of media young people consume in the United States varies substantially by age, with those in the 11-to-14-year-old and 15-to-18 year-old groups exposed to the most media, up to nearly 12 hours (11:53) in a typical day, which is about 3½ and 4 hours more than for 8-to-10-year olds (Rideout, Foehr, and Roberts, 2010: 11). Boys are exposed to almost an hour more of media each day than girls (11:12 v 10:17), with most of the difference coming from console video games (0:56 vs 0:14) (Rideout, Foehr, and Roberts, 2010: 11). The other large demographic difference in media exposure is that between White youth and Black or Hispanic youth. These latter two groups consume nearly 4½ hours more media per day than do white youth, about which we will have more to say shortly.

In the United States, texting is the dominant mode of communication between those with whom they communicate (Lenhart, 2012: 2). Seventy-five percent of U.S. teens text, and sixty-three percent of teens say they exchange text messages *every day* with people in their lives, which far surpasses the frequency with which teens say they engage in other forms of daily communication, *including face-to-face socializing* outside of school (Lenhart, 2012). Those teens who text estimate that they send an average of 118 text messages and spend about an hour and a half (1:35) engaged in sending and receiving texts in a typical day (Rideout, Foehr, and Roberts, 2010: 18). Among black teens, the amount of time spent sending and receiving texts every day is over two hours (2:03) and among Hispanic teens it is over an hour and a half (1:42) (Rideout, Forhr, and Roberts, 2010: 18). Girls are the more enthusiastic gender when it comes to texting, with a median of 100 texts a day in 2011, compared with 50 for boys of the same age (Lenhart, 2012: 11). The daily average number of texts is moving upward, with Hispanic teens and African-American teens leading the way. (See Table 5.1, Number of Text Messages Sent/Received Per Day by U.S. Teens, by Race and Ethnicity).

TABLE 5.1 NUMBER OF TEXT MESSAGES SENT/RECEIVED PER DAY BY U.S. TEENS, BY RACE AND ETHNICITY AMONG TEENS WHO TEXT

Race and Ethnicity	Mean	Median
White, Non-Hispanic	149	50
Black, Non-Hispanic	186	80
Hispanic	202	100

Adapted from Amanda Lenhart, *Teens, Smartphones & Texting* (Washington, D.C.: Pew Research Center's Internet & American Life Project, March 19, 2012), p.12.

Blacks and Hispanic youth also lead the way in the amount of time youth spend with media each day. Black youth and Hispanic youth consume an average of 13 hours worth of media content *per day* (12:59 for Blacks and 13:00 for Hispanics), compared with about 8 and a half hours for White youth, a difference of about four and a half hours per day. In recent years this gap in media usage between White and Black youth has *doubled* and between White and Hispanic youth it has *quadrupled* (Bennett, 2012). These racial and ethnic differences are robust and remain strong even after researchers control for social class and family structure (Rideout, Lauricella, and Wartella, 2011: 1).

The biggest difference in media consumption among American youth is in the amount of time spent with TV. Black youth spend nearly six hours daily watching TV and Hispanics spend 5:21, compared to 3:36 for Whites (Rideout, Foehr, and Roberts, 2010: 37). In other words, Black youth spend an average of 2 hours 18 minutes more per day with TV than do white youth. Other substantial differences emerge for time spent with music and video games (Rideout, Foehr, and Roberts, 2012:39). Black (3:00) and Hispanic (3:08) youth spend about an hour more per day with music than do white youth (1:56). Black and Hispanic youth also spend more time each day than white youth playing video games. Black (1:25) and Hispanic (1:35) youth spend about an hour and a half each day playing video games, compared to just under an hour (0:56) for white youth (Rideout, Foehr, and Roberts, 2010: 37).

One big difference in the home environments of young people in the United States is that Black and Hispanic youth are much more likely to have TVs, DVD players, and video game consoles in their bedrooms than others in their age group. For example, 86 percent of Black and 77 percent of Hispanic youth have a TV in their bedroom, compared with 64 percent of white youth (Ridebout, Lauricella, and Wartella, 2011:7). In their bedrooms, black youth are also more likely to have DVD/VCR players and more likely to have a videogame system than their white counterparts (Bennett, 2012). In their bedrooms, black youths (20%) are more than twice as likely as white youths (8%) to have TiVo/DVR access; black youths are also more likely to have internet access in their bedrooms (33%) than white youths. Black youths (42%) and Hispanic youths (28%) are also more likely than white youths (17%) to have cable and premium channels in their bedrooms (Bennett, 2012; Rideout, Lauricella, and Wartella, 2011: 2). Analysis of data from children age six and younger shows that these differences begin to emerge at a young age. For example, in this age group over half of Black children (54%) have a TV in their bedroom compared with 27% of White and 39% of Hispanic children (Bennett, 2012; Rideout, Lauricella, and Wartella, 2011: 7).

Another difference is that Black youth (54%) are more likely than White youth (43%) to live in homes where the TV is left on in the background most of the time, even if no one is watching. Also, both Black and

Hispanic youth are more likely to report that the TV is usually on during meals (78% for Blacks, 67% for Hispanics, and 58% for Whites) (Rideout, Lauricella, and Wartella, 2011: 7).

Young people who grow up in homes where the TV is usually on during meals; where the TV is left on as background, whether anyone is watching or not; and where they have TVs in their bedrooms, spend a great deal more time watching live TV than their peers. See Table 5.2.

TABLE 5.2 TIME SPENT WATCHING TV AMONG 8-TO-18-YEAR-OLDS IN THE UNITED STATES, BY BACKGROUND TV CONDITIONS IN THE HOME

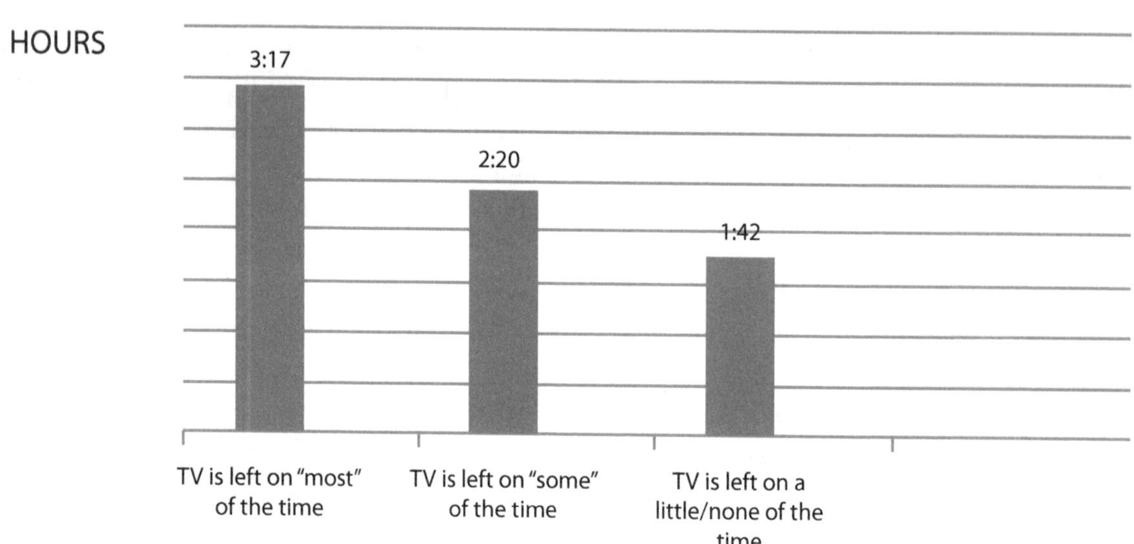

Adapted from Victoria J. Rideout, Ulla G. Foehr, and Donald F. Roberts, *Generation M²–Media in the Lives of 8-to-18-Year-Olds* A Kaiser Family Foundation Study (Menlo Park, CA: The Henry J. Kaiser Family Foundation, January 2010), p. 35.

Parents make numerous decisions about their children's media environment—e.g., how many TVs, video games, and computers to buy for the home; whether there are TVs and video game players in their children's bedrooms; whether the TV is left on as background when no one is watching; whether the TV is on during meals; whether there are limits set on the amount of time or content of the media their children use. All of these decisions, put together, create a media environment for young people. The media environment that young people grow up in is strongly related to the amount of time they spend with media (Rideout, Foehr, and Roberts, 2010: 35).

Sixteen percent of young people grow up in homes where the parents set no rules of any kind about either content or amount of time spent with media (Rideout, Foehr, and Roberts, 2010: 35). At the other end of the continuum, about one youth in four (26 percent) says that their parents have media rules for them and that their parents generally enforce those rules most of the time. In between are the plurality of youth, the 39 percent who report that their parents have some rules regarding their media use but that those rules are not always enforced (Rideout, Foehr, and Roberts, 2010: 35). In general parents are more likely to put limits

on the types of content their children can consume than on the amount of time they can spend consuming it. Thus, while 46 percent of young people say their parents have rules about what they can watch on TV, only 28 percent say they have rules about how long they can watch it (Rideout, Foehr, and Roberts, 2010:35).

What difference does it make whether parents make and enforce rules about their children's media use? When parents set limits, youth spend less of their time with media. Children whose parents *don't* leave the TV on during meals or in the background when no one is watching or *do* impose media-related rules spend substantially less time with media than do children with more media-lenient parents (Rideout, Foehr, and Roberts, 2010: 4). Those whose parents set rules about their media use consume an average of nearly 3 hours (2: 52) less media content *per day* than those who say their parents don't have rules (Rideout, Foehr, and Roberts, 2010: 36).

There is a wealth of research indicating that media are a powerful influence on young people's development. Research indicates that there is a negative relationship between media use and health outcomes--including violence, sexual activity, tobacco use, and obesity (Rideout, Lauricella, and Wartella, 2011: 1). There also is an inverse relationship between social class and media consumption, with persons of lower social class consuming more than their higher social-class counterparts (Rideout, Foehr, and Roberts, 2010; Lenhart, 2012; Bennett, 2012). This inverse relationship holds, no matter what the method used for measuring social class. Likewise, there is an inverse relationship among school-aged youth between the number of hours spent with media and grades in school. Youth who spend a lot of time with media earn lower grades in school than their lighter-media-use counterparts. Heavy media users also are more likely to say they get into trouble a lot, are often unhappy or sad, and are often bored (Rideout, Foehr, and Roberts, 2010: 4). These robust relationships between media exposure and grades, between media exposure and personal contentment, remain even after researchers control for other possibly relevant factors such as age, sex, social class, and single vs two-parent households.

SONGS WITH VIOLENT LYRICS

Several experimental studies have investigated the effects of aggressive music videos and the effects of listening to violent songs with no videos. For example, Waite, Hillbrand, and Foster (1992) report a significant decrease in aggressive behavior on a forensic inpatient ward after removal of Music Television (MTV). Johnson, Jackson, and Gatto (1995) report that males randomly assigned to view violent rap music videos became more accepting of the use of violence as a legitimate means of resolving interpersonal problems. And Anderson, Carnagey, and Eubanks (2003) demonstrate that male and female college students who heard violent songs felt more hostile than those who heard similar but nonviolent songs.

Studies indicate that African American youth (2:52) and Hispanic youth (2:42) age 8-18 spend about an hour more a day with music than white youth (1:17) (Rideout, Foehr, and Ropberts, 2010: 5). As a musical form Hip Hop has permeated deep into the African American culture. According to Cynthia E. Griffin (2012), the majority of its content is skeptical of traditional school achievement, distrustful of the traditional educative process, and resistant to a masculine identity based on school achievement. For Black youth in the United States, at every grade-point average, being into Hip Hop is associated with higher self-esteem, but it is also associated with more problem behaviors in school (Griffin, 2012).

TELEVISION VIOLENCE

Dozens of studies have documented that 58 percent of television programs contain violence (Seppa, 1997; Cantor et. al., 2001); and, of those, more than 75 percent contain not even a jot of remorse, criticism, or penalty for that violence. It has been estimated that by the time the average child in the United States has completed *elementary* school, she or he has witnessed more than 8,000 murders and more than 100,000 other acts of violence on television (Eron, 2001).

A large body of scientific research spanning more than four decades has endeavored to ascertain what children learn from viewing violence on television (e.g., Anderson, Carnagey and Eubanks, 2003; Bushman and Anderson, 2001; Anderson and Bushmman, 2002). A number of long-term studies indicates that the more violence individuals watch on TV as children, the more violence they exhibit as teenagers and as young adults (Eron, 1982, 1987; Eron, Huesmann, Lefkowitz, and Walder, 1996). The thrust of experimental research also demonstrates that watching violence on television increases the frequency of aggressive behavior in children (e.g., Cantor et. al., 2001; Geen, 1998, 1994; Huesmann and Miller, 1994). For example, in an early experiment on this by Liebert and Baron (1972), the experimental group of children viewed a violent police drama, while the control group watched an exciting but nonviolent sporting event on television for the same length of time. Then, each child played in another room with a group of other children. Those who had watched the violent television programming showed far more aggression against their playmates than those who had watched the sporting event.

RACIAL AND ETHNIC SOCIALIZATION

In a study of nine to ten year olds attending a public school in a large city in England, Michael J. Boulton observed British Asian and British white boys and girls on the playground during recess. He wanted to discover their spontaneous peer preferences. He found that Asian males, Asian females, white males, and white females each exhibited a highly significant tendency to play with own-gender and own-race/ethnicity peers more than with any other type of peer (Boulton, 1996; Boulton and Smith, 1993). This preference for own-race over other-race peers is evident in both observational (e.g., Urberg and Kaplan, 1989) and verbal self-report data (Boulton and Smith, 1996), and it emerges during the preschool stage of development and persists until early adolescence (Finkelstein and Haskins, 1983).

Researchers have discovered that own race and other race awareness and ethnic and racial attitudes and values are apparent in very young children (Marger, 1994). On the basis of experimental evidence, Lawrence Hirschfeld (1996) proposes that young children do *not* form beliefs about race from simple observation of surface cues (color of skin, hair texture). Instead, we seem to pick up the idea of race from our *discursive environment*--from hearing people talk (Hirschfeld, 1996: 193). Young children "initially do not see race; they hear it" (Hirschfeld, 1996: 195). This position is consistent with other research. Branch and Newcomb find that parents are an important source of influence regarding racial attitudes among children below eight years of age (1986).

In the first study examining the influence of racial socialization on the development of very young children, Margaret O'Brien Caughy and her colleagues (2002) conducted home visits with 200 African American families with children between 3 and 4.5 years of age in Baltimore, Maryland. They interviewed primary caregivers and their children, and administered surveys to measure cognitive and behavioral skills, social development, and racial socialization. The survey measured several components of racial socialization, including racial pride, preparation for racial bias, and the extent to which parents influenced their children to mistrust other ethnicities, and spirituality. The researchers also measured racial socialization in the home by noting the presence of items such as Afro-centric toys, fabrics, and prints.

The researchers found that racial socialization is a major component of parenting. Some types of socialization are more popular than others. Nearly 90 percent of parents conveyed racial or cultural pride messages, and sixty-four percent reported promoting mistrust of other ethnicities. The child study participants were equally likely to get racial socialization messages whether their parents were rich or poor, well educated or not, or whether the children were male or female. The researchers also found that while most of the families they interviewed had Afro-centric items in their homes, the wealthier families had more of them, including Afro-centric toys, books, magazines, and music. Children from homes rich in African American culture had greater factual knowledge and better problem-solving skills, a finding that held true even when the researchers took family income into account. Racial pride was associated with fewer behavioral problems.

TABLE 5.3 AVERAGE ACT COMPOSITE TEST SCORE, UNITED STATES, 2012, BY RACE AND ETHNICITY

Race/Ethnicity	Average ACT Composite Test Score
Asian	23.6
White	22.4
Hispanic	18.9
American Indian	18.4
African American	17

Adapted from ACT, *The Condition of College & Career Readiness 2012 National* (Iowa City, Iowa: ACT, 2012), p. 18.

Let us now turn our attention to an arena of American life, educational outcomes and their variation by race and ethnicity, that brings together a lot of the processes we have examined in terms of socialization in this chapter—family, school, peers, and media. Please see Table 5.3. This excursion offers us an opportunity to exercise our growing sociological imagination so that we may better perceive the connections between the micro- and macro-levels of human experience.

There are many ways to measure educational outcomes, just one of which is the average composite test score on the ACT. The range of scores on this particular test is 1 – 36. The average composite test scores in 2012 in the United States for Asian students was 23.6; for Whites, 22.4; for Hispanic students, 18.4, and for African American students, 17 (ACT, 2012). These are large, significant differences (ACT, 2013) between Asian and Whites on the one hand and African Americans and Hispanics on the other. By the time Latino and African-American students graduate from high school, their math and reading skills are roughly the same level as 13-year-old white students (Nevarez, 2012; Haycock, 2011). Researchers find these educational achievement gaps between white students on the one hand and black and Hispanic students on the other on virtually *every* measure of educational outcomes, including standardized test scores, grade point average, the drop-out rate, and the extent to which students are left back a grade (e.g., Jeynes, 2011: 27). These differences also reveal themselves in the extent to which students say they understand the assigned readings in school. When Harvard economist Ronald F. Ferguson surveyed middle- and high-school students in fifteen affluent school districts, he found that *half* of all black students report that they don't understand the assigned readings "very well" most of the time, which is almost double the figure (27 percent) reported by their white peers (Ferguson, 2002).

Professor John U. Ogbu of University of California at Berkeley endeavors to understand these diverse outcomes (e.g., Ogbu, 2008; Ogbu, 2003; Gibson and Ogbu, 1991). Ogbu himself grew up in a remote village with no roads and no running water in rural Nigeria. His parents could not read or write. His father had three wives and seventeen children with those women (Goldsmith, 2003).

Professor Ogbu went to school in Nigeria and to university in the United States, earning his B.A., M.A., and Ph. D. from University of California, Berkeley. Ogbu spent decades researching how members of different ethnic groups perform academically (e.g., Ogbu, 2008; Ogbu, 2003; Gibson and Ogbu, 1991; Fordham and Ogbu, 1986). He studied student coping strategies in inner-city schools of Washington, D.C. Ogbu studied African Americans and Latinos in Oakland and Stockton, California, and he examined how they compare to racial and ethnic minorities in other countries—India, Japan, New Zealand, Britain, and Israel. His research often focused on why some groups are more successful than others.

With this breadth of background, he received a formal invitation from the school district in the affluent Cleveland, Ohio, suburb of Shaker Heights. Affluent black parents there wanted an explanation. These black parents were doctors, lawyers, judges, and insurance brokers. Many of them had moved to this upscale suburb precisely because of its stellar public school district. Yet most of their children were performing poorly there, lagging far behind their white counterparts on every measure of academic success—grade-point average, standardized test scores, and enrollment in advanced-placement courses. For example, on average, black students earned a 1.9 grade point average while their white counterparts held down a 3.45 grade point average (Goldsmith, 2003: 1). The other indicators were similarly dismal.

Ogbu went to Shaker Heights and proposed a research project to find out just what was happening. The school district financed the study and the parents offered him unlimited access both to their children and their homes. The Professor and his research assistant moved to Shaker Heights for nine months, where they observed 110 different classes, from kindergarten all the way through high school. They examined tests and test scores. The research team conducted exhaustive interviews with school personnel, black parents, and students.

Their study reached an unexpected and perhaps unwelcome conclusion. It wasn't socio-economics, school funding, or racism that accounted for the students' lagging academic performance. It was the students' own attitudes as well as those of their parents that drove the train of academic disengagement. By and large, educational researchers define parents as highly involved in their children's education if they communicate with their children about their school work requirements and about what took place during the school day, are almost always available to help their children with their school work, are aware of class assignments and activities, and communicate their academic expectations to their children (Jeynes, 2011: 86). Researchers find that there is a positive relationship between the level of parental involvement and the educational outcomes of their children (Jeynes, 2011).

Ogbu observes that the average black student in Shaker Heights put little effort into his or her schoolwork. Ogbu contends that that orientation was part of a peer culture that looked down on high academic performance as "acting white." As for the black parents, they, too, were academically disengaged, defining their own role as fulfilled by moving to Shaker Heights and paying the higher taxes that funded their children's education so that their children could graduate from Shaker. In the black parental definition of the situation, the school system should take care of the rest. The result? The black parents themselves did

not supervise their children that much, didn't make sure their children did their homework, did not show up at school events, and failed to motivate their children to engage in school work. In fact, the black middle-class parents of Shaker Heights spent no more time on homework or tracking their children's schooling than poor white parents" (Lee, 2002).

In the language of educational researchers, the black middle-class parents of Shaker Heights manifested low levels of parental involvement in the education of their children. Ogbu concludes that this, too, is a cultural norm. The black middle-class parents, but not the white middle-class parents, thought or believed "that it was the responsibility of teachers and the schools to make their children learn and perform successfully" (Goldsmith, 2003: 5). Similarly, black middle-class parents were less likely than their white counterparts to stock children's books in the home. The average white kindergartner has ninety-three children's books, the average black child less than half as many These differences persist through the 12th grade (Thernstrom and Thernstrom, 2003: 135, 146).

Laurence Steinberg has studied 20,000 students in nine affluent public high schools in California and Wisconsin (1996: 91, 161). Intriguing group differences emerge from a question asking students about the "trouble threshold" in their families: What is the lowest grade they could earn without their parents getting angry? Black and Hispanic youth tended to get into trouble only when their grades fell below C-. For whites, it was a full grade higher. By contrast, Asian students felt that receiving anything below A- would generate parental wrath (Steinberg, 1996: 91, 161).

It is also worth noting that Asian students cut classes less often and report higher levels of concentration and attention during class (Steinberg, 1996: 87). Additionally, Asian students spend only about half as much time hanging out with their peers (Steinberg: 87, 180-181), are far more likely to enroll in the most academically demanding courses, and from the fourth through twelfth grades spend twice as much time doing homework each day compared to their non-Asian peers (Thernstrom and Thernstrom, 2003: 93-94).

When Ogbu asked black students what it took to do well in the Shaker district schools, the students knew that they had to work hard to succeed. That knowledge alone, however, did not translate into their putting in the needed work. Instead, their approach was characterized by what Ogbu terms "low effort syndrome." For instance, Ogbu found near consensus among black students of almost every grade level that they and their peers did not work hard in school. Actually, the effort these students put into their schoolwork *decreased* markedly from elementary school to high school. Students gave many reasons for their academic disengagement. Some say they simply didn't want to do the work. Others told Ogbu that "it was not cool be successful" (Goldsmith, 2003: 4). Almost all of the students admitted they had other priorities. They put other pursuits—such as TV, work, playing sports, or talking on the phone-- ahead of academic ones. That system of personal priorities is also corroborated by the research of Stephan Thernstrom, who is the Winthrop Research Professor of History at Harvard and Abigail Thernstrom, who is Vice Chair of the U.S. Commission on Civil Rights, (Thernstrom and Thernstrom, 2003). The Thernstroms' research identifies "the special role of television in the life of black children" and the lack of parental involvement in education as keys to understanding why black children lag behind their white contemporaries in almost any measure of academic performance. With regard to the special role of television in the lives of black children, nearly half of African American fourth graders, but less than twenty percent of White fourth graders spend *five hours* or more staring at a TV screen on a typical school day (Thernstrom and Thernstrom, 2003: 142.

Why are African American youth so heavily time-invested in television? On the basis of a detailed analysis of the Shaker Heights' data, Harvard economist Ronald R. Ferguson (2001) reports that African American youth regard watching television as their "social homework" and felt left out of the conversation if they had not seen all of the programs that all their chums had viewed the night before. One youth told him, "you have to watch television to get your material to be funny" (as cited in Thernstrom and Therndstrom, 2003: 144). Television was thus a crucial unifying element in the black adolescent peer culture of Shaker Heights, a key source of its group cohesion (Thernstrom and Thernstrom, 2003: 144).

Indeed, Ogbu characterizes the black adolescent peer culture in Shaker Heights as an "oppositional peer culture" that rejects certain behaviors as "acting white." These behaviors include making good grades, speaking Standard English, being overly involved in class, and enrolling in honors or advanced-placement courses. Ogbu concludes that the adolescent African-American peer culture of Shaker Heights pressures black students *not* to do well in school. By embracing that peer culture, black students also embrace orientations to schoolwork that do not serve them well if their goal is academic success. The oppositional peer culture sees no connection between good grades and finding a job.

Other research extends the concept of oppositional peer culture to well beyond the age reach of adolescence so that it embraces the parental generation as well. Thus, John McWhorter is the author of *Losing the Race: Self-Sabotage in Black America* (2000) and *Winning the Race: Beyond the Crisis in Black America* (2006). McWhorter observes that "(t)here is an element of black identity today that sees doing well in school as being outside the core of black identity" (as quoted in Goldsmith, 2003: 7). One consequence is ambivalence on the part of many black middle-class parents to confront the "acting white syndrome" because those parents, too, harbor ambivalence about mainstream culture. This ambivalence impedes them from effectively encouraging their children to pursue academic excellence.

Ogbu and others (e.g., Blauner, 1969, 1972) identify a core distinction, which Ogbu contends is central to understanding why some minority groups embrace an oppositional peer culture while others do not. It is the idea of voluntary versus involuntary minority. A voluntary immigrant is someone who comes to this country by her or his own choosing. An involuntary immigrant is someone who comes to this country against her or his own will. Migration is one of the ways that minority groups are formed. Sociologists use the term ***minority group*** to refer to any "recognizable ethnic, racial, religious, or gender group that has experienced an ingrained pattern of prejudice and discrimination" (Donovan and Gonzales, 2010: 291). People who voluntarily immigrate to the United States tend to have different orientations to the world and tend to do better in terms of educational and occupational attainment than the involuntary immigrants (e.g., Blauner, 1969, 1972; Gonzales, 2003). Obbu calls Asian Americans "voluntary minorities" because they came to this country by their own choosing. Ogbu calls Chicanos (Mexican Americans), blacks, and Native Americans (American Indians) "involuntary minorities" because they joined the United States against their will (Goldsmith, 2003:6), either by being conquered or enslaved. Ogbu sees the distinction between voluntary and involuntary minority as critical for long-term success in or out of school. These differing histories of inclusion into the fabric of the United States—voluntary or involuntary-- have the unintended consequence (latent function) of creating subcultures whose cultural content also differs markedly.

Whereas some blacks say that Standard English is being imposed on them, that tends *not* to be the case among the Chinese, or among blacks from the Caribbean, or among the Ibo from Nigeria. These latter groups are all voluntary immigrants to this country. If you come voluntarily to the United States, there is a strong tendency positively to value education as a means of bettering your life chances and to know that you need to master Standard English, which is the language of the global economy, or you won't do well either in school or in the workforce. Steinberg made a fascinating discovery in his educational research (1996: 91-94). He finds that in the United States, Asian parents and their children do not think of academic success as due to any sort of innate ability. Likewise, they do not see teacher biases as playing a role in their grades.

Instead, they embrace the position that their academic performance depends almost entirely on their own level of effort, on how hard they worked at it. Sociologists would term this an **internal locus of control**. People with an internal locus of control views themselves as masters of their own fate. If we were to think of ourselves as a vehicle, say, a car, then the issue of "locus of control" concerns *where* you perceive yourself as being situated *in* the vehicle. If you perceive yourself as being behind the steering wheel, then you have an internal locus of control. You perceive yourself as having some control over where the vehicle goes and at what speed. If, however, you view yourself as baggage in the trunk of the car, you would be viewing yourself as having an **external locus of control**. People with an external locus of control view themselves as lacking in free will or agency and view their own actions as having little impact on their lives. Asian voluntary migrants to this country by and large embrace an internal locus of control.

By contrast, since at least the late 1960s, a differing mindset has grown and flourished among involuntary minorities, so that now some Native Americans and blacks say, "Whites took away our heritage and our language and forced us to learn their heritage and their language. *They* caused the problem." Some observe that this idea is part of an ideology of abdication of personal responsibility and forms part of the nucleus of a subculture of victimhood and of entitlement that is highly ambivalent about mainstream culture in the United States (e.g., Steele: 2006, 2008, 1991; Thernstrom and Thernstrom, 1999).

SUGGESTED READINGS

Bhutto, Benazir, *Reconciliation: Islam, Democracy, and the West* (New York: HarperCollins, 2008).

D'Souza, Dinesh, *The Roots of Obama's Rage* (Washington, D.C.: Regnery Publishing, Inc., 2010).

Hirsi Ali, Ayaan, *Infidel* (New York: Free Press, 2007).

Horowitz, David, *Radical Son; A Generational Odyssey* (New York: Touchstone, 1997).

Isaacson, Walter, *Steve Jobs* (New York: Simon & Schuster, 2011).

Kallen, Stuart A., *We Are Not Beasts of Burden: Cesar Chavez and the Delano Grape Strike, California, 1965-1970* (Minneapolis, MN: Twenty-First Century Press, 2011).

Lipsky, David, *Absolutely American: Four Years at West Point* (New York: Vintage Books, 2003).

Liu, Eric, *The Accidental Asian: Notes of a Native Speaker* (New York: Vintage Books, 1998).

Marable, Manning, *Malcolm X: A Life of Reinvention* (New York: Viking, 2011).

Noor, Queen, consort of Hussein, King of Jordan, 1951-, *Leap of Faith: Memoirs of an Unexpected Life* (New York: Miramax Books, 2003).

Pinker, Steven, *The Blank Slate: The Modern Denial of Human Nature* (New York: Viking, 2002).

Radosh, Ronald, *Commies: A Journey Through the Old Left, the New Left, and the Leftover Left* (San Francisco, CA: Encounter, 2001).

Rice, Condoleezza, *Extraordinary, Ordinary People: A Memoir of Family* (New York: Crown Publishers, 2010).

Roker, Al, *Never Goin' Back: Winning the Weight-loss Battle for Good* (New York: Penguin, 2012).

Steele, Shelby, *The Content of Our Character* (New York: Harper Perennial, 1991).

Stiles, T.J., *The First Tycoon: The Epic Life of Cornelius Vanderbilt* (New York: Alfred A. Knopf, 2009).

BIBLIOGRAPHY

Abbey, Antonia, "Acquaintance Rape and Alcohol Consumption on College Campuses: How Are They Linked?" *Journal of American College Health*, Vol. 39, 1991a: 165-169.

Abbey, Antonia, "Misperceptions as an Antecedent of Acquaintance Rape: A Consequence of Ambiguity in Communication Between Women and Men," in A. Parrot (Ed.), *Acquaintance Rape* (New York: John Wiley, 1991b).

Abbey, Antonia, "Misperceptions of Friendly Behavior as Sexual Interest: A Survey of Naturally Occurring Incidents," *Psychology of Women Quarterly*, Vol. 11, 1987: 173-194.

Abbey, Antonia; McAuslan, P.; and Ross, L.T., "Sexual Assault Perpetration by College Men: The Role of Alcohol, Misperception of Sexual Intent, and Sexual Beliefs and Experiences," *Journal of Social and Clinical Psychology*, Vol. 17, 1998: 167-195.

ACT, *Scores. National Ranks for Test Scores and Composite Score* As of January 28, 2013, available online at www.actstudent.org/scores/norms1.html

ACT, *The Condition of College & Career Readiness 2012 National* (Iowa City, Iowa: ACT, 2012).

Adams, Susan; Kuebli, Janet; Boyle, Patricia A., and Fivush, Robyn, "Gender Differences in Parent-Child Conversations about Past Events: A Longitudinal Investigation," *Sex Roles*, Vol. 33, Nos. 5/6, 1995: 309-323.

Ainsworth, Mary D., "Attachment: Retrospect and Prospect," in C.M. Parkes and J. Stevenson (Eds.), *The Place of Attachment in Human Behavior* (London: Tavistock, 1982).

Ainsworth, Mary, D., "Attachments Beyond Infancy," *American Psychologist*, Vol. 44, 1989: 709-716.

Alwin, D.F., "Historical Changes in Parental Orientations to Children," in N. Mandell (Ed.), *Sociological Studies of Child Development*, Vol. 3, (Greenwich, CT: JAI Press, 1990).

Amato, Paul R. and Alan Booth, *A Generation at Risk: Growing Up in an Era of Family Upheaval* (Cambridge, MA: Harvard University Press, 1997).

Anderson, C.A., and Bushman, B.J., "The Effects of Media Violence on Society," *Science*, Vol. 295, March 29, 2002: 2377-2378.

Anderson, Craig A.; Carnagey, Nicholas L.; and Eubanks, Janie, "Exposure to Violent Media: The Effects of Songs With Violent Lyrics on Aggressive Thoughts and Feelings," *Journal of Personality and Social Psychology*, Vol. 84, No. 5, 2003: 960-971.

Anderson, M.L., *Thinking About Women* Fourth Edition (Boston: Allyn Bacon, 1997).

Argyle, Michael, *The Psychology of Social Class* (London: Routledge, 1994).

Aronson, Elliot, "Applying Social Psychology to Prejudice Reduction and Energy *Conservation,"* Personality and Social Psychology Bulletin, Vol. 16, 1990: 118-132

Aronson, Elliot, and Gonzales, M.H., "Desegregation, Jigsaw, and the Mexican-American Experience," in P. A. Katz and D. Taylor (Eds.), *Towards the Elimination of Racism: Profiles in Controversy* (New York: Plenum, 1988): 310-330.

Aronson, Elliot; Wilson, Timothy; and Akert, Robin M., *Social Psychology* Fifth Edition (Upper Saddle River, NJ: Pearson/Prentice Hall, 2005).

Aronson, Elliott, and Patnoe, S., *Cooperation in the Classroom: The FMethod* (New York: Longman, 1997).

Baron, Robert, and Byrne, Donn, "Interpersonal Attraction: Getting Acquainted, Becoming Friends," in B. Allen and G. Smith (Eds.), *Social Psychology: Understanding Human Interaction* (Boston: Allyn

and Bacon, 1994): 262-303. Baron, Robert, and Byrne, Donn, "Interpersonal Attraction: Getting Acquainted, Becoming Friends," in B. Allen and G. Smith (Eds.), *Social Psychology: Understanding Human Interaction* (Boston: Allyn and Bacon, 1994): 262-303.

Barry, Dave, "Bored Stiff," *Funny Times* (January 1995), page 5, as cited in David Myers, *Social Psychology* ninth edition (Boston: Mc Graw Hill, 2008), page 170.

Baumrind, Diana, "The Influence of Parenting Style on Adolescent Competence and Substance Use," *Journal of Early Adolescence*, Vol. 11, No. 1, 1991: 56-95.

Bennett, John, "Victimology and the Phony 'Digital Divide,'" *American Thinker*, January 3, 2012. As of January 22, 2013, available online at www.americanthinker.com/2012/01/victimology_and_the_phony_digital_divide.html

Berndt, T.J., "The Features and Effects of Friendship in Early Adolescence," *Child Development*, Vol. 53, 1982: 1447-1460.

Berscheid, Ellen, "Interpersonal Attraction," in Gardner Lindzey and Elliott Aronson, *The Handbook of Social Psychology* Third Edition (New York: Random House, 1985).

Beutel, Ann M., and Marini, Margaret Mooney, "Gender and Values," *American Sociological Review*, Vol. 60, (June) 1995: 436-448.

Blauner, Robert, "Internal Colonialism and Ghetto Revolt," *Social Problems*, Vol. 16, 1969: 393-408.

Blauner, Robert, *Racial Oppression in America* (New York: Harper & Row, 1972).

Bloch, M.N., "Young Girls and Boys Play at Home and in the Community: A Cultural-Ecological Framework," in M.N. Block and A.D. Pellegrini (Eds.), *The Ecological Context of children's Play* (Norwood,NJ: Ablex, 1989), 120-154.

Boivin, Michael, and Hymel, Shelley, "Peer Experiences and Social Self-Perceptions: A Sequential Model," *Developmental "Psychology*, Vol. 33, No. 1, 1997: 135-145.

Boulton, Michael J., "Partner Preferences of British and Asian White Girls and Boys on the Middle School Playground," *Journal of Research in Childhood Education*, Vol. 11, No. 1, 1996: 25-34.

Boulton, Michael J., "Partner Preferences of British and Asian White Girls and Boys on the Middle School Playground," *Journal of Research in Childhood Education*, Vol. 11, No. 1, 1996: 25-34.

Boulton, Michael J., and Smith, P.K., "Ethnic, Gender Partner, and Activity Preferences in Mixed Race Schools in the UK: Playground Observations," in C. Hart (Ed.), *Children on Playgrounds: Research Perspectives and Applications* (Albany: New York: State University of New York Press, 1993): 210-237.

Boulton, Michael J., and Smith, P.K., "Liking and Peer Perceptions Among Asian and White British Children," *Journal of Social and Personal Relation*, Vol. 13, 1996: 163-177.

Bowlby, John, *Attachment and Loss* Second Edition (New York: Basic Books, 1982).

Branch, C.W., and Newcomb, "Racial Attitude Development Among Young Black Children as a Function of Parental Attitudes: A Longitudinal and Cross-Sectional Study," *Child Development*, Vol.56, 1986: 712-721

Bridges, J.S., "Pink or Blue: Gender Stereotypic Perceptions of Infants as Conveyed by Birth Congratulations Cards," *Psychology of Women Quarterly*, Vol. 17, 1993: 193-205.

Brody, Leslie R., and Hall, Judith A., "Gender and Emotion," in Michael Lewis and Jeannette Haviland (Eds.), *Handbook of Emotions* (New York: Guilford Press, 1993).

Browning, J., and Dutton, D., "Assessment of Wife Assault with the Conflict Tactics Scale: Using Couple Data to Quantify the Differential Reporting Effect," *Journal of Marriage and the Family*, Vol. 48, 1986: 375-379.

Bushman, B.J., and Anderson, C.A., "Media Violence and the American Public: Scientific Facts Versus Media Misinformation," *American Psychologist*, Vol. 56, 2001: 477-489.

Caldwell, M. A., and Peplau, L.A., "Sex Differences in Same-Sex Friendships," Sex Roles, Vol. 8, 1982: 721-731.

Cann, Arnie, and Vann, Elizabeth D., "Implications of Sex and Gender Differences for Self: Perceived Advantages and Disadvantages of Being the Other Gender," *Sex Roles*, Vol. 33, Nos. 7/8, 1995: 531-541.

Cantor, J., et. al., "Some Hazards of Television Viewing: Fears, Aggression, and Sexual Attitudes," in D. G. Singer and J.L. Singer (Eds.), *Handbook of Children and the Media* (Thousand Oaks, CA: Sage, 2001): 207-307.

Carpenter, C.J.; Houston, A.C.; and Serpa, L., "Children's Use of Time in their Everyday Activities During Middle Childhood," in M.N. Bloch and A.D. Pellegrini (Eds.), *The Ecological Context of Children's Play* (Norwood, NJ: Ablex, 1989).

Caughy, M.; O'Campo, P.; Randolph, S.; and Nickerson, K., "The Influence of Racial Socialization Practices on the Cognitive and Behavioral Competence of African American Pre-Schoolers," *Child Development*, Vol. 73, No. 5, 2002: 1611-1625

Charon, Joel M., *Symbolic Interactionism: An Introduction, An Interpretation, An Integration* Upper Saddle River, NJ: Prentice Hall, 2000).

Clark, R.M., *Family Life and School Achievement: Why Poor Black Children Succeed or Fail* (Chicago, Illinois: University of Chicago Press, 1983).

Colarossi, Lisa G., "Adolescent Gender Differences in Social Support: Structure, Function, and Provider Type," *Social Work Research*, Vol. 25, 2001: 233-241.

Crabb, Peter B., and Bielawski, Dawn, "The Social Representation of Material Culture and Gender in Children's Books," *Sex Roles*, Vol. 30, 1994: 69-79.

Crosnoe, Robert, "Friendships in Childhood and Adolescence: The Life Course and New Directions," *Social Psychology Quarterly*, Vol. 63, No. 4, 2000: 377-391.

Crosnoe, Robert, "High School Curriculum Track and Adolescent Association with Delinquent Friends," *Journal of Adolescent Research*, Vol. 17, 2002: 143-167.

Crosnoe, Robert, and Needham, "Holism, Contextual Variability, and the Study of Friendship in Adolescent Development," *Child Development*, Vol. 75, No. 1 (January) 2004: 264-279.

Crosnoe, Robert; Erikson, Kristan; and Dornbusch, Sanford, "Protective Functions of Family Relationships and School Factors on the Deviant Behavior of Adolescent Boys and Girls: Reducing the Impact of Risky Friendships," *Youth and Society*, Vol. 33, 2002: 515-544.

Curtiss, Susan, *Genie: A Psycholinguistic Study of a Modern-Day "Wild Child"* (New York: Academic Press, 1977).

Davis, Kingsley, "The Sociology of the Parent-Youth Conflict," *American Sociological Review*, Vol. 5, 1940: 523-535.

Davis, Kingsley, *Human Society* (New York: The Macmillan Company, 1948).

Davis, M.H., Franzoi, S.L., and Wellinger, P., "Personality, Social Behavior, and Loneliness," presented at the American Psychological Association Annual Meeting, Los Angeles, CA, (August) 1985.

De Maris, Alfred; Pugh, Meredith D.; and Harman, Erika, "Sex Differences in the Accuracy of Witnesses of Portrayed Dyadic Violence," *Journal of Marriage and the Family*, Vol. 54, (May) 1992: 335-354.

Donovan, Marjorie, and Gonzales, Juan L., Jr., *Sociology: Fundamentals for the Twenty-First Century* Third Edition (Dubuque, Iowa: Kendall/Hunt Publishing Company, 2010).

Dornbusch, "The Sociology of Adolescence," *Annual Review of Sociology*, Vol. 15, 1989: 233-259.

Douvan, E., and Adelson, J., *The Adolescent Experience* (New York: Wiley, 1966).

DuBois, David and Hirsch, Barton, "School and Neighborhood Friendship Patterns of Blacks and Whites in Early Adolescence," *Child Development*, Vol. 61: 1990: 524-536.

Dunn, Judy, "The Beginnings of Moral Understanding: Development in the Second Year," in Jerome Kagan and Sharon Lamb (Eds.), *The Emergence of Morality in Young Children* (Chicago: University of Chicago Press, 1987): 91-112.

Dunn, Judy, *The Beginnings of Social Understanding* (Oxford: Blackwell, 1988).

Eccles, Jacquelynne S., Jacobs, Janise E., and Harold, Rena D., "Gender Role Stereotypes, Expectancy Effects, and Parents' Socialization of Gender Differences," *Journal of Social Issues*, Vol. 46, 1990: 183-201.

Edelson, J.L., and Brygger, M.P., "Gender Differences in Reporting of Battering Incidences," *Family Relations*, Vol. 25, 1986: 377-382.

Edwards, C.P., "Behavioral Sex Differences in Children of Diverse Cultures: The Case of Nurturance to Infants," in M. Pereira and L. Fairbanks (Eds.), *Juveniles: Comparative Sociology* (Oxford: Oxford University Press, 1991).

Elder, Glen; Tri Van Nguyen; and Avshalom Caspi, "Linking Family Hardship to children's Lives," *Child Development*, Vol. 56, 1885: 361-375.

Ellis, Albert, "Techniques of Handling Anger in Marriage," *Journal of Marriage and Family Counseling*, Vol. 2, No. 4 (October), 1976: 305-315.

Ellis, Albert, *How to Live with and without* (New York: Reader's Digest Press, 1977).

Ellis, Albert, *Humanistic Psychotherapy: The Rational-Emotive Approach* (New York: McGraw-Hill, 1973).

Emde, R.N., "Individual Meaning and Increasing Complexity: Contributions of Sigmund Freud and Rene Spitz to Developmental Psychology," *Developmental Psychology*, Vol. 22, No. 3, 1992: 347-359.

Erikson, Erik, *Childhood and Society* (New York: W.W. Norton and Company, Inc., 1963). Originally published in 1950.

Erikson, Erik, *Identity and the Life Cycle* (New York: W.W. Norton and Company, Inc., 1994).

Erikson, M.F., Sroufe, L.A., and Egeland, B., "The Relationship Between Quality of Attachment and Behavior Problems in Preschool in a High Risk Sample," in I. Bretherton and E. Waters (Eds.), *Monographs of the Society for Research in Child Development*, Vol. 50, 1985.

Eron, L.D., "Parent-Child Interaction, Television Violence, and Aggression of Children," *American Psychologist*, Vol. 37, 1982: 197-211.

Eron, L.D., "Seeing Is Believing: How Viewing Violence Alters Attitudes and Aggressive Behavior," in A.C. Bohart and D.J. Stipek (Eds.), *Constructive and Destructive Behavior: Implications for Family, School, and Society* (Washington, D.C.: American Psychological Association, 2001): 49-60.

Eron, L.D., "The Development of Aggressive Behavior from the Perspective of a Developing Behaviorism," *American Psychologist*, Vol. 42, 1987: 425-442.

Eron, L.D., Huesmann, L.R.; Lefkowitz, M.M.; and Walder, L.O., "Does Television Violence Cause Aggression?," in D.F. Greenberg (Ed.), *Criminal Careers* Volume 2 (Aldershot, England: Dartmouth, 1996): 311-321.

Ferguson, Ronald F., "A Diagnostic Analysis of Black-White GPA Disparities in Shaker Heights, Ohio," *Brookings Papers on Education Policy: 2001* (Washington, D.C.: Brookings Institution Press, 2001).

Ferguson, Ronald F., "Responses from Middle School, Junior High, and High School Students in Districts of the Minority Student Achievement Network," Weiner Center for Public Policy, John F. Kennedy School of Government, Harvard University, November 18, 2002).

Figurski, Thomas J., "Moral Development," in Edgar F. Borgatta and Marie L. Borgatta (Eds.), *Encyclopedia of Sociology* Vol. 3 (New York: Macmillan Publishing Company, 1992), pp. 1310-1318.

Finkelstein, N.W., and Haskins, R., "Kindergarten Children Prefer Same-Color Peers," *Child Development*, Vol. 21, 1983: 502-508.

Fordham, Signithia, and Ogbu, John, "Black Students' School Success: Coping with the 'Burden' of 'Acting White,'" *The Urban Review*, Vol. 18, No. 3, 1986: 176-206.

Freud, Sigmund, *Civilization and Its Discontents* (London: Hogarth Press, 1930).

Freud, Sigmund, *Gesammelte Werke* (Frankfurt am Maine, Germany: S. Fisher, 1938-1985). *Beyond the Pleasure Principle*, in Vol. 18 of Sigmund Freud, *Standard Edition of the Complete Psychological Works of Sigmund Freud* (New York: Norton, 1920).

Freud, Sigmund, *The Future of an Illusion* (New York: Doubleday Anchor Books, 1957). (Originally published, 1927).

Frey, Conrad, and Rothlisberger, Christoph, "Social Support in Healthy Adolescents," *Journal of Youth and Adolescence*, Vol. 25, 1996: 17-31.

Gecas, Victor, "Socialization," in Edgar F. Borgatta and Marie L. Borgatta, (Eds.), *Encyclopedia of Sociology* (New York: Macmillan Publishing Company, 1992), pp. 1683-1872).

Geen, R. G., "Aggression and Antisocial Behavior," in D.T. Gilbert, S.T. Fiske, and G. Lindzey (Eds.), *The Handbook of Social Psychology* (4th Edition) Vol. 2 (New York: McGraw-Hill, 1998): 317-356.

Geen, R.G., "Television and Aggression: Recent Developments in Research and Theory," in D. Zillmann, J. Bryant, and A.C. Huston (Eds.), *Media, Children, and the Family* (Hillsdale, NJ: Erlbaum, 1994).

Gibson, Margaret, and Ogbu, John U. (Eds.), *Minority Status and Schooling: A Comparative Study of Immigrant and Involuntary Minorities* (New York: Garland, 1991).

Gilligan, Carol, *In a Different Voice Psychological Theory and Women's Development* (Cambridge, MA: Harvard University Press, 1993).

Gilligan, Carol, *Joining the Resistance* (Malden, MA: Polity, 2011).

Gilligan, Carol, *Making Connections: The Relational Worlds of Adolescent Girls at Emma Willard School* (Cambridge, MA: Harvard University Press, 1990).

Goldberg, Susan, and Lewis, Michael, "Play Behavior in the Year-Old Infant: Early Sex Differences," *Child Development*, Vol. 40, 1969: 21-31.

Goldsmith, Susan, "Rich, Black, Flunking," East Bay Express, May 21, 2003. As of January 27, 2013, available online at http://www.eastbayexpress.com/ebx/rich-black-flunking/Content?oid=1070459

Gonzales, Juan L., Jr., *Racial and Ethnic Groups in America* Fifth Edition (Dubuque, Iowa: Kendall/Hunt Publishing Company, 2003)

Griffin, Cynthia E., "STAR Report Shows California Black Students Still Lagging in English, Math," *Our Weekly*, September 19, 2012. As of January 29, 2013, available online at http://www.ourweekly.com/los-angeles/star-report-shows-california-black-students-still-lagging-english-math

Grotpeter, Jennifer K., and Crick, Nikki R., "Relational Aggression, Overt Aggression, and Friendship," *Child Development*, Vol. 67, 1996:2 328-2338.

Haigler, V.F., Day, H.D., and Marshall, D.D., "Parental Attachment and Gender-Role Identity," *Sex Roles*, Vol. 33, 1995: 203-220.

Harlow, Harry F., "The Heterosexual Affectional System in Monkeys," *American Psychologist*, Vol. 17, 1962: 1-9.

Harlow, Harry F., and Harlow, Margaret Kuenne, "Social Deprivation in Monkeys," *Scientific American*, Vol. 207, 1962: 137-146.

Harlow, Harry F., and Zimmerman, R.R., "Affectional Responses in the Infant Monkey," *Science*, Vol. 130, 1959: 421-432.

Harré, Rom, and Lamb, Rogers (Eds.), *The Dictionary of Personality and Social Psychology* (Cambridge, MA: MIT Press, 1986),

Harrison, A.O.; Wilson, M. N.; Pine, C. J.; Chan, S.Q.; and Buriel, R., "Family Ecologies of Ethnic Minority Children," *Child Development*, Vol. 61, No. 2, 1990: 347-362.

Hartup, Willard, and Stevens, Nan, "Friendships and Adaptation in the Life Course," Psychological Bulletin, Vol. 121, 1997: 355-370.

Haycock, Kati, *Raising Achievement and Closing Gaps Between Groups: Lessons from Schools and Districts on the Performance Frontier* (Reno, NV: The Education Trust, November 2011).

Hazan, Cindy, "Attachment," in David Levinson (Ed.), *Enclopedia of Marriage and the Family* Vol. 1 (New York: Simon and Schuster Macmillan, 1995), pp. 40-50.

Hinde, R.A., "Why Do Sexes Behave Differently in Close Relationships," *Journal of Social and Personal Relations*, Vol. 1, 1984: 471-501.

Hirschfeld, Lawrence A., *Race in the Making: Cognition, Culture, and the Child's Construction of Human Kinds* (Cambridge, MA: MIT Press, 1996).

Huesmann, L. R., and Miller, L.S., "Long-term Effects of Repeated Exposure to Media Violence in Childhood," in L.R. Huesmann (Ed.), *Aggressive Behavior: Current Perspectives* (New York: Plenum, 1994): 153-186.

Intons-Peterson and Reddel, M., "What Do People Ask About a Neonate?," *Developmental Psychology*, Vol. 20, 1984: 358-359.

Itard, Jean Marc Gaspard, *The Wild Boy of Aveyron* (New York: Appleton-Century Crofts, 1962).

Jeynes, William H., "The Salience of Subtle Aspects of Parental Involvement and Encouraging that Involvement: Implications for School-Based Programs," *Teachers' College Record*, Vol. 112, No. 3, 2010: 747-774.

Jeynes, William H., *Parental Involvement and Academic Success* (New York: Routledge, 2011).

Johnson, C.B.; Stockdale, M.S.; and Saal, F.E., "Persistence of Men's Misperceptions of Friendly Cues Across A Variety of Interpersonal Encounters," *Psychology of Women Quarterly*, Vol. 15, 1991: 463-475.

Johnson, J.D.; Jackson, L.A.; and Gatto, L., "Violent Attitudes and Deferred Academic Aspirations: Deleterious Effects of Exposure to Rap Music," *Basic and Applied Social Psychology*, Vol. 16, 1995: 27-41.

Johnson, Monica K.; Crosnoe, Robert; and Elder, Glen H., "Student Attachment and Academic Engagement: The Role of Ethnicity," Sociology of Education, Vol. 74, 2001: 318-340.

Jouriles, E.N., and O'Leary, K.D., "Interspousal Reliability of Reports of Marital Violence," *Journal of Marriage and the Family*, Vol. 53, 1985: 419-421.

Juergen-Lohman, J.; Borsch, F.; and Giesen, H., "Kooperatives Lernen an der Hochschule: Evaluation des Gruppenpuzzlesin Seminaren der Paedagogischen Psychologie," *Zeitschrift fuer Paedagogische Psychologie*, Vol. 15, 2001: 74-84.

Karraker, Katherine Hildebrandt; Vogel, Dena Ann, and Lake, Margaret Ann, "Parents' Gender-Stereotyped Perceptions of Newborns: The Eye of the Beholder Revisited," *Sex Roles*, Vol. 33, Nos. 9/10, 1995: 687-701.

Knight, G.P., and Chao, C., "Gender Differences in Cooperative, Competitive, and Individualistic Values of Children," *Motivation and Emotion*, Vol. 13, 1989: 125-141.

Kohn, M. L.; Naoi, A.; Schoenbach, C.; Schooler, C.; and Slomczynski, K. M., "Position in the Class Structure and Psychological Functioning in the United States, Japan, and Poland," *American Journal of Sociology*, Vol. 95, 1990: 964-1008.

Kowalski, Robin M., "Inferring Sexual Interest from Behavioral Cues: Effects of Gender and Sexually Relevant Attitudes," *Sex Roles*, Vol. 29, Nos. 1/2, 1993: 13-36.

Kuttler, Ami Flam; La Greca, Annette; and Prinstein, Mitchell, "Friendship Qualities and Socio-Emotional Functioning of Adolescents with Close Cross-Sex Friendships," *Journal of Research on Adolescence*, Vol. 9, 1999: 339-366.

Lachmann, Richard (Ed.), *The Encyclopedic Dictionary of Sociology* fourth edition (Guilford, CT: The Dushkin Publishing Group, 1991).

Laumann, E.O.; Gagnon, J.H.; Michael, R.T.; and Michaels, S., *The Social Organization of Sexuality: Sexual Practices in the United States* (Chicago: University of Chicago Press, 1994).

Lee, Felicia R., "Why Are Black Students Lagging?" The New York *Times*, November 30, 2002. As of January 28, 2013, available online at http://www.nytimes.com/2002/11/30/arts/why-are-black-students-lagging.html?pagewanted=all&src=pm

Lenhart, Amanda, *Teens, Smartphones & Texting* (Washington, D.C.: Pew Research Center's Internet & American Life Project, March 19, 2012.) As of January 24, 2013, available online at http://pewinternet.org/~/media/Files/Reports/2012/PIP_Teens_Smartphones_and_Texting.pdf

Lewis, M., Feiring, C., McGuffog, C., and Jaskir, J., "Predicting Psychopathology in Six-Year-Olds from Early Social Relations," *Child Development*, Vol. 55, 1984: 123-136.

Liebert, R.M., and Baron, R.A., "Some Immediate Effects of Televised Violence on Children's Behavior," *Developmental Psychology*, Vol. 6, 1972: 469-475.

Maccoby, E. E., and Martin, J.A., "Socialization in the Context of the Family: Parent-Child Interaction," in P.H. Mussen (Ed.), and E.M. Hetherington (Vol. Ed.), *Handbook of Child Psychology* Vol. 4 *Socialization, Personality, and Social Development* (4th Ed.) (New York: Wiley, 1983: 1-101.

Maccoby, Eleanor, and Jacklin, Carol Nagy, "Gender Segregation in Childhood," in H. Reese (Ed.), *Advances in Child Development and Behavior* (New York: Academic Press, 1987), pp. 239-287.

Maccoby, Eleanor, *The Two Sexes: Growing Up Apart, Coming Together* (Cambridge, MA: Harvard University Press, 1998).

Marger, Martin R., *Race and Ethnic Relations: American and Global Perspectives* (Belmont, CA: Wadsworth, 1994).

Maslow, A., "A Theory of Human Motivation," *Psychological Review*, Vol. 50, 1943a: 370-396.

Maslow, A., *Motivation and Personality* (New York: Harper, 1943b).

McLeod, Jane D.; and Michael J. Shanahan, "Poverty, Parenting, and Children's Mental Health," *American Sociological Review*, Vol. 58, 1993: 351-366.

McLeod, Jane D.; Candace Kruttschnitt; and Maude Dornfeld, "Does Parenting Explain the Effects of Structural Conditions on Children's Antisocial Behavior? A Comparison of Blacks and Whites," *Social Forces*, Vol. 73, 1994: 575-604.

McWhorter, John, *Losing the Race: Self-Sabotage in Black America* (New York: Free Press, 2000).

McWhorter, John, *Winning the Race: Beyond the Crisis in Black America* (New York: Gotham Books, 2006).

Miller, N.B.; Cowan, P.A.; Cowan, C.P.; and Hetherington, E.M., "Externalizing in Preschoolers and Early Adolescents: A Cross-Study Replication of a Family Model," *Developmental Psychology*, Vol. 29, No. 1, 1993: 3-18.

Miyake, K., Chen, S., and Campos, J.J., "Infant Temperament, Mother's Mode of Interaction, and "Attachment in Japan: An Interim Report," in I. Bretherton and E. Waters (Eds.), *Monographs of the Society for Research in Child Development*, Vol. 50, 1985.

Money, John, and Wiedeking, C., "Gender Identity/Role: Normal Differentiation and Its Transposition," in B.B. Wolman and John Money (Eds.), *Handbook of Human Sexuality* (Englewood Cliffs, NJ: Prentice Hall, 1980), 269-284.

Morris, William (Ed.), *The American Heritage Dictionary of the English Language* (New York: Houghton Mifflin Company, 1969).

Munroe, R.L., and Munroe, R.H., "Effect of Environmental Experience on Spatial Ability in an East African Society," *Journal of Social Psychology*, Vol. 83, 1971: 15-22.

Myers, David G., *Social Psychology* ninth edition (Boston: McGraw Hill, 2008).

Nerlove, S.B., Munroe, R.J., and Munroe, R.L., "Effects of Environmental Experiences on Spatial Ability: A Replication," *Journal of Social Psychology*, Vol. 84, 1971: 3-10.

Nevarez, Griselda, "Latino and African American Students Lagging in Math and Reading," *Voxxi*, September 12, 2012. As of January 28, 2013, available online at http://www.voxxi.com/latino-african-american-students-lagging-math-and-reading/

Ogbu, John U. (Ed.), *Minority Status, Oppositional Culture, and Schooling* (New York: Routledge, 2008).

Ogbu, John U., *Black American Students in an Affluent Suburb: A Study of Academic Disengagement* (Mahwah, NJ: L. Erlbaum Associates, 2003).

Otnes, Cele; Kyungseung, Kim; and Kim, Young Chan, "Yes, Virginia, There Is a Gender Difference: Analyzing Children's Requests to Santa Claus," *Journal of Popular Culture*, Vol. 28, 1994: 17-29.

Pomerleau, A., Bolduc, D., Malcuit, G., and Cossette, L., "Pink or Blue: Environmental Gender Stereotypes in the First Two Years of Life," *Sex Roles*, Vol. 22, 1990: 359-367.

Pryor, J.B.; De Souza, E.R.; Fitness,J.; Hutz, C.; Kumpf, M.; Lubbert, K.; Pesonen, O.; and Erber, M.W., "Gender Differences in the Interpretation of Socio-sexual Behavior: A Cross-Cultural Perspective on Sexual Harassment," *Journal of Cross-Cultu8ral Psychology*, Vol. 28, 1997: 509-534.

Range, Lillian M., and Stringer, Traci A., "Reasons for Living and Coping Abilities Among Older Adults," *International journal of Aging and Human Development*, Vol. 43, No. 1, 1996: 1-5.

Richardson, D.; Hammock, G.; Smith, S.; and Gardner, W., "Empathy As a Cognitive Inhibitor of Interpersonal Aggression," Aggressive Behavior, Vol. 20, 1994: 275-289.

Richey, M.H., and Richey, H.W., "The Significance of Best-Friend Relationships in Adolescence," *Psychology in the Schools*, Vol. 17, 1980: 536-540.

Rideout, Victoria, Ulla G. Foehr, and Donald F. Roberts, *Generation M^2: Media in the Lives of 8-to-18 Year Olds* (Menlo Park, CA: Henry J. Kaiser Family Foundation, January 2010). As of January 13, 2013, available online at http://www.kff.org/entmedia/8010.cfm

Rideout, Victoria; Lauricella, Alexis, and Wartella, Ellen, *Children, Media, and Race: Media Use Among White, Black, Hispanic, and Asian American Children* (Evanston, IL: Center on Media and Human Development, School of Communication, Northwestern University, June 2011).

Rossi, Alice A. and Rossi, Peter H., *Of Human Bonding: Parent-Child Relations Over the Life Course* (New York: Aldine de Gruyter, 1991).

Rymer, Russ, *Genie* (New York: Harper Perennial, 1994).

Saal, F.E.; Johnson, C.B.; Weber, N., "Friendly or Sexy? It May Depend on Whom You Ask," *Psychology of Women Quarterly*, Vol. 13, 1989: 263-276.

Schneider-Rosen, K., Braunwald, K.G., Carlson, V., and Cicchetti, D., "Current Perspectives in Attachment Theory: Illustration from the Study of Maltreated Infants," in I. Bretherton and E. Waters (Eds.), *Monographs of the Society for Research in Child Development*, Vol. 50, 1985.

Schofield, Janet, "Promoting Positive Peer Relations in Desegregated Schools," *Educational Policy*, Vol. 7, 1993: 297-317.

Schultz, D.P., and Schultz, S.E., *A History of Modern Psychology,* (Orlando, FL: Harcourt-Brace, 1987).

Seppa, N., "Children's TV Remains Steeped in Violence," *APA Monitor*, Vol. 28, 1997: 36.

Shaken, M., Shakin, D., and Sternglanz, S.H., "Infant Clothing: Sex, Labeling for Strangers," *Sex Roles*, Vol. 12, 1885: 955-964.

Sharan, S., "Cooperative Learning in Small Groups," *Review of Educational Research*, Vol. 50, 1980: 421-271.

Slavin, R.E., and Cooper, R., "Improving Intergroup Relations: Lessons Learned from Cooperative Learning Programs," *Journal of Social Issues*, Vol. 55, 1999: 647-663.

Spitz, "Hospitalism," *The Psychoanalytic Study of the Child*, Vol. II, 1947: 113-117.

Spitz, René, "Hospitalism," *The Psychoanalytic Study of the Child*, Vol. I 1945: 53-74.

Sroufe, L., "Infant-Caregiver Attachment and Patterns of Adaptation in Preschool: The Roots of Maladaptation and Competence," in M. Permutter (Ed.), *Minnesota Symposium in Child Psychology*, 1984.

Steele, Shelby, *A Bound Man* (New York: Free Press, 2008).

Steele, Shelby, *White Guilt: How Blacks and Whites Together Destroyed the Promise of the Civil Rights Era* (New York: Harper Collins, 2006).

Steinberg, Laurence, *Beyond the Classroom: Why School Reform Has Failed and What Parents Need to Do* (New York: Simon & Schuster, 1996).

Stelter, Brian, "Ownership of TV Sets Falls in U.S.," The New York *Times*, May 3, 2011, page B1. As of January 23, 2013, available online at http://www.nytimes.com/2011/05/03/business/media/03television.html

Stokes, J., and Levin I., "Gender Differences in Predicting Loneliness from Social Network Characteristics," *Journal of Personality and Social Pscychology*, Vol. 51, 1986: 1069-1074.

Szinovacz, M.E., and Egly, L.C., "Comparing One-Partner and Couple Data on Sensitive Marital Behaviors: The Case of Marital Violence," *Journal of Marriage and the Family*, Vol. 57, 1995: 995-1010.

Thernstrom, Abigail, and Thernstrom, Stephan, *America in Black and White: One Nation, Indivisible* (New York: Touchstone, 1999).

Thernstrom, Abigail, and Thernstrom, Stephan, *No Excuses: Closing the Racial Gap in Learning* (New York: Simon & Schuster, 2003).

Thompson, Elizabeth; Thomas L. Hanson, and Sara S. McLanahan, "Family Structure and Child Well-Being: Economic Resources vs. Parental Behaviors," *Social Forces*, Vol. 73, 1994: 221-242.

Thorne, B., *Gender Play: Girls and Boys in School* (Buckingham, England: Open University Press, 1993).

Turner-Bowker, Diane, "Gender Stereotyped Descriptors in Children's Picture Books," *Sex Roles*, Vol. 35, Nos. 7/8, 1996: 461-488.

Urberg, K.A., and Kaplan, M.G., "An Observational Study of Race-, Age-, and Sex-Heterogeneous Interaction in Preschoolers," *Journal of Applied Developmental Psychology*, Vol. 10, 1989:299-311.
Urberg, K.A., and Kaplan, M.G., "An Observational Study of Race-, Age-, and Sex-Heterogeneous Interaction in Preschoolers," *Journal of Applied Developmental Psychology*, Vol. 10, 1989:299-311.

Waite, B.M.; Hillbrand, M.; and Foster, H.G., "Reduction of Aggressive Behavior After Removal of Music Television," *Hospital and Community Psychiatry*, Vol. 43, 1992: 173-175.

Weiss, L.H., and Schwarz, J.C., "The Relationship Between Parenting Types and Older Adolescents' Personality, Academic Achievement, Adjustment, and Substance Use," *Child Development*, Vol. 67, No. 5, 1996: 2101-2114.

Werner, Emmy E., "Vulnerability and Resiliency: A Longitudinal Study of Asian Americans from Birth to Age 30," Invited Address at the IX Biennial Meeting of the International Society for the Study of Behavioral Development, Tokyo, July 15, 1987.

Werner, Emmy E., and Smith, Ruth S., *Vulnerable But Invincible: A Longitudinal Study of Resilient Children and Youth* (New York: Adams, Bannister, Cox, 1989).

Whitbeck, Les B.; Simons, Ronald L.; Conger, Rand D.; Wickrama, K.A.S.; Ackley, Kevin A., and Elder, Glen H. Jr., "The Effects of Parents' Working Conditions and Family Economic Hardship on Parenting Behaviors and Children's Self-Efficacy," *Social Psychology Quarterly*, Vol. 60, No. 4, 1997: 291-303.

Wilcox, Bradford, "Conservative Protestant Childrearing: Authoritarian or Authoritative?" *American Sociological Review*, Vol. 63, No. 6, (December) 1998: 796-809.

Wilson, James Q., and Herrnstein, Richard J., *Crime and Human Nature* (New York: Simon and Schuster, 1985).

Zhou, Min, "Growing Up American: The Challenge Confronting Immigrant Children and Children of Immigrants," *Annual Review of Sociology*, Vol. 23, 1997: 63-95.

CHAPTER 6

The Family and Social Structure

THE FAMILY—BASIC CONCEPTS

As you learned in the first chapter of this textbook, sociology may be defined as the study of social structure. The family is an important component of the social structure of all human societies, past and present. The famous British anthropologist, George Peter Murdock, appreciated this. His classic book, *Social Structure*, is all about family and kinship. In order to understand human society, Murdock needed to understand family and kinship. In the types of societies he was looking at— hunting and gathering or folk societies—the family *is* the social structure, in a very literal sense. The family remains a key institution in all known societies.

This chapter presents a sociological analysis or portrait of the dynamic, reciprocal relationship between the institution of the family and social structure. What goes on in families touches, influences, and shapes all the other parts of social life. What goes on the other parts of society—politics, economics, technical innovation, the cultural milieux, education, religion, and so forth—influences the family as an institution. That's what a "reciprocal" relationship between or among them means. The institutions of society are dynamically interdependent.

From a sociological perspective the **family** is a basic unit of kinship consisting of persons related by blood (consanguinity), marriage (affinal ties), or adoption, whose adult members are responsible for the rearing and socialization of any children they may have. The institution of the family is found in all human societies (e.g., Murdock, 1949; Fisher, 1992: 65-66). **Marriage** is a socially and legally recognized relationship between two people, the unique trait of which is "social recognition and approval ... of a couple's engaging in sexual intercourse and bearing and rearing offspring" (Davis, 1985: 5; Malinowski, 1930). When people marry, they become kin to one another. When people marry, it is expected that they will bear children. This normative expectation is known as pronatalism. Marriage traditionally is, and historically has been, the basis of a family of procreation.

In the United States and other highly developed modern (OECD) societies during the past five decades a de-linking for many people has occurred between marriage and family. The family album now includes ensembles without marriage between the adult partners. For example, most Americans say a single parent raising a child is a family, that parents do not have to be married to be a family and that the parents do not even need to be of the opposite sex. In 2010 the Pew Research Center, in association with TIME magazine, conducted a study of a nationally representative sample of adults in the United States regarding their attitudes about marriage, family, and kinship (Taylor, 2010). Please see Table 6.1 for Americans' responses in this survey regarding what is a family. Virtually all respondents agree that a married couple with children fits their definition of family. Other arrangements have joined the family circle. Nearly nine in ten Americans (88 percent) say a childless married couple is a family and nearly as many say a single parent rearing at least one child is a family (86 percent) and that an unmarried couple with children (80 percent) is a family. A smaller majority say a gay or lesbian couple with a child is a family (63 percent).

TABLE 6.1 WHAT IS A FAMILY? PERCENT SAYING THIS IS...

Percent saying this is...	a family	not a family
Married couple with children	99	01
Married couple without children	88	10
Single parent with children	86	12
Unmarried parent with children	80	18
Same-sex couple with children	63	34
Same-sex couple without children	45	52
Unmarried couple without children	43	54

Source: Paul Taylor, *The Decline of Marriage and the Rise of New Families* (Washington, D.C.: Pew Research Center, 2010), p. 40. Note: "Don't know/Refused" responses are not shown. Question wording: "As I read you a list of different arrangements, please tell me whether you consider each to be a family or not." Pew Research Center

Perceptions about what is a family vary by the age of the perceiver. It is among the young that the greatest acceptance of newer family forms resides. In other words, different generations define families differently. For example, 80 percent of those aged 18-29 but only 37 percent of those aged 65 and older perceive a same-sex couple with children as a family (Taylor, 2010: 41). Likewise, fifty-one percent of those aged 18-29 but only 30 percent of those aged 65 or older view a same-sex couple without children as a family. Similarly, almost half (47 percent) of those aged 18-29 but only 25 percent of those aged 65 or older view an unmarried couple without children as a family (Taylor, 2010: 42).

Perceptions of what is a family also vary by sex of the perceiver. Males are significantly less likely than females to say same-sex living arrangements are families. Fewer than six-in-ten males (57 percent) say that a gay or lesbian couple with children is a family, compared with 70 percent of women. Similarly, 37 percent of men but 51 percent of women say that same-sex couples without children are a family. When it comes to unmarried couples without children, the sexes are in agreement: 42 percent of men and 44 percent of women say they are a family.

It is worth noting that marriage does figure into in the American public's calculus of what is a family. Fully 88 percent of Americans believe that a married couple without children is a family, while less than half think of an *unmarried* couple without children as a family (43 percent) or that a that a same-sex couple without children is a family (45 percent) (Taylor, 2010: 40).

Another way to explore the boundaries of family is by asking people how obligated they would feel to help out various people with financial assistance or caregiving in time of need. Americans' responses agree with the old maxim that "you can choose your friends but you can't choose your family." In other words, even if people do not like their family members very much, many feel obligated to help them out in time of need while they do not feel a similar obligation toward their best friend. More than eight in ten Americans feel "very obligated" to help their parents in time of need. Grown children come next, with 77 percent feeling obligated to help them get over hard times, and then come grandparents (67 percent), a sibling (64 percent), or the parent of a partner or spouse (62 percent) (Taylor, 2010).

"Blended" family members—stepchildren, stepparents, and step or half siblings-- do not fare as well (Taylor: 2010, 45) and friends fare even worse. Parents are 17 percentage points more likely to feel obligated to a grown child (77 percent) than to a grown stepchild (60 percent). Similarly, adults are more likely to help a parent (83 percent) than a stepparent (55 percent) and a brother or sister (64 percent) rather than a step or half sibling (43 percent) (Taylor, 2010: 45). When asked about one's best friend, just 39 percent say they would feel a similar sense of obligation.

Kinship is a relationship that links people based on blood ties, marriage, or adoption, and it is culturally defined (Theodorson and Theodorson, 1969: 221; Giddens, et. al., 2013: 333). Kinship relations are, by definition, part of marriage and the family, but kinship relations extend more broadly. While in many modern highly developed (OECD) countries, few social obligations are involved in kinship relations extending beyond the immediate family, in traditional cultures an intricate fabric of rights, duties, and obligations bind the members of the kinship. Kinship relations in these societies are vitally important in social life.

SOME MAJOR FAMILY TYPES—POLYGAMOUS, MONOGAMOUS, EXTENDED, NUCLEAR

The family into which a person is born is that person's **family of orientation.** The **family of procreation** is the family an individual starts when she or he gets married or has children. The family is the basic institution of status ascription in human societies. The newborn child is given the status of her or his married parents. Even as adults, one's family of orientation is, and remains, an ascriptive retreat. Thus, during the Great Recession, many grown children moved into their parents' home, often bringing their own children with them.

There has been a large increase in the number of three-generational households in the United States in recent years due to the harsh dislocations cause by hard economic times (Kochhar and Cohn, 2011). Thus, in 2009, 13.7 percent of Hispanic Americans and 13.5 percent of Asian Americans lived in three-generation households (e.g., grandparents, their grown children, and their children's children). Similarly, 11.9 percent of black Americans and 5 percent of non-Hispanic white Americans lived in three-generation households in 2009 (Taylor, 2011: 29). This growth in the prevalence of three-generation households represents a big turnaround from a retreat from multi-generational households that had characterized the United States for more than a century and a half (Ruggles, 2007, 2009). In the years of the Great Recession, the multi-generational population of the United States increased by 4.9 million people, or 10.5 percent. By contrast, the number of people in other households rose by only 333,000 (Kochhar and Cohn, 2011: 5). During this same period, the population of the nation increased only 1.8 percent. As a result, the share of the population living in multi-generational households increased to 16.7 percent in 2009, up from 15.4 percent in 2007 (Kochhar and Cohn, 2011: 2).

Moving in with the parents has been a boon to the unemployed during the Great Recession. For example, among the unemployed in 2009, the poverty rate among people in multi-generational households was 17.5 percent, compared with 30.3 percent for those living in other households (Taylor, Kochhar, Cohn, et. al., 2011:14). Also, Economist Thomas DeLeire and his colleague Ariel Kalil, using data from the National Educational Longitudinal Study (NELS) document that three-generational households have salutary effects on teenagers' developmental trajectories. In particular, in comparison with teenagers living in single-parent households and in comparison with teenagers living in cohabiting households in the United States, teenagers living with their single mothers and with at least one grandparent in multi-generational households have better developmental outcomes. Indeed, their developmental outcomes that are at least as good, and often are better than, the outcomes of teenagers in married families (DeLeire and Kalil, 2005). These findings hold when the researchers control for a wide range of economic resources, parenting behavior, and home and school characteristics. Family structure matters.

CHART 6.1 FAMILY ARRANGEMENTS FOR CHILDREN UNDER 18 YEARS OF AGE IN THE UNITED STATES, 2011, BY RACE AND ETHNICITY

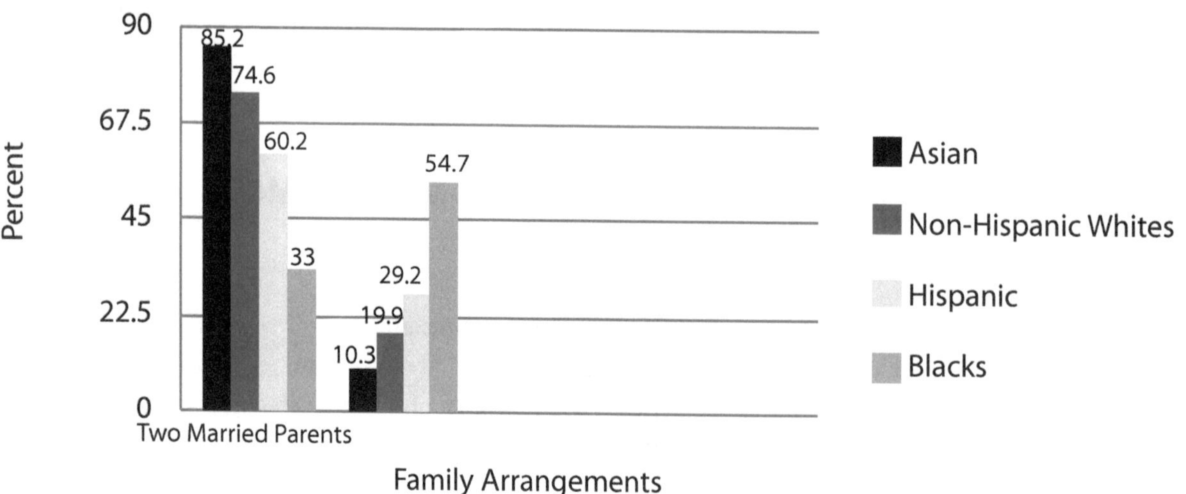

Source: U.S. Parents, Race, and Hispanic Origin, 2011. Census Bureau, *Current Population Survey, 2011 Annual Social and Economic Supplement,* Table C9, Children by Presence and Type of Parents, Race, and Hispanic Origin, 2011. As of September 30, 2012, available online at http://www.census.gov/population/www/socdemo/hh-fam/cps2011.html

The family arrangements for children under 18 years of age in the United States vary by race and ethnicity. See Chart 6.1 on family arrangements for children under age 18 by race and ethnicity. Of Asian-American children under 18 years of age, only 10 percent live in one-parent families, while 20 percent of non-Hispanic white children, about 30 percent Hispanic children, and over half (54.7 percent) of black children live in one-parent families. Likewise, over 80 percent of Asian-American children under the age of 18 live in families with two married parents, as do 75 percent of non-Hispanic white children and 60 percent of Hispanic children. One-third (33 percent) of black children under the age of 18 live in families with two married parents (U.S. Census Bureau, U.S. Parents, Race, and Hispanic Origin, 2011).

Keeping the meaning of a few simple root words in mind helps us to understand, and to be able to recall, some of the forms of marriage and family. -Gamy is a root word meaning "marriage." "Poly" is a Greek root word meaning "many" and "mono" is a root word meaning "one." "Andr" is a root word meaning "male" and "gyny" is a root word meaning female. In the United States, we have a form of marriage known as **monogamy**, wherein people may have only one spouse at any given time. This form of marriage is known as monogamous marriage. Other societies and other cultures permit a person to have more than one spouse at a time, which is known as **polygamy**. This form of marriage is known as polygamous marriage. With regard to the distribution of polygamy around the world, Africa and the Middle East are regions of the world that have the most polygyny.

There are several types of polygamy. In **polygyny,** the most prevalent form of polygamy, a man has more than one wife at the same time. A common form of polygynous marriage is **sororal polygyny**, in which a man marries two or more sisters at the same time. If we define a society as polygynous if the *ideal* is for a man to have more than one wife at a time, then a majority have been polygynous. In George Peter Murdock's classic study of family structures around world, 193 out of 234 tribal societies (82%) were polygynous (Goode, 1982: 96). Of course, most of these societies were small, some of them numbering only a few hundred people or less. *The Ethnographic Atlas* is a database on over a thousand societies coded by George Peter Murdock and it was published in 29 successive installments in the journal, Ethnology, between 1962 and 1980. As of 2010, *The Ethnographic Atlas* included information on marriage in over 1200 societies and shows that exclusive monogamy occurs in about 15.1 percent of the sample, polygyny in about 84.6 percent of these societies, and polyandry in less than one-half of one percent (Henrich, 2010: 14). Of course, a majority of the world's societies does not necessarily embrace a majority of the world's population; as noted above, many of these societies are small, numbering only a few hundred people or less.

Polygamy sometimes is found in societies even when it legally is not permitted. Thus, from time to time, you will find an article in the news media about a "scandal" involving a polygynous marriage or a polygynous community in the United States (e.g., Hlad and Beardsley, 2012; Salem, 2012; Lambe, 2009; Barksdale, 2008; McDonald, 2008). In the United States, if a person already is married and marries another person, the second marriage is bigamous. In a legal system where monogamy is the only legal form of marriage, **bigamy** is the condition of having two wives or two husbands at the same time. Bigamy is a crime in the United States. A person who knowingly enters into a bigamous marriage can be found guilty of the crime of bigamy. One can be found guilty of multiple counts of bigamy. Occasionally, people commit bigamy accidentally, usually in the belief that a prior marriage had been dissolved legally. Perhaps the most famous case in the United States is that of Andrew Jackson (who subsequently became the 7thPresident of the United States) and his wife Rachel Robards née Donelson (Brands, 2005). Rachel's husband, Captain Lewis Robards, had applied for a divorce but it had not been granted – it required legislative approval—at the time of her marriage to Andrew Jackson. When Rachel Robards became aware of the bigamous nature of her marriage to Andrew Jackson, she secured a divorce, after which she and Andrew Jackson remarried in 1794 (Brands, 2005).

Some societies, of course, permit polygyny even though it is not the ideal. However, most of the great civilizations have not permitted polygyny (Goode, 1982). Islam did, and today in many majority Muslim

countries a man may have up to four wives simultaneously; but China, India, Japan, and the West did not, for most of their last thousand years of history. Polygyny as an ideal was more widespread in Africa than in any other region of the globe. In Murdock's sample, it appeared in about nine out of ten of the Sub-Saharan tribes for which data were available (Goode, 1982: 96; Dorjahn, 1959: 102-105).

Sociologist Azar Gat (2006: 68) concludes that in most human societies, including those of hunter-gatherers, polygyny was legitimate. It was legitimate among all the Aborigine tribes of Australia and highly desired by the men there (Gat, 2006:70). Sociologists and anthropologists agree that even in those societies where it was or is legitimate, most married males at any given point in time are not in polygynous marriages (e.g., Gat, 2006: 68; Long, 1970; Megitt, 1965a; Keen, 1982). The common pattern in these societies is that only a few, select, well-to-do males of fairly high social status could afford to support, and thus have, the extra wives and children. The average married man would have only one wife for most of his life, while men of wealth, nobility, and power typically would have more wives and thus more offspring. For example, the Bible tells us that King Solomon had 700 wives and 300 concubines (Potts and Hayden, 2008: 10). Among the Egyptian Pharohs, the Aztec Kings, the African Kings, Chinese Emperors, and Turkish Sultans, large harems were the order of the day (Betzig, 2008). The comparative studies among the Aboriginal tribes of Australia show that men with only one wife comprised the largest category of married men, often the majority. Only 10-15 percent of married men had three or more wives, and the figures declined with every additional wife (Megitt, 1965b; Long, 1970; Daly and Wilson, 1983). Among the Aka pygmies of central Africa, the leaders were found to be more than twice as polygynous as the non-leader males (Betzig, 1991). Among the Xavante horticulturalists of Brazil, 16 of the 37 men (43%) in one village had more than one wife, and a larger survey of the Xavante found that 42% of married males (74 of 184) had more than one wife (Daly and Wilson, 1983: 88-89, 332-333; Symons, 1979: 143; Chagnon, 1979: 380). Among the native Indian tribes of the resource-rich environment of the American Northwest, while most married men were monogamous, the rich, strong, and powerful were mostly polygynous (Rosman and Rubel, 1971: 16-17, 32, 110; Drucker, 1951: 301; Drucker, 1965: 54; Krause, 1970 [1885]: 154).

In some cultures, there is the social custom known as the **levirate**, whereby a widow must marry a brother of her deceased husband. The levirate, of course, is an engine that can generate polygynous marriages. If the deceased husband's brother already is married, his marriage to the widow of his deceased brother transforms his previously monogamous marriage into a polygynous one. While ancient Hebrew society practiced the social custom known as the levirate, it is found in other societies and regions as well. In many African societies, the social security "safety net" of the levirate existed (Goode, 1982: 105). Anthropologists also have found that the levirate has been practiced in certain areas of Mexico (Guiteras-Holmes, 1947: 12), that it was an expected social practice among well-to-do Aztecs, and that most of the polygynous relationships in Mesoamerican societies were due to the practice of the levirate (Soustelle, 2002:112).

The levirate served a number of functions. It was a cultural solution to what some might term "the widow problem," the challenge of "who is going to take care of the widow and her dependent children?" If the dead husband had no brother, his kinship would appoint someone to act as the deceased husband's brother, a practice known by anthropologists and sociologists as fictive kin. Sociologists and anthropologists use the term **fictive kin** to refer to the cultural practice of treating non-family members as if they were in fact members of the family. A high level of acceptance of the cultural practice of fictive kin is found in a great many societies—hunting and gathering, horticultural, urban-agrarian, industrial, and post-industrial—past and present around the globe (e.g., van den Berghe, 1979: 210-211). In the case of the levirate, if the deceased husband had no living brother, his kinship would appoint someone to act in that capacity and the widow would marry him. If the widow were still of child-bearing age, she would be required to bear children by her new husband and these children would remain in the family line of her deceased husband's brother. The levirate helped ensure the survival of any dependent children that the widow may have had when her husband died. This was a vital concern in traditional societies that lacked a state-sponsored "social safety net" paid for by tax-payers to secure the care and safety of children when one or more of their parents had experienced an untimely death. In the social practice of the levirate, the family took care of the widow and her children.

The rarest form of polygamy is **polyandry**, wherein a woman has more than one husband at the same time. In his classic study of marriage and the family in various societies around the world, British anthropologist George Murdock found only two societies that allowed for the practice of polyandry (Murdock: 1949: 26-28). When polyandry does occur, it usually occurs due to a skewed sex ratio.

The study of population structure is known as **demography.** Demography is one of the sub-fields of sociology. Demographers use the term **sex ratio** to refer to the number of males per 100 females in a population. Many aspects of social life are predicated upon a balanced sex ratio. 100 is a balanced sex ratio. When the sex ratio is balanced, there are equal numbers of males and females in the population. When the sex ratio departs significantly from 100, it is said to be characterized by skew. If the sex ratio is high—say 116 or 120—there are a lot more males than females in the society. Likewise, if the sex ratio is low—say, 80—there is a shortage of males in the population or an overabundance of females, depending on the point of view.

When there is a shortage of females in the population (a high sex ratio), males may become more willing to "share" a wife. In fact, when polyandry does occur, it most frequently takes the form of two brothers sharing a wife, a family form known as **fraternal polyandry**. Sex ratios may be skewed in the form of a high sex ratio for a number of reasons, one of which is female infanticide (van den Berghe, 1979: 62).

Anthropologists make a distinction between harem polygyny and hut polygyny. Harem polygyny is rare. In ***harem polygyny*** a man of high station has many wives who are not economically active in the paid labor force and who are guarded by males who pose no threat in terms of sexual trespass relative to the wives whom he is guarding because he has been castrated; the guardian is a eunuch. Much more common, historically and cross-culturally, is ***hut polygyny***, in which each wife has her own home or "hut" in which live the wife and her dependent children of the common husband/father (Ingoldsby, 2005: 103). The common husband/father has his own hut, generally situated in the center of a compound. The compound contains the husband's hut in the center, around which are located a hut for each of his wives. In the hut of each wife live that wife and her dependent children of the common husband/father. In a hut-polygynous village, the village is composed of several such compounds. Not infrequently, the various wives are economically active and each wife may have a plot of ground outside the village compound in which she grows things for trade. The economic productivity of the various wives makes this form of polygyny more cost-affordable for the husband.

In systems of hut polygyny, normative structures help regulate the relations among the various wives, children, and the common husband/father of the children. Rules of rotation (rotation rules) inform the various wives when they need to be sexually available to husband, when they need to cook for the common husband, and so forth. Rules of etiquette regulate relations among the wives, and inform them who must defer to whom, with the first wife generally being accorded greater deference and respect by the higher-order wives.

There are many types of family. The nuclear family is the smallest family type. The **nuclear family** consists of husband, wife, and their dependent children. As such, the nuclear family contains, at most, two generations—the parents (generation #1) and their dependent children (generation #2). Anthropologists and sociologists have documented the presence of the nuclear family in virtually all societies; and, as such, we may think of it as the fundamental building block of other family types (e.g., Shapiro, 2012; Shapiro, 2011). The concept of the nuclear family is an ideal type. Sociologists use the term **ideal type** to refer to a theoretical construct that contains all the major elements of a recognized social phenomenon. Other family types may be thought of as either adding one or more elements to, or subtracting one or more elements from, this basic type of family. Thus, Andrew Billingsley (1968) observes that the ***incipient nuclear family*** consists of husband and wife and he uses the term ***simple nuclear family*** to refer to husband, wife, and their dependent children. Sometimes friends or other relatives are incorporated into the nuclear family, sometimes as fictive kin. In such cases, Billingsley (1968) refers to the nuclear family as ***augmented***. The augmented nuclear family consists of husband, wife, one or more children, and one or more relatives or non-relatives.

Sometimes the term ***conjugal family*** is used instead of nuclear family. The two terms may be used interchangeably when referring to the family unit. In the conjugal family, the primary focus is on the spousal relationship and their unmarried children. If other relatives are found in the conjugal family, their position tends to be peripheral (Theodorson and Theodorson, 1969:147). Conjugal families usually do not form extended families.

The ***extended family*** consists of three or more generations of relatives operating as a family. The extended family is found in many traditional societies. For example, in pre-revolutionary China, when a woman married, she and her husband moved in with the groom's parents. Who else would live in that household? In addition to the bride, groom, and the groom's parents, that household would consist of the groom's unmarried brothers and unmarried sisters; the groom's married brothers and their wives and their dependent children, and, of course any grandchildren or great-grandchildren in the paternal line. All would function as a family. They might live together in a great compound, in a great house, or in tents close together. The important point is that these generations of family functioned together as a family. The concept of the extended family thus refers to social structure, not architecture. It is possible for three or more generations of family to operate as a family without living in the same house or in the same compound.

The term extended family can also be applied to the ***stem family*** common in feudal Europe, post-feudal Europe, Tokugawa Japan, and elsewhere, including among some farmer groups here and there in the United States. (Goode, 1982: 94). The term stem family (*famille souche*) was coined by Frédéric Le Play (1855, 1884) to describe a type of patriarchal family in which the family estate is passed on intact to one son chosen by the father (Theodorson and Theodorson, 1969:150). In this way, the property is not constantly subdivided from generation to generation, nor is it automatically inherited by the eldest son as is the case in ***primogeniture***. The sons not inheriting the family estate usually are given aid in establishing a livelihood elsewhere and may return to the family home in time of need. The family remains an ascriptive retreat in the stem family system.

The ***joint family***, common in traditional India, is an extended family that also extends laterally across siblings in any generation (Chandrasekhar, 1943; Goode, 1963: 238-247). In India, its principle members are brothers who have a right to the products of the family property, which is supposed to be passed down intact from one generation to the next. The joint family consists of the brothers in any generation, with their sons in the next generation, plus the sons of the next generation. The household would include, of course,

any in-marrying brides and their dependent children. When a daughter married, she would become a member of her husband's joint household. The emphasis was placed on brothers in India, since according to Hindu tradition the male child from birth had rights in the family property. In other societies, such as the United States, joint households may be formed on the basis of siblings—brothers and sisters. Nonetheless, sociologist Steven Ruggles (2010) has shown that at least for the past century and a half, people in the United States (and in most of Europe) have had a strict aversion to forming joint families.

KINSHIP ORGANIZATION: DESCENT, INHERITANCE, AUTHORITY, RESIDENCE, AND MATE SELECTION PATTERNS

Some Descent Patterns—Bilateral, Matrilineal, Patrilineal

Families in all known societies and cultures are structured around a number of principles including descent, inheritance, authority, residence, and mate selection. All known societies have normative structures, called **rules of descent**, that inform people about which of their biological relatives are to be considered as sociological relatives, how those relationships are to be traced, what those relationships are, and what the reciprocal rights, duties, and obligations are for each of the relationships so specified. This bundle of norms is known as rules of descent. All societies have them.

There are many ways in which a biological canvas of possible relatives may be parceled out into a sociological canvas of actual relatives. One way of tracing descent is the lineage; the adjectival form of this word is -lineal. The **lineage** is a type of corporate kin group that contains the descendants of a common ancestor, considered to be the founder of the line or lineage. Sometimes, the founding ancestor is a famous historical figure, or a mythical figure symbolized by a clan name, or a figure shrouded in the mist of history, or even is considered to be a god or an animal. Lineages tend to be exogamous—which mean that when one marries, one must marry outside of one's lineage.

Two major modes of tracing descent in the lineage are *unilineal* and *omnilineal* (Goode: 1982: 113). As the names suggest, in a unilineage, descent is traced through one line only (father's or mother's). while in an omnilineage, descent is traced through both the mother's and the father's lines. In the United States, the custom is to use a form of omnilineal descent known as **bilateral descent** wherein descent and inheritance are regarded as determined equally by the mother's and father's line. One's father's and mother's relatives are accepted equally as kin. The culture determines which relatives (how far removed or how far a circle) are socially significant, but the social significance extends to the same degree of relationship on the mother's and the father's side (Theodorson and Theodorson, 1969: 29). Thus, if Suzie were to say that she has a favorite uncle, and that is all she tells us, then we would not know whether he is the brother of her father or the brother of her mother. Either one would equally be her uncle. In a system of bilineal or bilateral descent, close biological relatives on both sides of the family equally are relatives. In George Murdock and Douglas White's Standard Cross-Cultural Sample, 69 out of 186 societies (37 percent) have a bilateral rule of descent (Murdock and White, 2006: 340).

Patrilineal descent, also known as ***agnatic descent*** or ***patrilineality***, follows the unilineal principle and traces descent through the father and the male line. Patrilineal descent is the most prevalent rule of descent in George Murdock and Douglas White's Standard Cross-Cultural Sample, with 76 out of 186 societies (40.8

percent) having patrilineal descent (Murdock and White, 2006: 340). Since many people in the United States have no experience of living even briefly in a lineage, let's use an exercise of the imagination to help us understand it. Let us suppose we had a patrilineage in this country. Who would be in *your* lineage? You would include all your male ancestors in the direct line. The men's wives are not members. Your father's brothers (if he had any) would be included, and his sons and daughters. Also included would be your father's father, his brothers, and their descendants. Only the descendants of the males would be included. The descendants of females would be included in the lineages of the men these women married. In effect, the lineage is composed of all the descendants of a founding father.

If the United States were patrilineal, your relatives through your mother's family would play a smaller part in your life. You would expect, and get, less help from them and you might be less anxious about incurring their displeasure. The father in your nuclear family would have more authority than at present. If you were old enough to marry, the patrilineage would play a large role in the marriage—setting rules concerning whom you might marry, when you marry, helping to amass the money for the marriage celebration and setting up the household, and, perhaps, even picking out your spouse (who might be your cousin). If you were male, you would claim your children for your lineage in the event of divorce because they have been members of your patrilineage from birth. If you were female and got a divorce, you would return to your family of orientation without your children. If you traveled to another town, you would expect to be received with open arms by members of your lineage, even if they had not met you before. If you had a serious disagreement with another member of the lineage, the elders of the lineage would adjudicate the issue rather than permit you to go to court. If the serious dispute were with someone outside the lineage, your lineage would take your side of the quarrel. In general, in your relations outside your own household, you would be treated more as a member of a lineage than as an independent individual. Under this system, you would lose some of your freedom to make gifts to your kin through your mother's line or to will property to them.

In **matrilineal descent** (also known as ***uxorial descent*** or ***matrilineality***) utilizes the unilineal principle and traces descent through the female line. In matrilineal descent, males on the female line are particularly important. Matrilineal systems make up only about 17 percent of the world's societies (Mattison, 2011: 65; Murdock and White, 1969). In George Murdock and Douglas White's Standard Cross-Cultural Sample, 31 out of 186 societies (16.7 percent) have matrilineal descent (Murdock and White, 2006: 340). Even though matrilineal societies are found in only a small percentage of the world's societies, these societies can be found in many parts of the world. Thus, historically, a great belt of matrilineal tribes ran from west Africa eastwards through the continent. The Zuni and Navajo of the southwestern United States traditionally have been matrilineal. On the Indian subcontinent, there once were many matrilineal groups along the entire south-western coast of the Indian peninsula. Some matrilineal groups are found in Melanesia in the South Pacific, including the Trobrianders who were extensively studied by Bronislaw Malinowski (1987).

In matrilineal descent, one is part of a descent group whose members are linked through successive generations of females. A girl and her brother are part of their mother's lineage. The mother and *her* brothers and sisters are part of *their* mother's lineage. Every matrilineage contains males (brothers and sons of the women through whom descent is traced) who hold the most important positions (Mattison, 2011: 65). Thus, there in built-in tension in matrilineal descent systems because authority is vested in men while descent is traced through females. Matrilineal descent systems are known for their high levels of divorce (marital dissolution).

In a matrilineal society, when a woman marries, she marries a man who is outside of her lineage. (Lineages are exogamous.) Likewise, when a man marries, he marries a woman who is outside of his lineage.

A given matrilineage, then, excludes the women who are married to the male member *in* it as well as the "outside" men who have married its female members.

In a matrilineal society, the mother's brother acts as the sociological father of her children. Since many people in the United States have no experience of living even briefly in a matrilineage, let's use an exercise of the imagination to help us understand it. Let us suppose that we had a matrilineage in this country, that Mary and Mark are married to each other, and that they have children. Mary also has a brother, Tim. In this situation, who is it who fills the role of sociological father of Mary's children? It is not Mary's husband, Mark. The role of sociological father of Mary's children is filled by the mother's brother, Tim. What if Mary has no brother (because her brothers have died or she didn't have any in the first place)? Her kinship appoints someone—let's name him "Bob"—to fill the role of Mary's brother, which is an example of fictive kin. Bob, then, acts as the sociological father of Mary's children.

In a matrilineal society, the mother's brother not only is an authority figure, he also is the person from whom a boy inherits. A man's property goes to his sister's sons in a matrilineage. As an authority figure, the mother's brother also figures significantly in the ritual life of the family, being the person who represents the family in ritual matters. Since the mother's brother also tends to be married and to have fathered children with his wife, he may feel a desire to give gifts to his own children or even to leave property to his own children, much to the annoyance of his nephews specifically and to his lineage. In a matrilineal society, in case of divorce, the children remain with the mother, because they have been part of her lineage since birth.

Inheritance Patterns

All cultures have norms regarding to whom property is to be distributed to upon the death of the parents. In some cultures, the cultural expectation is that of **primogeniture**, wherein the eldest son inherits the entire estate (and the royal title, if any) upon the death of the father, with none of the inheritance going to the other children. Primogeniture was practiced by the upper classes in western Europe during the Middle Ages. It provided a means of keeping large estates, and thereby the position of the family to whom the estate belonged, intact across generational lines. As we have seen, a modified version of primogeniture has been found in other societies and among other classes. This was the case, for instance, with the stem family, in which the father chooses who, among all his sons, shall be the heir. In yet other cultures, only persons of a particular faith community may inherit property. In yet other cultures, the expectation is that all children shall inherit equally. Historically in many societies, issues related to inheritance have been viewed as so vital that they are regulated and stipulated by law rather than being left up to the choice of individuals.

Residence Patterns

All known cultures, past and present, have normative structures, which sociologists and anthropologists term ***rules of residence,*** that shape people's preferences regarding where the ideal place to reside is once they get married. In the United States today, the most common pattern for newly married couples is **neolocal residence** (also known as neolocality), wherein the newly married couple reside in an abode of their own, separate from that of the family of the groom and separate from that of the family of the bride. In many traditional societies, however, the preferred place for a newly married couple to live is with the family of the groom, a practice known as **patrilocal residence** (or patrilocality). In these cultures, the newly married bride and groom move in with the groom's father's family. The least common rule of residence is that of **matrilocal residence**, wherein the newly married couple moves into the household of the bride's mother.

Authority Patterns

In terms of authority relations within the family, ***patriarchy*** has played a central role in many traditional societies and continues to do so today. Many of the family patterns we have discussed so far—patrilocality, patrilineal descent, polygyny—reflect a common global pattern known as patriarchy. Patriarchy refers to a system of male supraordination, a system in which males tend to rank higher than females in terms of class, status, and power. Within the family in a patriarchal system, the male head of household wields great authority and influence and is accorded great deference by other members of the household, both male and female. Even in OECD countries today, the head of household typically is a male. Even in the United States, most parents give the children the last name of the father.

Matriarchy is the least common form of marital authority in families around the world, both today and in the past. In a matriarchal system, a female is the main authority figure in the family and she is accorded respect and deference by the other family members. To the extent that this authority pattern occurs, it usually does so when a female becomes a single parent or when the eldest male of the extended family dies and the eldest female (e.g., the grandmother) is the sole survivor of that generation. Under these circumstances, the grandmother may assume a position of authority in the extended family, if only symbolically. The grandmother matriarch is viewed by the other family members as the "glue" that holds the family together.

In the United States and other OECD countries, the ***egalitarian*** authority structure is emerging. In the egalitarian family, authority tends to be shared fairly equally between the husband and the wife.

Mate Selection Patterns

Sociologists have devoted a lot of study to understand how people select marriage partners from the potential pool of persons available for selection. There are two major norms of mate selection, endogamy and exogamy. **Endogamy** is a norm that says that mate selection should occur *within* a particular group or groups. Common bases of endogamy are class, race, ethnicity, religious affiliation, education, and noble status. Many cultures encourage their members to marry within certain group or groups; in other words, they encourage their members to marry endogamously.

A cultural norm that sets a limit on the extent of endogamy is the incest taboo. The incest taboo is the major norm of exogamy and it is found in all known societies, past and present (Parsons, 1954). **Exogamy** is a norm that says that marriage should occur outside of a certain group or groups. The **incest taboo** prohibits marriage and intimate sexual relations within prohibited degrees of kinship. Precisely what those prohibited degrees of kinship are varies from one culture to another. Thus, while first-cousin marriage is legal within the United Kingdom under Civil Law, in the United States 31 of the fifty states prohibit marriage between first cousins (Bittles, 2003: 137). In contrast to the situation in the United States, in many other countries the preferred marriage partner *is* a first cousin. In many traditional societies, children may not know exactly whom they will marry when they grow up, but they know that person will most likely be one of their first cousins (either a cross-cousin or a parallel-cousin).

There is a form of marriage known as ***consanguineous marriage***, consanguine marriage, cousin marriage, or cross-cousin marriage. The terms are often used interchangeably or synonymously. The term consanguine marriage comes from the Latin word "sanguineus," literally meaning "of blood" and frequently translated into English as "of the same blood." The consanguine family is not necessarily an extended family, although it forms a basis for the extended family. In one form of the consanguine family, the preferred spouse is one's close family relative, frequently one's first or second cousin. This form of marriage is the preferred form of marriage in many traditional societies both historically and today (Bittles and Black, 2010). In fact, the consanguine form of marriage and family is extensively practiced in various parts of the global community (Tadmouri, et. al., 2009; El Mouzan, et. al., 2007). The highest rates of consanguineous marriage are found in Africa and the Middle East.

The concept of **marriage rate** refers to the number of marriages per 1,000 unmarried females aged fifteen and older. For example, in Pakistan, 70 percent of all marriages are between first cousins (Sennels, 2010), as are 54 percent in Qatar (Benner and Alali, 2006), 47 percent in Mauritania (Hammami, et. al., 2005) and 24 percent in Oman (Rajab and Patton, 2000). In Iraq, as in much of the region, nearly half of all married couples are first or second cousins. Perhaps the most prominent example of an Iraqi first cousin marriage was that of the late Saddam Hussein and his first wife Sajida (Sailer, 2001). In Saudi Arabia, as in other countries, the rates of consanguineous marriage tend to be higher in the countryside than in urban areas. In Saudi Arabia, between 34 percent to 67 percent of marriages are consanguineous (El Mouzan, et. al., 2007), between 32 percent to 45 percent in Yemen (Jurdi and Saxena, 2003; Gunaid, et. al., 2004), between 20 percent to 64 percent in Jordan (Hamamy, et. al, 2005; Sueyoshi and Ohtsuka, 2003), between 24 percent to 56 percent in Oman (Rajab and Patton, 2000), and between 11 percent to 34 percent in Algeria (Zaoui and Biémont, 2002).

In some countries and cultures, consanguineous marriage takes the form of ***avunculate marriage***, which refers to uncle-niece marriage or to aunt-nephew marriage. For example, uncle-niece marriage is still practiced in Dravidian southern India. In many Sephardic Jewish communities, it is a meritorious thing for a man to marry his sister's daughter (Bittles and Black, 2010). In other countries and in other cultures, however, uncle-niece marriage is prohibited, which is the case in the United States, England, and Wales.

For many people in Western countries, consanguineous marriage arouses curiosity and even disapproval, despite the fact that until the mid-nineteenth century cousin marriages were quite common and widely favored both in Europe and in the United States, particularly among the more privileged classes (e.g., Bittles, 2010; Boetsch, et. al., 2003; Frankenberg, 1990; Pattison, 2003; Huth, 1875). Attitudes towards consanguineous marriages are more favorable in northern and in Sub-Saharan Africa, the Middle East, Turkey, central Asia and South Asia where between 20% to over 50% of current marriages are between biological relatives, with first cousins being particularly preferred (Bittles, 2010: 507). In these areas, a large majority of marriages may also occur within long-established lineages—for instance, within the tribe and clan (hamula) in Arab societies, within the caste in India, and within the *biraderi* in Pakistan.

The ***biraderi*** ("brotherhood," a patrilineal kinship group) forms an important locus of authority, identity, and endogamy among people from the central areas of the Punjab, including among those who emigrate from Pakistan to the United Kingdom (UK). It is a manifestation of patrilineal descent among people from Kashmir, many of whom have migrated to what is now Pakistan. When they emigrate to, say, the United Kingdom, their brothers and sisters who still live in Pakistan expect offers of marriage from their brother's and sister's children who live in the United Kingdom. From the point of view of the brothers still in Pakistan, this improves the family's economic situation by sponsoring young men to work in the UK.

There has been a lot of global migration during the past two generations. Millions of individuals, families, and occasionally entire communities have moved both within as well as between continents (Bittle, 2010: 507). Against this backdrop, consanguinity has re-emerged as an important feature of community, of community health, and as a topic of general interest. For instance, it is estimated that at least 55 percent of British Pakistanis are married to first cousins (Rowlatt, 2005). British Pakistanis are 13 times more likely to have children with genetic disorders than the general population in the United Kingdom. Accounting for just over 3 percent of all births, British Pakistanis are just under a third of all British children with genetic disorders. In fact, in Birmingham, a large city in the United Kingdom, the Birmingham Primary Care Trust estimates that one in ten of all children born to first cousins in that city either dies in infancy or goes on to develop serious disability as a result of a recessive genetic disorder (Rowlatt, 2005).

SOCIOLOGICAL PARADIGMS AND THE FAMILY

Sociological paradigms offer an array of lenses for perceiving and understanding families.

Structural Functionalism

The family as an institution is found in all human societies (e.g., Fukuyama, 2011). Why? According to structural functional theory, the family helps societies to exist across time by performing essential functions or tasks, which include the following:

- **REGULATION OF SEXUAL ACTIVITY** Every culture endeavors to regulate sexual activity and child bearing. As discussed earlier in this chapter, for example, the incest taboo prohibits sexual relations and marriage between persons within prohibited degrees of kinship.
- **SOCIALIZATION** As discussed in Chapter 5 (Socialization), the family is a primary context, institution, or agent of socialization. The family is the first and most important setting for rearing children. It is within the family that most children grow up. Ideally, parents help children to develop into well integrated and contributing members of the community.
- **STATUS ASCRIPTION** The family is the primary institution of status ascription. Families provide an initial status or position to the newborn. Parents pass on their own status to their children. Parents pass on their identities—for example, in terms of race, ethnicity, religious affiliation, social class, noble status—to their own children at birth. As we have discussed, families are an ascriptive retreat for their members later on in life as well. The family's "ascriptive business" is not finished early in life but persists across the life course.
- **MATERIAL AND EMOTIONAL RETREAT** For many people, the family is a "retreat," a haven in a heartless world. As discussed in this chapter, even as adults, the members of one's family of orientation tend to feel an obligation to help and assist its members in difficult times. Maybe that is why married people tend to be healthier, happier, and wealthier than single people or people who cohabit (e.g., Goldstein and Kenney, 2001; Waite and Gallagher, 2000).
- **UNIT OF ECONOMIC PRODUCTION** In many types of societies—including hunting and gathering societies—the family was an essential unit of economic production. In contemporary highly-developed societies the family as a unit of production by no means has disappeared. Think of the family farm, the family hardware store, the family restaurant; the family roofing, electrical, or

plumbing business; or the family-owned car repair shop. Although the family as a unit of economic production still is important in many societies, in many of the OECD countries the family as a unit of economic production has decreased in prevalence.

Conflict Theory

Like structural-functionalist theory, conflict theory views the family as a basic part of human social organization. Conflict theory, however, views the family as a primary institution of oppression—on the bases of gender, class, race, and ethnicity. For instance, Friedrich Engels, in The Origins of the Family, Private Property and the State (1975 [1884]), traces the origin of the institution of the family to men's need to be able to identify their heirs so that they, as fathers, could hand down property to their son or sons. In this way, property and wealth could be "reproduced" across generational lines. In addition, Engels (1884) sees the oppression of females by males in monogamous marriage as the first case of class antagonism in human history. To the extent that racial and ethnic groups persist across time only to the extent that they engage in endogamy—marry people like themselves—then it could be said that racial and ethnic endogamy support stratification on the bases of race and ethnicity.

Feminist theorists perceive a link between the family as an institution and patriarchy. Feminists perceive that family and kinship systems transform females into the economic and sexual property of males. The mechanisms used to achieve this end are varied and include, among others, the doctrine of coverture, female genital cutting, purdah, and honor killing. The general principle that links these various forms of the social control of females together is the answer to the question, "Qui bono?"—Who benefits? Feminist theorists take the perspective that males benefit by these practices. You may want to keep the feminist-theorist response in mind as we briefly look at the following practices:

- **Coverture** is the doctrine that upon marriage the husband and wife become a single legal identity, that of the husband. The doctrine of coverture is an English common-law concept. Derived, at least in part, from Roman and feudal Norman custom, it dictated a woman's legal subordination to her husband during marriage (Zaher, 2002; Bailey, 2002). Prior to marriage, an adult woman (*feme sole*, from the Norman French, meaning "single woman") could freely enter into contracts; she could sell or give away her real estate or personal property as she wished. In contrast, a married woman (*feme covert*) was under the protection or cover of the husband. Her legal existence as an individual was suspended. Coverture renders a married woman unable to own property in her own name, unable to enter into contracts without her husband's consent, unable to obtain a loan without her husband's consent, and she is unable to execute a will without her husband's consent. If she works for income, the income she earns belongs to her husband. Under coverture, marital assets were considered the property of the husband (Cavallo and Warner, 1999).

  Even under coverture, however, women had some control over property (Brand, 2001). Thus, at the death of her husband, a widow was entitled to one-third of his property as her dower. Because of this entitlement, a husband could not transfer or sell property without his wife's consent. Were he to do so, after his death she could claim that the transfer or sale was illegal and demand return of the property. It is for this reason that wives usually signed their husband's deeds of sale or of transfer, to show their consent. Often a statement that the woman was signing of her own free will and was not being coerced by her husband accompanied her signature.

The doctrine of coverture was imported from England into Colonial America. In the United States, coverture began to be disassembled through legislation at the state level beginning in Mississippi in 1839 (Brand, 2001).

- **Female genital mutilation (FGM)**, also known as female genital cutting, refers to all procedures involving the total or partial removal of the external female genitalia and includes such practices as female circumcision, clitoridectomy, and infibulation.

  FGM is an umbrella term that refers to several practices that are deeply embedded in the cultures of various groups around the world. One practice, common in Egypt, is *sunnna circumcision*, after the Arabic word for tradition. In this procedure, the clitoral foreskin (or prepuce) is removed. Sometimes part or all of the clitoris is removed as well. A second practice involves the excision of the clitoris with partial or total excision of the labia minora. A third practice called *infibulation* (or pharonic circumcision) is more severe. It involves the removal of the clitoris, the labia minora, and most of the labia majora, leaving only an opening large enough for the passage of urine and menses. Infibulation is most common in Africa. The infibulated female must be cut open, so that she can have sexual relations with her husband. She may be sewn up again if he leaves for an extended period of time, as for a business trip abroad. The infibulated female must be cut open further, if she is to give birth vaginally. Then, following childbirth, she will again be infibulated, only to be cut open again to resume sexual relations with her husband. Over time, these repeated procedures can lead to a buildup of scar tissue, resulting in menstrual and urinary-tract complications.

  According to the World Health Organization (2012), about 140 million girls and women currently living have been subjected to FGM. How many people is that? It's a number of females equivalent in size to 44 percent of the entire population of the United States in 2012 (U.S. Census Bureau, 2012). In Africa alone an estimated 92 million females currently living and aged 10 years or older have undergone FGM (World Health Organization, 2012). The practice is most common in the western, eastern, and north-eastern regions of Africa, in some countries in Asia and the Middle East and among migrants from these areas.

  FGM is mostly carried out on young girls sometime between infancy and age 15 by local traditional circumcisers. The trend is increasing, however, whereby the procedures are performed by modern health-care providers. The World Health Organization estimates that today about 18 percent of all FGM is performed by modern health-care providers.

- **Purdah** refers to the seclusion of females from public observation and it takes various forms in different cultures. It frequently is accomplished, at least in part, by females wearing concealing clothing from head to toe; and by the use of high-walled enclosures, curtains, and screens within the home.

  In India, the word *purdah* stems from the Hindi *parda*, which translates into English as screen or veil. The practice of purdah is said to have originated in the Persian culture and to have been acquired in the seventh century by the Muslims during the Arab conquest of what is now Iraq (Ahmed, 1992). In turn, Muslim domination of northern India influenced the practice of Hinduism, which is an example of **cultural diffusion.** Cultural diffusion is the transmission of cultural traits or social practices from one culture or subculture to another through such mechanisms as exploration, military conquest, social interaction, tourism, migration, immigration, the mass media, and so forth. Purdah became widely observed among upper caste Hindus in northern India.

  Purdah flourished in ancient Babylon, where no woman could go outside the home unless she was masked and accompanied by a male from her family. Even parts of the household were

separated as a practice of segregation. The Prophet Muhammad incorporated the practice of purdah as part of the Islamic tenets of faith. During the British hegemony in India, purdah observance was widespread among both the Muslim minority and among upper caste and affluent Hindus. Since then, purdah has become less widespread among Hindus in India but the seclusion and veiling of women is still practiced to a greater or lesser degree in many Islamic countries today. The limits imposed by purdah vary according to different cultures and class levels.

- **Honor killing** refers to killing in order to restore the family honor; found as a familial obligation in some patriarchal societies and among migrants from such societies even today. All cultures provide their members with culturally approved ways of restoring honor. For instance, in feudal Japan and in ancient Rome, suicide was defined as an honorable and or redemptive ritual. Persons who had behaved dishonorably and thereby had brought dishonor not only upon themselves but upon their family could cleanse the stain by committing suicide in a prescribed ritualistic manner.

  The cultural practice or institution known as honor killing fulfills a similar function and is found in many cultures. For example, in the Roman Empire, the male head of household could kill a family member who had dishonored the family and the state would take no legal action against the male head of household. Quite generally, in societies that have the institution of honor killing, if a person is perceived as dishonoring her or his family, a member of the family thus dishonored has the *obligation* to kill the perpetrator. It is a heavy obligation. The killing of the perpetrator is a symbolic act that is viewed by the culture as having the effect of restoring the family's honor. The killing itself is viewed as an honorable act and no action is taken against the perpetrator or perpetrators. The person who had brought dishonor to the family is stricken from the family lineage; the fiction thus created is that the person never existed.

  The idea that females embody the "virtue" or "honor" of the family is particularly widespread in patriarchal societies, past and present. Feminist theorists point out that female virtue is a "symbolic marker of men's group boundaries" (Epstein, 2007: 13; Douglas, 1966). Female conformity to the norms of the group is regarded as a manifestation of the honor of the group, while males generally are given greater latitude than females to engage in deviant behavior. To maintain female virtue and purity, female behavior is closely monitored and restricted.

  During the past few decades there has been a lot of international movement of peoples. When people migrate they take their customs with them, including the custom of honor killing. There have been many cases of honor killing in OECD countries in recent years. For instance, in January, 2012, three Afghan Canadians were convicted of first-degree murder for the drowning deaths of four family members in an honor killing. Mohammad Shafia had immigrated to Canada from his native Afghanistan with his two wives. He apparently was a typical immigrant that many countries would want: he started his own business, he was a law-abiding citizen, a family man (Dhillon, 2012). The fact that his three teenage daughters would put on make-up, have a boyfriend, and lead a lifestyle that to many Canadians is normal led the father—with the assistance of his son and his second wife—to drown his three daughters along with his first wife (who had been supportive of his daughters' Western lifestyle and who wanted a divorce) in the family's Nissan Sentra which was found submerged at the bottom of the Rideau Canal in eastern Ontario, Canada (Tripp, 2012). The father, son, and second wife each received a life sentence in prison with no possibility of parole for 25 years, after which it is expected that they all will be deported to Afghanistan (Tripp, 2012).

Conflict theory brings into particular focus the role of the family in perpetuating social privilege—e.g., on the bases of sex or gender, class, race, and ethnicity. As seen through the lenses of conflict theory, the family as an institution is in the stratification business and part of its business is to perpetuate into the future the system of stratification that exists today. Maybe that is why conflict theories tend to be hostile to the continued existence of the family as an institution. And it also helps to explain why some males in these cultures might be hostile to those who seek fundamentally to change the sexually stratified order. A case in point is that of Fern L. Holland of Miami, Oklahoma. Fern Holland was an American civilian who founded women's shelters in Iraq so that there would be safe havens for females who wanted to flee abusive family situations. Fern Holland also promoted women's political empowerment in Iraq and helped to draft sections of the Iraqi interim constitution, sections intended to ensure a role for women in Iraq's still evolving system of governance. On March 9, 2004, Fern L. Holland, age 33, was shot to death near Hilla, a town about 35 miles south of Baghdad, the nation's capitol, by elements in Iraq vehemently opposed to women's rights (Chan and Murphy, 2004).

Microlevel Theories

While structural functionalist and conflict theories view the family as part of a larger social system, micro-level theories are interested in the ways in which individuals experience and shape family life and the meanings that family life has for them.

FAMILY DYNAMICS: MICRO-LEVEL PROCESSES Studies of the day-to-day activities in the average household in the United States document that when it comes to household tasks, things look pretty much like what Arlie Hochschild described almost a quarter of a century ago in The Second Shift (1989). The **second shift** is Arlie Hochschild's term for the extra time that working women spend doing household chores at home after working at a paid job in the extra-familial labor force. The point that Hochschild made was that child-care and house work still are primarily done by females.

The U.S. Department of Labor conducts an annual time-use survey of Americans 15 years of age and older. The most recent results show that on an average day, 19 percent of men do housework—such as cleaning or doing laundry—compared with 48 percent of women. And, on an average day, men who do housework spend less than half as much time at it (14 minutes) compared with women (32 minutes) (U.S. Bureau of Labor Statistics, 2012). As with housework, so, too, with child care. The U.S. Bureau of Labor Statistics documents that on an average day, among adults with children under the age of 6, women spend 1.1 hours providing physical care (such as bathing and feeding a child) while men spend 26 minutes providing such care (U.S. Bureau of Labor Statistics, 2012).

SOCIAL EXCHANGE THEORY Social exchange theory is a micro-level approach to understanding social life and it perceives both courtship and marriage as forms of negotiation (Blau, 1964). The different parties may bring different assets table, as it were. Traditionally men bring power and wealth to the table and women bring youth and beauty. An old, wealthy, influential man who is not physically attractive may nonetheless be attractive as a potential spouse to a young female, because she perceives in him someone who would be able to be a "good provider" for her and any children they may have. For instance, Larry King was a successful talk-show host on CNN for many years. He had many wives, many of whom were substantially younger than himself. Another example is provided by Donald Trump, the American business magnate.

Donald Trump has had several wives who have been significantly younger than himself. What assets do you think they brought to the table?

Social exchange theorists perceive social life, including family and kinship processes, as a series of negotiations. In traditional societies, a family—or a middle-man or go-between on their behalf-- negotiates with another family or families for spouse for their child. In modern societies that have courtship and dating as a way of finding spouses, people strike negotiations on their own behalf.

TRENDS IN MARRIAGE AND FAMILY

As you already have learned in this chapter, many family forms exist in the world. In some areas of the globe, traditional family systems are essentially unchanged. In most developing countries, however, changes are afoot. Among the complex origins of these changes are the spread of Western ideals of romantic love. Another factor is the spread of nation-building, the spread of a centralized government in areas that previously were smaller and fairly autonomous and fairly sovereign societies. People's lives are changed in many ways by their involvement in a larger, national political system. Governments may try to alter traditional ways. Governments may dissuade nomadic peoples from nomadicism and institute policies to transform their way of life into one that is sedentary. Governments may institute policies designed to reduce the fertility of the population by advocating the use of contraception and by increasing both its availability and affordability. The one-child policy of the Peoples Republic of China is but one extreme example of such policies. As countries develop economically, urban centers, where most of the new jobs are, grow rapidly due to large-scale migration from the rural hinterland and, sometimes, due to large scale immigration from other countries as well. In all these cases, traditional family forms and kinship systems may come under stress, and weaken. A growing diversity of family forms may proliferate. This process of change was first documented by sociologist William J. Goode in *World Revolution and Family* Patterns (1963) and has been substantiated by other research.

During the period from roughly the mid 1960s to the early 1990s, the United States and other economically advanced societies underwent a profound transformation from industrial to information societies (Bell, 1976; Fukuyama, 1999b). At the same time, Western societies experienced, and continue to experience, a quiet revolution (Taylor, 2010), a retreat or flight from marriage and family (e.g., Eberstadt, 2012; Marcus, 2012; Banks, 2011; Pew Research Center, 2010; Hymowitz, 2006; Fukuyama, 1999a, 1999b). Francis Fukuyama, the Oliver Nomellini Senior Fellow at Stanford University's Freeman Spogli Institute for International Studies, identifies the birth control pill as one of the most revolutionary of human technologies, without which many of the changes in marriage and family that we analyze in this chapter would not have been conceivable (Fukuyama, 1999b). What are some indices of this perceived retreat or flight from marriage and family? There are several of them, including

- The age at first marriage has risen significantly
- The marriage rate has fallen
- The postponement of family formation has increased significantly
- The divorce rate has risen a lot
- The prevalence of non-marital cohabitation has increased a lot
- The fertility rate has fallen-- to below replacement levels in many developed countries
- One-person households have increased in prevalence
- Single parent households have increased in prevalence
- Much child bearing occurs outside of marriage rather than in it

Age at First Marriage

In Japan, Taiwan, South Korea and Hong Kong, the mean age at first marriage is 29-30 for women and 31-33 for men (The Economist, 2011). In the United Kingdom, the mean age at first marriage increased from 27.2 for males and 24.7 for females in 1970 to 36.2 for males and 33.6 for females in 2010 (Office for National Statistics, 2010). In the United States, the median age at first marriage increased from 20 for females and 23 for males in 1960 to 26.5 and 28.7, respectively, in 2011 (Wilcox and Marquardt, 2011: 60; U.S. Census Bureau, 2011), the highest ever recorded in this country (Taylor, 2010). In the United States, the age at first marriage has risen by roughly six years in the past half century. It is worth noting, that as high as the current age at first marriage is in the United States, our age at first marriage, both for males and for females, appears "young" if we compare it with the comparable figures for age at first marriage in many OECD countries. See Table 6.2 on mean age at first marriage for males and females in various European countries.

TABLE 6.2 MEAN AGE AT FIRST MARRIAGE FOR MALES AND FEMALES IN VARIOUS OECD EUROPEAN COUNTRIES, BY SELECTED YEARS

Country	Sex		Year
	Male	Female	
Austria	31.7	28.9	2008
Czech Republic	30.3	27.6	2008
Denmark	34.8	32.4	2008
Estonia	29.6	27.2	2008
Finland	32.5	30.2	2008
France	31.6	29.6	2008
Germany	33.0	30.0	2008
Greece	31.8	28.9	2008
Iceland	34.3	32.1	2008
Ireland	32.1	30.4	2006
Italy	32.8	29.7	2007
Norway	33.4	31.1	2008
Poland	27.7	25.6	2008
Portugal	31.0	29.5	2011
Sweden	35.1	32.5	2008
Switzerland	31.4	29.1	2008
Turkey	26.7	23.4	2011
United Kingdom[a]	36.2	33.6	2010

Source: A UK data are from Office for National Statistics, Statistical bulletin "Marriages in England and Wales, 2010." As of September 19, 2012, available online at http://www.ons.gov.uk/ons/rel/vsob1/marriages-in-england-and-wales--provisional-/2010/marriages-in-england-and-wales--2010.html#tab-Age-at-marriage The data on the other countries are from United Nations Economic Commission for Europe, "Mean age at first marriage by sex" As of September 19, 2012, available online at http://w3.unece.org/pxweb/Dialog/varval.asp?ma=052_GEFHAge1stMarige_r&ti=Mean+Age+at+First+Marriage+by+Sex%2C+Country+and+Year&path=../DATABASE/Stat/30-GE/02-Families_households/&lang=1

Decline in the Marriage Rate

In the United States, the yearly number of marriages per 1,000 unmarried females aged 15 and older has dropped nearly by half since 1970, from 76 to 36 in 2009 (Wilcox and Marquardt, 2010: 61). Today, just 20 percent of people aged 18-29 are married, compared with 72 percent in 1960 (Francis, 2011). It is worth noting, however, that as low as the marriage rate is today in the United States, ours looks high in comparison with the marriage rate in a lot of other OECD countries. See Table 6.3 on the number of marriages per 1,000 unmarried females in various OECD countries in the 1990s and 2000s and the percent change between those two time periods.

TABLE 6.3 THE MARRIAGE RATE IN VARIOUS OECD COUNTRIES AND THE UNITED STATES IN THE 1990S AND 2000S AND PERCENT CHANGE

Country	1990s		2000s		Percent Change
Australia	1996	33.4	2006	32.0	-4.3
Canada	1995	24.0	2006	22.2	-34.7
Denmark	1994	36.0	2005	31.2	-13.4
France	1994	22.3	2005	20.8	-6.8
Germany	1994	29.3	2005	23.0	-21.5
Italy	1994	27.3	2001	22.1	-19.1
Netherlands	1994	28.9	2005	22.6	-21.8
New Zealand	1991	42.7	2006	24.8	-41.9
Norway	1994	23.0	2002	25.0	8.6
Spain	1994	47.2	2001	38.7	-18.1
Sweden	1994	17.2	2005	20.0	16.1
United Kingdom	1994	30.6	2005	27.2	-11.2
United States	1995	50.8	2005	40.7	-19.9

Source: David Popenoe, *Cohabitation, Marriage and Child Wellbeing: A Cross National Perspective* (New Brunswick, NJ: The National Marriage Project at Rutgers University, 2008), Table 2 on Page 5

Postponement of Family Formation

In Italy, seven out of 10 adults aged 18-39 live at home with their parents. Such children are known as "***bamboccioni***," which translates roughly into English as "big baby"—the ever growing number of young adults who are still living in their parents' home in the same bedroom they have slept in since they were in diapers (Steyn, 2010). Italy's bamboccioni have their equivalents in other OECD countries. In Canada in 2006, 43.5 percent of adults aged 20-29 lived with their parents and between 1981 and 2006, the percentage of men in their late twenties living at home doubled while the percentage of women living at home nearly tripled. In Germany, the bamboccioni are called "***Nesthockers***;" in Great Britain, they are called "***KIPPERS***"

(Kids in Parents' Pockets Eroding Retirement Savings). In Japan they are called "***Parasite Singles.***" In 2010, a third of Japanese women entering their 30s were single (Steyn, 2010). In 2010, 37 percent 37 percent of all women in Taiwan aged 30-34 were single. In Thailand, the number of women entering their 40s without being married increased from 7 percent in 1980 to 12 percent in 2000 (The Economist, 2011).

In Sweden, the proportion of women in their late 30s who are single is higher than in Asia, at 41 percent. In Britain and the United States, only about 11-15 percent of those in their late 30s are single (The Economist, 2011). As with many of the other measures of the flight or retreat from marriage, the United States is situated at mid-range. The United States is not leading the pack; it is in the middle of the pack. Nonetheless, in 2010, just 48 percent of working-class white males in this country were married, down from 84 percent in 1960 (Murray, 2012b). That people in the United States are less likely to marry than previously is reflected in a decline of more than 50 percent, from 1970 to 2010, in the annual number of marriages per 1,000 unmarried adult females (Wilcox and Marquardt, 2011: 60).

The percentage of adults who are currently married in the United States has shrunk. Among all persons aged 15 and older, the percentage who are married has declined about 16 percentage points since 1960. The decline has been 30 percentage points among black females (Wilcox and Marquardt, 2011: 61-62.) In fact, black women have become "only half as likely as white women to be married, and more than three times as likely as white women never to marry" (Banks: 2011: 7). As Richard Ralph Banks, the Jackson Eli Reynolds Professor of Law at Stanford Law School, puts it, "[o]ver the past half century, African Americans have become the most unmarried people in our nation. By far. We are the least likely to marry and the most likely to divorce." (Banks, 2011: 2).

In 1970, 72 percent of American adults were married. By 2008, about half (52 percent) of all adults in this country were married (Taylor, 2010). There are variations in the tendency to marry by race and ethnicity. See Graph 6.1 on the share of never-marrieds, by race and ethnicity, in the United States, 1960 to 2008. According to U.S. Census Bureau data, fewer than one-third of adult blacks (32%) are currently married, compared with half of Hispanics and 56 percent of non-Hispanic whites (Taylor, 2010). The flip side reveals that today 44 percent of blacks never have been married, compared with 23 percent of whites (Taylor, 2010). The size of the racial and ethnic marriage divide did not used to be this large. In 1960, 17 percent of adult blacks and about 14 percent of adult whites were not married, a gap of 3 percentage points.

GRAPH 6.1 PERCENT OF NEVER-MARRIED ADULTS AGED 18 AND OLDER, BY RACE AND ETHNICITY, IN THE UNITED STATES, SELECTED YEARS, 1960-2008

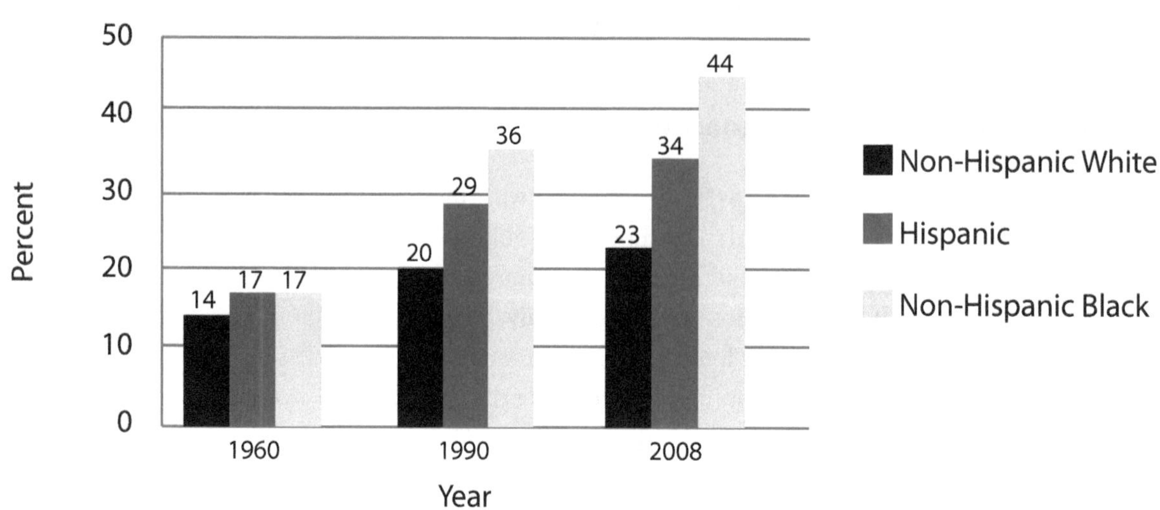

It is worth noting that in recent years a marital educational divide has emerged in our country. Those who are college educated—those with at least a Bachelor's degree—make up 30 percent of the adult population. Fully 64 percent of them are married (Taylor, 2010; Wilcox and Marquardt, 2010). Among the well educated, marriage is strong and stable, and appears to be getting even stronger. The big change has been happening in the broad center of our society, among those with a high-school but not a four-year college degree. This moderately educated middle of America constitutes 58 percent of the adult population in the United States, and it is here that marriage is foundering (Wilcox and Marquardt, 2010). In 2008, only 48 percent of adults with a high-school education were married, compared with 76 percent of them in 1960 (Taylor, 2010). Moderately educated Americans have become less like likely to form stable, high-quality marriages.

Divorce

The **divorce rate** is the number of divorces per 1,000 married women. After the introduction of no-fault divorce laws in the late 1960s, the divorce rate in the United States increased so much that many analysts refer to the large increase in divorce as the divorce revolution (Brown and Lin, 2012). California's no-fault divorce law was signed by Governor Ronald Reagan on September 4, 1969 and it became effective on January 1, 1970. By late 1977, nine states had adopted no-fault divorce laws (Baskerville, 2007); and by late 1983, every state but South Dakota and New York had no-fault divorce. Today, all fifty states and the District of Columbia have no-fault divorce. The United States has the highest divorce rate in the world (Brown and Lin, 2012; Amato, 2010; Cherlin, 2010).

The American divorce rate today is nearly double that of 1960 (Wilcox and Marquardt, 2011: 67), even though it has declined since hitting its highest point in our history in the early 1980s. See Graph 6.2 on the number of divorces Per 1,000 married women aged 15 and older in the United States in selected years, 1960 to 2009.

GRAPH 6.2 NUMBER OF DIVORCES PER 1,000 MARRIED WOMEN AGED 15 AND OLDER IN THE UNITED STATES, BY SELECTED YEARS, 1960-2009

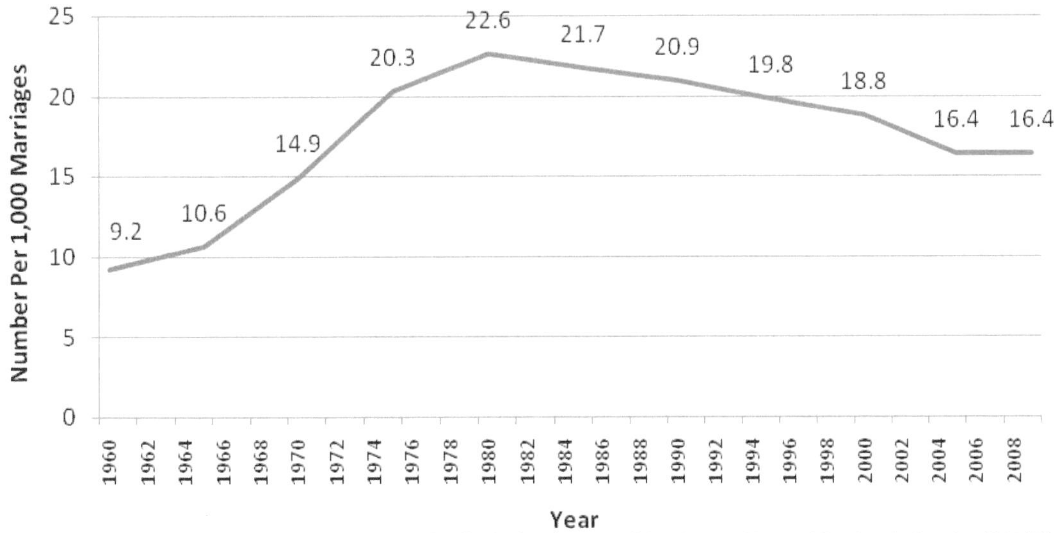

Source: Adapted from Wilcox, W. Bradford, and Marquardt, Elizabeth, *The State of Our Unions, Unions Marriage in America 2011* (Charlottesville, VA: The National Marriage Project, December, 2011), p. 68, Figure 5. U.S. Census Bureau: *Statistical Abstract of the United States* for 2001 (Table 117), available online at www.census.gov/prod/www/abs/statab.html; *Current Population Report* for 2000 (Table 3), available online at www.census.gov/cps; Centers for Disease Control and Prevention: "Births, Marriages, Divorces, and Deaths: Provisional Data" for 2000 (in *National Vital Statistics Report 49*) and 2009 (in NVS Report58) (Table 2), available online at www.cdc.gov/nchs/products/nvsr.htm.

The growth of divorce has lead to a steep increase in the percent of all adults who are currently divorced. This percentage, which was only 1.8 percent for males and 2.6 percent for females in 1960, had quadrupled by the year 2000. By 2008, 14 percent of adults aged 15 or older were currently divorced (Taylor, 2010).

The likelihood of divorce varies considerably among different segments of the American population. In 2010, the rate of divorce was 2.5 times higher for those in remarriages versus first marriages (Brown and Lin, 2012). Also, divorce rates are higher for blacks than for whites, and higher in the South and West than in other parts of the country. These variations have been diminishing. The trend toward a greater similarity of divorce rates between whites and blacks is largely due to the fact that fewer blacks are marrying (Teachman, 2002). You can't get divorced if you're not married.

At the same time, there still are large divorce rate differences between those who marry when they are teenagers compared to those who marry after age 21 and between those who perceive themselves as non-religious and the religiously committed. Teenagers and the non-religious have considerably higher divorce rates (Raley and Bumpass, 2003).

There is a growing educational divide in divorce in the United States. Less educated Americans have much higher divorce rates than their college-educated counterparts. For instance, among Americans with a high-school but not a four-year college degree, 37 percent divorce or separate within the first ten years of marriage, compared with 11 percent of their more highly educated counterparts with a 4-year college degree (Wilcox and Marquardt, 2010).

In many other OECD countries, the divorce rate also has increased a lot since 1970. For example, in Japan, the divorce rate nearly tripled between 1970 and 2009 (Eberstadt, 2012). From the mid-1990s to the early 2000s, the divorce rate increased by 28 percent in Germany, 31 percent in France, and 27 percent in Spain (Popenoe, 2008: 9).

Adult children of divorced parents are 47 percent more likely to be currently cohabiting, compared to those who were reared in intact, married families (Wilcox, 2009:87). Let us now look at cohabitation which has emerged in OECD countries as a serious competitor to marriage in the social organization of sex, intimacy, child bearing and even child rearing.

Cohabitation

Cohabitation refers to living together in a sexual relationship without marriage. At the midpoint of the twentieth century, 75 percent of children in this country lived in nuclear families of two biological parents who were married to each other, with only full siblings (if they had brothers or sisters), and no other household members until they reached adulthood (Cavanagh and Fomby, 2012:81). Today, about 40 percent of all children in the United States spend some time living in a cohabiting family by age 12 (Kennedy and Bumpass, 2008; Bumpass and Lu, 2000).

One of the biggest changes in marriage and family in OECD countries is the growth in prevalence of cohabitation (Brown, Bulanda, and Lee, 2012; Beaujouan and Bhrolcháin, 2011; Gabrielli and Hoem, 2010; Philipov and Jasilioniene, 2008; Popenoe, 2008; Sobotka and Toulemon, 2008; Murphy, 2000). See Table 6.4 on cohabitors as a percent of all couples in various European countries and the United States from the 1990s to the first decade or so of the twenty-first century. Since 1970, cohabitation has shifted from being a relatively rare phenomenon to being part of the familial tapestry that shows no sign of going away. Between 1995 and 2010, the prevalence of cohabitation among people aged 30-44 years old in the United States doubled, from 3 percent to 7 percent (Fry and Cohn, 2011).

TABLE 6.4 COHABITORS AS A PERCENT OF ALL COUPLES IN VARIOUS EUROPEAN COUNTRIES AND THE UNITED STATES, 1990S-2000S AND PERCENT CHANGE

Country	1990s		2000s		Percent Change
Australia	1996	10.1	2006	15.0	48.5
Canada	1995	13.9	2006	18.4	32.4
Denmark	1995	24.7	2006	24.4	-1.2
France	1995	13.6	2001	17.2	26.5
Germany	1995	8.2	2005	11.2	36.6
Italy	1995	3.1	2003	3.8	22.6
Netherlands	1995	13.1	2004	13.3	1.5
New Zealand	1996	14.9	2006	23.7	59.1
Norway	2001	20.3	2007	21.8	7.4
Spain			2002	2.7	NA
Sweden	1995	23.0	2005	28.4	23.5
United Kingdom	1995	10.1	2010	17.0	68.3
United States	1995	5.1	2005	7.6	49.0

Source: Adapted from David Popenoe, *Cohabitation, Marriage and Child Wellbeing: A Cross National Perspective* (New Brunswick, NJ: The National Marriage Project at Rutgers University, 2008), Table 1 on Page 2; United Kingdom: for 2010, data are from p. 2 of Éva Beaujouan and Máire Bhrolcháin, "Cohabitation and Marriage in Britain Since the 1970s," Population Trends, Nr. 145, (Autumn) 2011, Office for National Statistics.

In the United States, among adults aged 30-44 years of age, cohabitation is more prevalent among the less educated, among whom 8 percent lived with an opposite-sex partner in 2009 (Fry and Cohn, 2011). The share among those with at least a Bachelor's degree was half that rate (4 percent) (Fry and Cohn, 2011). Among people with at least a Bachelor's degree in the United States, marriage rates have held steady as cohabitation has grown (Fry and Cohn, 2010; Murray, 2012a). So, in the United States an educational divide exists in terms of relationship status, whereby the less educated—those with a high-school degree or less--tend either to have no partner or to cohabit while the highly educated tend to marry.

Of course, the percentage of adults who *ever* have cohabited is much larger than the share *currently* cohabiting and it has grown to be a majority in recent decades in this country. According to data from the National Survey of Family Growth, among females aged 19-44, 58 percent have ever lived with an opposite-sex unmarried partner in 2006-2008, up from 33 percent of a comparable group in 1987 (National Center for Marriage and Family Research, 2010). Among females aged 19-44 without a high school degree, 73 percent have ever cohabited, compared with 47 percent of those with a college degree (National Center for Marriage and Family Research, 2010).

More than half (58 percent) of women who marry for the first time in the United States have lived with their husbands before the wedding (Kennedy and Bumpass, 2008). Survey findings by the Pew Research Center indicate that most, but not all, adults who cohabit view it as a step toward marriage. In a 2010 Pew Research Center Survey, nearly two-thirds (64 percent) of respondents who ever had cohabited say they thought of it as a step toward marriage. Among those currently cohabiting, 53 percent say so (Fry and Cohn,

2011). For many people, then, the meaning of cohabitation is that it is a stage in the process of relationship building that precedes marriage. This close connection between cohabitation and marriage for many people is indicated in Figure 6.1, which shows that the most important reason for cohabiting for both males and females is so that "couples can be sure they are compatible before marriage" (Bumpass, Sweet, and Cherlin, 1991: 920).

FIGURE 6.1 REASONS FOR COHABITING

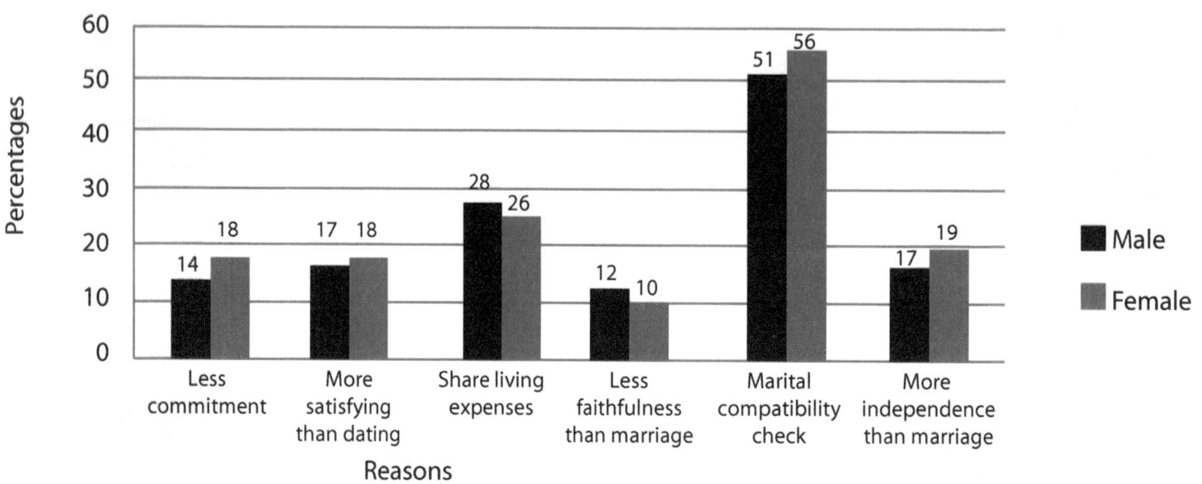

Source: Larry L. Bumpass, James A. Sweet, and Andrew Cherlin, "The Role of Cohabitation in Declining Rates of Marriage," *Journal of Marriage and Family*, Vol. 53 (November) 1991: 913-927.

But whatever the motivations and expectations and of those who cohabit, these relationships tend to be short-lived in comparison to marriages (e.g., Taylor, et. al., 2007; Amato, 2005; Manning, Smock, and Majumdar, 2004; Landale and Hauan, 1992). Cohabiting unions have become less tied both to marriage and longer duration (Kennedy and Bumpass, 2011) even as they have become increasingly tied to child bearing. A recent Pew survey finds that about half of all non-marital births are to cohabiting couples (Taylor, Funk, and Clark, 2007).

The Fragile Families Study follows a cohort of about 5,000 children born between 1998-2000 in medium to large cities in the United States (Hymowitz, 2010). One of the study's findings is that 80 percent of the unmarried couples were romantically involved at the time of their child's birth and 50 percent of them were living together. Fathers almost always visited the mothers and children in the hospital and usually provided financial support. Most of these new parents said there was a 50-50 chance they would eventually marry each other and they spoke highly of their partners' commitment to their children and of their supportiveness. But one-year after the birth of their child, one-fourth of the cohabiting biological parents no longer lived together (Carlson, McLanahan, and England, 2003; McLanahan, 2004). Within five years, only 15 percent of the unmarried couples had taken wedding vows, while 80 percent of them had split up (Hymowitz, 2010).

Other studies indicate that in the United States, about half of all cohabiting relationships end within five years (Bramlett, and Mosher, 2002; Taylor, 2010) and that people—both males and females--increasingly reside in multiple cohabiting unions (Bumpass and Lu, 2000; Kennedy and Bumpass, 2008; Lichter, Turner and Sassler, 2010), one after the other. Thus, by the time the children born to the unmarried cohabiting couples in the Fragile Families Study were five years old, 20 percent of their mothers had given birth to a child by a different man and 27 percent of the kids were living with their mother's new live-in partner (Hymowitz, 2010).

Total Fertility Rate

The **total fertility rate** is the number of births per woman during her reproductive years, often measured as the number of births per female aged 15-45. A rate of about 2.1 will produce a stable population, a population that does not increase or decrease in size. A total fertility rate of 2.1 results, in other words, in a population reproducing itself, which is why a total fertility rate of 2.1 is called a "replacement-level" fertility rate. A total fertility rate less than 2.1 will result in a declining population unless the difference is made up for by immigration.

Currently, few OECD countries have a total fertility rate at or above 2.1. As of 2012, the OECD countries with replacement-level or higher fertility rates include Mexico (2.27), Israel (2.6), Greenland (2.1), and Turkey (2.13) (CIA World Factbook, 2012). In the United States, the total fertility rate was 3.4 from 1960-1964, 2.6 from 1965-1969, 2.1 from 1970 to 1974, and 1.8 from 1975-1979 (Wattenberg, 1985: 63). Currently, the total fertility rate in the United States is about 2.06, which is just below replacement level (CIA World Factbook, 2012). The total fertility rate of the United States seems "high" in comparison with the total fertility rate of most European OECD countries. See Table 6.5 on the total fertility rate of various OECD Countries in 2012.

In Italy, Spain, and Germany, total fertility has dropped so dramatically that these countries stand to lose up to 30 percent of their population each generation, absent new net immigration (Fukuyama, 1999a). The Germans, who saw their population shrink by 700,000 in just the years from 2000 to 2009, have a term for this new phenomenon, ***schrumpfende Gesellschaft***, which translates into English as shrinking society (Ebertadt, 2012). In a couple of generations, most Europeans and Japanese may be related only to their ancestors (Fukuyama: 1999b: 13) and 60 percent of Italy's children will have no siblings, cousins, uncles, or aunts (Eberstadt, 2012).

Though the dearth of relatives can be presented in statistics, the human meaning of this dramatic change may better be captured through anecdote. In Japan, these include the following (Eberstadt, 2012):

- "Rental relatives" are now readily available throughout the country, both for formal rituals like weddings and funerals, as well as for more informal occasions (McCurry, 2009). For instance, a mother may rent someone to act as the uncle of her child or children at a school sports day. This rented relative would cheer his "nephew" and "niece" on, record their efforts on his hand-held video camera, and join in the adult-and-child races. In essence, rental relatives are a non-familial, private-sector solution for providing "fictive kin" when the family, quite literally, has disappeared. If does not want it to appear to others that he or she lacks family members, unbeknownst to others, one rents them. Human needs do not "go away." People simply find innovative ways of satisfying those needs with the resources available to them.

- In a recent government survey in Japan, fully one-third of boys aged 16 to 19 years of age described themselves as "uninterested in or positively averse" to sexual intimacy (Eberstadt, 2012)
- "Babyloids"—small, furry robotic "dolls" that mimic some of the sounds and gestures of real babies are being marketed to help older Japanese ameliorate depression and loneliness
- Rental pets and robotic pets—are available for those who want the affection of an animal and the comfort of interacting with one without taking care of one (Villar, 2012). There are cat cafes, dog cafes, and even bunny cafes in Japan. There also are robotic pets, some of the soft, furry variety and some that look more like "robots." One of the soft, furry robotic pets is named "Paro." Paro is a popular robotic baby seal. Another soft, furry robotic pet is "Aibo," which means "pal" in Japanse. Aibo is made and marketed by Sony and he is particularly popular among the elderly in Japan (Rose, 2005).

TABLE 6.5 TOTAL FERTILITY RATE IN VARIOUS OECD COUNTRIES, 2012

COUNTRY	TOTAL FERTILITY RATE
United States of America	2.06
United Kingdom	1.91
Netherlands	1.78
Norway	1.77
Belgium	1.65
Russia	1.61
Canada	1.59
China	1.55
Switzerland	1.53
Spain	1.48
Austria	1.41
Germany	1.41
Japan	1.39
Greece	1.39
Czech Republic	1.27
South Korea	1.23

Source: CIA World Factbook 2012. The total fertility rates are 2012 preliminary data. As of September 24, 2012, total fertility rate preliminary data are available online at www.cia.gov

In cultures in which kin relations are important social actors who come to one another's aid, a steep decline fertility poses difficult challenges to social cohesion by, quite literally, eliminating an important source of what sociologists term "social capital." ***Social capital*** refers to social networks within, between, and among groups. These social networks are important vehicles for providing their members with access to important resources, including emotional support in good times and in hard times. Social capital encompasses one's

relationships, support systems, and access to important community resources. Members of social networks share important values, meanings, and norms that facilitate belonging to society (Fukuyama 1999b: 113; Flavin, 2004; Jarrett, Sullivan, and Watkins, 2005). Family and kin are important elements of social capital. Falling fertility poses difficult problems for social cohesion (social solidarity) by weakening family and kinship as a source of social capital.

One-Person Households

A growing number of people are living alone for long stretches of their lives. In Japan, one-person households are 30 percent of all households, while the corresponding figure is 36 percent in Germany and 34 percent in the Netherlands (OECD Family Database).

Less than ten percent of households in the United States in 1950 consisted of just one person. Today, over 30 million adults live alone —about one out of every 7 adults—and they constitute 28 percent of all households (Klineberg, 2012). Single people living alone are more than 40 percent of all households in San Francisco, Seattle, Atlanta, Denver, and Minneapolis and almost 50 percent in Washington, D.C. and Manhattan, New York (Klineberg, 2012). The numbers are even higher in European OECD countries. In Scandinavia, almost half of all households are composed of single individuals (Fukuyama, 1999b: 114). In Oslo, the number of people living alone rises to some 75 percent of all households (Tiger, 1999).

In the Netherlands, **lat-relationships** are a significant part of the intimate relationship landscape. "Lat" is an acronym for living apart together. In a lat-relationship, single people maintain a relationship with each other without moving in with each other. Among older people, this type of relationship is particularly popular: more than 40 percent of people over 40 in the Netherlands and nearly 70 percent of people over 50 with a lat-partner do not want to be living with that partner at any point in the future. About half of all people currently living alone who want to continue living alone in the future in the Netherlands list preserving their freedom as their main reason for wanting to do so (Latten, 2004).

Single-Parent Families

One-parent families, over 80 percent of which are headed by a single mother in the United States, may result from divorce, widowhood, death of a partner, or a decision by an unmarried female to bear a child. According to the U.S. Census Bureau, thirty-four percent of children under the age of 18 live in single-parent unmarried families in the United States, which is a 6 percent increase since 2005 (Annie E. Casey Foundation, 2012: 18-19). There is significant variation by race and ethnicity, with 16 percent of Asian and Pacific Islander children under the age of 18 living in single-parent homes, compared with 24 percent of non-Hispanic white children, 41 percent of Hispanic children, 52 percent of American Indian children, and 66 percent of African American children under the age of 18 who live in single-parent homes in the United States (Annie E. Casey Foundation, 2012: 19).

One of the fastest-growing forms of single-parent families in the United States are those headed by single fathers (Lawrence and Hesse, 2010: 71), which now account for about 15 percent of all single-parent families in the United States. Stephen Demuth and Susan L. Brown of the Center for Family and Demographic Research at Bowling Green University, using data from the 1995 National Longitudinal Survey of Adolescent Health, find that levels of delinquency are significantly greater among youth residing in single-parent families than among their counterparts residing with two married, biological parents (Demuth and Brown, 2004). They also find that rates of delinquency are significantly higher among youth in single-father homes than among youth in single-mother homes, due to greater shortfalls in parental supervision and discipline of the youths in single-father homes (Demuth and Brown, 2004).

Janet L. Lauritsen (2003) analyzes data from the National Crime Victimization Survey, which is based on a national probability sample of U.S. households. Lauritsen documents that youth in single-parent homes are at far greater risk of violent criminal victimization than are youth in two-parent married families. Approximately 60 out of every 1,000 children aged 12-17 in single-parent families report at least one violent criminal victimization during a 6-month period, compared with 40 out of every 1,000 children in two parent families. In other words, the overall risk for violence is 50 percent higher among youth living in single-parent homes than among youth living in two-parent families (Lauritsen, 2003: 4).

The difference in risk for neighborhood violence is even more pronounced. Youth in single parent families are about twice as likely as youth in two-parent families to become a victim of violence in their own neighborhood (40.8 versus 19.9 per 1,000 youth). These levels of risk are significantly higher than those found for most Americans. Children "living in single-parent homes have an overall risk for violent victimization that is about three times higher than the average American (60 versus 18 per 1,000") (Lauritsen, 2003: 4). The increased risk of violent victimization on the basis of family structure and processes (e.g., adequacy of parental supervision and discipline) does not disappear when we control for social class, race, and ethnicity.

Regardless of family structure, the quality of parenting is one of the strongest predictors of children's emotional and social well-being (Amato, 2005). A large body of research indicates that many single parents find it difficult to function effectively in their parental roles. Thus, compared with continuously married parents, single parents are less emotionally supportive of their children, have fewer rules, dispense harsher discipline, are more inconsistent in dispensing discipline, provide less supervision, and engage in harsher discipline with their children (Amato, 2005: 83; Aseltine, 1996; Simons and Associates, 1996; Morrison and Cherlin, 1995; Amato, 1994).

Many studies link inept parenting by single parents with a variety of negative outcomes including poor academic achievement, emotional problems, conduct problems, low self-esteem, and problems forming and maintaining relationships (Amato, 2005: 83; Buchanan, Maccoby, and Dornbusch, 1996; Simons and Associates, 1996; McLanahan and Sandefur, 1994).

Non-Marital Childbearing

Childbearing increasingly occurs outside of marriage. In Iceland 66 percent of all births are to unmarried females, while in Sweden the share is 55 percent (The Economist, 2011). In France (50.5 percent) and Norway (53 percent) more than half of all births are to unmarried females (Popenoe, 2008: 6) and in the Netherlands, the comparable figure is 40 percent (Latten, 2004). In the United States, 41 percent of all births are to unmarried females (Martin, Hamilton, and Ventua, et. al., 2011), up from 5 percent in 1960. The likelihood of not being married when giving birth varies significantly by race and ethnicity. Among non-Hispanic whites, less than a third (29 percent) of all births occur to females who are not married. Comparable figures are 73 percent of black births, 65 percent of births to American Indians or Alaska natives, and 53 percent of births to Hispanics (Martin, Hamilton, Ventura, et. al., 2011: 8). See Table 6.6 on the percent of all births to non-married females by race and ethnicity in the United States in 2009.

TABLE 6.6 PERCENT OF ALL BIRTHS TO UNMARRIED FEMALES IN THE UNITED STATES, 2009, BY RACE AND ETHNICITY

All Races	Non-Hispanic Whites	Non-Hispanic Blacks	American Indian or Alaska Natives	Asian or Pacific Islander	Hispanic
41.0	29.0	72.8	65.4	17.2	53.2

Source: Joyce A. Martin, Bradley E. Hamilton, Stephanie J. Ventura, et. al., "Births: Final Data for 2009" *National Vital Statistics Reports*, Vol. 60, No. 1 (Hyattsville, MD: National Center for Health Statistics, 2011).

Level of education matters, too, in the probability of not being married when giving birth in the United States. Let us use the term "highly educated" to refer to those who have earned a four-year college degree, "moderately educated" to refer to those with a high-school but not a four-year college degree, and "least educated" to refer to those who lack a high-school degree or its equivalent (GED). In the late 2000s, only 6 percent of babies born to highly educated mothers in the United States were born outside of marriage, compared to 44 percent of babies born to moderately educated mothers and 54 percent of the babies born to the least educated mothers (Wilcox and Marquardt, 2010).

ARE VARIOUS FAMILY FORMS EQUAL IN TERMS OF OUTCOMES OR DO FAMILY STRUCTURE AND PROCESS MATTER? A LOOK AT THE EVIDENCE

Does it really matter that the marriage rate has fallen and that there has been a large increase in the prevalence of divorce, non-marital births, and cohabitation? Many people think not. For instance, a Pew Research survey reveals that 65 percent of people aged 18-29 in the United States (and 52 percent of those aged 30-49 but only 36 percent of those aged 65 or older) believe that "one parent can bring up a child as well as two parents together" (Kohut, 2012: 27). In the United States, there are sizeable gender differences in this belief, with 62 percent of women but only 39 percent of men agreeing that "one parent can bring up a child as well as two parents" (Kohut, 2012: 30). Likewise, a 2006 AC Nielsen global survey finds that 77 percent of Europeans agree with the statement "I consider a stable, long-term relationship just as good as marriage" (Global Consumer Confidence Survey, 2006). And fully two-thirds of adults in Great Britain agree that there is "little difference socially between being married and living together as a couple" (Beaujouan and Bhrolcháin, 2011: 2).

We may well ask whether it is true that various family forms are equal in their outcomes, that they are, essentially, functional equivalents of each other. To arrive at an answer, we will summarize the scholarly evidence about the impact that cohabitation is having on marriage, family life, and the welfare of children and about the impact that divorce, stepfamilies and single parenthood have on children, adults, and the larger commonweal. We accomplish this by looking at five major themes that emerge from the scholarship on family outcomes.

Five Major Themes

Several major themes emerge from the scholarship on family outcomes (Wilcox, et. al., 2011: 7-9). First, children are less likely to thrive in cohabiting households, compared with intact, married families consisting of the two biological parents of the children. Children in cohabitating households do significantly worse on numerous social, educational, and psychological outcomes than children in intact, married families. For instance, when it comes to abuse, federal data indicate that children in cohabiting households are markedly more likely to be physically, sexually, and emotionally abused than children in both intact, married families and in single-parent families. See Figure 6.2 on the incidence per 1,000 children of physical abuse, sexual abuse, and emotional abuse by family structure and living arrangement in the United States, 2005-2006 (Sedlak, Mettenburg, Basena, Petta, McPherson, Greene, and Li, 2010: 5-22).

FIGURE 6.2 INCIDENCE PER 1 ,000 CHILDREN OF HARM STANDARD ABUSE BY FAMILY STRUCTURE AND LIVING ARRA

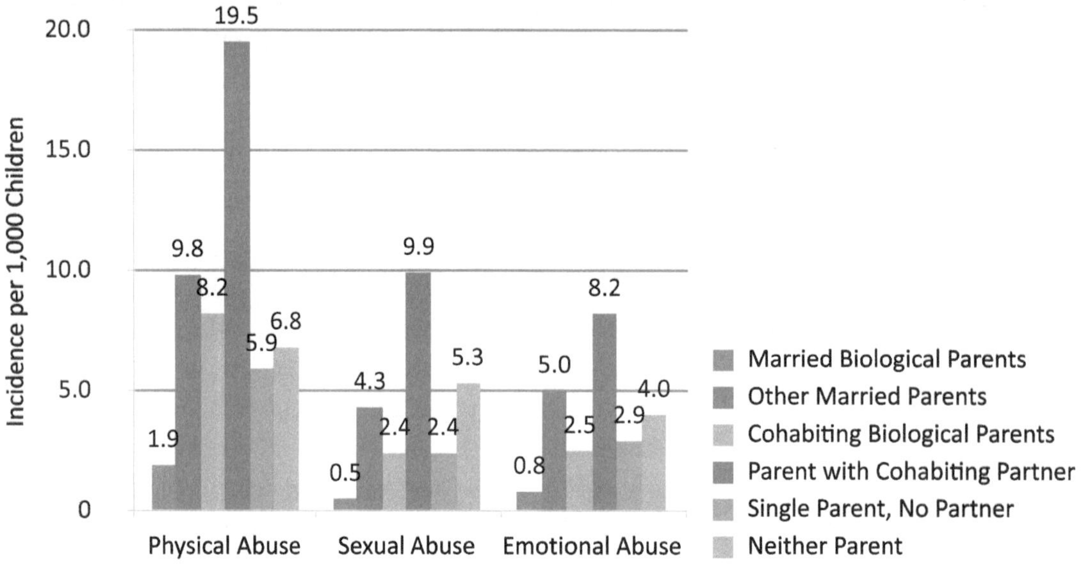

Source: Figure 5.2 in A.J. Sedlak, J. Mettenburg, M. Basena, I. Petta, K. McPherson, A. Greene, and S. Li, *Fourth National Incidence Study of Child Abuse and Neglect (NIS-4): Report to Congress* (Washington, D.C.: U.S. Department of Health and Human Services, Administration for Children and Families, 2010), page 5-22.

In comparison with children who grow up in stable, two-parent families, children who grow up outside of marriage commit more delinquency, have lower grade-point averages as teens, and have significantly lower test scores in adolescence on nationally standardized tests in mathematics, reading, science, and social studies (Jeynes, 2011: 136; Manning and Lamb, 2003); and they reach adulthood with less education, more delinquency, earn less income, have lower occupational status, are more likely to be "idle" (i.e., not employed and not in school), have more troubled marriages, experience higher rates of divorce, and report more symptoms of depression (Amato, 2005: 78; Teachmen, 2004; Teachman, 2002; Haveman, Wolf, and Pence, 2001; McLanahan and Sandefur, 1994).

Second, family instability is generally bad for children. Transitions—especially multiple transitions--into and out of marriage, cohabitation, single-parenthood and other intimate relationships (boyfriends, girlfriends) are linked with negative outcomes for the children in such unions. What types of negative outcomes? Research consistently shows that, even when researchers control for economic status, race, and ethnicity, these transitions are linked to higher rates of a wide range of cognitive, emotional, health, and social problems, not only in childhood but also in adulthood, including school failure, behavioral problems, drug use, depression, and incarceration (e.g., Amato, 2005; Harper and McLanahan, 2004). For instance, social scientists consistently have documented the downward pressure that divorce exerts on children's academic achievement (e.g., Jeynes, 2002: 119; Amato, 1993). Sociologist Paul R. Amato, who is the Arnold and Bette Hoffman Professor of Family Sociology and Demography at The Pennsylvania State University as well as the 2012 Chair of the Family Section of the American Sociological Association and the 2013 President of the National Council of Family Relations estimates that if the United States enjoyed the same level of family stability today as it did in 1960, the nation would have 750,000 fewer children repeating grades in school, 1.2 million fewer school suspensions, approximately 500,000 fewer acts of teenage delinquency, about 600,000 fewer kids receiving therapy, and about 70,000 fewer suicide attempts *each year* (Wilcox, 2009: 85). In their book, *Growing Up with a Single Parent: What Hurts, What Helps*, sociologists Sara McLanahan and Gary Sandefur find that 31 percent of adolescents with divorced parents dropped out of high school, compared with 13 percent of children from intact homes (McLanahan and Sandefur, 1994). Sara McLanahan and Gary Sandefur also conclude that one third (33 percent) of divorced parents become teen mothers compared to 11 percent of girls from continuously married families (McLanahan and Sandefur, 1994). McLanahan and her colleagues have also found that 11 percent of boys who come from divorced families end up spending time in prison before the age of 32, compared with 5 percent of boys who come from continuously married families (Wilcox, 2009: 84; Harper and McLanahan, 2004).

Pew Research Center finds that there is a correlation between the kinds of family arrangements that people experience while growing up and their own behaviors in adulthood (Taylor, Funk, and Clark, 2007). For instance, among people who are themselves products of parents who never married, about a third (32 percent) are themselves never-married parents. By comparison, just 6 percent of the general public are themselves the children of never married parents (Taylor, Funk, and Clark, 2007: 10).

A large body of research demonstrates that adults with divorced parents, when compared to adults with continuously married parents, report greater unhappiness, a weaker sense of personal control, less satisfaction with life, more symptoms of anxiety and depression, and a greater use of mental health services (e.g., Amato and Sobolewski, 2001; Biblarz and Gottainer, 2000; Amato and Booth, 1997, 1991). Similar findings appear in national samples from Britain, Canada, and Australia (Cherlin, Chase-Lansdale, and McRae, 1998; Le Bourdais and Marcil-Gratton, 1998; Amato, 1988). The great majority of studies demonstrate a link between childhood family structure and adult psychological well-being (Amato, 2010; Amato and Sobolewski, 2001). In short, it's not just family structure that is important in terms of outcomes; the level of stability matters as well. Children who are born to two married parents are least likely to be exposed to family instability.

Third, family life is becoming increasingly unstable for children. As we already have discussed in this chapter, one of the reasons that children's lives are increasingly turbulent is because they are being born into or raised in cohabiting families that are much more fragile—more prone to splitting apart—than married families and that they experience these transitions multiple times while growing up. Compared with offspring with two continuously married parents, offspring with divorced parents are more likely to drop out of high school, less likely to attend college, more likely to be unemployed, and more likely to experience economic hardship as adults (Amato and Cheadle, 2005; Amato and Keith, 1991; McLanahan and Sandefur, 1994).

Fourth, contemporary adults and children are more likely to live and to have lived in what scholars term "complex households" or "blended families," where children and adults are living with people who are step-parents, half-siblings, stepsiblings, step-children, or other persons unrelated to them by birth or marriage.

Many Americans believe that parental marriage following divorce generally benefits children (Jeynes, 2002: 120). After all, remarriage introduces an additional caregiver into the family. Re-marriage also tends substantially to raise the economic position of the family and it is assumed that the effect of this would be beneficial. Nonetheless, research consistently documents that in the United States the introduction of a nonbiological caregiver into a family exerts downward pressure on the academic achievement of the child or children (e.g., Jeynes, 1998a, 1998b, 2002, 2011; McLanahan and Sandefur, 1994). Even though remarriage raises the socio-economic status of the family, remarriage exerts a negative effect on the academic achievement of children, a negative effect that persists even if parental engagement in the education of the children is high (e.g., Jeynes, 2011: 151). It is not that parental involvement has no impact on the academic achievement of the children of divorce and remarriage. High parental engagement in the education of the children of divorce and remarriage does somewhat compensate for the downward pressure that is exerted by parental divorce and remarriage. It does not eliminate the negative effects of parental divorce and remarriage on the academic achievement of the children, even when the researchers control for race, ethnicity, and social class (Jeynes, 2011; Cavanagh and Fomby, 2012).

Multiple-partner fertility, where one or more parents has children by more than one romantic partner (whether married to them at some point or not), is one way that complex or blended families are formed in the United States. Even when researchers control for social class, race, and ethnicity, children from these relationships are more likely to report poor relationships with their parents, to have behavioral as well as health problems, and to experience a variety of academic problems including failure in school (Cavanagh and Fomby, 2012; Jeynes, 2011; Cherlin, 2009; Cavanagh and Huston, 2008, 2006; Fomby and Cherlin, 2007; Osborne and McLanahan, 2007; Wu and Thomson, 2001). Children in step families are more likely to experience school failure, delinquency, teen pregnancy, and incarceration than children growing up in intact, married families (Wilcox, et. al, 2011:16-17; Harper and McLanahan, 2004; Aseltine, 1996; Morrison and Cherlin, 1995; McLanahan and Sandefur, 1994).

Fifth, cohabitation is not the functional equivalent of marriage, either for the adults or for the children (Wilcox, et. al., 2011: 17-18; Smock and Manning, 2004). Adults who cohabit are more similar to singles than to married people in terms of mental health and emotional well-being (e.g., Brown, 2000), physical health (e.g., Pienta, Hayward, and Jenkins, 2000), and earnings and assets (e.g., Daniel, 1995). Children living with cohabiting parents have outcomes more similar to children living with single or remarried parents than children from intact marriages (Jeynes, 2000, 2011; Morrison and Ritualo, 2000). In other words, children in cohabiting households do not fare as well as children in married families. For instance, sociologist Susan L. Brown of the Department of Sociology and Center for Family and Demographic Research at Bowling Green State University finds that children and adolescents living in cohabiting families are significantly more likely to experience emotional, behavioral and academic difficulties than are their counterparts in intact, married families, even after controlling for a range of socio-economic and parenting factors (Brown, 2004). In another study, Brown uses data from the National Longitudinal Study of Adolescent Health to examine the linkages between relationship type (dating, cohabiting, marriage) and relationship violence perpetration and victimization among young adults. She finds that among women in this nationally representative sample, cohabitors report significantly higher levels of relationship violence than either daters or marrieds. This pattern persists even after controlling for individual socio-demographic factors and relationship quality indicators (Brown, 2008). Using the same database in another study (Brown, 2006), Brown examines the influence of parental marital and cohabitation transitions on adolescent delinquency, depression, and school engagement. Adolescents who experienced a family transition report decreased well-being relative to those in stable, two-biological parent families. Moving *out of* a cohabiting stepfamily into a single-mother family was actually associated with *improvements* in school engagement, while moving *into* a cohabiting stepfamily from a single-mother family *decreased* adolescent well-being (Brown, 2006).

Other studies that also utilize nationally representative samples find similar results. For instance, Thomas De Leire, who holds a Ph.D. in Economics from Stanford University and who currently is the Director of the LaFollette School of Public Affairs at the University of Wisconsin, Madison, and Ariel Kalil of the Harris Graduate School of Public Policy Studies at University of Chicago, using data from the National Educational Longitudinal Study (NELS) find that teenagers who live in non-married cohabiting families are less likely to graduate from high school or to attend college, more likely to smoke or drink, and more likely to initiate sexual activity (DeLeire and Kalil, 2002).

In another study, DeLeire and Kalil (2005) use the Consumer Expenditure Survey to see if cohabiting couples with children spend their income on a different set of goods than either married-parent families or single parents. Cohabiting couples with children spend a substantially larger share of their total expenditure on alcohol and tobacco than do either married parent families or single parents. Cohabiting couples with children also spend less on education than do married parents (DeLeire and Kalil, 2005). One reason for this may be because, in comparison with married couples, cohabiting couples are less committed to each other as partners and to their future together (Stanley, Whitton, and Markman, 2004). One manifestation of this lesser commitment is that cohabiting couples are less likely than their married counterparts to pool their income (Oropesa and Landale, 2005; Lerman, 2002). The greater instability and lower levels of commitment in cohabiting relationships also pose hardships for the elderly who appear to be more likely to be institutionalized or abandoned if they are cohabiting rather than married (Wilcox, et. al., 2011; Moustgaard and Martikainen, 2009).

Cohabiting parents are more than twice as likely as married parents to break up (Wilcox and Marquardt, 2011). One recent study estimates that 65 percent of parents who had a child while cohabiting will break up by the child turns 12 years of age, compared with just 24 percent of parents who had a child while married (Kennedy and Bumpass, 2011). Growing up with two continuously cohabiting biological parents is rare in the United States. How rare? An analysis of the 1995 Adolescent Health Study reveals that one-half of one percent of adolescents aged sixteen to eighteen had spent their entire childhoods living with two continuously cohabiting biological parents (Amato, 2011: 79).

Economist Benjamin Scafidi has calculated the costs to U.S. taxpayers of the high rates of divorce and unmarried child bearing and rearing. See Table 6.7 on the estimated annual cost to U.S. taxpayers due to family fragmentation. Family fragmentation costs U.S. taxpayers *at least* $112 billion dollars *each year*, or over a trillion dollars per decade (Scafidi, 2008: 17-18). The changes in family structure and process that we have documented in this chapter have broad economic implications, including larger expenditures for both federal and state governments. Private choices can and do carry heavy public price tags. This is an example of the dynamic interdependence of institutions in the modern age.

TABLE 6.7 ESTIMATED ANNUAL COST FOR U.S. TAXPAYERS OF FAMILY FRAGMENTATION* IN THE UNITED STATES

*These costs include federal, state, and local costs	In Billions
Justice System	$19.3
Temporary Assistance for Needy Families (TANF)—Cash Assistance	$ 5.1
Food Stamps	$ 9.6
Housing Assistance	$ 7.3
Medicaid	$27.9
State Children's Health Insurance Program (SCHIP)	$ 2.8
Child Welfare	$ 9.2
Women, Infants, and Children (WIC) Assistance	$ 1.6
Low Income Home Energy Assistance Program (LIHEAP)	$ 0.7
Head Start	$ 2.7
School Lunch and Breakfast Program	$ 3.5
Additional U.S. Income Taxes Paid	$ 6.1
Additional FICA (Social Security and Medicare) Taxes Paid	$ 9.4
Additional State & Local Taxes Paid	$ 6.8
Total Annual U.S. Taxpayer Cost of Family Fragmentation	$112.0

Source: Table 7 on page 18 of Benjamin Scafidi, *The Taxpayer Costs of Divorce and Unwed Childbearing: First-Ever Estimates for the Nation and All Fifty States* (New York: Institute for American Values, 2008).

CONCLUSION

This chapter provides a brief sociological overview of the social structure of the family and thereby reveals that the family is a dynamic institution capable of evolving to help individuals solve their survival needs. As conditions change for the individual, family form manages to evolve and to change to accommodate and satisfy human needs as best it can with the limited resources at its disposal. Today some of these adaptations seem to have a "satisficing" quality about them, in the sense that the solutions the evolving family forms provide may be far from optimal, even in countries that have generous "social safety nets." The evolving forms of the family, however, help people to move forward with their lives with the limited resources at their disposal. The social structure of the family, then, both influences the social, economic, political, and cultural worlds in which it is situated and is affected by them. The relationship between the structure of the family and other aspects of society is one of dynamic interdependence.

SUGGESTED READINGS

Banks, Ralph Richards, *is Marriage for White People? How the African American Marriage Decline Affects Everyone* (New York: Dutton, 2011).

Cross, Gary S., *Men to Boys: The Making of Modern Immaturity* (New York: Columbia University Press, 2008).

Eberstadt, Mary, *Adam and Eve After the Pill* (San Francisco: Ignatius Press, 2012).

Eller, Cynthia, *The Myth of Matriarchal Prehistory: Why an Invented Past Will Not Give Women a Future* (Boston, MA: Beacon Press, 2000).

Fukuyama, Francis, *The Great Disruption* (New York: The Free Press, 1999).

Hymowitz, Kay S., *Marriage and Caste in America: Separate and Unequal Families in a Post-Marital Age* (Chicago, Illinois: Ivan R. Dee Publisher, 2006).

Murray, Charles, *Coming Apart: The State of White America, 1960-2010* (New York: Crown Forum, 2012).

Nagle, Jeanne, *Same Sex Marriage: The Debate* (New York: Rosen Publishing Group, Inc. 2010).

Regnerus, Mark, "How Different Are the Adult Children of Parents Who Have Same-Sex Relationships? Findings from the New Family Structures Study," *Social Science Research*, Vol. 41, 2012: 752-770.

Rodriguez, Richard T., *Next of Kin: The Family in Chicano -- A Cultural Politics* (Durham, NC: Duke University Press, 2009).

West, Diana, *The Death of the Grownup: How America's Arrested Development is Bringing Down Western Civilization* (New York: St. Martin's Press, 2007).

Wilcox, W. Bradford, et. al., *Why Marriage Matters* Third Edition (New York: Institute for American Values, 2011).

BIBLIOGRAPHY

Ahmed, Leila, *Women and Gender in Islam: Historical Roots of a Modern Debate* (New Haven, CT: Yale University Press, 1992).

Amato, Paul R., "Children's Adjustment to Divorce: Theories, Hypotheses, and Empirical Support," *Journal of Marriage and the Family*, Vol. 55, No. 1, 1993: 23-28.

Amato, Paul R., "Long-Term Implications of Parental Divorce for Adult Self-Concept," *Journal of Family Issues*, Vol. 9, 1988: 201-213.

Amato, Paul R., "Research on Divorce: Continuing Trends and New Developments," *Journal of Marriage and Family*, Vol. 72, 2010: 650-666.

Amato, Paul R., "The Impact of Family Formation Change on the Cognitive, Social, and Emotional Well-Being of the Next Generation," *The Future of Children*, Vol. 15, No. 2 (Fall) 2005: 75-96.

Amato, Paul R., "The Implications of Research on Children in Stepfamilies," in Alan Booth and Judy Dunn (Eds.), *Stepfamilies: Who Benefits? Who Does Not?* (Hillsdale, NJ: Lawrence Erlbaum, 1994).

Amato, Paul R., and Booth, Alan, "Consequences of Parental Divorce and Marital Unhappiness for Adult Well-Being," *Social Forces*, Vol. 69, 1991: 895-914.

Amato, Paul R., and Booth, Alan, *A Generation at Risk: Growing Up in an Era of Family Upheaval* (Cambridge, MA: Harvard University Press, 1997).

Amato, Paul R., and Cheadle, Jacob, "The Long Reach of Divorce: Divorce and Child Well-Being across Three Generations," *Journal of Marriage and Family*, Vol. 67, (February) 2005: 191-206.

Amato, Paul R., and Keith, B., "Separation from a Parent During Childhood and Adult Socio-economic Attainment," *Social Forces*, Vol. 70, 1991: 187-206.

Amato, Paul R., and Sobolewski, Juliana M., "The Effects of Divorce and Marital Discord on Adult Children's Psychological Well-Being," *American Sociological Review*, Vol. 66 (December), 2001: 900-921.

Annie E. Casey Foundation, *Kids Count Data Book 2012* (Baltimore, MD: The Annie E. Casey Foundation, 2012).

Aseltine, Robert H., "Pathways Linking Parental Divorce with Adolescent Depression," *Journal of Health and Social Behavior*, Vol. 37, 1996: 133-148.

Bailey, Joanne, "Favored or Oppressed? Married Women, Property, and 'Coverture' in England, 1660-1800," *Continuity and Change*, Vol. 17, No. 3, (December) 2002: 351-372.

Banks, Ralph Richard, *is Marriage for White People? How the African Marriage Decline Affects Everyone* (New York: Dutton, 2011).

Baskerville, Stephen, *Taken into Custody: The War Against Fathers, Marriage, and the Family* (Nashville, TN: Cumberland House, 2007).

Beaujouan, Éva, and Bhrolcháin, Máire Ni, "Cohabitation and Marriage in Britain Since the 1970s," *Population Trends*, Nr. 145, (Autumn) 2011. Office for National Statistics.

Bell, Daniel, *The Coming of Post-Industrial Society* (New York: Basic Books, 1976).

Bener, A., and Alali, K.A., "Consanguineous Marriage in a Newly Developed Country: the Qatari Population," *Journal of Biosocial Science*, Vol. 38, 2006: 239-246.

Betzig, Laura L., "Comment," *Current Anthropology*, Vol. 32, 1991: 410.

Betzig, Laura L., *Despotism and Differential Reproduction: A Darwinian View of History* (Piscataway, NJ: Aldine Transaction, 2008). Originally published (New York: Aldine Publishing Company, 1986).

Biblarz, Timothy, and Gottainer, Greg, "Family Structure and Children's Success: A Comparison of Widowed and Divorced Single Mother Families," *Journal of Marriage and the Family*, Vol. 62, 2000: 342-349.

Billingsley, Andrew, *Black Families in White America* (Englewood Cliffs, NJ: Prentice Hall, 1968).

Bittles, Alan H., "Consanguinity, Genetic Drift, and Genetic Diseases in Populations with Reduced Numbers of Founders," in Friedrich Vogel and Arno G. Motulsky (Eds.), *Human Genetics* Fourth Edition (Berlin: Springer-Verlag: 2010), pp. 507-528.

Bittles, Alan H., "The Bases of Western Attitudes to Consanguineous Marriage," *Developmental Medicine & Child Neurology*, Vol. 45, 2003: 135-138.

Bittles, Alan H., and Black, M.L., "Consanguineous Marriage and Human Evolution," *Annual Review of Anthropology*, Vol. 39, (October) 2010: 193-207.

Blau, Peter M., *Exchange and Power in Social Life* (New York: Wiley, 1964).

Boetsch, G., Prost, M., and Rabino-Massa, "Evolution of Consanguinity in a French Alpine Valley: The Vallouise in the Brianfon Region (17th -19th Centuries)," *Human Biology*, Vol. 73 (2002): 285-300.

Bramlett, Matthew D. and Mosher, William D., "Cohabitation, Marriage, Divorce, and Remarriage in the United States," *Vital and Health Statistics*, Series 23, No. 22, 2002. Centers for Disease control and Prevention, National Center for Health Statistics Journal of Gerontology: Social Sciences

Brand, Paul, "Deserving and 'Undeserving' Wives: Earning and Forfeiting Dower in Medieval England," *Journal of Legal History*, Vol. 22, No. 1 (April) 2001: 1-20.

Brands, H.W., *Andrew Jackson: His life and Times* (New York: Doubleday, 2005).

Brown, Susan L., "Family Structure and Child Well-Being: The Significance of Parental Cohabitation," *Journal of Marriage and the Family*, Vol. 66, No. 2, (May) 2004: 351-367.

Brown, Susan L., "Family Structure Transitions and Adolescent Well-Being," *Demography*, Vol. 43, 2006: 447-461.

Brown, Susan L., "The Effect of Union Type on Psychological Well-Being: Depression Among Cohabitors Versus Marrieds," *Journal of Health and Social Behavior*, Vol. 41, No. 3, (July) 2000: 241-255.

Brown, Susan L., and Bulanda, Jennifer Roebuck, "Relationship Violence in Early Adulthood: A Comparison of Daters, Cohabitors, and Marrieds," *Social Science Research*, Vol. 37, 2008: 73-87.

Brown, Susan L., and Lin, I-Fen, "The Gray Divorce Revolution: Rising Divorce among Middle-Aged and Older Adults, 1990-2010," *Journals of Gerontology Series B: Psychological Sciences and Social Sciences*, Vol. 67, No. 6, 2012: 731-741.

Brown, Susan L., Bulanda, Jennifer Roebuck, and Lee, Gary R., "Transitions into and out of Cohabitation in Later Life," *Journal of Marriage and Family*, Vol. 74, 2012: 774-793.

Buchanan, Christine, Maccoby, Eleanor, and Dornbusch, Sanford M., *Adolescents after Divorce* (Cambride, MA: Harvard University Press, 1996).

Bumpass, Larry L.; Sweet, James A.; and Cherlin, Andrew, "The Role of Cohabitation in Declining Rates of Marriage," *Journal of Marriage and Family*, Vol. 53, No. 4, (November) 1991: 913-927.

Bumpass, Larry, and Lu, H., "Trends in Cohabitation and Implications for Children's Family Contexts in the United States," *Population Studies*, Vol. 54, 2000: 29-41.

Carlson, M.; McLanahan, Sara; and England, Paula, "Union Formation and Dissolution in Fragile Families," *Fragile Families Research Brief*, No. 4 (Bendheim-Thoman Center for Research on Child Wellbeing, Princeton University, January, 2003).

Cavallo, Sandra, and Warner, Lyndham (Eds.), *Widowhood in Medieval and Early Modern Europe* (New York: Addison Wesley Longman, 1999).

Cavanagh, Shannon and Fomby, Paula, "Family Instability, School Context, and the Academic Careers of Adolescents," *Sociology of Education*, Vol. 85, No. 1, 2012: 81-97.

Cavanagh, Shannon and Huston, Althea, "Family Instability and Children's Early Problem Behavior," *Social Forces*, Vol. 85, 2006: 575-605.

Cavanagh, Shannon and Huston, Althea, "The Timing of Family Instability and Children's Social Development," *Journal of Marriage and the Family*, Vol. 70, 2008: 1258-1269.

Cavanagh, Shannon E., Schiller, Kathryn, and Riegle-Crumb, Catherine, "Marital Transitions, Parenting, and Schooling: Exploring the Linkage between Family Structure History and Adolescents' Academic Status," *Sociology of Education*, Vol. 79, 2006: 329-354.

Chagnon, Napoleon, *Evolutionary Biology and Human Social Behavior* (North Scituate, MA: Duxbury, 1979).

Chan, Sewell and Murphy, Caryle, "Civilian Killed in Iraq Worked on Constitution," *The Washington Post*, March 12, 2004. As of October 18, 2012, available online at http://www.spokesmanreview.com/news-story.asp?date=031204&ID=s1498530

Chandrasekhar, S., "The Hindu Joint Family," *Social Forces*, Vol. 21, 1943: 328-333.

Cherlin, Andrew J., "Demographic Trends in the United States: A Review of Research in the 2000s," *Journal of Marriage and Family*, Vol. 72, 2010: 403-419.

Cherlin, Andrew J., Chase-Lansdale, Lindsay, and McRae, 1998, "Effects of Divorce on Mental Health throughout the Life Course," *American Sociological Review*, Vol. 63, 1998: 239-249.

Cherlin, Andrew J., *The Marriage-Go-Round: The State of Marriage and Family in America Today* (New York: Alfred A. Knopf, 2009).

CIA World Factbook, 2012. Total Fertility Rate data, as of September 24, 2012, available online at *www.cia.gov*

Daly, Martin, and Wilson, Margo, *Sex, Evolution, and Behavior* (Boston, MA: Willard Grant, 1983).

Daniel, Kermit, "The Marriage Premium," in Mariano Tommasi and Kathryn Ierulli (Eds.), *The New Economics of Human Behavior* (New York: Cambridge University Press, 1995), pages 113-125.

Davis, Kingsley (Ed.), *Contemporary Marriage: Comparative Perspectives on a Changing Institution* (New York: Russell Sage Foundation, 1985).

DeLeire, Thomas, and Kalil, Ariel, "Good Things Come in Threes: Single-Parent Multigenerational Family Structure and Adolescent Adjustment," *Demography*, Vol. 39, No. 2 (May) 2002: 393-413.

DeLeire, Thomas, and Kalil, Ariel, "How Do Cohabiting Couples with Children Spend Their Money?" *Journal of Marriage and Family*, Vol. 67, No. 2, (May) 2005: 286-295.

Demuth, Stephen, and Brown, Susan L., "Family Structure, Family Processes, and Adolescent Delinquency: The Significance of Parental Absence Versus Parental Gender," *Journal of Research in Crime and Delinquency*, Vol. 41, No. 1, (February) 2004: 58-81.

Dhillon, Sunny, "Ayaan Hirsi Ali: from Muslim 'Infidel' to Mother," *The Globe and Mail*, March 16, 2012. As of October 18, 2012, available online at http://www.theglobeandmail.com/arts/books-and-media/ayaan-hirsi-ali-from-muslim-infidel-to-mother/article542380/

Dorjahn, Vernon R., "The Factor of Polygamy in African Demography," in William R. Bascom and Melville J. Herskovits (Eds.), *Continuity and Change in African Cultures* (Chicago: University of Chicago Press, 1959), pp. 102-105.

Douglas, Mary, *Purity and Danger: An Analysis of Concepts of Pollution and Taboo* (London, England: Routledge and Kegan Paul, 1966).

Drucker, Philip, *Cultures of the North Pacific Coast* (San Francisco, CA: Chandler, 1965).

Drucker, Philip, *The Northern and Central Nootkan Tribes* (Washington, D.C.: Smithsonian Institute, 1951).

Eberstadt, Mary, *Adam and Eve After the Pill: Paradoxes of the Sexual Revolution* (San Francisco: Ignatius Press, 2012).

El Mouzan, M.I., et. al., "Regional Variations in the Prevalence of Consanguinity in Saudi Arabia," *Saudi Medical Journal*, Vol. 28, No. 12, 2007: 1881-1884.

Engels, Friedrich, *The Origins of the Family, Private Property and the State* (New York: International Press, 1975). (Originally published, 1884).

Epstein, Cynthia Fuchs, "2006 American Sociological Association Presidential Address—Great Divides: The Cultural, Cognitive, and Social Bases of the Global Subordination of Women," *American Sociological Review*, Vol. 72, No. 1, (February) 2007: 1-22.

Fisher, Helen, *Anatomy of Love: A Natural History of Mating, Marriage, and Why We Stray* (New York: Fawcett Columbine, 1992).

Flavin, Jeanne, "Employment, Counseling, Housing Assistance…and Aunt Yolanda? How Strengthening Families' Social Capital Can Reduce Recidivism," *Fordham Urban Law Journal*, Vol. 3, No. 2, 2004: 209-216.

Frankenberg, S.R., "Kinship and Mate Choice in a Historic Eastern Blue Ridge Community, Madison County, Virginia," *Human Biology*, Vol. 62, 1990: 817-835.

Fry, Richard, and Cohn, D'Vera, *Living Together: The Economics of Cohabitation* (Washington, D.C.: Pew Social and Demographic Trends, 2011).

Fry, Richard, and Cohn, D'Vera, *Women, Men, and the New Economics of Marriage* (Washington, D.C.: Pew Research Center, 2010).

Fukuyama, Francis, "The Great Disruption," *The Atlantic Monthly*, Vol. 283, No. 5, (May) 1999a: 55-80.

Fukuyama, Francis, *The Great Disruption* (New York: The Free Press, 1999b).

Fukuyama, Francis, *The Origins of Political Order: From Prehuman Times to the French Revolution* (New York: Farrar, Straus, and Giroux, 2011).

Gabrielli, G., and Hoem, J.M., "Italy's Non-negligible Cohabitational Unions," *European Journal of Population*, Vol. 26, 2010: 33-46.

Galloway, Lindsey, "Feline Fun in Japan's Cat Cafes," *BBC Travel*, April 3, 2012. As of September 24, 2012, available online at http://www.bbc.com/travel/blog/20120402-worldwide-weird-feline-fun-in-japans-cat-cafes

Gat, Azar, *War in Human Civilization* (New York: Oxford University Press, 2006).

Giddens, Anthony, Duneier, Mitchell, Appelbaum, Richard P., and Carr, Deborah, *Essentials of Sociology* Fourth Edition (New York: Norton, 2013).

Global Consumer Confidence Survey (New York: A.C. Nielsen, June 2006).

Goldstein, Joshua r., and Kenney, Catherine T., "Marriage Delayed or Marriage Forgone? New Cohort Forecasts of First Marriage for U.S. Women," *American Sociological Review*, Vol. 66, No. 4, (August) 2001: 506-519.

Goode, William J, *The Family* Second Edition (Englewood Cliffs, NJ: Prentice-Hall, 1982).

Goode, William J., *World Revolution and Family Patterns* (New York: The Free Press, 1963).

Guiteras-Holmes, Calixta, "Clanes y Sistema de Parentesco de Cancuc Mexico," *Acta Americana, Vol 5, 1947: 1-17.*

Gunaid, A. A., et. al., "Consanguineous Marriages in the Capital City Sana'a, Yemen," *Journal of Biosocial Science*, Vol. 36, 2004: 111-121.

Hamamy, H., et. al., "Consanguineous in Jordan: Why is the Rate Changing with Time?" *Clinical Genetics*, Vol. 67, 2005: 511-516.

Harper, Cynthia C., and McLanahan, Sara, "Father Absence and Youth Incarceration," *Journal of Research on Adolescence*, Vol. 14, No. 3, (September) 2004: 369-397.

Haveman, Robert, Wolf, Barbara, and Pence, Karen, "Intergenerational Effects of Non-Marital and Early Childbearing," in Lawrence L. Wu and Barbara Wolf (Eds.), *Out of Wedlock: Causes and Consequences of Nonmarital Fertility* (New York: Russell Sage Foundation, 2001), pages 287-316.

Henrich, Joseph, "Polygyny in Cross-Cultural Perspective: Theory and Implications," a requested paper submitted to the Supreme Court of British Columbia on July 15, 2010. As of September 16, 2012, available online at http://www.vancouversun.com/pdf/affidavit.pdf

Hetherington, E. Mavis, and Clingempeel, W. Glenn, "Coping with Marital Transitions," *Monographs of the Society for Research in Child Development*, Vol 57, Nos. 2-3 (University of Chicago Press, 1992).

Hetherington, E. Mavis, and Jodl, K.M., "Sepfamilies as Settings for Child Development," in Alan Booth and Judy Dunn (Eds.), *Stepfamilies: Who Benefits? Who Does Not?* (Hillsdale, NJ: Lawrence Erlbaum, 1994), pages 55-79.

Hlad, Jennifer, and Beardsley, Steven, "Outrage Over Perceived Light Sentence for Convicted Colonel," *Stars and Stripes*, June 18, 2012. As of October 21, 2012, available online at http://www.military.com/daily-news/2012/06/18/outrage-over-perceived-light-sentence-for-colonel.html

Hochschild, Arlie, *The Second Shift: Working Parents and the Revolution at Home* (New York: Viking, 1989).

Huth, A.H., *The Marriage of Near Kin, Considered with Respect to the Laws of Nations, the Results of Experience, and the Teachings of Biology* (London, England: Churchill, 1875).

Hymowitz, Kay S., "The Fragile Family Effect: It's Family Instability, Not Poverty, that Does Greater Damage to Children," *Los Angeles Times*, November 11, 2010. As of October 2, 2012, available online at http://articles.latimes.com/2010/nov/11/opinion/la-oe-hymowitz-families-20101111

Hymowitz, Kay S., *Marriage and Caste in America: Separate and Unequal Families in a Post-Marital Age* (Chicago: Ivan R. Dee, 2006).

Ingoldsby, Bron, "Marital Structure," in Bron Ingoldsby and Suzanne D. Smith, *Families in Global and Multi-Cultural Perspective* Second Edition (Thousand Oaks, CA: Sage, 2005), pp. 99-112.

Jarrett, R.L.; Sullivan, P.J.; and Watkins, N.D., "Developing Social Capital Through Participation in Organized Youth Programs: Qualitative Insights From Three Programs," *Journal of Community Psychology*, Vol. 33, No. 1, 2005: 41-55.

Jeynes, William H., "A Historical Overview of the Research on the Effects of Remarriage Following Divorce on the Academic Achievement of Children," *School Community Journal*, Vol. 8, No. 1, 1998a: 23-30.

Jeynes, William H., "Does Divorce or Remarriage Following Divorce Have the Greater Negative Impact on the Academic Achievement of Children?" *Journal of Divorce and Remarriage*, Vol. 29, Nos. 1-2, 1998b: 79-101.

Jeynes, William H., *Divorce, Family Structure, and the Academic Success of Children* (New York: The Haworth Press, 2002).

Jeynes, William H., *Parental Involvement and Academic Success* (New York: Routledge, 2011).

Jeynes, William H., The Effects of Several of the Most Common Family Structures on the Academic Achievement of Eighth Graders," *Marriage and Family Review*, Vol. 30, Nos. 1-2, (2000): 73-97.

Jurdi, R., and Saxena, P.C., "The Prevalence and Correlates of Consanguineous Marriages in Yemen: Similarities and Contrasts with Other Arab Countries," *Journal of Biosocial Science*, Vol. 25, 2003: 1-13.

Keen, I., "How Some Murngin Men Marry Ten Wives," *Man*, Vol. 17, 1982: 620-642.

Kennedy, Sheela, and Bumpass, Larry, "Cohabitation and Trends in the Structure and Stability of Children's Family Lives," presented at the 2011 Annual Meeting of the Population Association of America, Washington, D.C. As of September 25, 2012, available online at http://paa2011.princeton.edu/download.aspx?submissionid=111757

Kennedy, Sheela, and Bumpass, Lawrence, "Cohabitation and Children's Living Arrangements: New Estimates from the United States," *Demographic Research*, Vol. 19, 2008: 1663-1692.

Klineberg, Eric, *Going Solo: The Extraordinary Rise and Surprising Appeal of Living Alone* (New York: Penguin Press, 2012).

Kochhar, Rakesh, and Cohn, D' Vera, "Fighting Poverty in a Bad Economy, Americans Move in with Relatives," Executive Summary. (Washington, D.C.: Pew Research Center, Pew Social & Demographic Trends, October 3, 2011). As of September 15, 2012, available online at http://www.pewsocialtrends.org/2011/10/03/fighting-poverty-in-a-bad-economy-americans-move-in-with-relatives/

Kohut, Andrew, *Trends in American Values: 1987-2012* (Washington, D.C.: Pew Researech Center for the People and the Press, 2012).

Krause, Aurel, *The Tlingit Indians* (Seattle, WA: University of Washington, 1970 [1885]).

Lambe, Joe, "Bigamy earns ex-cop 18 months probation; restitution likely," *Kansas City Star*, December 12, 2009. McClatchy Washington Bureau. As of October 21, 2012, available online at http://www.mcclatchydc.com/2009/12/12/v-print/80565/bigamy-earns-ex-cop-18-months.html

Landale, Nancy S. and Hauan, Susan M., "The Family Life Course of Puerto Rican Children," *Journal of Marriage and the Family*, Vol. 54, 1992: 912-924.

Latten, Jan, *Trends in Cohabiting and Marriage* (Voorburg, The Netherlands: Central Bureau voor de Statistiek, 2004).

Lauritsen, Janet L., "How Families and Communities Influence Youth Victimization," Office of Juvenile Justice and Delinquency Prevention *Juvenile Justice Bulletin* (November) 2003, pp. 1-11. As of October 8, 2012, available online at http://www.ncjrs.gov/pdffiles1/ojjdp/201629.pdf

Lawrence, Richard and Hesse, Mario, *Juvenile Justice: The Essentials* (Thousand Oaks, CA: 2010).

Le Bourdais, and Marcil-Gratton, Nicole, "The Impact of Family Disruption in Childhood on Demographic Outcomes in Young Adulthood," in Corak, M. (Ed.), *Labour Markets, Social Institutions, and the Future of Canada's Children* (Ottawa, Canada: Statistics Canada and Human Resources Development Canada, 1998), pages 91-205.

Le Play Frédéric, *Les ouvriers européens: Etudes sur les travaux, la vie domestique et la condition morale des populations ouvrières de l'Europe, précédées d'un exposé de la méthode d'observation* (Paris: Imprimerie impériale; 1855).

Le Play, Frédéric, *L'organisation de la famille selon le vrai modèle signalé par l'histoire de toutes les races et de tous les temps.* Third. (Tours: A. Mame; 1884).

Lerman, Robert L., *Impacts of Marital Status and Parental Presence on the Material Hardship of Families with Children* (Washington, D.C.: Urban Institute, 2002).

Lichter, Daniel T., Turner, R.N., and Sassler, S., "National Estimates of the Rise in Serial Cohabitation," *Social Science Research*, Vol. 39, Issue 5, (September) 2010: 754-765.

Long, Jeremy, "Polygyny, Acculturation, and Contact: Aspects of Aboriginal Marriage in Central Australia," in R. M. Berndt (Ed.), *Australian Aboriginal Anthropology* (Nedland: University of Western Australia, 1970), p. 293.

Malinowski, Bronislaw, "The Principle of Legitimacy: Parenthood, the Basis of Social Structure," in V.F. Calverton and S.D. Schmalhausen (Eds.), *The New Generation* (New York: Macauley Co., 1930), pp. 113-168.

Malinowski, Bronislaw, *Sexual Life of Savages in Northwestern Melanesia: An Ethnographic Account of Courtship, Marriage, and Family Life Among the Natives of the Trobriand Islands, British New Guinea* (Boston, Beacon Press, 1987). Introduction by Annette B. Weiner, with a preface by Havelock Ellis. (Originally published London: G. Rutledge, 1929).

Manning, Wendy D., and Lamb, Kathleen, "Adolescent Well-Being in Cohabiting, Married, and Single-Parent Families," *Journal of Marriage and Family*, Vol. 65, (November) 2003: 876-893.

Manning, Wendy; Smock, Pamela; and Majumdar, Debarun, "The Relative Stability of Marital and Cohabiting Unions for Children," *Population Research and Policy Review*, Vol. 23, 2004: 135-159.

Marcus, Ruth, "A Costly Marriage Crisis," *The Week*, December 30-January 6, 2012, p. 12.

Martin, Joyce A.; Hamilton, Bradley E.; Ventura, Stephanie J., et. al., "Births: Final Data for 2009," *National Vital Statistics Reports*, Vol. 60, No. 1 (Hyattsville, MD: National Center for Health Statistics, 2011).

Mattison, Siobhán, "Evolutionary Contributions to Solving the 'Matrilineal Puzzle' A Test of Holden, Sear, and Mace's Model," *Human Nature*, Vol. 22, 2011: 64-88.

McCurry, Justin, "Lonely Japanese Find Solace in 'Rent a Friend' Agencies," *The Guardian*, September 20, 2009. As of September 24, 2012, available online at http://www.guardian.co.uk/world/2009/sep/20/japan-relatives-professional-stand-ins

McDonald, Thomasi, "N.C. man charged with bigamy after 2 wives turn him in," May 8, 2008, McClatchey Newspapers. As of October 21, 2012, available online at http://www.ecollegetimes.com/student-life/n-c-man-charged-with-bigamy-after-2-wives-turn-him-in-1.489199#.UIRoFG_R7Qk

McLanahan, Sara and Sandefur, Gary, *Growing Up with a Single Parent: What Hurts, What Helps* (Cambridge, MA: Harvard University Press, 1994).

McLanahan, Sara, "Diverging Destinies: How Children Are Faring under the Second Demographic Transition," *Demography*, Vol. 41, 2004: 606-627.

Meggitt, M.J., "Marriage Among the Walbiri of Central Australia: A Statistical Examination," in R.M. Berndt and C.H. Berndt (Eds.), *Aboriginal Man in Australia* (Sydney: Angus & Robertson, 1965a), pp. 146-159.

Meggitt, M.J., *Desert People* (Chicago: University of Chicago Press, 1965b).

Morrison, Donna R., and Cherlin, Andrew J., "The Divorce Process and Young Children's Well-Being: A Prospective Analysis," *Journal of Marriage and the Family*, Vol. 57, 1995: 800-812.

Morrison, Donna R., and Ritualo, Amy, "Routes to Children's Economic Recovery after Divorce: Are Cohabitation and Remarriage Equivalent?" *American Sociological Review*, Vol. 65, No. 4 (August 2000): 560-580.

Moustgaard, Heta, and Martikainen, Pekka, "Nonmarital Cohabitation Among Older Finnish Men and Women: Socioeconomic Characteristics and Forms of Union Dissolution," *Journal of Gerontology: Social Sciences*, Vol. 64, No. 4 (2009): 507-516.

Murdock, George Peter, and White, D.R., "Standard Cross-Cultural Sample," *Ethnology*, Vol. 8, No. 4, 1969: 329-369.

Murdock, George Peter, and White, D.R., "Standard Cross-Cultural Sample: online edition," July 19, 2006. Working Paper Series. Social Dynamics and Complexity, Institute for Mathematical Behavioral Sciences, University of California, Irvine. As of September 16, 2012, available online at http://escholarship.org/uc/item/62c5c02n#page-1 Originally published in *Ethnology*, Vol. 8 (1969): 329-369.

Murdock, George Peter, *Social Structure* (Toronto: The Macmillan Company, 1949).

Murphy, M., "The Evolution of Cohabitation in Britain, 1960-95," *Population Studies*, Vol. 54, 2000: 43-56.

Murray, Charles, "Why Economics Can't Explain Our Cultural Divide," *The Wall Street Journal*, March 16, 2012b.

Murray, Charles, *Coming Apart: The State of White America, 1960-2010* (New York: Crown Forum, 2012a).

National Center for Family & Marriage, 2010. *Trends in Cohabitation: Twenty Years of Change, 1987-2008.* October NCFMR FP-10-07.

OECD Family Database, *www.oecd.org/els/social/family/database* OECD- Social Policy Division- Directorate of Employment, Labour and Social Affairs SF1.1: Family Size and Household Composition. Table SF1.1A "Types of Household in Percent of All Households" Latest Year. As of September 25, 2012, available online at http://www.oecd.org/els/socialpoliciesanddata/41919509.pdf

Office of National Statistics, Statistical bulletin, "Marriages in England and Wales, 2010" As of September 19, 2012, available online at http://www.ons.gov.uk/ons/rel/vsob1/marriages-in-england-and-wales--provisional-/2010/marriages-in-england-and-wales--2010.html#tab-Age-at-marriage

Oropesa, R.S., and Landale, Nancy S., "Equal Access to Income and Union Dissolution among Mainland Puerto Ricans," *Journal of Marriage and the Family*, Vol. 67, No. 1, (February) 2005: 173-190.

Osborne, Cynthia, and McLanahan, Sara, "Partnership Instability and Child Well-Being," *Journal of Marriage and the Family*, Vol. 69, 2007: 1065-1083.

Parsons, Talcott, "The Incest Taboo in Relation to Social Structure," *The British Journal of Sociology*, Vol. 5, 1954: 101-117.

Pattison, J.E., "Effects of the Bubonic Plague Epidemics on Inbreeding in 14th Century Britain," *American Journal of Human Biology*, Vol. 15, 2003: 101-111.

Philipov, D., and Jasilioniene, A., "Union Formation and Fertility in Bulgaria and Russia: A Life Table Description of Recent Trends," *Demographic Research*, Vol. 19, 2008:

Pienta, Amy Mehraban, Hayward, Mark D., and Jenkins, Kristi Rahrig, "Health Consequences of Marriage for the Retirement Years," *Journal of Family Issues*, Vol. 21, No. 5, (July) 2000: 559-586.

Popenoe, David, *Cohabitation, Marriage, and Child Wellbeing: A Cross-National Perspective* (New Brunswick, NJ: The National Marriage Project at Rutgers University, 2008).

Potts, Malcolm and Hayden, Thomas, *Sex and War: How Biology Explains Warfare and Terrorism and Offers a Path to a Safer World* (Dallas;TX: Benballa Books, Inc., 2008).

Rajab, A., and Patton, M.A., "A Study of Consanguinity in the Sultanate of Oman," *Annals of Human Biology*, Vol. 27, No. 3, 2000: 321-326.

Raley, R. Kelley and Bumpass, Larry, "Topography of the Divorce Plateau: Levels and Trends in Union Stability in the United States After 1980," *Demographic Research*, Vol. 8, (April) 2003: 246-260.

Rose, Lacey, "Nanto City, Japan: Robotic Companions," *Forbes.com*, June 8, 2005. As of September 24, 2012, available online at http://www.forbes.com/2005/06/08/cx_lr_0608japan.html

Rosman, Abraham, and Rubel, Paula, *Feasting with the Enemy: Rank and Exchange among Northwest Coast Societies* (New York: Columbia University Press, 1971).

Rowlatt, Justin, "The Risks of Cousin Marriage," BBC News, November 16, 2005. As of September 15, 1012, available online at http://news.bbc.co.uk/2/hi/programmes/newsnight/4442010.stm

Ruggles, Steven, "Reconsidering the Northwest European Family System: Living Arrangements of the Aged in Comparative Historical Perspective," *Population and Development Review*, Vol. 35, No. 2, (June) 2009: 249-273.

Ruggles, Steven, "Stem Families and Joint Families in Comparative Historical Perspective," *Population and Development Review*, Vol. 36, No. 3, 2010: 563-577.

Ruggles, Steven, "The Decline of Intergenerational Coresidence in the United States 1850 to 2000," *American Sociological Review*, Vol. 72, No. 6, 2007: 964-989.

Sailer, Steve, "Cousin Marriage Conundrum: An Ancient Iraqi Custom Will Foil Nation-Building," *The American Conservative*, January 13, 2003: 20-22. As of September 15, 2012, available online at http://www.isteve.com/cousin_marriage_conundrum.htm

Salem, Dina Abu, "Texas Bigamist Led a Double Life for Three Years, Police Say," ABC News, October 19, 2012. As of October 21, 2012, available online at http://abcnews.go.com/blogs/headlines/2012/10/texas-bigamist-led-a-double-life-for-three-years-police-say/

Scafidi, Benjamin, *The Taxpayer Cost of Divorce and Unwed Childrearing: First Ever Estimates for the Nation and All Fifty States* (New York: Institute for American Values, 2008).

Sedlack, A.J., Mettenburg, J., Basena, M., Petta, I., McPherson, K., Greene, A., and Li, S., *Fourth National Incidence Study of Child Abuse and neglect (NIS-4): Report to Congress* (Washington, D.C.: U.S. Department of Health and Human Services, Administration for Children and Families, 2010).

Sennels, Nicolai, "Muslim Inbreeding: Impacts on Intelligence, Sanity, Health and Society," *EuropeNews*, August 9, 2010. As of September 3, 2012, available online at http://europenews.dk/en/node/34368/

Shapiro, Warren, "Anti-Family Fantasies in 'Cutting-Edge' Anthropological Kinship Studies," *Academic Quesitons*, Vol. 25, No. 3, 2012: 394-402.

Shapiro, Warren, "The Nuclear Family *Versus* the Men's House: A Re-Examination of Mundurucú Sociality," *Anthropological Forum*, Vol. 21, No. 1, (March) 2011: 57-75.

Simons, Ronald L., and Associates, *Understanding Differences between Divorced and Intact Families* (Thousand Oaks, CA: Sage, 1996).

Smock, Pamela J., and Manning, Wendy D., "Living Together Unmarried in the United States: Demographic Perspectives and Implications for Family Policy," *Law and Policy*, Vol. 26, No. 1 (January) 2004: 87-117.

Sobotka, T., and Toulemon, L., "Changing Family and Partnership Behaviour: Common Trends and Persistent Diversity across Europe," *Demographic Research*, Vol. 19, 2008: 85-138.

Soustelle, Jacques, *The Daily Life of the Aztecs on the Eve of the Spanish Conquest* (Mineola, New York: Dover Publications, 2002). Translated from the French by Patrick O'Brian.

Stanley, Scott M., and Whitton, Sarah W., and Markman, Howard J., "Maybe I Do: Interpersonal Commitment Levels and Premarital or Nonmarital Cohabitation," *Journal of Family Issues*, Vol. 25, No. 4 (May) 2004: 496-519.

Sueyoshi, Ohtsuka R., and Ohtsuka, Ryutaro, "Effects of Polygyny and Consanguinity on High Fertility in the Rural Arab Population in South Jordan," *Journal of Biosocial Science*, Vol. 35, 2003: 513-526.

Symons, Donald, *The Evolution of Human Sexuality* (New York: Oxford University Press, 1979)

Tadmouri, Ghazi O., Pratibha Nair, Tasneem Obeid, Mahmoud T. Al Ali, Najib Al Khaja, and Hanan A. Hamamy, "Consanguinity and Reproductive Health Among Arabs," *Reproductive Health*, Vol. 6, 2009. As of September 3, 2012, available online at http://www.reproductive-health-journal.com/content/6/1/17#B14

Taylor, Paul (Ed.), *The Decline of Marriage and Rise of New Families* (Washington, D.C.: Pew Research Center, 2010).

Taylor, Paul, and Kochhar, Rakesh; Cohn, D' Vera; Passel, Jeffrey, S., et. al., in *Fighting Poverty a Tough Economy, Americans Move in with Their Relatives* (Washington, D.C.: Pew Social and Demographic Trends, October 3, 2011).

Taylor, Paul, Funk, Carey, and Clark, April, *As Marriage and Parenthood Drift Apart, Public Is Concerned about Social Impact: Generation Gap in Values, Behaviors* (Washington, D.C.: Pew Research Center, 2007).

Teachman, Jay D., "Childhood Living Arrangements and the Intergenerational Transmission of Divorce," *Journal of Marriage and Family*, Vol. 64, 2002: 717-729.

Teachman, Jay D., "Stability across Cohorts in Divorce Risk Factors," *Demography*, Vol. 39, 2002: 331-351.

Teachman, Jay D., "The Childhood Living Arrangements of Children and the Characteristics of Their Marriages," *Journal of Family Issues*, Vol. 25, 2004: 86-96.

The Economist, "Asian Demography: The Flight from Marriage," *The Economist*, August 20, 2011.

Theodorson, George A., and Theodorson, Achilles G., *A Modern Dictionary of Sociology* (New York: Barnes and Noble Books, 1969).

Tiger, Lionel, *The Decline of Males* (New York: Golden Books, 1999).

Tripp, Rob, "Shafia Family Sentenced to Life for Four Counts of First-Degree Murder," The Gazette, January 31, 2012. As of October 18, 2012, available online at http://www.montrealgazette.com/news/Shafia+family+sentenced+life+four+counts+first+degree+murder/6069325/story.html

U.S. Bureau of Labor Statistics, "Table 1. Time spent in primary activities (1) and percent of the civilian population engaging in each activity, averages per day by sex, 2011 averages" in U.S. Department of Labor News Release USDL-12-1246, June 22, 2012, *American Time-Use Survey—2011 Results*. As of October 18, 2012, available online at http://www.bls.gov/news.release/atus.t01.htm and at http://www.bls.gov/news.release/pdf/atus.pdf

U.S. Census Bureau, *U.S. & World Current Population Clocks*, 2012. As of October 19, 2012, available online at http://www.census.gov/main/www/popclock.html

U.S. Census Bureau, Current Population Survey, March and Annual Social and Economic Supplement, 2011. Table MS-2 Estimated Age at First Marriage by Sex: 1890 to the Present."

U.S. Census Bureau, U.S. Parents, Race, and Hispanic Origin, 2011. As of September 30, 2012, available online at Census Bureau, *Current Population Survey, 2011 Annual Social and Economic Supplement*, Table C9, Children by Presence and Type of Parents, Race, and Hispanic Origin, 2011, at http://www.census.gov/population/www/socdemo/hh-fam/cps2011.html

Van den Berghe, Pierre, *Human Family Systems: An Evolutionary View* (New York: Elsevier, 1979).

Villar, Ruairidh, "Tokyo's Cat Cafes Threatened by Changes to Japan's Animal Protection Laws," *Weird News*, March 1, 2012, Reuters. As of September 25, 2012, available online at http://www.huffingtonpost.com/2012/03/02/tokyo-cat-cafes-new-law_n_1315355.html

Waite, Linda J., and Gallagher, Maggie, *The Case for Marriage: Why Married People Are Happier, Healthier, and Better Off Financially* (New York: Doubleday, 2000).

Wattenberg, Ben J., *The Good News Is the Bad News Is Wrong* (New York: Simon and Schuster, 1985).

Wilcox, W. Bradford, "The Evolution of Divorce," *National Affairs*, Issue No. 1 (Fall) 2009: 81-94.

Wilcox, W. Bradford, and Marquardt, Elizabeth, *The State of Our Unions: Marriage in America 2011* (Charlottesville, VA: The National Marriage Project, 2011).

Wilcox, W. Bradford, and Marquardt, Elizabeth, *The State of Our Unions Marriage in 2010 When Marriage Disappears* (Charlottesville, VA: The National Marriage Project, 2010).

Wilcox, W. Bradford, et. al., *Why Marriage Matters* Third Edition (New York: Institute for American Values, 2011).

World Health Organization, "Female genital mutilation," *Fact sheet* No. 241, (February) 2012. As of October 18, 2012, available online at http://www.who.int/mediacentre/factsheets/fs241/en/

http://www.who.int/mediacentre/factsheets/fs241/en/

Wu, Lawrence L., and Thomson, Elizabeth, "Race Differences in Family Experience and Early Sexual Initiation: Dynamic Models of Family Structure and Family Change," *Journal of Marriage and Family*, Vol. 63, 2001: 682-696.

Zaher, Claudia, "When a Woman's Marital Status Determined Her Legal Status," *Law Library Journal*, Vol. 94, No. 3, 2002: 459-486.

Zaoui, Salah, and Biémont, Christian, "Frequency of Consanguineous Unions in the Tiemcen Area (West Algeria)," *Sante*, Vol. 12, No. 3, 2002: 289-295.

CHAPTER 7

Stratification

STRATIFICATION

Stratification refers to the persistent and inheritable unequal access to scarce yet widely-valued goods and services. It is found in all human societies. It is universal. It is a fundamental part of the social structure of all known human societies, past and present. Stratification is one of the main sources of variation in human behavior (Domhoff, 2014; Zweigenhaft and Domhoff, 2010; Argyle, 2008; Grusky, 2008; Veblen, 2007; Zweigenhaft and Domhoff, 2006). However it is defined, stratification affects other aspects of social life, including values (e.g., Dalrymple, 2001), consumption, extent of civic engagement (Smith, 2013) and of saving money (Elliott and Beverly, 2011), access to health care, education, political participation (Smith, 2013: 15, 18, 21), religious practice (e.g., Hoge, Dinges, Johnson, and Gonzales, Jr., 2001), food choice, number of hours spent watching television, as well as the probability of incarceration (Walsh, 2012), marriage, social mobility, visiting art galleries or archeological sites and visiting the public library within the past four weeks (e.g., Argyle, 1994:103).

In this chapter we examine stratification in industrialized and post-industrial societies and variation in inequality around the world. Then we focus on stratification in the United States, including the distribution of wealth and income, the class structure and the extent of both upward and downward movement in it. Throughout, we use sociological theory to understand stratification in human societies.

There are many types or bases of stratification, among which are caste, social class, gender, age, sex, race, ethnicity, religious affiliation, and noble status. In sociology, the various paradigms define stratification differently, measure it differently, and conceive its nature and effects and even its history differently.

Stratification has many different names—including social stratification and structured social inequality, and many of these terms are used interchangeably. How does a person get a place or position in a system of stratification? Sociology identifies two ways that an individual gets a place in a system of stratification—ascription and achievement. We speak of **ascription** and say that a position is **ascribed** to the extent that a person gets a place in a system of stratification through no efforts of his or her own. Common bases of ascription are age, sex, social class, race, ethnicity, and noble status. We speak of **achievement** and say that a position or status is **achieved** to the extent that a person gets a position or status through her or his own efforts. For instance, when Ben finally earns his Bachelor of Arts or Bachelor of Science degree from whatever college or university he is attending, he will have *done* lots of things—taken and scored acceptably well on numerous examinations, constructed many work products, read many books and other pertinent material in his chosen field of endeavor, and so forth. His educational degree is an achieved status.

Ascription and achievement are not mutually exclusive ways of attaining a position in a system of stratification. Why not? Any particular status tends to be neither purely ascribed nor purely achieved but rather is a combination of the two. Any particular status tends to be either more ascribed than achieved (e.g., sex—being male or female) or more achieved than ascribed (e.g., educational degree). Which is it? If you want to know the answer to that question, you need to investigate to discover the answer. It is an empirical question that only can be answered empirically.

STRATIFICATION IN INDUSTRIAL SOCIETIES: FROM INVERTED U TO N

Industrialization is a process that transforms societies from a reliance on agriculture and hand-made goods as the major forms of economic production to a reliance on factory or mechanized economic production. Industrial capitalism began in England in the 1750's, driven at first by textile production (Clark, 2011), and by the nineteenth century it had spread to Western Europe, Russia, Japan, and North America.

GRAPH 7.1 KUZNETS CURVE

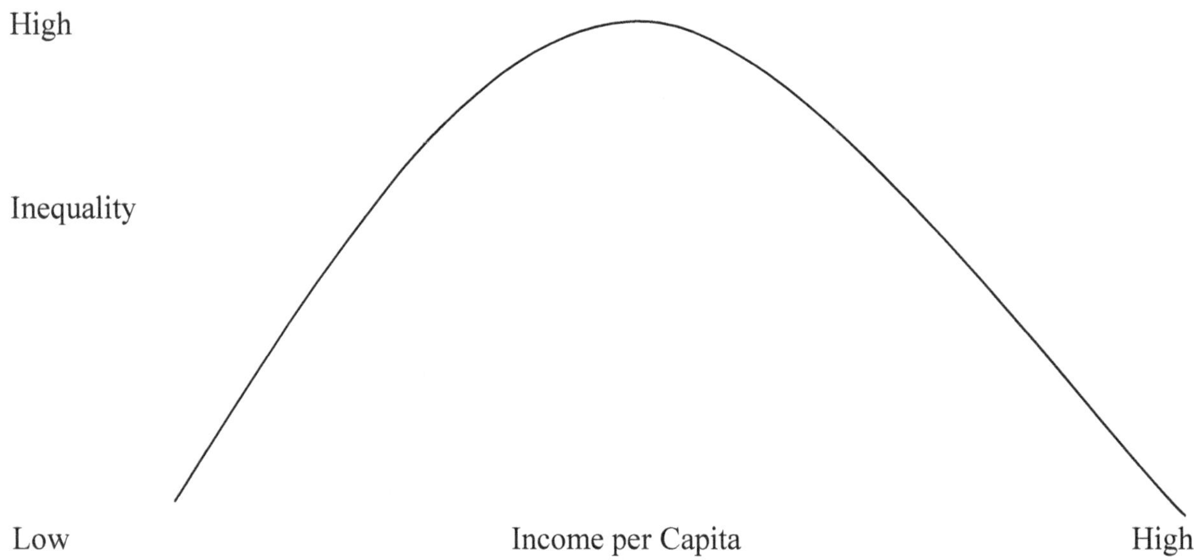

American sociologist Daniel Bell formulated the concept of **post-industrial society** in 1962 to refer to societies in which the majority of the labor force is in engaged in economic production in the service sector of the economy (Abercrombie, Hill, and Turner, 1994: 325). Shortly after World War II, the United States became the first nation to employ more than half of its labor force in the service sector. By 1960, all of the industrialized countries had reached this level. By 2012, four out of five members of the labor force in the United States (79.1 percent) worked in the service sector (computed from CIA World Factbook, 2012a).

In large part this rapid change in the composition of the labor force in the latter part of the twentieth century and during the first decades of the twenty-first century was made possible by the introduction and growth of computer technology. Computers automated many manufacturing and office procedures, creating jobs in the service sector of the economy, while they quickly eliminated jobs in the manufacturing sector.

Over the long haul, industrial capitalism has reduced and lessened the extent of stratification, including global inequality. This historical pattern characterized much of the twentieth century, when inequality lessened in many countries of the world. In fact, the lessening of social stratification seemed so inevitable that Simon Kuznets, a Belarusian-born Harvard economist, in 1955 famously described the relationship between inequality and the prosperity brought by industrialization as having the graphical shape of an upside-down or inverted U, known as the Kuznets curve. See Graph 7.1. According to the **Kuznets curve**, the market forces of industrial capitalism cause inequality at first to increase during the early stages of industrialization, as poor people from rural areas move to the cities, become more productive by working in factories, and earn more in factories. Inequality increases at this early stage because of the growing gap in average earnings between industrial and agricultural workers. For example, in Rhode Island, when times were good, industrial workers in the early 19th century earned two or three times what they had earned as agricultural workers (Davies, 1962: 8); and the situation was similar in late 19th century Russia (Davies, 1962: 11). Then, as industrialization advances, although different countries may take different paths, mass political parties emerge, education becomes more widespread, the state begins to play a redistributive role, and inequality goes down (Milanovic, 2011: 7; The Economist, October 13, 2012c) eventually stabilizing at low levels.

For the purpose of cross-country comparisons, the most frequently used measure of inequality is the **Gini coefficient**, named after the Italian statistician and economist Corrado Gini who defined it in 1914 (Milanovic, 2011: 30). The Gini coefficient aggregates the gaps between people's incomes into a single measure. The range of the Gini coefficient is from 0, where everyone has the same income and there is no inequality to 1, where all income goes to one person and everybody else has none, which would be the maximal possible inequality. Because of the way the Gini is constructed, a modest-sounding difference in the Gini ratio implies a big difference in inequality.

For simplicity, the Gini often is presented in percentages. For example, instead of saying that Country X's Gini is 0.43, we say that the inequality is 43 Gini points. In these instances, rather than referring to the Gini as a coefficient, it is termed an index. Thus, the CIA computes a Gini index for many countries of the world and these may be found in the Economy sections of the CIA's World Factbook. The more unequal a country's income distribution, the higher its Gini Index—e.g., a Sub-Saharan country with a Gini index of 50 or higher. If income were distributed with perfect inequality, the Gini index would be 100 and one person would have all the income and everybody else in that country would have none. The more nearly equal a country's income distribution, the lower the Gini index, e.g., a Scandinavian country with a Gini index of 23 or 25. Theoretically, the range of the Gini index is from 0, where there is perfect equality of income, to 100, where one person has all the income and everybody else has none.

Global inequality—the income gaps between all people on the planet—has declined as poorer countries successfully played catch up with the richer more industrialized ones in a process that some observers have termed "the great convergence" (e.g., Mahbubani, 2013; Young, 2009; Clark, 2007; Dowrick and DeLong, 2003). For instance, the Gini coefficient for the whole world declined from 0.6 in 1968 to 0.52 in 1997, a reduction of more than 10 percent (Norberg, 2003: 57). Since 1980, the twin forces of globalization and technical innovation have *narrowed* the income gaps *between* countries, while *within* many countries income gaps have *widened.* For example, in the United States, the share of national income going to the richest 1 percent of Americans has doubled, from 10 percent to 20 percent (The Economist, October 13, 2012a) since 1980.

This newer trend of increasing inequality *within* countries is not confined to the United States. Many countries, including Canada, Britain, China, India, and even egalitarian Sweden have seen a rise in the share of national income that goes to the top 1 percent. These days, the inverted U of the Kuznets curve has been transformed into a shape that more closely resembles an italicized *N*, with the final stroke pointing ominously upward. Today, more than two-thirds of the world's people live in countries where income disparities have risen since 1980 (The Economist, October 13, 2012b). A 2011 study from the Organization for Economic Co-operation and Development (OECD) reports that from the mid-1980s to the late 2000s, income inequality increased in seventeen of the 22 OECD countries for which long-term data are available. Seven of the most advanced OECD economies—Canada, Finland, Germany, Luxembourg, Israel, New Zealand, and Sweden—experienced grater increases in inequality than had the United States (OECD, 2012).

Levels of inequality differ widely around the world. Emerging economies (such as the BRICS—Brazil, Russia, India, China, and South Africa) are more unequal than rich ones. Scandinavian countries have the smallest income disparities, with a Gini coefficient for disposable income of around 0.25 (The Economist, October 13, 2012a). At the other end of the continuum are the world's most unequal societies that have Ginis of around 0.60 or higher. With an income Gini of .70 in 2008, South Africa stands as one of the most unequal countries in the world (World Bank, September 2012).

Where is the United States in terms of the Gini coefficient? The United States has a Gini that is mid-range. The Gini for disposable income for the United States is up by almost 30 percent since 1980 and is 0.39 (The Economist, October 13, 2012a). Sweden's is up by 25 percent in the same time period, to 0.24. China's is up by 50 percent in the same time period, to 0.42 (and by some measures to 0.48 (The Economist, October 13, 2012a).

The biggest possible exception to the general upward trend in inequality within countries since 1980 is Latin America, where Gini coefficients in several countries there have fallen sharply in the past dozen years (The Economist, October 13, 2012a). Nonetheless, South American Gini coefficients by and large remain in the medium-high range, which thus far is "normal" for emerging economies, and the Gini coefficients of several countries in Latin America have increased markedly in recent years. See Table 7.1.

TABLE 7.1 DISTRIBUTION OF FAMILY INCOME—THE CENTRAL INTELLIGENCE AGENCY'S GINI INDEX FOR SELECTED COUNTRIES BY MOST RECENT YEAR AVAILABLE AND BY COMPARISON YEAR

Country	Direction of Trend—Increase or Decrease in Inequality	Distribution of Family Income—Gini Index	Year
Colombia	Increase	56 53.8	(2010) (1996)
Ecuador	Decrease	47.3 50.5	(2011) (2006)
Bolivia	Increase	58.2 57.9	(2009) (1999)
Brazil	Decrease	51.9 60.7	(2012) (1998)
Chile	Decrease	52.1 57.1	(2009) (2007)
Costa Rica	Increase	50.3 45.9	(2009) (1997)
Uruguay	Increase	45.3 44.8	(2010) (1999)
Venezuela	Decrease	39 49.5	(2011) (1998)
European Union	Increase	30.7 26.8	(2011 estimate) (2008)
United States	Increase	45 40.8	(2007) (1997)
Canada	Increase	32.1 31.5	(2005) (1994)
China (Peoples Republic of)	Increase	48 41.5	(2009) (2007)
India	Decrease	36.8 37.8	(2004) (1997)
Russia	Increase	42 39.9	(2010) (2001)
South Africa	Increase	65 59.3	(2005) (1994)

Source: Compiled from CIA World Factbook. Distribution of Family Income—Gini Index. As of February 21, 2013, available online at https://www.cia.gov/library/publications/the-world-factbook/fields/2172.html#xx

SOCIOLOGICAL THEORY AND STRATIFICATION

The various sociological paradigms help us to understand stratification in human societies.

Functionalist Theory

About seven decades ago, American sociologists Kingsley Davis and Wilbert Moore enunciated the best known functionalist explanation as to why stratification exists in virtually all human societies (1945). As the attentive reader may recall, when functionalist theorists want to understand why we have some part of society, the question they ask is "Qui bono?" (Who benefits?) by this arrangement and the answer they come up with is "society as a whole." With regard to stratification, the position of functionalist theorists is that stratification benefits society as a whole. In other words, we all benefit.

Kingsley Davis and Wilbert Moore's functionalist answer to the question of "Qui bono?" by stratification is simple and consists of four basic points. If a society is to exist across time, it must do at least two things: (1) fill certain positions and (2) see that the rights, duties, and obligations attached to those positions are performed with some minimally acceptable amount of competence and diligence. In order to accomplish these ends, all positions have rewards attached to them.

What strikes students of stratification, however, is not that all positions have rewards attached to them, but that some positions have far more rewards attached to them than do other positions. Why do some positions have more rewards attached to them? According to Davis and Moore, the amount of rewards attached to a position is a function of the *interaction* of two variables: (3) how important a position is and (4) how hard it is to fill.

As an example of this theoretical relationship let us look at parenting. Parenting is an important position. After all, without people willing to be parents, the human species would cease to exist. Nonetheless, the rewards of class, status and power that attach to parenting are fairly modest. By and by far the greatest reward attached to parenting is status (esteem, honor, deference). This raises the question as to why such a modest reward structure exists in our society for such an important position. Davis and Moore's answer is simple: while parenting is important, the position is easy to fill. There is no shortage of people willing to become parents. Many people even become parents by accident. The position, while important, is not difficult to fill; hence, the rewards do not need to be very high.

The functionalist theory of stratification reminds us of the otherwise easily overlooked point that stratification benefits society as a whole. How? It is a mechanism that enables societies to exist across time by attaching rewards to positions so that those positions will be filled and the responsibilities and duties that attach to them will be executed with some minimally acceptable amount of competence and diligence.

How do functionalist theorists explain the staying power of ascription in human societies? Ascription involves using a pre-established structure-- e.g. the family, the existing workers on a job--- as a resource for allocating people to positions, rather than creating a new specialized structure for the same purpose. Developing new structures is costly and tends to be done only if it is sufficiently productive to justify the costs involved in creating and maintaining them.

Conflict Theory

How do conflict theorists explain the staying power of ascription in human societies? They view it as a mechanism to help those on top stay on top. There are many types of sociological conflict theory. What they have in common is that in constructing a sociological understanding of social life they focus on the **dialectics** of social life, the clashes of contradictions. Dialectical dynamics can operate at various levels of analysis. For instance, have you ever argued with *yourself*? Were you to do so, that's an example of intra-individual dialectics. Two people may argue with each other. That's an example of inter-personal or inter-individual dialectics. Groups conflict, as when one urban gang fights for turf or territory or for markets with a rival gang or cartel. Organizations can conflict, as can value systems, nations, even groupings of nations. Classes can conflict. Males and females can conflict. When we try to understand social life by focusing on the dialectics of social life, we are taking or using a conflict perspective.

From the point of view of conflict theory, stratification is a mechanism that benefits the supraordinate, those who are on top of the stratification system, and the rest of the people pay the price. Different conflict theories see different groups, aggregates, or collectivities as being "on top." For instance, Karl Marx sees the capitalists (bourgeoisie) as being on top. Feminist conflict theorists see males as being on top. World system theory sees "the core" as being on top. In all of these instances, the conflict-theory position is that it is those who are *not* on top who pay the price.

Karl Marx (1818-1883) frequently is called as the father of conflict theory. Karl Marx lived in the age of laissez-faire capitalism. Laissez faire are French words that translate into English as "leave it alone." In laissez-faire capitalism, the government does not interfere with the workings of the economy. Marx also lived at a time when the government in England and in most other industrialized countries provided very few "social safety nets" to the people.

For Marx, the most important part of society is the economy, that part of society that is responsible for creating and distributing goods and services. The economy is so important that Marx called it the substructure (the foundation) of society. The substructure influences everything else. Everything else is situated in the superstructure (also known as the suprastructure). Thus, the family, education, the political order, law, the arts and sciences, gender relations, religion and so forth, are all located in the superstructure. According to Marx, if you want to change anything in the superstructure, you need to change the substructure.

According to Marx, stratification is rooted in people's relationship to the **economic means of production**, the property necessary for economic production to occur. In hunting and gathering societies, the economic means of production can consist of bows, arrows, spears, and digging sticks. In an industrial society, the economic means of production might consist of factories. For Marx, a person's objective social class position is defined in terms of one's objective relationship to the economic means of production. Marx thought that a person could have only one of two possible objective relationships to the economic means of production. One either owned the economic means of production and thereby was a member of the capitalist class, also known as the **bourgeoisie** or one sold one's labor to those who owned the economic means of production, in which case one was a member of the **proletariat**. Marx views the objective interests of these two classes as opposite and as antagonistic to each other. For instance, the bourgeoisie want to pay their workers as little as possible, thereby maximizing their own profit and workers want to be paid more so that they can take care of the needs of themselves and their families.

Of course, it is possible for people to lack a subjective awareness of their objective relationship to the economic means of production, which Marx terms **false consciousness**. For instance, members of the proletariat may vote *for* and identify with the candidates of the political parties that represent the interests of the capitalists. To use an example from the United States, a factory worker might vote for the candidates of the Republican political party. Marx would say that such a worker has false consciousness. False consciousness can prevent workers from banding together with their proletarian brothers and sisters to overthrow the capitalists.

Marxists do not like profit because they see profit as what results when workers do more labor than is necessary to pay the cost of hiring their labor-power. To Marxists, capitalist profit results from paying workers less than the value the products of their labor are worth. Profit results from exploiting the labor of the workers; as such, it is the fruit of the poisoned tree and the tree is the capitalist mode of economic production. The owners of the economic means of production exploit the labor of the workers and then reinvest some of the profit in their business, which grows their business; and they use some of it to live comfortable, fashionable, and luxurious life styles. Thus, in the late 19th century, at the height of the first Gilded Age in the United States, the grandson and heir of business tycoon Cornelius Vanderbilt built a country estate, named Biltmore, in the Blue Ridge Mountains of North Carolina. With 250 rooms and 175,000 square-feet, this home was 300 times larger than the average dwelling of its day (The Economist, October 13, 2012a; Stiles, 2009). Industrialist Andrew Carnegie earned more than $20 million in 1900 at a time when the average worker in the United States earned about $500 a year (Macionis, 2013:195).

According to Marx, while industrial capitalism enriches the bourgeoisie, it impoverishes the workers. Workers become poorer and poorer. In Marxian economic theory, this is the **immiseration thesis**: the nature of capitalist economic production logically requires both an ever greater reduction in real wages and a worsening of labor conditions for the proletariat. The proletariat become immiserated. Immiseration is the train that drives the proletariat to revolt against the bourgeoisie.

Another characteristic of industrial capitalism is that the proletariat have little control over what they make, how they make it, or how many hours of work are available to them. According to Marx, in the economic system of industrial capitalism, work produces **alienation**, the estrangement of individuals from themselves, from others, and from the products of their own labor. In other words, one feels distant, removed, and disconnected from oneself, from others, and from the products of one's own labor. Have you ever looked at something you have created and felt a separation, a "disconnect" between it and yourself? If so, that's an example of alienation.

Because Marx emphasizes material conditions i.e., economic factors, as the basic causal forces determining human history, his conflict theory of stratification sometimes is called **dialectical materialism.** Marx interpreted the entirety of human history, social change, as a series of class struggles. At any given point in time, there is a dominant economic class. In time, conflict breaks out between the dominant class and a rising class, resulting in the overthrow of the old ruling class and the establishment of a new dominant class. According to Karl Marx, it was in this fashion, that the capitalist class replaced the feudal aristocracy as the dominant class in the West.

Marx thought that since capitalists and proletarians have objective economic interests that are opposite and antagonistic to each other and since these two classes are separated by vast differences in class, status, and power, that class conflict and revolution were inevitable. Marx believed that the immiserated workers would band together with their proletarian brothers and sisters to overthrow the owners of capital. Proletarians would make revolution and they would be victorious. After the revolution, the economic

means of production would be placed equally in the hands of all workers, a state of affairs which Marxists refer to as the dictatorship of the proletariat (Lenin, 1918). At this point the state would disappear. It would be the end of history.

Why No Marxist Revolution in Capitalist Industrial Societies?

We may well ask, why did proletarian revolutions not break out across industrial capitalistic Western Europe and in England? Sociologists, economists, political scientists and others have suggested the following five reasons:

1. **IMPERIALISM** Vladimir Illyich Lenin, political theorist, founder of the Communist Party, leader of the Bolshevik Revolution, architect and first leader of the Union of Soviet Socialist Republics (USSR) from 1917 until his death at the age of 53 from a series of strokes, finds the answer in imperialism (Lenin, 1916). Let us use England as an example. Capitalist England engaged in imperial ventures, so many of them that by 1897 the British Empire covered 25 percent of the world's land surface and controlled about the same proportion of the world's population (Ferguson, 2002: 240). Imperialism, according to Lenin, delays revolution. By conquering other peoples, the capitalists exploit their labor and resources and then again exploits those countries as markets for goods manufactured in the mother country. Imperialism develops enormous wealth, a small portion of which goes to the proletarians in the mother country, making them more prosperous and more content.

2. **CAPITALIST CLASS IS FRAGMENTED** In other words, how we define the central concept of social class influences how likely we perceive revolution to be. Sociologist Ralf Dahrendorf (1959) rejects Marx's two class system both as too simplistic and as overly focused on property ownership (Ritzer, 2008: 16). Due to the rise of the joint stock company, ownership in modern capitalist countries does not necessarily mean control of economic production in those societies. Instead, day-to-day corporate decisions are in the hands of a large class of managers who may or may not be major stockholders.

   Moreover, stockholding (ownership) is widely dispersed in the United States. About half of all families directly own at least some stocks, which means that more and more people perceive themselves as having a direct stake in the capitalist system (Bricker, Kennickell, Moore, and Sabelhaus, 2012: 41). In the United States, the median value of directly held stocks for families with stock holdings in 2010 was $20,000; the mean value of directly held stocks for families with stock holdings in 2010 was $209,700 (Bricker, Kennickell, Moore, and Sabelhaus, 2012: 30, 31).

3. **NOT IMMISERATION BUT A HIGHER STANDARD OF LIVING** A century ago, most workers in the United States either were on farms or in factories in **blue-collar** occupations, lower-prestige jobs that involve manual labor. Today, most workers are in **white-collar** occupations, higher prestige jobs that involve mainly mental activity. These jobs are in sales, education, customer support, professional and other service occupations. Most of these workers do not think of themselves as members of the industrial proletariat.

   The standard of living has risen dramatically during the past 100 years in the United States. Today, the average full-time employee works about 40 hours per week rather than 60 and the average family spends just 15 percent of its income on food today, compared to 44 percent in 1900 (Edwards and Landau, 1999). Just as important, the average wage has increased more than tenfold between 1900 ($4,748) and 2011 ($50,054) (Edwards and Landau, 1999; DeNavas-Walt, Proctor, and Smith, 2012). The term **income** refers to wages and salaries earned from paid occupations plus unearned money from investments (Giddens, Duneier, Applebaum, and Carr, 2012: 201). The term **real income** refers to income after controlling for inflation; thus, real income provides a fixed standard that we may use to make comparisons from year to year. Blue-collar workers in Western societies "now earn three to four times as much in real income as their counterparts in the early 1900s" (Giddens, Duneier, Applebaum, and Carr, 2012: 201). Gains of white-collar workers have been even higher. Thus, despite recent tough economic times, the typical worker today in the United States is far better off, economically, than the typical worker of a century ago. One consequence of the rising standard of living is that people tend to support the economic system that supports them.

Similarly, economist and economic historian Gregory Clark has tracked the position of the unskilled laborer over time in England relative to the rest of the population. In 1770 the typical unskilled laborer earned £10.4 (a little over 10 pounds sterling, the currency of England). These earnings represented 47 percent of the average income per adult in that country. This ratio remained unchanged by 1851. However, by 2004, the unskilled worker was earning 57 percent of the average income per adult in England (Clark, 2007: 282). Once again, industrialization had increased the standard of living of the average worker rather than increasingly immiserating him or her.

4. **IMPROVED WORKING CONDITIONS** Over the past century, workers have gained the right to engage in collective bargaining and to join unions. Labor unions have made demands on the owners of the economic means of production and on management with regard to working conditions. One result is that disputes are settled without overthrowing the capitalist system. Also, laws have changed. For instance, the **Occupational Safety and Health Act** is the primary federal law which governs occupational health and safety in both the private sector and federal government in the United States. It was enacted by Congress in 1970 and signed into law by President Richard Nixon in December of that year. Its main goal is to ensure that employers provide employees with an environment free from recognized hazards, such as exposure to toxic chemicals, excessive noise levels, mechanical dangers, excessive heat or cold, and unsanitary conditions. Among other things, the Act created the Occupational Safety and Health Administration (OSHA), an agency of the U.S. Department of Labor. OSHA was given the authority both to set and enforce workplace health and safety standards. In this way, governmental agencies, such as OSHA, stipulate and enforce health and safety standards in the private sector and federal government in the United States. The result is that rather than deteriorating, working conditions have improved. Revolution is improbable when there is continued improvement in working conditions coupled with an objective improvement in living standards (Davies, 1962).

5. ***WHEN* IS REVOLUTION MORE LIKELY TO OCCUR: IMMISERATION OR DAVIES J-CURVE?** Revolution also is improbable when society is generally impoverished, or, to use Marx's term, immiserated. In that condition, people's physical and mental energies tend to be totally focused and expended on satisfying the basic Maslovian needs, the needs that must be satisfied for life itself to be possible.

Revolution is more likely to occur when a prolonged period of objective economic and social improvement is followed by a short period of sharp reversal (Davies, 1962: 6). The long period of improvement produces an expectation, which continues to rise, of a continued ability to satisfy higher-order Maslovian needs. The short period of sharp reversal produces a mental state of anxiety and frustration when real life departs significantly and abruptly from anticipated life. People then subjectively fear that the ground they gained with great effort will be quite lost and their mood becomes revolutionary. The intolerable gap between what people want (rising expectations) and what they get is the engine that drives the train of revolution (Gurr, 2010, 1970; Davies, 1962).

This relationship between need satisfaction and revolution has been termed **the Davies J-curve**, deriving its name from James C. Davies, the sociologist who enunciated this hypothesis in 1962 (Davies, 1962). More colloquially, it sometimes is termed the revolution of rising expectations. The French Revolution, the American Revolution, and the Russian Revolution of 1917, among others, all fit the Davies J-curve. While Karl Marx said that *absolute deprivation*—immiseration-- would spur the proletariat to revolution, the Davies J-Curve posits that *relative deprivation* fills, or can fill, that crucial role. When we speak of an intolerable gap between our expectations and actual reality, we are speaking of **relative deprivation**, deprivation or disadvantage measured not by objective standards but by comparison with the relatively superior advantage of some other standard, such as our former selves, whom one desires to emulate. The term was used originally by Samuel A. Stauffer in *The American Soldier* (1950) (Theodorson and Theodorson, 1969).

FIGURE 7.1 **DAVIES J-CURVE**

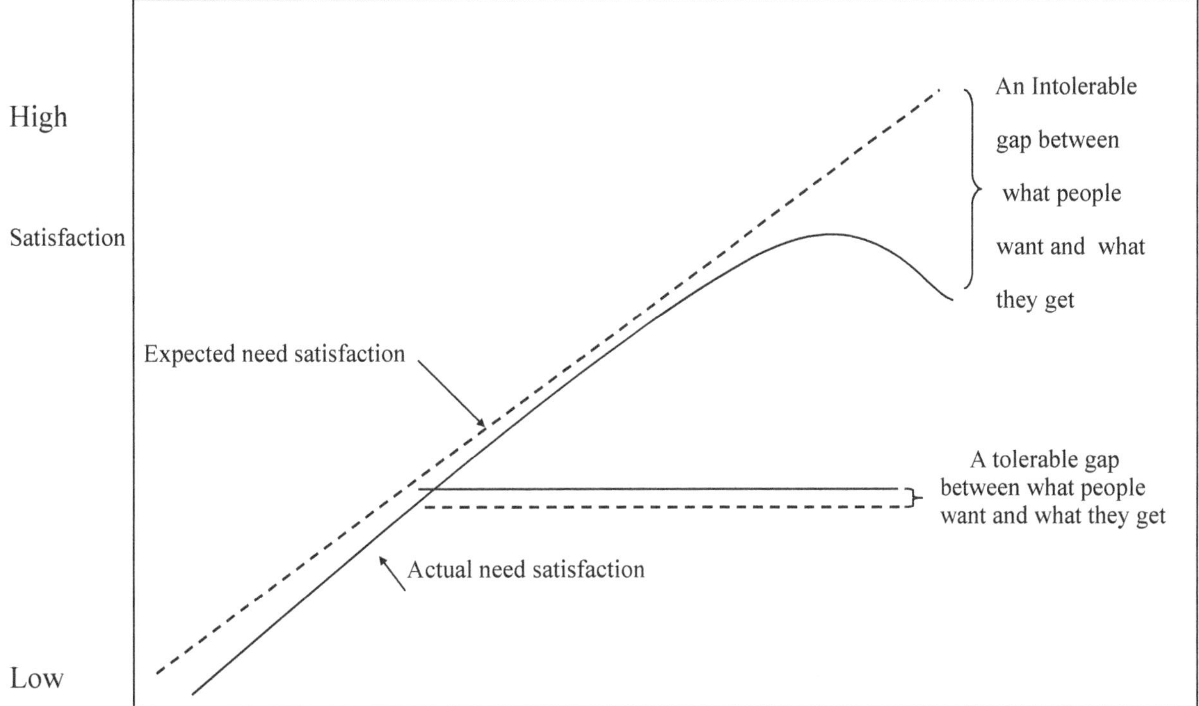

WORLD SYSTEM THEORY

Some conflict theories take a global perspective in the attempt to understand stratification. This is the case with **world-system theory** which has several intellectual antecedents including Marxian conflict theory and **dependency theory**. Dependency theory is a body of social-science theories predicated on the notion that scarce and widely-valued resources flow from a "periphery" of poor and underdeveloped states to a "core" of wealthy states, enriching the latter at the expense of the former. It is a central tenet of dependency theory that poor states are impoverished and rich ones are enriched by the way that poor states are integrated into the "world system." Basic premises of dependency theory are that poor nations ("the periphery") provide natural resources, cheap labor, a destination for obsolete technology, and markets for developed nations, without which the developed nations ("the core") would not have the high standard of living that they enjoy. *Andre Gunder Frank* (1929-2005) is a German-American sociologist and economic historian who developed and promoted both dependency theory and world-system theory (e.g., Frank, 1967; Frank and Gills, 1993).

World-system theory is a macro-level approach to understanding stratification, social change, and history that stresses that the world-system (and not nation states) should be the primary unit of social analysis. World-system theory is a Marxian-influenced macro-level theory that argues that the organization of modern capitalism occurs on a global, not a national, basis. The interlocking nature of the global economy became apparent in visceral ways to many ordinary people of the world during the global economic recession of 2007-2009. The world-system refers to a trans-national division of labor, which divides the world into core countries, semi-periphery countries, and periphery countries.

American sociologist Immanuel Wallerstein has developed the best-known version of world-system theory (e.g., Wallerstein, Aguirre Rojas, and Lemert, 2012; Wallerstein, 1983, 1989, 2004). Wallerstein traces the roots of the global economic order to Europe in the fifteenth century, when Europeans began to colonize distant parts of the world, gathering raw materials, bringing them back to Europe where, among other things, they fueled the industrial revolution.

In the world economic system, **core countries** are the most advanced industrial capitalist countries to whom flow the lion's share of profits in the world economic system. Core countries include but are not limited to the United States, Germany, France, Great Britain, Switzerland, Norway, Finland, Denmark, Sweden, and Japan (Chase-Dunn, Kawano, and Brewer, 2000). See Box 7.1. According to the tenets of world-system theory, countries of the core exploit the countries of the semi-periphery and of the periphery. Japan, which at one time was a country of the semi-periphery, has joined the core. Countries of the core are high-income countries.

Low-income countries are the **periphery countries**. Countries of the periphery provide countries of the core with inexpensive labor, large quantity of raw material, and a vast market for industrial and high-technology products produced by the core (Chirot, 1986). According to the tenets of world-system theory, countries of the periphery are exploited by countries of the core and semi-periphery but they are too weak to exploit other countries of the global economy themselves.

The remaining countries in the global economy are the **semi-periphery countries**. These include middle-income countries, such as the emerging economies known as the BRICs—Brazil, Russia, India, and China-- that have close ties to the core countries. Countries of the semi-periphery also include Mexico as well as the Four Tigers or Asian Dragons--Hong Kong, South Korea, Taiwan, and Singapore. The Four Asian Tigers or Asian Dragons at one time had been countries of the periphery. Each succeeded in developing particular sectors of their economies and industries that were competitive on world markets. These

WHAT IS THE G-8?

BOX 7.1

The **G-8**, also known as the Group of 8, is an annual forum at which the heads of state of the major industrial democracies, or their representatives, have been meeting annually to deal with the major economic and political issues facing their respective nations and the world as a whole. The G-8 is a magnet for anti-globalization protesters and other activists such as the regulars of the Occupy Wall Street movement and **the Occupy movement**, an international protest movement against social and economic inequality, whose primary goal is to make the economic and political relations in all societies less vertically hierarchical and more flatly distributed.

The forum originated in 1975 with a summit hosted by France that brought together representatives of six governments: the United States, France, Germany, the United Kingdom, Italy and Japan, which lead to the name Group of Six or G-6. The next year, with the addition of Canada, the group became known as the Group of Seven or G-7. In 1997 Russia was added to the group for essentially political reasons and the group then became known as the G-8 or Group of 8. The G-7 still is active after the creation of the G-8. The European Union is represented within the G8 but cannot host or chair its summits. G-8 or the Group of 8 can refer to the member states in aggregate or to the annual summit meeting of the G-8 heads of government or their representatives. G8 ministers also meet throughout the year, such as the G7/G8 finance ministers, who meet four times a year; the G8 environment ministers, or the G8 foreign ministers. Each calendar year, the responsibility of hosting the G8 rotates through the member states in the following order: France, United States, United Kingdom, Russia, Germany, Japan, Italy, and Canada.

Collectively the G8 nations comprise 53 percent of the 2011 global nominal GDP (Gross Domestic Product) and 42.5 percent of global GDP (PPP). PPP stands for purchasing power parity.

The G-7/G-8 consistently has addressed macro-economic management, international trade, and relations with developing countries.

Sources: Nicholas Bayne and Robert D. Putnam, *Hanging in There: The G7 and G8 Summit in Maturity and Renewal* (Aldershot, England: Ashgate Publishing, Ltd., 2000) and "G8" as of March 7, 2013, available online at http://en.wikipedia.org/wiki/G8

industries and sectors created enough capital accumulation within their countries to raise income levels not just for a small elite but across the population of their countries more broadly (Goldstein and Pevenhouse, 2010: 280) and they have moved from the periphery to the semi-periphery of the world economic system. Their growth shows that it is possible to rise out of poverty to relative prosperity. If they continue on their current trajectory, they may become countries of the core one day.

According to world-system theory, countries of the semi-periphery are exploited by the core and they, in turn, exploit the countries of the periphery. Semi-peripheries can come into existence from developing peripheries (as in the case, for example, of the Four Asian Tigers) and from declining cores. Russia is an example of a former core country that, after the breakup of the Soviet Union, fell to the periphery and now is a country of the semi-periphery.

Rich countries dominate the system. It is important to note that there is an elite (core) in every country. This elite becomes wealthy by serving the core countries, not their own people. It is also important to note that, according to world-system theory, the global economic system is set up to advantage the rich countries, not to help the poor countries to converge. This arrangement is a world-system theory explanation for why the countries on the bottom of the global system of stratification are on the bottom.

Alternative Explanation for the Immiseration of Those in the Bottom Position of the Global Stratification System

In *The Bottom Billion* (Collier, 2007), economist Paul Collier presents an alternative explanation for the immiseration of countries at the bottom of the global stratification system. Collier reckons that there are just under sixty countries on the bottom of the global system of stratification and that and these countries are home to about a billion people. Life expectancy for the bottom billion is 50 years and one in seven children there dies before the age of five. Not all of these people are in Africa. Some live in North Korea, Cambodia, Myanmar, Haiti, and Yemen; but 70 percent of the bottom billion lives in Africa (Collier, 2007, 2010) and there is good reason to expect that proportion to rise. Four features that characterize the countries of the bottom billion and that account for their lack of development are these (Collier, 2007, 2010):

1. **POLITICAL VIOLENCE** There is a lot of political violence in the countries of the bottom billion. Usually the violence is internal. 73 percent of those who live in the bottom billion live in countries that have had sustained, endemic civil conflict. Civil wars in the countries of the bottom billion are nasty, brutish, and long: their victims are mainly civilians and they last more than ten times as long as international wars (Collier, 2010: 7). Three economic characteristics globally make a country prone to civil war: low income, slow economic growth, and dependence upon primary commodity exports (e.g., oil, gas, diamonds, etc.). Countries of the bottom billion have all three characteristics and civil wars are endemic in many of these small poor countries. The bulk of countries that fall into civil war are from the bottom billion (Colllier, 2007: 35).

   The most common form of political violence often is successful without any deaths at all: it is the **coup d'état**, the seizure of political power by domestic military forces, i.e., a change of political power outside of the state's constitutional order (Goldstein and Pevehouse, 2010: 159). Outside the bottom billion, coups are very rare; inside the bottom billion, they are common. The political instability they manifest is known to be detrimental to economic development (Collier, 2007: 35).

   Why do so many of the bottom billion become mired in internal conflict. Collier has spent years trying to figure this out. Civil war, it turns out, has nothing much to do with the legacy of colonialism, or income inequality, or political repression of minorities. Three things tend to increase the risk of conflict: (1) a relatively high proportion of young, uneducated men; (2) an imbalance between ethnic groups, with one tending to outnumber the rest; and (3) a supply of natural resources (e.g., gold, diamonds, oil), which helps simultaneously to encourage and to finance rebellion.

2. **BAD NEIGHBORHOOD** Neighbors matter. Geography matters. Why is Uganda poor and Switzerland rich? Both are landlocked countries. Switzerland's access to the sea (and to global trading that the sea

affords) depends upon German and Italian infrastructure, while Uganda's access to the sea depends upon Kenyan infrastructure. Which do you imagine is better? If you are a landlocked country and your country has poor transport links to the coast and those transport links are, in any event, beyond your control, it is difficult for you to integrate into global markets with products that require a lot of transport. That leaves out manufacturing; and, to date, manufacturing has been the most reliable driver of rapid economic development (Ferguson, 2011; Goldstein and Pevenhouse, 2010; Collier, 2007: 55).

Your neighbors also are potential markets for your goods. Some neighbors are better markets than others. Switzerland has Germany, Italy, Austria, and France as neighbors. Uganda has Kenya, whose economy has been fairly stagnant for decades due to corruption, reliance upon several primary goods whose prices have remained low, and low infrastructure investment (CIA World Factbook, 2013b); South Soudan, whose economy and infrastructure are severely underdeveloped after decades of civil war with Sudan (CIA World Factbook 2013b); Rwanda, which had a state-orchestrated genocide (CIA World Factbook, 2013c); the Democratic Republic of the Congo, marred by systemic corruption and country-wide instability and conflict that has resulted in more than 5 million deaths from violence, famine, and disease since the mid-1990s, and whose people have an annual income of $400 per capita in 2012 US dollars and where 71 percent of the people are below the poverty line (CIA World Factbook, 2013d) ; Somalia, which completely collapsed and whose citizens enjoy a GDP per capita income of $600 a year, in 2012 U.S. dollars –which works out to living on $1.64 a day (CIA World Factbook, 2013e); and Tanzania, which invaded it (Collier, 2007: 55). In recent years, you could say that Switzerland has been in the better neighborhood.

Countries benefit from the growth of their neighbors. Nice neighborhoods, in the sense of fast growth, are good for everyone. Landlocked countries like Switzerland orient their economies to serve the markets provided by their neighbors. This works well if you are Switzerland but not so well if you are Uganda, stuck in one or more of the growth traps, with neighbors in a similar position as yourself. Uganda cannot access the global market due to the high transport costs of hauling along neglected Kenyan roads nor rely on reorienting its economy to its neighbors, because they are stuck in the development traps, too.

3. **RESOURCE CURSE** This trap may seem counter-intuitive. Countries that are rich in natural resources (e.g., diamonds, gold, natural gas, oil) are paradoxically more prone to conflict than those lacking such resources. Collier attributes this to three causes. First, resources make conflict over, or for control of, the resources likely. Second, natural resources, as a source of revenue for the state, mean that a government does not have to tax its citizens. Consequently, the citizenry are less likely to demand financial accountability from government. Hence, there are fewer checks and balances on the governmental system, fewer political restraints on how power is used. Third, the exploitation of valuable natural resources can result in what economists term Dutch disease: a country's other industries become less competitive and wither.

4. **BAD GOVERNANCE AND BAD POLICIES** Bad governance and bad policies, from corruption to excessive government planning rather than using markets to run the economy, can destroy an economy with startling speed.

   China is a good example. Between 1958-1962, China, under the leadership of Mao Zedong, adopted economic policies that became known as the **Great Leap Forward**, an attempt to catch up with, and to surpass, Britain economically in less than fifteen years. The peasant masses would be mobilized to transform both agriculture and industry simultaneously. Everything was collectivized in this Chinese version of **a command economy**. Instead of allowing dispersed buyers and sellers to determine their own economic activities according to what economists call the laws of supply and demand, a higher authority would issue commands determining the overall direction of the economy according to a master plan (Dikötter, 2010: 127). For the greater good, all economic decisions were centralized. The state decided what would be produced, in what amount, when and where and at what price, and what price could be charged for materials, goods, and services. Central planning replaced the market. The results were nothing short of swift catastrophe, with 45 million people dead as a result, one-third of all housing demolished, and the transportation system in collapse, unable to cope with the demands created by a command economy (Dikötter, 2010).

It was against this background that, two years after the death of Chairman Mao, Deng Xiaoping, China's new ruler, embarked on policies of economic reform that transformed China's southern coastal provinces into *free economic zones* open to foreign investment and run on capitalist principles; allowed peasants to work their own fields instead of working on collective farms and to get rich (by Chinese standards if they did it well). (Goldstein and Pevehouse, 2010: 281).

These agrarian reforms paid off well. Crop yields rose between 1978 and 1984 by 7.7 percent annually. The same country that twenty years earlier had been hit by the worst famine in human history now had a food surplus. Policies matter.

BOX 7.2

GROSS DOMESTIC PRODUCT PER CAPITA (PPP)

In comparing levels of well-being, including social stratification, across countries we need to use measures that are comparable. Let us tell you about a measure called **gross domestic product per capita (PPP)** that most economists find useful in studying stratification and levels of well-being across countries.

Gross domestic product (GDP) is the value of all final goods and services produced within a nation in a given year. A nation's GDP per capita is the value of all final goods and services produced in a nation in a given year divided by the population of the country. A nation's GDP at purchasing power parity (PPP) is the sum value of all goods and services produced in the country valued at prices prevailing in the United States in the year noted. Purchasing power parity takes into account the relative cost of living and the inflation rates of the countries, rather than just using the official exchange rates of their countries' currencies. A nation's GDP per capita (PPP) is the sum value of all goods and services produced in the country valued at prices prevailing in the United States in the year noted, divided by the population as of July 1 of the same year.

GDP per capita (PPP) is the measure most economists prefer when looking at per-capita welfare and when comparing living conditions or use of resources across countries.

Sources: Nicholas Bayne and Robert D. Putnam, *Hanging in There: The G7 and G8 Summit in Maturity and Renewal* (Aldershot, England: Ashgate Publishing, Ltd., 2000) and "G8" as of March 7, 2013, available online at http://en.wikipedia.org/wiki/G8

The free enterprise zones allowed Chinese entrepreneurs to engage in foreign trade. Foreign investment flooded into southern China. Entrepreneurs started companies, hired workers, generated profits. Other areas of China gradually opened up to capitalist principles as well (Goldstein and Pevehouse, 2010:281). Trade was permitted in the countryside and also between town and country. The formerly self-sufficient villages became integrated with regional and even national markets (Norberg, 2003: 48). Unprofitable state-run industries laid off 10 million workers in the 1990s (Goldstein and Pevehouse, 2010: 281).

The changes in economic policy that China started in 1978 enabled 800 million Chinese farmers to double their incomes in only six years (Norberg, 2003: 48). In twenty years, half a billion Chinese had left absolute poverty behind them (Yao, 2000). Between 1981 and 2001, the proportion of the population living in poverty in China fell from 53 percent to 8 percent (Martin Ravallion, 2005) and the mean income of the population had quadrupled (Ravallion and Chen, 2004: 16). Economic policies matter.

India provides another example of policy and its influence on development and social stratification. Bad policies can destroy an economy. For instance, one way to avoid becoming dependent on other states that might seem attractive to a weaker country whose trading partners tend to be more powerful, is to avoid trading externally altogether and instead to try to produce everything it needs by itself. Such a policy is called self-sufficiency or **autarky** (Goldstein and Pevehouse, 2010: 171; Elias, 1982). The policy of autarky has proven ineffective, as the experience of India demonstrates.

India followed a policy of nearly total economic autarky for decades after its establishment as an independent state in 1947. During this period, economic growth barely kept pace with its population growth, and the proportion of its population falling below the poverty line actually grew from 50 percent at Independence to 62 percent in 1966 (Norberg, 2003: 51). In the mid-1970s, India began a slow re-ordering of its economy and these policies gained speed in the early 1990s. India pretty much abandoned autarky and replaced it with economic policy that relied on the country's advantage in labor-intensive industry. Tariff levels, which had averaged a crippling 87 percent, were lowered to 27 percent (Norberg, 2003: 51-52). India opened itself to world trade.

India's niche in the globalized world economy is in the service and information sectors. Capitalizing on its large, educated English-speaking population, India has become a major exporter of information-technology services and software workers (Goldstein and Pevenhouse, 2010: 284). For instance, multi-national corporations widely use India's labor force to answer phone calls from around the world, including technical support calls for the companies' products. In short, by abandoning autarky and adopting economic policies that integrated India into the global economic system, India propelled itself from the periphery to the semi-periphery of the global economic and stratification systems. The percentage of the population below the Indian poverty line has fallen to under 30 percent (CIA World Factbook, 2013f), which is less than half of what had been in 1966 when India embraced autarkic policies. Economic policies matter.

Let us turn our attention to the issue of poor governance and its relation to economic development and stratification. Poor countries that are below the cut-off point in terms of economic policies and effective governance are termed failing states or **failed states** (e.g., Piazza, 2008; Collier, 2007: 64-75; Stewart, 2007; Mallaby, 2002; Rotberg, 2002; Helman and Ratner, 1992-1993). A failed state is one that has lost control of its territory or of a monopoly on the legitimate use of physical force therein. These states no longer perform basic functions such as governance, security, education, and provision and maintenance of infrastructure, including roads, railways, and so forth; and in these states, criminality and corruption are rampant and endemic. These factors make economic development a low probability occurrence.

An example of corruption in government in a failed state is provided by the results of a 2004 survey that tracked money released by the Ministry of Finance in Chad intended for rural health clinics (Collier, 2007: 66). The survey had the modest purpose of finding out how much of the money actually made it to the clinics. Amazingly, less than one percent of it reached the clinics, which means that 99 percent of it failed to reach its destination. Bad governance matters. See Box 7.2 Gross Domestic Product Per Capita (PPP). The people of Chad are poor: their GDP per capita (PPP) is $2000, in 2012 U.S. dollars. Chad's only option is for the government to provide services and corruption has closed off that option. In the 2012 Transparency International ratings of corruption, Chad ties with three other countries (Haiti, Burundi, and Venezuela) for 6th place from the bottom. In other words, Chad is the sixth most corrupt country on Planet Earth (Transparency International, 2012) and has been among the top five failed states for years on end as well. High levels of corruption impede economic development.

SOCIAL STRATIFICATION IN THE UNITED STATES

An understanding of a few basic concepts helps us better to understand social stratification in the United States. **Income** refers to earnings from work or investments, while **wealth** refers to the total value of money and other assets, minus outstanding debts. For many Americans, income is the salary or wages they earn at their jobs. Quite generally income tends to be more equally distributed in a population than is wealth. Phrased somewhat differently, wealth tends to be more unequally distributed than income. This tendency is quite widespread across countries.

Let us now look at the distribution of income and wealth in the United States, social class in the United States, and the extent of upward and downward social mobility.

Income Distribution in the United States

Our discussion of the distribution of income is facilitated by understanding a couple of basic statistical concepts, one of which is quintile and another of which is percentile. In statistics, a **quintile** is one of four points dividing a frequency distribution into five equal parts. The first quintile is the 20th percentile, the second quintile is the 40th percentile, the third quintile is the 60th percentile, and the fourth quintile is the 80th percentile.

A **percentile** is one of one hundred points dividing a frequency distribution into one hundred equal parts. A particular percentile tells us the percent of the total number of cases in a frequency distribution that falls below that point. For example, the tenth percentile is the point below which 10 percent of the cases lie, the 90th percentile is the point below which ninety percent of the cases lie, and so forth. Thus, if you scored in the 97th percentile on a test, then 97 percent of the people who took the test scored lower on it than you did.

TABLE 7.2 DISTRIBUTION OF HOUSEHOLD INCOME BY QUINTILE IN THE UNITED STATES, 2000-2011

Percentage of Total Household Income						
Year	Bottom	Second	Third	Fourth	Fifth	HiLo
2000	3.6	8.9	14.8	23.0	49.8	13.8
2001	3.5	8.7	14.6	23.0	50.1	14.3
2002	3.5	8.8	14.8	23.3	49.7	14.2
2003	3.4	8.7	14.8	23.4	49.8	14.6
2004	3.4	8.7	14.7	23.2	50.1	14.7
2005	3.4	8.6	14.6	23.0	50.4	14.8
2006	3.4	8.6	14.5	22.9	50.5	14.9
2007	3.4	8.7	14.8	23.4	49.7	14.6
2008	3.4	8.6	14.7	23.3	50.0	14.7
2009	3.4	8.6	14.6	23.2	50.3	14.8
2010	3.3	8.5	14.6	23.4	50.3	15.2
2011	3.2	8.4	14.3	23.0	51.1	16.0

Source: Data on household income quintiles extracted from Table A-2 of DeNavas-Walt, Carmen, Bernadette D. Proctor, and Jessica C. Smith, "Income, Poverty, and Health Insurance Coverage in the United States: 2011," *Current Population Reports*, P60-243 (Washington, D.C.: U.S. Government Printing Office, 2012). As of April 3, 2013, available online at http://www.census.gov/prod/2012pubs/p60-243.pdf HiLo data computed from data in Table 7.2.

Most discussions of income inequality rely on data collected by the U.S. Census Bureau (Browning, 2008: 19), which annually conducts a survey of about 60,000 American households carefully selected to be representative of the entire population. In this survey, the U.S. Census Bureau collects a wide array of information about these households, including their incomes for the previous year. On the basis of this survey, the U.S. Census Bureau publishes a variety of measures that describes the distribution of money income in the United States. One of the most common measures is presented in Table 7.2. Because this presentation is so widely used, both in scholarly studies and in the news media, it is worthwhile explaining how it is constructed.

First, the households are ranked ordered by income from highest to lowest. Then they are separated into five equal-sized portions, each containing one-fifth (20 percent) of all households in the sample. (These fifths are called quintiles.) The bottom-income fifth contains the twenty percent of households that have the lowest incomes. The second-income fifth contains the twenty percent of households with incomes between the twentieth and fortieth percentiles, and so on. Then, we add up the total income of all the households in the entire sample. Then, we add up the total income of the households within each fifth and express that sum as a percentage of the total income of all the households (in all five groups together). The result is five percentages, each of which gives us the share of the total income received by that fifth of households. By definition, these percentages add up to 100 percent.

What does the distribution of income look like in the United States? See Table 7.2. As shown in the first quintile column of Table 7.2, the bottom fifth of households in 2011 received 3.2 percent of total income, while the highest fifth received 51.1 percent; the other fifths received shares falling between these.

The Internal Revenue Service is another source of data on income in the United States and it also provides data on tax shares by income. Let us now look at income and tax shares by income in the United States for 2010, the most recent year for which data are available from the Internal Revenue Service (data extracted from Table 5, pages 56-58 and from Table 8 on page 63 of Dungan and Parisi, 2013):

- **THE TOP 1/10TH OF 1 PERCENT:** Americans who earned an adjusted gross income of $1,634,386 or more accounted for 9.2 percent of all wages in 2010, but they paid 17.9 percent of total reported income taxes. The average tax rate for the top 1/10th of 1 percent of wage earners in 2010 was 22.8 percent. When people talk about the super rich, these are the folks they are talking about.
- **THE TOP 1 PERCENT:** Americans who earned an adjusted gross income of $369,691 or more accounted for 18.9 percent of all wages in 2010, but they paid 37.4 percent of total reported income taxes. The average tax rate for the top 1 percent of wage earners in 2010 was 23.4 percent.
- **THE TOP 5 PERCENT:** Americans who earned an adjusted gross income of $161,579 or more accounted for 33.8 percent of all wages in 2010, but they paid 59.1 percent of total reported income taxes. The average tax rate for the top 5 percent of wage earners in 2010 was 20.6 percent.
- **THE TOP 10 PERCENT:** Americans who earned an adjusted gross income of $116,623 or more accounted for 45.2 percent of all wages in 2010, but they paid 70.6 percent of total reported income taxes. The average tax rate for the top 10 percent of wage earners in 2010 was 18.5 percent.
- **THE TOP 25 PERCENT:** Americans who earned an adjusted gross income of $69,126 or more accounted for 67.6 percent of all wages in 2010, but they paid 87.1 percent of total reported income taxes. The average tax rate for the top 25 percent of wage earners in 2010 was 15.2 percent.
- **THE TOP 50 PERCENT:** Americans who earned an adjusted gross income of $34,338 or more accounted for 88.3 percent of all wages in 2010, but they paid almost all (97.7 percent) of the income tax for 2010. The average tax rate for the top 50 percent of wage earners in 2010 was 13.1 percent.
- **THE BOTTOM 50 PERCENT** of wage earners accounted for 11.4 percent of all wages in 2010 and they paid 2.5 percent of the income tax for 2010. The average tax rate for the bottom 50 percent of wage earners in 2010 was 2.4 percent.

  It is worth noting that of all federal income tax filers in 2011, 46.6 percent were exempt from paying any federal income tax at all (Eichler, 2011). *More than half* of those exempt from federal income tax in 2011 are in the lowest income quintile. In 2011, those in the bottom quintile have incomes of less than $16, 812, and 93.3 percent of the bottom quintile pay no federal income tax whatsoever in 2011 (Bartlett, 2011); moreover, 60.3 percent of those in the next to the bottom quintile pay no federal income tax whatsoever in 2011 (Bartlett, 2011). The bottom two income quintiles are 82.8 percent of those persons who pay no federal income tax whatsoever (Bartlett, 2011).

Internal Revenue Service data document that there is significant income concentration in the United States. They also document that federal individual income tax in the United States is a progressive tax. In a **progressive tax**, the tax rate increases as the amount subject to taxation increases. Higher income earners pay a *higher* tax rate than do lower income earners. In fact, a study on inequality by researchers at the Organization for Economic Cooperation and Development (OECD) in Paris reveals that when it comes to income taxes and employee social security contributions, the United States "has the most progressive tax system and collects the largest share of taxes from the richest 10% of the population" in the world (OECD, 2008: 112).

While taxes rise with the advance of industrialization, the way that governments spend these revenues varies greatly (The Economist, 2012c). In the United States, where government has been more interested in equality of opportunity than of income, the most transformative shift has been to bring in mass education. Thus, between 1870-1910, free public high school education became democratized in this country. The free, public comprehensive high school prepared the great mass of 14-17-year olds for work and life. To accomplish this task, the United States made huge investments in secondary education. Then, after World

War II, the G.I. bill offered returning soldiers the chance of higher education. Harvard economists Claudia Goldin and Lawrence F. Katz (2007) view this dramatic investment in education as the main cause of the narrowing of inequality in the United States during the mid-twentieth century. Investment in education boots social mobility (e.g., Aaronsen and Mazumder, 2011).

The general principle is that in England and Europe, governments were far slower to invest heavily in mass education (Ben-David, 1963-1964). For instance, in England free secondary education was not available until 1944, when The Education Act of 1944 made secondary education free for all pupils in England and Wales and raised the school leaving age to 15. In England, as in Europe, the emphasis is on equality of outcomes, to be achieved with big government transfers. Particularly after the Second World War, continental governments invested heavily in creating and sustaining large social safety nets, with generous child subsidies, income support, jobless benefits, and access to health care. In virtually all rich countries other than the United States, such benefits (rather than progressive tax systems) have become the most important vehicles or paths for reducing income inequality.

Let us now consider data on individual earnings. Economists expect more skilled (more economically productive) workers to have higher earnings in a free market economy (Browning, 2008:29). Economists also expect that productivity is related to the educational level achieved by workers. Hence, it is not surprising that more educated workers have higher earnings. Taken from the same U.S. Census Bureau database that produces the distributional data presented in Table 7.2, here are the median 2011 earnings for male workers aged 25 and older who worked full time, year round, in relation to their educational attainments (data extracted from Table P-24, United States Census Bureau, Historical Tables: People):

- 9th to 12th Grade (No Diploma): $ 30,423
- High School Graduate (Includes Equivalency): $ 40,447
- Some College, No Degree: $ 47,072
- Bachelor's Degree: $ 66,196
- Master's Degree: $ 83,027
- Doctoral Degree: $100,766

We see in these data that a college graduate earns 2.2 times as much as a high-school dropout. One with a master's degree earns twice as much as a high-school graduate. One with a PhD earns 3.3 times as much as a high-school dropout and 2.5 times as much as a high-school graduate. Keep in mind that these figures are earnings before payment of taxes and receipt of government transfers. After-tax and after-transfer earnings differences would be even smaller (Browning, 2008: 209). Do these differences seem unfair to you?

Before leaving the topic of income distribution in the United States, let us consider the question regarding how much income inequality there is in the United States. Box 7.3, "How Much Income Inequality Is There in the United States?" focuses on this important issue.

BOX 7.3 HOW MUCH INCOME INEQUALITY IS THERE IN THE UNITED STATES?

How much income inequality is there, according to the income-quintile numbers in Table 7.2, which show the distribution of household income by quintiles in the United States for 2011 and for the eleven previous years? Because many people experience difficulty juggling and interpreting five income shares meaningfully, Professor of Economics at Texas A&M University Edgar K. Browning suggests that we focus instead on just one number to summarize the extent of income inequality in these data, a measure that he terms the HiLo ratio (Browning, 2008: 20-36).

That number is simply the ratio of average income in the top quintile to average income in the bottom quintile. This is the ratio of the top and bottom quintile shares. In 2011, 51.1/3.2 = 16.0, which tells us that the average high-income household in 2011 had an income 16 times as large as that of the average low-income household. A HiLo ratio of 16 suggests that there is a wide disparity of incomes separating the highest and lowest income categories.

It is important to keep in mind that these data on income shares tell us nothing about absolute levels of income. For instance, if all incomes were to double, the shares remain unchanged, even though everyone is better off. In short, these numbers are indicative only of relative income position, how households stand relative to one another.

The U.S. Census also collects income data on families. You might think that families and households are the same thing. There is a lot of overlap; but, according to U.S. Census definitions, there is an important difference. A household can be a single person living alone, whereas a family must be composed of at least two people. What this means is that household quintile data display far more income inequality than the family quintile data. In short, the two data sets paint very different pictures of income inequality in America. This in part is the case because the number of persons per household varies widely among the fifths. The number of households is the same in each fifth but the number of persons is not. In fact, "the top fifth of households contains 72 percent more people than the lowest fifth" (Browning, 2008: 21).

In 2011, income shares for families were 3.8, 9.3, 15.1, 23.0, and 48.9 (United States Census Bureau, Historical Income Tables, Families). The family-inccome quintile HiLo ratio in 2011 is 12.8, which is 20 percent lower than that for the same year using household-quintile data. People who want to exaggerate the extent of income differences in America will often use household income data without correcting for, or mentioning, the large differences in household size, which has the effect of exaggerating the amount of measured inequality. In any given year, what the United States Census Bureau's income quintile data on households or families actually measures is one year's before-tax income (Browning, 2008: 22-28). Income quintile data overstate income inequality for six reasons:

(1) **Before tax income** In terms of economic well-being, what is important is after-tax income. In the United States, after-tax income is more equally distributed than before-tax incomes because the relevant taxes fall more heavily on higher-income earners.

(2) **Much income is received in non-monetary form** A lot of real income that people receive is in non-monetary form and is not counted as income. Particularly important are government in-kind (non-cash) transfers that add to people's incomes but are not counted as income. Examples are food stamps, Medicaid, and housing assistance. Even one important cash transfer, the Earned Income Tax Credit (EITC), is not counted as income. Nationwide in 2012, 27 million families received over $60 billion in EITC (Internal Revenue Service, 2013). An estimated 26 million households received a total of $55 billion in EITC payments in 2010 (Tax Policy Center, page II-1-8). The Internal Revenue Service reports that in 2009 EITC lifted nearly 7 million people out of poverty, including over 3 million children (Tax Policy Center, page II-1-8). In short, much income at the bottom of the income distribution simply is not defined as "income" by the government. This situation makes the income distribution look more unequal than actually is the case.

(3) **Differences in number of persons per family/household** Higher income households and families, as we have seen, have more people to support. Not taking this into account creates the impression that these families are better off, financially speaking, than they actually are. One way to take this into account is to measure income per person, not income per household or income per family. When individual income measures are used, there is less inequality among the quintiles than when comparing family or household quintiles.

(4) **Differences in amount of work done** There are vast differences in the amount of work done among the quintiles (Browning, 2008: 11). Suppose we compare the work effort of households whose income places them in the bottom income quintile with the work effort of those in the top quintile. How much greater do you suppose the hours of work are for the high income group? One university professor who has been surveying students' opinions on this question for years finds that the modal response, the most frequently occurring response, falls within the 25 to 50 percent range (Browning, 2008: 11). However, the correct answer is that "the high-income group works around *700 percent more*," that is, nearly eight times as much as the low-income group (Browning, 2008: 11; italics in original). Most people would agree that it is fair for people who work eight times longer hours to have a substantially higher income.

Of course, the highest and lowest income quintiles differ on factors other than the number of hours worked. The lowest income quintile has a higher percentage of retired and young households, as well as single-parent households and those on welfare. The high-income quintile has more than twice as many people of working age (18-64) than the bottom group. So, to an extent we are comparing apples and oranges; but that is exactly what people do when they focus on income inequities by quintile. They pretend that the highest and lowest groups are pretty much alike in all respects except that one tends to earn a lot more money.

(5) **How much people consume** It may be inappropriate to focus on in income. People's standard of living is better evaluated by consumption. How much economic inequality is there as measured by consumption?

The United States Department of Labor provides much of our knowledge about consumption. In its Consumer Expenditure Survey, which is conducted by the Bureau of the Census for the

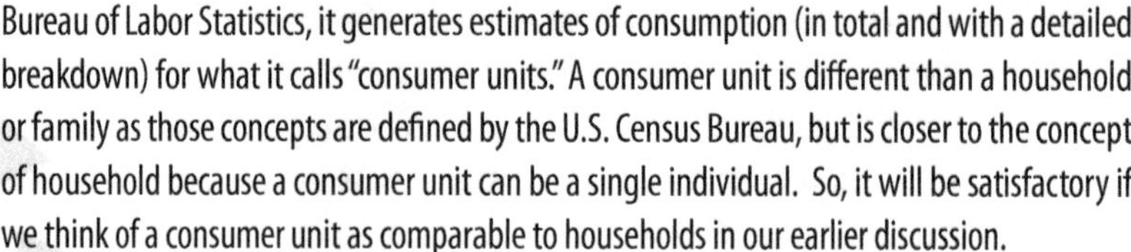

Bureau of Labor Statistics, it generates estimates of consumption (in total and with a detailed breakdown) for what it calls "consumer units." A consumer unit is different than a household or family as those concepts are defined by the U.S. Census Bureau, but is closer to the concept of household because a consumer unit can be a single individual. So, it will be satisfactory if we think of a consumer unit as comparable to households in our earlier discussion.

In 2011, according to the Bureau of Labor Statistics, in terms of consumer expenditures (not exactly the same as consumption, but close), the wealthiest quintile spent 4.3 times as much as the lowest quintile (data extracted and computed from U.S. Bureau of Labor Statistics, 2012), which is a HiLo ratio of about 4.3 for consumption. Consumer expenditures are far more equally distributed than is income. (The consumption shares for the quintiles of consumer units in 2011 are 8.9, 12.9, 17.1, 23.1, and 38.0.) In 2011, the HiLo ratio for household income data was 3.7 times larger than the HiLo ratio for consumption units. Stated somewhat differently, the HiLo ratio for consumption units in 2011 is 86 percent lower than the similar figure using household quintile income data.

The consumption data presented above take no account of the fact that there are fewer persons per consumer unit in the lowest consumption quintile than in the highest consumption quintile. In the lowest consumption quintile unit there are only 1.7 persons per consumer unit, while in the highest consumer quintile there are 3.2. The top quintile thus supports 88 percent more people with its expenditures than does the lowest quintile. There also are four times as many wage earners per consumer unit in the top consumer quintile (2.0) than in the lowest consumer quintile unit (0.5) (U.S. Bureau of Labor Statistics, 2012). Adjusting for these factors would produce an even more equal distribution.

(6) **Ignores intra-generational mobility** People move around, both up and down, in the income distribution from year to year. This is termed intragenerational vertical mobility. When many people see a data array such as that of our Table 7.2, which shows income quintile data for twelve years in the United States, what strikes them is the extent to which the figures don't change much from year to year. Year to year changes are small. This gives the mistaken impression of a static, unchanging distribution: that poor people stay poor and rich people stay rich over time.

That is a very mistaken impression. As you will see in our discussion of intragenerational mobility, there is a lot of upward and downward movement of persons, at the top of the income distribution, at the bottom of the income distribution, and in the middle, too.

Source: Internal Revenue Service, EITC Statistics (Washington, D.C.: Internal Revenue Service, 2013). As of April 4, 2013, available online at http://www.eitc.irs.gov/central/eitcstats/; Tax Policy Center, *The Tax Policy Briefing Book: Taxation and the Family.* As of April 4, 2013, available online at http://www.taxpolicycenter.org/upload/Elements/II-1KEYELEMENTS_TAXATIONANDTHEFAMILY.final.pdf; data on consumption extracted and computed from "Table 1, Quintiles of Income Before Taxes: Average Annual Expenditures and Characteristics, *Consumer Expenditure Survey, 2011*," U.S. Bureau of Labor Statistics, Consumer Expenditure Survey, 2011 (Washington, D.C.: U.S. Bureau of Labor Statistics, September, 2012).

Wealth Distribution in the United States

Data regarding the distribution of wealth (otherwise known as net worth) in the United States are limited. The U.S. Census Bureau's Survey of Income and Program Participation (SIPP) is one source of data on the distribution of wealth in the United States. SIPP is a longitudinal survey designed to follow nationally representative samples of the non-institutionalized, civilian population over several years (Taylor, 2011:35). A second, and the most comprehensive source of information about the distribution of wealth in the United States, is the national Survey of Consumer Finances (SCF) conducted every three years by the governors of the Federal Reserve Bank (Levine, 2012:1).

Both data sets show that wealth is highly concentrated. SIPP data show that, adjusted for inflation, the median wealth of U.S. households was $70,000 in 2009, which is a 28 percent drop in wealth since 2005, when the median wealth of U.S. households had been $96,894 (Taylor, 2011: 13). The size of that drop hints at the magnitude of wealth destruction that occurred in the downturn of the global economy during 2007-2009, which often is termed the Great Recession. It is worth noting that in the Great Recession the U.S. economy contracted less than the world's other advanced economies (Hagopian and Ohanian, 2012). For instance, the U.S. GDP shrunk 3.5 percent in 2009, which was 25 percent less than the 4.7 percent contraction experienced by the non-U.S. G-7; and in 2010, the U.S. economy grew 3.0 percent, which is 42 percent more than the 2.1 percent grown for the non-U.S. G-7 (Hagopian and Ohanian, 2012).

The precipitous decline in wealth in the United States was not evenly distributed across demographic groups. Minority households—Hispanics, blacks, and Asians—experienced far steeper declines than white households because minority households are more dependent on home equity as a source of their wealth and—in the case of Hispanics and Asians-- because they are disproportionately likely to reside in states that have been among the hardest hit by the housing crisis—California, Florida, Nevada, and Arizona. Hispanics and blacks also have been more susceptible to home foreclosures and their home ownership rates have dropped more than for other groups (e.g., Taylor, 2011: 13; Sowell, 2010; Norberg, 2009).

SIPP data indicate that in 2009, the median net worth of white households was $113,149 (Taylor, 2011:13). In sharp contrast, the median net worth of Hispanic and black households was $6,325 and $5,677, respectively (Taylor, 2011: 13). In other words, in 2009 the median net worth of white households was more than 17 times as great as the median net worth of Hispanic households. Similarly, in 2009, the median net worth of white households was 20 times as great as the median net worth of black households.

Prior to the Great Recession of 2007-2009, the racial and ethnic disparities in wealth were much smaller in the United States. Thus, SIPP data indicate that in 2005, the median net worth of white households was $134,992 (Taylor, 2011: 13). In contrast, the median net worth of Hispanic and black households in 2005 was $18,359 and $12,124, respectively (Taylor, 2011: 13). In other words, in 2005, the median net worth of white households was 7 (not 17) times as great as the median net worth of Hispanic households. Similarly, in 2005, the median net worth of white households was 11 times (not 20 times) as great as the median net worth of black households. The effects of the Great Recession still are being felt.

While all ethnic and racial groups in the United States experienced drops in wealth from 2005-2009, the drop was particularly precipitous among those for whom home equity is the lion's share of their wealth. Thus, Hispanic median net worth fell 66 percent, from $18,359 in 2005 to $6,325 in 2009 (Taylor, 2011: 14). Black median net worth fell 53 percent, from $12,124 in 2005 to $5,677 in 2009 (Taylor, 2011: 14). The drop in the median net worth of white households was 16 percent, declining from $134,992 in 2005 to $113,149 in 2009 (Taylor, 2011: 14).

How concentrated is the wealth in the United States and what factors influence wealth accumulation? The national Survey of Consumer Finances (SCF) conducted every three years by the governors of the Federal Reserve Bank documents that the wealthiest 10 percent of families in 2010 had a median net worth of $1,864,000, which is more than 186 times as much as the lowest quintile of families, whose median net worth in 2009 was $10,000 (Bricker, Kennickell, Moore, and Sabelhaus, 2012: 13, 17). Education matters. For instance, the median net worth of college graduates is more than twelve times greater than that of high school dropouts (Bricker, Kennickell, Moore, and Sabelhaus, 2012: 17). Owning a home makes a big difference, because homes are the principal wealth asset for most families. For instance, the median net worth of homeowners in 2010 was $713,400, which is 12.5 times as large as the $57,200 median net worth of renters (Bricker, Kennickell, Moore, and Sabelhaus, 2012: 18).

Net worth has become more concentrated in recent decades. The share of wealth held by the top 10 percent of wealth owners grew from 67.2 percent in 1989 to 74.5 percent in 2010 (Levine, 2012: 4). Declines occurred in the remaining 90 percent of households (Levine: 2012:4).

TABLE 7.3 SHARE OF WEALTH HELD BY THE WEALTHIEST TEN PERCENT OF HOUSEHOLDS IN THE UNITED STATES AND THRESHOLD FOR ENTRY INTO TOP TEN PERCENT OF WEALTH HOLDERS, 2005 AND 2009, BY RACE AND ETHNICITY

Race/Ethnicity	Wealth Share Held by the Wealthiest 10 Percent of Households in United States		Threshold for Entry Into Top 10 Percent of Wealth Holders, in 2009 US Dollars	
	2005	2009	2005	2009
All	49%	56%	$646,327	$598,435
Whites	46%	51%	$719,983	$702,950
Hispanics	56%	72%	$395,667	$236,161
Blacks	59%	67%	$290,486	$234,252

Source: Adapted from page 32 of Paul Taylor, *Twenty-to-One: Wealth Gaps Rise to Record Highs Between Whites, Blacks and Hispanics* (Washington, D.C.: Pew Research Center, Pew Social and Demographic Trends, July 26, 2011).

An increased concentration of wealth characterizes all racial and ethnic groups in the United States. See Table 7.3. The share of total wealth held by the top 10 percent of households increased from 2005 to 2009 among whites, Hispanics, and Black Americans. This did *not* happen because the rich got richer, because they did not. As you can see in Table 7.3, the threshold for entry into the wealthiest 10 percent of households, *decreased* from 2005 to 2009 for all racial and ethnic groups. For all U.S. households, the threshold decreased 7 percent, from $646,327 to $598,435. Among Hispanics, the drop was more dramatic, from $395,667 to $236,161, which is a drop of 40 percent in just four years. The threshold fell 19 percent among blacks and 2 percent among whites.

As you can also see in Table 7.3, the increase in the degree of concentration of wealth at the top was the greatest among Hispanics. The share of the top 10 percent went up from 56 percent to 72 percent among Hispanics, a sixteen percent increase in just four years. Among blacks, the wealth share increased from 59 percent to 67 percent, an 8 percent increase in just four years. The increase in wealth disparity from 2005 to 2009 was *lowest* among whites, with the share of the top 10 percent increasing from 46 to 51 percent, an increase of five percent in just four years.

Social Class in the United States

Most sociologists identify social classes in terms of income, wealth, occupation, and education. The idea of social class is familiar: society is seen as consisting of a number of layers of people in a hierarchy. Within each of the layers, people accept one another on equal terms and are more likely to marry or to select one another as intimate significant others (Murray, 2013). There are no sharply defined or universally agreed upon boundaries between social classes, but a number of social classes generally are recognized—the "middle class" and "working class," for example. The following discussion describes the broad landscape of social class in the United States.

THE UPPER CLASS

The wealthiest Americans, families earning about $205,200 or more are about 5 percent of the population (U.S. Census Bureau, 2012) and they belong to the upper class. The upper class is a diverse lot. Most people in the upper class are wealthy but not super rich. Only a small portion of the upper class are super-rich. About 1/10 of 1 percent of Americans are super rich, with incomes of $1,634,386 or more a year (Dungan and Parisi, 2013). The super rich would include the 442 billionaires in this country in 2013 (Kroll and Dolan, 2013).

By and large, the more a family's income exceeds $200,000 a year, the stronger would be its claim to upper-class position (Macionis, 2013: 203). More than *size* of income is involved in upper-class membership. *Source* of income also is important. The larger the portion of income that comes from *inherited* wealth in the form of stocks, bonds, real-estate, and other assets, the stronger is a person's or a family's claim to upper-class membership. This distinction—between earning and inheriting money—is part of the distinction between the upper-upper class and lower-upper class. In the upper-upper class, more than money is important. Family lineage is important (Amory, 1947).

THE UPPER-UPPER CLASS The upper-upper class inherits its wealth, generation after generation, and this wealth tends to be enormous. For this reason, the upper-upper class sometimes is called "old money." In the United States, old-money families include the Rockefellers, Vanderbilts, Mellons, Du Ponts and many others not well known to the general population. Upper uppers are one percent or less of the population in this country and they live in exclusive neighborhoods such as Nob Hill in San Francisco, Beacon Hill in Boston, and the Gold Coast of Chicago. Their children typically attend schools, largely private, with others of similar background and continue their formal education at elite colleges and universities. In the pattern of European aristocrats, they tend to study liberal arts rather than engage in vocationally-oriented studies (Ben-David, 1963-1964). Upper-upper class families tend to marry into other upper-upper class families. Family lineage is highly valued among upper-upper class people.

THE LOWER-UPPER CLASS In contrast, the lower-upper class is new money and about 3 to four percent of the U.S. population belongs to this class. The lower-upper class sometimes is called the "new rich." Bill Gates is a self-made man whose 2013 net worth of $67 billion makes him the 2nd wealthiest person on the planet and the wealthiest man in the United States (Kroll and Dolan, 2013). Bill Gates made his fortune with the company he founded, Microsoft, and he is at the top rung of the lower-upper class in the United States. In similar fashion, in the United Kingdom, J.K. Rowling, a poor, divorced mother on welfare became famous and wealthy by the success of the Harry Potter books she authored and the associated movie franchise. Hers is a "rags to riches" life course. She earned her way to the higher rungs of the lower-upper class. The wealth of quondam upstart entrepreneurs such as Bill Gates or J.K. Rowling often exceeds that of persons in the upper-upper class.

The new rich families often live in large homes in expensive neighborhoods. For instance, American movie actor Nicolas Cage once owned a six-bedroom home in the Garden District of New Orleans where, in the nineteenth century, wealthy newcomers built opulent homes (Starr, 2005). Other new-rich American movie actors who have owned large homes in this expensive neighborhood include John Goodman and Sandra Bullock. The new rich often also own vacation homes near the water or in the mountains, or both. Their children often attend private schools and attend good colleges.

THE MIDDLE CLASS

The middle class is diverse, encompassing 40-50 percent of all American households (Giddens, Duneier, Applebaum, and Carr, 2012: 210). Middle-class people earn stable incomes at largely white-collar and professional jobs. **White-collar jobs** are occupations where the work is largely non-manual and primarily mental in character; this term sometimes is used to refer to all jobs where the labor required is largely non-manual in character.

THE UPPER-MIDDLE CLASS People near the top of the middle class are called *upper-middle class* and they earn incomes in the range of 114,000 – 200,000 a year (Macionis, 2013: 204). Occupations typical of the upper-middle class include successful doctors, lawyers, professors, engineers, stock brokers, mid-level corporate managers, owners or managers of small business or retail shops, and some large farm owners. They live in comfortable homes in fairly expensive areas, own multiple motor vehicles and are likely to be college graduates, often with advanced degrees, as are their children. Their occupations tend to be secure and to provide retirement benefits and health benefits. They own comfortable homes, drive and own late model vehicles, have investments and savings and are civically engaged. They tend to marry and to bear children within marriage. About 20 percent of American households belong to the upper-middle class.

Many people, including many minorities, have moved into the upper-middle class by acquiring higher levels of education which qualify them for professional jobs that have both high prestige and high incomes. A good education is one way of attaining the American Dream.

The middle-middle and lower-middle classes together constitute about thirty percent of the U.S. population.

THE MIDDLE-MIDDLE CLASS People near the middle or center of the U.S. class structure work at less prestigious white-collar jobs. Examples would be bank branch managers and high-school teachers. Family income falls between$48,000 and $114,000 a year (Macionis: 2013: 204). Middle middle-class people generally build up a small amount of wealth over the course of their working lives, largely in the form of a home and retirement funds.

THE LOWER-MIDDLE CLASS Lower-middle class people work in the lower-rungs of white-collar occupations and the upper rungs of blue-collar occupations. Examples of occupations typical of this class are elementary-school teachers, book keepers, and others who provide skilled services such as nurses, police officers, fire fighters, and dental technicians. Some small business owners are also members of this class. Members of this class tend to have fairly high status; it is their lower income and educational attainment that determine their class position. Almost all have graduated from high school, and some have some college, more likely from a community college than from a four-year college or university. If they have a college degree, it more frequently is an Associate of Arts degree (AA) from a community college.

IS THE MIDDLE CLASS STAGNANT OR DISAPPEARING? Before departing our discussion of the middle class in the United States, let us briefly explore the matter as to whether the middle class is stagnant or "disappearing." What do the data show?

Over the period 1979-2007, the income of the lower-middle class grew by 37 percent, the income of the upper-middle class grew by 40 percent and median income in the United States grew by 37 percent (Moore, 2012: 30; Burkhauser, Larrimore, and Simon, 2012). The conclusion of Richard V. Burkhauser of the Department of Policy Analysis and Management at Cornell University at Ithaca, New York, is that "the real, inflation-adjusted income of middle class households as measured by median household income has consistently grown over time" (Burkhauser, Larrimore, and Simon, 2012: 7). Moreover, since 1980, the average income of black families rose by 44 percent, Hispanic families by 28 percent, and white families by 38 percent (Moore, 2012: 42).

The Federal Reserve Bank of Dallas looked at income data from 1975-1991 (Federal Reserve Bank of Dallas, 1995) and finds that 98 percent of poor households in 1975 were not poor by 1991. Seventy-five percent of those in the bottom 20 to 40 percent of family income in 1975 had climbed into the middle class or higher over this fifteen-year period (Federal Reserve Bank of Dallas, 1995). Over the period 1982-2012, the net worth of Americans rose from roughly $18 trillion to $ 66 trillion according to data from the U.S. Federal Reserve Bank (Moore, 2012: 26; Board of Governors of the Federal Reserve System, 2013). More financial wealth was created in the twenty-five year period of 1982-2007 than in the previous two hundred years (Moore: 2012). This was a genuine rising tide that lifted nearly all boats. Then, too, the Congressional Budget Office documents that the middle class in the United States is growing (Congressional Budget Office, 2012, 2011). For instance, in the 31-year period of 1979-2009, which are the most recent data available, after tax, inflation-adjusted income for the middle three income quintiles *grew* by almost 40 percent, which is a rate of a little over 1 percent per year (Congressional Budget Office, 2012). In short, the data are inconsistent with an interpretation of decline, stagnation, or disappearance of the middle class in the United States.

THE WORKING CLASS

About thirty percent of the U.S. population belongs to the working class, largely as blue-collar and pink-collar laborers. Occupations typical of this class include restaurant, hotel, and casino workers as well as sales clerks, mechanics, and factory workers. **Blue-collar workers** are manual laborers whose work is primarily physical rather than mental and deals with things rather than with ideas; this category encompasses skilled, semi-skilled, and unskilled workers, including farm workers, miners, and construction workers (Theodorson and Theodorson, 1969: 32). **Pink-collar** laborers work in semi-skilled occupations that have a high concentration of females and low pay. Day-care workers, wait-persons, cashiers, and check-out clerks are examples of pink-collar laborers.

In terms of Marxian conflict theory, the working class is the heart of the proletariat. Low-skilled and semi-skilled factory workers and a variety of pink-collar workers are the core of the working class (Derks, 2010).

These workers have little room for deciding what to do, when, while they are on the job since they tend to be closely and continually supervised at work. These job characteristics correlate highly with workers developing an instrumental attitude toward their work: work is viewed or defined by workers as a way to earn a paycheck rather than as something that is intrinsically worthwhile (Macionis, 2013: 204; Argyle, 1994). Household income is about $29,000 to $49,000 a year (United States Census Bureau, 2012), which just covers basic living expenses and perhaps a summer vacation (Giddens, Duneier, Appelbaum, and Carr, 2012: 210). While older members of the working class may own a home, typically in a less expensive neighborhood, younger working-class people are more likely to rent a home or an apartment. The household vehicle rarely is new and tends to be a lower-priced model. Working-class families accumulate little or no wealth during their working lives and are particularly vulnerable to financial difficulties posed by economic downturns or illness.

The creative destruction characteristic of capitalism and economic globalization (Schumpeter, 2008) particularly threatens the jobs of the working class. For instance, in the first two years of the Great Recession, about 1 in 12 (or 8 percent of) white-collar jobs in sales, administrative support, and non-managerial office work vanished, while one of every six (or 17 percent of) blue-collar jobs in production, craft, repair and machine operation did the same (Wehner and Beschel, Jr., 2012). In other words, twice the percentage of working-class as middle-class jobs disappeared. Working-class children who graduate from high school are more likely to seek employment right away rather than to go to college. Members of the working class tend to feel more insecure about the future. Nonetheless, although they may vote, most members of the working class are not politically or civically active, even in their own communities (Smith, 2013).

THE LOWER CLASS

About 15 percent of the U.S. population is a member of the lower class. In 2011, the federal government classified 46.2 million people, including 16 million children, as poor, which is 15.1 percent of the total U.S. population (Gabe, 2012: 2). Family structure matters. More than a third of single-parent families with children are poor, compared to 7 percent of families with married parents (Rector and Marshall, 2013). Children of married parents are 82 percent less likely to be poor than are the children of single mothers. This inverse relationship between marriage and poverty persists across lines of race and educational attainment (Rector and Marshall, 2013; Shattuck and Kreider, 2013: 4-5). Of females who gave birth in 2011 and who listed their race as Black or African American, 67.8 percent, the highest percentage, were unmarried (Shattuck and Kreider, 2013: 5); and among those who listed their race as Asian alone, 11.3 percent were unmarried, the lowest percentage (Shattuck and Kreider, 2013: 5). Forty-three percent of Hispanic births and 26 percent of births to non-Hispanic White females in 2011 were to unmarried females (Shattuck and Kreider, 2013:5). In short, unmarried mothers are less educated, have lower incomes, are predominantly Black and Hispanic and the rate of poverty for unmarried mothers is 5 times higher than for married couple families (Shattuck and Kreider, 2013; Crouse, 2013).

There is an inverse relationship between amount of education and probability of giving birth while unmarried (Shattuck and Kreider, 2013:4). Among females with less than a high school degree who gave birth in 2011, 57 percent were unmarried. In contrast, among females with a four-year college degree who gave birth in 2011, 8.8 percent were unmarried (Shattuck and Kreider, 2013: 4).

In the United States, the percentage of unmarried females who gave birth in 2011 decreased as their income level increased (Shattuck and Kreider, 2013: 5). Thus, among females who earned less than $10,000 a year who gave birth in 2011, 68.9 percent were unmarried. In contrast, among females with household incomes of $200,000 or greater, just 9 percent who gave birth were unmarried.

Let us now turn our attention to other aspects of life in the lower class. Somewhat less than half of lower-class families own their own homes (Macionis, 2013: 204). The average home owned by a person classified as poor by the U.S. Census Bureau is a 3-bedroom house with one-and-a half baths, a garage, and a porch or patio (Rector and Sheffield, 2011). The typical poor American lives in a house or apartment that is in good repair and not over crowded. In fact, the average home of a *poor* American is *larger* than the home of *the average citizen* of the United Kingdom, France, or Germany (Rector and Marshall, 2013). For instance, the average poor American has 515 square feet of living space per person, which is 40 percent *more* living space than the average citizen in every European nation except Luxembourg (714 square feet per person) and Denmark (553 square feet per person) (Rector and Sheffield, 2011: 12). While America's poor do experience real material hardship, ninety-six percent of poor parents in the United States state that their children were never hungry at any time during the past year (Rector and Marshall, 2013).

THE WORKING POOR Of people who were in the labor force for 27 or more weeks in 2010, about 10.5 million persons are classified as the working poor (U.S. Bureau of Labor Statistics, 2012: 1). Hispanics and Blacks continue to be much more likely than Whites and Asians to be among the working poor. In 2010, 14.1 percent of Hispanics and 12.6 percent of Blacks were among the working poor, compared with 6.5 percent of Whites and 4.8 percent of Asians (U.S. Bureau of Labor Statistics, 2012: 1). Educational attainment matters. The chances of being among the working poor greatly diminishes with education: For instance, among persons with less than a high-school diploma, 21.4 percent of those who were in the labor force for at least 27 weeks were classified as working poor, compared with 2.1 percent of those who were college graduates. In other words, those with less than a high-school diploma were more than ten times as likely to be among the working poor, compared with college graduates (U.S. Bureau of Labor Statistics, 2012: 1). Similarly, occupation matters. The likelihood of being among the working poor varies widely by occupation. People who work in occupations that require higher education and that are characterized by relatively high earnings—such as managers and professionals—are far less likely to be classified as working poor (2.4 percent) than those who work in occupations that require little education and that have relatively low earnings attached to them. For instance, in 2010, 13.1 percent of service workers were classified as working poor, as were 19.5 percent of workers employed in farming, fishing, and forestry occupations and 12.8 percent of those in construction and extraction occupations (U.S. Bureau of Labor Statistics, 2012: 3).

THE UNDERCLASS Within the lower class, some sociologists and other social scientists recently have identified a segment of society that they term the underclass, sometimes also called the new urban poor or the truly disadvantaged (e.g., Wilson, 2012, 1996; Clark, Marcin, Abu-Sneneh, Chow, Mo-Jung, Marek, and Williams, 2013). Of course, members of the underclass can also be found in rural areas and in other societies (e.g., Hu, 2011; Welshman, 2006). Estimates of the size of the underclass vary from 1.5 percent to about five percent of the U.S. population. These individuals are seldom employed and they are under educated. The underclass includes many single mothers and their children, and many of the homeless. Racial and ethnic minorities are over represented among the underclass. American sociologist William Julius Wilson argues that changes in the global economy have contributed to the formation and growth of a largely unemployed class of persons in the United States, largely concentrated in our inner cities (Wilson, 2012).

To summarize the preceding discussion, the percentage distribution of the population of the United States by social class looks like this--

Upper Class:	5 percent
(Upper Upper	1 percent)
(Lower Upper	4 percent)
Middle Class	50 percent
(Upper Middle	20 percent)
(Middle Middle, Lower Middle	30 percent)
Working Class	30 percent
Lower Class	15 percent
Total:	100 percent

Social Mobility in the United States

The upward, downward, or lateral (horizontal) movement of individuals, groups, or collectivities in a system of stratification is termed **social mobility**. **Vertical mobility** refers to movement up or down a hierarchy of positions in a system of social stratification. Vertical mobility is also known as vertical social mobility, upward or downward mobility, upward or downward economic mobility, or upward or downward social mobility. Sociologists use these terms interchangeably and synonymously. **Horizontal mobility** refers to a change in one's social position without a corresponding change in one's general position in a prestige hierarchy or social-class level (Theodorson and Theodorson, 1969: 259-260). For instance, this might occur in the case of a change from one type of pink-collar occupation to another, both of which are at the same general prestige level.

The amount of vertical social mobility is often used as an indicator of the degree of openness or fluidity of a society and of its system of stratification. The study of social mobility looks at mobility rates and mobility patterns, both short-range (between adjacent hierarchical levels) and long-range (between more widely separated levels).

INTERGENERATIONAL MOBILITY

Intergenerational mobility compares the present position of individuals with those of their parents. Stated somewhat differently, intergenerational mobility looks at mobility across generational lines. For instance, if Bob is a shoe salesperson and his dad had been a ditch digger, that would be termed upward intergenerational social mobility for Bob. If Bob's dad had been the president of the college or university you are attending, it would be termed downward intergenerational social mobility for Bob the shoe salesperson.

There are numerous studies of intergenerational mobility. One way to assess how much intergenerational mobility there is in the United States is to ask people whether they are better off than their parents were at the same age—i.e., whether they experience *absolute* upward social mobility. What does the intergenerational absolute mobility picture look like in the United States? In comparison with other core countries and emerging econonomies (such as Peoples Republic of China and Brazil), the United States is situated mid-range in terms of the amount and extent of intergenerational mobility (Clark, 2013; Corak, 2013; Hertz, Jayasundera, Piraino, Selcuk, Smith, and Verashchagina, 2007).

The Pew Economic Mobility Project (EMP) shows that 80 percent of adults in the United States today are better off than their parents were at the same age (DeLeire and Lopoo, 2010). Other research shows similar results. For instance, research by Julia Isaacs and her colleagues at the Brookings Institution shows that two-thirds of 40-year-old Americans are in households with larger incomes than their parents had at the same age (Isaacs, Sawhill, and Haskins, 2008). A recent study by the Pew Charitable Trusts finds that 84 percent of adult Americans today, across all levels of the income distribution, have higher real incomes than their parents did at the same age, adjusted for inflation. Moreover, fully 93 percent of Americans whose parents were in the bottom quintile exceed their parents' income as adults today (Butler, 2013; The Economist, October 13, 2012c).

Culture matters. Evidence suggests, for example, that the habit of saving, even in small amounts, is a key to intergenerational mobility in the United States (Cramer, O'Brien, Cooper, and Luengo-Prado, 2009). Thus, children of low-saving (i.e., below the median), low-income parents are significantly less likely to be upwardly mobile than children of high-saving, low-income parents. According to the Pew Economic Mobility Project, 71 percent of children born to high-saving, low-income parents move up from the bottom income quartile over a generation, compared to only 50 percent of children from similarly low-income households whose parents do not save (Butler, 2013; Cramer, O'Brien, Cooper, and Luengo-Prado, 2009: 2).

Stuart M. Butler (2013) identifies several reasons why savings are helpful to mobility. First, savings can prevent a setback, such as encountering unanticipated bills, from becoming a catastrophe. Second, a great deal of research shows that, from early childhood onward, successfully handling setbacks, rather than being paralyzed or deflected from pursuing one's goal by them, is associated with building the perseverance at task that is needed for long-term success and mobility (Myers, 2010; Werner and Smith, 1989). Third, savings enable people to take advantage of opportunities for economic mobility, such as buying a car in order to take a job or a better job. Fourth, savings can also make it easier to invest in acquiring human capital, such as education or starting a business, steps also likely to increase social mobility (Elliott and Beverly, 2011).

Among households with similarly low incomes, wide and important differences exist in the rate and extent of saving money. Culture matters. For instance, modest-income Asian Americans and whites are much more likely to enroll in 401(k) plans than are African Americans or Hispanics with similar incomes (Butler, 2013). Savings rates are consistently higher in many other countries than in the United States.

In a review of multiple studies, University of Kansas professor William Elliott finds that among children from low-income households, forming the habit of saving money early in life, even in small amounts, is connected with later success in completing college (Butler, 2013; Elliott, 2012). Professor Elliott's research on savings, culture, and economic mobility helps to illuminate how savings influences the way low-income children think about college, their extent of academic engagement, and the probability that they will attend and graduate from college. Low-income and minority students are reluctant to borrow to pay for college due to concerns about their ability to pay back loans (Burdman, 2005). Personal savings that can be used to help pay for college reduce the need for student loans and therefore are likely to have effects on student college expectations similar to those of grants and scholarships (Elliott, 2012). If children grow up knowing they have financial resources to help pay for schooling, they are more likely to have more positive college expectations, which in turn foster educational engagement. Greater educational engagement fosters better academic preparation and achievement (Tough, 2012; Jeynes, 2011). These attitudinal and behavioral effects of savings are important: poor children with savings in their name are more likely to attend college and to persist through graduation (Elliott, 2012).

Research by Scott Winship of the Brookings Institution also documents that there is a lot of intergenerational mobility in America. Scott Winship recently examined data from a national longitudinal survey of children born between 1962 and 1964 and children born between 1980 and 1982. Winship compared these cohorts' income when they reached the age of twenty-six to twenty-eight with their parents' incomes at similar ages. Winship finds that upward mobility from poverty to the middle class rose from 51 to 57 percent over these two periods (Moore, 2012: 47). Although Winship is reluctant to conclude that the extent of absolute upward economic mobility has increased, he is emphatic that the data provide absolutely no evidence to support an interpretation that economic mobility has declined.

With regard to race and absolute mobility, among African Americans whose parents had been at the bottom of the income distribution, 82 percent now have greater family income than their parents had at the same age (Winship, 2011). Family structure matters. Among African American children who start in the bottom third of the income distribution, 53 percent of those with divorced parents exceed their parents' income in adulthood, compared to 87 percent with continuously married parents (De Leire and Lopoo, 2010: 16). Among African American children who start in the middle third of the income distribution, 58 percent exceed their parents' income in adulthood. In short, among African Americans, there is a lot of absolute upward intergenerational mobility, both from the bottom and from the middle of the income distribution.

INTRAGENERATIONAL MOBILITY

Intragenerational mobility compares the position attained by a person at two different points in that person's life course. Stated somewhat differently, intragenerational mobility looks at mobility within generational lines. For example, if Germaine's first job was as a janitor at the local hospital and now she is a high-school teacher, that's upward intragenerational mobility for Germaine. What does the intragenerational mobility picture look like in the United States?

There are many studies of intragenerational mobility. Andrew Rettenmaier and Donald Deere use data from the National Longitudinal Study of Youth to examine how individual workers move around in the quintile distribution of *individual earnings* for periods of up to fifteen years (Rettenmaier and Deere, 2003; Rettenmaier, 2003). Of the workers in the lowest quintile in one year, 32 percent had moved to a higher quintile just one year later, with 1 percent jumping all the way to the top quintile. Of workers in the top quintile in one year, fully 25 percent had fallen to a lower quintile one year later, with 2 percent falling all the way to the lowest quintile. So, even over a short period of time, there is a lot of intragenerational movement from the bottom *and* from the top of the income distribution.

Rettenmaier and Deere (2003) generate estimates of the amount of intragenerational mobility not just from one year to the next, but also for 5-, 10-, and 15-year intervals as well. They find that the longer the interval studied, the greater the amount of intragenerational mobility. The findings for the 15-year interval are particularly dramatic. Of those in the bottom quintile in one year, fully two-thirds are in a higher income quintile 15 years later. Fully 24 percent move from the bottom income quintile to one of the top two quintiles, with 10 percent moving all the way to the top income quintile. At the other extreme, of those at the top income quintile in one year, 61 percent were in a lower income quintile fifteen years later, with 18 percent falling from the top to one of the two bottom income quintiles.

The U.S. Treasury released a study in November 2007 that examines income mobility in the United States from 1996 to 2005 using data from individual income tax returns (Garrett, 2010). This study finds that 58 percent of the households that were in the lowest income quintile in 1996 had moved to a higher income quintile by 2005. Similarly, nearly 50 percent of the households in the second-lowest quintile in 1996 had moved to a higher income quintile by 2005. Likewise, a study by economists at the Federal Reserve Bank of Minneapolis finds that nearly half of the families in the lowest fifth of income earners in 2001 had moved up within six years (Diaz-Giménez, Glover, and Ríos-Rull, 2011). This is hardly surprising: a business school student, for example, may have little money and high debts, but nine years later she or he could be earning a big salary and bonuses. In the United States, education is an important way for many people to attain the American Dream, and hence an effective tool for creating intragenerational mobility.

Numerous studies document that "the rich" in the United States are not a monolithic, unchanging class. There is a lot of movement out of the top. For instance, a study by Thomas A. Garrett, an economist at the Federal Reserve Bank of St. Louis, found that less than half of the richest one percent of households in 1996 were still there in 2005 (Wilson, 2010). Likewise, a study by economists at the Federal Reserve Bank of Minneapolis finds that more than a third of those in the highest income quintile in 2001 had moved down within six years (Diaz-Giménez, Glover, and Ríos-Rull, 2011).

The Internal Revenue Service also documents that there is a lot of turnover at the top of the income distribution (Browning, 2008: 26-27) in the United States. The 400 people who occupy the exalted position of being the richest people in the country are not the same people from one year to another. For instance, over a nine-year period, 2,218 taxpayers were in the top 400 for at least one year. Of these 2, 218 taxpayers, three-fourths were among the top 400 for just one year. Fewer than 23 persons were in the top 400 for all nine years. Thus, there is a lot of movement both into, and out of, the top of the income distribution. There are people such as Bill Gates or Warren Buffet who are ensconced in the top tier, but far more common are people who are rich only for short periods of time.

SUGGESTED READINGS

Beenstock, Michael, *Heredity, Family, and Inequality: A Critique of Social Sciences* (Cambridge, Massachusetts: The MIT Press, 2012).

Beito, David, *From Mutual Aid to the Welfare State: Fraternal Societies and Social Services, 1890-1967* (Chapel Hill, NC: North Carolina Press, 2000).

Carson, Ben, *America the Beautiful: Rediscovering What Made this Nation Great* (Grand Rapids, Michigan: Zondervan, 2012).

Carson, Ben, *Gifted Hands: The Ben Carson Story* 20th Anniversary Edition (Grand Rapids, Michigan: Zondervan, 2011).

Daniel, Kermit, "The Marriage Premium," in Mariano Tommasi and Kathryn Ierulli (Eds.), *The New Economics of Human Behavior* (New York: Cambridge University Press, 1995), pp. 113-125.

Dhingra, Pawan, *Life Behind the Lobby: Indian American Motel Owners and the American Dream* (Stanford, CA: Stanford University Press, 2012).

Eberstadt, Nicholas, *The Poverty of the Poverty Rate: Measure and Mismeasure of Want in Modern America* (Washington, D.C.: The AEI Press, 2008).

Farrell, Warren, *Why Men Earn More: The Startling Truth Behind the Pay Gap—And What Women Can Do About It* (New York: American Management Association, 2005).

Furchtgott-Roth, Diana, *Women's Figures: An Illustrated Guide to the Economic Progress of Women in America* 2012 Edition (Washington, D.C.: AEI Press, 2012).

Hayward, David R., and Kemmelmeier, Markus, "Weber Revisited: A Cross-National Analysis of Religiosity, Religious Culture, and Economic Attitudes," *Journal of Cross-Cultural Psychology*, Vol. 42, No. 8, 2011: 1406-1420.

McWhorter, John, *Losing the Race: Self-Sabotage in Black America* (New York: Harper Perennial, 2001).

McWhorter, John, *Winning the Race: Beyond the Crisis in Black America* (New York: Gotham Books, 2005).

Milanovic, Branko, *The Haves and the Have-Nots: A Brief and Idiosyncratic History of Global Inequality* (New York: Basic Books, 2011).

Nieli, Russell K., *Wounds That Will Not Heal: Affirmative Action and Our Continuing Racial Divide* (New York: Encounter Books, 2012).

Page, Benjamin I., and Jacobs, Lawrence R., *Class War: What Americans Really Think About Economic Inequality* (Chicago, IL: University of Chicago Press, 2009).

Sowell, Thomas, *Affirmative Action Around the World: An Empirical Study* (New Haven, CT: Yale University Press, 2004).

BIBLIOGRAPHY

Aaronsen, Daniel, and Mazumder, Bhashkar, "The Impact of Rosenwald Schools on Black Achievement," *Journal of Political Economy*, Vol. 119, No. 5, (October) 2011: 821-888.

Abercrombie, Nicholas; Hill, Stephen; and Turner, Bryan S., *The Penguin Dictionary of Sociology* (New York: Penguin Books, 1994).

Amory, Cleveland, *The Proper Bostonians* (New York: E.P. Dutton, 1947).

Argyle, Michael, *The Psychology of Social Class* (New York: Routledge, 1994).

Argyle, Michael, *The Social Psychology of Everyday Life* (New York: Routledge, 2008).

Bartlett, Bruce, "Who Doesn't Pay Federal Income Taxes (Legally)," New York Times, April 6, 2013. As of April 6, 2013, available online at http://economix.blogs.nytimes.com/2011/06/28/who-doesnt-pay-federal-income-taxes-legally/

Ben-David, Joseph, "The Growth of the Professions and the Class System," *Current Sociology*, Vol. 12, 1963-1964: 256-277.

Board of Governors of the Federal Reserve System, "Flow of Funds Accounts of the United States: Flows and Outstandings, Fourth Quarter 2012," *Federal Reserve statistical release*. Z.1. (Washington, D.C.: Board of Governors of the Federal Reserve System, March 7, 2013). As of May 5, 2013, available online at http://www.federalreserve.gov/releases/z1/current/z1.pdf

Bricker, Jesse; Kennickell, Arthur B.; Moore, Kevin B.; and Sabelhaus, John, "Changes in U.S. Family Finances from 2007 to 2010: Evidence from the Survey of Consumer Finances," *Federal Reserve Bulletin*, June 2012, Vol. 98, No. 2. As of February 23, 2013, available online at http://www.federalreserve.gov/pubs/bulletin/2012/pdf/scf12.pdf

Browning, Edgar K., *Stealing from Each Other: How the Welfare State Robs Americans of Money and Spirit* (Westport, CT: Praeger, 2008).

Burdman, Pamela, "The Student Debt Dilemma: Debt Aversion as a Barrier to College Access," Center for Studies in Higher Education. University of California, Berkeley. October 2005. As of April 29, 2013, available online at http://cshe.berkeley.edu/publications/docs/ROP.Burdman.13.05.pdf

Burkhauser, Richard V.; Larrimore, Jeff; and Simon, Kosali I., "A 'Second Opinion' on the Economic Position of the American Middle Class," *National Tax Journal*, Vol. 65, No. 1, (March) 2012: 7-32.

Butler, Stuart M., "Can the American Dream Be Saved?" *National Affairs*, No. 14, Winter 2013. As of April 29, 2013, available online at http://www.nationalaffairs.com/publications/detail/can-the-american-dream-be-saved

Chase-Dunn, Christopher; Kawano, Yukio; and Brewer, Benjamin, "Trade Globalization Since 1795," *American Sociological Review*, Vol. 65, (February) 2000: 77-95.

Chirot, Daniel, *Social Change in the Modern Era* (San Diego, CA: Harcourt Brace Jovanovich, 1986).

CIA World Factbook, 2012a. Computed from labor force by occupation data for the United States. As of February 17, 2013, available online at https://www.cia.gov/library/publications/the-world-factbook/geos/us.html

CIA World Factbook, 2013a. Kenya. As of March 8, 2013, available online at https://www.cia.gov/library/publications/the-world-factbook/geos/ke.html

CIA World Factbook, 2013b. South Sudan. As of March 8, 2013, available online at https://www.cia.gov/library/publications/the-world-factbook/geos/od.html

CIA World Factbook, 2013c. Rwanda. As of March 8, 2013, available online at https://www.cia.gov/library/publications/the-world-factbook/geos/rw.html

CIA World Factbook, 2013d. Democratic Republic of the Congo. As of March 11, 2013, available online at https://www.cia.gov/library/publications/the-world-factbook/geos/cg.html

CIA World Factbook, 2013e. Somalia. As of March 9, 2013, available online at https://www.cia.gov/library/publications/the-world-factbook/geos/so.html

CIA World Factbook, 2013f. India. As of March 10, 2013, available online at https://www.cia.gov/library/publications/the-world-factbook/geos/in.html

Clark, Gregory, "What is the True Rate of Social Mobility? Evidence from the Information Content of Surnames," conference paper presented at the Annual Meeting of the American Economic Association, January 4, 2013, San Diego, CA

Clark, Gregory, *A Farewell to Alms: A Brief Economic History of the World* (Princeton, New Jersey: Princeton University Press, 2011).

Clark, Gregory; Marcin, Daniel; Abu-Sneneh, Firas; Chow, Wilfred M.; Mo-Jung, Kuk; Marek, Ariel M.; and Williams, Kevin, "Social Mobility Rates in the U.S.A., 1920-2010: A Surname Analysis," 2013. As of May 6, 2013, available online at http://www.econ.ucdavis.edu/faculty/gclark/papers/Social%20Mobility%20Rates%20in%20the%20USA.pdf

Collier, Paul, *The Bottom Billion: Why the Poorest Countries Are Failing and What Can Be Done About It* (New York: Oxford University Press, 2007).

Collier, Paul, *Wars, Guns, and Votes* (New York: Harper Perennial, 2010).

Congressional Budget Office, *Trends in the Distribution of Household Income, 1979-2009* Presentation to the NBER Conference on Research and Wealth (Washington, D.C.: Ed Harris and Frank Samartino, August 6, 2012). As of May 5, 2013, available online at http://www.cbo.gov/sites/default/files/cbofiles/attachments/Trends_in_household_income_forposting.pdf

Congressional Budget Office, *Trends in the Distribution of Household Income Between 1979 and 2007* Publication No. 4031. A CBO Study. October 2011. As of May 5, 2013, available online at http://www.cbo.gov/sites/default/files/cbofiles/attachments/10-25-HouseholdIncome.pdf

Corak, Miles, "Inequality from Generation to Generation: The United States in Comparison," in Robert S. Rycroft (Ed.), *The Economics of Inequality, Poverty, and Discrimination in the 21st Century* (Santa Barbara, CA: Praeger, 2013).

Cramer, Reid; O'Brien, Rourke; Cooper, Daniel; and Luengo-Prado, Maria, *A Penny Saved is Mobility Earned: Advancing Economic Mobility Through Savings* (Washington, D.C.: The Pew Charitable Trusts. Economic Mobility Project, November, 2009).

Crouse, Janice Shaw, "Census Report Shocker," *American Thinker*, May 3, 2013. As of May 6, 2013, available online at http://www.americanthinker.com/2013/05/census_report_shocker.html

Dahrendorf, Ralf, *Class and Class Conflict in Industrial Society* (Stanford, CA: Stanford University Press, 1959).

Dalrymple, Theodore, *Life at the Bottom: The Worldview That Makes the Underclass* (Chicago, IL: Ivan R. Dee, 2001).

Davies, James C., "Toward a Theory of Revolution," *American Sociological Review*, Vol. 27, No. 1, (February) 1962: 5-19.

Davis, Kingsley, and Moore, Wilbert, "Some Principles of Stratification," *American Sociological Review*, Vol. 7, 1945: 242-249.

DeLeire, Thomas and Lopoo, Leonard M., *Family Structure and the Economic Mobility of Children* (Washington, D.C.: The Pew Charitable Trusts, Economic Mobility Project, May 3, 2010). As of April 28, 2013, available online at http://www.pewstates.org/uploadedFiles/PCS_Assets/2010/Family_Structure.pdf

DeNavas-Walt, Carmen, Bernadette D. Proctor, and Jessica C. Smith, "Income, Poverty, and Health Insurance Coverage in the United States: 2011," *Current Population Reports*, P60-243 (Washington, D.C.: U.S. Government Printing Office, 2012). As of April 3, 2013, available online at http://www.census.gov/prod/2012pubs/p60-243.pdf

Derks, Scott, *Working Americans, 1880-2009: The Working Class* (Lakeville, CT: Grey House Publishing, 2010).

Diaz-Giménez; Glover, Andy; and Ríos-Rull, José-Victor, "Facts on the Distribution of Earnings, Income, and Wealth in the United States: 2007 Update," Federal Reserve Bank of Minneapolis *Quarterly Review*, Vol. 34, No. 1, (February) 2011. As of May 3, 2013, available online at http://www.minneapolisfed.org/research/QR/QR3411.pdf

Dikötter, Frank, *Mao's Great Famine: The History of China's Most Devastating Catastrophe, 1958-1962* (New York: Walker & Co., 2010).

Domhoff, G. William, *Who Rules America?: The Triumph of the Corporate Rich* (New York: Oxford University Press, 2007).

Dowrick, Steve, and DeLong, J. Bradford, "Globalization and Convergence," in Michael D. Bordo, Alan M. Taylor, and Jeffrey G. Williamson (Eds.), *Globalization in Historical Perspective* (Chicago, IL: University of Chicago Press, 2003), pp. 191-220.

Dungan, Adrian, and Parisi, Michael, "Individual Income Tax Rates and Shares, 2010," *Statistics of Income (SOI) Bulletin* A Quarterly Statistics of Income Report, Vol. 32, Number 3, Winter 2013: 18-63. (Washington, D.C.: Internal Revenue Service, Winter 2013). As of April 25, 2013, available online at http://www.irs.gov/pub/irs-soi/13winbul.pdf

Edwards, Chris and Landau, David, *The U.S. Economy at the Beginning and End of the 20th Century* (Washington, D.C.: United States Congress, December 1999). Prepared by the Joint Economic Committee, Office of the Chairman, U.S. Senator Connie Mack. As of February 23, 2013, available online at http://infousa.state.gov/economy/overview/docs/century.pdf

Eichler, Alexander, "46 Percent of Americans Exempt From Federal Income Tax in 2011," The Huffington Post, June 28, 2011, 9:04 PM ET, Updated: August 28, 2011, 06:12 AM ET. As of April 6, 2013, available online at http://www.huffingtonpost.com/2011/06/28/46-percent-of-americans-e_n_886293.html.

Elias, Norbert *The Civilizing Process* Volume II (New York: Pantheon Books, 1982).

Elliott, W., and Beverly, S., "Staying on Course: The Effects of Savings and Assets on the College Progress of Young Adults," *American Journal of Education*, Vol. 117, No. 3, 2011: 343-374.

Elliott, W., *We Save, We Go To College* (Washington, D.C.: New America Foundation; St. Louis, MO: Washington University, Center for Social Development. January, 2012). As of April 29, 2013, available online at http://assets.newamerica.net/sites/newamerica.net/files/policydocs/Elliott_III_final1.4.12.pdf

Federal Reserve Bank of Dallas, *By Our Own Bootstraps: Economic Opportunity & the Dynamics of Income Distribution* Annual Report, 1995. W. Michael Cox and Richard Alm. As of May 5, 2013, available online at http://www.dallasfed.org/assets/documents/fed/annual/1999/ar95.pdf

Ferguson, Niall, *Civilization: The West and the Rest* (New York: The Penguin Press, 2011).

Ferguson, Niall, *Empire: The Rise and Demise of the British World Order and the Lessons for Global Power* (New York: Basic Books, 2002).

Foreign Policy, *Failed State Index, 2012*. 2012. As of March 9, 2013, available online at http://www.foreignpolicy.com/failed_states_index_2012_interactive

Frank, Andre Gunder and Gills, Barry K. (Eds.), *The World System: Five Hundred Years or Five Thousand* (New York: Routledge, 1993).

Frank, Andre Gunder, *Capitalism and Underdevelopment in Latin America: Historical Studies of Chile and Brazil* (New York: Monthly Review Press, 1967).

Gabe, Thomas, "Poverty in the United States: 2011," Congressional Research Service Report for Congress, 7-5700, RL33069. September 27, 2012. As of April 28, 2013, available online at http://www.fas.org/sgp/crs/misc/RL33069.pdf

Garrett, Thomas A., "U.S. Income Inequality: It's Not So Bad," *Inside the Vault*, Spring 2010. As of May 3, 2013, available online at http://www.stlouisfed.org/education_resources/assets/lesson_plans/10ITV_IncomeInequality.pdf

Giddens, Anthony; Duneier, Mitchell; Applebaum, Richard P.; and Carr, Deborah, *Introduction to Sociology* Eighth Edition (New York: W.W. Norton & Company, 2012).

Goldin, Claudia and Katz, Lawrence F., *The Race Between Education and Technology: The Evolution of U.S. Educational Wage Differentials, 1890-2005* (Cambridge, MA: National bureau of Economic Research 2007).

Goldstein, Joshua S., and Pevehouse, Jon C., *International Relations* Brief Fifth Edition (New York: Longman, 2010).

Grabb, Edward, *Theories of Social Inequality* (Toronto, Ontario, Canada: Thomson/Nelson, 2007).

Grusky, David B. (Ed.), *Social Stratification: Class, Race, and Gender in Sociological Perspective* Third Edition (Boulder, CO: Westview Press, 2008).

Gurr, Ted Robert, *Why Men Rebel* Fortieth Anniversary Edition (Boulder, CO: Paradigm Publishers, 2010). Originally published in 1970 by Princeton University Press.

Hagopian, Kip, and Ohanian, Lee, "The Mismeasure of Inequality," *Policy Review*, August 1, 2012, No. 174. As of May 3, 2013, available online at http://www.hoover.org/publications/policy-review/article/123566

Helman, Gerald B., and Ratner, Steven R., "Saving Failed States," *Foreign* Policy, No. 89, (Winter) 1992-1993: 3-20.

Hertz, Tom; Jayasundera, Tamara; Piraino, Patrizio; Selcuk, Sibel; Smith, Nicole; and Verashchagina, Alina, "The Inheritance of Educational Inequality: International Comparisons and Fifty-Year Trends," *The B.E. Journal of Economic Analysis & Policy*: Vol. 7, No. 2, 2007, Article 10.

Hoge, Dean R.; Dinges, William D.; Johnson, Mary; and Gonzales, Juan L., *Young Adult Catholics: Religion in the Culture of Choice* (Notre Dame, Indiana: University of Notre Dame Press, 2001).

Hu, Xinying, *China's New Underclass: Paid Domestic Labor* (New York: Routledge, 2011).

Isaacs, Julia; Sawhill, Isabel V.; and Haskins, Ron, *Getting Ahead or Losing Ground: Economic Mobility in America* (Washington, D.C: The Brookings Institution. The Pew Charitable Trusts. Economic Mobility Project, 2008).

Jeynes, William H., *Parental Involvement and Academic Success* (New York: Routledge, 2011).

Kroll, Luisa, and Dolan, Kerry A., "The World's Billionaires: The Richest People on the Planet, 2013," *Forbes*, March 4, 2013. As of April 25, 2013, available online at http://www.forbes.com/billionaires/

Lenin, Vladimir I., "The Proletarian Revolution and the Renegade Kautsky," in Jim Riordan (Translator and Editor), *Lenin's Collected Works*, Vol. 28 (Moscow, Russia: Progress Publishers, 1974), pp. 227-325. (Originally published, 1918.) As of February 23, 2013, available online at http://www.marxists.org/archive/lenin/works/1918/prrk/index

Lenin, Vladimir I., *Imperialism, the Highest Stage of Capitalism* (London England: Penguin Books, 2010). Originally published in 1916. As of February 23, 2013, available online at http://www.marxists.org/archive/lenin/works/1916/imp-hsc/

Levine, Linda, "An Analysis of the Distribution of Wealth Across Households, 1989-2010," Congressional Research Service Report for Congress, 7-5700, RL33433. July 17, 2012. As of April 1, 2013, available online at http://www.fas.org/sgp/crs/misc/RL33433.pdf

Macionis, John J., *Society: The Basics* (New York: Pearson, 2013).

Mahbubani, Kishore, *The Great Convergence: Asia, The West, and the Logic of One World* (New York: Public Affairs, 2013).

Mallaby, Sebastian, "The Reluctant Imperialist: Terrorism, Failed States, and the Case for American Empire," *Foreign Affairs*, Vol. 81, No. 2, (March/April) 2002: 2-27.

Milanovic, Branko, *The Haves and the Have-Nots: A Brief and Idiosyncratic History of Global Inequality* (New York: Basic Books, 2011).

Moore, Stephen, *Who's The Fairest of Them All? The Truth About Opportunity, Taxes, and Wealth in America* (New York: Encounter Books, 2012).

Murray, Charles A., *Coming Apart: The State of White America, 2960-2010* (New York: Crown Forum, 2013).

Myers, David G., *Social Psychology* Tenth Edition (NY: McGraw Hill, 2010).

Norberg, Johan, *Financial Fiasco: How America's Infatuation with Homeownership and Easy Money Created the Economic Crisis* (Washington, D.C.: Cato Institute, 2009).

Norberg, Johan, *In Defense of Global Capitalism* (Washington, D.C.: Cato Institute, 2003).

OECD, *Divided We Stand: Why Inequality Keeps Rising* (Paris, France: OECD Publishing, January 26, 2012). As of March 21, 2013, available online at http://dx.doi.org/10.1787/9789264119536-en

OECD, *Growing Unequal? Income Distribution and Poverty in OECD Countries* (Paris, France: OECD Publishing, October 2008). As of March 31, 2013, available online at http://www.oecd-ilibrary.org/social-issues-migration-health/growing-unequal_9789264044197-en

Piazza, James A., "Incubators of Terror: Do Failed and Failing States Promote Transnational Terrorism?" *International Studies Quarterly*, Vol. 52, No. 3, (September) 2008: 469-488.

Prince, Rosa, "Forbes List: J.K. Rowling Fortune Under Vanishing Spell," *The Telegraph*, March 7, 2012, 10:01 PM GMT. As of April 25, 2013, available online at http://www.telegraph.co.uk/culture/books/booknews/9129981/Forbes-list-JK-Rowling-fortune-under-vanishing-spell.html

Ravallion, Martin, "Fighting Poverty: Findings and Lessons from China's Success," Research at the World Bank, 2005. As of March 10, 2013, available online at http://econ.worldbank.org/WBSITE/EXTERNAL/EXTDEC/EXTRESEARCH/0,,contentMDK:20634060~pagePK:64165401~piPK:64165026~theSitePK:469382,00.html

Ravallion, Martin, and Chen, Shaohua, "Learning from Success: Understanding China's (Uneven) Progress Against Poverty," *Finance and Development,* (December) 2004: 16-19. As of March 10, 2013, available online at http://www.imf.org/external/pubs/ft/fandd/2004/12/pdf/ravallio.pdf

Rector, Robert and Marshall, Jennifer, "The Unfinished Work of Welfare Reform," *National Affairs,* Issue No. 14, Winter 2013. As of April 28, 2013, available online at http://www.nationalaffairs.com/publications/detail/the-unfinished-work-of-welfare-reform

Rector, Robert, and Sheffield, Rachel, *Understanding Poverty in the United States: Surprising Facts About America's Poor* (Washington, D.C.: The Heritage Foundation. Backgrounder No. 2607. September 13, 2011). As of May 3, 2013, available online at http://www.heritage.org/research/reports/2011/09/understanding-poverty-in-the-united-states-surprising-facts-about-americas-poor

Rettenmaier, Andrew J., "Economic Mobility," National Center for Policy Analysis, *Brief Analyses*, No. 449, Wednesday, July 23, 2003. As of May 3, 2013, available online at http://www.ncpa.org/pub/ba449

Rettenmaier, Andrew J., and Deere, Donald R., *Climbing the Economic Ladder* (Washington, D.C.: National Center for Policy Analysis, 2003).

Ritzer, George, *Sociological Theory* (New York: McGraw Hill, 2008).

Rotberg, Robert I., "Failed States in a World of Terror," *Foreign Affairs*, Vol. 81, No. 4, (July/August) 2002: 127-140.

Schumpeter, Joseph A., *Capitalism, Socialism, and Democracy* (New York: Harper Perennial Modern Thought, 2008).

Shattuck, Rachel M., and Kreider, Rose M., "Social and Economic Characteristics of Currently Unmarried Women With a Recent Birth: 2011," *American Community Survey Reports*, ACS-21, May 2013. United States Census Bureau. As of May 6, 2013, available online at http://www.census.gov/prod/2013pubs/acs-21.pdf

Smith, Aaron, *Civic Engagement in the Digital Age* (Washington, D.C.: Pew Research Center's Internet and American Life Project, April 25, 2013). As of April 25, 2013, available online at http://pewinternet.org/~/media//Files/Reports/2013/PIP_CivicEngagementintheDigitalAge.pdf

Sowell, Thomas, *The Housing Boom and Bust* Revised Edition (New York: Basic Books, 2010).

Starr, S. Frederick, *Southern Comfort: The Garden District of New Orleans* (New York: Princeton Architectural Press, 2005).

Staufer, Samuel A. (Ed.), *The American Soldier* (Princeton, NJ: Princeton University Press, 1950).

Stewart, Patrick, "Failed States and Global Security: Empirical Questions and Policy Dilemmas," *Internal Studies Review*, Vol. 9, No. 4, 2007: 644-662.

Stiles, T.J., *The First Tycoon: The Epic Life of Cornelius Vanderbilt* (New York: Alfred A. Knoff, 2009).

Taylor, Paul, *Twenty to One: Wealth Gaps Rise to Record Highs Between Whites, Blacks, and Hispanics* (Washington, D.C.: Pew Research Center, Pew Social and Demographic Trends, July 26, 2011).

The Economist, "As You Were: After a Period on the Wane, Inequality Waxing Again," *The Economist*, October 13, 2012c. As of March 31, 2013, available online at http://www.economist.com/node/21564413

The Economist, "For Richer, For Poorer," *The Economist*, October 13, 2012a. As of February 19, 2013, available online at http://www.economist.com/node/21564414

The Economist, "Inequality and the World Economy-True Progressivism," *The Economist*, October 13, 2012b. As of February 19, 2013, available online at http://www.economist.com/node/21564556

The Economist, "Like Father, Not Like Son: Measuring Social Mobility," *The Economist*, October 13, 2012c. As of April 28, 2013, available online at http://www.economist.com/node/21564417

The World Bank, "South Africa Overview," The World Bank, September 2012. As of February 19, 2013, available online at http://www.worldbank.org/en/country/southafrica/overview

Theodorson, George A., and Theodorson, Achilles G., *A Modern Dictionary of Sociology* (New York: Barnes & Noble Books, 1969).

Tough, Paul, *How Children Succeed: Grit, Curiosity, and the Hidden Power of Character* (Boston: Houghton Mifflin, 2012).

Trow, Martin, "The Second Transformation of American Secondary Education," *The International Journal of Comparative Sociology*, Vol. 2, 1961: 144-166.

U.S. Bureau of Labor Statistics, U.S. Department of Labor, *A Profile of the Working Poor, 2010*. Report 1035. March 2012. Re-issued on January 23, 2013 to reflect corrections to table 4. As of April 28, 2012, available online at www.bls.gov/cps/cpswp2010.pdf

United States Census Bureau, *Historical Income Tables: People*. Data extracted from Table P-24, "Educational Attainment—Full-Time, Year-Round Workers 25 Years Old and Over by Median Earnings and Sex: 1991-2011." As of April 4, 2013, available online at http://www.census.gov/hhes/www/income/data/historical/people

United States Census Bureau, Mean Household Income by Each Fifth and Top 5 Percent of Households (All Races): 1967 to 2011. Historical Income Tables: Income Inequality. Table H-3. *Current Population Survey, Annual Social and Economic Supplements*, 2012. Retrieved April 27, 2013, online at http://www.census.gov/hhes/www/income/data/historical/inequality/index.html

Veblen, Thorstein, *Theory of the Leisure Class* (New York: Oxford University Press, 2007).

Wallerstein, Immanuel, *Historical Capitalism* (London: Verso, 1983).

Wallerstein, Immanuel, *The Modern World-System III: The Second Era of Great Expansion of the Capitalist World-Economy, 1730s-1840s* (San Diego: Academic Press, 1989).

Wallerstein, Immanuel, *World-Systems Analysis: An Introduction* (Durham, NC: Duke University Press, 2004).

Wallerstein, Immanuel; Aguirre Rojas, Charles Antonio; and Lemert, Charles C., *Uncertain Worlds: World-Systems Analysis in Changing Times* (Boulder, CO: Paradigm Publishers, 2012).

Walsh, Anthony, *Criminology: The Essentials* (Thousand Oaks, CA: SAGE Publications, 2012).

Wehner, Peter, and Beschel, Jr., Robert P., "How to Think About Inequality," *National Affairs*, Issue No. 11, Spring, 2012. As of April 27, 2013, available online at http://www.nationalaffairs.com/publications/detail/how-to-think-about-inequality

Welshman, John, *Underclass: A History of the Excluded, 1880-2000* (New York: Hambledon Continuum, 2006).

Werner, Emmy E., and Smith, Ruth S., *Vulnerable But Invincible: A Longitudinal Study of Resilient Children and Youth* (New York: Adams, Bannister, Cox, 1989).

Wilson, James Q., "Angry About Inequality? Don't Blame the Rich," *The Washington Post*, January 26, 2012. As of May 3, 2013, available online at http://articles.washingtonpost.com/2012-01-26/news/35441854_1_incomes-rise-inequality-high-school-diploma

Wilson, William Julius, *Truly Disadvantaged: The Inner City, the Underclass, and Public Policy* (Chicago, IL: University of Chicago Press, 2012). Originally published in 1987.

Wilson, William Julius, *When Work Disappears: The World of the New Urban Poor* (New York: Knopf, 1996).

Winship, Scott, "Mobility Impaired," *Brookings*. November 09, 2011. As of April 29, 2013, available online at http://www.brookings.edu/research/articles/2011/11/09-economic-mobility-winship

Yao, Shuije, "Economic Development and Poverty Reduction in China over 20 Years of Reform," *Economic Development and Cultural Change*, Vol. 48, No. 3, 2000: 447-474.

Young, Cristobal, "Religion and Economic Growth in Western Europe: 1500-2000." Paper presented at the annual meeting of the American Sociological Association Annual Meeting," Hilton San Francisco, San Francisco, CA, August 8, 2009. As of February 23, 2013, available online at http://www.stanford.edu/~cy10/public/Religion_and_Economic%20Growth_Western_Europe.pdf

Zweigenhaft, Richard L., and Domhoff, G. William, *Diversity in the Power Elite: How It Happened, Why It Matte4rs* (Lanham, Maryland: Rowman & Littlefield Publishers, 2006).

Zweigenhaft, Richard L., and Domhoff, G. William, *The New CEOs: Women, African American, Latino and Asian American Leaders of Fortune 500 Companies* (Lanham, Maryland: Rowman & Littlefield Publishers, 2010).

CHAPTER 8

Sex and Gender

by
Gary D. Wilson

INTRODUCTION

Gender stratification refers to males' and females' unequal access to a society's power, property, and prestige. Each society establishes a structure that, on the basis of sex and gender, permits or limits access to privileges. *Sex* refers to biological distinctions between males and females; *gender* refers to what a society considers to be proper behaviors and attitudes for its males and females. In the "*nature versus nurture*" debate, almost all sociologists take the side of nature.

Sociologists suggest that one is born a male or female but becoming a man or a woman is the result of social and cultural expectations that pattern the behavior of men and women. From birth, gender expectations influence how boys and girls are treated. Some researchers argue that biological factors (two X chromosomes in females, one X and Y in males) results in differences in male (more aggressive and domineering) and female (more comforting and nurturing) conduct. The dominant sociological position is that gender differences result from sex being used to mark people for special treatment. Symbolic interactionists stress that society interprets the physical differences: males and females take the relative positions that society assigns to them.

Globally, gender is the primary division between people. Because society sets up barriers to deny women equal access, they are referred to as a minority even though they outnumber men. Murdock (1935) surveyed hundreds of primitive societies and found activities to be sex-typed in all of them, although activities considered female in one society may be male in another (Murdock, 1935). Universally greater prestige is given male activities regardless of the details. If caring for cattle is men's work, it carries high prestige; if it is women's work, it has less prestige. Although the origin of patriarchy (male dominance) is unknown, two theories have emerged, both assuming patriarchy to result from universal conditions.

1. As a result of pregnancy and breast-feeding, women were limited for much of their lives. They assumed tasks associated with the home and child care; men took over tasks requiring greater speed and longer absences, such as hunting animals. This enabled men to make contact with other tribes, trade with those other groups, and wage war and gain prestige by returning home with prisoners of war or with large animals to feed the tribe; little prestige was given to women's more routine tasks.

2. In prehistoric times, each group was threatened with annihilation by other groups, and each had to recruit members to fight enemies in dangerous, hand-to-hand combat. Men, who were bigger and stronger, were coaxed into this bravery by promises of rewards, including sexual access to females. Thus, men were trained for combat; women were conditioned from birth to acquiesce in male demands. The drudge work was assigned to women since men preferred to avoid those tasks.

3. Either theory may be correct but the answer is buried in human history and there is no way of testing either.

A society's culture and institutions both justifies and maintains its customary forms of gender inequality. In the past, women in the United States did not have the right to vote, hold property, testify in court, or serve on a jury. If a woman worked outside the home, she handed her wages over to her father or husband. Males did not willingly surrender their privileges; rather, women's rights resulted from a prolonged and bitter struggle. While women enjoy more rights today, gender inequality still exists. Patterns of *gender discrimination* persist in everyday life. Females' capacities, interests, attitudes, and contributions are not taken as seriously as those of their male counterparts. Patterns of conversation reflect inequalities between men and women. Men are more likely than women to interrupt a conversation and to control a change in topics. Most victims of rape are females. Males are more likely to commit murder than females. Feminists use symbolic interactionism to understand violence against women. They stress that U. S. culture promotes violence by males. It teaches men to associate power, dominance, strength, virility and superiority with masculinity. Men use violence to try and maintain higher status.

Feminists advocate for a restructuring of social institutions to meet the needs of all groups, not just those who already have enough power and privilege to make social institutions work for them. The successes of the women's movement demonstrate that change is possible, but only when people are vigilant about their needs.

GENDER AS A SOCIAL CONSTRUCTION

Sex is a biological concept. Gender is a sociological concept. It describes the social and cultural differences a society assigns to people based on their biological sex. There is a set of social expectations (norms) for females and for males. These expectations are known as *gender roles*. Society expects certain behaviors of females, femininity, and certain behavior of males, masculinity. Gender therefore, may be described as a social construction. How we behave as females and males is not pre-determined by our biology but is guided by society's expectations based on whether we are female or male. We learn about these expectations as we grow and develop a gender identity. Our gender identity reflects our beliefs about ourselves as females and males.

Femininity and masculinity are reflected in our language particularly adjectives, both positive and negative, that are used to describe females and males. Adjectives traditionally ascribed to women include: gentle, sensitive, nurturing, delicate, graceful, cooperative, decorative, dependent, emotional, passive and weak. Adjectives traditionally ascribed to men include: strong, assertive, brave, active, independent, intelligent, competitive, insensitive, unemotional and aggressive. The use of such adjectives contributes to the social construction of gender and perpetuates traditional gender roles.

Biology and Gender

Several biological explanations for gender roles exist. One explanation is from the related fields of sociobiology and evolutionary psychology (Workman and Reader, 2009) and argues an evolutionary basis for traditional gender roles. Scholars advocating this view reason that in prehistoric societies, few social roles existed. A major role centered on relieving hunger by hunting or gathering food. The other major role centered on bearing and nursing children. Because only women could perform this role, they were also the primary caretakers for children for several years after birth. Since women were frequently pregnant, their roles as mothers confined them to the home for most of their adulthood. Men, meanwhile, were better suited than women for hunting because they were stronger and quicker than women. In prehistoric societies, then, biology was indeed destiny: for biological reasons, men in effect worked outside the home (hunted), while women stayed at home with their children.

Evolutionary reasons also explain why men are more violent than women. In prehistoric times, men who were more willing to commit violence against and even kill other men would win competitions for female mates. Such men were much more likely than less violent men to produce offspring who would then carry forward the violent tendencies.

If humans evolved along these lines, socio-biologists and evolutionary psychologists contend that natural selection favored societies with stronger men and more fertile and nurturing women. Such traits over time became fairly instinctual leading to different evolutionary paths for men and women. Men became more assertive, daring and violent than women, while women became more gentle, nurturing and maternal than men. Traditional gender roles for women and men make sense from an evolutionary point of view. This implies that existing gender inequality must continue because it is rooted in biology.

Critics challenge the evolutionary explanation on several grounds (Hurley, 2007; Begley, 2009). First, much greater gender variation in behavior and attitudes existed in prehistoric times than the evolutionary explanation assumes. Second, even if biological differences did influence gender roles in prehistoric times, these differences are mostly irrelevant in today's world since physical strength is not necessary for survival. Third, human environments over time have been too diverse to permit the simple biological development that the evolutionary explanation assumes. Fourth, evolutionary arguments implicitly justify existing gender inequality by implying the need to confine women and men to their traditional roles.

A second biological explanation for traditional gender roles centers on hormones and specifically on testosterone. One of the most important differences between boys and girls and men and women in the Unites States and many other societies is their level of aggression. Males are much more physically aggressive than females and in the United States and commit about 85% - 90% of all violent crimes. Why? This gender difference is often attributed to higher levels of testosterone in males (Mazur, 2009).

Several studies have found that higher levels of testosterone appear to contribute to increased amounts of violence and aggression. A widely cited study of Vietnam-era male veterans found that those with higher levels of testosterone had engaged in more violent behavior (Booth and Osgood, 1993). This correlation however, does not necessarily prove that testosterone increased violence since some studies have suggested that violent behavior may increase testosterone levels.

Biological evidence for gender differences certainly exists but its interpretation remains very controversial. It must be carefully weighed against the evidence that supports cultural variations and how they affect experiences that contribute to gender socialization.

Culture and Gender

Anthropologists offer compelling evidence against a strong biological determination of gender roles. Anthropological studies of preindustrial societies demonstrate some striking gender variation from one culture to another. Anthropologist Margaret Mead (1935) studied cultural differences related to gender issues. Mead's work focused on three tribes in New Guinea: the Arapesh, the Mundugumor, and the Tchambuli. Gender roles varied among the three tribes. Both sexes displayed gentle and nurturing traits in the Arapesh tribe. Both men and women spent time with the children and exhibited behavior that would be considered "maternal." Distinct gender roles did not exist among the Arapesh because both sexes displayed behavior similar to modern female gender roles. Mead found the reverse among the Mundugumor. Both men and women were aggressive and competitive, even violent. Both sexes distanced themselves from the children. Mead's conclusion was that as with the Arapesh, the Mundugumor had no gender roles. Both sexes displayed behavior similar to modern male gender roles (Mead, 1935).

Mead's observation of the Tchambuli revealed very distinct differences from the other two tribes. She found that distinct gender roles existed among the Tchambuli. One sex was dominant, assertive and assumed leadership positions among the tribe. The other sex used make-up, dressed in elaborate clothing and even spent time giggling with other members of the tribe. Mead reported that she had found a society with gender roles similar to those found in the society of the United States, but there was an unexpected difference. In the Tchambuli women were the dominant, aggressive sex in leadership positions while men were submissive and focused on superficial details such as clothing and make-up (Mead, 1935).

Mead's research was of great interest among scholars because it challenged the biological view on gender that was very prevalent at the time. Today Mead's work is controversial. It is supported by some anthropologists and refuted by some anthropologists. Some argue that Mead may have applied an over simplified idea regarding gender roles among the three societies, (Scheper, 1987). Others defend Mead's work by citing numerous subsequent studies that also suggest that cultural forces powerfully influence gender roles (Morgan, 1989).

Sexual Orientation

Sexual orientation describes a person's preference for sexual relationships with individuals of the other sex (heterosexuality), one's own sex (homosexuality), or both sexes (bisexuality). The term also increasingly refers to transgendered individuals, those whose behavior, appearance, and/or gender identity fails to conform to conventional norms. Transgendered individuals include transvestites (those who dress in the clothing of the opposite sex) and transsexuals (those whose gender identity differs from the psychological sex and who sometimes undergo a sex change).

While most people learn stable sexual identities, over the course of one's life, sexual identity evolves. Heterosexual identity is thus strongly encouraged by the dominant culture, and young people growing up shape their sexual identity in this context. Sometimes, one's sexual identity may change. For example, a person who has always thought of himself or herself as a heterosexual may decide at a later time that he or she is gay or lesbian. In more unusual cases, people may actually undergo a sex change operation, changing their sexual identity in the process. In the case of bisexuals, a person might adopt a dual sexual identity.

Within the United States, the social construction of sexual identity is also revealed by studies of the "coming out" process. Coming out - the process of defining oneself as gay or lesbian - is a series of events and redefinitions in which a person comes to see herself or himself as having a gay identity. In coming out, a person consciously labels that identity either to oneself or others (or both). Coming out is usually not the result of a single homosexual experience. If it were, there would be far more self-identified homosexuals than there are, because researchers find that a substantial portion of both men and women have some form of homosexual experience at some time in their lifetime. A person may even change between gay, straight, and bisexual identities (Rust, 1993). This indicates, as the social construction perspective suggests, that identity is created not fixed, over the course of a life.

Sociological understanding of sexual identity has developed largely through new studies of lesbian and gay experience. Long thought of only in terms of social deviance, gays and lesbians have been much stereotyped in traditional social science, but the feminist and gay liberation movements have discouraged this approach, arguing that gay and lesbian experience is merely one alternative in the broad spectrum of human sexuality. Now there is a growing research literature examining different aspects of gay life (Nardi and Schneider, 1997; Seidman, 1994).

The institutional context of sexuality within the United States, as well as other societies, was historically one where homophobia permeated the culture. *Homophobia* is the fear and hatred of homosexuality. It is manifested in prejudiced attitudes toward gays and lesbians, as well as in overt hostility and violence directed against people suspected of being gay. Homophobia is a learned attitude, as are other forms of negative social judgments about particular groups. Homophobia is deeply embedded in people's definitions of themselves as men and women. Boys are often raised to be "manly" by repressing so-called feminine characteristics in themselves. Being called "fag" or a "sissy" is one of the peer sanctions that socialize a child to conform to particular gender roles. Similarly, verbal attacks on lesbians are a mechanism of social control, because ridicule can be interpreted as encouraging social conformity.

Homophobia plays an important role in gender socialization because it encourages stricter conformity to traditional expectations, especially for men and young boys. Slurs directed against gays encourage boys to act more masculine as a way of affirming for their peers that they are not gay. As a consequence, homophobia also discourages so-called feminine traits in men, such as caring, nurturing, empathy, emotion, and gentleness.

Because of homophobia in the culture, there are numerous misleading myths about gays and lesbians. One is that gay men have large discretionary incomes who work primarily in artistic areas and personal service jobs (such as hairdressing). This stereotype prevents people from recognizing that there are gays and lesbians in all racial-ethnic groups, some of whom are working class or poor, and who are employed in a wide range of occupations (Gluckman and Reed, 2007). Some lesbians and gays are also old people, even though the stereotype defines them as mostly young or middle aged (Smith, 2103).

Heterosexism refers to the institutionalization of heterosexuality as the only socially legitimate sexual orientation. Heterosexism is rooted in the belief that heterosexual behavior is the only natural form of sexual expression and that homosexuality is a perversion of "normal" sexual identity. Heterosexism is reinforced through institutional mechanisms that project the idea that only heterosexuality is normal. Institutions also structure the unequal distribution of privileges to people presumed to be heterosexual. Historically businesses and communities for example, rarely recognized the legal rights of those in homosexual relationships, although this is changing. Heterosexism is an institutional phenomenon although people's beliefs can reflect heterosexist assumptions. Thus a person may be quite accepting of gay and lesbian people (that is, not be homophobic), but still benefit from heterosexual privileges or engage in heterosexist practices that have the unintentional effect of excluding lesbians and gays, such as by talking with co-workers about their dating activities on the assumption that everyone is interested in a heterosexual partner.

The heterosexist framework of social institutions enforced situations in which gay and lesbian relationships lack the institutional support of heterosexual relationships. In the absence of such socially sanctioned institutions, lesbians and gays have invented their own rituals and communities to support these relationships. The absence of institutionalized roles for lesbians and gays affects the roles they adopt within relationships. Despite popular stereotypes, gay partners typically do not assume roles as the dominant or subordinate sexual partner. They are more likely to adopt roles as equals. Gay and lesbian couples are also more likely than heterosexual couples to both be employed, another source of greater equality within the relationship. Researchers have also found that the quality of relationships among gay men is positively correlated with the social support the couple receives from others (Smith and Brown, 2011).

Gender Identity

Gender identities are the conceptions we have of ourselves as being male or female. As such they are invisible, something that cannot be established by appearance. For most people, there is a good fit between their anatomy and their gender identity. Boys generally come to behave in ways their culture labels "masculine," and girls learn to be "feminine." But there are some individuals for whom this is not the case. The most striking examples are *transsexuals* – individuals who have normal sexual organs, but who psychologically feel like members of the opposite sex. In some cases medical science has found a way, through surgery and hormones, to reduce the incompatibility by modifying the person's anatomy to conform to the gender identity.

Learning plays a key part in the acquisition of gender identities. However, the exact nature of this learning has been the subject of considerable debate. According to Sigmund Freud and his followers, gender identity and the adoption of sex-typed behaviors are the result of an *Oedipus conflict* that emerges between the ages of 3 and 6. During this period, children discover the genital differences between the sexes. According to Freudians, this discovery prompts children to see themselves as rivals of their same-sex parent for the affection of the parent of the other sex. Such desires and feelings give rise to considerable anxiety. Freud said the anxiety is resolved through complicated psychological maneuvers in which children come to identify with the parent of the same sex. By virtue of this identification, boys acquire masculine self-conceptions and girls learn feminine self-conceptions. However, research that has tried to test Freud's theory has been either inconclusive or at odds with it. Additionally cross-cultural research suggests that the Oedipus conflict does not occur among all peoples.

Unlike Freud and his followers, *cultural transmission* theorists contend that the acquisition of gender identities and behaviors is not the product of an Oedipus conflict, but rather is a gradual process of learning that begins in infancy (Bandura, 1971). They suggest that parents, teachers, and other adults shape a child's behavior by reinforcing responses that are deemed appropriate to the child's gender role and discouraging inappropriate ones. Moreover, children are motivated to attend to, learn from, and imitate same-sex models as more like themselves. Children are given cues to their gender roles in a great variety of ways. Parents often furnish boys' and girls' rooms differently, decorating those of boys with animal motifs and those of girls with floral motifs, lace, fringe, and ruffles. The toys found in the rooms also differ. Boys are provided with more vehicles, military toys, sports equipment, toy animals, and mechanical toys; girls, more dolls, doll houses, and domestic toys (Caldera, Huston and O'Brien, 2009).

Cultural-transmission theory draws our attention to the part socialization plays in shaping the sex-typed behavior of children. However, the image we gain from the theory is one of essentially passive individuals who are programmed for behavior by adult bearers of culture. *Labeling theory* (also called cognitive-developmental theory) provides a corrective to this perspective by calling our attention to the fact that children actively seek to acquire gender identities and roles. According to developmental psychologist Lawrence Kohlberg (1966, 1969; Kohlberg and Ullian 1974), children come to label themselves as "boys" or "girls" when they are between 18 months and 3 years of age. Once they have identified themselves as males or females, they want to adopt behaviors consistent with their newly discovered status. This process is called *self-socialization*. According to Kohlberg, children form a stereotyped conception of maleness and femaleness - an oversimplified, exaggerated, cartoon-like image. Then they use this stereotyped image in organizing behavior and cultivating the attitudes and actions associated with being a boy or a girl.

Both the cultural-transmission and labeling theories of gender-role learning have received research support (Maccoby and Jacklin, 1974; Bem, 1981; Serbin and Sprafkin, 1986). Increasingly, social and behavioral scientists are coming to the view that any full explanation of gender-role acquisition must incorporate elements from both theoretical approaches.

Gender Socialization

Gender socialization begins in infancy since most parents socialize their children into traditional gender roles without even knowing it (Snider, 2009). Parents typically describe their infant sons as big, strong and assertive while they refer to their infant daughters as pretty and delicate. Parents typically play more roughly with their sons and more quietly with their daughters. When infant daughters cry, they are comforted but infant sons are often allowed to cry for longer periods of time and they receive less comforting treatment.

Clues to proper gender roles surround children in materials produced by corporations (books, toys, games), in mass media images, in educational settings, and in religious organizations and beliefs. Agents of socialization play a major role in teaching children proper gender roles. Corporations, for example, produce materials that help to socialize children into proper conduct. Publishers produce books that present images of expected gender behavior. Language and pictures in preschool picture books, elementary children's books, and school textbooks are steeped in gender role messages, reflecting society's expectations and stereotypes.

Producers of toys and games also contribute to traditional messages about gender. Such toys fill rooms in the homes of children in the western world and it is usually quite clear which are boys' rooms and which are girls' rooms. Boys' rooms are filled with sports equipment, army toys, building and technical toys, and cars and trucks. Girls' rooms have fewer toys and most are related to dolls and domestic roles. Boys have more experience manipulating blocks, Tinker Toys, Legos, and Erector sets, all of which parallel masculinized activities outside the home in the public domain, from constructing and building trades to military roles and sports. Girls prepare for domestic roles with toys relating to domestic activities. Barbie dolls stress physical appearance, consumerism, and glamour. Only a few Barbies are in occupational roles. In contrast, the Ken dolls that Mattel designed to match Barbie (and have now been discontinued) were often doctors or other professionals.

In 2009, Mattel produced Barbie's online dream house, a virtual house that can be decorated and furnished. Barbie's house was designed with girls as the target market. A complementary target boy program features Hot Wheels cars with car races and uses virtual tools to customize cars. These models differed in more than simple appearance. The life lessons learned from such computer games reinforce gender stereotypes (Snider, 2009). Each toy or game prepares children through anticipatory socialization for future gender roles. Toys that require building, manipulating, and technical skills provide experiences for later life. Choices ranging from college major and occupational choice to activities that depend on visual-spatial and mathematical abilities appear to be affected by these early choices and childhood learning experiences (Tavris & Wade, 1984).

Television is also a very powerful agent of socialization. By school age typical U. S. children will have spent more time in front of a television than they will classrooms in the coming twelve years of school, a behavior that contributes to obesity in the United States (Randerson, 2008). Television presents a simple, stereotyped view of life, from advertisements to situation comedies to soap operas. Women in soap operas and ads, especially those working outside the home, are often depicted as having problems in carrying out their role responsibilities (Benokraitis & Feagin, 1995). See Box 8.1 – The Boy Code – for additional information on gender socialization.

Gender Differences: Having v. Doing

Ideas regarding what is not "normal" for a particular gender are not based on biological traits; it is the product of social behavior. Childhood is the primary time for developing and understanding these standards. Children follow the cultural rules and try to meet the expectations of the gender that they perceive themselves to be. This results in the formation of gender identity. Once children learn the appropriate behaviors for their particular gender, they are more likely to fit in with peers and be accepted by family members and authority figures (West and Zimmerman, 2007).

In their work, *Doing Gender*, Sociologists West and Zimmerman suggest that there are distinctions between "doing gender" and "having gender" (West and Zimmerman, 2007). Specific body parts do not necessarily ensure that a child will be biologically forced to "do" that gender. "Doing gender" refers to the act of matching one's behavior to a certain set of gender-related standards. "Having gender" refers specifically to the biological characteristics that result in the attachment of labels, male or female. We all have a gender but the way we behave is the doing of gender. When little girls put on their mother's make-up or little boys pick up their father's tools, they are learning gender roles or doing gender. Gender constructs become so fixed that children who do not fit the model are often treated as outcasts and may experience negative sanctions including teasing, isolation, harsh words, and stigma. To avoid such informal sanctions, children usually conform to traditional gender expectations, at least in public situations.

THE BOY CODE

BOX 8.1

Boys and girls begin to conform to gender expectations once they are old enough to understand that their sex is permanent. They then become even more conscious of adhering to the norms of others in their gender category.

The so-called "Good Old Boy" network that has traditionally favored men in American society actually starts with "the boy code." Young boys learn the code from parents, siblings, peers, teachers, and society in general. They are praised for following the code and punished for violating it. William Pollack (1999) suggested that boys learn several stereotyped behavior models exemplifying the boy code:

1. "The sturdy oak" – men should be stoic, stable, and independent -- a man never shows weaknesses.
2. "Give 'em hell" – from athletic coaches and movie heroes, the consistent theme is extreme daring, bravado, and attraction to violence.
3. "The big wheel" – men and boys should achieve status, dominance, and power – they should avoid shame, wear the mask of coolness, and act as though everything is under control.
4. "No sissy stuff" – boys are discouraged from expressing feelings or urges perceived as feminine – dependence, warmth , empathy.

The boy code is ingrained in society. By five or six years of age boys are less likely than girls to express hurt or distress. They have learned to be ashamed of showing feelings and of being weak. The gender straitjacket, according to Pollack, causes boys to conceal feelings in order to fit in and be accepted and loved. As a result some boys , especially in adolescence, become silent, covering any vulnerability and masking their true feelings. This affects boys' relationships, performance in school, and the ability to connect with others. It also causes young males to put on what Jackson Katz (2006) calls the "tough guise" – when young men and boys emphasize aggression and violence to display masculinity.

Pollack (1999) suggests that we can help boys reconnect to non-gendered norms by doing the following:

1. Giving some undivided attention each day just listening to boys.
2. Encouraging a range of emotions.
3. Avoiding language that taunts, teases, or shames.
4. Looking behind the veneer of "coolness" for signs of problems.
5. Expressing love and empathy.
6. Dispelling the "sturdy oak" image.
7. Advocating a broad, inclusive model of masculinity.

With the women's movement and shifts in gender expectations have come new patterns of male behavior. Some men are forming more supportive and less competitive relationships with other men, and there are likely to be continued changes in the broadening of "appropriate" behavior for men (Kimmel & Messner, 2009).

As children reach school age, the lifelong process of gender socialization continues through activities separate from parents. Others in the community including teachers, religious leaders, coaches, and other children become influential in the lives of young people. Many activities involve boys versus girls, we versus they, us and them and so forth. Even if parents are not highly traditional with regard to gender expectations, children still experience many influences at the micro level to conform to traditional gender notions.

Adulthood involves new forms of gender stratification in which men have traditionally had more networks and statuses as well as greater access to resources outside the home. This has resulted in women having less power because they depend more on husbands or fathers for resources. Consider the following example: When the question arises of who walks through the door first, the answer is that in most western societies, "she" does. The strong man steps back and defers to the weaker female, graciously holding the door for her (Walum, 2004). Yet when it comes to who walks through the metaphorical door to professions, it is the man who goes first. Women are served first at restaurants and other micro-level settings, but this seems little compensation for the fact that doors have traditionally been closed to them in other situations in society. See Table 8.1 for information on gender segregation in the workplace.

TABLE 8.1 GENDER SEGREGATION IN THE WORKPLACE FOR SELECTED OCCUPATIONS (2010)

Occupation	Female Workers (%)	Male Workers (%)
Dental Hygienists	99.2	0.8
Speech-language pathologists	98.0	2.0
Pre-school and Kindergarten Teachers	97.3	2.7
Secretaries and Administrative Assistants	96.7	3.3
Registered Nurses	91.7	9.3
Food Servers	74.0	26.0
Lawyers	32.6	67.4
Physicians	30.0	70.0
Dentists	28.2	71.8
Computer Software Engineers	20.8	79.2
Carpenters	1.9	98.1
Electricians	1.7	98.3

Source: Data from U.S. Census Bureau (2010). Statistical abstract of the United States 2010. Washington, DC: U.S. Government Printing Office.

FEMINISM

Feminist theorists suggest that gender stratification is based on power struggles rather than biology. A distinguishing characteristic of most feminist theory is that it actively advocates a change in the social order. There are a range of feminist theories all of which argue for bringing about a new and equal ordering of gender relationships to eliminate the *patriarchy* and *sexism* of current gender stratification systems (Kramer, 2007).

WOMEN'S HISTORY MONTH

BOX 8.2

National Women's History Month's roots go back to March 8, 1857, when women from New York City factories staged a protest over working conditions. International Women's Day was first observed in 1909, but it wasn't until 1981 that Congress established National Women's History Week to be commemorated the second week of March. In 1987, Congress expanded the week to a month. Every year since, Congress has passed a resolution for Women's History Month, and the President has issued a proclamation.

158.3 million

The number of females in the United States in 2011. The number of males was 153.3 million.
Source: Population Estimates: 2011, Table NC_EST2011_01
At 65 and older, there were 13.3 percent more women than men in 2011. Source: Population Estimates: 2011, Table NC_EST2011_01

Jobs

57.7%

Percentage of females 16 and older who participated in the labor force, representing about 72.6 million women in 2012.
Source: U.S. Bureau of Labor Statistics, Current Population Survey, Table A-2

41.7%

Percent of employed females 16 and older who worked in management, professional and related occupations, compared with 35.1 percent of employed males in December 2012.
Source: U.S. Bureau of Labor Statistics, Current Population Survey, Table A-19

Military

204,973

Total number of active duty women in the military, as of Nov. 30, 2012. Of that total, 38,378 women were officers, and 164,021 were enlisted.
Source: U.S. Department of Defense, Selected Manual Statistics, annual, and unpublished data.

Earnings

$37,118

The median annual earnings of women 15 or older who worked year-round, full time in 2011. In comparison, the median annual earnings of men were $48,202.
Source: Income, Poverty, and Health Insurance Coverage in the United States: 2011, Page 7 & 11.

0.77

The female-to-male earnings ratio in 2011. The number of men and women with earnings who worked year-round in 2011 was not statistically different from the ratio in 2010.
Source: Income, Poverty, and Health Insurance Coverage in the United States: 2011, Page 12.

Education

31.4 million

Number of women 25 and older with a bachelor's degree or more in 2011, higher than the corresponding number for men (30 million). Women had a larger share of high school diplomas (including equivalents), as well as associate, bachelor's and master's degrees. More men than women had a professional or doctoral degree.
Source: Educational Attainment in the United States: 2011, Table 3

30.1%

Percent of women 25 and older who had obtained a bachelor's degree or more as of 2011.
Source: Educational Attainment in the United States: 2011, Table 3

11.3 million

Number of college students in fall 2011 who were women age 15 and older.
Source: School Enrollment in the United States: 2011, Table 5

Businesses

$1.2 trillion

Revenue for women-owned businesses in 2007.
Source: 2007 Survey of Business Owners

7.8 million

The number of women-owned businesses in 2007.
Source: 2007 Survey of Business Owners

7.5 million

Number of people employed by women-owned businesses in 2007.
Nearly half of all women-owned businesses (45.9 percent) operated in repair and maintenance; personal and laundry services; health care and social assistance; and professional, scientific and technical services. Women-owned businesses accounted for 52.0 percent of all businesses operating in the health care and social assistance sector.
Source: 2007 Survey of Business Owners

4

Number of states with at least 500,000 women-owned businesses in 2007 was California, Texas, New York and Florida. California had 1,039,208 women-owned businesses or 13.3 percent of all women-owned businesses in the United States, Texas had 609,947 or 7.8 percent, New York had 594,517 or 7.6 percent, and Florida had 581,096, or 7.5 percent.
Source: 2007 Survey of Business Owners

Voting

46.2%

Percentage of female citizens 18 and older who reported voting in the 2010 congressional election. 44.8 percent of their male counterparts cast a ballot. Additionally, 66.6 percent of female citizens reported being registered to vote.
Source: Voting and Registration in the Election of November 2010, Table 1

Motherhood

85.4 million

Estimated number of mothers in the United States in 2009.
Source: Unpublished data from the Survey of Income and Program Participation, 2008 1.9
Average number of children that women 40 to 44 had given birth to as of 2010, down from 3.1 children in 1976, the year the Census Bureau began collecting such data.
Source: Fertility of American Women: 2010 table 2 and Historical table 2
The percentage of women in this age group who had given birth was 81 percent in 2010, down from 90 percent in 1976.
Source: Fertility of American Women: 2010 table 1 and Historical table 2

Marriage

64.9 million

Number of married women 18 and older (including those who were separated or had an absent spouse) in 2011.
Source: Families and Living Arrangements: 2011, Table A1

5.1 million

Number of stay-at-home mothers nationwide in 2012.
Source: Families and Living Arrangements: 2012, Table FG8

Feminist theorists try to understand the causes of women's lower status and seek ways to change the systems to provide more opportunities, to improve the standard of living, and to give women control over their bodies and reproduction. Feminist theorists also feel that little change will occur until group consciousness is raised so that women understand the system that limits their options and do not blame themselves, or men, for their situations - a systemic social problem (Kramer, 2007).

As societies become technologically advanced and need an educated workforce, women of all social classes and ethnic groups around the world are likely to gain more equal roles. Women are entering institutions of higher education in record numbers, and evidence indicates they are needed in the world economic system and the changing labor force of most countries. Societies in which women are not integrated into the economic sphere generally lag behind other countries. Feminist theorists examine these global and national patterns, but they also note the role of patriarchy in interpersonal situations.

Feminist analysis finds gender patterns embedded in social institutions of family, education, religion, politics, economics, and health care. If the societal system is patriarchal, ruled by men, the interdependent institutions are likely to reflect and support the system. See Box 8.2 for information about Women's History Month and Box 8.3 for information on Betty Friedan, a leader of the modern women's movement who maintained that women and men must forge relationships as allies, not enemies.

BOX 8.3

FOCUS ON BETTY FRIEDAN (1921 – 2006)

"Man is not the enemy here, but the fellow victim." – Betty Friedan

"It is easier to live through someone else than to complete yourself. The freedom to lead and plan your own life is frightening if you have never faced it before. It is frightening when a woman finally realizes that there is no answer to the question 'who am I' except the voice inside herself." – Betty Friedan

"You can have it all, just not all at the same time." – Betty Friedan

"The problem lay buried, unspoken, for many years in the minds of American women. It was a strange stirring, a sense of dissatisfaction, a yearning that women suffered in the middle of the twentieth century in the United States. Each suburban wife struggled with it alone. As she made the beds, shopped for groceries, matched slipcover material, ate peanut butter sandwiches with her children, chauffeured Cub Scouts and Brownies, lay beside her husband at night -she was afraid to ask even of herself the silent question- "Is this all?" – Betty Friedan

Betty Friedan was born Bettye Naomi Goldstein in 1921 to Harry Goldstein, a Russian immigrant and owner of a jewelry store, and Miriam (Horowitz) Goldstein. Her mother gave up her position as editor of the women's page of the local paper to raise her family.

Bettye Goldstein majored in psychology and edited the college newspaper at Smith College. Under her guidance, the paper became a forum for the fight against fascism abroad and promoted the organization of unions at home. She graduated summa cum laude in 1942. Bettye, dropped what she thought was the pretentious "e" at the end of her given name when she became a psychology research fellow at the University of California in Berkeley. One year later she moved to New York to work as a reporter and she became involved in labor union activity. She worked for union publications as a labor journalist and pamphlet writer and developed an intense interest in working women's issues. In 1947, she married Carl Friedan. The marriage produced three children and ended after twenty-two years. Friedan received maternity leave and continued working after her first child was born in 1949, but she was forced to leave her job during her second pregnancy in 1953. She spent the next decade raising her two sons and a daughter. She continued to work as a writer for middle-class women's magazines.

In 1957, Betty Friedan surveyed two hundred of her Smith College classmates and found that many of them suffered from "the problem that has no name." They were supposed to be happy

in their suburban paradises, with working husband and smiling children, but many were bored, depressed and anxious. She was not satisfied by the women's explanation that their unhappiness was their own fault so she continued to explore the matter. She received widespread response to an article she published in *Good Housekeeping* in September of 1960, entitled "Women Are People Too!" The reaction to the article helped her to realize that the malaise she found was not limited to women from prestigious eastern colleges.

The results of her research formed the basis of her book *The Feminine Mystique*, published in 1963, throughout which Friedan encouraged women to seek new opportunities for themselves. In *The Feminine Mystique*, Friedan described a type of depression experienced by many middle-aged, college-educated women, and she suggested its cause. She argued that the media and educators had created an image of women's proper role as appendages of their husbands and children: "as Tom's wife or Mary's mother." The effect of this "feminine mystique" was that women denied their own desires for the sake of familial harmony. Their lack of excitement about their own lives made them smother their children and cling to their husbands. They were bored and ineffectual. The book quickly became a sensation, and created a social revolution by dispelling the myth that all women wanted to be happy homemakers, and marking the start of what would become Friedan's incredibly significant role in the women's rights movement (Friedan, 1963).

As a feminist revolutionary, Betty Friedan was considered by many to be the "mother" of the second wave of modern feminism. Her struggles against the "feminine mystique" and in favor of gender equality led to the establishment of a common cause and a fundamental transformation in the way American women view themselves. Betty Friedan did more though, than write about confining gender stereotypes. She became a force for change. She encouraged women to become more involved in the political process and co-founded the National Organization for Women in 1966. She served as its first president. She also fought for abortion rights by establishing the National Association for the Repeal of Abortion Laws (now known as NARAL Pro-Choice America) in 1969.

Friedan published *The Second Stage* in 1982, in which she presented a more moderate feminist position from her earlier work. Friedan later explored the later stages of a woman's life in *The Fountain of Age*, published in 1993, when she was in her 70s.

Betty Friedan died of heart failure on February 4, 2006, in Washington, D.C. She is remembered as one of the leading voices of the women's rights movement of the 20th century. The work that she started is still being carried on by the organizations that she helped to establish.

Selected Works by Betty Friedan –
The Feminine Mystique (1963, reprinted, 2001); *It Changed My Life* (1976); *The Second Stage* (1981); *The Fountain of Age* (1993); *Life So Far: A Memoir* (2000).

Sources: Friedan (1963, 1976, 1981, 1993, 2001), National Organization of Women (NOW) (2013).

Feminism and Sexism

"Just wait until your father gets home!" The statement suggests that Father is the supreme authority figure and that a severe punishment will occur upon his arrival. The threat was used historically to create fear in children. The statement indicates that a mother has less influence than a father on the behavior of children and reinforces an enduring stereotype that the man is the dominant member of the family. Such family dynamics are common in a patriarchy, a social system in which men dominate and exert power and authority over women and children. In patriarchal societies, men manage public affairs in government, business, religion and education. No pure matriarchy exists even though some women may seem to have more power than men. In most cultures there are clear lines of male dominance in the social systems. Women, in general, have less power.

Income and Workplace Inequality and the Gendered Wage Gap

Such systems typically result in sexism, the belief that one sex is superior to the other. Patriarchal societies view women as weak and no match for a man's physical or intellectual prowess. Even in societies that give women the same civil rights as men, there are still different standards for women. Even after years of fighting for equal rights in the United States, women still earn less money than men. A man with a bachelor's degree earns about $71,000 annually while a woman with a bachelor's degree earns about $51,000 annually. Men with doctorates average $113,000 while women with doctorates average $82,000. The variations in salaries between men and women illustrate a gendered wage gap. See Table 8.2 for information comparisons of educational attainment based on gender. The gendered wage gap primarily results from sex segregation in the workplace (see Table 8.1). While labor force participation has increased significantly for women in recent years, the workplace remains segregated by gender. See Table 8.4 for information regarding labor force participation. Almost half of all women work in a few low-paying clerical and service –type jobs, such as retail or food, while men work in a much greater variety of jobs, including high paying jobs. Table 8.1 shows that many jobs are held primarily by either women or men. Part of the reason for this segregation is that socialization affects job choices for young people and women and men do not typically want to encounter difficulties including social disapproval that may result if they pursue a job that is traditionally assigned to the other sex. Compounding the problem, sex-segregated jobs often discriminate against applicants who are not the correct sex for the job. Employers may either consciously refuse to hire someone who is the wrong sex for the job or have job requirements and workplace rules that unintentionally make it more difficult for women to qualify for certain jobs. Such practices are of course, illegal, but they persist due to an institutionalized sexism that exists in societies. The sex-segregation that results contributes to the continuing gendered wage gap between female and male workers. Occupations dominated by women tend to pay lower wages and salaries and since women are concentrated in low paying jobs, their earnings continue to be much lower than earnings for men (Reskin and Padavic, 2002).

TABLE 8.2 EDUCATIONAL ATTAINMENT OF THE POPULATION 25 YEARS AND OVER BY SEX, FOR BLACK ALONE AND WHITE ALONE, NOT HISPANIC: 2011

(Numbers in thousands. Civilian noninstitutionalized population.[1])

Sex and educational attainment	Total		Race and Hispanic origin[2]					
			Black alone		White alone, not Hispanic		Other[3]	
	Number	Percent	Number	Percent	Number	Percent	Number	Percent
Both sexes	201,543	100.0	23,364	100.0	139,146	100.0	39,034	100.0
Less than 9th grade	10,277	5.1	965	4.1	3,202	2.3	6,111	15.7
9th to 12th grade (no diploma)	14,763	7.3	2,664	11.4	7,366	5.3	4,733	12.1
High school graduate	61,911	30.7	8,133	34.8	42,960	30.9	10,819	27.7
Some college or associate's degree	53,249	26.4	6,953	29.8	38,290	27.5	8,006	20.5
Bachelor's degree	39,286	19.5	3,079	13.2	30,082	21.6	6,124	15.7
Advanced degree	22,057	10.9	1,570	6.7	17,247	12.4	3,240	8.3
Less than high school graduate	25,040	12.4	3,629	15.5	10,567	7.6	10,844	27.8
High school graduate or more	176,503	87.6	19,735	84.5	128,578	92.4	28,190	72.2
Less than bachelor's degree	140,200	69.6	18,714	80.1	91,817	66.0	29,669	76.0
Bachelor's degree or more	61,343	30.4	4,649	19.9	47,329	34.0	9,365	24.0
Male	97,220	100.0	10,411	100.0	67,420	100.0	19,390	100.0
Less than 9th grade	5,117	5.3	426	4.1	1,705	2.5	2,986	15.4
9th to 12th grade (no diploma)	7,443	7.7	1,256	12.1	3,664	5.4	2,522	13.0
High school graduate	30,370	31.2	3,983	38.3	20,820	30.9	5,567	28.7
Some college or associate's degree	24,319	25.0	2,872	27.6	17,645	26.2	3,802	19.6
Bachelor's degree	19,017	19.6	1,268	12.2	14,884	22.1	2,865	14.8
Advanced degree	10,954	11.3	606	5.8	8,701	12.9	1,647	8.5
Less than high school graduate	12,560	12.9	1,682	16.2	5,369	8.0	5,509	28.4
High school graduate or more	84,660	87.1	8,728	83.8	62,051	92.0	13,881	71.6
Less than bachelor's degree	67,249	69.2	8,537	82.0	43,835	65.0	14,877	76.7
Bachelor's degree or more	29,971	30.8	1,874	18.0	23,585	35.0	4,512	23.3
Female	104,323	100.0	12,953	100.0	71,726	100.0	19,644	100.0
Less than 9th grade	5,160	4.9	539	4.2	1,497	2.1	3,125	15.9
9th to 12th grade (no diploma)	7,320	7.0	1,408	10.9	3,701	5.2	2,211	11.3
High school graduate	31,541	30.2	4,150	32.0	22,139	30.9	5,252	26.7
Some college or associate's degree	28,930	27.7	4,081	31.5	20,645	28.8	4,204	21.4
Bachelor's degree	20,269	19.4	1,812	14.0	15,198	21.2	3,259	16.6
Advanced degree	11,103	10.6	964	7.4	8,546	11.9	1,593	8.1
Less than high school graduate	12,480	12.0	1,946	15.0	5,198	7.2	5,336	27.2
High school graduate or more	91,843	88.0	11,007	85.0	66,528	92.8	14,309	72.8
Less than bachelor's degree	72,951	69.9	10,177	78.6	47,982	66.9	14,792	75.3
Bachelor's degree or more	31,372	30.1	2,776	21.4	23,744	33.1	4,852	24.7

[1]Plus armed forces living off post or with their families on post.

[2]Hispanic refers to people whose origin is Mexican, Puerto Rican, Cuban, Spanish-speaking Central or South American countries, or other Hispanic/Latino, regardless of race.

[3]Includes American Indian and Alaska Native; Asian alone; Native Hawaiian and Other Pacific Islander alone; White alone, Hispanic; and Two or More Races.

SOURCE: U.S. Census Bureau, Current Population Survey, Annual Social and Economic Supplement, 2011. Internet release Date: November 2012

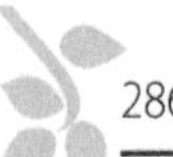

TABLE 8.3 EARNINGS BY SEX OF FULL-TIME, YEAR-ROUND WORKERS 15 YEARS AND OVER BY SEX, FOR BLACK ALONE AND WHITE ALONE, NOT HISPANIC: 2010

(Numbers in thousands. Civilian noninstitutionalized population.[1])

Sex and earnings[3]	Total		Race and Hispanic origin[2]					
			Black alone		White alone, not Hispanic		Other[4]	
	Number	Percent	Number	Percent	Number	Percent	Number	Percent
Both sexes	99,246	100.0	10,987	100.0	68,382	100.0	19,876	100.0
Under $5,000	657	0.7	57	0.5	496	0.7	104	0.5
$5,000 to $9,999	1,127	1.1	149	1.4	664	1.0	314	1.6
$10,000 to $14,999	3,756	3.8	523	4.8	1,936	2.8	1,296	6.5
$15,000 to $19,999	6,187	6.2	915	8.3	3,196	4.7	2,076	10.4
$20,000 to $24,999	8,348	8.4	1,307	11.9	4,648	6.8	2,393	12.0
$25,000 to $34,999	17,164	17.3	2,494	22.7	10,682	15.6	3,988	20.1
$35,000 to $49,999	21,223	21.4	2,561	23.3	14,913	21.8	3,750	18.9
$50,000 to $74,999	21,162	21.3	1,895	17.2	16,108	23.6	3,159	15.9
$75,000 to $99,999	8,850	8.9	625	5.7	6,937	10.1	1,287	6.5
$100,000 and over	10,772	10.9	462	4.2	8,802	12.9	1,508	7.6
Male	56,412	100.0	5,167	100.0	39,334	100.0	11,910	100.0
Under $5,000	373	0.7	30	0.6	278	0.7	64	0.5
$5,000 to $9,999	571	1.0	62	1.2	318	0.8	190	1.6
$10,000 to $14,999	1,697	3.0	229	4.4	806	2.0	662	5.6
$15,000 to $19,999	2,730	4.8	321	6.2	1,255	3.2	1,154	9.7
$20,000 to $24,999	3,979	7.1	578	11.2	2,054	5.2	1,347	11.3
$25,000 to $34,999	8,558	15.2	1,138	22.0	5,134	13.1	2,286	19.2
$35,000 to $49,999	11,197	19.8	1,174	22.7	7,809	19.9	2,215	18.6
$50,000 to $74,999	13,031	23.1	1,003	19.4	10,030	25.5	1,998	16.8
$75,000 to $99,999	6,020	10.7	345	6.7	4,808	12.2	867	7.3
$100,000 and over	8,255	14.6	286	5.5	6,841	17.4	1,127	9.5
Female	42,834	100.0	5,820	100.0	29,048	100.0	7,967	100.0
Under $5,000	284	0.7	27	0.5	217	0.7	39	0.5
$5,000 to $9,999	556	1.3	87	1.5	345	1.2	123	1.6
$10,000 to $14,999	2,059	4.8	294	5.1	1,130	3.9	634	8.0
$15,000 to $19,999	3,457	8.1	593	10.2	1,941	6.7	922	11.6
$20,000 to $24,999	4,369	10.2	729	12.5	2,594	8.9	1,046	13.1
$25,000 to $34,999	8,606	20.1	1,355	23.3	5,548	19.1	1,702	21.4
$35,000 to $49,999	10,026	23.4	1,387	23.8	7,104	24.5	1,535	19.3
$50,000 to $74,999	8,131	19.0	891	15.3	6,078	20.9	1,162	14.6
$75,000 to $99,999	2,829	6.6	280	4.8	2,129	7.3	420	5.3
$100,000 and over	2,517	5.9	175	3.0	1,961	6.7	381	4.8

[1]Plus armed forces living off post or with their families on post.

[2]Hispanic refers to people whose origin is Mexican, Puerto Rican, Cuban, Spanish-speaking Central or South American countries, or other Hispanic/Latino, regardless of race.

[3]Earnings is the sum of wage and salary income and self-employment income.

[4]Includes American Indian and Alaska Native; Asian alone; Native Hawaiian and Other Pacific Islander alone; White alone, Hispanic; and Two or More Races.

SOURCE: U.S. Census Bureau, Current Population Survey, Annual Social and Economic Supplement, 2011. Internet release Date: November 2012

TABLE 8.4 LABOR FORCE AND EMPLOYMENT STATUS OF THE CIVILIAN POPULATION 16 YEARS AND OVER BY SEX, FOR BLACK ALONE AND WHITE ALONE, NOT HISPANIC: 2011

(Numbers in thousands. Civilian noninstitutionalized population.)

Sex, labor force status, and employment status[2]	Total		Race and Hispanic origin[1]					
			Black alone		White alone, not Hispanic		Other[3]	
	Number	Percent	Number	Percent	Number	Percent	Number	Percent
Both sexes	238,999	100.0	29,004	100.0	161,145	100.0	48,850	100.0
In civilian labor force	152,868	64.0	17,611	60.7	103,316	64.1	31,940	65.4
Employed[4]	138,410	90.5	14,812	84.1	95,286	92.2	28,312	88.6
Unemployed[4]	14,458	9.5	2,799	15.9	8,031	7.8	3,628	11.4
Not in civilian labor force	86,131	36.0	11,393	39.3	57,828	35.9	16,910	34.6
Male	115,986	100.0	13,108	100.0	78,319	100.0	24,559	100.0
In civilian labor force	81,294	70.1	8,245	62.9	54,849	70.0	18,199	74.1
Employed[4]	72,732	89.5	6,671	80.9	50,008	91.2	16,053	88.2
Unemployed[4]	8,562	10.5	1,574	19.1	4,841	8.8	2,147	11.8
Not in civilian labor force	34,692	29.9	4,863	37.1	23,470	30.0	6,360	25.9
Female	123,012	100.0	15,896	100.0	82,826	100.0	24,291	100.0
In civilian labor force	71,574	58.2	9,366	58.9	48,467	58.5	13,741	56.6
Employed[4]	65,679	91.8	8,141	86.9	45,278	93.4	12,260	89.2
Unemployed[4]	5,895	8.2	1,225	13.1	3,189	6.6	1,481	10.8
Not in civilian labor force	51,438	41.8	6,530	41.1	34,359	41.5	10,550	43.4

[1]Hispanic refers to people whose origin is Mexican, Puerto Rican, Cuban, Spanish-speaking Central or South American countries, or other Hispanic/Latino, regardless of race.
[2]Civilian labor force data for 2011 in this table differ slightly from data for 2011 published by the Bureau of Labor Statistics (BLS) due to the use by BLS of a composite estimation procedure that reduces sampling error, especially in estimates of month-to-month change. In addition, the data in this table differ from annual-average data and from seasonally adjusted data published by BLS.
[3]Includes American Indian and Alaska Native; Asian alone; Native Hawaiian and Other Pacific Islander alone; White alone, Hispanic; and Two or More Races.
[4]Percent based on persons in the civilian labor force.
SOURCE: U.S. Census Bureau, Current Population Survey, Annual Social and Economic Supplement, 2011. Internet release Date: November 2012

"The glass ceiling keeps women from reaching the highest level of corporate and public responsibility and the sticky floor keeps the vast majority of the world's women stuck in low-paid jobs" (Hunter College Women's Studies Collective, 2005). Men, on the other hand, face the glass escalator, especially in traditionally female occupations. Even if they do not seek to climb in the organizational hierarchy, occupational social forces push them up the job ladder to the higher echelons (Wingfield, 2009). Women around the world do two thirds of the work, receive 10% of the world's income, and own 1% of the world's means of production (Robbins, 2005). They make up more than 40% of the world's paid workforce but hold only about 20% of the managerial jobs, and for those, they are often compensated at lower pay than their male counterparts. Only 5% of the top corporate jobs are held by women. However, companies with women in leadership positions do realize high profits (Hunter College Women's Studies Collective 2005). See Table 8.5 for information on wages and poverty rates for women.

TABLE 8.5 POVERTY STATUS OF THE POPULATION BY SEX AND AGE, FOR BLACK ALONE AND WHITE ALONE, NOT HISPANIC: 2010

(Numbers in thousands. Civilian noninstitutionalized population.[1])

Sex, age, and poverty status [3,4]	Total		Race and Hispanic origin[2] Black alone		White alone, not Hispanic		Other[5]	
	Number	Percent	Number	Percent	Number	Percent	Number	Percent
Both sexes	305,688	100.0	38,965	100.0	197,203	100.0	69,520	100.0
Below poverty	46,180	15.1	10,675	27.4	19,599	9.9	15,905	22.9
At or above poverty	259,508	84.9	28,289	72.6	177,604	90.1	53,615	77.1
Under 18 years	74,494	100.0	11,145	100.0	40,494	100.0	22,855	100.0
Below poverty	16,401	22.0	4,362	39.1	5,002	12.4	7,037	30.8
At or above poverty	58,093	78.0	6,784	60.9	35,492	87.6	15,817	69.2
18 to 64 years	192,015	100.0	24,425	100.0	125,657	100.0	41,933	100.0
Below poverty	26,258	13.7	5,702	23.3	12,481	9.9	8,075	19.3
At or above poverty	165,757	86.3	18,723	76.7	113,176	90.1	33,857	80.7
65 years and over	39,179	100.0	3,394	100.0	31,052	100.0	4,732	100.0
Below poverty	3,520	9.0	612	18.0	2,116	6.8	793	16.7
At or above poverty	35,658	91.0	2,783	82.0	28,936	93.2	3,940	83.3
Male	150,413	100.0	18,211	100.0	97,035	100.0	35,167	100.0
Below poverty	21,012	14.0	4,643	25.5	8,741	9.0	7,628	21.7
At or above poverty	129,401	86.0	13,567	74.5	88,294	91.0	27,539	78.3
Under 18 years	38,112	100.0	5,645	100.0	20,773	100.0	11,694	100.0
Below poverty	8,454	22.2	2,242	39.7	2,532	12.2	3,680	31.5
At or above poverty	29,658	77.8	3,403	60.3	18,241	87.8	8,014	68.5
18 to 64 years	95,220	100.0	11,244	100.0	62,551	100.0	21,425	100.0
Below poverty	11,406	12.0	2,214	19.7	5,529	8.8	3,663	17.1
At or above poverty	83,814	88.0	9,030	80.3	57,022	91.2	17,761	82.9
65 years and over	17,081	100.0	1,321	100.0	13,711	100.0	2,049	100.0
Below poverty	1,153	6.7	188	14.2	680	5.0	285	13.9
At or above poverty	15,928	93.3	1,133	85.8	13,031	95.0	1,764	86.1
Female	155,275	100.0	20,754	100.0	100,168	100.0	34,352	100.0
Below poverty	25,167	16.2	6,032	29.1	10,858	10.8	8,277	24.1
At or above poverty	130,107	83.8	14,722	70.9	89,310	89.2	26,075	75.9
Under 18 years	36,382	100.0	5,500	100.0	19,721	100.0	11,160	100.0
Below poverty	7,947	21.8	2,120	38.5	2,470	12.5	3,357	30.1
At or above poverty	28,434	78.2	3,380	61.5	17,251	87.5	7,803	69.9
18 to 64 years	96,795	100.0	13,181	100.0	63,106	100.0	20,508	100.0
Below poverty	14,852	15.3	3,488	26.5	6,952	11.0	4,412	21.5
At or above poverty	81,943	84.7	9,693	73.5	56,154	89.0	16,096	78.5
65 years and over	22,098	100.0	2,073	100.0	17,341	100.0	2,684	100.0
Below poverty	2,368	10.7	424	20.5	1,436	8.3	508	18.9
At or above poverty	19,730	89.3	1,649	79.5	15,905	91.7	2,176	81.1

[1]Plus armed forces living off post or with their families on post.

[2]Hispanic refers to people whose origin is Mexican, Puerto Rican, Cuban, Spanish-speaking Central or South American countries, or other Hispanic/Latino, regardless of race.

[3]Poverty status is described in the CPS glossary of subject concepts at www.census.gov/population/www/cps/cpsdef.html.

[4]Poverty statistics exclude unrelated individuals under 15.

[5]Includes American Indian and Alaska Native; Asian alone; Native Hawaiian and Other Pacific Islander alone; White alone, Hispanic; and Two or More Races.

SOURCE: U.S. Census Bureau, Current Population Survey, Annual Social and Economic Supplement, 2011. Internet release Date: November 2012

Sexual Harassment

Sexual harassment is a common workplace problem. It is defined by federal guidelines and legal rulings and statutes as unwelcome sexual advances, requests for sexual favors, or physical conduct of a sexual nature used as a condition of employment or promotion or that interferes with an individual's job performance and creates an intimidating or hostile environment.

Although men can be, and are, sexually harassed, women are more often the targets of sexual harassment, which is often considered a form of violence against women. This gender difference exists for at least two reasons, one cultural and one structural. The cultural reason centers on the depiction of women and the socialization of men. Women are depicted by mass media as sexual objects that exist for men's pleasure. At the same time our culture socializes men to sexually assertive. These two cultural beliefs combine to make men believe that they have the right to make verbal and physical advances to women in the workplace. When these advances meet the guidelines previously mentioned, they become sexual harassment.

The second reason that most targets of sexual harassment are women is more structural. Reflecting the gendered nature of the workplace and of the educational system, typically the men doing the harassment are in a position of power over the women they harass. A male boss harasses a female employee, or a male professor harasses a female student or employee. These men realize that subordinate women may find it difficult to resist their advances for fear of reprisals.

Title IX

In 1972, the Patsy T. Mink Equal Opportunity in Education Act, commonly known as Title IX, was passed in Congress. A revolutionary document, Title IX prohibits exclusion of any person from participation in an educational program on the basis of gender. The most extreme effect, and the one that gave the act its controversial reputation, was the allocation of funding to female extracurricular activities, particularly sports.

Before 1972, very few girls were involved in sports, partly because very few organized athletic programs existed for them. In the decades since Title IX was passed, the number of female athletes has increased dramatically. While women's participation in athletics has increased, the goal of equality has still not been met. Although girls have more opportunities now than they did forty years ago, they still fail to receive equal funding for sports programs for their schools. Even though women outnumber men on college campuses, they receive 45 percent of Division I scholarship money and only 32 percent of recruiting dollars on average. Even though Title IX requires equal treatment of male and female teams, it does not require schools to spend equal amounts of money on male and female athletes (National Women's Law Center). Many school districts are reluctant to invest in sports that have historically been of little interest to the public. Every dollar that is allocated to female sports has to be taken away from male sports.

BOX 8.4

CONSIDER THE THEORETICAL PERSPECTIVES

Structural Functionalism – Functionalists view society as a system of many parts working together to form a whole. When studying gender, functionalists examine how different gender roles complement each other and help society run smoothly. If Mother does the laundry and Father mows the lawn, the house remains in good shape. Children watch and learn from their parents and step into these roles early in life. Girls are often expected to help their mothers with domestic chores while boys are primed to work outside the house (Parsons, 1942).

Gender roles can be rigid, but often complement each other. Does this help or hinder the lives of men and women?

Social Conflict – Conflict theorists are interested in the struggle for power between groups, especially economic power. In general, women are more likely to be poor than their male counterparts, a trend referred to as the feminization of poverty. This is a result of the job and wage discrimination present in the system. While it is true that globally inequality trends show that we are moving toward greater equality, studies show that all nations continue to have gender inequality in all areas of life (Dorius and Firebaugh, 2010).

According to conflict theory, those with power often use it to dominate others. Even in today's world, the majority of societal power still lies in the hands of men. Can men benefit by keeping women in a subordinate position?

Symbolic Interactionism – Symbolic interactionists look at the micro-interactions of daily life and how they influence the ways in which we perceive an issue. Do we define certain tasks as "men's" or "women's" work? If a man prepares dinner for his family, does that make him less of a man? Gender roles in today's society are much more fluid than they were 50 years ago. What has changed? Over time, societal views on household labor have been modified. How does this affect the lives of present-day men and women?

How we define the roles of men and women determines how they act in society. What does it mean if a man stays home while his wife goes to work?

VIDEO SUGGESTIONS

In My Country: An International Perspective on Gender. A resource for studying cultural attitudes related to gender, this set covers division of household labor, types of discipline for boys and girls, marriage decisions, control of money, society's view of rape, care for the elderly, and attitude toward gays. It features interviews with people from Zaire, El Salvador, St. Vincent, England, Taiwan, Sweden, Lebanon, Japan, India, China, the Fiji Islands, and Mexico. (Volume 1=45 min./Volume 2=47min.). Insight Media, 2162 Broadway, New York, NY 10024-0621. Web: www.insight-media.com

Chore Wars. Featuring commentary by John Goffman, a psychologist, and Arlie Hochschild, a sociologist and author of *The Second Shift*, this video provides insights into the sociological and emotional meaning of chores and suggests reasons why there is such a struggle over who does chores in the contemporary U.S. household. First Run/Icarus Films, 153 Waverly Place, New York, NY 10014.

Man Oh Man. Looks at socialization of men in regard to definitions of masculinity, self-worth, and gender stereotyping. 18 min. n/d. New Day Films, Dept. CA, 22-D, Hollywood Ave., Hohukus, NJ 07423. Web: www.newday.com

Men, Women, and the Sex Difference: Boys and Girls Are Different. This ABC News special featuring John Stossel looks at the question of nature versus nurture and includes interviews with parents who have tried to foster gender-neutral behavior in their children. 43 min. n/d. Films for the Humanities and Sciences, P.O. Box 2053, Princeton, NJ 08543-2053.
Web: www.films.com

Killing Us Softly 3: Advertising's Image of Women. This film examines the messages portrayed in media advertising and their relationship to women, self-image, eating disorders, and violence. 2000. 34 min. Media Education Foundation, 60 Masonic Street, Northampton, MA 01060.
Web: www.mediaed.org/

Tough Guise. This film examines the relationship between media violence and masculinity in addition to the social construction of masculinity. 82 min. or 57 min. Media Education Foundation, 60 Masonic Street, Northampton, MA 01060.
Web: www.mediaed.org/

Boys Don't Cry. (1999) The true story of the life of Brandon Teena, a transgendered teen who preferred life in a male identity until it was discovered he was born biologically female.

Transamerica. (2005) A film that provides insight into what it means to be male or female and to be caught between the two identities.

SUGGESTED READINGS

Benokraitis, N. V. *Subtle Sexism: Current Practices and Prospects for Change.* (Thousand Oaks, CA: Sage, 1997).

Higginbotham, E., and Romero, M., (eds.). *Women and Work: Exploring Race, Ethnicity, and Class.* Thousand Oaks, CA: Sage, 1997).

LeMoncheck, L., and Hajdin, M. *Sexual Harassment: A Debate.* (Lanham, MD: Rowman & Littlefield, 1997).

Lorber, Judith. 1995. Paradoxes of Gender. New Haven, CT: Yale University Press.

Journal: Gender & Society, published bimonthly by the Sociologists for Women in Society, and available from SAGE Publications, Inc., 2455 Teller Road, Thousand Oaks, CA 91320.

Messner, M. A. *Politics of Masculinity*. (Thousand Oaks, CA: Sage, 2007).

Reese, R. R. *American Paradox: Young Black Men*. (Raleigh, NC: Carolina Academic Press, 2003).

Zinn, M., Messner, M., and Hondagneu-Sotelo, P. "Gender Through the Prism of Difference (2nd ed.). (Boston: Allyn and Bacon, 2000).

BIBLIOLGRAPHY

Aulette, J.R., Wittner, J., and Blakeley, K. *Gendered Worlds*. (New York, NY: Oxford University Press, 2009).

Bandura, A. *Psychological Modeling: Conflicting Theories*. (Chicago, IL: Aldine-Atherton, 1971).

Barash, D.P. *Natural Selections: Selfish Altruists, Honest Liars, and Other Realities of Evolution*. (New York, NY: Bellevue Literary Press, 2006).

Barkan, S.E. *Criminology: A Sociological Understanding* (5th ed.). (Upper Saddle River, NJ: Prentice Hall, 2012).

Baron, L., and Straus M.A. *Four Theories of Rape in American Society: A State Level Analysis*. (New Haven, CT: Yale University Press, 1989).

Barry, K.L. *Susan B. Anthony: Biography of a Singular Feminist*. New York, NY: New York University Press, 1988).

Behling, L.L. *The masculine woman in America, 1890-1935*. (Urbana, IL: University of Illinois Press, 2001).

Begley, S. "Pink Brain, Blue Brain: Claims of Sex Differences Fall Apart." *Newsweek* 28, 2009, September 14).

Begley, S. "Don't Blame the Caveman." *Newsweek* 52-62, 2009, June 29).

Bem, S. "Gender Schema Theory: A Cognitive Account of Sex Typing." *Psychological Bulletin*. (Vol. 88: 354-364, 1981).

Benokraitis, N., and Feagin, J. *Modern Sexism: Blatant, Subtle, and Covert Discrimination*. 2nd Ed. (Englewood Cliffs, NJ: Prentice Hall, 2005).

Booth, A., and Osgood, D.W. The Influence of Testosterone on Deviance in Adulthood: Assessing and Explaining the Relationship. *Criminology, 31* (1), 93-117, 1993).

Browne, K. *Biology at Work: Rethinking Sexual Equality*. (New Brunswick, NJ: Rutgers University Press, 2002).

Bureau of Labor Statistics. Employment and Earnings Online, 2012. Retrieved from http://www.bls.gov/opub/ee/home.htm

Bureau of Labor Statistics. Employment and Earnings Online, 2012. Retrieved from http://www.bls.gov/opub/ee/home.htm

Caldera, Y., Huston, A., and O'Brien, M. "Social Interactions and Play Patterns of Parents and Toddlers with Feminine, Masculine, and Neutral Toys. *Child Development*. (Vol. 70: 70-76, 2009).

Card, N.A., Stucky, B.D., Sawalani, G.M., and Little, T.D. "Direct and Indirect Aggression During Childhood and Adolescence: A Meta-Analytic Review of Gender Differences, Inter-correlations, and Relations to Maladjustment." *Child Development, 79* (5), 1185-1229 (2008).

Dow, B.J. and Wood, J.T. (Eds) *The Sage handbook of gender and communication*. (Thousand Oaks, CA: Sage, 2006).

Engle, M.J., McFalls, J.A., Gallagher, B.J., and Curtis, K. "The attitudes of American Sociologists Toward Causal Theories of Male Homosexuality." *The American Sociologist*, (37 (1), 66-67, (2006).

Fackler, M. "Career Women in Japan Find a Blocked Path." *The New York Times*, (1-A, 2007, August 6).
Faludi, S. *Backlash: the unclaimed war against American women.* New York, NY: Crown, 1991).
Federal Bureau of Investigation. *Crime in the United States.* Washington, D.C: FBI, (2012).
Gluckman, A., and Reed, B. *Homo Economics: Capitalism, Community, and Lesbian and Gay Life.* (New York, NY: Routledge, 2007).
Hochschild, A. *The Second Shift: Working Parents and the Revolution at Home.* (New York, NY: Viking, 1989).
Hunter College Women's Studies Collective. *Women's Realities, Women's Choices: An Introduction to Women's Studies,* 3rd Ed. (New York, NY: Oxford University Press, 2012).
Hurley, S. "Sex and the Social Construction of Gender: Can Feminism and Evolutionary Psychology Be Reconciled?" In J. Browne (Ed), *TheFuture of Gender.* 98-115. (New York, NY: (Cambridge University Press, 2007).
Kimmel, M.S. and Messner, M.A. (Eds). *Men's Lives* (8th ed.). (Boston, MA: Ally and Bacon, 2010).
Klein, S.S. (Ed.). *Handbook for Achieving Gender Equity Through Education* (2nd ed.). (Mahwah, NJ: Lawrence Erlbaum Associates, 2007).
Kohlberg, L. "A Cognitive Development Analysis of Children's Sex-Role Concepts and Attitudes." (Stanford, CA: Stanford University Press, 1966).
Kohlberg, L. "Stage and Sequence: The Cognitive-Developmental Approach to Socialization." (Chicago, IL: Rand McNally, 1969).
Kohlberg, L., and Ullian, D. "Stages in the Development of Psychosexual Concepts and Attitudes." (New York, NY: Wiley, 1974)
Kramer, R., and Brewer, M. "Effects of Group Identity on Resource Use in a Simulated Commons Dilemma." *Journal of Personality and Social Psychology.* (Vol. 46: 1044-1057, 2007)
Lindsey, L.L. *Gender Roles: A Sociological Perspective* (5th ed.). (Upper Saddle River, NJ: Prentice Hall, 2011).
Maccoby, E. *The Psychology of Sex Differences.* (Stanford, CA: Stanford University Press, 1974).
Magee, P. "USM Settles with Ex-student." *Hattiesburg American.* (2009, September 22).
Magnuson, C. "Gender, Occupational Prestige, and Wages: A Test of Devaluation Theory." *European Sociological Review,* (25 (1), 87-101, 2009).
Mazur, A. "Testosterone and Violence Among Young Men." In A. Walsh and K.M. Beaver (Eds.), *Biosocial Criminology: New Directions in Theory and Research,* 190-204. (New York, NY: Routledge, 2009).
McIntosh, P. "White-privilege and Male Privilege: A personal Account of Coming to See Correspondence Through Work in Women's Studies." In M.L. Andersen and P. H. Collins (Eds.). *Race, Class and Gender: An Anthology* (6th ed.). (Belmont, CA: Wadsworth, 2007).
Mead, M. *Sex and Temperament In Three Primitive Societies.* (New York, NY: William Morrow, 1935).
Miedzian, M. *Boys will be Boys: Breaking the Link Between Masculinity and Violence.* (New York: NY: Lantern Books, 2002).
Morgan, S. (Ed.). *Gender and Anthropology: Critical Reviews for Research and Teaching.* (Washington, DC: American Anthropological Association, 1989).
Murdock, G. "Comparative Data on the Division of Labor by Sex." *Social Forces.* (15, 551-553, 1937).
Nardi, P., and Schneider. *Social Perspective on Lesbian and Gay Studies.* (New York, NY: Routledge, 1997).
National Center for Education Statistics. *The Condition of Education.* (2012) Retrieved from http://nces.ed.gov/programs/2012//Section4/indicator/34.asp

Pollack, W. *Real Boys: Rescuing our Sons from the Myths of Boyhood.* New York, NY: (Owl Books, 1999).

Rand, M. R. *Criminal Victimization, 2008.* (Washington, DC: Bureau of Justice Statistics, U.S. Department of Justice, 2009).

Randerson, J. "Cutting TV Time Makes Children Healthier, says U.S. study." *The Guardian* 2008, March 4).

Reskin, B. and Padavic, I. *Women and Men at Work* (2nd ed.). (Thousand Oakes, CA: Pine Forge Press, 2002).

Robbins, R. H. *Global problems and the culture of capitalism.* 3rd Ed. (Boston, MA: Allyn & Bacon, 2005).

Rospenda, K. M., Richman, J. A. and Shannon, C. A. "Prevalence and Mental Health Correlates of Harassment and Discrimination in the Workplace: Results from a National Study." *Journal of Interpersonal Violence,* (24 (5), 819-843, 2009).

Rust, P. "Coming Out in the Age of Social Constructionism: Sexual Identity Formation Among Lesbian and Bisexual Women." *Gender and Society.* (Vol. 7: 50-77, March, 1993).

Sadker, M., and Sadker, D. *Failing at Fairness: How America's Schools Cheat Girls.* (New York, NY: Charles Scribner's, 1994).

Scheper-Hughes, N. "The Margaret Mead Controversy: Culture, Biology and Anthropological Inquiry." *Perspectives in Cultural Anthropology.* (Albany, NY: State University of New York Press, 1987).

Schneider, L., and Silverman, A. *Global Sociology: Introducing Five Contemporary Societies* (5th ed.). (New York, NY: McGraw-Hill, 2010).

Seidman, S. "Symposium: Queer Theory/Sociology: A Dialogue." *Sociological Theory.* (Vol. 12: 178-187, July, 1994).

Serbin, L., and Sprafkin, C. "The Salience of Gender and the Process of Sex Typing in Three to Seven Year Old Children." *Child Development.* (Vol. 57: 1188-1199, 1986).

Smith, J. "The Paradox of Women's Poverty: Wage-Earning Women and Economic Transformation." *Signs.* (Vol. 10: 290-310, 2013).

Smith, R.B., and Brown, R.A. "The Impact of Social Support on Gay Male Couples." *Journal of Homosexuality.* (Vol. 33: 39-61, 2011).

Snider, M. "Mattel Gives Barbie Online Dream House," (USA Today, 2009, January 27).

Tavris, C., and Wade, C. *The Longest War.* 2nd Ed. (San Diego, CA: Harcourt Brace Jovanovich, 1984).

Walum, L. R. "The Changing Door Ceremony: Some Notes on the Operation of Sex Roles in Everyday Life." *Urban Life and Culture.* (2 (4) pp. 506-515, 1974).

West, C., and Zimmerman, D.H. "Doing Gender." *Gender and Society.* (Vol. 12: 125-151, 1987).

Wingfield, A. H. "Racializing the Glass Escalator: Reconsidering Men's Experiences with Women's Work." *Gender and Society.* (23 (5). pp 5-26, 2009).

Workman, L., and Reader, W. *Evolutionary Psychology.* (2nd Ed.) (New York, NY: Cambridge University Press, 2009).

CHAPTER 9

Race and Ethnicity

by

Gary D. Wilson

INTRODUCTION

Race refers to a category of people who share certain inherited physical characteristics such as skin color, facial features, and stature. A key question about race is whether it is more of a biological category or a social category. Most people think of race in biological terms, and for more than 300 years, or ever since white Europeans began colonizing populations of color elsewhere in the world, race has indeed served as the "premier source of human identity" (Smedley, 1998, p. 690). It is certainly easy to see that people in the United States and around the world differ physically in some obvious ways. The most noticeable difference is skin tone: some groups of people have very dark skin, while others have very light skin. Other differences also exist. Some people have very curly hair, while others have very straight hair. Some have thin lips, while others have thick lips. Some groups of people tend to be relatively tall, while others tend to relatively short. Using such physical differences as their criteria, scientists at one point identified as many as nine races: African, American Indian or Native American, Asian, Australian Aborigine, European (white), Indian, Melanesian, Micronesian, and Polynesian (Smedley, 1998).

Although people certainly do differ in many physical features that led to the development of such racial categories, anthropologists, sociologists, and many biologists question the value of these categories and thus the value of the biological concept of race (Smedley, 2007). For one thing, we often see more physical differences within a race than between races. For example, some "white" people, such as those with Scandinavian backgrounds, have very light skins, while others, such as those from some Eastern European backgrounds, have much darker skins. In fact, some "whites" have darker skin than some "blacks," or African Americans. Some whites have very straight hair, while others have very curly hair; some have blonde hair and blue eyes, while others have dark hair and brown eyes. Because of interracial reproduction going back to the days of slavery, African Americans also differ in the darkness of their skin and other physical characteristics. In fact it is estimated that about 80% of African Americans have some white ancestry; 50% of Mexican Americans have European or Native American ancestry; and 20% of whites have African or Native American ancestry. If clear racial differences ever existed hundreds or thousands of years ago, and some scientists doubt such differences ever existed, in today's world these differences have become increasingly blurred.

Another reason to question the biological concept of race is that an individual or a group of individuals is often assigned to a race on arbitrary or even illogical grounds. A century ago, for example, Irish, Italians, and Eastern European Jews who left their homelands for a better life in the United States were not regarded as white once they reached the United States but rather as different, inferior (if un-named) race (Painter, 2010). The belief in their inferiority helped justify the harsh treatment they suffered in their new country. Today, of course, we call people from all three backgrounds white or European.

The reasons for doubting the biological basis for racial categories suggest that race is more of a social category than a biological one. Another way to say this is that race is a social construction, a concept that has no objective reality but rather is what people decide it is (Berger and Luckman, 1963). In this view race has no real existence other than what and how people think of it.

This understanding of race is reflected in problems in placing people with multiracial backgrounds into any one racial category. A well-known, and now somewhat infamous, example of this issue involves golfer, Tiger Woods. Woods was typically called African American by the news media when he burst onto the golfing scene in the 1990s, but in fact his ancestry is one-half Asian (divided evenly between Chinese and Thai), one quarter white, one eighth Native American, and only one eighth African American (Leland and Beals, 1997).

If race is a social construction and since the social construction of reality suggests that things perceived as real are real in their consequences, then because people do perceive race as something real, it has real consequences. Even though so little of DNA accounts for the physical differences associated with racial differences, that low amount leads us to classify people into different races and to treat them differently, and unequally, based on their classification. Modern evidence shows that there is little scientific basis for the racial classification that is the source of so much inequality.

Ethnicity Defined

In the 1960s, words such as ethnic group, ethnic identity, and ethnicity became increasingly common in both academia, the social world, and in the mass media. The words however, are difficult to define even though most people probably believe that they know their meaning. The word *ethnic* has a long history. It is derived from the Greek word *ethnos*, meaning, nation. The reference is not to a political unity, but to the unity of persons of common blood or descent: a people. As an adjective, *ethnikos*, eventually entered Latin as *ethnicus* referring to heathens, those others who did not share the dominant faith. This is basically the meaning that the word carried when it was first used in English around the 15th century. In English, ethnic referred to someone who was neither Christian nor Jew: a pagan, or heathen. The matter of belief though, is much less important than the drawing of a boundary. Ethnic clearly referred to others, to those who were not us (Just, 1989). By the 20th century, the meaning of the word had changed again but some of the original Greek conception re-emerged. The specific reference to religion was gone but the emphasis on other, not us, was emphasized. Only others, and certainly not us, could be ethnics. Ethnicity then, became a way of defining others, and ourselves at the same time, and thus, became a widely used sociological concept.

TABLE 9.1 RACE DISTRIBUTION OF THE POPULATION BY SEX AND REGION: 2011

(Numbers in thousands. Civilian noninstitutionalized population.[1])

Sex and region[3]	Total		Race and Hispanic origin[2]					
			Black alone		White alone, not Hispanic		Other[4]	
	Number	Percent	Number	Percent	Number	Percent	Number	Percent
Both sexes	306,110	100.0	39,031	12.8	197,423	64.5	69,656	22.8
Northeast	54,782	100.0	6,789	12.4	38,220	69.8	9,774	17.8
Midwest	66,104	100.0	6,765	10.2	52,204	79.0	7,135	10.8
South	113,275	100.0	21,894	19.3	68,190	60.2	23,191	20.5
West	71,949	100.0	3,583	5.0	38,809	53.9	29,557	41.1
Male	150,643	100.0	18,237	12.1	97,166	64.5	35,241	23.4
Northeast	26,713	100.0	3,141	11.8	18,675	69.9	4,897	18.3
Midwest	32,506	100.0	3,146	9.7	25,632	78.9	3,727	11.5
South	55,465	100.0	10,180	18.4	33,597	60.6	11,689	21.1
West	35,959	100.0	1,770	4.9	19,262	53.6	14,928	41.5
Female	155,466	100.0	20,794	13.4	100,256	64.5	34,416	22.1
Northeast	28,069	100.0	3,648	13.0	19,545	69.6	4,876	17.4
Midwest	33,599	100.0	3,619	10.8	26,572	79.1	3,408	10.1
South	57,810	100.0	11,714	20.3	34,593	59.8	11,502	19.9
West	35,989	100.0	1,814	5.0	19,547	54.3	14,629	40.6

[1]Plus armed forces living off post or with their families on post.
[2]Hispanic refers to people whose origin is Mexican, Puerto Rican, Cuban, Spanish-speaking Central or South American countries, or other Hispanic/Latino, regardless of race.
[3]Regions are described in the CPS glossary of subject concepts at www.census.gov/population/www/cps/cpsdef.html.
[4]Includes American Indian and Alaska Native; Asian alone; Native Hawaiian and Other Pacific Islander alone; White alone, Hispanic; and Two or More Races.
SOURCE: U.S. Census Bureau, Current Population Survey, Annual Social and Economic Supplement, 2011. Internet release Date: November 2012

Majority and Minority Groups

Different racial and ethnic groups can be classified as majority or minority groups. For example, in 2010, whites made up 63.7 percent of the U.S. population (U.S. Census Bureau, 2010). This makes them a majority group that not only has a greater numerical representation in society but also holds significant power and privilege. A *minority group* refers to any group that holds less power than the majority group. Minorities often experience unequal treatment compared to the dominant group, giving them a collective sense of being discriminated against (Wirth, 1945). See Table 9.1 for information regarding race distribution in the United States.

With the aid of migration patterns, minority groups are gaining greater representation within the U.S. population. More than half of the growth in the total population of the United States between 2000 and 2010 was the result of the increase in the number of Latinos. The Latino population grew by 43 percent, while the non-Latino population grew by only 5 percent. This pattern of growth is expected to continue in the next 10 years (U.S. Census Bureau, 2010).

Several factors characterize minority groups and their relations with dominant groups in society (Dworkin and Dworkin, 1999):

1. Minority groups can be distinguished from the group that holds power by factors that make them different – physical appearance, dress, language, or religion.

2. Minority groups are excluded or denied full participation in society in economic, political, educational, religious health, and recreational institutions.

3. Minority groups have less access to power and resources within the nation and are evaluated less favorably based on their characteristics as minority group members.

4. Minority groups are stereotyped, ridiculed, condemned, or otherwise defamed, allowing dominant group members to justify and not feel guilty about unequal and poor treatment.

5. Minority group members develop collective identities to insulate themselves from the unaccepting world; this in turn perpetuates their group identity by creating ethnic or racial enclaves, intragroup marriages, and segregated group institutions such as religious congregations.

While there has historically been, and continues to be, much conflict and division associated with ethnic and racial diversity, that was not the whole story in the 20th century. Ethnic and racial diversity and identity were also sources of pride, unity and achievement. The United States often celebrated its immigrant origins and the cultural pluralism that resulted (Kallen, 1924). Various groups proudly celebrated their own cultures and identities even as they struggled to live the American Dream. The Kwanzaa festival became an annual African American celebration. In corporations, on college campuses, and in major cities, leaders dealing with ethnic and racial issues argued that diversity should be an asset, not a liability. The U.S. women's gymnastics team exemplified ethnic diversity when they won a gold medal at the 1996 Olympic Games in Atlanta. The team included an Asian American, an African American, and white girls with names like Miller and Moceanu, (Lexington, 1996). The team itself was viewed as a great American accomplishment and a source of pride.

The rise of multiculturalism and its focus on the positive aspects of diversity showed little sign of changing at the start of the 21st century. The horrors of September 11, 2001, changed all of that by placing the Arab population of the United States on the defensive. Arab Americans, many of whom were born and raised in places from Detroit to Los Angeles and with no direct experience with the Middle East, suddenly became the targets of suspicion and ridicule in their communities. Four years later, Hurricane Katrina exposed a stark racial divide in New Orleans, bringing attention once again to the default penalties associated with being Black in the United States.

There was much hope that ethnicity and race would become obsolete as sources of division and conflict in the modern world. Many social scientists predicted such change. Robert Park, in 1926, observed that certain forces were at work in the world that seemed likely to dismantle the prejudices and boundaries that separated races and people. Park argued that powerful global factors including trade, migration, new

communication technologies, and even motion pictures, were bringing about a vast "interpenetration of peoples" (Park, 1926: 150). Such factors, Park suggested, "enforce new contacts and result in new forms of competition and of conflict, but out of this confusion and ferment, new and more intimate forms of association arise" (Park, 1926: 150). Park wrote,

> In the relations of races there is a cycle of events which tends everywhere to repeat itself. The race relations cycle which takes the form, to state it abstractly, of contrasts, competition, accommodation and eventual assimilation, is apparently progressive and irreversible (Park, 1926: 150).

Park wrote at a time when the term "race" included categories that are no longer issues of concern. His conception of "races" treated separately, for example, the Slavic peoples, Jews, Chinese, Japanese, Puerto Ricans, Portuguese, and others (Park, 1934). Current classifications emphasize ethnic groups and combine them into inclusive racial categories: Japanese and Chinese as Asians, for example, and Slavic peoples and Portuguese as Whites.

There is a clear sense of transformation embedded in Park's ideas. The forces of history appeared to be having an effect on the process and the rest of the 20th century would only serve to accelerate the process. The impact would integrate people and lead to universal participation in a common life and culture. According to Park, "if America was once in any exclusive sense the melting pot of races, it is no longer. The melting pot is the world," (Park, 1934, 149).

Not everyone agreed with Park and none was more vocal than W.E.B DuBois, who in 1905 claimed that the color line would be the paramount problem of humankind in the 20th century (DuBois, 1903). But most sociologists seemed to subscribe to Park's view of the future. The melting pot, at both local and global levels, would work to forge new arrangements; ethnic and racial bonds would be forgotten; and the peoples of the world would be integrated into a broad stream of shared cultures and social relations. "Everywhere there is competition and conflict; but everywhere the intimacies which participation in a common life enforces have created new accommodation, and relations which once were merely formal or utilitarian have become personal and human" (Park, 1926: 149). For additional information on W.E.B DuBois see box 9.1.

Park's life experiences and observations influenced his thinking. He and his colleagues at the University of Chicago studied the immigrant population in North America as streams of migrants from the various countries of Europe poured into the growing cities and labor markets of the rapidly industrializing United States. They observed that over time and across generations, the migrants learned English, sent their children to school, struggled for economic and political success, spread across the continent, replaced customs from the old country with customs from the new, and even began to marry across the ethnic boundaries that originally separated them. These early students of European immigration frequently found evidence of Park's proposed sequence: contact with other groups; competition and conflict among them over territory and opportunities; eventual accommodation to one another's presence, character, and interests; and gradual assimilation as newcomers began to participate more and more in the dominant society and its institutions and came to share in "a common culture and a common historical life" (Park, 1926: 149).

The expectation that ethnic and racial attachments would decline was even supported by classical sources of sociological thought. Karl Marx's radical historical vision saw capitalism as the tool that would eventually eliminate ties of nationality or tribe by replacing them with the iron bonds of class which would link people to each other on the basis of their positions in the process of economic production. In the 1960s, a body of work developed in the social sciences that supported Marx's predictions that class interests would become the foundation of collective identity and political consciousness. As capitalism developed around the world, other sources of group ties such as language, religion, and national origin would become

BOX 9.1

FOCUS ON W.E.B. DU BOIS

William Edward Burghardt Du Bois (pronounced "Due-Boyss") was born February, 23, 1868, and died August 27, 1963. DuBois was born just after the Civil War and died as the Vietnam War was well under way. He was born a few years after the defeat of slavery, and died the night before Martin Luther King, Jr., delivered his famous "I Have a Dream" speech. Du Bois received a B.A. in 1888, from Fisk University, a second B.A. from Harvard in 1890, and an M.A. from Harvard in 1892. He went on to earn a Ph.D. from Harvard in 1895. He was an Assistant Instructor of Sociology at the University of Pennsylvania from 1896 to 1897 (though he was barred from teaching any classes!). He was Chair of the Sociology Department at Atlanta University from 1934 to 1944. DuBois was a prolific writer, publishing more than twenty books and thousands of essays and articles throughout his life.

He was a prominent founder of the National Association for the Advancement of Colored People (NAACP) and served as its chairman for many years. He publicly fought against lynching, discrimination, and colonial exploitation. A socialist (and later communist), he fought for women's rights, Jewish rights, and workers' rights. Not only was he a principal architect of the civil rights movement, but he also supported the arts and various critical cultural expressions as a founder of the American Negro Academy and one of the supporting pillars of the Harlem Renaissance. Du Bois was a pioneer of urban sociology. Du Bois's *The Philadelphia Negro: A Social Study* is, in the words of Charles Lemert "the first great work of American urban ethnography." Julius Lester dubbed it "the first sociological study done in America."

Du Bois was one of the nation's first criminologists and he was the first American sociologist of religion. DuBois was also the first sociologist of race. Du Bois was one of the earliest proponents of sociology in the United States, publicly advocating its strengths and establishing a department of sociology at Atlanta University at a time when the discipline was still met with substantial suspicion. "Sociology," he argued, "cannot be characterized merely as a science of human action. Nor is it to be understood as simply a field which takes as its subject of study a certain metaphysical entity called society" (Dubois, 1935).

Du Bois emphasized sociology's concern with social problems; he defined a social problem as "the failure of an organized social group to realize its group ideals, through the inability to adopt a certain desired line of action to given social conditions." "Sociology," he insisted, "must bridge this chasm between generalizations and facts. It must bring theory and practice nearer together, and in so doing, discover if indeed there is rhythm and law in the mass of the deeds of men and if so how can it best be measured and stated" (DuBois, 1935).

DuBois's sociological work was thickly permeated with original research resulting from participant observation, questionnaire and survey data, ethnographic field work, interviews, and content analyses of archival material, census information, and government documents. DuBois's sociological output was characterized by a hands-on, empirical research methodology. He studied, documented, and theorized about what many would rather ignore or sidestep: "racism, that disturbing disease of American culture so readily denied and dismissed by those it infects" (Dubois, 1935). In recent years Du Bois has finally gained the attention of a wider (and whiter) audience.

Similar to Emile Durkheim, Du Bois resisted narrow psychological or biological explanations of human behavior, choosing instead to emphasize the enormous impact social institutions and historical circumstances have in shaping individual actions and beliefs. Du Bois argued throughout his writings that racial inequality is not to be explained as a result of innate differences or genetic predispositions, but rather as the result of social, economic, historical, and political forces. Du Bois disallowed any inherent or inherited racial superiority of white over black. Du Bois similarly emphasized the social in religious life, stressing the importance of group ties and communal bonding as being central to the religious enterprise.

Du Bois's writing was often social-psychological in nature. *The Souls of Black Folk* spoke of the peculiar identity of a black man in white America:

> . . . a world which yields him no true self-consciousness, but only lets him see himself through the revelation of the other world. It is a peculiar sensation, this double-consciousness, this sense of always looking at one's self through the eyes of others, of measuring one's soul by the tape of a world that looks on in amused contempt and pity. One ever feels his twoness,-an American, a Negro; two souls, two thoughts, two unrecognized strivings; two warring ideals in one dark body, whose dogged strength alone keeps it from being torn asunder (Dubois, 1935).

"Double-consciousness" is one of Du Bois's most famous concepts, which artfully articulates the notion not only that identity is often fractured by numerous social identities and social roles within one being but also that these social identities and roles can sometimes even be at odds with one another.

In the tradition of Max Weber, Du Bois infused his sociological writings with detailed historical analysis. Both Weber and Du Bois emphasized the ability of ideals and beliefs to influence and affect social life. Weber focused on the role particular Protestant Calvinist beliefs played in the development of modern Western capitalism. Throughout his work, Du Bois focused on the role racist beliefs and ideas held by the powerful white majority played in the real-life oppressive experiences of blacks. Both Weber and Du Bois wrote about the dynamics of power, stratification, conflict, and domination.

Du Bois's social theory is directly linked to the work of Karl Marx, usually in explicit and direct ways. He generally agreed with Marx that underlying economic conditions and how people organize themselves in relationship to the means of production and distribution shape and often institutionalize components of a given society:

> ". . . the wealth which the working masses produce and which is supplied by nature, has been and is being dishonestly taken from them by forced sale of their labor at less than its real value; this reduces the laborer to poverty while the surplus value of their work thus exploited goes to increase the wealth and power of the employing class" (DuBois, 1935).

Like Marx, Du Bois believed that a truly just society could be realized only if democracy was extended to the realm of industry; raw materials, tools, technology and land. According to Dubois, "political power is curtailed by organized capital in industry and that in this industry, democracy does not prevail; and that until wider democracy does prevail in industry, democracy in government is seriously curtailed and often quite ineffective" (Du Bois, 1935).

Du Bois recognized that racial distinctions and racial constructs are supremely important and crucially central to how human beings experience the world. Du Bois linked racial analysis with class analysis. Du Bois systematically dealt with the intertwined nature of class and race. He believed that race is ultimately a social construction, involving matters of economics, history, politics, heritage, and culture much more than simple biology or physicality. Race could not be reduced to merely a scientific category or biological determinant.

One of the most militant male feminists of the early twentieth century, he did not always incorporate gender into his analysis to a degree we might expect of a social theorist today. Du Bois was, in the words of Martin Luther King, Jr. "a tireless explorer gifted discoverer of social truths" (King, 1963). In *The Sociological Imagination*, C. Wright Mills offered the ideal portrait of a sociologist. The ideal sociologist, according to Mills, is one who consistently recognizes the intersections of biography within history and society. The ideal sociologist is one who avoids grand theorizing for the mere sake of grand theorizing, and who resists conveying his or her thoughts in obtuse, obscure language. The ideal sociologist is one who avoids abstract empiricism, collecting facts and figures outside of a critical theoretical framework. The work of the ideal sociologist is comparative, historical, and interdisciplinary. The ideal sociologist utilizes empirical data within a clear theoretical vision marked by an ever-present sensitivity to social justice. The ideal sociologist is one who, through a careful coupling of research and theory, strives to make the world a better place. Du Bois fits Mill's ideal perfectly.

Source: NAACP, 2013

insignificant. Groups would discover that their true interests were defined by their positions in productive processes or markets and would reorganize along class lines.

Another classical voice, Max Weber, agreed that ethnicity would decline in importance. For Weber though, the rationalization of human action and organization was the hallmark of modernity. Ethnicity, in contrast, was a communal relationship. It was based not on the rational calculation of interest, but on subjective feelings among group members "that they belong together" (Weber, 1968: 40). Weber predicted that as modernity and rationalization progressed communal relationships would be displaced. Only where "rationally regulated action is not widespread" would such relationships remain compelling (Weber, 1968: 389). Weber's and Marx's ideas had similar implications even though they were very different. Both predicted that over time ethnicity and race would decline as significant social forces in the modern world.

See Box 9.2 for information regarding debates of English Only Laws.

ENGLISH ONLY LAWS

BOX 9.2

Proponents of "English Only" laws say these policies encourage assimilation. The American Civil Liberties Union, however, argues that such laws harm immigrants by restricting or cutting funding for multi-lingual programs that some U.S. residents cannot do without, such as health services, voting assistance, and driver's licensing tests, (ACLU, 2008).

Social policies dealing with assimilation, such as the so-called "English Only" laws draw passionate responses from both sides of the issue. What does each side have to say?

Pro	Con
Having an official language unites the country by giving us commonality.	"English Only" laws are anti-immigrant because they make it harder for immigrants to obtain driver's licenses, find work, and so forth.
Having an official language provides an incentive for new immigrants to assimilate.	The fear of losing English as the national language is unfounded. U.S. Census Bureau projections suggest that by 2050, approximately 24% of the U.S. population will be Latino. Even if all these people were to speak only Spanish, it still means that almost three-fourths of Americans would speak English.
"English Only" laws potentially save costs because government documents will no longer need to be printed in multiple languages.	Such laws can be used to weaken the educational opportunities of non-English-speaking children.
With waves of immigration, such laws ensure that the history of the country, and its language, remains intact.	
Such laws are unnecessary – people must learn English in order to work, shop, and interact with society anyway.	

Source: ACLU, 2012

Prejudice and Discrimination

When minority groups are present within a society, *prejudice* influences dominant-minority group relations. Prejudice refers to attitudes that prejudge a group, usually negatively and based on facts. Prejudiced individuals lump together people with certain characteristics as an undifferentiated group without considering individual differences. While prejudice can be stimulated by events such as conflicts at the institutional level and war at the societal level, attitudes are held by individuals and can be best understood as a micro-level phenomenon.

When prejudiced attitudes are manifested in actions, they are referred to as discrimination. *Discrimination* includes differential treatment and harmful actions against minorities. These actions at the micro level might include refusal to sell someone a house because of their religion, race, or ethnicity of the buyer or employment practices that treat groups differently based on minority status (Feagin and Feagin, 2007).

If race is an invention of society, a social construction, then why does discrimination happen? John Dollard suggests that frustration leads to prejudice (Dollard, 1939). In situations in which we feel powerless, we tend to scapegoat, or unfairly accuse, another group as being the cause of our problem. Blaming a racial or ethnic minority for issues such as poverty or unemployment will not increase one's salary, but it might keep one from having to accept blame for his or her situation. Generally, studies support the idea that prejudice is learned so assuming that prejudice is a learned behavior, it can also be unlearned (Tatum, 1987).

Explanations of Prejudice

What is the source of racial and ethnic prejudices? Why are some people more prejudiced than others? Scholars have tried to answer these questions at least since the 1940s, when the horrors of Nazism were still fresh in people's minds. For information on one of the most notorious members of the Nazi Party see Box 9.3 – Focus on Amon Goth.

One of the first social-psychological explanations of prejudice focused on the *authoritarian personality* (Adorno, 1950). According to this view, authoritarian personalities develop in childhood in response to parents who practice harsh discipline. Individuals with authoritarian personalities emphasize such things as obedience to authority, a rigid adherence to convention, and low acceptance of people they perceive as different from themselves. Many studies find strong racial and ethnic prejudice among such individuals (Sibley and Duckitt, 2008). But whether their prejudice stems from their authoritarian personalities or instead from the fact that their parents were probably prejudiced themselves remains an important question.

According to *frustration-aggression* theory, many of the perpetrators of racially motivated violent actions feel angry and frustrated because they cannot achieve their work or other goals. They blame any vulnerable minority group – religious, ethnic, sexual-orientation – and members of that group become targets of their anger. Frustration-aggression theory focuses largely on poorly adjusted people who displace their frustration with aggressive attacks on others. Hate groups evolve from like-minded individuals, often because of prejudice and frustration.

When it is impossible to vent one's frustration on the real target, this frustration can take the form of aggressive action against minority group members, who are vulnerable because of their low social status. They become *scapegoats*. The word scapegoat comes from the Bible, Leviticus 16:5-22. Once a year, a goat (which was obviously innocent) was laden with parchments on which people had written their sins. The

FOCUS ON AMON GÖTH

BOX 9.3

Amon Leopold Göth was born on 11 December 1908 in Vienna. He was married twice, divorced in 1934 and again in 1944. He had two children. He studied agriculture in Vienna until 1928, then from 1928 until 1939 he was employed by the company of 'Verlag fur Militar und Fachliteratur' in Vienna. Göth joined the NSDAP in 1932 and the SS in 1940. In March of 1940 he was drafted into the Wehrmacht, with the rank of Unterfeldwebl. He was promoted in succession to SS-Obersturmfuhrer in 1940, and Untersturmfuhrer with the letter "F" denoting professional officer in war time, in 1941. The final rank Göth obtained was SS-Hauptsturmfuhrer in 1944, and he was a holder of the Cross of Merit with swords. After serving at Cieszyn and the Volksdeutsche Mittlestelle in Kattowice, Goth was transferred to Odilo Globocnick's staff in Lublin in June 1942, for participation in "Judenumseidlung". (Jewish Deportations). In February 1943 he left Lublin after conflict with SS Major Hermann Hofle, Globocnik's, Chief of Staff for Aktion Reinhard, and was transferred to Krakow with the rank of SS-Unterscharfuhrer, as the Commandant of Plaszow Labour camp. Göth's service in Krakow was from February 1943 until September 1944. It was clear that Göth had arrived in Krakow with a brief to destroy the remaining Jews of Krakow. In order to exterminate the Jews of Krakow, the Germans chose a most symbolic site – the new Jewish cemetery on the outskirts of the city, in the suburb of Plaszow. There huts were constructed in desecration of the freshly-dug graves and a sign was hung up 'Arbeitslager' (Labour Camp).

According to survivor's accounts he was, "A hideous and terrible monster who reached the height of more than two meters. He set the fear of death in people, terrified masses and accounted for much chattering of teeth. He ran the camp through extremes of cruelty that are beyond the comprehension of a compassionate mind – employing tortures which dispatched his victims to hell." (USHMM, 2012). For even the slightest infraction of the rules he would rain blow after blow upon the face of the helpless offender, and would observe with satisfaction born of sadism, how the cheek of his victim would swell and turn blue, how the teeth would fall out and the eyes would fill with tears. Anyone who was being whipped by him was forced to count in a loud voice, each stroke of the whip and if he made a mistake was forced to start counting over again. During interrogations, which were conducted in his office, he would set his dog on the accused, whom was strung by his legs from a specially placed hook in the ceiling. In the event of an escape from the camp, he would order the entire group, from which the escapee had come, to form a row, would give the order to count ten and would, personally kill every tenth person. At one morning parade, in the presence of all the prisoners he shot a Jew, because, as he complained, the man was too tall. Then as the man lay dying he urinated on him. Once he caught a boy who was sick with diarrhea and was unable to restrain himself. Göth forced him to eat all the excrement and then shot him." Another survivor reported that women prisoners were also treated very harshly by Göth: "My sister was in a group of women sitting, breaking tombstones into tiny pieces for building roads. Another older woman was working with them, when Göth appeared and told the older woman she was not doing it right. Göth showed her how to do it. When the older woman returned to her work, Göth shot her" (USHMM, 2012).

Göth played a leading role in the destruction of a number of Jewish Ghettos, including the Rzeszow Ghetto in 1942, where the Jews were deported to the death camp at Belzec, the Krakow ghetto on 13 – 14 March 1943, where he personally shot about 50 children and he supervised the liquidation of the Tarnow Ghetto in early September 1943. 10,000 Jews were deported to Plaszow, and 4000 were killed. During the liquidation of the Tarnow Ghetto, he shot a girl who asked him for a transfer to a different working group to be together with her fiancé. Leon Leser, testified at Göth's trial: There was Ghetto 'A' for those working and Ghetto' B' for those that were unemployed. Göth ordered everyone employed from Ghetto 'A' to go to Ghetto 'B' and assemble there in groups, according to their employer. Every group had a board indicating the name of the employer. Then Göth selected a group of 300 persons as a Sauberungskolonne (clearing up column). The Jews assembled once again separately. At that point a fiancé of one of the Jewish men approached Göth, her name was Batista, begging him to allow her to stay with her fiancé, who was remaining. He refused, she begged him once again, he ordered her to turn around and fired into her head. She fell dead and after that he separated all the people again, he took out those that should go to Plaszow, and those that were left behind remained on the Magdeburger Square."

During the clearance of the Tarnow Ghetto, Göth misappropriated Jewish property, furniture, furs, clothing, jewelry, tobacco and alcohol, which were later found by the Gestapo in storage, at Brunnlitz. Also at Brunnlitz was Göth's mistress, Ruth Irene Kalder, also known as 'Majola.' Göth also supervised the progressive liquidation of the forced labor camp in Szebnie near Jaslo. The liquidation began in September of 1943 with the killing of 700 Jewish prisoners who were driven in trucks to a forest in Tarnowiec, 3km from the camp, where they were shot. This action was carried out by SS-Hauptscharfuhrer Grzymek and supervised by the commandant Kellermann, acting on Göth's orders. Göth also prepared under the leadership of Willi Haase, plans for the liquidation of ghettos in Bochnia, Rzeszow and Przemysl. In September of 1944 Göth was arrested by the SS und Polizeigericht VI (Police Court) in Krakow for large- scale fraud.

Göth was also interrogated by the Sicherheitspolizei (Security Police) for giving information to the engineer, Grunberg, about the liquidation of the Krakow Ghetto. Grunberg, a German, was sympathetic to the Jews and closely associated with Stern, Pemper and Schindler. He passed the information on to Schindler, who in turn warned the ghetto leaders. Göth was released from prison in January of 1945, due to his diabetes and was moved to a sanatorium in Bad Tolz. There he was arrested by the Americans. The Americans agreed to the request to extradite Göth to Poland following a request by the Polish authorities and Göth was tried before the Polish Supreme Court on charges of committing mass murder during the liquidations of the ghettos in Krakow and Tarnow and the camps at Plaszow and Szebnie. He was sentenced to death in Krakow in September of 1946 and hanged in the former camp at Plaszow, defiantly saluting Hitler.

Source: Former Camp Plaszow website – www.cekie.krakow.pl/oboz_plaszow

goat was then sent out to the desert to die. This was part of a ritual of purification, and the creature took the blame for others.

Scapegoating occurs when a minority group is blamed for the failures of others. It is difficult to look at oneself to seek reasons for failure but easy to transfer the blame for one's failure to others. Individuals who feel they are failures in their jobs or other aspects of their lives may blame minority groups. From within such a prejudiced mindset even violence toward the out-group becomes acceptable.

Today, jobs and promotions are harder for young adults to obtain than they were for the baby boom generation, but the reason is mostly demographic. The baby boom of the 1940s and 1950s resulted in a bulge in the population. There are so many people in the workforce at each successive step on the ladder that it will be another few years before those baby boomers retire in large numbers. Until that happens, there will be a good deal of frustration about the apparent occupational stagnation. It is easier, and safer, to blame minorities or affirmative action programs than to vent frustration at the next oldest segment of the population or at one's grandparents for having a large family. Blacks, Hispanics, and other minorities become easy scapegoats.

Although these theories help to explain some situations, they do not predict when frustration will lead to aggression or explain why only some people who experience frustration vent their feelings on the vulnerable and why some groups become targets (Marger, 2009).

Ethnocentrism and Ethnic Enclaves

Anti-immigrant sentiment is often justified through ethnocentric thinking. *Ethnocentrism* is thinking about or defining another culture on the basis of one's own culture. Most of us are ethnocentric in some way. We view the world from our point of view and generally see groups with greater differences from us more negatively.

Facing discrimination often encourages a sense of solidarity among members of a single racial or ethnic group. In a sense, being "outsiders" bonds people together in *ethnic enclaves*, neighborhoods where people from similar cultures live together, for three main reasons:

1. Their differences from the dominant group often lead to discrimination;

2. The shared values of similar people make adjustment easier; and

3. Their social capital increases their chances of success, (Brooks, 1993).

This means that a person who enters a new country with very little money, few resources, and limited knowledge of the new culture can increase his or her chances of success by living in an enclave. This has always been the case in the United States as new immigrants seek out locations with others from their same country. Of course, belonging to a group that looks like the dominant group tends to decrease discrimination. Yet, many groups who are now considered "white" initially suffered from discrimination. Groups such as Italians, Germans, Poles, and Russians were all at one time or another singled out for discrimination. In response to this, such people often let go of their ethnic heritage because their appearance makes it easier to assimilate into the dominant culture. See Boxes 9.4 and 9.5 for information on celebrations of ethnic heritage.

BOX 9.4

HISPANIC HERITAGE MONTH: SEPT. 15 - OCT. 15

In September 1968, Congress authorized President Lyndon B. Johnson to proclaim National Hispanic Heritage Week, observed during the week that included Sept. 15 and Sept. 16. The observance was expanded in 1989 by Congress to a month long celebration (Sept. 15 - Oct. 15), America celebrates the culture and traditions of those who trace their roots to Spain, Mexico and the Spanish-speaking nations of Central America, South America and the Caribbean.

Sept. 15 was chosen as the starting point for the celebration because it is the anniversary of independence of five Latin American countries: Costa Rica, El Salvador, Guatemala, Honduras and Nicaragua. In addition, Mexico and Chile celebrate their independence days on Sept. 16 and Sept. 18, respectively.

Population

53 million

The Hispanic population of the United States as of July 1, 2012, making people of Hispanic origin the nation's largest ethnic or racial minority. Hispanics constituted 17 percent of the nation's total population.
Source: 2012 Population Estimates

1.1 million

Number of Hispanics added to the nation's population between July 1, 2011, and July 1, 2012. This number is close to half of the approximately 2.3 million people added to the nation's population during this period.
Source: 2012 Population Estimates

128.8 million

The projected Hispanic population of the United States in 2060. According to this projection, the Hispanic population will constitute 31 percent of the nation's population by that date. Source: Population Projections

2nd

Ranking of the size of the U.S. Hispanic population worldwide, as of 2010. Only Mexico (112 million) had a larger Hispanic population than the United States (50.5 million).
Source: International Data Base

65%

The percentage of Hispanic-origin people in the United States who were of Mexican background in 2011. Another 9.4 percent were of Puerto Rican background, 3.8 percent Salvadoran, 3.6 percent Cuban, 3.0 percent Dominican and 2.3 percent Guatemalan. The remainder was of some other Central American, South American or other Hispanic/Latino origin.
Source: U.S. Census Bureau, 2011 American Community Survey: Table B03001

States and Counties

Florida

The state with the highest median age, 34, within the Hispanic population.
Source: 2012 Population Estimates
State Characteristics: Median Age by Race and Hispanic Origin

10 million

The estimated population for those of Hispanic-origin in Texas as of July 1, 2012.
Source: 2012 Population Estimates
State Characteristics: Population by Sex, Race, and Hispanic Origin

8

The number of states with a population of 1 million or more Hispanic residents in 2012 — Arizona, California, Colorado, Florida, Illinois, New Jersey, New York and Texas.
Source: 2012 Population Estimates

More than 50%

The percent of all the Hispanic population that lived in California, Florida, and Texas as of July 1, 2012. Source: 2012 Population Estimates

47%

The percentage of New Mexico's population that was Hispanic as of July 1, 2012, the highest of any state.
Source: 2012 Population Estimates
State Characteristics: Population by Race and Hispanic Origin

14.5 million

The Hispanic population of California. This is the largest Hispanic population of any state as well as the largest numeric increase within the Hispanic population since July 1, 2011 (232,000).
Source: 2012 Population Estimates

4.8 million

The Hispanic population of Los Angeles County, Calif., in 2012. This is the highest of any county and the largest numeric increase since 2012 (55,000).
Source: 2012 Population Estimates

21

Number of states in which Hispanics were the largest minority group. These states were Arizona, California, Colorado, Connecticut, Florida, Idaho, Illinois, Iowa, Kansas, Massachusetts, Nebraska, Nevada, New Hampshire, New Jersey, New Mexico, Oregon, Rhode Island, Texas, Utah, Washington and Wyoming.
Source: American FactFinder: United States DP-1

Families and Children

11.6 million
The number of Hispanic family households in the United States in 2012.
Source: Families and Living Arrangements

62.3%
The percentage of Hispanic family households that were married couple households in 2012.
Source: Families and Living Arrangements

60.4%
The percentage of Hispanic married-couple households that had children younger than 18 present in 2012.
Source: Families and Living Arrangements

65.7%
Percentage of Hispanic children living with two parents in 2012.
Source: Families and Living Arrangements

45.3%
Percentage of Hispanic married couples with children under 18 where both spouses were employed in 2012.Source: Families and Living Arrangements

Spanish Language

37.6 million
The number of U.S. residents 5 and older who spoke Spanish at home in 2011. This is a 117 percent increase since 1990 when it was 17.3 million. Those who hablan español en casa constituted 12.9 percent of U.S. residents 5 and older. More than half of these Spanish speakers spoke English "very well." Source: U.S. Census Bureau, 2011 American Community Survey

74.3%
Percentage of Hispanics 5 and older who spoke Spanish at home in 2011.
Source: U.S. Census Bureau, 2011 American Community Survey

Income, Poverty and Health Insurance

$38,624
The median income of Hispanic households in 2011.
Source: Income, Poverty, and Health Ins. Coverage in the United States: 2011

25.3%
The poverty rate among Hispanics in 2011, down from 26.5 percent in 2010.
Source: Income, Poverty, and Health Insurance Coverage in the United States: 2011

30.1%

The percentage of Hispanics who lacked health insurance in 2011.

Source: Income, Poverty, and Health Insurance Coverage in the United States: 2011

Education

63.2%

The percentage of Hispanics 25 and older that had at least a high school education in 2011.

Source: American Community Survey: 2011 Table S0201 (crossed with Hispanic origin)

13.2%

The percentage of the Hispanic population 25 and older with a bachelor's degree or higher in 2011.

Source: American Community Survey: 2011 Table S0201 (crossed with Hispanic origin)

3.7 million

The number of Hispanics 25 and older who had at least a bachelor's degree in 2011.

Source: American Community Survey: 2011 Table S0201 (crossed with Hispanic origin)

1.2 million

Number of Hispanics 25 and older with advanced degrees in 2011 (e.g., master's, professional, doctorate).

Source: American Community Survey: 2011 Table S0201 (crossed with Hispanic origin)

14.5%

Percentage of students (both undergraduate and graduate students) enrolled in college in 2011 who were Hispanic.

Source: School Enrollment Data Current Population Survey: October 2011

22.5%

Percentage of elementary and high school students that were Hispanic in 2011.

Source: School Enrollment Data Current Population Survey: October 2011

Jobs

67.4%

Percentage of Hispanics or Latinos 16 and older who were in the civilian labor force in 2011.

Source: U.S. Census Bureau, 2011 American Community Survey

19.2%

The percentage of civilian employed Hispanics or Latinos 16 and older who worked in management, business, science, and arts occupations in 2011.

Source: U.S. Census Bureau, 2011 American Community Survey

Voting

8.4%

The percentage of voters in the 2012 presidential election who were Hispanic. Hispanics comprised 7 percent of voters in 2010.

Source: News Release: Census Bureau Reports Hispanic Voter Turnout Reaches Record High for Congressional Election and Voting and Registration in the Election of November 2012: Table 2

Serving our Country

1.2 million

The number of Hispanics or Latinos 18 and older who are veterans of the U.S. armed forces.

Source: U.S. Census Bureau, 2011 American Community Survey

BOX 9.5

BLACK (AFRICAN-AMERICAN) HISTORY MONTH: FEBRUARY

To commemorate and celebrate the contributions to our nation made by people of African descent, American historian Carter G. Woodson established Black History Week. The first celebration occurred on Feb. 12, 1926. For many years, the second week of February was set aside for this celebration to coincide with the birthdays of abolitionist/editor Frederick Douglass and Abraham Lincoln. In 1976, as part of the nation's bicentennial, the week was expanded into Black History Month. Each year, U.S. presidents proclaim February as National African-American History Month.

Note: The reference to the black population in this publication is to single-race blacks ("black alone") except in the first section on "Population." There the reference is to black alone or in combination with other races; in other words, a reference to respondents who said they were one race (black) or more than one race (black plus other races).

Population

43.9 million

The number of blacks, either alone or in combination with one or more other races, on July 1, 2011, up 1.6 percent from the census on April 1, 2010.

Source:Population Estimates

77.4 million

The projected black population of the United States (including those of more than one race) for July 1, 2060. On that date, according to the projection, blacks would constitute 18.4 percent of the nation's total population.

Source: Population projections

3.7 million
The black population in New York, which led all states as of July 1, 2011. Texas had the largest numeric increase since April 1, 2010 (84,000). The District of Columbia had the highest percentage of blacks (52.2 percent), followed by Mississippi (38.0 percent).
Source: Population Estimates

1.3 million
The black population in Cook, Ill., which had the largest black population of any county in 2011. Fulton, Ga., had the largest numeric increase since 2010 (13,000). Holmes, Miss., was the county with the highest percentage of blacks in the nation (82.9 percent).
Source: Population Estimates

Serving Our Nation

2.3 million
Number of black military veterans in the United States in 2011.
Source: 2011 American Community Survey

Education

82.5%
The percentage of blacks 25 and older with a high school diploma or higher in 2011.
Source: 2011 American Community Survey

18.4%
The percentage of blacks 25 and older who had a bachelor's degree or higher in 2011.
Source: 2011 American Community Survey

1.6 million
Among blacks 25 and older, the number who had an advanced degree in 2011.
Source: 2011 American Community Survey

3.1 million
Number of blacks enrolled in college in 2011, a 74.0 percent increase since 2001.
Source: 2011 American Community Survey

Voting

11.1 million
The number of blacks who voted in the 2010 congressional election, an increase from 10 percent of the total electorate in 2006 to 12 percent in 2010.
Source: Voting and Registration in the Election of 2010

55%
Turnout rate in the 2008 presidential election for the 18- to 24-year-old citizen black population, an 8 percentage point increase from 2004. Blacks had the highest turnout rate in this age group.
Source: Voting and Registration in the Election of 2008

65%
Turnout rate among black citizens regardless of age in the 2008 presidential election, up about 5 percentage points from 2004. Looking at voter turnout by race and Hispanic origin, non-Hispanic whites and blacks had the highest turnout levels.
Source: Voting and Registration in the Election of 2008

Income, Poverty and Health Insurance

$32,229
The annual median income of black households in 2011, a decline of 2.7 percent from 2010.
Source: U.S. Census Bureau, Income, Poverty and Health Insurance Coverage in the United States: 2011

27.6%
Poverty rate in 2011 for blacks.
Source: U.S. Census Bureau, Income, Poverty and Health Insurance Coverage in the United States: 2011

80.5%
Percentage of blacks that were covered by health insurance during all or part of 2011.
Source: U.S. Census Bureau, Income, Poverty and Health Insurance Coverage in the United States: 2011

Families and Children

61.9%
Among households with a black householder, the percentage that contained a family in 2012. There were 9.7 million black family households.
Source: 2012 Current Population Survey, Families and Living Arrangements, Table F1 and Table HH-2

45.2%
Among families with black householders, the percentage that were married couples in 2012.
Source: 2012 Current Population Survey, Families and Living Arrangements, Table F1

1.2 million
Number of black grandparents who lived with their own grandchildren younger than 18 in 2011. Of this number, 48.5 percent were also responsible for their care.
Source: 2011 American Community Survey

Homeownership

43.4%
Nationally, the percentage of households with a householder who was black who lived in owner-occupied homes in 2011.
Source: 2011 American Community Survey

Jobs

28.2%
The percentage of blacks 16 and older who worked in management, business, science and arts occupations.
Source: 2011 American Community Survey

Businesses

$135.7 billion
Receipts for black-owned businesses in 2007, up 53.1 percent from 2002. The number of black-owned businesses totaled 1.9 million in 2007, up 60.5 percent.
Source: 2007 Survey of Business Owners

37.7%
Percentage of black-owned businesses in 2007 in health care and social assistance, repair and maintenance, and personal and laundry services.
Source: 2007 Survey of Business Owners

10.6%
Percentage of all black-owned firms operating in 2007 in New York, which led all states or state-equivalents. Georgia and Florida followed, at 9.6 percent and 9.4 percent, respectively.br />
Source: 2007 Survey of Business Owners

Multiculturalism and Assimilation

One possible solution to the problem of racial and ethnic conflict is the rise of multiculturalism, a concept that supports the inherent values of different cultures within society. Proponents of multiculturalism think that immigrants should maintain links to their original culture including language, cultural beliefs and traditions, and religion, while also integrating into their new culture. Opponents however, worry that this practice keeps groups from adapting to the dominant culture.

Assimilation is the process by which minority groups adopt the patterns of the dominant culture. Assimilation can be voluntary, but it can also be enforced by social policies. "English Only" laws are an example of one such policy. In recent years, several states have adopted these laws, which range from merely declaring English as the official state language to limiting government services in languages other

than English. Looking at longitudinal data of immigrants, however, research shows that Latinos speaking Spanish at home in school showed no effect on the acquisition of the English language by second-generation youth, (Van, 2010). (See Box 9.2 on English Only Laws.)

Rapid assimilation occurs when a minority group completely abandons its previous culture in favor of a new one. One method by which the U.S. government tried to force rapid assimilation involved taking Native American children from their parents and placing them in boarding schools to teach them "white ways." However, many Native American students left the boarding schools unprepared to live in either the dominant culture or their own culture, (David, 1995).

The fact is that most immigrant groups practice segmented assimilation, which means that there is more than one way to adapt to a new land and become economically and socially successful. Traditional thought has held that the faster immigrants become acculturated to the United States, the faster they will achieve successful assimilation. Alejandro Portes argues that this is not necessarily so. He states that the cultural elements to which immigrants are exposed are of particular importance, (Portes, 2006). That is, successful assimilation depends on being exposed to a new culture. For example, poor immigrants who are acculturated to the culture of poor inner-city residents do not learn a culture that leads to successful assimilation. However, poor immigrants who are exposed to the culture of the poor have a better chance of success if they maintain a close connection with the culture of their home countries, such as the connection that are established in ethnic enclaves. The connection protects immigrants from a culture that is detrimental, and is an alternative path to assimilation. By taking this path, immigrants are able to develop the social capital necessary to achieve social and economic success without giving up traditional cultural practices.

THE COSTS OF RACISM

Individual victims of racism suffer from the destruction of their lives, health, and property, especially in societies where racism leads to poverty, enslavement, conflict, or war. Poor self-concept and low self-esteem result from constant reminders of a devalued status in society.

Prejudice and discrimination result in costs to organizations and communities as well as to individuals. First, they lose the talents of individuals who could be productive and contributing members. Because of poor education, sub-standard housing, and inferior medical care, these citizens cannot use their full potential to contribute to society.

Many cultural costs also result from continued attempts to justify racism by stereotyping and labeling groups. There are many talented African American athletes who are stars on college sports teams, but very few of them have been able to break into the ranks of coaches and managers (Eitzen and Sage, 2003). The number of African American and Mexican American actors and artists has increased, but the number of minority playwrights and screenwriters who can get their works produced or who have become directors remains limited. African American musicians have found it much more difficult to earn royalties and therefore cannot compose full-time (Alexander, 2003). Because these artists must create and perform their art as a sideline, they are less able to contribute their talents to society. The rest of us in society are the poorer for it. See Table 9.2 for information regarding income earned by members of minority groups.

TABLE 9.2 TOTAL MONEY INCOME OF HOUSEHOLDS BY TYPE, FOR BLACK ALONE AND WHITE ALONE, NOT HISPANIC HOUSEHOLDS: 2010

(Numbers in thousands. Civilian noninstitutionalized population.[1])

Household type and money income[3]	Race and Hispanic origin[2]							
	Total		Black alone		White alone, not Hispanic		Other[4]	
	Number	Percent	Number	Percent	Number	Percent	Number	Percent
Total households	118,682	100.0	15,065	100.0	83,471	100.0	20,147	100.0
Under $5,000	4,176	3.5	1,126	7.5	2,138	2.6	912	4.5
$5,000 to $9,999	5,055	4.3	1,352	9.0	2,721	3.3	982	4.9
$10,000 to $14,999	7,061	5.9	1,404	9.3	4,365	5.2	1,291	6.4
$15,000 to $19,999	7,260	6.1	1,094	7.3	4,882	5.8	1,284	6.4
$20,000 to $24,999	6,937	5.8	1,127	7.5	4,399	5.3	1,411	7.0
$25,000 to $34,999	12,878	10.9	1,917	12.7	8,505	10.2	2,455	12.2
$35,000 to $49,999	16,464	13.9	2,192	14.6	11,362	13.6	2,909	14.4
$50,000 to $74,999	21,051	17.7	2,284	15.2	15,289	18.3	3,478	17.3
$75,000 to $99,999	13,567	11.4	1,146	7.6	10,385	12.4	2,036	10.1
$100,000 and over	24,235	20.4	1,422	9.4	19,424	23.3	3,388	16.8
Family households[5]	78,613	100.0	9,418	100.0	53,909	100.0	15,287	100.0
Under $5,000	1,825	2.3	550	5.8	741	1.4	534	3.5
$5,000 to $9,999	1,807	2.3	539	5.7	772	1.4	497	3.2
$10,000 to $14,999	2,552	3.2	601	6.4	1,243	2.3	708	4.6
$15,000 to $19,999	3,133	4.0	565	6.0	1,705	3.2	863	5.6
$20,000 to $24,999	3,784	4.8	712	7.6	2,056	3.8	1,016	6.6
$25,000 to $34,999	7,698	9.8	1,221	13.0	4,620	8.6	1,857	12.1
$35,000 to $49,999	10,767	13.7	1,421	15.1	7,084	13.1	2,262	14.8
$50,000 to $74,999	15,193	19.3	1,641	17.4	10,728	19.9	2,824	18.5
$75,000 to $99,999	10,968	14.0	938	10.0	8,301	15.4	1,729	11.3
$100,000 and over	20,886	26.6	1,231	13.1	16,659	30.9	2,996	19.6
Nonfamily households	40,069	100.0	5,647	100.0	29,562	100.0	4,860	100.0
Under $5,000	2,351	5.9	576	10.2	1,397	4.7	378	7.8
$5,000 to $9,999	3,247	8.1	813	14.4	1,949	6.6	485	10.0
$10,000 to $14,999	4,508	11.3	802	14.2	3,123	10.6	583	12.0
$15,000 to $19,999	4,128	10.3	529	9.4	3,178	10.7	421	8.7
$20,000 to $24,999	3,153	7.9	415	7.4	2,343	7.9	395	8.1
$25,000 to $34,999	5,180	12.9	696	12.3	3,885	13.1	598	12.3
$35,000 to $49,999	5,696	14.2	772	13.7	4,278	14.5	647	13.3
$50,000 to $74,999	5,858	14.6	643	11.4	4,561	15.4	654	13.5
$75,000 to $99,999	2,600	6.5	209	3.7	2,084	7.1	307	6.3
$100,000 and over	3,349	8.4	192	3.4	2,765	9.4	392	8.1

[1]Plus armed forces living off post or with their families on post.
[2]Hispanic refers to people whose origin is Mexican, Puerto Rican, Cuban, Spanish-speaking Central or South American countries, or other Hispanic/Latino, regardless of race. Household type is shown by the race and Hispanic origin of the householder.
[3]Total money income is the sum of wages and salaries, net income from self-employment, and income other than earnings.
[4]Includes American Indian and Alaska Native; Asian alone; Native Hawaiian and Other Pacific Islander alone; White alone, Hispanic; and Two or More Races.
[5]Households in which at least one member is related to the person who owns or rents the occupied housing unit (householder).
SOURCE: U.S. Census Bureau, Current Population Survey, Annual Social and Economic Supplement, 2011.
Internet release Date: November 2012

Policies

Discrimination's influence is widespread, from slavery and subjugation to unequal educational and work opportunities, to legal and political arenas, and every other part of the social world. If one accepts the premise that discrimination is destructive to both individuals and societies, then ways must be found to address the root problems effectively. However, finding solutions to ethnic tensions around the world leaves many experts baffled. Consider the ethnic strife in Bosnia and Croatia in Eastern Europe; conflicts between Palestinians and Israelis in the Middle East; conflicts between Shiites and Sunni Muslims in Iraq; tribal genocide in Kenya, Sudan, and Rwanda in Africa; and conflicts between religious groups in Northern Ireland. In places such as these, each new generation is socialized into the prejudice and antagonisms that perpetuate the animosity and violence. Social scientists and policymakers have made little progress in resolving conflicts that rest on century-old hostilities. Table 9.3 shows types of programs that have been enacted to combat prejudice, racism, and discrimination at the individual, group, societal, and global levels.

TABLE 9.3 PROBLEMS AND SOLUTIONS

Types of Problems at Each Level	Types of Solutions or Programs at Each Level
Individual Level: stereotypes and prejudice	Therapy, tolerance-education programs
Group Level: negative group interaction	Positive contact, awareness by majority of their many privileges
Societal Level: institutional discrimination	Education, media, legal-system revisions
Global Level: deprivation of human rights	Human rights movements, international political pressure

Source: ACLU, 2012.

Programs to address prejudice, racism, and stereotypes through human relations workshops, group encounters, and therapy can achieve goals with small numbers of people. For instance, African American and White children who are placed in interracial classrooms in schools are more likely to develop close interracial friendships (Ellison and Powers, 1994). Also, the higher the people's education level, the more likely they are to respect and like others and appreciate and enjoy differences. Education gives a broader, more universal outlook; reduces misconceptions and prejudice; shows that many issues do not have clear answers; and encourages multicultural understanding and focus on individuals, not judging of groups.

Two groups of strong multicultural education programs are the Anti-Defamation League and the Southern Poverty Law Center's Teaching Tolerance Program. Both groups provide schools and community organizations with literature, videos, and other materials aimed at combatting intolerance and discrimination toward others.

Many social scientists advocate organized group contact between dominant and minority group members to improve relations and break down stereotypes and fears. Although not all contact reduces prejudice, many studies have shown the benefits of contact. Some essential conditions for success are equal status for participants, noncompetitive and nonthreatening contact, and projects or goals on which to cooperate (Farley, 2009).

In a classic study of group contact, social psychologists Muzafer Sherif and Caroline Sherif (1953) and their colleagues ran summer camps for boys of ages 11 and 12 and studied how groups were established and reestablished. On arrival, the boys were divided into two groups that competed periodically. The fiercer the

competition, the more hostile the two cabins of boys became toward each other. The experimenters tried several methods to resolve the conflicts and tensions:

1. Appealing to higher values (be nice to your neighbors): This proved to be of limited value.

2. Talking with the natural leaders of the groups (compromises between group leaders): The group leaders agreed, but their followers did not go along.

3. Bringing the groups together in a pleasant situation (a mutually rewarding situation): This did not reduce competition; if anything, it increased it.

4. Introducing a superordinate goal that could be achieved only if everyone cooperated: This technique worked. The boys were presented with a dilemma: The water system had broken, or a fire needed to be extinguished, and all were needed to solve the problem. The groups not only worked together, but their established stereotypes eventually began to fade away. Such a situation in a community might arise from efforts to get a candidate elected, a bill passed, or a neighborhood improved. At the global macro level, hostile countries sit together to solve issues (Sherif and Sherif, 1953).

Programs involving group contact to improve conditions for minorities have been tried in many areas of social life, including integrated housing projects, job programs to promote minority hiring, and busing children to schools, to achieve higher level of racial and socioeconomic integration. For example, the Chicago Housing Authority opened a refurbished mixed-income housing experiment with resident participation in decision making. Although many predicted failure, the project thrived, with long waiting lists of families wanting to participate (McCormick, 1992). Positive contact experiences tend to improve relations in groups on a micro level by breaking down stereotypes, but to solidify these gains, we must also address institutionalized inequalities.

Sociologists contend that institutional and societal approaches to reduce discrimination get closer to the core of the problems and affect larger numbers of people than do micro-level strategies. For example, voluntary advocacy organizations pursue political change through lobbying, watchdog monitoring, educational information dissemination, canvassing, protest marches, rallies, and boycotts (Minkoff, 1995). Groups such as the NAACP and ACLU have filed lawsuits and lobbied legislators for changes in laws that they believed were discriminatory.

THE FUNCTIONALIST AND CONFLICT PERSPECTIVES

THE FUNCTIONALIST PERSPECTIVE. Functionalists conceive of society as resembling a living organism in which the various parts of a system contribute to its survival. Accordingly, they look to the functions and dysfunctions associated with given social patterns. Although at first sight racial and ethnic conflict would seem to impair social solidarity and stability, functionalists point out that conflict may nonetheless be functional for a society (Coser, 1956). First, conflict promotes group formation, and groups are the building blocks of a society. It facilitates a consciousness of kind, an awareness of shared or similar values. The distinction between "we," or the in-group, and "they," or the out-group, is established in and through conflict. Groups in turn bind people together within a set of social relationships. And they define the statuses people occupy in the social structure, particularly positions that are ascribed.

Second, not only is a group defined and its boundaries established through conflict, but conflict also promotes group cohesion. It makes group members more conscious of their group bonds and may increase their social participation. Some social scientists have pointed out that anti-Semitism and anti-black sentiment may be functional in that they provide dominant group members who lack a sense of cohesion within the society with an anchor-with a sense of group membership (Adorno et al., 1950). It highlights their racial and ethnic membership, providing them with a means of identification in an uncertain, alienated world.

Third, ethnic and racial conflict may function as a safety valve for the society as a whole (Berkowitz, 1989). Prejudice provides for the safe release of hostile and aggressive impulses that are culturally tabooed within other social contexts. By channeling hostilities from within family, occupational, and other crucial settings onto permissible targets, the stability of existing social structures may be promoted. This is the well-known scapegoating mechanism.

And fourth, functionalists point out that a multiplicity of conflicts between large numbers of differing groups within a society may be conducive to a democratic as opposed to a totalitarian order. The multiple group affiliations of individuals contribute to a variety of conflicts crisscrossing society. The groups thus operate as a check against one another. A person's segmental participation in numerous groups, rather than total absorption by one group, results in a kind of balancing mechanism and prevents deep cleavages along one axis (for instance, it prevents cleavage along rigid class lines that results in class struggle). In contrast, in totalitarian societies, there is a maximum concentration of power in one institution - the state.

The dysfunctions of racial and ethnic conflict are often more readily apparent than its functions. Conflict may reach a frequency and intensity that imperils a larger social system, as has occurred with the collapse of the central regimes in Yugoslavia, the Soviet Union, and Lebanon. Further, energy and resources are drained and dissipated by friction that might otherwise be directed within more productive channels and cooperative activities. Fears and expectations of conflict may lead to an inefficient and ineffective employment of human resources and individual talents.

THE CONFLICT PERSPECTIVE. While functionalists emphasize social stability and the mechanisms that promote or interfere with it, conflict theorists see the world as in continual struggle. Conflict theorists contend that prejudice and discrimination can best be understood in terms of tension or conflict among competing groups.: ethnocentrism, competition, and unequal power.

Ethnocentrism involves the tendency to judge the behavior of other groups by the standards of one's own. Individuals assume that it is the nature of things that all people should be organized according to the same assumptions that characterize their own group. When individuals are strongly ethnocentric, they find it easy to perceive the out-group as an object of loathing, as a symbol of strangeness, evil, and even danger. Ethnocentrism provides a fertile soil for prejudicial attitudes and stereotypes.

Competition intensifies ethnocentric sentiments and may lead to intergroup strife. In human affairs, conflict theorists point out that people typically seek to improve their outcomes with regard to those things, particularly privilege, prestige, and power, that they define as good, worthwhile, and desirable. When they perceive their group outcomes as mutually exclusive and legitimate, so that each group can realize its goals only at the expense of the other, intergroup tensions are likely to mount (Beck and Tolmay, 1990; Belanger and Pinard, 1991). For the most part, the attitudes people have toward out-groups tend to reflect their perceptions of the relationships they have with the groups. Where the relations between two groups are

viewed as competitive, negative attitudes (prejudice) will be generated toward the out-group. The boys' camp experiment undertaken by Muszafer Sherif and described earlier documents this process.

Competition provides the motivation for systems of social inequality, and ethnocentrism channels competition along racial and ethnic lines, but power determines which group will subordinate the other (Noel, 1972). Without power, prejudices cannot be translated into discrimination, and groups cannot turn their claims on scarce resources into institutional discrimination. In brief, power is the mechanism by which domination and subjugation are achieved.

Marxists take the conflict thesis even further. They say that racial prejudice and exploitation were aroused in the Western world with the rise of Capitalism (Cox, 1948; Szymanski, 1976, 1978;). Marxist theorists contend that racist notions serve the economic interests of the capitalist class in four ways. First, ideologies of racial superiority make colonialism and racist practices palatable and acceptable to the white masses. Second, racism is profitable, since capitalists can pay minority workers less and thus generate greater profits for themselves. Third, racist ideologies divide the working class by pitting white workers and minority workers against one another, a tactic of "divide and conquer." And fourth, capitalists require minority workers as an industrial reserve army that can be fired during times of economic stagnation and re-hired when needed for producing profits during times of prosperity.

Marxists blame capitalists for generating racism, but some contend that economic competition within a split labor market underlies the development of tensions among ethnic groups. A split labor market is an economic arena in which large differences exist in the price of labor at the same occupational level. When a group sells its labor at rates substantially lower than the prevailing ones, higher-paid labor faces severe competition to maintain its advantage. When the cheaper labor is of a differing racial or ethnic group, the resulting class antagonism takes the form of racism. The antagonism focuses on racial or ethnic issues, although the source of the conflict is one of class.

The more expensive labor resists displacement through exclusion or a caste system. The anti-Chinese movement, which flourished in California in the 1870s, illustrates an exclusion strategy. White workers sought to drive the Chinese from their communities through harassment and violence and to shut off the entry of new immigrants. The racial caste system was the strategy employed in the post-Civil War period. White labor erected social and legal barriers -Jim Crow segregation arrangements to avoid competition with black workers.

Regardless of the precise form that conflict theories take, and they do differ substantially from one another, they nonetheless contrast sharply with functionalist theories that look to the forces that contribute to stability rather than those that divide.

See Box 9.6 for additional information on theoretical perspectives on race and ethnicity.

BOX 9.6

CONSIDER THE THEORETICAL PERSPECTIVES

Functionalism – Racism supports in-group biases and causes groups that see themselves as alike to unite strongly. The ability of these groups to unite ties them together. In this way, self-segregation helps immigrants and minorities. Of course there are latent consequences of this. Self-segregation can be dysfunctional when societies limit the opportunities of minority groups, and thereby miss recognizing strengths that could help improve society.

When immigrants move to ethnic enclaves, they strengthen their in-group connections, and also improve their odds of successfully adapting to the new country. Can voluntary segregation be functional for both the minority and the majority? How?

Social Conflict – Conflict theory deals with racial and ethnic divisions within society, and shows how these divisions also relate to social class. According to conflict theorists, racism potentially creates a willing "underclass" to provide cheap labor to the elites. Consider racial stratification in terms of education, income and poverty, and opportunities. Conflict theorists might view the inequalities experienced by minority groups as a way for the powerful majority to keep racial and ethnic minorities in a subordinate position. For example, in the United States, business owners may be tempted to hire undocumented immigrant workers who are willing to work for a lower wage. Factors such as low wages, inferior education, and lack of access to public assistance keep many immigrants in subordinate positions. As a result, business owners have a constant supply of cheap labor.

According to conflict theory, those with power often use it to dominate others. How does the dominant group benefit by keeping minorities in a subordinate position?

Symbolic Interactionism – Symbolic interactionists look at the micro-interactions of daily life and how they support or attack an issue. For example, consider the prevalence of racial slurs 100 years ago versus today. Years ago, teachers may have been willing and able to utter racial slurs in the classroom. But today, a teacher who did so would most likely be reprimanded and could even lose his or her job. What has changed? Over time, society's tolerance for racial slurs has decreased dramatically. Symbolic interactionists would suggest that by changing the acceptable terms, we can change the reality. Perhaps we can eliminate racial slurs altogether.

Interactionists suggest that eliminating racial slurs puts the world on more equal terms. Over the last 100 years, we have made strides toward creating a more equal society. How much of this progress is due to the fact that racial slurs are no longer socially acceptable?

SUGGESTED READINGS

Churchill, W. *Indians Are Us? Culture and Genocide in Native North America.* (Monroe, ME: Common Courage Press, 1994).

Doob, C. B. *Racism: An American Cauldron.* (New York: Longman, 1999).

Feagin, J. R., and Hernan V. *White Racism: The Basics.* (New York: Routledge, 1995).

Feagin, J. R., and Sikes, M. 1994. *Living with Racism: The Black Middle-Class Experience.* (Boston: Beacon Press, 1994).

Frankenberg, R. *White Women, Race Matters: The Social Construction of Whiteness.* (Minneapolis, MN: University of Minnesota Press, 1993).

Smith, B., (ed.). *Neither Separate Nor Equal: Women, Race, and Class in the South.* (Philadelphia: Temple University Press, 1999).

Takaki, Ronald. *A Larger Memory: A History of Our Diversity, with Voices.* (Boston: Little, Brown, 1998). See also "The New Immigrant Series" from Allyn and Bacon (http://www.abacon.com) which includes short books on the experiences of recent immigrant groups such as Vietnamese Americans, Jews from the former Soviet Union, Sudanese refugees, Salvadorians, and Dominicans, among others.

VIDEO SUGGESTIONS

Affirmative Action and Reaction -This video shows that African Americans and white Americans typically have differed in their understanding of affirmative action and poses the question of whether affirmative action is still necessary to remedy past discrimination. 27 min. 2006. Films for the Humanities and Sciences, P.O. Box 2053, Princeton, NJ, (800) 257-5126.

Casting Calls: Hollywood and the Ethnic Villain - This program examines how filmmakers portray villains in films that reinforce ethnic stereotypes. 46 min. 2003. Films for the Humanities and Sciences, Princeton, NJ 08543-2053, (800) 257-5126. Web: http://www.films.com

Color Adjustment - Marlon Riggs provides outstanding examples of how network television reluctantly—and selectively—integrated African Americans into prime time shows such as Amos 'n' Andy, Good Times, Roots, and The Cosby Show. Provides an excellent starting point for the discussion of how current programs depict people from diverse racial and ethnic categories. 87 min. 2009. California Newsreel, 149 Ninth Street, San Francisco, CA 94103, (415) 621-6196.

Crash - Through a complex interweaving of multiple subplots, this 2004 film provides powerful insight into our responses to differences in race and ethnicity that are part of our everyday lives.

Horizons and Homelands: Integrating Cultural Roots - This video shows the lives of two families - a Native American family, which has recently moved from a reservation to the city; and a family from Laos, who recently immigrated to the same city. The video not only makes viewers aware of the distinctive nature of these two cultures but also shows how people work to integrate their differences with their new lives in an urban setting. 24 min. 2006. Films for the Humanities and Sciences, P.O. Box 2053, Princeton, NJ, (800) 257-5126.

Legislating Morality: Affirmative Action and the Burden of History - This video examines opposing viewpoints on the question of whether affirmative action promotes racial balance or is a form of reverse discrimination. 26 min. 2012. Films for the Humanities and Sciences, P.O. Box 2053, Princeton, NJ, (800) 257-5126.

Overcoming Prejudice - This documentary focuses on what prejudice is, where it comes from, and how to deal with it successfully. It employs the experiences of numerous people from a variety of walks of life who have survived the prejudice of others, overcome their own prejudices, or succeeded at breaking the destructive chain of prejudice in their relationships. (60 min./CC Closed captioned). Insight Media, 2162 Broadway, New York, NY 10024-0621, (800) 233-9910. Web: www.insight-media.com

The Triumph of Evil - This film provides an in-depth analysis of genocide in Rwanda and the reaction to genocide by thc international community and the United States. PBS Video, P.O. Box 609, Melbourne, FL 32902-0609, (877) PBS-SHOP.

Women of Hope: Latinas Abriendo Camino - The story of Latina women in the United States is told through portraits of twelve women who have broken new ground in their lives and made achievements. The video also shows historical footage and features a soundtrack of Latin music from the 1940s through today. 28 min. 2006. Films for the Humanities and Sciences, P.O. Box 2053, Princeton, NJ, (800) 257-5126.

BIBLIOGRAPHY

Adorno, T.W., Frenkel-Brunswick, E., Levinson, D., and Sanford, R.N. *The Authoritarian Personality.* (New York, NY: Harper, 1950).

Alexander, J. "Theorizing the Modes of Incorporation." *Sociological Theory.* (Vol. 19:237-49, 2001).

American Civil Liberties Union. "ACLU Briefing paper number 6: English only laws." (*The Lectric Law Library,* 2012).

Beck, E.M., and Tolnay S. E. "The Killing Fields of the Deep South: The Market for Cotton and the Lynching of Blacks, 1882-1930." *American Sociological Review.* (Vol. 55: 526-539, 2001).

Belanger, S., and Pinard, M. "Ethnic Movements and the Competition Model: Some Missing Links. *American Sociological Review.* (Vol. 56: 446-(457, 1991).

Begley, S. "Race and DNA." *Newsweek.* (p 52-54 2008, Feb. 29).

Berger, P., and Luckman, T. *The Social Construction of Reality.* (New York, NY: Doubleday, 1963).

Berkowitz, L. "Frustration-Aggression Hypothesis: Examination and Reformulation." *Psychological Bulletin,* 106: 59-73, 1989).

Brooks-Gunn, J., Duncan. "Adolescent Development?" *American Journal of Sociology,* (Volume 99, pp. 353-395, 1993).

Coser, L. A. *The Functions of Social Conflict.* (New York: Free Press, 1956).

Cox, O. C. *Caste, Class and Race.* (Garden City, N.Y.: Doubleday, 1948).

David, W.A. *Education for Extinction: American Indians and the Boarding School Experience.* (Lawrence, KS: University of Kansas Press, 2008).

Dollard, J. *Frustration and Aggression.* (New Haven, CT: Yale University Press, 1939).

Dworkin, S. L., and Messner, M. A. "Just Do...What?" *Revisioning Gender*. Thousand Oaks, CA: Sage, 1999).

Eitzen, D., and Sage, G. *Sociology of North American Sport.* (Boston, MA: McGraw-Hill, 2003)

Ellison, C., and Powers, D. "The Contact Hypothesis and Racial Attitudes Among Black Americans." *Social Science Quarterly*. (Volume 75(2), pp. 385-400, 1994).

Farley, J. *Majority-Minority Relations.* 6th Ed. (Englewood Cliffs, NJ: Prentice Hall, 2009).

Feagin, J. R., and Feagin, C. *Racial and Ethnic Relations.* 7th ed. (Upper Saddle River, NJ: Prentice Hall, 2003).

Just, R. "Triumph of the Ethnos." *History and Ethnicity*, (London: Routledge, 1989).

Kallen, H. *Culture and Democracy in the United States.* (New York: Boni and Liverright, 1924).

Leland, J., and Beals, G. "In Living Colors: Tiger Woods is the Exception that Rules." *Newsweek.* pp. 58-60, 1997, May 5).

Lexington. 1996. "A Cheer for Olympo-Americans." *Economist.* (August 3, 1996)

Marger, M.N. *Race and Ethnic Relations: American and Global Perspectives.* 8th Ed. (Belmont, CA: Wadsworth, 2009).

McCormick, J. "A Housing Program that Actually Works." *Newsweek.* (June 22, 1992) p. 61.

Noel, D. M. *The Origins of American Slavery and Racism.* (Columbus, Ohio: Charles E. Merrill, 1972).

Painter, N.I. *The History of White People.* (New York, NY: W.W. Norton, 2010).

Park, R. E. "Race Relations and Certain Frontiers." *Race and Culture Contracts.* (New York: McGraw-Hill, 1934).

Park, R. E. "Our Racial Frontier on the Pacific." *Race and Culture.* (Glencoe, IL: Free Press, 1926, 1950).

Portes, A., and Stepick, A. *City on the Edge: The Transformation of Miami.* (Berkeley, CA: University of California Press, 2006).

Portes, A., and Rumbaut, R.G. *Immigrant America.* (Berkeley, CA: University of California Press, 1996).

Sherif, M., and Sherif, C. "Groups in Harmony and Tension." (New York, NY: Harper and Row, 1953).

Sibley, C.G., and Duckitt, J. "Personality and Prejudice: A Meta-Analysis and Theoretical Review." *Personality and Social Psychology Review.* (Volume 12, pp. 248-279, 2008).

Smedley, A. "Race and the Construction of Human Identity." American Anthropologist. (Volume 100, pp. 690- 702, 1998)

Smedley, A. (2007). "Race in North America: Evolution of a Worldview." (Boulder, CO: Westview Press, 2007).

Tatum, B.D. *Assimilation Blues: Black Families in a White Community.* (Westport, CT: Greenwood Press, 1987).

Szymanski, A. "Racial Discrimination and White Gain." *American Sociological Review*, (Vol. 41: 403-414, 1976).

Szymanski, A. "White Workers' Loss from Racial Discrimination." *American Sociological Review*, (Vol. 43: 776-782, 1978).

Van, C.T. "English Gain vs. Spanish Loss? Language Assimilation Among Second-Generation Latinos in Young Adulthood." *Social Forces.* (Volume 89(1), pp. 257-284, 2010).

U.S. Census Bureau. "Population Projections." (2012). http://www.census.gov/ipc/www/usinterimproj.

U.S. Census Bureau. "Overview of Race and Hispanic Origin, 2010."

http://www.census.gov/prod/cen2010/briefs/c2010-02.pdf.

Weber, M. *Economy and Society*. Edited by Guenther Roth and Claus Wittich. (Berkley: University of California Press, 1968).

Wirth, L. "The Problem of Minority Groups," in *The Science of Man in the World Crisis*. (New York, NY: Columbia University Press, 1945).

CHAPTER 10

Crime and Deviance

INTRODUCTION TO CRIMINOLOGY AND DEVIANCE

Criminology is a subfield of sociology. Edwin Sutherland, a past President of the American Sociological Association and a well-known criminologist, defines criminology as the scientific study of law making, law breaking, and the enforcement of the law (Sutherland, Cressey, and Luckenbill, 1992: 3). Criminology is an interdisciplinary science whose practitioners have been trained in many fields, including psychology, political science, history, philosophy, biology, the brain sciences, and, of course, sociology. Criminology has developed into an independent field of study, even though it sometimes is confused with related disciplines, such as criminal justice, justice studies, and deviance. **Deviance** refers to the violation of social norms, whether folkways or mores. Deviance as a field of study refers to the scientific study of behavior that departs from social norms. Not all forms of deviance have been written into law as crimes.

The various paradigms in sociology define the concept of crime differently. For instance, consensus theorists tend to define **crime** in terms of law violation. Thus, from the point of view of consensus theory, crime is an intentional act or omission of an act that violates the provisions of criminal statutory or case law, occurs without defense or justification, and is deemed by the state to be a felony or misdemeanor (Reid, 2006). See Table 10.1 for the distinction between misdemeanor and felony.

In contrast, conflict theory stresses that crime is a politically defined concept and that the law that defines crimes is a tool that the ruling class uses to maintain its supraordinate position at the expense of the poor.

In the symbolic interactionist view, "moral entrepreneurs" define crime; no acts are inherently either good or bad, and crimes are illegal simply because influential audiences or stakeholders define them that way. Howard S. Becker, an American symbolic interactionist, defines a **moral entrepreneur** as a social actor who generates and enforces a definition of morality. **Morality** is a doctrine or system of right human conduct. Symbolic interactionists are particularly interested in the meanings that social actors attribute to themselves, others, things, occurrences, situations, and to their own and others' behaviors.

In this chapter we examine crime and crime trends, focusing on violent crime, first in the long sweep of human history and then in shorter frames of time. Next, we examine crime, punishment, and law in the United States today. Throughout, we use sociological theory to illuminate an understanding of crime and deviance in human society.

TABLE 10.1 MISDEMEANOR AND FELONY

Type of Crime	Seriousness of the Offense	Sentence	Confinement	
			Type of Facility	Length of Confinement
Misdemeanor	Less serious	Fine, secure confinement	Local—such as County Jail	Less than a year
Felony	More serious	Fine, secure confinement, capital punishment	Prison—State or Federal	More than a year

CRIME TRENDS: WE'RE LIVING IN A MORE PEACEFUL WORLD

We may be living in the most peaceable era in the entire history of our species (Pinker, 2011). This decline in violence has not been smooth and it is not guaranteed to continue, but it is an unmistakable and empirically demonstrable development (e.g., Human Security Report Project, 2012; Eisner, 2008, 2003; Clark, 2007; Gat, 2006; Elias, 2000, 1939; Keeley, 1996; Cockburn, 1991; Gurr, 1989: 21-54; Daley and Wilson, 1988). No aspect of life is untouched by this retreat from violence: violence has diminished in the family, in the neighborhood, between tribes and other armed collectivities, and among nations and states (Pinker, 2012).

Outline of the Retreat from Violence

Harvard Professor Steven Pinker (2011: xxiv, 31- 481) identifies the following six major trends that mark our species' retreat from violence:

1. **THE RISE OF THE STATE AND RULE OF LAW** The first is the rise of the state and rule of law and it took place on scale of millennia, beginning around 5,000 years ago. With this change came a reduction in chronic raiding and feuding that had characterized life in hunting and gathering and horticultural societies (Hobbes, 1985, 1651; Gat, 2006: 409), resulting in a more or less fivefold decrease in rates of violent death (Pinker, 2012: 35).

2. **THE CIVILIZING PROCESS** The second transition spanned more than half a millennium (e.g., Pinker, 2011, 2012; Wood, 2004) and is best documented in Europe. With a nod to sociologist Norbert Elias who authored a book named *The Civilizing Process* (1939, 2000), Pinker terms the

second transition the civilizing process (Pinker, 2011: xxiv). Between the late Middle Ages and the twentieth century, European countries experienced a tenfold-to-fiftyfold decrease in their rates of violent homicide. Sociologist Norbert Elias attributes this decline to the consolidation of a patchwork of feudal territories into large kingdoms with both centralized authority and an infrastructure of commerce (Elias, 1939, 2000). The consolidation of smaller political entities into larger states was huge. For instance, according to military historian Quincy Wright, Europe had 5,000 independent political units—mainly baronies and principalities—in the 15th century, 500 at the time of the 30Years War (1618-1648) in the 17th century, 200 at the time of Napoleon in the early 19th century, and fewer than 30 in 1953 (Wright, 1942: 215; Richardson, 1960: 168-169).

With the advent of the consolidation of the state, many rules changed. For instance, for centuries in England, the legal system had treated homicide as a tort, i.e., as a private wrong, for which the perpetrator or the perpetrator's family had to pay monetary compensation to the victim's family. This custom of atonement for wrongs by payment to appease the victim's family or tribe became known as **lex salica** or **wergeld** or wergild in Europe. It is still in effect in many Far Eastern and Middle Eastern countries, with the amount of payment varying according to the injured person's age, sex, and rank or position in the social group (Allen and Simonson, 2001:7). For example, under the sixth century English legal code (Churchill, 1956, Vol. I: 66-67), a "prince... was worth 1500 shillings, a shilling being the value of a cow in Kent, or of a sheep elsewhere; an eorl, or nobleman, 300 shillings; ...a yeoman farmer, was worth 100 shillings; a laet, or agricultural serf, 40-80 shillings".

King Henry I (1100-1135) of England "redefined homicide as an offense against the state and its metonym, the crown" (Pinker, 2011: 74-75). In this way homicide was moved from the arena of being a personal wrong to being a matter of state interest. Murder cases no longer were *Benjamin Doe vs Alexander Stewart*; now they became *The Crown vs Alexander Stewart* (or later, in the United States, *The People vs Alexander Stewart* or *The State of Kansas vs Alexander Stewart*). The wergild often was the offender's assets in their entirety, together with additional money rounded up from the offender's family and it went to the King instead of to the family of the victim. Wergild thus became a de facto method of revenue generation for the crown. To ensure that each death was reported to the courts, each death was investigated by a local agent of the crown, the coroner (Daly and Wilson, 1988: 241-245).

With the advent of the consolidation of the state, there was a large reduction in *elite* violence. Thus, economist Gregory Clark's study of the deaths of English aristocrats from the late Middle Ages to the Industrial Revolution demonstrates that in the late 14th and 15th centuries (1330-1479) 26 percent of male English aristocrats died from violence (Clark, 2007: 122), which is about at the same rate as is the average for preliterate tribes (Keeley, 1996; Gat, 2006; Bowles, 2009). The violent aristocratic death rate fell to the single digits by the turn of the 18th century, to a level not much above those for the general population (Clark, 2007: 122) and later to a level well below that for the general population (Cooney, 1997).

In The Civilizing Process, Norbert Elias writes a socio-political-economic history of the consolidation of states in Europe and also analyzes the pacification, the civilizing, of the aristocracy that occurred during that period of time. The aristocracy was civilized at court because they were increasingly dependent on the king's favor for their social standing. The middle classes followed suit; they were civilized not by the royal court but by employment in factories and in businesses which enticed or required them to acquire habits of decorum. Then, too, an increasingly democratic political process enabled the middle classes to identify with mainstream culture which opened up the court system to them as a way legitimately to pursue their grievances (Pinker, 2011: 82). By and large, the middle classes embraced the legal system as a way to pursue grievances.

Today, statistics from Western countries show that the overwhelming majority of homicides and other violent crimes are committed by people in the lowest socioeconomic classes. Part of the reason for this is that while elites and middle classes largely pursue justice within the legal system, segments of the lower classes are more likely to resort to "self-help" (e.g., Pinker, 2011: 83; Wilkinson, Beaty and Lurry, 2009; Wood, 2003; Katz, 1988; Black, 1983). From the point of view of consensus theory, **self-help** is another term for vigilantism, "taking the law into your own hands," and retaliation, by means of which people themselves secure justice instead of relying on the state to do it for them. From the point of view of the perpetrators, much of what we call "crime" is actually the pursuit of justice and a code of honor (Katz, 1988). This is a point made by sociologist Donald Black in an influential article entitled "Crime as Social Control" (Black, 1983) and it is a point that is made by many perpetrators of violent crimes (e.g., Harris, 1995) when they talk about *why* they did what they did.

Black begins with a statistic that long has been known to students of criminology: only a small percent of homicides, perhaps as low as ten percent, are committed as a means to a practical end, like murder for hire, killing the victim of a crime because dead people tell no tales, killing a police officer to avoid being arrested, and so forth (Eisner, 2009). The most common motives for homicide are moralistic: retaliation after an insult, punishing an unfaithful or deserting romantic partner, and other acts of jealousy, revenge, and self defense (Pinker, 2011: 83). Black argues that most homicides are really instances of capital punishment, with the private citizen acting as judge, jury, and executioner.

Black's interpretation of murder reminds us of the importance of the definition of the situation in coming to an understanding of crime. American sociologist W. I Thomas observed that if we define something as real, it is real in its consequences, and this observation is known as the **Thomas theorem**. Symbolic interactionists remind us that not everyone defines a given situation similarly. For instance, consider a man who is arrested and brought to criminal trial for aggravated assault or even attempted murder because he wounded his wife's lover. From the point of view of the law, the aggressor is the husband and the victim is society, which is now pursuing justice. From the point of view of the wounded lover, he himself is the victim and the husband is both the perpetrator and the aggressor; were the husband to "get off" on an acquittal or a mistrial or a plea bargain, there is no justice because the legal system enjoins the lover from engaging in "self-help justice." From the point of view of the husband, he himself is the victim (because he has been cuckolded), the lover is the aggressor, and justice has been done by his attack on the lover; but now he (the husband) is the victim of a second act of aggression, in which the state is the aggressor and the lover is an accomplice.

These observations challenge several conceptions or myths about violence. One is that violence is due to a deficit of morality and justice. On the contrary, violence often is due to an abundance of justice or morality, at least as these are defined and implemented by the perpetrators of violence. Another belief about violence that is embraced by some consensus theorists is that lower-class people engage in violent crime because they are financially needy (for instance, they need money to buy drugs or to feed their children). Yet another belief about violence that is embraced by some conflict theorists is that lower-class people commit crime because they are expressing rage against society or against the capitalist class. The violence of a lower-class or otherwise marginalized person may indeed express rage, but it tends to be rage against someone who dishonored him or his family and the actions he took serve to restore that honor. His rage tends not to be against society or the capitalist class but is aimed more narrowly at the person whose actions besmirched his or his

family's (or his tribe's) honor. In short, the historical civilizing process did not eliminate violence, but it relegated it to the socio-economic margins.

3. **THE HUMANITARIAN REVOLUTION** The third transition unfolded on the scale of centuries, taking off around the time of the Age of Reason and the Enlightenment, and Pinker and some historians terms this transition "the humanitarian revolution" (Pinker, 2012: 35). This age saw the first organized movements to abolish slavery, despotism (including monarchy), dueling, judicial torture, witch hunts, sadistic punishment, and even cruelty to animals.

4. **THE LONG PEACE** The fourth transition has taken place since the end of World War II and historians refer to it as "the long peace," a term coined by historian John Lewis Gaddis (1987). For more than two-thirds of a century, the great states have not waged war on each other, which, historically, is an unprecedented development.

5. **THE NEW PEACE** The fifth transition is more tenuous and Pinker terms it "the new peace." As hard as it may be to believe, since the end of the Cold War in 1989, organized conflicts of all kinds—civil wars, genocides, repressions by autocratic governments, coups d'état, and even terrorist attacks—have declined throughout the world.

6. **THE RIGHTS REVOLUTIONS** Finally, since the end of World War II, symbolically begun by the Universal Declaration of Human Rights in 1848, there has been a growing revulsion against aggression on smaller scales, including violence against sexual and gender minorities, religious minorities, ethnic minorities, women, children, and animals. These spin-offs from the concept of human rights have been, and continue to be, asserted in a cascade of social movements since the late 1950s to the present day, which Pinker collectively refers to as "the rights revolutions."

Explaining the Retreat from Violence

Why is violence decreasing in the world? Steven Pinker (2011, 2012) identifies five reasons why violence is decreasing: leviathan, commerce, feminization, cosmopolitanism, and reason.

1. **LEVIATHAN** Thomas Hobbes called the state leviathan in a famous book which he authored of the same name (Hobbes, 1985, 1651). Max Weber reminds us that the state successfully holds claim to monopoly on the legitimate use of physical force (Weber, 1968: 54, 904). However, a claim to monopoly over legitimate force, even a successful one, never actually amounts to a 100 percent monopoly on all force. Existing around and even inside leviathan are social actors who do not always leave the use of force to the state. Bandits are an example. Pirates are another example. The perpetrators of intimate partner violence, in societies where such violence is illegal, are another example. Nonetheless, by penalizing violence and providing alternative modes of dispute resolution (e.g., the courts), the state can inhibit the impulse for revenge. For instance, after bands, tribes, and chiefdoms came under the control of the first states, violent feuding and raids diminished dramatically (Pinker, 2012: 35).

BOX 10.1

EUROPEAN SOCIOLOGIST NORBERT ELIAS (1897-1990) ON THE CIVILIZING PROCESS

Norbert Elias is an influential European sociologist. Elias' most important work is the two-volume *The Civilizing Process* (2000), originally published in 1939. In 1969 its first volume was translated into English. Volume I traces the historical developments of the European *habitus*, or "second nature," the particular individual psychological structures which Freud would term the Superego, and which many people would call a conscience and which American Sociologist Travis Hirschi (1969) would call "the social bond." The second volume *The Civilizing Process* (1982) looks into the causes of the emergence of the European *habitus*, and Elias finds them in an increasingly differentiated and interconnected web of complex social networks. Elias documents that Western norms regulating the control of bodily functions, from eating and sleeping to blowing one's nose, arose in the Middle Ages as the courts consolidated their power over feudal societies and exported the standards of courtly behavior to the countryside. Such behavior became a symbol that a person was a member of the upper classes and not a serf or "a savage."

Elias' major interest has been in understanding the pacification of European medieval society through the development of individual, moral forms of restraint found in codes, such as table manners and other forms of etiquette (e.g., nose blowing, coughing, etc.) The emergence of the nation state as a system of social regulation has been accompanied by the emergence of civilized systems of self-control. Table manners and other forms of etiquette, then, are not just personal matters; they are important manifestations of social control, part of the richly-textured tapestry that makes the modern nation state possible. These codes are embedded in networks of social relations.

Elias traces how Post-medieval European standards regarding violence, sexual behavior, bodily functions, table manners, and forms of speech were gradually transformed by increasing thresholds of shame and repugnance, working outward from a nucleus in court society.

In *The Court Society (Hoefische Gesellschaft)* (2006), Elias studied the evolution of ceremony in the French Court before the Revolution in the 18th century, the economic decline of aristocratic society, and the emergence of bourgeois society. The internalized "self restraint" imposed by increasingly complex networks of social connections developed the psychological self-perceptions that Freud called the "superego," and which most of us might call a "conscience." For Elias, the conscience is a social construct, and it is embedded in networks of social relations.

In short, Elias argues that the functional complexity of post-medieval Europe went hand-in-hand with a sublimation of people's baser instincts. In other words, Elias is keenly interested in a sociological understanding of social life and of social change.

The reader, at first glance, might wonder at the relevance to an understanding of modern social life-- including crime, criminology, and deviance-- of such observations as "in medieval society people generally blew their noses into their hands" (Elias, 2000: 126). The dominant sociological explanations for the rise of the nation state, after all, usually have been based in economics (e.g., Marx) rather than in the sort of etiquette, manners and social customs that are the key independent variables in Elias' work. However, Elias makes a convincing case that such customs deserve predominant explanatory power, being vehicles of social control that lay the psychological groundwork for the rise of the nation state.

Such an explanation also helps political scientists and others answer the perplexing question of why Western political institutions fail when placed into unfamiliar countries of the periphery or semi-periphery, such as via military conquest or collapse of empire. Many analysts have chalked this up to unequal economic development, but Elias would probably favor an explanation emphasizing the lack of a "civilizing" process in these cases.

It is important to appreciate that the state does not rely on coercion or threat of coercion alone to inhibit violence. Refraining from violence can become a habit, or, as Norbert Elias phrases it, "second nature" or *habitus.* See Box 10.1. As Elias might phrase it, civilized parties will inhibit a temptation to aggress even when leviathan's back is turned. Then, too, soft power can inhibit violence.

Joseph S. Nye, Jr., former Dean of the Kennedy School of Government at Harvard University, coined the term **soft power** to refer the ability to affect others through the co-optive means of framing the agenda, persuading, and eliciting positive attraction (Nye, 2011: 20-21). In other words, soft power is the power of attraction. Hard power is push. Soft power is pull. The types of resources associated with soft power include the intangible factors such as institutions, ideas, values, culture, and the perceived legitimacy of policies (Nye, 2011: 21).

It is important to appreciate that here are segments of the population that lay beyond the reach of the state, zones that the civilizing process has not fully penetrated--such as some peripheral and mountainous backwaters of Europe; the frontiers of the American West and of the American South, both of which retained their violent cultures of honor; the countries of the bottom billion, and swaths of the unassimilated population.

2. **COMMERCE** A second factor contributing to the historical decline in violence is commerce, a positive-sum game in which everybody can win (Pinker, 2012: 36; Durkheim, 1964, 1895). As technological changes enable the exchange of ideas and goods over larger and larger distances and over larger and larger groups of trading partners, other people become more valuable alive (they can buy your goods) than dead. Society comes to devalue violence.

3. **FEMINIZATION_** A third factor promoting our species' retreat from violence has been a growing respect for the values, interests, and education of females. Since violence is largely a young, male pastime, societies that empower their female populations tend to move away from a glorification of violence.

4. **COSMOPOLITANISM** A fourth factor promoting the historical decline in violence is cosmopolitanism (e.g., Beck, 2006; Fukuyama, 2006; Brock and Brighouse, 2005; Chea and Robbins, 1998). In the traditional sense, **cosmopolitanism** refers to loyalty to the good of humanity as a

whole even if it conflicts with loyalty to the interests of one's own nation (Robbins, 2012). The word derives from the Greek words *cosmos*, which can be translated into English as "the universe" and *polites*, which can be translated into English as "citizen." Put these two words together and you get "citizen of the world" or "world citizen." A person who embraces or adheres to the idea of cosmopolitanism in any of its various forms is called a **cosmopolitan** or **cosmopolite**.

When cosmopolitans look at the social world they see not only many states, they see a global society of states, a global society of individuals. When we speak about justice, say the cosmopolitans, we should speak about justice for individuals. In Immanuel Kant's influential essay "Perpetual Peace" (Kant, 1795), the dogma is asserted that all the individuals of the world have equal right to "use the right to the earth's surface which belongs to the human race in common". In other words, cosmopolitans tend to be *redistributionist*—they assert as a basic human right that the bounty of the planet should be distributed equally among all of the peoples on the planet. In short, cosmopolitans are focused on issues of redistributive justice—i.e., on issues of who gets what (Nye, 2005:27). Cosmopolitans also assert that national boundaries have no moral standing and merely serve to defend inequalities that should be abolished (Nye, 2005: 27). In other words, for cosmopolitans, national boundaries are illegitimate and peoples of the world have the right, as a basic human right, to move when and where they want to. For instance, the peoples living in failed states have the basic human right to emigrate, to immigrate to and to live in any state in the world. This free movement of peoples and redistribution of resources, say the cosmopolitans, would result in less violence in the world. Others, of course, argue that the radical redistribution espoused by cosmopolitans is likely to result in *increased* violent conflict because people tend not to give up their wealth and privileged position easily (Nye, 2005: 27).

Cosmopolitanism is an ancient school of thought or philosophy, dating back to the Cynics of the fourth century B.C. (Appiah, 2006) and it influenced the ethical legacies of the Enlightenment (e.g., Kant, 1784, 1795), the French Revolution, and it is embodied in the United Nations' (UN) Universal Declaration of Human Rights (UDHR), which was adopted by the UN General Assembly in 1948. While the UN Charter commits states to respect fundamental freedoms, the UDHR does not have the force of international law; rather, the UDHR enunciates or sets forth hoped-for international norms regarding the behavior of governments toward both their own citizens and foreigners alike (Goldstein and Pevehouse, 2010: 250-251). The declaration roots itself in the principle that violations of human rights upset international order by causing outrange, sparking rebellion, and so forth. The declaration proclaims that "all human beings are born free and equal" without regard to race, sex, language, religion, or political affiliation, or the status of the territory in which they were born (Goldstein and Pevehouse, 2010: 250). It goes on to promote norms in a wide variety of areas, including banning torture, guaranteeing religious and political freedom, and ensuring the "right of economic well-being."

Enforcing norms of human rights is difficult because it involves interfering in a state's internal affairs. Nonetheless, in recent years international norms have shifted against, or away from, sovereignty (i.e., the right of a state to do what it wants within its own borders without interference from other states). In fact, a major summit of world leaders in 2005 enshrined the concept of **responsibility to protect** (R2P), which holds that governments worldwide "must act to save civilians from genocide or **crimes against humanity** perpetrated by their own governments" (Goldstein and

Pevehouse, 2010: 252). Crimes against humanity are defined as "inhumane acts and persecutions against civilians on a vast scale in the pursuit of unjust ends" (Goldstein and Pevehouse, 2010: 252).

Abuses of human rights often occur on a large scale during war. Serious violations of human rights are considered **war crimes**. War crimes are violations of the law governing the conduct of warfare, such as unnecessarily targeting civilians or mistreating prisoners of war (Goldstein and Pevehouse, 2010: 360). In 1998 many of the world's states signed a treaty to create a permanent **International Criminal Court** (ICC), which is a permanent tribunal for war crimes and crimes against humanity. The ICC is located in The Hague, the third largest city of the Netherlands. The ICC hears cases of genocide, war crimes, and crimes against humanity from anywhere in the world.

Factors that promote cosmopolitanism include literacy, the movement of peoples (geographical mobility), and mass media. Each of these can prompt people to take on the role of the other, i.e., to take the perspective of people unlike themselves, to expand their circle of "we-ness," of sympathy. It is more difficult to de-humanize people and to aggress against them if we feel sympathy and empathy with them, if we identify with them.

5. **REASON** A final factor that has helped to move our species away from violence is the triumph of reason over superstition in the structuring of our affairs. For instance, Peace Studies reframes war and violence as problems to be solved rather than as contests to be won. How we frame things matters. Intensifying the application of reason and knowledge to human affairs can encourage people to recognize the futility of cycles of violence.

   Let us now turn our attention to a consideration of crime in the United States today.

CRIME IN THE UNITED STATES TODAY

To be convicted of a crime in the United States, a person must be found guilty of having violated the criminal law.

How Much Crime Is There?

There are three major sources of data on how much crime there is in the United States—the Uniform Crime Reports (UCR), the National Crime Victimization Survey (NCVS), and self-report data. The most widely cited source of crime data in the United States is the Uniform Crime Report, which is published annually by the Federal Bureau of Investigation, and these data are based on crime known to the police.

UNIFORM CRIME REPORTS

The Uniform Crime Reports express crime data in three ways. First, raw figures express the numbers of crimes known to the police. For example, 14,612 murders occurred in 2011. This is 2,317 *fewer* homicides than in 2007 (Federal Bureau of Investigation, 2012). Second, crime rates are reported as the number of crimes per 100,000 population. The number of reported crimes divided by the number of people in the total United States population multiplied by 100,000 is the crime rate per 100,000 population. In equation form, the formula looks like this:

$$\frac{\text{Number of Reported Crimes}}{\text{Total U.S. Population}} \times 100{,}000 = \text{Rate per 100,000}$$

The 2011 murder rate was 4.7 murders per 100,000 population, while it was 5.6 just four years previously in 2007. Third, the Uniform Crime Report expresses crime data as percentage change from one year to another. Thus, the 2011 murder rate of 4.7 offenses per 100,000 inhabitants is 17.4 percent lower than the rate for 2007 (Federal Bureau of Investigation, 2012). That is a sizeable drop in a short amount of time.

TABLE 10.2 DEFINITIONS OF UCR PART I OFFENSES

The Crime	Definition
Criminal Homicide	1. Murder and nonnegligent manslaughter: the willful (nonnegligent) killing of one human being by another. Deaths caused by negligence, attempts to kill, assaults to kill, suicides, and accidental deaths are excluded. Justifiable homicide is limited to a) the killing of a felon by a law enforcement officer in the line of duty, b) the killing of a felon, during the commission of a felony, by a private citizen 2. Manslaughter by negligence: the killing of another person through gross negligence. Deaths of persons due to their own negligence, accidental deaths not resulting from gross negligence, and traffic fatalities are not included in the category Manslaughter by negligence.
Forcible Rape	The carnal knowledge of a female forcibly and against her will. Rapes by force and attempts or assaults to rape regardless of the age of victim are included. Statutory offenses (no force used—victim under age of consent) are excluded.
Robbery	The taking or attempting to take anything of value from the care, custody, or control of a person or persons by force or threat of force or violence and/or by putting the victim in fear.
Aggravated assault	An unlawful attack by one person against another for the purpose of inflicting severe or aggravated bodily injury. This type of assault usually is accompanied by the use of a weapon or by means likely to produce death or great bodily harm.
Burglary (breaking or entering)	The unlawful entry of a structure to commit a felony or a theft. Attempted forcible entry is included.
Larceny-theft (except motor vehicle theft)	The unlawful taking, carrying, leading, or riding away of property from the possession or constructive possession of another. Examples are thefts of bicycles or automobile accessories, shoplifting, pocket-picking, or the stealing of any property or article which is not taken by force and violence or by fraud. Attempted larcenies are included. Embezzlement, confidence games, forgery, worthless checks, etc., are excluded.

Motor vehicle theft	The theft or attempted theft of a motor vehicle. A motor vehicle is self-propelled and runs on the surface and not on rails. Specifically excluded from this category are motorboats, construction equipment, airplanes, and farming equipment.
Arson	Any willful or malicious burning or attempt to burn, with or without intent to defraud, a dwelling house, public building, motor vehicle or aircraft, personal property of another, etc.

Source: U.S. Department of Justice, Federal Bureau of Investigation, *Crime in the United States 2010* Offense Definitions. Released September 2011. As of May 25, 2013, available online at http://www.fbi.gov/about-us/cjis/ucr/crime-in-the-u.s/2010/crime-in-the-u.s.-2010/offense-definitions

TABLE 10.3 UCR CRIME CLOCK STATISTICS, 2011

Violent	**Crime**	every	26.2	Seconds
One	Murder	every	36.0	Minutes
One	Forcible Rape	every	6.3	Minutes
One	Robbery	every	1.5	Minutes
One	Aggravated Assault	every	42.0	Seconds
Property	**Crime**	every	3.5	Seconds
One	Burglary	every	14.4	Seconds
One	Larceny-Theft	every	5.1	Seconds
One	Motor-Vehicle Theft	every	44.1	Seconds

Source: Uniform Crime Reports 2011. As of May 13, 2013, available online at http://www.fbi.gov/about-us/cjis/ucr/crime-in-the-u.s/2011/crime-in-the-u.s.-2011/offenses-known-to-law-enforcement/crime-clock

The UCR classifies crimes into two large groups, Part I Offenses (also known as Index Offenses or Index Crimes) and Part II Offenses. Part I Offenses include the four violent crimes of murder and nonnegligent manslaughter, forcible rape, robbery, and aggravate assault, and the four property crimes of burglary, larceny/theft, motor vehicle theft, and arson. Thus, there are eight Part I Offenses. See Table 10.2 for definitions of these UCR crimes. See Table 10.3 for summary measures of how much crime there is in America. Table 10.3 reports the figures derived from the UCR's 2011 "Crime Clock." For each of the index offenses, the total number of crimes is divided by the number of hours or minutes or seconds in a year, to tell us how many of each crime happens per each unit of time. UCR data indicate that violent crime has been on the decrease in this country for several years. See Table 10.4. UCR data also indicate that property crime also has been decreasing in the United States. See Table 10.5.

The UCR program collects and publishes data on "clearance rates" for the Part I offenses. Crimes may be "cleared" in the UCR program in one of two ways. A crime is ***cleared by arrest*** when a person is arrested, charged with the commission of the offense, and turned over for prosecution. A crime is ***cleared by exceptional means*** when a person would have been arrested, charged with the commission of the offense and turned over for prosecution, except that the law-enforcement agency encountered circumstances outside of its control, which prohibited the agency from arresting, charging, and prosecuting the offender.

Examples of exceptional circumstances include, but are not necessarily limited to, the death of the offender; the victim's refusal to cooperate with the prosecution after the offender had been identified; the denial of extradition of the offender who had fled the jurisdiction in which the crime was committed. See Table 10.6.

TABLE 10.4 UNIFORM CRIME REPORTS: VIOLENT CRIME RATES IN THE UNITED STATES, SELECTED YEARS, 1990-2011 (NUMBER OF CRIMES PER 100,000 INHABITANTS)

Year	Violent Crime	Murder and Non-Negligent Homicide	Forcible Rape	Robbery	Aggravated Assault
1990	729.6	9.4	41.1	256.3	422.9
2000	506.5	5.5	32.0	145.0	324.0
2005	469.0	5.6	31.8	140.8	290.8
2006	480.6	5.8	31.7	150.6	292.6
2007	472.0	5.7	30.5	148.4	287.4
2008	457.5	5.4	29.7	145.7	276.7
2009	429.4	5.0	28.7	133.0	262.8
2010	403.6	4.8	27.5	119.1	262.3
2011	386.3	4.7	26.8	113.7	241.1

Source: U.S. Department of Justice, Federal Bureau of Investigation. *Uniform Crime Reports* 2011. As of May 13, 2013, available online at http://www.fbi.gov/about-us/cjis/ucr/crime-in-the-u.s/2011/crime-in-the-u.s.-2011/tables/table-1; Uniform Crime Reports 2009 at http://www.fbi.gov/ucr/cius2009/data/table_01.html ;Uniform Crime Reports 2010, as of July 17, 2012, available online at http://www.fbi.gov/about-us/cjis/ucr/crime-in-the-u.s/2010/crime-in-the-u.s.-2010/tables/10tbl01.xls Reports 2011

TABLE 10.5 UNIFORM CRIME REPORTS: PROPERTY CRIME RATES, SELECTED YEARS 1990-2011 (NUMBER OF CRIMES PER 100,000 INHABITANTS)

Year	Property Crime	Burglary	Larceny Theft	Motor Vehicle Theft
1990	5073.1	1232.2	3185.1	655.8
2000	3618.3	728.8	2477.3	412.2
2005	3431.5	726.9	2287.8	416.8
2006	3357.7	735.2	2221.4	401.1
2007	3276.8	726.0	2186.3	364.6
2008	3211.5	732.1	2164.5	315.0
2009	3036.1	716.3	2060.9	258.8
2010	2941.9	699.6	2003.5	238.8
2011	2908.7	702.2	1976.9	229.8

Source: U.S. Department of Justice, Federal Bureau of Investigation. *Uniform Crime Reports* 2011. As of May 13, 2013, available online at http://www.fbi.gov/about-us/cjis/ucr/crime-in-the-u.s/2011/crime-in-the-u.s.-2011/tables/table-1; Uniform Crime Reports 2009 at http://www.fbi.gov/ucr/cius2009/data/table_01.html ;Uniform Crime Reports 2010, as of July 17, 2012, available online at http://www.fbi.gov/about-us/cjis/ucr/crime-in-the-u.s/2010/crime-in-the-u.s.-2010/tables/10tbl01.xls Reports 2011

TABLE 10.6 UNIFORM CRIME REPORTS CLEARANCE RATES FOR VIOLENT AND FOR PROPERTY CRIMES, 2011

Year	Violent Crime	Murder and Non-Negligent Homicide	Forcible Rape	Robbery	Aggravated Assault
2011	47.7%	64.8%	41.2%	28.7%	56.9%
	Property Crime	Burglary	Larceny Theft	Motor Vehicle Theft	Arson
	18.6%	12.7%	21.5	11.9	18.8%

Source: U.S. Department of Justice, Federal Bureau of Investigation. Uniform Crime Reports 2011. As of May 13, 2013, available online at http://www.fbi.gov/about-us/cjis/ucr/crime-in-the-u.s/2011/crime-in-the-u.s.-2011/tables/table_25

Nationwide in 2011, 47.7 percent of violent crimes were cleared by arrest or exceptional means, and 18.6 percent of property crimes. As a general rule, the more serious a crime, the higher the clearance rate. Of the violent crimes, murder had the highest clearance rate—64.8 percent.

NATIONAL CRIME VICTIMIZATION SURVEY

Crime that occurs but that is not reported to the police is known as **the dark figure of crime**. The National Crime Victimization Survey (NCVS) provides data that shed light on the dark figure of crime. The NCVS is based on a national probability sample of households in the United States, and the U.S. Bureau of Justice Statistics (BJS) publishes it each year. With the exception of murder, the NCVS asks respondents whether they have experienced any of the Part I Offenses as well as other specific crimes. The national probability survey method of the NCVS allows the BJS to estimate the likelihood of victimization by rape, sexual assault, robbery, assault, theft, household burglary, and motor-vehicle theft for the population as a whole as well as for segments of the population, such as women, the elderly, members of various racial groups, city dwellers, rural dwellers, and other groups.

What do NCVS data tell us about the amount of crime in the United States? According to 2011 NCVS data, violent crime rates *declined* 30 percent between 2002-2011 (Truman and Planty, 2012: Table2, page 3). For instance, between 2002-2011, the number of rapes *declined* 30 percent, the number of robberies *declined* 11 percent, and the number of aggravated assaults *declined* 21 percent (Truman and Planty, 2012: Table 1, page 2). These are large declines in a short period of time and the direction of the changes (i.e., downward) is the same as is indicated by Uniform Crime Report data. Similarly, according to 2011 NCVS data, and the number of property crimes declined 8 percent between 2002-2011 (Truman and Planty, 2012: Table 2, page 3). For instance, between 2002-2011, the number of motor-vehicle thefts *declined* 38 percent (Truman and Planty, 2012: Table 3, page 4), the number of larceny thefts *declined* 10 percent (Truman and Planty, 2012: Table 9, page 9), as did the number of burglaries (Truman and Planty, 2012: Table 8, page 8). Once again, these are large declines in a short period of time and the direction of the changes (i.e., downward) is the same as is indicated by the Uniform Crime Report data.

It is worth noting that declines in the rate of crime victimization occurred in all measured demographic groups in the United States. For instance, with respect to the rate of violent crimes, the NCVS data indicate that between 2002-2011, Blacks experienced a *decline* of 27 percent in the rate of violent crime victimizations and Hispanics a decline of 20 percent, American Indian and Alaskan Natives a decline of 28 percent, and Asian Americans experienced a decline of 4 percent in the rate of violent crime victimizations (Truman and Planty, 2012: Table 5, page 5).

SELF-REPORTS AND VALIDITY OF SELF-REPORTS

A third source of information about the extent and incidence of crime and deviant behavior is provided by self-report surveys. Self-report surveys are based on the principle that if the researcher guarantees respondents anonymity or confidentiality, that people will accurately report their illegal or deviant behaviors. The types of items typically included on self-report surveys are not comparable to the Index Crimes of the Uniform Crime Reports. Instead, self-report surveys tend to ask people about lesser offenses— truancy, shoplifting, alcohol use, fighting, damaging school property, and so forth. Self-reports tend to be used largely to ask juveniles in school about their minor offending and deviant behaviors.

In what is probably the most thorough analysis of the validity of self-report survey methodologies, sociologists Michael Hindelang, Travis Hirschi, and Joseph Weis (1981) document that self-report surveys are differentially valid by race by sex. Among young African-American males, the results of self-report surveys that ask about serious offending, such as the crimes included in the UCR Index Offenses, lack validity. Thus, for "serious offenses...the white" male "nonreporting rate was 20 percent compared to a rate of 57 percent" among black males (Hindelang, Hirschi, Weis, 1981: 173). African American males "are less likely to report delinquent offenses at all levels" of severity and especially for serious offenses. On self-report instruments, African American males failed to report 67 percent of their arrests for burglary and robbery, 62 percent of arrests for weapons offenses, and 57 percent of arrests for motor-vehicle theft. Among African-American males, the failure to self-report significant offenses remains pronounced whatever the method of administration of the self-report instrument (Hindelang, Hirschi, and Weis, 1981: 123,172, 178). In summary, a method of data collection (i.e., self reports) shown to be clearly false in so important a respect loses all claim to validity as a measure of crime and delinquency.

Hate Crimes

Attacks on individuals because of how they are perceived to look, pray, or behave long have been part of the human experience. In 1990 the federal government of the United States gave it a name, **hate crime** and decided to monitor it by giving law enforcement the task of identifying and responding to hate crime. Hate crimes, also known as bias crimes, are offenses determined by law enforcement to have been driven by bias against race, religion, ethnicity, sexual orientation and, since 1994, disability.

The Uniform Crime Reporting Program has been a primary source of crime statistics for the use of law enforcement since the Program's establishment in 1929. When the Hate Crimes Statistics Act of 1990 was enacted, the UCR Program became the clearinghouse for the collection and dissemination of data regarding these crimes. See Table 10.7.

TABLE 10.7 HATE CRIMES IN THE UNITED STATES, BY OFFENSE TYPE, 2011

Crimes Against the Person	Number	Percent
Intimidation	1,720	45.82
Simple Assault	1,336	35.59
Aggravated Assault	677	18.03
Murder and Nonnegligent Homicide	4	0.11
Forcible Rape	7	0.19
Other	10	0.27
Total*	**3,754**	**100.00**
Crimes Against Property	Number	Percent
Destruction/Damage/Vandalism	2,125	81.39
Larceny-Theft	152	5.82
Robbery	131	5.02
Burglary	124	4.75
Arson	42	1.61
Other	31	1.19
Motor-Vehicle Theft	6	0.23
Total	**2,611**	**100.00**

Source: Federal Bureau of Investigation, *Hate Crimes Statistics 2011* (Washington, D.C.: Government Printing Office, 2012), Table 2. As of May 26, 2013, available online at http://www.fbi.gov/about-us/cjis/ucr/hate-crime/2011/tables/table-2

* Percents may not add to 100 due to rounding. The total number of incidents is 6,222. However, the column figures will not add to the total because incidents may include more than one offense type and these are counted in each appropriate offense type category.

In 2011, law enforcement agencies reported over 6,222 hate crime offenses, which is a decline of 31.9 percent since 2007. This is a large decrease in a short period of time.

Of the 6,222 hate crimes reported in 2011, racial bias accounted for 46.9 percent of the single-bias incidents. Sexual-orientation bias motivated 20.8 percent of the incidents, religious bias provoked 19.8 percent of incidents, and bias against ethnicity or national origin caused 11.6 percent. Bias against a physical or mental disability was the basis of 0.9 percent of the single-bias incidents (Federal Bureau of Investigation, Hate Crime Statistics 2011).

Of the 1,233 reported incidents rooted in religious bias, anti-Jewish bias accounted for 62.5 percent of these offenses, anti-Islamic bias made up 12.7 percent of these offenses, and bias against other, unspecified religious groups made up 10.5 percent. Of the remainder, 5.4 percent of the offenses were anti-Catholic, 3.5 percent anti-Protestant, 4.8 percent anti-multiple-religions, and 0.34 percent was anti-atheism or anti-agnosticism (Federal Bureau of Investigation, Hate Crimes Statistics 2011, Table 1).

White-Collar Crime

The term white-collar crime was originally coined by Edwin Sutherland in an address to the American Sociological Association in 1939. As originally used by Sutherland, the term **white-collar crime** refers to activities of moral or administrative disrepute committed by respectable individuals of high social status during the course of their professions. Sutherland's original definition has been widely rejected today.

Two points are worth noting. First, most of the offenses that Sutherland and other sociologists term white-collar crimes actually were not, and many still are not, violations of statutory criminal law. To the extent white-collar "crimes" tend to result in court action, many of these court actions tend to take place either in civil or administrative law proceedings. Second, due to changes in technology and mass communication, not only the upper classes, but the lower classes as well, have access to opportunities to commit white-collar crime.

Another definition of white-collar crime that is widely accepted comes from ***Herbert Edelhertz***, who defines white-collar crime as an illegal act or a series of illegal acts committed by non-physical means for the purpose of obtaining money and property (Edelhertz, 1970). White-collar crime is distinguishable conceptually from corporate crime. **Corporate crime** is committed by individuals in formal organizations for the benefit of the formal organization. Thus, financial embezzlement by employees for their *own* benefit is white collar crime, while false advertising of a company's products is corporate crime. Some examples of corporate crimes are corporate income tax evasion, bribery, extortion, insider trading, and anti-trust violations. Examples of white-collar crime are employee theft, embezzlement, and Ponzi schemes. See Box 10.2.

Sociologists, particularly those of a conflict orientation, tend to lament the fact that white-collar crime often generates very little attention. It is an axiom of conflict theory that the financial and social costs to society occasioned by white-collar crime exceed those occasioned by "street" property crimes which receive a lot of attention in the Uniform Crime Reports. Conflict theorists proffer four reasons for a putative lack of attention to white-collar crime.

The first factor is the group-serving bias. The dominant classes in the country downplay deviance and crime committed by their own group and concentrate instead on the crimes committed disproportionately by the lower classes. The dominant classes do not like to think ill of themselves and hence they tend not to focus on crimes perpetrated by their own members. In a classic article, sociologist ***Alexander Liazos*** (1972) criticizes American sociologists for concentrating on norm breaking among the powerless and oppressed segments of the population--nuts, sluts, and perverts--to the neglect of more serious and harmful deviance among the powerful and affluent groups. Examples of deviance among the affluent include inequitable taxation, racism, sexism, and environmental pollution. Sociologists, Liazos laments, have tended to ignore unethical, illegal, and socially destructive activities of powerful groups and individuals.

Second, conflict theorists perceive the interests of the dominant classes as differing from those of the working classes. Hence, all the institutions of society preserve the interests of those in positions of power and control. As part of this effort, crime committed by the members of the upper classes is either ignored or is not taken seriously. Hence, quite generally crime by the powerful results in very little stigma for the perpetrator.

Third, the type of crime that elicits fear and dread of injury is street crime. Even though injury from a faulty product may result in far more serious injury, there traditionally has been a widespread lack of dread about white-collar criminal activities.

Fourth, the costs of white-collar crime are diffused. Although the economic cost of white collar crime is enormous, this cost is diffused over thousands or many millions of people, and therefore usually is not even perceived directly or significantly by individuals.

Let us now turn our attention to sociological theories about why people commit crime and deviance.

OF PONZI SCHEMES AND THE PUNISHMENT OF WHITE-COLLAR CRIMES IN THE UNITED STATES AND PEOPLES REPUBLIC OF CHINA

BOX 10.2

The Ponzi scheme gains its name from a fraud conducted by Charles Ponzi (1882-1949), an Italian who immigrated to Boston, Massachusetts, almost a century ago. Within a six-month period during the spring and summer of 1920, Ponzi went from obscure poverty to being a Boston millionaire (Zuckoff, 2005) by promising to double investors' money in three months. Profits were supposed to come from exchanging international postal reply coupons. At the peak of his success, Ponzi was taking in more than 2 million dollars a week. In a Ponzi scheme, the criminal pays off early investors with the money that comes in from later investors.

Ponzi's scheme came tumbling down but not before thousands of investors were bilked out of $15 million (THE WEEK, January 30, 2009: 11). When the dust settled, six banks had failed due to the Ponzi scheme and Ponzi's 40,000 investors were practically wiped out, losing more than two of every three dollars they had invested with Ponzi (Zuckoff, 2005). Federal authorities charged Ponzi with 86 counts of mail fraud for sending letters to his "marks" notifying them that their notes had matured. He pleaded guilty to a single count and was sentenced to five years in federal prison (Zuckoff, 2005). Upon his release, Ponzi was tried on Massachusetts state charges of larceny, was found guilty and was sentenced to 7 to 9 years in prison. He served 7 years in prison and was released in 1934.

After word got around that, although Ponzi had lived in the United States for most of the time since 1903, he never obtained American citizenship, federal officials deported him to Italy. He died penniless in a charity hospital in Rio de Janeiro on January 18, 1949.

In March, 2009, Bernard Madoff, former NASDAQ stock market Chairman, pleaded guilty to having run a world-wide Ponzi scheme for over twenty years. NASDAQ is an acronym for the National Association of Securities Dealers Automated Quotations, an American stock exchange (Terrell, 2006). NASDAQ is the largest electronic stock market in the world, having more trading volume per hour than any other stock exchange (Ingebretsen, 2002). So, Bernie Madoff, as former NASDAQ Chairman, was a highly influential financier.

Madoff orchestrated his Ponzi scheme by telling clients that he could earn steady returns of 10 percent to 15 percent a year using a secret stock trading strategy. There were many eager investors. Bernie Madoff bilked more than 4,800 client accounts for as much as $65 billion dollars (McCool and Graybow, March 12, 2009). Madoff's malfeasance was brought to light when the worldwide financial crisis prompted many of his investors to liquidate. Madoff simply was unable to bring in the funds to meet the redemption requests.

In March, 2009, Madoff, 71 years of age, pleaded guilty to 11 federal charges including securities fraud, mail fraud, wire fraud, three counts of money laundering, making false statements and perjury. In June of the same year, Bernard Madoff was sentenced to 150 years in prison for his crimes (McCool and Graybow, June 29, 2009), the stiffest sentence possible under the federal sentencing guidelines.

In contrast to the situation in the United States, in the Peoples Republic of China, people who commit serious white-collar crimes may be sentenced to death. According to human-rights groups, China carries out more court-ordered executions than the rest of the world combined (Kahn, 2007). For example, in 2006 the Government claimed that 1,010 people were executed in China, while human-rights groups have credible reports putting "the actual figure closer to 8,000. During that same year, the rest of the world combined executed about 1,591 people" (Amnesty International Australia, 2008). Precisely how many court-ordered executions China carries out each year—-and, of those, how many are for white-collar crimes—-are unknowns, because the government of China says the statistics are state secrets.

We now briefly examine three highly publicized white-collar crimes in the Peoples Republic of China during the past few years that resulted in the death penalty being carried out against the offenders.

In January, 2009, two men were given the death penalty for their involvement in China's contaminated and watered-down baby-milk scandal. Melamine is a chemical used to make plastics and fertilizers. This chemical is toxic if ingested, and if it is ingested in large amounts it can cause kidney stones and kidney failure. It can also give the appearance of higher protein levels when mixed into watered-down milk. Twenty-two companies sold the melamine-contaminated watered-down milk and major dairy companies in China bought the contaminated milk from such dealers, failing to test the milk for purity and nutritional value. This toxic milk killed at least six children in China, made nearly 300,000 ill, and led to product recalls across the globe (BBC NEWS, 2009; MSNBC World News, January 22, 2009).

In February, 2009, a Chinese court sentenced Li Peiying, 59 years old, the former Chairman of the state-owned holding company that was responsible for overseeing 30 airports, including Beijing International, to death for bribery and embezzlement amounting $14.6 million during an eight year period from 1995. Li was also found guilty of having misappropriated $12 million in funds for personal use during a three-year period from 2000. In handing down its sentence, the court said that Li's actions had resulted in large economic losses for the nation and that the amounts involved were extraordinary (MarketWatch, 2009).

On July 10, 2007, China executed Zheng Xiaoyu, the former head of Beijing's version of the Food and Drug Administration in the United States (Barboza, 2007). Mr. Zheng had helped to create and then he headed this important agency from 1998 to 2005. Mr. Zheng was found guilty of dereliction of duty in personally approving unsafe and unproven medicines after having accepted $850,000 in bribes--in a country where the average worker at the time earned less than $2,000 a year (Kahn, 2007). During his eight-year reign as the head of China's ministry of food and drug safety, Zheng personally ordered approvals of more than 150,000 new medicines. That is an approval rate that is 134 times higher than that of the FDA in the United States which only approves 140 or so new medicines each year. Most of these 150,000 new medicines were produced by the eight pharmaceutical companies that bribed Zheng (Barboza, 2007).

THEORIES OF CRIME AND DEVIANCE

Many people want to understand why people engage in crime, delinquency, and deviance. Sociologists tend to use the same theories to explain why people engage in crime, delinquency, and deviance. We now examine some of these theories, roughly arranged by paradigm.

Consensus Theories

There are several consensus theories of criminal behavior, particularly structural theories, which consider society's social structure or organization. In these theories, folkways, mores, and laws are viewed as reflecting society's values. Some crime and deviance are seen as inevitable, even functional, or as due to a weakened bond between the individual and the conventional (law-abiding) social order. The consensus approach is illustrated by the contributions of Durkheim, Merton, and Hirschi.

EMILE DURKHEIM—CRIME AND DEVIANCE AS NORMAL

Emile Durkheim, the noted French sociologist, made significant contributions to the study of all human behavior. Perhaps his greatest contribution to the study of crime and deviance was his observation that these phenomena are normal, have functional consequences, and that no society can be free from them (1964:66).

What are the functions of crime/deviance? First, crime and deviance and the social response to them can serve to increase group solidarity. For example, one summer's night in 1969, the police raided a gay bar in Greenwich Village, New York, called the Stonewall Inn. In the past, police had raided gay bars across this nation with impunity, meeting no overt resistance. On this night, however, the gays in this particular bar resisted the rousting, resisted arrest, and thereby sparked a riot. The riot is known as the Stonewall riot, and it touched off a gay rights movement in the United States.

Second, crime and deviance serve to clarify and maintain boundaries between acceptable and unacceptable behavior. This is called a boundary maintenance function. For example, the responses of the United States to the atrocities of September 11, 2001, served to let terrorists around the globe know that such acts would not be tolerated by the government of these United States.

Third, crime and deviance may serve an innovative function. When Rosa Parks refused to sit at the back of a public bus in an era of de jure racial segregation, she helped to spark the civil-rights movement in the United States. Sometimes crime and deviance are a catalyst for inspiring social actors to change their social systems in fundamental ways.

ROBERT K. MERTON'S STRAIN OR ANOMIE THEORY

Robert K. Merton (1910-1993) authored what is perhaps the best known explanation of crime and deviance, strain (or anomie) theory (Merton, 1938). This perspective provides an explanation for the concentration of crime in lower-class urban areas as well as for the overall high crime rate in American society. This theory leans heavily on the insights of Emile Durkheim, whose ideas Merton adapts to build anomie or strain theory.

As we have previously seen, Durkheim used the term anomie to refer to norms being in flux, guidelines for behavior no longer being clear. Merton adapts this concept to the conditions of modern industrial societies in general and the United States in particular. To Merton, an integrated society maintains balance between culture (approved goals) and social structure (access to legitimate means). Merton used the term anomie to refer to a form of societal malintegration, wherein there is strain or disjunction between the culturally approved goal of financial success and access to legitimate means, such as education and jobs, for its attainment.

FIGURE 10.1 ROBERT K. MERTON'S TYPOLOGY OF MODES OF ADAPTATION

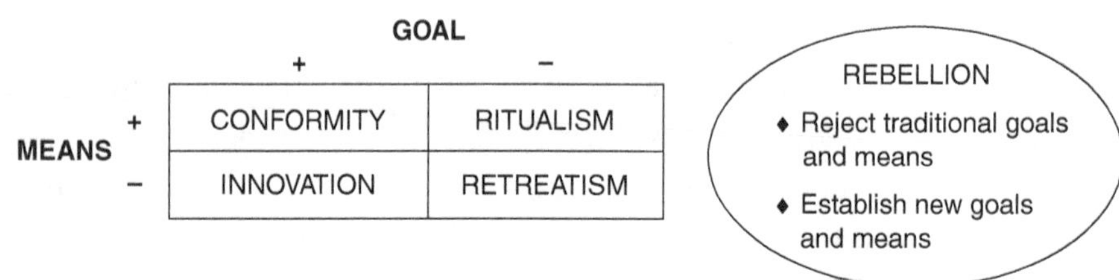

There are various ways that individuals may respond to the problem of anomie. Merton describes these options as conformity, innovation, ritualism, retreatism, and rebellion. See Figure 10.1. In *conformity* one uses legitimate means to attain the goal of financial success. This is the most frequently used adaptation. In contrast, *innovation* represents an acceptance of the goal but rejection of legitimate means to attain it. In innovation, one uses illegitimate means to attain the goal of financial success. Robbing a store or selling illegal drugs are examples of innovation. Most crimes and delinquency belong to this adaptive mode, according to Merton. Another deviant mode, *rebellion*, rejects the system altogether, both means and goals, and establishes new goals and new means in their place. Yet another, *retreatism*, refers to an escapist response: one becomes a societal "dropout," giving up on both the goals and the effort to attain them through legitimate means. Merton perceived that drug addicts, vagrants, alcoholics, many of the homeless, and the severely mentally ill were located in this adaptive mode. In *ritualism*, one uses legitimate means but does not pursue the goal of financial success. For example, one performs one's job just well enough that one does not get fired. Some people use the term "burn out" to describe people who use this adaptation.

Strain theories have clear policy implications. If blocked legitimate opportunities are a cause of crime and deviance, then that activity can be countered by the provision of greater access to legitimate opportunities through educational and job-training programs and through programs and policies that prohibit discrimination on the basis of race, ethnicity, gender, and so forth. Strain theory has had a significant impact on federal policy toward crime and delinquency. A case in point is the Juvenile Delinquency Prevention and Control Act of 1961, which, among other things, improved education, created work opportunities, and provided services for youths and their families, particularly in lower-class urban areas.

Job Corps, established by the U.S. Department of Labor in 1964, is a job-training program for disadvantaged, unemployed youth that continues to this day, with 119 centers across the nation. Job Corps provides services to more than 60,000 new young people each year. Job Corp's main goal is to improve the employability of participants by offering vocational-skills training, basic education, and health care to youths aged 16-24. Of Job-Corps participants, 40 percent come from families on social assistance, 80 percent have dropped out of school, and their mean family income is $6,000 per year (Curtis, 1995).

The most comprehensive study to date of the Job Corps program (Burghardt, Schochet, McConnell, et. al., 2001) finds that it generates significant earnings gains for disadvantaged youth. Earnings gains, educational progress, and other positive changes were found across most groups of participants. Thus, in the fourth year after enrolling in the program, participants' earning power was up about $1500, or 12 percent. Improvements were noted for groups that many programs find hard to reach, including females with children, youth who had been arrested for nonserious crimes, and older students without a high school credential. Job Corps participation significantly reduced involvement with crime, on the order of 16 percent, as well as receipt of public assistance. Furthermore, this $1-billion per year education and job-training program is cost-effective, returning about $2 to society for every dollar spent (Burghardt, Schochet, McConnell, et. al, 2001).

Private-sector equal-opportunity and job-training programs for economically disadvantaged youth are important today as well. Boys and Girls Clubs of America (BGCA) is a case in point. BGCA has a membership today of over 1.3 million boys and girls nationwide, and it has many programs, including Power Hour, SMART Moves, and Project Learn. Power Hour is designed to raise the academic proficiency of club members aged six to twelve. Project Learn reinforces the skills and knowledge young people learn at school through high-yield learning activities at the Club and in the home. Based on Fr. Reginald Clark's research that shows fun but academically beneficial activities increase academic performance, these activities include leisure reading, writing activities, homework assistance, and board games that help develop young people's cognitive skills. Formally evaluated by Columbia University, Project Learn has been proven to boost the academic performance of club members. Similarly, Self-Management and Resistance Training (SMART Moves) provides education to children, parents, and the community at large to assist young people in learning about the dangers of substance abuse and strategies for resisting pressures to use drugs and alcohol. Evaluation results show that housing developments with BGCA have fewer damaged units, less delinquency, an overall reduction in substance abuse and drug trafficking than similar housing developments without the clubs (Schinke, Orlandi, and Cole, 1992; Siegal, Welsh, and Senna, 2003).

Merton points out that strain or anomie theory "is designed to account for some, not all, forms of deviant behavior customarily described as criminal or delinquent" (1968:195). Nonetheless, Merton's theory does not enlighten us as to why people choose one adaptation, such as innovation, over another, such as conformity. However, American sociologist Travis Hirschi (1969) sheds light on this matter in his theory of the social bond.

LOWER-CLASS FOCAL CONCERNS: WALTER B. MILLER

While ***Walter B. Miller*** (1970) accepts the existence of lower class delinquent subcultures, he proposes that lower-classes do not approach the world the same way as the more affluent classes. The question for Miller is not one of reversing or rejecting middle class values such as economic success, education, or happiness. The question for Miller is, "On what do youth focus or expend their attentional resources?"

Miller appreciates that *we* humans *have limited attentional resources.* For instance, research on memory and information processing indicates that people's short-term memory can hold or retain or process only seven "chunks" of information, plus or minus two, at any given time. This aspect of human memory was reported over a half century ago by George A. Miller, a cognitive psychologist at Princeton University (1956), and this characteristic of human memory functioning is so well established that it is known as ***Miller's Law.*** When our short-term attentional resources are filled up, they are not available for investment elsewhere.

Sociologist Walter B. Miller develops a class-based explanation of delinquency that utilizes Miller's Law. Walter B. Miller suggests that working-class youth fill their attentional resources--which he terms **focal concerns**--with very different material than do those in more affluent classes. Miller views the lower classes as characterized by unstable marriages, female-headed households, and a lack of economic and child-rearing support from fathers. The following are the lower class focal concerns identified by Miller:

1. **TROUBLE** Getting into trouble and getting out of trouble are major foci that consume a lot of time and energy for this group. Trouble may involve sexual entanglements, criminal behavior, accidents, problems at school and so forth.

2. **TOUGHNESS** refers to a maniacal emphasis on physical strength and masculinity, on using physical violence as a preferred mode of dispute resolution.

3. **SMARTNESS** refers to "street smartness"--the ability to manipulate and to outwit others.

4. **FATE** refers to an external locus of control. Lower classes tend to feel a lower sense of control over destiny. They feel like they are cargo on the ship of life (external locus of control) rather than captain of the ship of life (internal locus of control). Good and bad happenings in life do not have much correlation with personal ability or effort.

5. **AUTONOMY** refers to a low tolerance for being in a subordinate position in a status hierarchy. As a result, it manifests itself in a rejection of and hostility towards authority figures like parents, judges, teachers, police officers, supervisors, and so forth. Statements like "Don't tell me what to do" typify this approach to social life.

6. **EXCITEMENT** Compared to the more evenly regulated rhythm of middle-class life, which revolves around work or school, family, faith community, and conventional leisure activities, the lower classes are thrill seekers whose lives are characterized by long bouts of boredom alternating with periods of high excitement--fighting, drinking to excess, engaging in illegal activities, and so forth. Excitement can lead to trouble.

The main theme of Miller's lower-class focal concerns approach is that people who expend their attentional resources on trouble, toughness, smartness, excitement, fate, and autonomy have few attentional resources remaining to develop approaches to life that maximize the probability that one will be successful in the conventional social order. People who expend their attentional resources on Miller's focal concerns disqualify themselves from successful participation in the conventional social order and increase the probability that they will engage in deviant and law-violating behaviors.

CRITICISMS OF MILLER'S LOWER-CLASS FOCAL CONCERNS APPROACH

Miller's lower class focal concerns approach to understanding deviance has been criticized on a number of grounds, including the following (Vold and Barnard, 1986):

- Values of middle-class boys are no different than the values he ascribes to lower-class boys. In fact, in contemporary society, trouble, toughness, smartness, fate, autonomy, and excitement seem to be the values of all juveniles.
- Most research since Miller indicates that poor parents tend to raise their children with similar values as the middle classes.

- Miller ignores the effects of economic deprivation on these juveniles, and consequently he engages in what William Ryan terms blaming the victim (Ryan, 1971). ***Blaming the victim*** is an umbrella term used by sociologists to refer to that which social psychologists refer to with two concepts—the group-serving bias (ultimate attribution error) and fundamental attribution error.

  Attributions are explanations we give for things--for our own behavior, the behavior of others, and events in the world. When explaining the actions of others, we commit **the fundamental attribution error** when we overestimate the importance of personal dispositions (temperament, personality) and underestimate the importance of situational or social-structural factors. **Group-serving bias** (also known as the ultimate attribution error) refers to the tendency to perceive both the groups and social categories to which one belongs and which one uses as positive reference groups in favorable terms. One of its manifestations is a tendency to give members of the groups and social categories to which one belongs and which one uses as positive reference groups the benefit of the doubt in situations where the evidence may be perceived as ambiguous. In short, the sociological concept "blaming the victim" refers to locating the source or cause of an individual's (or group's) suffering within the person (or group) itself.
- In addition, this approach has been critiqued for ignoring the delinquency of upper classes and females.

TECHNIQUES OF NEUTRALIZATION

Gresham Sykes and ***David Matza*** (1957) provide a technique of neutralization approach that tries to explain how many youth manage to drift between conventional (i.e., law abiding) and law-violating behaviors. Sykes and Matza argue that many youths use techniques of neutralization to avert their responsibility in subjecting others to harm.

What Sykes and Matza discuss as techniques of neutralization, students of psychology might study under the rubric of ego defense mechanisms. **Techniques of neutralization** are procedures that people use to place their superego (conscience) on "hold," so that they may break norms; afterwards, people bring their conscience back "online" and resume living in the conventional moral order. There are five techniques of neutralization:

- ***Denial of responsibility*** is a technique wherein one assigns blame to something outside of one's self. One assigns blame to one's social class, home life, lack of affection, etc.
- ***Denial of victim*** is a technique wherein one argues that the victim "had it coming." Since the person who got hurt was also a criminal, or immoral, or a member of an out group, the behavior is justified or acceptable.
- ***Denial of harm*** is a technique wherein one admits to engaging in the behavior but denies that any harm was done. For instance, one redefines stealing as "borrowing," rape as "sewing wild oats," and property destruction as youthful enthusiasm (e.g., "Boys will be boys").
- ***Condemnation of the condemners*** is a technique which, in the field of logic, is known as an ***ad hominem argument***--an argument aimed against a person. "Ad" is Latin for "at" and "hominem" is Latin for "person" or "man." So, an ad hominem argument is one that appeals to personal prejudices, interests, or emotions rather than to reason. In other words, "If you don't like the message, attack the messenger." For example,
  - "The reason I got an F on the math exam is because I am not a "teacher's pet; only despicable people are teachers' pets."

- "The reason I got a low grade on the exam is because it was a poor examination constructed by an incompetent teacher."
- "Police officers are corrupt, and judges are crooked. I don't have an alcohol problem. The reason I got three tickets within the past four weeks for driving under the influence is because the cops have it in for me. Besides, the police have a monthly quota of tickets they must write and they have to give them to somebody. I am just unlucky."

- ***Appeal to higher loyalties*** One justifies one's action through appeals, for instance, to one's gang or neighborhood. That to which one is loyal is viewed as more important than law-abiding behavior.

Among the contributions of this theory is the idea of soft determinism--the notion that we cannot meaningfully divide juveniles into delinquents and nondelinquents.

TRAVIS HIRSCHI'S THEORY OF THE SOCIAL BOND

In the last third of the twentieth century, American sociologist Travis Hirschi applied Durkheim's insights about the importance of integration to explain crime, delinquency, and deviance in society (Hirschi, 1969). Hirschi wondered why most people, most of the time, refrain from engaging in crime and delinquency, and he found the answer in the strength of the social bond between the individual and the conventional (law-abiding) social order. Hirschi, following Durkheim, hypothesized that if the social bond is strong, crime and delinquency are less likely. However, if the social bond is weak, the individual is unconstrained, freer to engage in crime and deviance. This theory is known as *social control theory*, *control theory,* or as the theory of the social bond.

There are four parts or elements to the social bond, which Hirschi terms attachment, commitment, involvement, and belief. *Attachment* refers to reciprocal positive affect between the individual and the others in the conventional (i.e., law-abiding, non-deviant) social order by the age of six months... For juveniles, attachment has three parts: parents, school, and peers. Of these, attachment to parents at an early age is arguably the most important. This is because the early positive reciprocal attachment to parents is "about" more than mere reciprocal "liking" of each other. For the young person, the primary caregiver *is* a prime "kissy-face-huggy-bear" source, to be sure. Prolonged ventral clinging, being hugged and held by the primary caregiver, is an important source of comfort for the young person. It is also the primary caregiver who meets, or fails to meet, the basic Maslowian needs—for survival, shelter, security, and so forth. Additionally, the primary caregiver is one of the first sources of "No"--of normative and imperative order-- for the young person. In other words, the primary caregiver is a basic source for the young person to learn basic notions of right and wrong behavior. The primary caregiver, in the young person's perceptions of how the primary caregiver interacts with the young person, is a template or mirror from whence the young person formulates a conscience (superego). In effect, the parent is normative order and imperative order incarnate. Reciprocal positive attachment to parent who is grounded in the conventional, law-abiding social order is thus very important (e.g., Murray and Farrington, 2005).

Attachment to school is important, too, because a young person in the United States spends much time at school. The school, as Hirschi reminds us, is "an eminently conventional institution" (1969: 110). It is, among other things, an institution of social control. In order to be able to stay in school, a pupil must bring her/his behavior into conformity with an array of school rules. To the extent that one drops out of school, one also drops out of a major institution that constrains behavior, and one is freer to engage in deviant acts of a variety of sorts.

A third form of attachment for adolescents is that to peers. Delinquent children are likely to have delinquent friends. Non-delinquents are far less likely to have delinquent friends. Hirschi's research indicates that if the other elements of the social bond are strong-- particularly one's stake in conformity (commitment to conventional lines of action)—then one is unlikely to have delinquent friends. Even if a child with a large stake in conformity does have delinquent friends (which isn't very likely), the probability that he/she will commit delinquent acts is relatively low. The evidence strongly supports the view that a child's stake in conformity affects her/his choice of friends rather than the other way around.

Commitment refers to one's stake in conformity, the extent to which one has invested one's time, attentional and temporal resources in conventional lines of behavior—in building a reputation for doing well in school; for being an honest, hard-working, trustworthy person, and so forth. One's stake in conformity is what one has to lose by deviant, criminal, or delinquent behavior.

Involvement refers to the adequacy of supervision by someone well rooted in the conventional social order. This element of the social bond sometimes is called the adequacy of parental supervision, and its meaning is conveyed by the folk saying, "Idle hands are the devil's workshop." That folk saying conveys the sense that a person is more likely to get into trouble if no one is around who is watching out for their best interests all the time. Many traditional agrarian societies, both in Africa and in the former Soviet Union, have a similar saying: "It takes an entire village to raise a child." In these settings, all adults in the community are expected to watch out for, and to protect, all young persons, all of the time.

Belief refers to the extent to which one views traditional authority, and those who embody or represent it, as legitimate. When you think about it, we live and even thrive within layers and layers of imperative order. There are school teachers, principles, police officers, truant officers, judges, probation and parole officers, sheriffs, state troopers, judges, municipal regulations, state laws, federal laws, and so forth. Hirschi's research documents that the stronger one's attachment to parents at a young age, the stronger one's belief.

Hirschi's theory of the social bond has many policy implications. Hirschi's theory argues that juveniles are less likely to engage in delinquent behavior when they are more strongly attached to their parents at an early age, have more to lose from committing crime, have adequate parental supervision, and have stronger beliefs in the moral validity of the law. All these arguments have been linked to policies to reduce delinquency. Curfew laws require juveniles to be at home by a certain hour, and these may enhance parental supervision. Adult-supervised after-school activities and midnight basketball programs in school gyms increase involvement in legitimate activity in the hopes that idle hands will not become the devil's workshop. Moral education programs can strengthen beliefs in the legitimacy of the law by teaching that all persons and all groups benefit from an orderly society in which everybody obeys the rules. Other examples are programs designed to reduce out of wedlock births, that encourage two-parent families, and that provide education in effective parenting practices.

Early Head Start is a federal effort that today operates in 664 communities and serves some 55,000 families across the country. The Administration on Children, Youth, and Families (ACYF) designed Early Head Start to strengthen the family during the critical first three years of a child's life. In 1996 ACYF funded the first 143 programs and brought Early Head Start under the Head Start umbrella. Early Head Start programs are charged with tailoring their program services to meet the needs of low-income pregnant women and families with infants and toddlers in their communities. A comprehensive evaluation of Early Head Start (Love, et. al., 2002) indicates that participating children sustained positive impacts on cognitive and language development and on socio-emotional development. For example, at age 3, Early Head Start children were less negative to their parents, more attentive objects during play, and they were rated lower in aggressive behavior by their parents than control children. Similarly, Early Head Start parents were more emotionally supportive of their children, more likely to report reading daily to their children, and Early Head Start fathers were less likely to report spanking their children during the previous week than control-group parents. Early Head Start succeeded in increasing school attendance among teenage parents and reduced the proportion who had another baby during the first two years after enrollment.

Symbolic Interactionist Theories

There are several symbolic-interactionist theories of criminal behavior and deviant behavior, including labeling and differential association. With regard to crime and deviance there are treatment, prevention, and sentencing approaches based on or informed by symbolic interactionism. Among these is therapeutic jurisprudence. See Box 10.3, "Therapeutic Jurisprudence and the Municipal Court."

BOX 10.3 THERAPEUTIC JURISPRUDENCE AND THE MUNICIPAL COURT

By Bradley P. Cameron, EdD, JD, MCJ, LMSW

I have been municipal court judge of Carthage, Missouri, a town of about 13,000 people, since 1980. I still serve in that capacity. I am also a professor of Social Work at Pittsburg State University, Pittsburg, Kansas. I have been faculty there since 1987.

A few months into my position as municipal court judge, it became clear that I was going to have a number of persons who provided the court with repeat business. Based on this epiphany my social work inclinations began to influence my judicial decision-making process.

I noticed that my repeat customers were consistently appearing before me in court for drug and alcohol offenses, petit theft, assault, and *contempt of cop*, legally known as obstruction. Often alcohol was involved in all of these cases.

Those persons on the repeat list were poor; many were homeless and tended to couch-surf with the repeaters who had a place to live. Fining them became an exercise in futility and when they were assigned community service, they rarely showed up and even when they did there was a lack of supervision to insure they did what they were supposed to do. Putting them in jail was not an option because to do so would require that I provide them with an attorney. The city was not willing to pay for that constitutional requirement.

Because of their socio-economic situation and the legal constraints, I decided that another approach with this population was needed.

I, along with the chief of police, appeared before the city council and lobbied them for a new position of court service officer to aid this group that had taken up residence in municipal court. The council reluctantly agreed to a half-time position and thus began my feeble attempt to utilize a therapeutic approach in municipal court.

Municipal law is divided into those laws that pertain to the operation of the municipality (civil) and those that pertain to offenses dealt with by law enforcement (criminal or quasi-criminal). The municipal court in which I serve deals with the latter.

The types of offenses normally dealt with in municipal courts include:

1. Traffic
2. Driving while intoxicated
3. Possession of a controlled substance
4. Minor in possession of alcohol
5. Simple assaults and domestic violence
6. Petit theft
7. Animal violations
8. Property code violations

A therapeutic approach would be most appropriate for two through six of the above-named offenses.

The general legal assumptions regarding legal intervention at any level are these:

- there is a causal link between legal intervention and positive outcome
- punitive intervention brings about positive behavioral change
- the law affects all citizens in the same way

Empirical scrutiny of these assumptions suggests to me that none of these assumptions holds up.

Many cities rely on the fines generated in municipal court to contribute significantly to the city's coffers. In this way, many cities and towns financially come to rely on a punitive approach to any and all violations of their ordinances.

Often mayors, city managers, and city councils take the view that helping the municipal defendant is a waste of time because these are "just minor offenses." Their attitude is that the offender should just pay the "two dollars" and be on his/her way. The problem with this viewpoint is that the majority of people who are defendants in municipal court are poor, so paying a fine of any amount is a burden.

Even though, as municipal judge, I cannot constitutionally sentence people to jail upon a guilty plea or a finding of guilt, failure to pay the fine, which constitutes defying a court order, can result in people being incarcerated. This often results in the person losing a job should he or she have one, thus creating more problems in an already problem-laden life.

Another issue of which I became aware was that many people who start their offending career in municipal court continue and end up in state or federal prison. This reality might suggest that early intervention could make a difference in some of these future felons' lives and that a therapeutic approach with repeat offenders in municipal court may reduce the possibility of some of these people ending up in prison.

Because of my desire to use my position of municipal judge to provide intervention rather than just punishment with repeat offenders, I began to search for a theoretical framework upon which to base my effort. Through my research I came across a theoretical framework developed by David B. Wexler of the University of Arizona's Rogers College of Law and Bruce J. Winick, Professor of Psychiatry and Behavioral Sciences at University of Miami in Coral Gables, Florida.

Winick and Wexler are regarded as the founders of therapeutic jurisprudence. Bruce J. Winick suggests that therapeutic jurisprudence refers to the study of the role of law as a therapeutic agent (Wexler and Winick, 1996: xvii). Winick and Wexler suggest that therapeutic jurisprudence is an attempt to humanize the law and have it address not only the legal but also the human, emotional, and psychological implications of the legal process (Wexler & Winnick, 1996: xvii).

Wexler (2000) contends that the law is a social force that produces behaviors and consequences. Sometimes the law does contribute to therapeutic outcomes but on other occasions the application of the law can be anti-therapeutic. (Wexler & Winnick, 1996)

Wexler (2000) argues that the law can be applied in a therapeutic way that respects both legal values and due process. Therapeutic jurisprudence is not designed to replace a legalistic approach in dealing with people before the court but rather it is designed to enrich the process and provide heretofore unconsidered options.

Therapeutic jurisprudence is the application of mental health concepts to legal situations by using the criminal justice system as <u>leverage</u> to intervene therapeutically in a person's life.

From my perspective, therapeutic jurisprudence is a lens through which the legal system can view specific violations of the law and decide what outcome is in the best interest of society as well as the best interest of the defendant. If the defendant, through this process, curtails his or her offending and becomes consistently a law abiding and productive citizen then it is a "win, win." I believe that municipal court is as good a place as any to utilize this approach.

This belief is predicated on the notion that municipal courts are often a person's first encounter with the court system.

People who appear in municipal court are there on relatively minor offenses (e.g., petit theft, minor in possession of a controlled substance, chronic reckless driving). Repeated commission of these minor offenses can be an indicator of a mindset that leads to future major offenses. This being the case, therapeutic intervention in these minor offenses might preclude a person from graduating to major offenses.

The therapeutic jurisprudence process itself is rather straightforward. The ideal would be for the judge to have at her/his disposal, a court service officer who could facilitate the various interventions that might be needed. Since, in municipal court, that is unlikely, the judge would need to acquaint her/himself with the necessary available resources and then utilize them when appropriate. The defendant would be given an option at the time of the plea or finding of guilt. Face the legal consequences or submit to a therapeutic consequence and, if successfully completed, avoid the legal consequence. The court would maintain jurisdiction throughout the therapeutic process and would monitor the defendant's progress or lack thereof by periodic reappearances in court and contact with the service provider.

At the conclusion of the services or at a point where it is clear whether or not the defendant is making progress, the court could impose the punishment for those who did not take advantage of the therapeutic opportunity. For those who took the opportunity seriously, the court could waive the punishment, reduce the punishment, dismiss the charges, or give the defendant a suspended imposition of sentence, which means that if the defendant does not reoffend and continues therapeutic involvement for a specified period of time, the charges would be dismissed.

Since I am also a professor of social work, it dawned on me that perhaps social work students might be interested in doing their required practicum in a criminal justice setting. As it turned out, there was considerable interest and over the past several years I have had social work students from three different universities complete their social work practicum education in my court.

In conclusion, I want to provide two examples of cases that were handled by two of the students. Each of these cases illustrates the value of the therapeutic jurisprudence process.

Example 1 - A young adult female was arrested for possession of a controlled substance, pled guilty and was fined a substantial amount. This was her third guilty plea to possession so she already had fines that she was unable or unwilling to pay related to her substance misuse. A fine reduction was offered as incentive for participation with the social work student. The student provided assessment to identify counseling and vocational needs. The client's needs were identified and were met through referral to counseling. Also, a direct intervention by a social worker assisted the person in finding employment. The student met with the client on a weekly basis and monitored her progress. Toward the end of the time that the student was going to be in the practicum, the student recommended to me that the fine be forgiven. I followed her recommendation. The young woman in question has not reappeared in my court since that intervention took place.

Example 2 – A young mother of an infant was homeless. She was convicted of petit theft. She had stolen a gallon of milk and some other items. She attempted to return the stolen items to the store to obtain a refund so she could purchase diapers. She was arrested, detained and eventually appeared in municipal court. Since she was homeless and had no money I referred her to the social work student. The student assisted the person in locating local resources for basic needs, helped her get into subsidized housing, and arranged for child care so the client could seek employment. The student assisted the client in preparing to look for work by doing

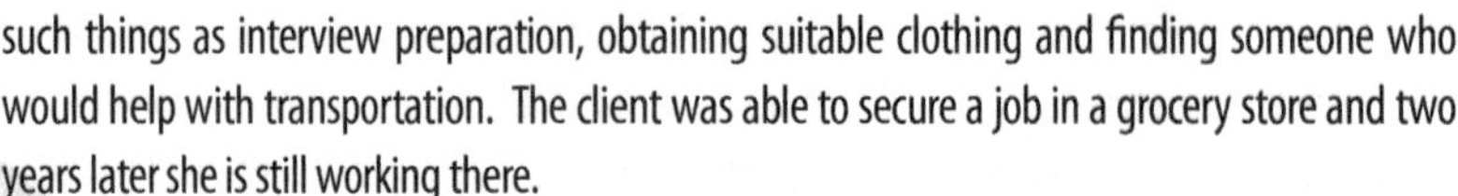

such things as interview preparation, obtaining suitable clothing and finding someone who would help with transportation. The client was able to secure a job in a grocery store and two years later she is still working there.

It is obvious that every therapeutic effort is not going to meet with the success that the above two examples did but without the excellent work of the practicum students both of these young women probably would have continued down the path that they were on prior to intervention. If even a few people profit from a therapeutic jurisprudence approach, it is good for them, good for the legal system and good for society.

Sources:
Wexler, David B., "Practicing Therapeutic Jurisprudence: Psychological Soft Spots and Strategies," in Dennis P. Stolle, David B. Wexler, and Bruce J. Winick, *Practicing Therapeutic Jurisprudence: Law as a Helping Profession* (Durham, NC: Carolina Academic Press, 2000): 45-68.

Wexler, David B., and Winick, Bruce J. (Eds.), *Law in a Therapeutic Key: Developments in Therapeutic Jurisprudence* (Durham, NC: Carolina Academic Press, 1996).

LABELING THEORY

Labeling theory, sometimes called *social reaction theory*, is so named because of its focus on the effects of the informal and formal application of stigmatizing deviant "labels" on people. A **stigma** is a stain or mark of disgrace, imposed by one social actor, whether an individual or collectivity, on another. A stigma is a discrediting attribution and it can serve to lower the esteem or honor in which a social actor is regarded by others and by the self (Fife and Wright, 2000; Goffman, 1963). Max Weber's term for a group that is highly stigmatized is **pariah group.** Labeling theory treats stigmatizing labels both as an independent variable (result) as well as an independent variable (cause).

Labeling theorists tend to view no act or behavior as inherently evil or bad. To a labeling theorist, prohibited acts are bad simply because they are prohibited (*mala prohibitum*). Other theoretical perspectives tend to view some acts (e.g., assault, rape, murder) as inherently bad or evil, as counter to core Western values (*mala in se*).

The earliest statements of modern labeling theory were made by American sociologist Frank Tannenbaum in the 1930s. In *Crime and the Community* (1938), Tannenbaum applies Charles Horton Cooley's concept of "the looking glass self," which looks at the self (our answers to "Who Am I?") as a social construct. As the attentive reader will recall, according to the concept of the looking glass self, we become that which we are addressed.

Tannenbaum was concerned that if we pay attention to behaviors that we want to discourage, that we may unintentionally thereby encourage those very behaviors. Tannenbaum urged us to be wary of the ***dramatization of evil***, the calling of attention to acts that we want to discourage. Tannenbaum thought that the process of making a criminal or a deviant is a process of "tagging, defining, identifying, segregating, describing, emphasizing" (Tannenbaum, 1938: 19-20). Doing those things "becomes a way of ...evoking the very traits that are complained of. ...The person becomes the thing he is described as being" (Tannenbaum, 1938: 20).

Building on Tannenbaum's insights, American sociologist Edwin Lemert formulated the concepts of primary and secondary deviance (1951). According to Lemert, ***primary deviance*** (also called primary deviation) refers to norm violation to which no one in a position of authority responds. Many people engage in primary deviation. Labeling theory is not interested in primary deviation, in what causes people to break norms in the first place.

In order to understand the concept of secondary deviation, let us approach the concept by means of an example. A child steals a piece of candy from the local grocery store, and nobody in a position of authority responds. This may happen several times. Eventually, someone in a position of authority responds when the child takes another child's sweater or mittens. This may happen several times. Eventually, the child comes to think of him or herself as someone who steals, as a thief. In other words, the child undergoes an identity transformation. This deviant identity becomes a core part of the self. The child then commits an act that is consistent with that deviant identity. Committing an act that is consistent with a deviant identity is ***secondary deviance*** (also known as secondary deviation).

Thus, if one were to view a videotape of a child stealing a pair of shoes, one would not know whether that was an act of primary or secondary deviance. One would need to know more about the child's personal identity history to determine whether a given act is primary or secondary deviation.

DIFFERENTIAL ASSOCIATION THEORY

Edwin H. Sutherland (1883-1950), heavily influenced by the ideas of George Herbert Mead, developed differential association theory over a period of many years as he attempted to create a general theory that could organize the many diverse facts then known about criminal behavior into some logical arrangement. Differential association theory consists of the following nine points (Sutherland, 1947: 6-7):

1. Criminal behavior is learned.
2. Criminal behavior is learned in a process of communication with others.
3. The principle part of the learning of criminal behavior occurs in intimate primary groups.
4. The learning of criminal behavior includes: (a) techniques of committing the crime, (b) the specific direction of motives, drives, rationalizations, and attitudes.
5. The specific direction of motives and drives is learned from definitions of the legal code as favorable or as unfavorable.
6. A person becomes criminal because of an excess of definitions favorable to violation of the law over definitions unfavorable to violation of the law. This is the principle of differential association.
7. Differential associations may vary in frequency, duration, priority, and intensity.
8. The process learning criminal behavior involves all of the mechanisms that are involved in any other learning.
9. While criminal behavior is an expression of general needs and values (e.g., economic ambition), it is not explained by those general needs and values, since noncriminal behavior is an expression of the same needs and values.

At the broadest level, differential association theory is untestable. That helps to explain why research testing its basic assumptions has been relatively sparse. Nonetheless, several research efforts have found correlations among (a) having delinquent friends, (b) holding deviant attitudes, and (c) committing deviant acts (e.g., Ploeger, 1997; Jackson, Tittle, and Burke, 1986; Bruinsma, 1992).

Conflict Theories

In the conflict perspective, values, norms, and laws are viewed as creating dissension, clash, and conflict. Conflict thinkers do not agree on the nature of this process. They do not even agree on what to call it.

Marxian conflict theory was first applied to criminology by Willem Bonger (1876-1949), a social scientist in Holland, in 1916. Bonger perceived that society is divided into economically powerful and powerless groups, and that penal law serves the interests of the powerful. No acts are inherently immoral or criminal. The acts of the powerless that threaten the interests of the powerful get written into law as crimes.

George Vold was one of the first American sociologists to apply conflict theory to criminology. Vold perceives that criminal acts are a consequence of direct contact between forces struggling to control society. (Burglars are engaging in class warfare.) Though the criminal content may obscure their political meaning, closer examination often reveals political undertones, according to Vold.

Feminist theorists view the cause of female crime as due to patriarchy, male supraordination (Brownmiller, 1975; Chesney-Lind and Shelden, 2004).

In summary, conflict theorists view society as in a constant state of internal conflict over valued resources, with various groups and collectivities striving to impose their will on others. Men use their economic power to subjugate women; the owners of the means of production use their position to pass laws that serve their interests at the expense of the proletariat. Conflict theory thus centers on a view of society in which the supraordinates use the law and the justice system to pursue and to solidify their own interests.

If conflict is a source of crime and crime control, perhaps conflict resolution may be a key to its solution. This, at least, is the aim of **restorative justice**, a movement in criminology that relies on nonpunitive strategies for crime control (Pranis, 1997; Daley and Immarigeon, 1998). The restorative justice movement has a number of sources, ranging from Quakerism to Zen.

To help us understand this orientation, it is useful to appreciate the distinction, common in traditional criminology, between general and specific deterrence. Deterrence refers to the effect of punishment as reducing the frequency of the occurrence of crime. The classical school of criminology, dating back to the nineteenth century, believes that punishment can deter crime. The classical school of criminology assumes that punishment can deter crime if the punishment is swift, certain, and, in terms of severity, if it outweighs the pleasure involved in committing the crime.

There are two types of deterrence, general and specific. Law-abiding others will refrain from breaking the law. Thus, if Jane steals a bicycle, and Jane is punished so that law-abiding others will not steal bicycles, we say that the aim or goal of the punishment is that of **general deterrence.** However, if Jane is punished for stealing a bicycle so that Jane will not steal bicycles anymore, we say that the aim of punishment is that of specific deterrence, also known as special deterrence. In **specific deterrence,** ego is punished so that ego will not commit crime anymore.

The restorative justice movement advocates a reliance on non-punitive strategies for crime prevention, control, and punishment (Braithwaite, 2001, 1995). Thus, John Braithwaite (1989, 1994) points out that low crime rates tend to prevail in countries like Japan where conviction for crimes brings with it a tremendous amount of shame. Shame is a powerful tool of social control. In contrast, in the United States there are some subcultures that do not view crime as shameful, and people in these subcultures tend not to internalize an abhorrence of crime. They tend not to view their crimes as shameful acts, and when they are punished for their crimes, they tend to view themselves as victims of the criminal justice system. Their punishment tends to come at the hands of neutral third parties, neutral "strangers"—the police, prosecutors, defense attorneys, and judges.

In contrast, in the restorative justice movement, shaming relies on the participation of both the perpetrator and victim. Braithwaite distinguishes between two types of shame, *stigmatization* and *reintegrative shaming*.

The most common form of shaming is stigmatization, which is an ongoing process of degradation wherein the offender is branded as an evil person and cast out of the community. Stigmatization may occur in many contexts—-in a school disciplinary hearing, at juvenile court, at criminal court, for instance. Stigmatization may have a general-deterrent effect: it makes law-abiding others afraid to engage in the punished acts because they do not want to experience like public humiliation and social rejection. However, Braithwaite contends that stigmatization is doomed to fail as a specific deterrent, because many people manifest a self-serving bias wherein they "reject their rejectors" and take refuge in a deviant subculture of like-minded people who resist social control. Some people who prefer a psychological-level of explanation might describe this adaptation as "authority defiant disorder."

Many jurisdictions in the United States appear to be making stigmatization both public and permanent. For example, in many states, convicted felons lose the right to vote and face major challenges in finding employment. Most states also have enacted sex-offender registry and notification laws (Petrosino and Petrosino, 1999). These make public the names of people convicted of sex offenses and warn people of their presence in the community.

Braithwaite argues that specific deterrence may be better achieved through reintegrative shaming which frames the offender's criminal deeds as evil but which respects the perpetrator of those deeds as a worthy person who can be reaccepted by the community. To be reintegrative, the shaming itself must be brief and followed by ceremonies of repentance, forgiveness, and acceptance (Braithwaite and Mugford, 1994). Sherman, Strang, and Woods (2002) compared the effects of standard court processing with the effects of reintegrative-shaming diversion for violent juvenile offenders in Australia. Those juveniles who received a disposition (sentence) of reintegrative shaming offended at a substantially lower level—-38 fewer offenses per year per 100 offenders—-than did the offenders assigned to court.

A critical element of reintegrative shaming occurs when the offenders "understand and recognize their wrongdoing and shame themselves" (Siegel, 2004:271). Some communities try to encourage this epiphany by bringing the offenders and victims together with the assistance of a third party.

SUGGESTED READINGS

Benell, Craig; Bloomfield, Sarah; Emeno, Karla; and Musolino, Evanya, "Classifying Serial Sexual Murderers: An Attempt to Validate Keppel and Walter's (1999) Model," *Criminal Justice and Behavior*, Vol. 40, No. 1 (January) 2013: 5-25.

Boisvert, Danielle; Stadler, William; Vaske, Jamie; Wright, John P.; and Nelson, Matthew, "The Interconnection Between Intellectual Achievement and Self-Control," *Criminal Justice and Behavior*, Vol. 40, No. 1, (January) 2013: 80-94.

Buntin, John, "The LAPD Remade," *City Journal*, Winter 2013.

Caldwell, Ryan Ashley, *Fallgirls: Gender and the Framing of Torture at Abu Ghraib* (Burlington, VT: Ashgate, 2012).

Franklin, Cortney A.; Bouffard, Leanna Allen; and Pratt, Travis, "Fraternity Affiliation, Male Peer Support, and Low Self-Control," *Criminal Justice and Behavior*, Vol. 39, No. 11, (November) 2012: 1457-1480.

Franklin, Cortney A.; Franklin, Travis W.; Nobles, Matt R.; and Kercher, Glen A., "Assessing the Effect of Routine Activity Theory and Self-Control on Property, Personal, and Sexual Assault Victimization," *Criminal Justice and Behavior*, Vol. 39, No. 10, (October) 2012: 1296-1315.

Grant, Judith, *Men and Substance Abuse: Narratives of Addiction and Recovery* (Boulder, CO: FirstForumPress, 2012).

Harris, Ellen, *Guarding the Secrets: Palestinian Terrorism and a Father's Murder of his Too-American Daughter* (New York: Scirbner, 1995).

Harris, Grant T.; Hilton, Zoe N.; and Rice, Marjorie E., "Explaining the Frequency of Intimate Partner Violence by Male Perpetrators: Do Attitude, Relationship, and Neighborhood Variables Add to Anti-Sociality?" *Criminal Justice and Behavior*, Vol. 38, No. 4, (April) 2011: 309-331.

Johnson, Richard R., "Suspect Mental Disorder and Police Use of Force," *Criminal Justice and_Behavior*, Vol. 38, No. 2 (February) 2011: 127-145.

Khan, Roxanne and Cooke, David, "Measurement of Sibling Violence: A Two-Factor Model of Severity," *Criminal Justice and Behavior*, Vol. 40, No. 1, (January) 2013: 26-39.

Klein, Jessie, *The Bully Society: School Shootings and the Crisis of Bullying in America's Schools* (New York: New York University Press, 2012).

Krohn, Marvin D.; Ward, Jeffrey T.; Thornberry, Terrence; Lizotte, Alan; and Chu, Rebekah, "The Cascading Effects of Adolescent Gang Involvement Across the Life Course," *Criminology*, Vol. 49, No. 4, 2011: 991-1028.

Kuhl, Danielle; Warner, Daniel F.; and Wilczak, Andrew, "Adolescent Violent Victimization and Precocious Union Formation," *Criminology*, Vol. 50, No. 4, 2012: 1089-1127.

Larson, Matthew and Sweeten, Gary, "Breaking Up is Hard to Do: Romantic Dissolution, Offending, and Substance Use During the Transition to Adulthood," *Criminology*, Vol. 50, No. 3, 2012: 605-636.

Mac Donald, Heather, "Courts v Cops: The Legal War on the War on Crime," *City Journal*, Winter 2013. As of May 30, 2013, available online at www.city-journal.org/printable.php?id=8788

Murray, Joseph; Loeber, Rolf; and Pardini, Dustin, "Parental Involvement in the Criminal Justice System and the Development of Youth Theft, Marijuana Use, Depression, and Poor Academic Performance," *Criminology*, Vol. 50, No. 1, 2012: 255-302.

Ratcliffe, Jerry H.; Taniguchi, Travis; Groff, Elizabeth R.; and Wood, Jennifer D., "The Philadelphia Patrol Experiment: A Randomized Controlled Trial of Police Patrol Effectiveness in Violent Crime Hotspots," *Criminology*, Vol. 49, No. 3, 2011: 795-832.

Reisig, Michael D.; Wolfe, Scott E.; and Pratt, Travis C., "Low Self-Control and the Religiosity-Crime Relationship," *Criminal Justice and Behavior*, Vol. 39, No. 9, (September) 2012: 1172-1191.

Steenbeek, Wouter and Hipp, John R., "A Longitudinal Test of Social Disorganization Theory: Feedback Effects Among Cohesion, Social Control, and Disorder," *Criminology*, Vol. 49, No. 3, 2011: 833-871.

BIBLIOGRAPHY

Allen, Harry E., and Simonsen, Clifford E., *Corrections in America: An Introduction* Ninth Edition (Upper Saddle River, NJ: Prentice Hall, 2001).

Amnesty International Australia, "The Death Penalty in China." April 2008. As of July 6, 2009, available online at http://www.amnesty.org.au/china/comments/10960

Appiah, Kwame Anthony, *Cosmopolitanism: Ethics in a World of Strangers* (New York: W.W. Norton & Company, 2006).

Barboza, David, "A Chinese Reformer Betrays His Cause, and Pays," *The New York Times*, July 13, 2007. Retrieved on July 7, 2009, from http://www.nytimes.com/2007/07/13/business/worldbusiness/13corrupt.html

BBC NEWS, "Chinese Milk Scam Duo Face Death," January 22, 2009, 12:02 GMT. Available online on July 8, 2009, at http://news.bbc.co.uk/2/hi/asia-pacific/7843972.stm

Beck, Ulrich, *The Cosmopolitan Vision* Translated by Ciaran Cronin (Malden MA: Polity Press, 2006).

Black, Donald, "Crime as Social Control," *American Sociological Review*, Vol. 48, No. 1, 1983: 34-45.

Bowles, Samuel, "Did Warfare Among Ancestral Hunter-Gatherers Affect the Evolution of Human Social Behaviors? *Science*, Vol. 324, No. 5932, (June) 2009: 1293-1298.

Braithwaite, *Crime, Shame, and Reintegration* (Melbourne, Australia: Cambridge University Press, 1989).

Braithwaite, John, "Applying Some Lessons from Japanese and Maori Culture to the Reintegrative Shaming of Criminal Offenders," *Japanese Journal of Criminal Psychology*, Vol. 32, 1994, 181-196.

Braithwaite, John, "Resolving Crime in the Community: Restorative Justice Reform in New Zealand and Australia," in C. Martin (Ed.), *Resolving Crime in the Community: Mediation in the Community* (London: Institute for the Study and Treatment of Delinquency, 1995).

Braithwaite, John, and Mugford, S., "Conditions of Successful Reintegration Ceremonies: Dealing with Juvenile Offenders," *British Journal of Criminology*, Vol. 34, 1994: 139-171.

Braithwaite, John, *Restorative Justice and Responsive Regulation* (New York: Oxford University Press, 2001).

Brock, Gillian, and Brighouse, Harry (Eds.), *The Political Philosophy of Cosmopolitanism* (New York: Cambridge University Press, 2005).

Brownmiller, Susan, *Against Our Will: Men, Women, and Rape* (NY: Simon and Schuster, 1975).

Bruinsma, Gerben J.N., "Differential Association Theory Reconsidered: An Extension and Its Empirical Test," *Journal of Quantitative Criminology*, Vol. 8, 1992: 29-46.

Burghardt, John; Schochet, Peter Z.; McConnell, Terry, et. al., *Summary Report: Does Job Corps Work? Summary of the National Job Corps Study* (Princeton, NJ: Mathematica Policy Research, Inc., 2001).

Chea, Pheng and Robbins, Bruce (Eds.), *Cosmopolitics: Thinking and Feeling Beyond the Nation* (Minneapolis: University of Minnesota Press, 1998).

Chesney-Lind, Meda; and Sheldon, Randall G., *Girls, Delinquency, and Juvenile Justice* (Belmont, CA: Thompson/Wadsworth, 2004).

Churchill, Winston, *A History of the English Speaking Peoples* Vol. I (New York: The Dorset Press, 1956).

Clark, Gregory, *A Farewell to Alms: A Brief Economic History of the World* (Princeton, New Jersey, Princeton University Press, 2007).

Cockburn, J.S., "Patterns of Violence in English Society: Homicide in Kent 1560-1985," *Past and Present*, Vol. 130, 1991: 70-106.

Cooney, Mark, "The Decline of Elite Homicide," *Criminology*, Vol. 35, No. 3, 1997: 381-407.

Curtis, Lyn A., *The State of Families: Family, Employment, and Reconstruction: Policy Based on What Works* (Milwaukee, WI: Families International, 1995).

Daly, Kathleen, and Immarigeon, Russ, "The Past, Present, and Future of Restorative Justice: Some Critical Reflections," *Contemporary Justice Review*, Vol. 1, 1998: 21-45.

Daly, Martin, and Wilson, Margo, *Homicide* (New York: Aldine De Gruyter, 1988).

Durkheim, Emile, *The Division of Labor in Society* (New York: Free Press, 1964). (Originally published, 1895).

Edelhertz, Herbert, *The Nature, Impact, and Prosecution of White-Collar Crime* (Washington, D.C.: U.S. Government Printing Office, 1970).

Eisner, M., "Long-Term Trends in Violent Crime," *Crime and Justice*, Vol. 30, 2003: 83-142.

Eisner, M., "Modernity Strikes BACK? A Historical Perspective on the Latest Increase in Interpersonal Violence 1960-1990," *International Journal of Conflict and Violence*, Vol. 2, 2008: 288-316.

Eisner, M., "The Uses of Violence: An Examination of Some Cross-Cutting Issues," *International Journal of Conflict & Violence*, Vol. 3, 2009: 40-59.

Elias, Norbert, *The Civilizing Process: Sociogenetic and Psychogenetic Investigations* Revised Edition (Malden, Massachusetts: Blackwell Publishers, 2000). Originally published 1939.

Federal Bureau of Investigation, *Crime in the United States 2011*. As of May 25, 2013, available online at http://www.fbi.gov/about-us/cjis/ucr/crime-in-the-u.s/2011/crime-in-the-u.s.-2011/violent-crime/murder

Federal Bureau of Investigation, *Hate Crime Statistics 2011*, Table 1. As of May 26, 2013, available online at http://www.fbi.gov/about-us/cjis/ucr/hate-crime/2011/tables/table-1

Federal Bureau of Investigation, *Hate Crimes Statistics, 2011* (Washington, D.C.: Government Printing Office, 2012). As of May 26, 2013, available online at http://www.fbi.gov/news/stories/2012/december/annual-hate-crimes-report-released/annual-hate-crimes-report-released

Fife, Betsy L., and Wright, E.R., "The Dimensionality of Stigma: A Comparison of Its Impact on the Self of Persons with HIV/AIDS and Cancer," *Journal of Health and Social Behavior*, Vol. 41, No. 1 (March 2000): 50-67.

Fukuyama, Francis, *The End of History and the Last Man Standing* (New York: Free Press, 2006).

Gaddis, John Lewis, *The Long Peace: Inquiries into the History of the Cold War* (New York: Oxford University Press, 1987).

Gat, Azar, *War in Human Civilization* (New York: Oxford University Press, 2006).

Goffman, Erving, *Stigma: Notes on the Management of Spoiled Identity* (Englewood Cliffs, NJ: Prentice Hall, 1963).

Goldstein, Joshua S., and Pevehouse, Jon C., *International Relations* Brief Fifth Edition (New York: Longman, 2010).

Gurr, Ted Robert, "Historical Trends in Violent Crime: Europe and the United States," in Ted Robert Gurr (Ed.), *Violence in America* Volume I The History of Crime (Newbury Park, CA: Sage, 1989), pp. 21-54.

Harris, Ellen, *Guarding the Secrets: Palestinian Terrorism and a Father's Murder of His Too-American Daughter* (New York: Scribner, 1995).

Hindelang, Michael; Hirschi, Travis Hirschi, and Joseph Weis, Joseph, *Measuring Delinquency* (Beverly Hills, CA: Sage, 1981).

Hirschi, Travis, *Causes of Delinquency* (Berkeley, CA: University of California Press, 1969).

Hobbes, Thomas, *Leviathan* (London: Penguin Books, 1985). Originally published 1651).

Human Security Report Project, *Human Security Report 2011. Sexual Violence, Education, and War: Beyond the Mainstream* (Vancouver, B.C., Canada: Human Security Press, 2012). As of May 14, 2013, available online at http://www.hsrgroup.org/human-security-reports/2012/text.aspx

Ingebretsen, Mark, *NASDAQ: A History of the Market That Changed the World* (Roseville, CA: Forum, 2002).

Jackson, Elton; Tittle, Charles; and Burke, Mary Jean, "Offense-Specific Models of the Differential Association Process," Social Problems, Vol. 33, 1986:335-356.

Kahn, Joseph, "China Executes the Former Head of Its Food and Drug Agency," *The New York Times*, July 10, 2007. Retrieved on July 7, 2009, from http://www.nytimes.com/2007/07/10/world/asia/10iht-china.1.6587520.html

Kant, Immanuel, "Idea for a Universal History from a Cosmopolitan Perspective," (1784), pp. 3-16 of Immanuel Kant, *Toward Perpetual Peace and Other Writings on Politics, Peace, and History* Pauline Kleingeld (Ed.) and Translated by David L. Colclasure (Binghamton, NY: Vail-Ballou Press, 2006).

Kant, Immanuel, "Toward Perpetual Peace," (1795), pp. 67-109 of Immanuel Kant, *Toward Perpetual Peace and Other Writings on Politics, Peace, and History* Pauline Kleingeld (Ed.) and Translated by David L. Colclasure (Binghamton, NY: Vail-Ballou Press, 2006).

Katz, Jack, *Seductions of Crime: Moral and Sensual Attractions of Doing Evil* (New York: Basic Books, 1988).

Keeley, Lawrence H., *War Before Civilization: The Myth of the Peaceful Savage* (New York: Oxford University Press, 1996).

Lemert, Edwin, *Social Pathology* (New York: McGraw Hill, 1951).

Liazos, Alexander "The Sociology of Deviance: Nuts, Sluts, and Perverts," *Social Problems*, Vol. 20, (Summer) 1972: 1-3-120).

MarketWatch, "China Airport Executive Sentenced to Death," MarketWatch, February 11, 2009, 12:00 AM EST. As of July 6, 2009, available online at http://www.marketwatch.com/story/china-airport-executive-sentenced-death-a?siteid=ybz

McCool, Grant, and Graybow, Martha, "Madoff Pleads Guilty, Is Jailed for $65 Billion Fraud," Reuters, March 12, 2009, 7:12 PM ET. Available on July 6, 2009, online at http://www.reuters.com/article/managementIssues/idUSN1234821920090312

Merton, Robert K., "Social Structure and Anomie," *American Sociological Review*, Vol. 3, 1938: 672-682.

Merton, Robert K., *Social Theory and Social Structure* (Glencoe, Illinois: The Free Press, 1968).

Miller, George A., "The Magical Number Seven, Plus or Minus Two: Some Limits on Our Capacity for Processing Information," *The Psychological Review*, Vol. 63, 1956: 81-97.

Miller, Walter B., "Lower Class Culture as Generating a Milieu of Gang Delinquency," in Marvin Wolfgang, Leonard Savitz, and Norman Johnson (Eds.), *The Sociology of Crime and Delinquency* (New York: Wiley, 1970). (Originally published, 1958).

MSNBC World News, "2 Face Execution Over China Poison Milk Scandal," MSNBC World News, January 22, 2009, 10:03 AM CT. As of July 7, 2009, available online at http://www.msnbc.msn.com/id/28787126

Murray, Joseph, and Farrington, David P., "Parental Imprisonment: Effects on Boys' Antisocial Behaviour and Delinquency through the Life-course," *Journal of Child Psychology and Psychiatry*, Vol. 46, No. 12, (December) 2005: 1269-1278.

Nye, Jr., Joseph S., *The Future of Power* (New York: Public Affairs, 2011).

Nye, Jr., Joseph S., *Understanding International Conflicts: An Introduction to Theory and History* Fifth Edition (New York: Pearson Longman, 2005).

Payne, James L., *A History of Force: Exploring the Worldwide Movement Against Habits of Coercion, Bloodshed and Mayhem* (Sandpoint, Idaho: Lytton Publishing Company, 2004).

Petrosino, Anthony, and Petrosino, Carolyn, "The Public Safety Potential of Megan's Law in Massachusetts: An Assessment from a Sample of Criminal Sexual Psychopaths," *Crime and Delinquency*, Vol. 43, 1999: 140-158.

Pinker, Steven, "Why the World Is More Peaceful," *Current History: A Journal of Contemporary World Affairs,* Vol. 111, Issue, 71, (January) 2012: 34-39.

Pinker, Steven, *The Better Angels of Our Nature: Why Violence Has Declined* (New York: Viking, 2011).

Ploeger, Matthew, "Youth Employment and Delinquency: Reconsidering a Problematic Relationship," *Criminology,* Vol. 35, 1997: 659-675.

Pranis, Kay, "Peacemaking Circles: Restorative Justice in Practice Allows Victims and Offenders to Begin Repairing the Harm," *Corrections Today*, Vol. 59, 1997: 72-76.

Reid, Sue Titus, *Crime and Criminology* eleventh edition (New York: McGraw Hill, 2006)

Richardson, Lewis Fry, *Statistics of Deadly Quarrels* Edited by Quincy Wright and Carl C. Lienau (Pittsburg, PA: Boxwood Press, 1960).

Robbins, Bruce, *Perpetual War: Cosmopolitanism from the Viewpoint of Violence* (Durham, NC: Duke University Press, 2012).

Ryan, William, *Blaming the Victim* (New York: Vintage Books, 1971).

Schinke, Steven P.; Orlandi, Mario A.; Cole, Kristin C., "Boys & Girls Clubs in Public Housing Developments: Prevention Services for Youth at Risk," *Journal of Community Psychology*, Office of Substance Abuse Prevention Special Issue, 1992: 118-128.

Sherman, Lawrence W.; Strang, Heather, and Woods, Daniel J., *Recidivism Patterns in the Canberra Reintegrative Shaming Experiments (RISE)* (Canberra, Australia: Center for Restorative Justice, 2002).

Siegel, Larry J., *Criminology* Eighth Edition (Belmont, CA: Wadsworth/Thompson Learning, 2003).

Siegel, Larry J.; Welsh, Brandon C.; and Senna, Joseph J., *Juvenile Delinquency: Theory, Practice, and Law* Eighth Edition (Belmont, Wadsworth/Thompson Learning, 2003).

Sutherland, Edwin H., *Criminology* Fourth Edition (Philadelphia, PA: Lippincott, 1947: 6-7).

Sutherland, Edwin H.; Cressey, Donald R., and Luckenbill, David F., *Principles of Criminology* Eleventh Edition (Dix Hills, New York: General Hall, Inc., Publishers: 1992).

Sykes, Gresham and Matza, David, "Techniques of Neutralization," American Sociological Review, Vol. 22, 1957: 664-670.

Tannenbaum, Frank, *Crime and the Community* (New York: Ginn and Company, 1938).

Terrell, Ellen, "History of the NASDAQ and American Stock Exchanges," in Library of Congress, *Business Reference Services*, September 2006. As of July 7, 2009, available online at http://www.loc.gov/rr/business/amex/amex.html

THE WEEK, "Briefing: The Scam That Keeps on Taking," THE WEEK, January 30, 2009: 11.

Truman, Jennifer L., and Planty, Michael, "Criminal Victimization, 2011," Bureau of Justice Statistics *Bulletin*, NCJ239437, October 2012. As of May 26, 2013, available online at http://www.bjs.gov/content/pub/pdf/cv11.pdf

U.S. Department of Justice, Federal Bureau of Investigation, *Crime in the United States 2010* Offense Definitions. Released 2011. As of May 25, 2013, available online at http://www.fbi.gov/about-us/cjis/ucr/crime-in-the-u.s/2010/crime-in-the-u.s.-2010/offense-definitions

Vold, George and Barnard, Thomas, *Theoretical Criminology* Third Edition (New York: Oxford University Press, 1986).

Weber, Max, *Economy and Society* Edited by Guenther Roth and Claus Wittich (New York: Bedminster Press, 1968).

Wilkinson, Deanna L.; Beaty, Chauncey C.; Lurry, Regina M., "Youth Violence—Crime of Self-Help? Marginalized Urban Males' Perspectives on the Limited Efficacy of the Criminal Justice System to Stop Youth Violence," *Annals* of the American Academy of Political and Social Science, Vol. 623, (May) 2009: 25-38.

Wood, John Carter, "Self-Policing and the Policing of the Self: Violence, Protection, and the Civilizing Bargain in Britain," *Crime, History, & Societies*, Vol. 7, 2003: 109-128.

Wood, John Carter, *Violence and Crime in Nineteenth-Century England: The Shadow of Our Refinement* (London: Routledge, 2004).

Wright, Quincy, *A Study of War* Volume I (Chicago: University of Chicago Press, 1942).

Zuckhoff, Mitchell, *Ponzi's Scheme: The True Story of a Financial Legend* (New York: Random House, 2005).

CHAPTER 11

Demography

INTRODUCTION

The subfield of sociology known as demography helps us to understand social life. In this chapter we explore the census, in the United States and elsewhere, as a source of data of interest to demographers, and the population pyramid, as a type of graph useful in displaying certain forms of population data. Next, we examine the origin of the field of demography, paying attention to its foundational theory. We then focus on the three main variables that demographers use in order to understand population structure—fertility, mortality, and migration. We conclude the chapter by considering the demographic patterns and divides that characterize this era of globalization

The term demography is derived from the Greek word "demo," meaning people or populace, and "graphy," meaning "to write," but which we can translate as meaning the "study of." **Demography** is the study of population structure (Giddens, Duneier, Appelbaum, and Carr, 2013: 492; Petersen, 1969). Those who engage in the study of population structure are called demographers. Demographers measure and analyze the size, composition, and distribution, density, vital statistics and characteristics of human populations and the patterns of change in them (Theodorson and Theordorson, 1969). See Table 11.1. Not all demographers are sociologists, but the majority of demographers are sociologists both by education and profession. Demographers have calculated that, throughout the entirety of human existence on earth, a total of 107,602,707,791 people have lived on this planet (Haub, 2011). The world's population today is 7,098,191,264 (U.S. Census Bureau, 2013) and thus constitutes about 6.6 percent of all the people who ever have lived on this planet.

TABLE 11.1 WORLD'S TEN LARGEST COUNTRIES, 2013, BY RANK ORDER, COUNTRY, AND POPULATION

Rank	Country	Population
1	China	1,349,585,838
2	India	1,220,800,359
3	United States	319,330,342
4	Indonesia	250,775,663
5	Brazil	207,964,531
6	Pakistan	193,238,868
7	Bangladesh	163,654,860
8	Nigeria	161,236,294
9	Russia	137,410,006
10	Japan	125,684,625

Source: U.S. Census Bureau, International Data Base. As of July 14, 2013, available online at http://www.census.gov/idb/ranks.html

Why do sociologists study demography? Sociologists are interested in demography because we want to understand social life. Demographic processes influence social life and social structure in a variety of ways. For instance:

- On March 21, 2010, as will happen every day for another two decades, 10,000 baby boomers became eligible for Social Security and Medicare in the United States (Will, 2010). In a democratic state, this creates a potentially strong lobby in favor of retaining, and not eroding, the social safety net for senior citizens.
- In the United Kingdom, According to the Office for National Statistics, the share of the foreign-born in the general population has doubled in the past two decades, to more than 11.3 percent of the English population (THE WEEK, 2011). That is a level approaching the percentage size of the foreign-born population of the United States today, which is about 13 percent of the population (Congressional Budget Office, 2013).
- In the United States, the immigrant population has doubled since 1990, tripled since 1980, and quadrupled since 1970 (Lowry, 2012).
- People's Republic of China has a shortage of females in its population (Poston, Conde, and De Salvo, 2011). For every 100 females who are born, 119 males are born and in some rural areas the figure rises to 130 males who are born for every 100 females (BBC News, 2010). What this gender imbalance means, according to a recent report by the Chinese Academy of Social Sciences, is that there are 24 million males in China who will be of marriageable age by 2020 who will never marry because of the sex ratio imbalance. This would be like the entire 2012 population of Australia (Central Intelligence Agency: Australia, 2013) or the entire 2012 population of the State of Texas never being able to marry. Stated somewhat differently, it would be like the entire population of the nine largest cities of the United States in 2012 never being able to marry: that's the entire population of New York City, Los Angeles, Chicago, Houston, Philadelphia, Phoenix, San Antonio, San Diego, and Dallas, Texas (InfoPlease, 2013). Imagine the social implications in a city or a nation that large where no one can marry. The Chinese Academy of Sciences reports that the number of kidnappings

> and trafficking of young girls has become rampant. Young girls are being kidnapped within China but also from neighboring countries such as Laos, Cambodia, Vietnam, Myanmar, and Thailand by organized gangs who sell them to families with boys of similar age. The girls will be raised by the families and given as brides to their sons as soon as they reach marriageable age. Others are shipped to brothels within China for a live as sex slaves (Steyn, 2010; Kong, 2010).

In the above examples, demographic processes are important independent variables. By studying demography, we attain an appreciably better understanding of the cultures and the world in which we live. A related reason for studying population is that social structure affects population processes in a number of ways. The birth and death of an individual are biological events that take place in a social setting. For instance, the theory of the demographic transition focuses on birth rates and death rates (and the resulting rate of population growth) as dependent variables that are influenced by the processes of industrialization. A sociologist might phrase this somewhat differently by saying that population processes are affected by social structure. Population processes, in this sense, are important dependent variables.

THE CENSUS

The **census** is an official, usually periodic, enumeration of population. The word is derived from the Latin word *censere*, meaning "to asses, tax" (Morris, 1969: 217). The first records of the census in human societies occur with the emergence of the state, thousands of years ago (Office for National Statistics, 2011). Ancient rulers wanted to know how many potential soldiers were available for military mobilization and how many persons were eligible for taxation purposes. For example, during the Roman Republic (509 BC-27 BC), the census was a list that kept track of all adult males fit for military service. Another example is the Domesday Book, which is a famous census undertaken in 1086 by William I of England (William the Conqueror) so that he could properly tax the land that he had recently conquered. Whatever the book said about who owned what and what it was worth, was the law of the land, with no appeal.

Historical demographers are trained to assess the validity and reliability of ancient and other census data, so that the inferences and conclusions that they draw about population trends based on historical census records are themselves reliable and valid. It is easy for the novice and others, unwittingly, to be hoodwinked or deceived. Since the census is conducted and published by governments, many people simply assume that the data are accurate, reliable, and valid. After all, the U.S. Constitution mandates that a census be taken in the United States every 10 years, in order to determine the number of seats each state is to receive in the U.S. House of Representatives. The data collected in the census also are used to provide states with the small-area data they use to redraw state legislative districts. Census data also are also used to distribute over $400 billion in federal program funding *each year* (United States Census Bureau, 2012). In these ways, there are political as well as economic and social benefits to accurate census enumeration.

Even those who are trained methodologists from time to time make mistakes in constructing the census instruments, in administering them, and in interpreting the data that are collected. For example, a seemingly simple matter of how the census questions were laid out on the page resulted in a 28 percent *over count* of the number of same-sex unmarried-partner households in the United States on the 2010 Census (United States Census Bureau, 2012). In other words, the actual number of same-sex unmarried-partner households is actually 28 percent lower than what is reported in the 2010 Census of the United States.

Scholars who are not demographers more readily make errors when using census data to understand social change over time. For example, in endeavoring to understand changes over the historical long-term in rates of death due to violence, cognitive psychologist Steven Pinker, in *The Better Angels of Our Nature* (2011), roots around the history books for wars and their death tolls. Pinker presents a table showing wars and their destructiveness in terms of loss of human life. At the crown, if you will, of this table is the An Lushan Revolt (755 AD-763 AD) in northern China, which, in a period of 8 years killed something like 36,000,000 (thirty-six million) Chinese, the equivalent of two-thirds (66 percent) of the T'ang Empire's population. Pinker arrived at this death toll on the basis of comparing two Chinese censuses, one that occurred pretty much right before the revolt and the other, right afterwards. Subtracting the two census figures renders the number of war dead.

Thirty-six million dead in eight years would be an astonishingly high death rate. Killing 66 percent of a population in eight years would be an astonishingly high death toll. The Nazi invasion of Soviet Russia killed 13 percent of Russia's population. The Black Death (plague) that swept Europe in 1348-1350 resulted in a 20 to 25 percent depletion of the population; and since it came in recurrent waves, the depletion conservatively amounted to 40 percent of the population of Europe by the end of the fourteenth century (Petersen, 1969: 390; Russell, 1948: 214-232; Russell, 1958: 40-45).

When assessing the impact of the An Lushan Revolt there are a number of difficulties. First, up until the modern age, population counts were sporadic and incomplete. The first census in the United States was not made until 1790. In the medieval Chinese era, the government counted households ("doors") and some or all of the people ("mouths") constituting them, but it did not attempt a full registration until 1953 (Twictchett, 1979; Durand, 1960). Chinese censuses in ancient times were for the purpose of levying troops and allocating tax burdens. Taxation records are frequently disrupted by war and the resulting administrative chaos. The figures for number of households are held to be more reliable than those for actual head count (Fitzgerald, 1973: 312-315). Second, the census figures vary wildly depending on level of governmental control (Fitzgerald, 1947: 4-11; Fitzgerald, 1932, 1947).

An Lushan was a garrison commanding general of ethnic-minority descent. His mother was descended from an important Turkic clan and his father was probably a soldier of Sogdian descent, medieval kin to Pashtuns who dominate Afghanistan today (White, 2012: 88). An Lushan rebelled against the T'ang Dynasty in 755 AD. This sparked a civil war across northern China for a period of eight years before the rebels were destroyed in 763 AD. The revolt had weakened central control, so that after the rebellion there was a lot more decentralization in the Empire than before it and census taking was affected, as had happened many times previously in China. For example, according to historian Richard Guisso, a census during the reign of Taizong from 626 AD to 640 AD shows 3 million households, while under the previous Sui dynasty (581-618 AD) the figure had been three times that large, at 9 million households (Guisso, 1979). This sensational decline was due not to loss of life during the civil warfare of the late Sui and early T'ang dynasties, but to simple failure of the local authorities to register the population in full. In times of trouble, the tax system broke down and half of the population would be omitted from the census.

After the An Lushan Revolt the situation reached crisis proportions. A new period of warlordism and regional autonomy emerged. The T'ang dynasty survived only by carrying out a widespread decentralization of administrative power, which became dispersed through a new tier of provincial governments. China broke into many regions. Each collected their own taxes and remitted only a small portion to the central government. The T'ang dynasty no longer could enumerate and impose taxes directly upon the majority of peasant households. This political weakening manifests itself in the decline of the registered population from approximately nine million households in 755 AD to less than two million in 760 AD (Graff, 2002: 240). What collapsed, then, was not the actual population but the ability of the government to find and count very taxpayer (White, 2012: 93).

How large was the loss of life in the An Lushan Revolt? White conservatively places the number of dead at 13 million (White, 2012: 13). This amounts to a decline, over a period of eight years, of 23.8 percent of the population of the T'ang Empire. As such, it still ranks, among the twenty deadliest "multicides"—human-made deadly events—in history.

CONSTRUCTING AND UNDERSTANDING A POPULATION PYRAMID

Demographers represent the distribution of a population by age and sex together in a special type of bar graph known as a **population pyramid**. A population pyramid is a technique of graphically portraying in the form of a pyramid the age and sex composition of a given population. The population pyramid of the United States in 2013 is presented in Graph 11.1. See Graph 11.1. The "boxy" shape of the 2013 population pyramid of the United States indicates an aging population. The median age of the United States population in 2013 is 37.2 years old.

On a population pyramid, the various bars, or rows, represent successive age groups. From the point of view of a person viewing the graph, the various bars or rows are divided between females to the right of center and males to the left of center. The male and female populations are broken down into 5-year age groups represented as horizontal bars along the vertical axis, with the youngest age groups at the bottom and the oldest at the top. The length of each bar indicates, according to the scale along the horizontal axis, the number of people, either in absolute figures or as a percentage. The shape of the population pyramid gradually evolves over time based on fertility, mortality, an international migration trends.

GRAPH 11.1 POPULATION PYRAMID OF THE UNITED STATES, 2013

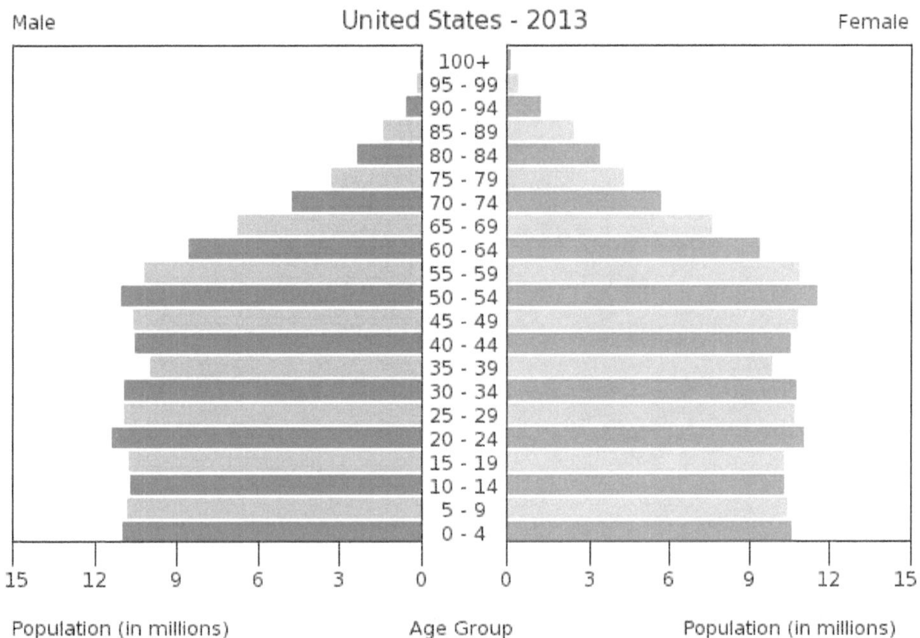

Source: U.S. Census Bureau, International Data Base. As of July 14, 2013, available online at http://www.census.gov/population/international/data/idb/region.php?N=%20Results%20&T=12&A=separate&RT=0&Y=2013&R=-1&C=US

The reason for the basic shape of the pyramid is that among those born, for example in 1990, some have died each year since then, changing the length of each bar representing successively higher ages. The shape is not ordinarily a perfect pyramid, because mortality varies from one year to another and because fertility and migration also affect the population structure. Whether recent fertility has been high or low is shown by the length of the bottom bar. If a society, like Afghanistan, for example, has a population pyramid with a large base, this indicates that the society has a high birth rate. See Graph 11.2.

The shape of Afghanistan's 2013 population pyramid is prototypical of a society that has a high fertility rate and a young population. How young is Afghanistan's population? The median age of the Afghani population is 17.9 years old (Central Intelligence Agency: Afghanistan, 2013). This contrasts with a median age of 37.2 years of age for the United States in 2013 (Central Intelligence Agency: United States, 2013). Afghanistan also has a high **total fertility rate**—the number of children a woman bears during her reproductive years, often measured as the number of births per female aged 15-45 years of age. In Afghanistan in 2013, mother's median age at first birth is 20.1 years of age. The total fertility rate in Afghanistan in 2013 is 5.54 children and the contraceptive prevalence rate is 21.8 percent. The **contraceptive prevalence rate** is the percent of women of reproductive age (15-49) who are married or in a union and are using, or whose sexual partner is using, a method of contraception. These figures contrast markedly with comparable figures for the United States in 2013, where the mother's median age at first birth is 25, the total fertility rate is 2.06 children, and the contraceptive prevalence rate is 78.6 percent.

GRAPH 11.2 POPULATION PYRAMID OF AFGHANISTAN, 2013

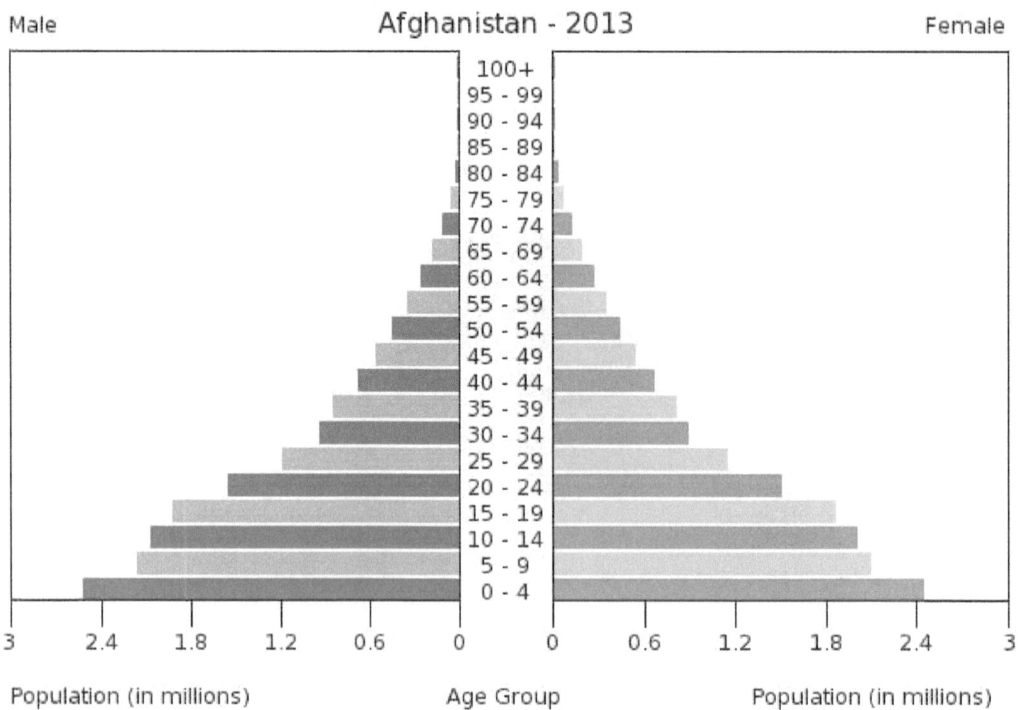

Source: U.S. Census Bureau, International Data Base. As of July 14, 2013, available online at http://www.census.gov/population/international/data/idb/region.php?N=%20Results%20&T=12&A=separate&RT=0&Y=2013&R=-1&C=AF

On a population pyramid, a depletion caused by a past famine, epidemic, pandemic, war, or by a period of particularly large emigration or low fertility, is represented by an indentation from a smooth pyramid pattern. In like fashion, a period of high fertility or of high immigration is represented by a corresponding protuberance in the population pyramid. These irregularities remain on population pyramids in successive dates, gradually moving to the top of the graph and disappearing only when the oldest cohorts eventually die off.

Usually the population represented in a population pyramid is broken down into five-year age groups, as can be seen in Graphs 11.1 and 11.2. Sometimes one population pyramid is superimposed on another, to illustrate the contrast between two populations or between the structures of one population at different times.

Let us now turn our attention to the origin of the field of demography and examine its foundational theory.

THOMAS ROBERT MALTHUS: THE RACE BETWEEN THE STORK AND THE PLOW

The first serious analysis of population structure began in England during the late 18th and early 19th centuries with the writings of Thomas Robert Malthus (1766-1834). Malthus is the one person whom most would consider the founding father of modern demography and he also was influential in the field of political economy, which has come to be known today as economics. Born in Surrey, England, in 1776, he was one of seven children and his father was a country gentleman. From his early childhood Malthus was known as "Robert." Malthus was an honor student at Jesus College in Cambridge. After he received his Masters degree he became an Anglican minister in 1797 and was a cleric and scholar for the remainder of his life. During his studies he took an interest in the relationship between economics and population growth in European societies. In fact, Malthus is one of the founders of nineteenth-century economics, a direct successor of Adam Smith (Petersen, 1969: 142); Petersen, 1979). He is now famous for his pioneering and controversial book titled *An Essay on the Principle of Population* published in 1798 (Malthus, 1798). *An Essay on the Principle of Population* was the first book he ever wrote, and it was an instant success, selling out of its first printing in a matter of days. It is interesting to note that Malthus first published *Essay on the Principle of Population* anonymously, because he was not sure how the general public would respond to the serious moral and social issues that he raised in the book. Between 1798 and 1826 Malthus wrote six editions of his book. Malthus was always fine tuning his thesis in light of the empirical evidence.

Malthus's basic thesis is that human populations tend to increase at a faster rate than the food supply. Malthus's thesis is sufficiently famous or well-known that the strain or tension between the rates of increase for population and food supply has been given a name. It is variously called "the Malthusian dilemma," the Malthusian trap, the Malthusian equilibrium, the pre-transition period, or "the race between the stork and the plow." These terms tend to be used interchangeably.

One thing that made Malthus's argument so convincing was his use of simple mathematical models to make his argument. Malthus was no stranger to statistics and in fact he was one of the co-founders of the Statistical Society of London in 1834 (Petersen, 1979). In *An Essay on the Principle of Population*, Malthus made the argument that human populations tend to grow or increase in *geometric progression*, i.e. in the following sequence: 1, 2, 4, 8, 16, 32, and so on. This geometric progression of population growth is captured by the demographic concept of **doubling time**—the amount of time it takes a population of a given size to double in size.

The formula used to calculate doubling time is 70 divided by the current growth rate. Thus, for example, Afghanistan in 2013 had a population growth rate of 2.25 percent (Central Intelligence Agency: Afghanistan, 2013). A population with a 2.25 percent growth rate will double in a little over three decades (31.1 years). By contrast, the United States in 2013 had a population growth rate of 0.9 percent (Central Intelligence Agency: United States, 2013). It will take a population with a 0.9 percent growth rate 77.8 years to double in size. Small differences make big differences.

Since the concept of geometric growth rate tends to be outside of the experience of many people, let us consider it for a moment through the lens of a thought experiment that involves a folktale about an Indian King, Sharim, and his vizier, Sissa Ben Dahir, the inventor of chess (Swirski, 2006:4). The story goes like this: The vizier, Sissa Ben Dahir, presents the Indian King with the game of chess. The King is so pleased with the gift that he offers a reward of sixty-four pieces of gold to the vizier, one for each square of the chessboard. The vizier counters with a request, instead, of a grain of rice for the first square, two for the second, three for the third, and so forth. Deceived by the apparent modesty of the proposal, the king accedes, unaware that all the grains of rice in the world—either then or now—would not be sufficient to supply the amount of rice needed. For instance, on the twenty-first square, more than a million grains would be needed, and more than a trillion would be needed on the forty-first square. There was not enough rice in the whole world for the final squares. On the entire chessboard there would be 2^{64} -1 = 18,446,744,073,709,551,615 grains of rice weighing 461,168,602,000 metric tonswhich would be a heap of rice larger than Mount Everest. This is about 1,000 times the global production of rice in 2010 (which was 464,000,000 metric tons) (MercoPress, 2011).

In contrast, Malthus argues that the size of the food supply tends to increase at a slower rate which he terms an *arithmetic rate*, that is, in the sequence of 1, 2, 3, 4, 5, and so forth. Malthus thought that people could increase food production only by slow, difficult methods such as reclaiming unused land or intensive farming. In contrast, Malthus thought that people could check population growth more effectively by marrying late, using contraceptives, emigrating, and so forth. In more extreme conditions, war, famine, pestilence, and disease bring population back into line with the available food supply.

Malthus on Positive Checks and Preventive Checks on Population Growth

Malthus predicted that human populations tend to outstrip their food supply, unless population growth were checked in some way. Malthus envisioned two typed of checks on population growth, which he termed **positive checks** and **preventive checks**. Malthus uses the term "positive checks" to refer to those factors that raise the death rate and the term "preventive checks" to refer to those factors that lower the birth rate. Thus, Malthus identifies illness, wars, natural catastrophes, pestilence, famine, and epidemics as positive checks on population growth. With regard to preventive checks on population growth—i.e., those factors that lower the birth rate--Malthus identifies two varieties, one of which he does not approve ("vice"), and the other of which he does approve ("moral restraint"). The principle moral restraint he identifies is the postponement of the age at first marriage, with no pre-marital sexual relations. He also advocated a life of celibacy for some, as a means of controlling population growth.

Some types of preventive checks Malthus viewed as human "vices," because they were methods of population control of which he did not approve. These included the use of contraception, abortion, promiscuous sexual relations (including prostitution), adultery, and homosexuality. These were all measures

or activities that would serve to reduce the birth rate in any population. However, his strong religious beliefs prohibited Malthus from supporting any of these methods as means of controlling population growth.

Ever since Malthus first published *An Essay on the Principle of Population*, people have wondered if he was correct in his thesis that population growth tends to outstrip the food supply. During the period of the most rapid growth in population on the planet—Stage Two of the demographic transition as it was experienced by the West, the food supply grew *faster* than population and the price of corn, rice, and wheat *decreased* markedly. We turn now to an examination of demographic transition theory. Malthusian theory and demographic transition theory, together, may be thought of as the foundational theory of demography.

DEMOGRAPHIC TRANSITION THEORY

Demographers have developed a number of models or theories for understanding population growth rates over the historical long term. One of the earliest and most famous of these is the theory of the demographic transition, first enunciated by American sociologist Warren S. Thompson in his doctoral thesis in sociology at Columbia University in 1915, published that year in book form (Thompson, 1915), and then refined by him and others ever since (e.g., Cummins, 2013; Clark and Cummins, 2012; Ferguson, 2011; Connelly, 2008; Clark, 2007; Riley, 2005; Petersen, 1969: 11; Petersen, 1960; Davis, 1945; Thompson, 1929). See Table 11.2.

TABLE 11.2 STAGES OF THE DEMOGRAPHIC TRANSITION

Stages of the Demographic Transition	Fertility	Mortality	Rate of Population Growth
I	High	High	Low
II	High	Low	High
III	Low	Low	Low

Warren S. Thompson thought that the two variables of fertility and mortality would be most useful in understanding the growth of populations over the long term. In his analysis of population growth Thompson therefore gave primary consideration to the fertility and mortality rates that were prevalent in various societies around the world. As a result of his studies, Thompson was able to see three distinct patterns or stages of population growth over time when he looked at the various nations of the world. **Demographic transition theory** conceptualizes the long-term changes in fertility, mortality, and rates of population growth as experienced by the societies of the West as they industrialized or modernized in the following manner—there is a transition from a situation of high birth rates and high death rates, with the associated low rates of population growth (First stage), to high birth rates and lowered death rates with the associated high rates of population growth (Second stage), to the low fertility and low mortality stage with its associated low rates of population growth (Third stage).

Since the early years of Thompson's research, many demographers have examined, debated, tested and developed demographic transition theory. Although some of its details have proved to be false and some of its implications misleading, "in its simplest form the theory of the demographic transition is nevertheless one of the best documented generalizations in the social sciences" (Peterson, 1969: 11).

The First Stage of the Demographic Transition

The first stage reflects the human condition that prevailed for most of the time that humans have lived on this planet. This first stage is recognized for its total dependency on food production. This can range from "simple" hunting and gathering societies (folk societies), to horticultural societies, to the more advanced societies of the agricultural revolution, where plow-based agriculture on irrigated ground transformed many aspects of social life.

This pre-transition period is marked by a combination of high fertility rates and high mortality rates. The high fertility and mortality rates tend to offset each other. The result is that, over the long term, a very slow rate of overall population growth results. In all of these societies, life indeed is "short and brutish," in that the overall **life expectancy** is no more than thirty-five to forty years of age, on the average. Life expectancy refers to the average number of years that persons in a given population born in a particular period of time can expect to live (Theodorson and Theodorson, 1969: 231; Giddens, Dineier, and Carr, 2013: 493). In many of these societies, almost as many people die in infancy and childhood as grow to maturity (Petersen, 1969:11). Causes of death were varied. In Asia, starvation seems to have been more important than disease as a cause of high mortality in this first stage of the demographic transition.

The Black Death, the bubonic plague caused by the flea-born bacterium *Yersinia pestis*, reached England in 1349 and reduced London's population from around 70,000 to around 40,000 (Ferguson, 2011: 23; Kelly, 2005: 215). Besides the plague, typhus, dysentery, and smallpox also were rife. Cities in the West in the medieval period were unhealthy, unsanitary places and would have lost population, had it not been for in-migration from the rural countryside.

Even in the absence of epidemics, poor sanitation made London, in the words of historian Niall Ferguson, "a death-trap" (Ferguson, 2011: 23). There was no functioning sewage system in London and the streets were the dumping ground for human excrement, both urine and feces (Ferguson, 2011: 23). Not surprisingly, therefore, death rates were much higher in London than in the countryside. For instance, English life expectancy at birth was on average thirty-seven years between 1540 and 1800. The corresponding figure for London was in the twenties. While roughly one in five (20 percent of) English children died in the first year of life, in London the corresponding figure was nearly one in three. Poor hygiene was widespread across the social hierarchy in Western Europe. Henry V himself became king at the age of twenty-six in fifteenth-century England and was dead from dysentery at the age of thirty-five (Ferguson, 2011: 24).

Economic historian Gregory Clark and others document the low standards of personal and community hygiene that prevailed in Europe during the preindustrial era (e.g., Clark, 2007; Cockayne, 2007: 180-205; Robinson, 2004). Europeans were, by modern standards and also by standards of preindustrial China and Japan, a filthy people, living in dirt and squalor. One crucial economic problem for hygiene in preindustrial Europe that is identified by Gregory Clark (Clark, 2007) is that human waste had little or no market value because it was not socially acceptable to use it as fertilizer for farm and garden purposes (Clark, 2007: 105). Alan Macfarlane documents that in preindustrial Japan, human waste (known as nightsoil) could be used in lieu of rent, but that in England one had to pay to have it taken away (Macfarlane, 2003: 173). Its removal and disposal were thus major social problems—or, at least, potential detriments to public health and human longevity. Samuel Pepys, for instance, complains in his diary on October 20, 1660, that while going down to his cellar, he put his feet "into a great heap of turds," by which he deduced that his neighbor's "house of office" (i.e., privy, outhouse) was full and its contents had overflowed into the cellar of Samuel Pepys. It took five days after this complaint for the neighbor to clean out the overflowing privy (Pepys, 2000).

In contrast, in China and Japan, human waste, both urine and feces, was a valuable property which householders *sold* to farmers and for which various groups competed for the right to collect (Macfarlane, 2003: 173; Clark, 2007: 106). In Japan and China, human waste was not dumped into cesspits, sewers, and streams, contaminating water supplies. Instead, in cities such as eighteenth-century Osaka, contractors found it profitable to provide public containers on street corners in order to profit from the waste deposits (Hanley, 1997: 104-129). In China and Japan, human waste seems to have been carried away daily, as opposed to being stored in cesspits below houses which were only periodically emptied, as was the tradition in London.

Cesspits were introduced to Europe in the sixteenth century when urban populations were growing at a faster rate than in the past (LaBerge, 2002). The cesspit or cesspool is a pit, conservancy tank, or covered cistern used to dispose of urine and feces. Their appearance was somewhat similar to a hand-dug water well, lined with loose-fitting brick or stone. Cesspits were often located or placed under cellar floors or in the yard of a house Some of them had wooden chutes to carry the excrement from the upper floors into the cesspit, sometimes flushed by rainwater (Hanawalt, 1995: 28-29). Cesspits were not watertight, allowing liquid waste to drain away and leaving only the solids to be collected (Cockayne, 2007: 143). Liquids leaked out through the soil as conditions allowed, contaminating water sources. (Hanawalt, 1995: 28-29). People also emptied their human waste from their chamber pots onto the streets each day (La Berge, 2002). Cesspits would get full, overflowing, as conditions permitted, into neighbors' cellars.

In Europe people paid workers, known as gong farmers, to clean out their cesspits. **Gong farmer** is a term that entered the English language in Tudor England (1485-1603) to describe someone who dug out and removed human excrement from privies (out houses) and cesspits. The word "gong" refers to the privies and cesspits as well as to their contents (Cockayne, 2007; Robinson, 2005; La Berge, 2002). Using shovels and horse-drawn wagons, the gong farmer dug out the cesspits and removed the excrement. For this labor in the late 15th century London gong farmers charged two shillings per ton of waste removed (Hanawalt, 1995: 28-29). Gong farmers employed at Hampton Court during the time of Queen Elizabeth I (1558-1603) were paid a sixpence a day, which was a good living for the time, but the working life of a gong farmer was spent "up to his knees, waist, and even neck" in human excrement (Robinson, 2005: 88). They were allowed to work only between 9 PM and 5 AM, to reduce the smell and annoyance to the public. Because they were allowed to work only at night, gong farmers also were known as nightmen.

In terms of personal hygiene, it is worth noting that in Europe bathing was not popular and in fact was regarded as an indulgence even in the early modern period (Clark, 2007). Data on soap production in eighteenth century England supports the idea that the washing of people and clothing was not a frequent activity (Clark, 2007: 107). In the 1710s, England's population was 5.7 million people and taxed soap output was 25 million pounds, which equates to less than 0.2 ounce per person per day for all uses of the product (Deane and Cole, 1967: 72; Clark, 2007: 107). To appreciate how meager this level of soap usage actually is, some comparisons are useful:

- The Southern Africa Food Security Operation currently aims to supply its destitute clients with 0.4 ounce of soap per day (Clark, 2007: 107);
- Transported convicts in Australia in the mid nineteenth century got a ration of 0.5 ounce of soap per day (Clark, 2007: 107);
- The ration of soap for both the Union and Confederate armies at the beginning of the U.S. Civil War was 0.64 ounce per day (Shannon, 1927: 479).

Another indication of the low attention paid to personal and community hygiene in the pre-industrial era in Europe and in England is expressed in their public toilet arrangements. Public latrines, known as "houses of easement," were a rarity. For instance, near the end of the 14th century, London had a population of roughly 30,000 people and only 16 houses of easement (Galloway, 2003: 78). When the Globe Theater was constructed on the south bank of the Thames in London in 1599, not one toilet was provided for the 1,500 audience members that the theater could accommodate. Theater goers did their toilet in the yard outside, or more likely, according to economic historian Gregory Clark, in the stairways and passages of the theater itself (Clark, 2007: 107).

It is important to point out that while we speak of these various types of societies in the past tense or as part of a model or theory, it is true that millions of people around the world today still live in societies like these. The fact is that millions of people today are situated in the first stage of the demographic transition.

The Second Stage of the Demographic Transition

The second stage of the demographic transition is noteworthy because countries break out of the Malthusian trap and world population grows significantly. These societies are more highly organized and more technologically advanced than the basic hunting and gathering and agricultural societies found in the first stage of the demographic transition. As a result of technological advances in food production, improved living conditions, and improved health, more and more people live instead of dying. There is, if you will, a health explosion, also known as a **health transition**—i.e., a reduction in mortality that manifests itself in an increase in life expectancy. At the same time, these pre-industrial societies still have high fertility rates. Declining mortality rates coupled with high fertility rates result in an increase in the rate of population growth. At this stage of the demographic transition, we see that people live longer and more of their children survive into reproductive ages. Hence we notice a dramatic increase in population growth over a relatively short period of time. It is at this stage that world population increased "at an unprecedentedly high rate to unprecedented totals" (Petersen, 1969: 11).

The Malthusian equilibrium held all societies in its grip before the latter half of the eighteenth century, which coincides with the first decades of industrialization (Petersen, 1969: 403). This transition is particularly well documented in the case of England, where, in the second half of the eighteenth century, in a series of individual acts of Parliament, the common land of villages was transferred to the private ownership of families in a process known as **enclosure** or inclosure (e.g., Petersen, 1969: 406-407; Chambers and Mingay, 1965; Thompson, 1964). The age of enclosure also was the age of new methods of draining fields, manuring, breeding and feeding cattle, which amounted to an agricultural revolution and to an astounding advance in English agriculture (Petersen, 1969: 407; Trevelyan, 1942; McKeown and Brown, 1965). Potatoes and other root crops became staples. New breeds of farm animals were developed. Feed was grown that could be stored over the winter, and so the older custom of converting a major part of the herd into salt meat was abandoned. These improved methods were also applied to what had been wasteland, thereby bringing about two million acres under cultivation in the eighteenth century alone (Petersen, 1969). These changes resulted in an improved food supply, both in quantity and quality (Drummond and Wilbraham, 1957). Population increased in both urban and rural areas. There is no question that population increased substantially from 1760 to 1840.

It was not until the last quarter of the nineteenth century that public sanitation became sufficiently established in England and Western Europe to cancel the biological hazards posed to human health and longevity by human excrement-disposal issues (Rosenberg, 1966; Hennock, 1957; Buer, 1926: 108). Even so important a step as the separation of sewage from drinking water was taken gradually. In 1831-1832 a cholera epidemic occurred in London that claimed over 3,800 lives (Higgins, 1979), at a time when urban sanitation in London was at its worst. Progress in urban sanitation remained slow in coming. It is worth noting in this regard that until 1850, one of London's drinking water companies had its intake within a few feet of the mouth of the Westbourne River which was a well-known common sewer (Buer, 1926). Even after the water closet (flushable toilet), was invented toward the end of the nineteenth century, it emptied either into large vaults under the houses (cesspits), or, later, into sewers that flowed into a river.

In England, from 1875 to 1945, medicine and public sanitation effected a rapid decline in mortality, particularly of infants and children. For earlier decades, the most important factor in the decline in mortality seems to have been the better food supply (Petersen, 1969: 428). Sociologist and demographer William Petersen suggests some changes in the environment, other than the improved food supply, may have contributed to the reduced mortality. Among these must be counted the shift from woolen to cotton clothing, and the improved cleanliness that this facilitated. Petersen credits this sartorial change as an important factor in the sharply reduced incidence of typhus during this period (Petersen, 1969: 417).

The timing of what might be termed the health explosion or the health transition—i.e., the beginning of sustained improvements life expectancy that is associated with the second stage of the demographic transition—is clear and coincides with industrialization. While average global life expectancy at birth around 1800 was just 18.5 years, two centuries later, in 2001, it had more than doubled to 66.6 years (Ferguson: 2011: 146). This health transition was not confined to the metropolitan areas of the world. It occurred in rural areas as well.

The timing of the health transition came at different times in different parts of the globe (Riley, 2005; Johansen, 2002; Szreter and Mooney, 1998; Woods, 1985). Thus, in Western Europe, it came between the 1770s and the 1890s, starting with Denmark in 1775, and Spain brought up the rear in the 1920s (Riley, 2005: 758). By the eve of the First World War, typhoid and cholera had been eliminated in Europe as a result of improvements in public health and sanitation (Ferguson, 2011: 147).

In twenty-three modern Asian countries for which long-term historical data are available, with one exception, the health transition came between the 1890s and the 1950s (Ferguson, 2011: 147). The one exception is Japan, where the health transition started around 1870 (Riley, 2005).

In most of the countries of Africa, the health transition came between the 1920s and the 1950s (Riley, 2005). Three things are worth noting. First, in nearly all Asian and African countries, improvements in life expectancy began *before* the end of European colonial rule (Ferguson, 2011: 147). Second, the rate of improvement in longevity has declined since independence, especially, but not exclusively, because of the HIV-AIDs epidemic (Ferguson, 201: 147). Third, the timing of the improvement in life expectancy *predated* the discovery and introduction of antibiotics, the insecticide DDT, and vaccines other than the simple ones for smallpox and yellow fever. Other than improvements in the quantity, quality, and lower price of the food supply and the change to cotton versus wool cloth for clothing, the evidence points to sustained improvements in public health along a broad front as the cause of the reduction in mortality, especially in mortality due to fecal disease, malaria, and even tuberculosis (Ferguson, 2011: 148).

The Third Stage of the Demographic Transition

The third stage of the demographic transition is characterized at by lower fertility rates and lower mortality rates. Consequently the overall rate of growth in these societies is low. A long-term decline in fertility began in the United States in 1810, in France probably even earlier, and among the middle and upper classes in England between 1760 and 1800 (Cummins, 2013; Clark and Cummins, 2012; Petersen, 1969: 420). In the industrialized Western countries, the upper and middle classes increased the age at marriage and had fewer children. In England, the net fertility of the affluent declined substantially. Within a forty year period, among the affluent in England an important and rapid decline in fertility was accomplished for marriages formed between 1760 and 1800. Up until then, the richest English men were producing four or more surviving children, at a time when men in general in England produced only 2.5 surviving children (Clark and Cummins, 2012). Within a generation the net fertility of the affluent fell. It became equal to, or even less than that of the general population in England, at a level of three serving children per family. Thus, in England, a demographic revolution accompanied the industrial revolution (Clark and Cummins, 2012: 38).

It is worth noting that this decline was accomplished *before* the creation of modern contraceptives. The age at first marriage increased among the affluent. And an increased age at first marriage, coupled with celibacy prior to marriage, can cut the fertility rate substantially. Then, too, the sheep-gut or animal-gut condom, also known as the skin condom, while not aesthetically appealing by modern standards, evidently worked with sufficient efficacy that it helped to curb the birth rate. Their popularity is attested to by the fact that in the eighteenth century they were sold at pubs, barbershops, chemist shops, open-air markets, and at the theater throughout Europe and Russia (Collier, 2007). Other contraceptive methods in use at this time included prolonged nursing, the sponge, *coitus interruptus*, and douche with an astringent solution (Petersen, 1969: 488; Knowlton, 1832; Owen, 1830; Place, 1822).

It was not until 1839 that Charles Goodyear discovered **vulcanization**, a process of making rubber stronger, more elastic, and more durable over time (Collier, 2007). The process is named after Vulcan, the Roman god of fire. The vulcanization of rubber was adapted to the manufacture of birth control technologies, including the condom and diaphragms, a form of birth control for females, which in the nineteenth century were called "womb veils" (Grigoriadis, 2010). The first rubber condom was produced in 1855. However, buying one of the earliest rubber condoms was not as simple as taking a trip to the local pharmacy, chemist shop, barber shop, or open-air market. Often, men had to visit doctors to be professionally fitted. But by the late 1850s, several major rubber companies were mass producing condoms of the one-size-fits-all variety, to be sold in pharmacies. In the 1870s, the first major condom manufacturing company was founded in England, E. Lambert and Son (Collier, 2007).

Between 1880 and 1900, in one area of Europe after another, the birth rate plummeted. All across England, it was most sudden and precipitous among professional families, but it soon spread to other segments of the class system, particularly to other segments of the middle class. The last two decades of the nineteenth century saw the reality of smaller families sweep across Europe, spurred on by the development of new or improved condoms and diaphragms (Connelly, 2008:20). Marital fertility rates in Denmark, Norway, Finland, Sweden, Britain, Germany, Belgium, Switzerland, the Netherlands, and Austria had all peaked by 1880. Once they began to fall, they never recovered. In fact, when plotted on a graph, they appear to have plunged off a cliff, with the countries of southern and eastern Europe following the pack (Coale and Treadway, 1986; Livi-Bacci, 1986; Connelly, 2008: 20).

In sum, demographic transition theory provides a useful model of how the rate of population growth can change over time and how population growth can affect the nature of a society. While no one has a crystal ball for accurately predicting the future, the expectation is that as more countries advance into the fields of high technology they will also move through the various stages of the demographic transition. The current population growth predictions for 2050 indicate that many nations will still find themselves in either the high growth or slow growth stages of the demographic transition, which will undoubtedly create a number of challenges for these, and for other nations, as well.

We now turn our attention, in turn, to three main variables that demographers use to understand population structure—fertility, mortality, and migration. These variables determine population growth and structure in any group. Fertility, the number of live births, adds to a population. Mortality, the number of deaths, subtracts from a population. Migration can either add to a population or deduct from it. Migration adds to a population as new immigrants arrive and settle into an adopted society. It is possible for migration to deduct from a population—as when, for example, immigrants return to their home country through a process of return migration. Emigration refers to the departure of individuals or groups from a country to take up residence in another country, and, as such it deducts from the population of the home country.

FERTILITY

Fertility refers to the number of births that occur in a population over a given period of time. **Fecundity** is the physiological ability, capacity, or potential to reproduce. **Fertility** refers to the realization of this potential, the actual birth rate, as measured by the number of offspring. Demographers describe fertility using the **crude birth rate**, which is the number of live births in a given year for every 1,000 people in the population. The formula for calculating the crude birth rate is

$$\text{Crude Birth Rate} = \frac{\text{Number of live births in year}}{\text{Total population at mid-year}} \times 1{,}000$$

The rate is "crude" because the denominator includes the entire population, even those too young (pre-pubertal) and too old (post-menopausal) to get pregnant as well as males, none of whom are able to get pregnant in the normal course of events. A more refined measure of the birth rate, therefore, would include in its denominator only those who are at risk of getting pregnant. One such measure is the **total fertility rate**, which is the number of births per woman during her reproductive years, often measured as the number of births per female aged 15-45 years of age.

If we consider only fertility and mortality as inputs into population size, the total fertility rate needed for a population to replace itself without either increasing or declining in size is termed **replacement-level fertility**. In highly economically developed societies, the replacement-level fertility rate is 2.1 children. Another name for replacement-level fertility is **zero population growth (ZPG)**, a term coined in 1967 by American sociologist and demographer Kingsley Davis to refer to a condition of demographic balance where the number of people in a specified population neither grows nor declines (Davis, 1967, 1973). Various social actors and stakeholders promote zero population growth as a social aim and as a social good, an ideal, towards which countries and the whole world should aspire, in the interests of accomplishing long-term environmental sustainability and social justice (e.g., Najam and Yusuf, 2013; Hoff, 2012; Laurie, 2010; Connelly, 2008; Ehrlich, 1975; Olson and Landsberg, 1973). The terms zero population growth and replacement-level fertility are used interchangeably and synonymously. In Europe five countries—Estonia, Austria, Monaco, Czech Republic, and Moldova—have achieved zero population growth as of 2012 (calculated using data from Population Reference Bureau, 2012).

Other countries, in Europe and elsewhere, have achieved **below replacement-level fertility**. In the economically advanced societies, below replacement-level fertility is a total fertility rate (TFR) below 2.1 children per couple. Absent immigration, below replacement-level fertility eventually will lead a population to shrink in size. It is for this reason that below replacement-level fertility is defined, conceptually, as a combination of fertility and mortality rates that leads to a negative population growth rate. At various times in modern history—during war or famine—birthrates have fallen below the replacement rates, to "low" or "very low" levels (Shorto, 2008). However, for the first time on record, a total fertility rate at or below 1.3 spread rapidly during the 1990s in Southern Europe, Eastern Europe, and the former Soviet Union, (e.g., Ortega, and Billari, 2002; Shorto, 2008; Steyn, 2008, 2007). For demographers, a TFR of 1.3 has a special mathematical significance. It is the level at which a country's population would be cut in half in 45 years, creating what some think of as a "cliff effect" from which it would be nearly impossible to recover. German demographer Hans-Peter Kohler and his colleagues created a new term for this phenomenon, **lowest-low fertility** Lowest-low fertility is a total fertility rate at or below 1.3 (Kohler, Billari, and Ortega, 2006; Kohler, Ortega, and Billari, 2002). Today there are only a handful of countries with TFRs below 1.3, compared to 21 countries in 2003 (Goldstein, Sobotka, and Jasilioniene, 2009). According to World Bank 2012 data, only five European countries have lowest-low fertility rates—Bosnia and Herzegovina (1.1), Hungary (1.2), Latvia (1.3), Poland (1.3), and Romania (1.3). In the whole of East Asia, only South Korea, Macao, and Singapore have lowest-low fertility rates (World Bank, 2012).

A number of social and demographic variables, other than fecundity, affect the fertility rate. First, the age at first sexual intercourse is a key variable in the fertility rate of a population. The younger the age of first intercourse, the higher the fertility rate. Sociologists would phrase this by saying that there is a positive relation between age at first sexual intercourse and fertility. Second, the age at first marriage is a key variable in the fertility of a population. The younger the age at first marriage, the higher the fertility rate. There is a positive relation between age at first marriage and fertility.

What these two factors have in common is the frequency of exposure to sexual intercourse. It is the frequency of exposure to sexual intercourse that increases the fertility rate. If a female lives in a traditional society that encourages early marriage and large families, she will have a long fecundity period. For instance, if a female has her fist menstruation, which is known as **menarche**, at, say, 12.5 years of age and does not enter menopause until 45 years of age, then she has a fecundity period of 32.5 years. On the other hand, if a female lives in a Western European country and waits until age thirty or older to marry, then she has a far shorter exposure to a likely pregnancy. The later in life a female marries and the later the onset of her first pregnancy, the fewer children she will produce. See Table 11.3, which lists those countries where the mean age of mother at first birth is older than 28.0 years of age.

Only a tiny percentage of females experience trouble conceiving prior to the age of 28. However, by the age of 35, fifty percent of women who are trying to get pregnant fail to get pregnant over the course of eight months, and after that the odds keep dropping (Grigoriadis, 2010). In vitro fertilization (IVF) is the gold standard of infertility treatments since 1978, the year in which Louise Brown, the first baby conceived by IVF, was born. In 2010, Robert Edwards, the British scientist who pioneered IVF, was awarded the Nobel Prize for physiology or medicine for his work in pioneering IVF, which, at that time had helped in the conception and birth of more than 4 million people worldwide (Jha,2010). Today, in a single cycle of IVF, about 64 percent of 30-year old women end up with a child. The success rate falls to 47 percent by age 35, and after that, the success rate drops markedly. At age 40, only 13 percent are successful, a rate which falls to 2 percent among those aged 44 and older (Grigoriadis, 2010).

TABLE 11.3 COUNTRIES WITH A MEAN AGE OF MOTHER AT FIRST BIRTH THAT IS GREATER THAN 28.0 YEARS OF AGE, BY RANK, COUNTRY, AND MOTHER'S MEAN AGE AT FIRST BIRTH

Rank	Country	Mother's Mean Age at First Birth
1	Australia	30.5
2	Switzerland	30.2
3	United Kingdom	30.0
4	Ireland	29.8
5	Hong Kong	29.8
6	South Korea	29.6
7	Japan	29.4
8	Singapore	29.4
9	Spain	29.3
10	Greece	29.2
11	Denmark	29.1
12	Germany	28.9
13	Slovenia	28.7
14	Sweden	28.6
15	France	28.6
16	Austria	28.5

Source: Adapted and compiled from CIA World Factbook. As of July 28, 2013, available online at https://www.cia.gov/library/publications/the-world-factbook/fields/2256.html#us

TABLE 11.4 COUNTRIES WITH A MEAN AGE OF MOTHER AT FIRST BIRTH THAT IS GREATER THAN 28.0 YEARS OF AGE, BY RANK, COUNTRY, AND MOTHER'S MEAN AGE AT FIRST BIRTH

Rank	Country	Total Fertility Rate
1	Niger	7.03
2	Mali	6.25
3	Somalia	6.17
4	Uganda	6.06
5	Burkina Faso	6.00
6	Burundi	5.99
7	Zambia	5.81
8	Afghanistan	5.54
9	South Sudan	5.54
10	Angola	5.49

Source: Adapted and compiled from Central Intelligence Agency, "Country Comparison: Total Fertility Rate," *The World Factbook.* As of July 14, 2013, available online at https://www.cia.gov/library/publications/the-world-factbook//rankorder/2127rank.html

Fertility rates vary greatly around the world. The most underdeveloped countries tend to have high total fertility rates. A sociologist might phrase this by saying that today there is an inverse relationship between level of economic development and fertility. In a financial sense, people in those countries least able to afford to have children and to rear them tend to have more of them. The number of births per 1,000 population is 11 in the more developed countries, 22 in the less developed, and 35 in the least developed countries (Population Reference Bureau, 2012: 6). See Table 11.4, on the ten highest total fertility rate countries in 2013, where the total fertility rate ranges from a low of 5.49 children in Angola to a high of 7.03 children in Niger. By contrast, in the highly economically developed countries of the world, total fertility rates tend to be far lower. See Table 11.5.

TABLE 11.5 TEN LOWEST TOTAL FERTILITY RATE COUNTRIES, 2013, BY RANK, COUNTRY, AND TOTAL FERTILITY RATE

Rank	Country	Total Fertility Rate
1	Singapore	0.79
2	Macau	0.93
3	Taiwan	1.11
4	Hong Kong	1.11
5	British Virgin Islands	1.24
6	South Korea	1.24
7	Bosnia and Herzegovina	1.25
8	Lithuania	1.28
9	Montserrat	1.28
10	Ukraine	1.29

Source: Adapted and compiled from Central Intelligence Agency, "Country Comparison: Total Fertility Rate," *The World Factbook*. As of July 14, 2013, available online at https://www.cia.gov/library/publications/the-world-factbook//rankorder/2127rank.html

The total fertility rate has been low in the People's Republic of China for decades. China's population is aging. In 1950 there were roughly 8.3 working-age people for every person over the age of 60. By 2050, there will be 1.6 working-age people for every aged person in China. More specifically, 31 percent, or some 400 million people, will be over sixty years of age (Kong, 2008). A retired population of this size—400 million people—is greater than the combined 2013 populations of the United States *and* Canada. Stated somewhat differently, it would be like *more than* every single person in Brazil (194.9 million), Mexico (113.4 million), South Africa (50.1 million) *and* Australia (22.3 million) were not working, were retired, and a single country had to support them all (Figures extracted and computed from Eurostat, 2012: 9). That is, essentially, the size of the **old-age dependency ratio** that China faces in 2050. The old-age dependency ratio is the term that demographers use for the population aged 65 and older as a percentage of the population aged 15 to 64. The population aged 15 to 64 years of age is considered the working-age population.

China's predicted population structure in 2050 structure would place a huge strain on the Chinese economic, social, and political systems. For instance, there is the issue of how China will fund the pension system necessary to take care of all these retired persons. And there is the issue of how China will fund a health-care system with the capacity to take care of the health-care needs of an elderly population that large. Health-care costs are higher for the elderly than for younger-aged persons.

To summarize, birth rates vary considerably around the world, with the more developed countries having lower fertility rates than the less developed countries. The lower birth rates of the more developed countries means that their populations are aging, including the population of the United States. For instance, a decade ago, in the United States, children under the age of 18 made up a significant component of annual population growth and exceeded growth of the population aged 65 and older. By 2011, however, those patterns had reversed. In the United States, the number of people under age 18 declined by 190,000 persons between 2010 and 2011, while the number of persons aged 65 and older increased by 917,000 (Population Reference Bureau, 2012: 5). Growth in the number of working-age adults, including those in the prime childbearing ages, is also down sharply. The aging population of the United States creates challenges regarding how the working-age population will finance the Social Security and Medicare costs that the baby-boom generation represents as it enters the retirement years.

MORTALITY

Mortality refers to the number of deaths that occur in a population over a given period of time. **Morbidity** refers to illness. Demographers are interested in morbidity because morbidity can be a big driver of mortality rates. Typhus, diphtheria, cholera, plague, flu, tuberculosis, and HIV-AIDS are examples of illnesses or diseases that have had large impacts on mortality rates around the world in various historical periods. War, famine, crime, and accidents also can be, and have been, large drivers of mortality in populations and subpopulations around the globe. Demographers describe mortality using the **crude death rate**, which is the number of deaths in a given year for every 1,000 people in the population. The formula for calculating the crude death rate is

$$\text{Crude Death Rate} = \frac{\text{Number of deaths in year}}{\text{Total population at mid-year}} \text{ X } 1{,}000$$

One reason the rate is called crude is because its denominator includes the entire population at mid-year, even though some age groupings of a population have higher death rates than others. For instance, the death rate among the elderly and among those within the first year of life tends to be higher than the death rate of the population as a whole. Nonetheless, the crude death rate has the advantage of being easy to compute with data that are fairly readily available.

Mortality rates vary greatly around the world. See Table 11.6, on the ten highest death-rate countries in the world. There is a tendency for more technologically underdeveloped countries tend to have higher mortality rates. A sociologist might phrase this by saying that there is an inverse relationship between level of economic development and mortality. Among the ten highest mortality rate countries in the world, the death rate per 1,000 population ranges from 13.65 in Estonia to 17.36 in South Africa, which has the distinction of having the highest mortality rate of any nation in the world as of 2013. These rates contrast markedly with those of the lowest death-rate countries. See Table 11.7. Among the 10 lowest death-rate countries, the death rate per 1,000 population ranges from 1.54 in Qatar to 3.41 in Singapore.

TABLE 11.6 TEN HIGHEST MORTALITY-RATE COUNTRIES, 2013, BY RANK, COUNTRY, AND DEATH RATE PER 1,000 POPULATION

Rank	Country	Death Rate per 1,000 Population
1	South Africa	17.36
2	Ukraine	15.75
3	Chad	14.85
4	Guinea-Bissau	14.77
5	Central African Republic	14.42
6	Bulgaria	14.31
7	Russia	13.97
8	Serbia	13.77
9	Belarus	13.68
10	Estonia	13.65

Source: Adapted and compiled from Central Intelligence Agency, "Death Rate," *The World Factbook*. As of July 14, 2013, available online at https://www.cia.gov/library/publications/the-world-factbook/fields/2066.html#xx

TABLE 11.7 TEN LOWEST DEATH-RATE COUNTRIES, 2013, BY RANK, COUNTRY, AND DEATH RATE PER 1,000 POPULATION

Rank	Country	Death Rate
1	Qatar	1.54
2	United Arab Emirates	2.01
3	Kuwait	2.14
4	Bahrain	2.65
5	Jordan	2.80
6	Turks and Caicos Islands	3.06
7	Gaza Strip	3.15
8	Saudi Arabia	3.32
9	Oman	3.40
10	Singapore	3.41

Source: Adapted and compiled from Central Intelligence Agency, "Death Rate," *The World Factbook*. As of July 14, 2013, available online at https://www.cia.gov/library/publications/the-world-factbook/fields/2066.html#xx

In some countries, there are more deaths per 1,000 population than there are births. These are **net-mortality** societies. In 2006, Japan became a net mortality society and it has remained so. See Table 12.8 for a ranking of the 15 net mortality countries of the world today. One of the net mortality societies (Japan) is in East Asia, two are in Northern Europe (Latvia, Lithuania), one is in Western Europe (Germany), six are located in Eastern Europe (Belarus, Bulgaria, Hungary, Romania, Russia, and Ukraine), and five are in

Southern Europe (Bosnia-Herzegovina, Croatia, Italy, Portugal, and Serbia). Most of the net-mortality countries, then, are European countries.

TABLE 11.8 NET-MORTALITY COUNTRIES, 2013, BY RANK, COUNTRY, AND BIRTH RATE AND DEATH RATE PER 1,000 POPULATION

Rank	Country	Birth Rate per 1,000 Population	Death Rate per 1,000 Population
1	Japan	9	10
2	Russian Federation	13	14
3	Bosnia-Herzegovina	8	9
4	Italy	9	10
5	Portugal	9	10
6	Lithuania	11	13
7	Germany	8	10
8	Belarus	11	13
9	Croatia	9	12
10	Hungary	9	13
11	Romania	9	13
12	Ukraine	11	15
13	Latvia	9	14
14	Bulgaria	10	15
15	Serbia	9	14

Source: Compiled, computed, and adapted from Population Reference Bureau, *2012 World Population Data Sheet* (Washington, D.C.: Population Reference Bureau, 2012: 8, 9).

Infant Mortality Rate

There are measures of mortality that are not crude. One of these is the **infant mortality rate**, which is the annual number of deaths of infants under 1 year of age per 1,000 live births (MacDorman, Hoyert, and Matthews, 2013). See Table 11.9. There are two components of the infant mortality rate: neonatal and postneonatal. **Neonatal mortality** is infant death that occurs within the first 27 days of life. The **neonatal mortality rate** is the number of deaths under 28 days of age per 1,000 live births (MacDorman, Hoyert, and Matthews, 2013: 6). **Postneonatal mortality** is infant death that occurs between 28 to 364 days of life. The **postneonatal mortality rate** is the number of deaths from age 28 days to under 1 year per 1,000 live births (MacDorman, Hoyert, and Matthews, 2013:6).

Most infant deaths occur within the first twenty-seven days of life. For instance, of all infant mortality in the United States, 67 percent of the infants die within the neonatal period, and 33 percent die within the postneonatal period (Centers for Disease Control and Prevention, 2012: 3).

TABLE 11.9 INFANT MORTALITY RATES FOR THE WORLD AND VARIOUS COUNTRIES AND GROUPINGS OF COUNTRIES, 2012

Geographical Entity	Infant Mortality Rate—Number of Deaths per 1,000 Births
World	41
More Developed	5
Less Developed	45
Less Developed, excluding China	49
Least Developed	72
United States	6
Canada	5.1
China	17
Taiwan	4.2
Hong Kong	1.3
Korea, North	28
Korea, South	3.2
European Union	4
Northern Europe	4
Denmark	3.5
Finland	2.4
Ireland	3.5
Norway	2.4
Sweden	2.1
United Kingdom	4.3
Western Europe	4
France	3.5
Germany	3.4
Netherlands	3.8
Switzerland	3.8
Eastern Europe	7
Moldova	11
Russia	7.5
Czech Republic	2.7
Poland	4.8
Southern Europe	4
Albania	18
South Central Asia	51
Afghanistan	129
Sri Lanka	12
Southeast Asia	27
Thailand	12
Western Asia	26
Azerbaijan	11
Bahrain	11

Source: Compiled and adapted from Population Reference Bureau, *2012 World Population Data Sheet* (Washington, D.C.: Population Reference Bureau, 2012).

The infant mortality rate is considered as a major indicator of societal health and well-being (e.g., Centers for Disease Control and Prevention, 2012: 3; Singh and van Dyck, 2010; Centers for Disease Control and Prevention, 2009: 1). Infant mortality also is the largest component of childhood mortality. Infant mortality rates are lower in the more developed countries (5 deaths per 1,000 live births), higher in the less developed countries (45 deaths per 1,000 live births), and highest in the least developed countries (72 deaths per 1,000 live births) (Population Reference Bureau: 2012).

The world infant mortality rate is 41 deaths per 1,000 live births (Population Reference Bureau, 2012). The infant mortality rate in the United States is 6 per 1,000 live births. The White Non-Hispanic infant mortality rate is 5.11 and for Non-Hispanic Blacks, 11.42 per 1,000 live births (Centers for Disease Control and Prevention, 2012:5). The comparable rate for the European Union is 4 per 1,000 live births. The rates for France (3.5), Czech Republic (2.7), Ireland (3.5), and Switzerland (3.8) are all lower than the comparable rate of the United States. One important reason for this discrepancy is methodological.

In the United States, all live births of any length, at any birth weight, and any gestational age are counted as live births (Centers for Disease Control and Prevention, 2009: 2). This is not the case in other countries (e.g., Anthopolos and Becker, 2010). The United States counts as live births what many other countries report as stillbirths (Healy, 2006). In Austria and Germany, fetal weight must be at least 500 grams (1 pound) to count as a live birth. In other parts of Europe, such as Switzerland, fetal length must be at least 30 centimeters (12 inches long). In Belgium and France, births at less than 26 weeks of pregnancy are registered as lifeless. And some countries do not register the birth of babies who die within the first 24 hours of life (Healy, 2006). This is important, because 40 percent of the infants who die in the United States do so within the first day of life. In France, Czech Republic, Ireland, the Netherlands, and Poland, live births under 500 grams (one pound) or 22 weeks gestation are not recorded as live births (Centers for Disease Control and Prevention, 2009). In contrast, the United States counts these live births as births and, if they die, they are counted as deaths. These reporting practices inflate the infant mortality rate for the United States in comparison with many European countries.

The United States also has teenage birth rates that are the highest in the industrialized world (Population Reference Bureau, April 2012). In the United States, there are 34.4 births per 1,000 females aged 15 to 19 (Population Reference Bureau, April 2012). This rate is more than twice as high as in Spain (12.2) and Ireland (16.3) and five times as high as in Italy. Lower infant mortality tracks with fewer teen pregnancies, married as opposed to single mothers, and less obesity and less smoking.

Totalitarianism and Mortality

In terms of the structure of imperative order at the level of the state, the most intensely controlled political form is **totalitarianism**, which American sociologist John J. Macionis defines as a highly centralized political system that extensively regulates people's lives (Macionis, 2013: 321). Totalitarian states are noteworthy for their excess mortality (e.g., Watson, 2010; Shore, 2005; Snyder, 2003, 1999; Gross and Grundzińska-Gross, 1981; Petersen, 1969). As the concept implies, totalitarian governments have or strive for a total concentration of power in all of the major institutions of social life and they allow no organized opposition or potential bases of loyalty that could compete with loyalty to the state. These governments closely control access to information—both in written as well as other forms, such as television, the internet, and so forth. For instance, in the former Soviet Union, voluntary associations—such as the Salvation Army, were banned, and most citizens had no access to telephone directories, copiers, fax machines, or even accurate city maps (Macionis, 2013: 321). Only in the last few years has the government of Cuba allowed ordinary citizens to own personal computers and cell phones (Macionis, 2013: 321).

Totalitarianism emerged in the twentieth century as a political form under various communist revolutions —the October Revolution of 1917 that created the Soviet Union and those that followed elsewhere around the globe, including but not limited to Poland, People's Republic of China, North Korea, Vietnam, Laos, Cambodia, Cuba, Nicaragua, Peru, Ethiopia, Angola, Mozambique, Pakistan (Macionis, 2013: 321; Rummel: 2008: 315-337), and Afghanistan (e.g., Rummel, 2008; Courtois, Werth, Panné, Paczkowski, Barto⊠ek, and Margolin, 2004). Other, non-communist but nonetheless totalitarian regimes could include, but are not limited to, Turkey's Young Turk government, which during World War I managed to exterminate virtually every Armenian in Turkey, all 2 million of them (Rummel: 2008: 209-239).

Some examples of excess mortality in authoritarian states would include the following:

- Soviet Union and Nazi Germany in The Bloodlands, 1933 to 1945 There is wide consensus that the Soviet Union under Joseph Stalin and Nazi Germany under Adolf Hitler were authoritarian states (e.g., White, 2012; Conquest, 2008, 2000, 1970). Within the span of 12 years (1933 to 1945), in deliberate killing policies unrelated to combat, the Nazi and Soviet regimes killed 14 million people between Berlin and Moscow, a geographical area which Yale University historian Timothy Snyder calls The Bloodlands. 14 million people is a very large number. It exceeds by more than 13 million all of the American battlefield losses in all of the foreign wars that the United States has ever fought (Snyder, 2010: 411). According to the World Bank, it exceeds the 2012 total population of the following eight countries: Denmark (5,590,478), Albania (3,162,083), Armenia (2,969,061), Estonia (1,339,396), Iceland (320,137), Barbados (283, 221), French Polynesia (273,814), and Greenland (56,840) (Compiled and computed from World Bank, 2013). In other words, it would be as if, in a 12 year period, every man, woman, child, and infant in all eight of these countries had been wiped off the face of the earth. This is the greatest human-made demographic catastrophe in European history (Snyder, 2010).
- People's Republic of China and the Great Leap Forward, 1958 to 1962 In 1958, Mao Zedong, Chairman of the Chinese Communist Party, began **The Great Leap Forward,** an attempt by the People's Republic of China to catch up with and overtake Great Britain in less than fifteen years (Dikötter, 2010). Mao tried to collectivize steel production and agriculture at the same time. Mao consolidated farming villages into great communes. All private land, animals, houses, and even trees were surrendered to the commune. Residents of the communes had to eat in communal canteens rather than at home. Their previous homes could be dismantled for parts, if need be. For a while, Mao tried to break up families and make the whole populace live in barracks sorted by age and gender (White, 2012: 433; Dikötter, 2010; Chang and Halliday, 2005)

  Because Mao thought that steel and iron production figures were the true measure of a nation's strength, he decreed that all people should make steel and mandated that the country must double its steel output in one year. If there were no factory at hand, the people should smelt metal at home. To meet the quotas of steel production, communes gathered metal tools, hair clips, cooking utensils, door handles, and so forth, to be melted down. By this massive effort, steel production was increased from 5.3 million tons to 10.7 million tons for one year. However, only the steel mills already in existence had produced anything that could be put to use. Three million tons of the new homemade steel was unusable (Chang and Halliday, 2005: 431-432; Chirot, 1994: 196).

This massive effort pulled 90 million peasants off the farms, thereby stripping the land not only of its agricultural workforce but also of its generations of learning about how to work the land effectively (Chirot, 1994: 195). Farm policy was set by Beijing (Dikötter, 2010). The amount of acreage under cultivation fell along with the number of farmers. Then a drought hit. Grain production dropped from 200 million tons in 1958 to 144 million in 1960. The number of pigs fell by 48 percent between 1957 and 1961. People scrounged meals from apricot pits, corn cobs, and rice husks. People died in great numbers. This particular famine is sufficiently famous to be known as the Great Famine of China. Beijing refused to admit that anything was wrong. To prove to the world that the Great Leap Forward was a success, China exported almost 5 million tons of grain in 1959 alone (Chang and Halliday, 2005: 428; Spence, 1991: 583).

Between 1958 and 1962, tens of millions of excess deaths occurred due to the famine. Estimates of the size of the excess death toll range from 18 million (Gráda, 2009: 241-253) to 45 million (Dikötter, 2010: xii, 333; Akbar, 2010), with Judith Banister, who is both a world demographer and a specialist on the demography of China and Asia, weighing in with an estimate of 30 million excess deaths due to famine in this 4 year period (Banister, 1987: 58, 118, 227). Matthew White also estimates the number of excess deaths in the Great Famine as 30 million (White, 2012: 438).

The Great Leap Forward continued to kill many years after it was stopped. During the Great Leap Forward, in 1961, a massive network of poorly planned and badly built dams and reservoirs was erected on the rivers in Henan Province (White, 2012: 434; Osnos, 2011; People's Daily Online, 2005). Then, in a single night in August of 1975, the entire network of sixty-two dams failed (Thibodeau and Williams, 1998). Human Rights Watch calls this event the largest known dam disaster in human history (Human Rights Watch, 1995). Estimates of the loss of life range from 86,000 (the government's internally-released figure) and 230,000, an estimate produced by eight senior Chinese critics of the Three Gorges project (Human Rights Watch, 1995). Evan Osnos, writing for *The New* Yorker, conservatively places his estimate in between these extremes, citing 171,000 as the death toll of this disaster (Osnos, 2011).

MIGRATION

Migration is a relatively permanent movement of a person, group, or a population across a political boundary to a new residential area or community. In demography a basic distinction is made between **international migration**, which refers to the relatively permanent movement of a person, group, or a population across a national boundary to a new or host country and **internal migration**, which is the relatively permanent movement of a person, group, or a population within a country. According to the United Nations, over 700 million people migrate within their own countries and more than 215 million people love outside their countries of birth (The World Bank, April 2013).

A distinction in terminology is used in the terms designating these two types of migrants. International migrants are said to be engaging in **emigration** when they depart from a country to take up residence in another country and they themselves are referred to as **emigrants**. Emigrants are persons, groups, or populations who are departing from a country to take up relatively permanent residence in another country. See Table 11.10. A **diaspora** is a mass movement of a people from a host society to a variety of other places within a relatively short period of time. The word stems from two Greek words: "dia" meaning "apart" in English and "speirein," meaning "to scatter." There have been countless diasporas in human history. For instance, in the 1840s in Ireland, in the wake of the potato blight, many people left Ireland to settle elsewhere, including the United States. So, one may speak of that particular movement of people as an Irish diaspora. Diasporas can be an important source of trade, capital, technology, and knowledge for countries of origin and destination.

TABLE 11.10 WORLD'S TOP TEN EMIGRATION COUNTRIES, 2010, BY RANK ORDER, COUNTRY, AND NUMBER OF IMMIGRANTS (IN MILLIONS)

Rank	Country	Number of Emigrants (In Millions)
1	Mexico	11.9
2	India	11.4
3	Russian Federation	11.1
4	China	8.3
5	Ukraine	6.6
6	Bangladesh	5.4
7	Pakistan	4.7
8	United Kingdom	4.7
9	Philippines	4.3
10	Turkey	4.3

Source: Adapted from World Bank, *Migration and Remittances Factbook 2011* (Washington, D.C.: World Bank, 2011), page 3. As of July 16, 2013, available online at http://siteresources.worldbank.org/INTPROSPECTS/Resources/334934-1199807908806/Top10.pdf

Immigration refers to the entrance into a country of individuals or groups who have left a different country to establish a new place of permanent residence and those who engage in this process are termed **immigrants**. See Table 11.11. Immigrants founded nearly half of top start-up companies in the United States: of the top 50 venture-backed companies today, 23 have at least one immigrant founder and 37 employ an immigrant in a key management position, such as chief technology officer (THE WEEK, 2012). Internal migrants are termed **in-migrants** when they arrive in the new area and **out-migrants** when they leave a specific area or region of a country. For instance, Sally was born in California and decides to move to New York for a new job. When she leaves California, she is an out-migrant and when she arrives in New York, she is an in-migrant.

International migration has enormous implications for poverty alleviation both in origin and destination countries (The World Bank, April 2013). International migration boots world incomes by allowing workers to move to where they are more productive. Also, money that international migrants send back to family members in their country of origin is called a **remittance**. Global remittance flows, including those to high-income countries, were an estimated $529 billion in 2012 (World Bank, April 2013). As a share of gross national product (GDP), remittances are larger in smaller and lower income countries. Remittances amount to 47 percent of GDP in Tajikistan. The corresponding figures are 31 percent of GDP in Liberia and 27 percent

TABLE 11.11 WORLD'S TOP TEN IMMIGRATION COUNTRIES, 2010, BY RANK ORDER, COUNTRY, AND NUMBER OF IMMIGRANTS (IN MILLIONS)

Rank	Country	Number of Immigrants (In Millions)
1	United States	42.8
2	Russian Federation	12.3
3	Germany	10.8
4	Saudi Arabia	7.3
5	Canada	7.2
6	United Kingdom	7.0
7	Spain	6.9
8	France	6.7
9	Australia	5.5
10	India	5.4

Source: Adapted from World Bank, *Migration and Remittances Factbook 2011* (Washington, D.C.: World Bank, 2011), page 1. As of July 16, 2013, available online at http://siteresources.worldbank.org/INTPROSPECTS/Resources/334934-1199807908806/Top10.pdf

of GDP in Lesotho (The World Bank, April 19, 2013: 2). Developing countries received about $401 billion in remittances during 2012 alone, which far exceeds the amount these governments receive in official development assistance (The World Bank, April 19, 2013: 1). India ($69 billion), China ($60 billion), the Philippines ($24 billion) and Mexico ($23 billion) are the four largest recipients of migrant remittances, even though smaller developing countries, such as Tajikistan, Liberia, Kyrgyz Republic, and Lesotho receive more as a share of GDP (The World Bank, April 19, 2013: 2). Remittances reduce the level and severity of poverty. Remittances also typically lead to higher human capital accumulation, better access to information and communication technologies, more entrepreneurship and reduced child labor (World Bank, April 2013).

Immigration is a focal point for the dialectics of social life, engendering controversies and encouraging debates about national identity, multiculturalism, citizenship tests, national canons, religious versus secular values, assimilation, terrorism, fairness, and tolerance, both in sending and receiving countries (Brinkley, 2013; Shorto, 2008). It is important to remember that not all terrorism, in the United States or elsewhere, is Islamic in nature and not all Islamic terrorism is Al-Qaeda related. Nonetheless, in the United Kingdom a total of 119 individuals have been found guilty of Islamism-related terrorist offenses between 1999 and 2009, and more than two-thirds of these convicted terrorists were British nationals. Just under a third of these convicted terrorists had attended an institute of higher education (e.g., college or university) and about the same percentage had attended a terrorist training camp (Simcox, Stuart, Ahmed, and Murray, 2011). Thus, in Great Britain in recent years, most persons convicted of this particular type of terrorism have not been immigrants. Many other countries, including Kazakhstan, Tanzania, the Philippines, Thailand, Austria, Egypt, and the United States also draw significant concern about Islamic terrorism.

In the United States, the Tsarnaev brothers charged with responsibility for the Boston Marathon bombings of April 2013 that killed three people and wounded more than two hundred and sixty others brought the specter of Islamic terrorism home again to Americans (Brinkley, 2013: 44). As in Great Britain, so, too in the United States: of the 171 individuals who have been convicted of Al-Qaeda-related offenses or who committed suicide attacks on U.S. soil between 1997 and 2011, the majority (54 percent) are U.S. citizens (Simcox and Dyer, 2013). Others, not Al-Qaeda related, also committed terrorist acts on U.S. soil. Thus, Dzhokar Tsarnaev, of Chechan ethnicity, became a U.S. citizen on September 11, 2012, about seven months prior to the Boston Marathon bombings (Ng, 2013). His deceased brother, Tamerlan, had applied for U.S. citizenship and his application was pending at the time of the Boston Marathon bombing (Bennett and Serrano, 2013).

Likewise, Major Nidal Malik Hasan is a U. S. citizen. Major Hasan has been charged with 3 counts of pre-meditated murder and 32 counts of attempted murder at the military reception center of Ft. Hood, Texas, where soldiers get medical attention before being deployed overseas. Major Hasan was born in Arlington, VA, to Palestinian parents who immigrated to the U.S. from al-Bireh, a community in the West Bank about 15 miles north of Jerusalem (McKinley and Dao, 2008). Major Hasan committed the terrorist acts less than one month before he himself was scheduled to be deployed to Afghanistan. While the U.S. Department of Defense (DOD) classifies the events at Fort Hood as "workplace violence," a U.S. Senate report characterizes the same event as "the worst terrorist attack on U.S. soil since September 11, 2001" (U.S. Senate Committee on Homeland Security and Governmental Affairs, 2011: 7). The decision by the U.S. Army not to charge Hasan with terrorism was itself controversial (McKinley and Dao, 2008).

DEMOGRAPHY TODAY: THE DEMOGRAPHIC DIVIDE

World population grew to 7.06 billion people in mid-2012, having passed the 7 billion mark in 2011 (Population Reference Bureau, 2012). Global population structure today is a picture of contrasts. The clear demographic contrasts between less developed and more developed countries—in birth rates, death rates, rates of population growth, and population structure—is known as **the demographic divide**. The highly developed countries of the world have low fertility rates, low death rates, and a low rate of population growth, with aging populations and long life expectancies. The least developed countries have high birth rates, relatively low death rates, high rates of population growth and a young population structure. Most of the world's increase in population is driven by the high birth rates of the less developed countries. See Table 11.12. The bulk of global immigration is from the less developed to the more developed countries.

The World Bank main criterion for classifying economies is gross national income (GNI) per capita. Based on its GNI per capita, every economy is classified as either high income, medium income, or low income. According to 2012 GNI per capita, the groupings are as follows (World Bank, 2013: *How we Classify Countries*):

- Low-income: $1,035 or less
- Medium-income: $1,036 to $12,615
- High-income: $12,616 or more

Low- and medium-income economies are sometimes referred to as developing economies. As you can see, most global population growth from 2010 to 2050 is projected to occur in the low-income countries, which are part of the developing countries. By far the largest regional percentage increase in population by 2050 will be in Africa, whose population is expected to double, at least, from 1.1 billion to about 2.3 billion people. That projection, however depends on the assumption that sub-Saharan Africa's total fertility rate (TFR) will decline from 5.1 to approximately 3.0 by 2050. That decline, in turn, assumes that the use of family planning in the region will rise significantly. However, recent surveys from many countries of Sub-

Saharan Africa have indicated that the decline in TFR is either slower than projected or is not happening at all (Population Reference Bureau, 2012). Only 20 percent of married women in Sub-Saharan Africa use a modern form of family planning, the lowest rate in the world (Population Reference Bureau, 2012).

TABLE 11.12 POPULATION PROJECTION OF HIGH-INCOME, MEDIUM-INCOME, AND LOW-INCOME COUNTRIES, 2010-2050

Category of Countries		Population, in Thousands		Percent Change in Population, 2010-2050
	Year:	2010	2050	
High income		1,126,237	1,253,791	11.3
Medium income		4,917,097	6,304,761	28.2
Low income		796,259	1,589,486	99.6

Source: Data compiled from, and percent change in population computed from data of The World Bank, Population Projection Tables by Country and Group. 2012. As of July 26, 2013, available online at http://web.worldbank.org/WBSITE/EXTERNAL/TOPICS/EXTHEALTHNUTRITIONANDPOPULATION/EXTDATASTATISTICSHNP/EXTHNPSTATS/0,,contentMDK:21737699~menuPK:3385623~pagePK:64168445~piPK:64168309~theSitePK:3237118,00.html

Asia currently has a population of 4.3 billion (Population Reference Bureau, 2012). Asia will likely experience a smaller proportional increase than Africa, but it will still add about a billion people by 2050. Much of what happens in terms of population growth in Asia depends on what happens in People's Republic of China and India, which together account for about 60 percent of the region's population (Population Reference Bureau, 2012). In India, the biggest unknown is the total fertility rate in the heavily populated northern states where TFRs of 3.5 are well above those of India's southern states.

Latin America and the Caribbean is the developing region where the smallest proportional growth is expected by 2050, from 599 million to about 740 million, due largely to fertility declines in several of its largest countries such as Brazil and Mexico. The region's TFR is about 2.2 children per woman. The contraceptive prevalence rate in the region is 67 percent, which rivals that of the developed countries (Population Reference Bureau, 2012).

As to the developed countries, Europe is likely to be the first region to see long-term population decline, largely as a result of the low fertility of Eastern Europe and Russia. Around the time that President Kennedy went to Germany and gave his famous "*Ich bin ein Berliner*" speech, Europe was 12.5 percent of the world's population. Today it is about 7.2 percent; and, if current trends continue, by 2050 only 5 percent of the world will be European (Shorto, 2008). The population of the 27-member European Union, around 502 million people, should roughly remain its current size, albeit with large increases in the elderly population compared with younger age groups (Population Reference Bureau, 2012). The Russian Federation has been undergoing depopulation since 1992. The U.S. Census Bureau expects its population to decrease from its 2010 population of 141.7 million to 109 million people by 2050, which is a 21 percent drop. Such a loss of population is even greater that what Russia suffered during World War II. Eastern Europe also is expected to shrink. Bulgaria has lost almost 8 percent of its population in the last ten years (Steyn, 2007) and its population is expected to shrink by 35 percent by 2050, Ukraine's by 33 percent (Steyn, May 5, 2008), and Poland's by 20.5 percent (Steyn, April 17, 2007).. By 2050, a fourth of all the people of Eastern Europe will have vanished (Steyn, May 5, 2008).

In short, the great bulk of population increase over the next four decades is expected to occur in developing countries, and the poorest of these countries will see the largest percentage increase. As defined by the United Nations these 48 countries have especially low incomes, high economic vulnerability, and low life-expectancy at birth (Population Reference Bureau, *World Population Data Sheet 2012*).

In sum, demography is the study of population structure. Sociologists study population structure because it helps us to understand social life. The issues that growing and shrinking populations pose will need to be dealt with in the next few years and we should expect them to play out as the impetus for pressures to engage in immigration reform and reform or restructuring of various social service policies.

SUGGESTED READINGS

Black, Edwin, *War Against the Weak: Eugenics and America's Campaign to Create a Master Race* (Washington, D.C.: Dialog Press, 2012).

Courtois, Stéphane; Werth, Nicolas; Panné, Jean-Louis; Paczkowski, Andrzej; Bartošek, Karel; and Margolin, Jean-Louis, *The Black Book of Communism: Crimes, Terror, Repression* (Cambridge, Massachusetts: Harvard University Press, 2004).

Davis, Robert C., *Christian Slaves, Muslim Masters: White Slavery in the Mediterranean, the Barbary Coast, and Italy, 1500-1800* (New York: Palgrave, 2003).

Dikötter, Frank, *Mao's Great Famine: The History of China's Most Devastating Catastrophe, 1958-1962* (New York: Walker & Co., 2010).

DiSalvo, Daniel, "The Great Remigration: Blacks are Abandoning the Northern Cities That Failed Them," *City Journal*, Summer 2012. As of July 16, 2013, available online at http://www.city-journal.org/2012/22_3_great-remigration.html

Inhorn, Marcia, *The New Arab Man: Emergent Masculinities, Technologies, and Islam in the Middle East* (Princeton, NJ: Princeton University Press, 2012).

Loyalka, Michelle Dammon, *Eating Bitterness: Stories from the Front Lines of China's Great Urban Migration* (Berkeley, CA: University of California Press, 2012).

Rosen, William, *Justinian's Flea: Plague, Empire, and the Birth of Europe* (New York: Viking, 2007).

Rummel, R.J., *Death by Government* (New Brunswick, NJ: Transaction Publishers, 2008).

Snyder, Timothy, *Bloodlands: Europe Between Hitler and Stalin* (New York: Basic Books, 2010).

BIBLIOGRAPHY

Akbar, Arifa, "Mao's Great Leap Forward 'killed 45 million in four years,'" The Independent, September 17, 2010. As of August 2, 2013, available online at http://www.independent.co.uk/arts-entertainment/books/news/maos-great-leap-forward-killed-45-million-in-four-years-2081630.html#

Anthopolos, Rebecca, and Becker, Charles M., "Global Infant Mortality: Correcting for Undercounting," *World Development*, Vol. 38, No. 4, 2010: 467-481.

Banister, Judith, *China's Changing Population* (Stanford, CA: Stanford University Press, 1987).

BBC News, "China Faces Growing Gender Imbalance," January 11, 2010, 14:34 GMT. As of July 21, 2013, available online at http://news.bbc.co.uk/2/hi/8451289.stm

Bennett, Brian and Serrano, Richard A., "Tamerlan Tsarnarv's Citizen Application Was Pending," *Los Angeles Times*, April 21, 2013. As of August 5, 2013, available online at http://articles.latimes.com/2013/apr/21/nation/la-na-nn-citizenship-ice-boston-20130421

Brinkley, Joel, "Islamic Terror—Decentralized, Franchised, Global," *World Affairs*, July/August 2013: 43-55. As of August 5, 2013, available online at http://www.worldaffairsjournal.org/article/islamic-terror-decentralized-franchised-global

Buer, M.C., *Health, Wealth, and Population in the Early Days of the Industrial Revolution* (London: Routledge, 1926).

Centers for Disease Control and Prevention, *Infant Mortality in the U.S.: Where We Stand* (Atlanta, GA: Centers for Disease Control and Prevention, October 16, 2012). As of July 31, 2013, available online at http://www.cdc.gov/about/grand-rounds/archives/2012/pdfs/GR_Infant_Mortality_Final_Oct16.pdf

Centers for Disease Control and Prevention, Marian F. MacDorman and T.J. Matthews, "Behind International Rankings of Infant Mortality: How the United States Compares with Europe," *NCHS Data Brief*, Number 23, November 2009.

Central Intelligence Agency, *The World Factbook*. Afghanistan. As of July 21, 2013, available online at https://www.cia.gov/library/publications/the-world-factbook/geos/af.html

Central Intelligence Agency, *The World Factbook*. Australia. As of July 21, 2013, available online at https://www.cia.gov/library/publications/the-world-factbook/geos/as.html

Central Intelligence Agency, *The World Factbook*. United States. As of July 21, 2013, available online at https://www.cia.gov/library/publications/the-world-factbook/geos/us.html

Chambers, J.D., and Mingay, G.E., *The Agricultural Revolution 1750-1880* (London: Batsford Books, 1965).

Chang, Jung, and Halliday, John, *Mao: The Unknown Story* (New York: Alfred A. Knopf, 2005).

Chirot, Daniel, *Modern Tyrants: The Power and Prevalence of Evil in Our Age* (Princeton, NJ: Princeton University Press, 1994).

Clark, Gregory, *A Farewell to Alms: A Brief Economic History of the World* (Princeton, NJ: Princeton University Press, 2007).

Clark, Gregory, and Cummins, Neil, "Malthus to Modernity: England's First Fertility Transition, 1760-1800," August 30, 2012. As of July 26, 2013, available online at http://www.econ.ucdavis.edu/faculty/gclark/papers/Malthus%20to%20Modernity%202012%20-%20AUG%20-%20%20Final.pdf

Coale, Ansley J., and Treadway, Roy, "A Summary of the Changing Distribution of Overall Fertility, Marital Fertility, and the Proportion Married in the Provinces of Europe," on pages 31-181 of Ansley J. Coale and Susan Cotts Watkins (Eds.), *The Decline of Fertility in Europe: The Revised Proceedings of a Conference on the Princeton European Fertility Project* (Princeton, NJ: Princeton University Press, 1986).

Cockayne, Emily, *Hubbub: Filth, Noise, and Stench in England: 1600-1770* (New Haven, CT: Yale University Press, 2007).

Collier, Aine, *The Humble Little Condom: A History* (Buffalo, New York: Prometheus Books, 2007).

Congressional Business Office, *A Description of the Immigrant Population—2013 Update* (Washington, D.C.: Congressional Budget Office, U.S. Congress, May 8, 2013). As of July 20, 2013, available online at http://www.cbo.gov/sites/default/files/cbofiles/attachments/44134_Description_of_Immigrant_Population.pdf

Connelly, Matthew, *Fatal Misconception: The Struggle to Control World Population* (Cambridge, Massachusetts: Harvard University Press, 2008).

Conquest, Robert, *Reflections on a Ravaged Century* (New York: W.W. Norton & Company, 2000).

Conquest, Robert, *The Great Terror: A Reassessment* (New York: Oxford University Press, 2008).

Conquest, Robert, *The Nation Killers: The Soviet Deportation of Nationalities* (London, England: Macmillan, 1970).

Courtois, Stephane; Werth, Nicolas; Panné, Jean-Louis; Paczkowski, Andrzej; Barto⊠ek, Karel; and Margolin, Jean-Louis (Eds.), *The Black Book of Communism: Crimes, Terror, Repression* (Cambridge, MA: Harvard University Press, 2004).

Cummins, Neil J., "Marital Fertility and Wealth During the Fertility Transition: Rural France, 1750-1850," *Economic History Review*, Vol. 66, No. 2, (May) 2013: 449-476.

Davis, Kingsley, "Population Policy: Will Current Programs Succeed?" *Science*, Vol. 158, No. 3802, (November 10) 1967: 730-739.

Davis, Kingsley, "The World Demographic Transition," *Annals of the American Academy of Political and Social Science*, Vol. 237, 1945: 1-11.

Davis, Kingsley, "Zero Population Growth: the Goal and the Means," on pages 15-30 of Mancur Olson and Hans H. Landsberg (Eds.), *The No-Growth Society* (New York: Norton, 1973).

Deane, Phyllis, and Cole, W.A., *British Economic Growth, 1688-1959* Second Edition (London, England: Cambridge University Press, 1967).

Dikötter, Frank, *Mao's Great Famine: The History of China's Most Devastating Catastrophe, 1958-1962* (New York: Walker & Co., 2010).

Drummond, J.C., and Wilbraham, Anne, *The Englishman's Food: A History of Five Centuries of English Diet* (London: Jonathan Cape, 1957).

Durand, John D., "The Population Statistics of China, A.D. 2-1953," *Population Studies*, Vol. 13, No. 3 (March) 1960: 209-256.

Ehrlich, Paul H., *The Population Bomb* (Rivercity, MA: Rivercity Press, 1975).

Eurostat, *The EU in the World 2013—A Statistical Portrait* (Luxembourg: Publications Office of the European Union, 2012). As of July 28, 2013, available online at http://epp.eurostat.ec.europa.eu/cache/ITY_OFFPUB/KS-30-12-861/EN/KS-30-12-861-EN.PDF

Ferguson, Niall, *Civilization: The West and the Rest* (New York: The Penguin Press, 2011).

Fitzgerald, Charles Patrick, "A New Estimate of the Chinese Population under the T'ang Dynasty in 618 A.D.," *The China Journal* (Shanghai), Vol. 16, No. 1 (January) 1932: 5-14 and (February) 1932: 62-72,

Fitzgerald, Charles Patrick, "The Consequences of the Rebellion of An Lu-Shan Upon the Population of the T'ang Dynasty in 618," *Philobiblon* (Nanking), Vol. 2, No. 1, 1947: 4-11.

Fitzgerald, Charles Patrick, *China: A Short Cultural History* (New York: Praeger, 1973).

Galloway, Priscilla, *Archers, Alchemists, and 98 Other Medieval Jobs You Might Have Loved or Loathed* (Buffalo, NY: Annick Press, 2003).

Giddens, Anthony; Duneier, Mitchell; Appelbaum, Richard P.; and Carr, Deborah, *Essentials of Sociology* Fourth Edition (New York: W.W. Norton & Company, 2013).

Goldstein, Joshua R.; Sobotka, Tomá⊠; and Jasilioniene, Aiva, "The End of 'Lowest-Low' Fertility?" *Population and Development Review*, Vol. 35, No. 4, (December) 2009: 663-699.

Gráda, Cormac Ó., *Great Leap into Famine* (Princeton, NJ: Princeton University Press, 2009).

Graff, David Andrew, *Medieval Chinese Warfare, 300-900* (New York: Routledge, 2002).

Grigoriadis, Vanessa, "Waking Up From the Pill," *New York Magazine*, November 28, 2010. As of July 28, 2013, available online at http://nymag.com/news/features/69789/

Gross, Jan T. and Grundzińska-Gross, Irena, *War Through Children's Eyes: The Soviet Occupation of Poland and the Deportations, 1939-1941* (Stanford, CA: Hoover Institution Press, 1981).

Guisso, Richard W.L., "The Reigns of the Empress Wu, Chung-tsung and Jui-tsung (648-742)," on pages 290-332 of Dennis Twitchett (Ed.), *The Cambridge History of China Volume 3. Sui and T'ang China 589-906 Part 1* (New York: Cambridge University Press, 1979).

Hanawalt, Barbara A., *Growing Up in Medieval London: The Experience of Childhood in History* (New York: Oxford University Press, 1993).

Hanley, Susan B., *Everyday Things in Premodern Japan: The Hidden Legacy of Material Culture* (Berkeley, CA: University of California Press, 1997).

Haub, Carl, *How Many People Have Ever Lived on Earth?* (Washington, D.C.: Population Reference Bureau, 2011). As of July 14, 2013, available online at http://www.prb.org/Articles/2002/HowManyPeopleHaveEverLivedonEarth.aspx

Healy, Bernadine, "Behind the Baby Count," *U.S. News and World Report*, September 24, 2006. As of July 17, 2013, available online at http://health.usnews.com/usnews/health/articles/060924/2healy.htm

Hennock, E.P., "Urban Sanitary Reform a Generation before Chadwick?" *Economic History Review* Second Series, Vol. 10, 1957: 113-119.

Higgins, Robert Mc R., "The 1832 Cholera Epidemic in East London," *East London Record*, No. 2, 1979. As of July 24, 2013, available online at http://www.mernick.org.uk/thhol/1832chol.html

Hoff, Derek S., *The State and the Stork: The Population Debate and Policy Making in U.S. History* (Chicago: University of Chicago Press, 2012).

Human Rights Watch, *The Three Gorges Dam in China: Forced Resettlement, Suppression of Dissent and Labor Rights Concerns*, Human Rights Watch Reports, Vol. 7, No. 1 (February) 1995. As of August 2, 2013, available online at http://www.hrw.org/legacy/summaries/s.china952.html

Infoplease, "Top 50 Cities in the U.S. by Population and Rank: 1990, 2000, 2005, 2010, and 2012," 2013. As of July 21, 2013, available online at http://www.infoplease.com/ipa/A0763098.html

Jha, Alok, "British IVF Pioneer Robert Edwards Wins Nobel Prize for Medicine," *The Guardian*, October 4, 2010, 7:23 EDT. As of July 28, 2013, available online at http://www.guardian.co.uk/science/2010/oct/04/ivf-pioneer-robert-edwards-nobel-prize-medicine

Johansen, Hans C., *Danish Population History 1600-1939* (Odense, Denmark: University Press of Southern Denmark, 2002).

Kelly, John, *The Great Mortality: An Intimate History of the Black Death, the Most Devastating Plague of All Time* (New York: HarperCollins Publishers, 2005).

Knowlton, Charles, *Fruits of Philosophy* (Mount Vernon, New York: Peter Pauper Press, 1937). Originally published 1832.

Kohler, Hans-Peter; Billari, Francesco; and Ortega, José Antonio, ⊠Low Fertility in Europe: Causes, Implications and Policy Options,⊠ on pages 48-109 of F.R. Harris (Ed.), *The Baby Bust: Who Will Do the Work? Who Will Pay the Taxes?* (Lanham, MD: Rowman & Littlefield Publishers, 2006).

Kohler, Hans-Peter; Ortega, José Antonio; and Billari, Francesco, ⊠The Emergence of Lowest-Low Fertility in Europe During the 1990s,⊠ *Population and Development Review*, Vol. 28, No. 4, (December) 2002: 641-680

Kong, Constance, "China's Cassandra Prophecy," *MercatorNet*, January 25, 2010. As of July 21, 2013, available online at http://www.mercatornet.com/articles/view/chinas_cassandra_prophecy/

Kong, Constance, "Titanic China has an Appointment with an Iceberg," *MercatorNet,* December 30, 2008. As of July 28, 2013, available online at http://www.mercatornet.com/articles/view/titanic_china_has_an_appointment_with_an_iceberg

La Berge, An Elizabeth Fowler, *Mission and Method: The Early Nineteenth Century French Public Health Movement* Second Edition (New York: Cambridge University Press, 2002).

Livi-Bacci, Massimo, "Social Group Forerunners of Fertility Control in Europe," on pages 182-200 of Ansley J. Coale and Susan Cotts Watkins (Eds.), *The Decline of Fertility in Europe: The Revised Proceedings of a Conference on the Princeton European Fertility Project* (Princeton, NJ: Princeton University Press, 1986).

Lowry, Rich, "Assimilation, Now More Than Ever," *National Review Online*, May 22, 2012. As of July 26, 2013, available online at http://www.nationalreview.com/articles/300667/assimilation-now-more-ever-rich-lowry

MacDorman, Marian; Hoyert, Donna L.; and Matthews, T.J., "Recent Declines in Infant Mortality in the United States, 2005-2011," *National Center for Health Statistics (NCHS) Data Brief*, No. 120, April 2013 (Hyattsville, MD: National Center for Health Statistics, 2013).

Macfarlane, Alan, *The Savage Wars of Peace: England, Japan and the Malthusian Trap* (New York: Palgrave, 2003).

Macionis, John J., *Society: The Basics* Twelfth Edition (New York: Pearson, 2013).

Malthus, Thomas Robert, *An Essay on the Principle of Population* (London: J. Johnson, 1798).

Mancur Olson and Hans H. Landsberg (Eds.). *The No-Growth Society* (New York: Norton, 1973).

Mazur, Laurie (Ed.), *A Pivotal Moment: Population, Justice, and the Environmental Challenge* (Washington, D.C.: Island Press, 2010).

McKeown, Thomas, and Brown, R.C., "Medical Evidence Related to English Population Changes in the Eighteenth Century," on pages 285-307 of D.V. Glass and D. E. C. Eversley, *Population in History* (Chicago: Aldine, 1965).

McKinley, James, and Dao, James, "Fort Hood Gunman Gave Signals Before His Rampage," *The New York Times*, November 9, 2009. As of August 5, 2013, available online at http://www.nytimes.com/2009/11/09/us/09reconstruct.html?_r=0&pagewanted=print

MercoPress.South Atlantic News Agency, "Global Rice Production Reaches 476 million tons in 2011: Strong Mercosur Recovery," June 27, 2011, 06:40 UTC. As of July 24, 2013, available online at http://en.mercopress.com/2011/06/27/global-rice-production-reaches-476-million-tons-in-2011-strong-mercosur-recovery

Morris, William (Ed.), *The American Heritage Dictionary* (New York: Houghton Mifflin, 1969).

Najam, Adil and Yusuf, Moeed (Ed.), *South Asia 2060: Envisioning Regional Futures* (New York: Anthem Press, 2013).

Ng, Christine, "Boston Bomb Suspect Became a U.S. Citizen on 9/11 Last Year," ABC News, April 19, 2013. As of August 5, 2013, available online at http://abcnews.go.com/US/boston-marathon-bombing-suspected-tsarnaev-brothers/story?id=19000426

Office for National Statistics, "Census-taking in the Ancient World," 2011. As of July 30, 2013, available online at http://www.ons.gov.uk/ons/guide-method/census/2011/how-our-census-works/about-censuses/census-history/census-taking-in-the-ancient-world/index.html

Osnos, Evan, "Faust, China, and Nuclear Power," *The New Yorker*, October 12, 2011. As of August 2, 2013, available online at http://www.newyorker.com/online/blogs/evanosnos/2011/10/faust-china-and-nuclear-power.html

Owen, Robert Dale, *Moral Physiology, or a brief and plain treatise on the population question* (London: James Watson, 1834). Originally published 1830.

People's Daily Online, "After Thirty Years, Secrets, Lessons of China's Worst Dams Burst Accident Surface," *People's Daily Online*, October 1, 2005. As of August 2, 2013, available online at http://english.peopledaily.com.cn/200510/01/print20051001_211892.html

Pepys, Samuel, *The Diary of Samuel Pepys* Edited by Robert Latham and William Matthews (Berkeley, CA: University of California Press, 2000).

Petersen, William, "The Demographic Transition in the Netherlands," *American Sociological Review*, Vol. 25, No. 3 (June) 1960: 334-347.

Petersen, William, *Malthus* (Cambridge, MA: Harvard University Press, 1979).

Petersen, William, *Population* Second Edition (New York: The Macmillan Company, 1969).

Pinker, Steven, *The Better Angels of Our Nature: Why Violence Has Declined* (New York: Viking, 2011).

Place, Francis, *Illustrations and Proofs of the Principle of Population including an examination of the proposed remedies of Mr. Malthus, and a reply to the objections of Mr. Godwin and others* (London: Longman, Hurst, Rees, Orme, and Brown, 1822).

Population Reference Bureau, "U.S. Teen Birth Rate Hits New Low, Still Higher Than Europe's," April 2012. As of August 1, 2013, available online at http://www.prb.org/Articles/2012/us-teen-birth-rate.aspx

Population Reference Bureau, *2012 World Population Data Sheet* (Washington, D.C.: Population Reference Bureau, 2012).

Population Reference Bureau, *World Population Data Sheet 2012.* Carl Haub, *Fact Sheet: World Population Trends 2012.* 2012. As of August 5, 2013, available online at http://www.prb.org/Publications/Datasheets/2012/world-population-data-sheet/fact-sheet-world-population.aspx

Poston, Jr., Dudley; Conde, Eugenia; De Salvo, Bethany, "China's Unbalanced Sex Ratio at Birth, Millions of Excess Bachelors and Societal Implications," *Vulnerable Children and Youth Studies: An International and Interdisciplinary Journal for Research, Policy, and Care*, Vol. 6, No. 4, (December) 2011: 314-320.

Riley, James C., "The Timing and Pace of Health Transitions around the World," *Population and Development Review*, Vol. 31, No. 4 (December) 2005: 741-764.

Robinson, Tony, *The Worst Jobs in History* (London, England: Pan Macmillan, 2005).

Rosenberg, Charles, "Cholera in Nineteenth-Century Europe: A Tool for Social and Economic Analysis," *Comparative Studies in Society and History*, Vol. 8, 1966: 452-463.

Rummel, Rudolph J., *Death by Government* With a foreword by Irving Louis Horowitz (New Brunswick, NJ: Transaction Publishers, 2008).

Russell, J.C., "Late Ancient and Medieval Population," *Transactions of the American Philosophical Society*, New Series Vol. 48, Part 3, 1958: 1-152.

Russell, J.C., *British Medieval Population* (Albuquerque, NM: University of New Mexico Press, 1948).

Shannon, Fred A., "The Life of the Common Soldier in the Union Army, 1861-1865," *Mississippi Valley Historical Review*, Vol. 13, No. 4, 1927: 465-482.

Shore, Marci, "Conversing with Ghosts," *Kritika: Explorations in Russian and Eurasian History*, Vol. 6, No. 2, (Spring) 2005: 345-374.

Shorto, Russell, "No Babies?," *The New York Times*, June 29, 2008. As of August 4, 2013, available online at http://www.nytimes.com/2008/06/29/magazine/29Birth-t.html?pagewanted=all&_r=0

Simcox, Robin, and Dyer, Emily, *Al-Qaeda in the United States—A Complete Analysis of Terrorism Offenses* Foreward by General Michael Hayden (London, England: The Henry Jackson Society, 2013).

Simcox, Robin; Stuart, Hannah; Ahmed, Houriya; and Murray, Douglas, *Islamist Terrorism: The British Connections* Revised Edition (London: The Henry Jackson Society, 2011).

Singh, G.K., and van Dyck, P.C., *Infant Mortality in the United States, 1935-2007: Over Seven Decades of Progress and Disparities* (Rockville, MD: U.S. Department of Health and Human Services, Health Resources and Services Administration, Maternal and Child Health Bureau, 2010).

Snyder, Timothy, "The Causes of Ukranian-Polish Ethnic Cleansing, 1943," *Past and Present*, Vol. 179, (May) 2003: 197-234.

Snyder, Timothy, "To Resolve the Ukranian Problem Once and for All: Polish Ethnic Cleansing of Ukranians in Poland: 1943-1947," *Journal of Cold War Studies*, Vol. 1, No. 2, 1999: 86-120.

Snyder, Timothy, *Bloodlands: Europe Between Hitler and Stalin* (New York: Basic Books, 2010).

Spence, Jonathan, D., *The Search for Modern China* (New York: W.W. Norton, 1991).

Steyn, Mark, "Apatalypse Now," *National Review Online*, May 5, 2008. As of August 5, 2013, available online at http://www.nationalreview.com/corner/162588/apatalypse-now/mark-steyn

Steyn, Mark, "Breaking China," *National Review Online*, January 25, 2010. As of July 21, 2013, available online at http://www.nationalreview.com/corner/193638/breaking-china/mark-steyn

Steyn, Mark, "Old Europe," *National Review Online*, October 10, 2007. As of August 4, 2013, available online at http://www.nationalreview.com/corner/150270/old-europe/mark-steyn

Steyn, Mark, "Unsustainable Levels of Overpopulationism," *National Review Online*, April 7, 2008. As of August 4, 2013, available online at http://www.nationalreview.com/corner/161252/unsustainable-levels-overpopulationism/mark-steyn

Suddath, Claire, "Census Update: What the World Will Look Like in 2050," *Time* Magazine, June 30, 2011. As of July 27, 2013, available online at http://www.time.com/time/nation/article/0,8599,2080404,00.html

Swirski, Peter, *Of Literature and Knowledge: Explorations in Narrative Thought Experiments, Evolution, and Game Theory* (New York: Routledge, 2006).

Szreter, Simon, and Mooney, Graham, "Urbanization, Mortality, and the Standard of Living Debate: New Estimates of the Expectation of Life at Birth in Nineteenth-Century British Cities," *Economic History Review*, Vol. 51, No. 1, 1998: 84-112.

THE WEEK, "Britain: Now a Land of Immigrants," THE WEEK, April 29, 2011: 18.

THE WEEK, "The bottom line," January 20, 2012: 34.

Theodorson, George A., and Theodorson, Achilles, G., *A Modern Dictionary of Sociology* (New York: Barnes & Noble Books, 1969).

Thibodeau, John G., and Williams, Philip B., *River Dragon Has Come!: The Three Gorges Dam and the Fate of China's Yangtse River and Its People* Compiled by Dai Qing, Translated by Yi Ming (Armonk, NY: M.E. Sharpe, 1998).

Thompson, Edward Palmer, *The Making of the English Working Class* (New York: Pantheon Books, 1964).

Thompson, Warren S., "Population," *American Journal of Sociology*, Vol. 34, No. 6, 1929: 959-975)

Thompson, Warren S., *Population: A Study in Malthusianism* (New York: Columbia University, 1915).

Trevelyan, G.M., *English Social History: A Survey of Six Centuries, Chaucer to Queen Victoria* (London: Longmans, Green: 1942).

Twitchett, Dennis (Ed.), *The Cambridge History of China Volume 3. Sui and T'ang China 589-906 Part 1* (New York: Cambridge University Press, 1979).

U.S. Census Bureau, *U.S. and World Population Clock*, 2013. As of July 14, 2013, available online at http://www.census.gov/popclock/?intcmp=sldr1

U.S. Senate Committee on Homeland Security and Governmental Affairs, *A Ticking Time Bomb: Counterterrorism Lessons from the U.S. Government's Failure to Prevent the Fort Hood Attack* A Special Report by Joseph I. Lieberman, Chairman and Susan M. Collins, Ranking Member. Washington, D.C.: February 3, 2011. As of August 5, 2013, available online at http://www.hsgac.senate.gov//imo/media/doc/Fort_Hood/FortHoodReport.pdf?attempt=2

United States Census Bureau. Daphne Lofquist, Terry Lugaila, Martin O'Connell, and Sarah Feliz, "Households and Families: 2010," *2010 Census Briefs*, C2010BR-14, April 2012.

Watson, George, *The Lost Literature of Socialism* Second Edition (Cambridge, England: Lutterworth Press, 2010).

White, Matthew, *The Great Big Book of Horrible Things: The Definitive Chronicle of History's 100 Worst Atrocities* Forward by Steven Pinker (New York: W.W. Norton & Company, 2012).

Will, George, "Searching for Obamacare's Silver Lining," *Townhall*, March 22, 2010. As of July 20, 2013, available online at http://townhall.com/columnists/georgewill/2010/03/22/searching_for_obamacares_silver_lining/page/full

Woods, Robert, "The Effects of Population Redistribution on the Level of Mortality in Nineteenth-Century England and Wales," *Journal of Economic History*, Vol. 45, No. 3, 1985: 645-651.

World Bank, *Data. Fertility rate, total (births per woman)* 2012. As of August 4, 2013, available online at http://data.worldbank.org/indicator/SP.DYN.TFRT.IN

World Bank, *Data. How we Classify Countries* 2013. As of August 5, 2013, available online at http://data.worldbank.org/about/country-classifications

World Bank, *Data. Population, total* 2013. As of August 1, 2013, available online at http://data.worldbank.org/indicator/SP.POP.TOTL

World Bank, *Migration and Development Brief 20*, April 19, 2013. As of August 3, 2013, available online at http://siteresources.worldbank.org/INTPROSPECTS/Resources/334934-1288990760745/MigrationDevelopmentBrief20.pdf

World Bank, *Migration and Remittances Factbook 2011* (Washington, D.C.: World Bank, 2011). As of July 16, 2013, available online at http://siteresources.worldbank.org/INTPROSPECTS/Resources/334934-1199807908806/Top10.pdf

World Bank, News & Broadcast- *Migration and Remittances* April 2013. As of August 3, 2013, available online at http://web.worldbank.org/WBSITE/EXTERNAL/NEWS/0,,contentMDK:20648762~menuPK:34480~pagePK:64257043~piPK:437376~theSitePK:4607,00.html

CHAPTER 12

Religion

by
Gary D. Wilson

INTRODUCTION

Religion involves socially shared ways of thinking, feeling, and acting that have as their focus the realm of the supernatural. As Emile Durkheim (1912) suggested, religion is centered in beliefs and practices that are related to the sacred as opposed to profane things. The *sacred* involves those aspects of social reality that are every day and commonplace but within certain contexts those things become extraordinary, mysterious, awe-inspiring, and even potentially dangerous. The sacred is distinct from normal, routine life (Berger, 1967). The same object or behavior can be profane or sacred depending on how people define it. A wafer made of flour when seen as bread is a profane object, but it becomes sacred to Catholics as the body of Christ when it is consecrated during the Mass. Because the sacred is caught up with strong feelings of reverence and awe, it can usually be approached only through rituals. In their religious behavior, human beings fashion a social world of meanings and rules that govern what they think, feel, and act, in much the same way that they do in other realms of life.

Historic Theories on the Origin of Religion

The question of the natural origin of religion before the time of the English Deists was raised first by the Roman skeptical philosopher and poet, Lucretius, who in his *de Rerum Natura* characterized all belief in gods as an illusion and ascribed its origin to fear. Hume, in 1755, in his *Natural History of Religion*, took essentially the position of Lucretius, saying that fear of the forces of nature led human beings to ascribe the phenomena of nature to powerful gods (Morris, 1902: 173-175). Sir John Lubbock, in his *Origin of Civilization*, published in 1870, cited considerable evidence to show that primitive humans personified nature and worshipped the ghosts of ancestors. More than that, he indicated that the worship of the ghosts of ancestors often grew out of the worship of living beings (Lubbock, 1870: 189-222). Long before that time Comte offered a theory on *animism*. He said, "The theological period of humanity could begin no otherwise than by a complete and usually very durable state of pure fetishism, which allowed free exercise to the tendency of our nature by which man conceived of all external bodies as animated by a life analogous to his own with differences of their intensity" (Martineau, 1870: 186). In concluding his argument he said, "This fetishism is the basis of the theological philosophy, deifying every substance or phenomenon which attracts the attention of humanity and remaining traceable through all its transformations to the very last" (Martineau, 1870: 199).

Development of Religious Servants

Today the ministry is recognized as a profession. Those who minister in religious matters are set apart for that particular work. In many primitive societies, ancient and modern, quite different arrangements existed. Men in savage tribes were often their own priests. Among the nomadic Semites no priesthood had been developed. Each member of the tribe among the ancient Arabs visited the tribal sanctuary and offered gifts of whatever was customary without intervention of a priest. Each sacrificed the animal and sometimes smeared the blood, which was the god's part of the sacrifice, on the sacred object, such as a stone pillar, and made pilgrimages to the sacred places. Among these primitive Arabs the keepers of the sanctuary developed into *soothsayers* because they kept the sacred lot and by it consulted the oracle for people. Out of this function developed the *seer*. Primitive human beings upon hearing an echo while rounding a bend in the river offered a sacrifice to the spirit, and civilized human beings offer a prayer when they feel the need of divine assistance. In spite of these similarities, there is a huge difference. In primitive societies the priestly function was often combined with that of head of the family, or the head of a wider group. In civilized societies usually the functions of ruler, head of the family, and priest or minister have been differentiated (Biblica, 1901: 211).

The *medicine man* was known among the most primitive people. An individual who was able to impress the people with his superior knowledge of supernatural beings, and with his ability to bring the feared powers under control, he occupied a place of unique importance. Once recognized as having superior power, he assumed a monopoly of influence over the spirits. Owing to the fact that it was thought that disease was an affliction of an evil spirit, the person who managed the evil spirit was the only one who could cure the disease, and so the services of priest and doctor were united in one person, the medicine man. Later these functions became divided and the priest attended to the affairs of religious worship and the medicine man to the cure of disease (Biblica, 1901: 213).

In the course of social development out of the functions of the medicine man developed those of *exorcist*, *fortune teller*, and *priest*, either as head of the household religion, ruler-priest, or specialized minister of a god worshipped at a particular spot, such as a sanctuary or temple. While the course of development in Israel does not parallel the development among other people, the source of information, the *Bible*, is familiar and accessible, and may therefore be cited as one type of change which has occurred in the character and number of religious servants but only the very general lines in the development are cited.

In I Samuel 9, 10, we have an account of the prophet Samuel. The donkeys of Saul's father had strayed away, and Saul sent out by his father to find them having failed, consulted Samuel as to where he should find them. He took with him a sum of money to pay Samuel for this service. The writer of the passage says that such a person was formerly called a seer. Samuel told him that the donkeys had been found, but took occasion to anoint Saul king of Israel. In this passage Samuel is represented as performing two different functions - those of fortune teller and those of political guide to the nation, such as were manifested by the later prophets of Israel. Here Samuel is described as a "man of God," and in his capacity as seer tells fortunes. From descriptions of practices among other peoples it is clear that he performs a function which finds parallels in many primitive peoples.

In chapter 10 of the same writing is found a description of a band of prophets who Saul meets. From the description it is clear that this band of prophets was composed of men possessed by a frenzy. Saul was seized with the same frenzy and "prophesied" with them. Says Cornill, "In these prophets of the time of Saul, where we first meet them, we have the type of the original form which prophesying assumed on Canaanite soil; they are men after the manner of Mohammedan fakirs, or dancing and howling dervishes, who express their religious exaltation through their eccentric mode of life" (Cornill, 1904: 27).

In the course of the next few centuries, however, in the history of Israel, the prophets became quite different functionaries. The other side of the prophetic office manifested by Samuel developed. They became the spiritual and social statesmen of the nation. Amos represents the development in the conception of the prophetic office, when to make clear the difference between his own functions and those of the mantic prophets which survived even to his time, and whom he despised, he says, "I was no prophet, neither was I a prophet's son."

The priesthood underwent a similar development. In the passage referred to above there seems to have been a connection between the band of mantic prophets and the sacred high place. The passage does not make clear whether they were ministers at the high place or not. In the Book of Judges, chapters, 17, 18, there is a very old record, which reveals practices of worship and priesthood which are very primitive. A man, Micah by name, who dwelled in the hill country of Ephraim built a house for the gods, made an ephod and teraphim, probably images of the god, and consecrated his son as a priest. A Levite from Bethlehem-Judah who came along to the house of Micah on a journey, Micah hired to become his priest.

This episode shows clearly two steps in the differentiation of the priesthood into a special class. The man delegates the priestly function of his "god's house" first to his son, and then to a Levite, a member of a tribe which early in the history of Israel had come to be looked upon as having special priestly functions. In the course of time the priests only may perform religious functions at the sanctuaries. While in the earlier accounts of the family of Eli, who with his sons serve the sacred Ark at Shiloh, there is no mention of their connection with the tribe of Levi, later the priests were thought of as Levites, and after the time of Solomon as sons of Zadok, i.e. a special class with increasingly specialized functions.

What were the functions of the priests among the Hebrews? In the early period, represented by the narrative in Judges, 17 and 18, the priest had charge of the house of god and consulted an oracle. Later he guarded the Ark, and when necessary carried it. With the growth in importance of the sanctuary at Jerusalem, culminating under King Josiah in the destruction of the local sanctuaries on high places, the priesthood developed a strength that came to an end only at the Exile, and revived again with the reestablishment of the Temple, and continued to be a mighty force to the destruction of Jerusalem in 70 A.D. Aside from the instance of Amaziah, the priest of the sanctuary at Bethel, there is no evidence of political functions discharged by the priests. However, since the oracle was consulted about all manner of things, those of public interest as well as those of private concern, the priests became early judges and lawmakers through the decisions they rendered after consulting the sacred lot. The Deuteronomic Code represents the priests' functions as having to do primarily with declaration of the divine will, and secondarily with ritual and sacrifice.

Down to the Exile the priests were subservient to the kings, as the prophets were not. As the ritual became more complex, and sacrifices multiplied, they became more important, and their fees increased. It was this ritual service of priests which excited the wrath of the great prophets. After the Exile, when the political organization of the Hebrews was finally destroyed, the priesthood became the center of the hopes of the future of Israel. From that time to Jesus the priests played a dominating part in the life of this people.

Among other peoples the development varied with the circumstances of national life. Out of these functionaries grew the minister of religion, the statesman, the educator, the physician, and the judge. At one time the medicine man was all of these and more. More skillful than others in legerdemain, ventriloquism, and in thought reading, he obtained great power over the people in every way. He was a master of sorcery at first, having power to help those who sought his aid or to injure those against whom he directed his machinations. Later one by one his many functions were assumed by others. Priest and healer he remained. Many survivals of his power still remain with us. Clairvoyance and fortune telling, as well as the nobler and entirely Christian act of intercessory prayer, are examples.

Conception of the Nature of the Gods

The conception of the nature of the supernatural varies from the vague conception of the "Great Dreadful," sometimes called mana or orenda, found among very low savages, to the just and loving Father of Jesus. This development takes place in response to the varying experiences of different peoples. With the growth of social organization and activities primitive man developed his pantheon. When one group conquered another or amalgamated peacefully with another, there occurred also a coalescence of the religious notions. If it was a case of conquest, the gods of the conquerors were exalted above those of the conquered and the latter became lesser deities in the pantheon or were outlawed and became the gods of secret cults and sectarians. An example is furnished of the former case by what occurred when the Latins conquered the adjacent tribes, of the latter by the history of Israel on the establishment of the Davidic kingdom. Finally, wherever the development went on to completion one god stands out supreme. How closely it may come to be associated with the earthly ruler is shown by the fact that sacrifice to the genius of the emperor, not to Jupiter, was the supreme test to which persecuted Jews and Christians ultimately were forced to submit. In the case of the Hebrews, owing to the peculiar circumstances of the Exile and to a few choice spirits among the prophets, monotheism pure and simple developed. Among most other peoples the development never went beyond henotheism, or a belief that there was only one god for each nation, but that each nation had a different god.

Socrates and a few others in other advanced nations seem to have reached a conception of a universal Deity. Thus, from the conception that all nature is peoples with awe-inspiring power there developed among some tribes the conception of many gods of special places and different functions, then one god for each tribe or nation, and finally one supreme God over all the earth. In his nature the divinity varies from something to be feared and to come to terms with by means of flattering praises or offerings to that of "God is a spirit; and they that worship must worship in spirit and truth."

Religious Forms and Ceremonies

In the early stages of religious development it was but natural for primitive man to think that if these spirits had power to do so much for the destruction or salvation of man, they must be sought out and managed. This brought about the idea of manipulating or exorcising the spirits for man's welfare. Offerings were chosen and actions observed that were supposed to please the spirit. Food was given, ceremonies performed, and the conduct of the tribe modified to please these unseen powers.

Then it appeared that there were good spirits who had the preservation of the tribe in view, and others who desired its destruction. The former must be worshiped and praised for their goodness and the latter appeased by gifts and offerings and turned away from their intended destruction. Religious rites, though influenced to a certain extent by individuals of superior gifts and extraordinary shrewdness, developed independently of them, as a social institution. The fact of death had great influence upon the development of religious ceremonies. The belief in the continued journey of the spirit after death led to the practice of burial ceremonies, and this practice aided development of social order. The custom of placing clothing and implements in the grave for the departed spirit, and the bringing of food to the grave for its sustenance brought the members of a community to a common meeting place, gave them a common social ideal, and developed more or less a regular order of procedure.

Whether originating in reverence and awe for some striking natural object, animal, or some natural function closely connected with the survival of the group, like a symbolic fruit or the reproductive process and organs, or in reverence rendered to the spirit of a departed ancestor, the group's religious activities were centered about a common object by means of common interests and from there developed common feelings and actions in other than religious concerns. Gradually these customs brought about permanent religious services because of the connection which the controlling spirit had with these ordinances. The idea of fear on the one hand and of worship on the other arose in the attempt to favor the spirit. In the case of ancestor worship an appeal to the spirit or god for safety of the departed led to prayer and the attempt to please him in order to receive favors gave rise to worship, while the attempt to manage an evil spirit led to necromancy. Sometimes the spirit of the mountain was identified with the spirit of a dead ancestor. Comparatively simple acts grew more and more into ceremony and were attended with increased pageantry. With the development of pomp and ceremonies in approaching the ruler and securing favors from him went growth in the richness of religious rites. The psychology of "the majesty that doth hedge a throne" has not yet been carefully worked out, but there is no doubt that very early in the history of social development the chief learned its practical value, how to create and enhance it in the eyes of his subjects, and the latter found ways of flattering the great by devising somewhat more elaborate forms of reverence and ever more extravagant terms of praise.

Sacred Places and Natural Phenomena

Animism, or the belief that the spirit life manifested itself in natural phenomena, let to the supposition that all the various forces appearing in nature were in activity in response to the will of various spirits, and was one idea from which developed the theory of sacred places. The worship of the several forms of nature was merely a worship of the spirits that dwelled in these forms, for nature worship was nothing more than spirit worship localized in the various objects of nature. Sometimes it was localized in a high mountain or hill. Again it was a lonely or majestic tree, in other cases in a rock standing out alone or of peculiar formation, and sometimes in an animal from which the tribe was supposed to be descended. First there developed clan sanctuaries, then a central sanctuary, and when the nation evolved there grew up the national sanctuary. There were also family sanctuaries connected with household worship. These meeting places were the foundations of the church or temple.

It is in accord with the habits of early man that Abraham, when he came out of Haran to Bethel, erected an altar of stones and placed thereon the burnt offering. It was a "house of God." He came to commune with the spirit of God and to worship him. When he returned out of Egypt he came to this place to meet God. Gradually the stone or tree was replaced by a tent sheltering some sacred casket containing sacred objects, and then an immovable chapel or temple located over or beside a sacred stone or spring or other object. Perhaps the best illustrations furnished by historic peoples of this evolution of the sacred place with all that it meant for the development of rite and ceremony, as well as of ideas of deity, are to be found in the evolution of the sanctuary in ancient Israel and in Rome. The people of Israel who as clansmen worshiped on every high hill and under every green tree, under the influence of the priests of the royal chapel and then of the eighth-century prophets came finally to concentrate their worship in the national sanctuary at Jerusalem so that ultimately sacrifice was permitted only there. The development among the Roman people is almost as clear and instructive. This primitive worship was at first merely an attempt to please God in order to receive his favor, or to appease his wrath in order to prevent the destruction of the tribe. Later it developed into worship, through prayer and appeal for strength and aid, not only for the individual, but for the tribe and nation. Primitive people prayed to their gods to give them victory in war, bountiful harvests, and prosperity in every way. Even yet most prayers have such "practical" ends in view. With the development, however, of an appreciation of the relation of religion to ethical conduct, less emphasis has been laid on the attainment of material benefits and more on character growth.

Where Is the Soul?

When the soul is in the body, the body is animated, that is alive, and when it, the soul, is out of the body, the body is dead. It has "given up the ghost." It has "expired." Historically the prevalent words for soul were words such as pneuma, signifying "breath" or "wind." The psyche was regarded as the energizing principle of the body. The body was the autos, or self. Hence it seems that the soul was a separate being for the continued possession of which an individual would strive. The soul and the individual were a sort of dual personality. There was a close bond between the individual and his or her soul. A strong person had a strong soul and a weak coward a contemptible one. The soul had various ways of leaving the body. In fainting it was breathed out to return apparently by the same way when recovery occurred. In death it departed regularly by way of the mouth, sometimes in a flow of blood or it followed the spear withdrawn from a wound. In all cases it flies in haste through the air, departing with mourning.

Existence in the beyond was conceived of in terms of existence during life, for the dead were supposed to retain the feelings of living men such as desire for property, love and pride, jealousy and pain, and they even bore their old wounds and by appearance and action indicated their station in their former life. When the soul of Patroclus appeared to Achilles in a dream, he was like the dead man even in the matter of clothing and that the dead retained human desires appears from the cry of Achilles to Patroclus, after the body of Hector had been ransomed. When Achilles in the dream tried to embrace the shade of his comrade, he did not take him but the soul fled with a shriek beneath the earth, like smoke, and Achilles was alarmed.

Thus the soul was identified with the body, the breath, and had most of the characteristics of the person. It was also recognized in dreams, identified with the inexplicable shadow that always skulks about when the sun shines, seen in the water when people stoop to drink, it appeared in photographs. "Tell me," asked an old woman whose photograph had been taken, "when I am dead, will my face disappear from that?" "No." "But if I move away from water, my image disappears." It assumed the form of animals and went wandering about; hence the belief in werewolves and dragons. It could take on the form of birds or insects and also dwell in trees, flowers, and rocks (Sumner, 1927: 795).

Countless theories have been suggested as to where the soul is located in human anatomy. Among the Seminoles of Florida, when a woman died in childbirth, the infant was held over her face to receive her parting spirit and thus acquire strength and knowledge for its future use. The Seminoles could have well understood why at the deathbed of an ancient Roman, the nearest kinsman would lean over to inhale the last breath of the departing (Sumner, 1927: 815).

Sometimes the soul is in the blood, hence, the almost universal preciousness of blood. Sometimes it is in the heart, sometimes in the head, in the hair, in the stomach, in the pupil of the eye, in the big toe, in the larynx, in the thigh, in the saliva, in the tongue, and so forth. Such beliefs explain numerous practices in connection with all of these parts such as head hunting, scalp taking, preserving hair, manipulating blood, and so forth (Biblica, 1901).

RELIGION AS A SOCIALIZING FORCE

Religious beliefs and religious ceremonies grow more complex with the development of social relationships and complexity of social organization. In the simple tribal life of the Semitic nomads each rock, tree and spring possessed its jinn or spirit. Mythology enabled them to account for every act of the tribe by reference to the deeds of ancestral spirits and every phenomenon of nature as produced by some spiritual being. The origin of the earth and the universe were thus accounted for. This developed numberless gods with different powers, capabilities, and services. Numerous stories or myths concerning the actions of gods and their relations to mankind arose. These stories occupied the minds and influenced not only the beliefs but the actions of men. With the settlement of the Hebrew tribes in Canaan, there developed a syncretism and the Hebrews took over sanctuaries of Canaan, beliefs, and gods. When a strong central government was imposed upon the separate, independent tribes, there grew up a national religion at Jerusalem, the capital, and the local sanctuaries were finally banned. With the appearance of the Assyrian world empire and their subsequent experiences in the Exile, the Hebrew leaders conceived of a universal god. The old desert religious conceptions suffered under the rise of a new agriculture and then a new commercialism. Out of the tragic social injustices in Hebrew society consequent on these changes and the national tragedy consummated in the Babylonian Exile the ethical religion of Judaism was born.

To the prophets of the eighth century Israel owed the development of an ethical religion. It was they who declared that Jahweh, their God, was more pleased with them for restoring the pledge to the poor, ceasing oppression, doing justice with loving-kindness, and walking in humbleness than for giving their firstborn to redeem their transgressions, the fruit of their bodies for the sin of their souls. With an assurance that carried conviction and an insistence which allowed no gainsaying, Amos urged Jahweh's ethical claims with, "Take thou away from me the noise of thy songs; for I will not hear the melody of thy viols. But let justice roll down as waters and righteousness as a mighty stream." The same conviction inspired Hosea, Isaiah, and Micah. Growing out of the insistence of these prophets and their followers we have the development of the legal-ethical religion of the Hebrew, in which the duty of individuals one to another finally is formally stated in the law of the nation. Out of the prophetic Hebrew religion grew a humanitarian, ethical religion in which the law of love prevails. Every primitive culture is closely interwoven with religious beliefs. During every time of crisis in the life of primitive man, religion was a most important spur to mental and physical activity. In the attempt of the individual to understand the phenomena of an unknown world, religion became a positive necessity. Imagine an individual suddenly brought into contact with the activities and appearances of natural life without any knowledge or experience or instruction. The effects are startling and appalling: he or she sees the flash of lightning, hears the thunder, observes the storm and the destructiveness of the roaring torrent, the change of seasons, the movement of the heavenly bodies, the growth of plants and animals, and all the manifestations of sun and air and moisture, and yet understands not one of all these phenomena. The moment the mind begins to inquire, the childish nature is satisfied by attributing these activities to the doings of an unseen power, a spirit, a god. The speculation as to the nature of the universe originated in primitive religion. And so in the childhood of the race, religion served a similar purpose to that of science in the more developed social life of the present. It provided a working hypothesis to groping minds and thus introduced order into the chaos of early thought.

Moreover, religion bound the energies of the savage which were being expended in anti-social ways, on the one hand, and on the other loosed those energies in activities, mental and physical which ministered to the welfare of the group. For example, by causing action in a crisis religion spurred a series of experiments with nature which have not yet been exhausted. It provided a foundation upon which significant attempts to alter the environment for the welfare of the people, and to bend other men to their will, not by physical force, but by spiritual devices. While from the modern standpoint it enthralled them in activities which later impeded their progress, in early history it gave spur to otherwise undeveloped tendencies to help others. The feelings, thoughts, and activities of primitive people clustered around religious life. The well-established customs of primitive society were all founded on religion. It called forth feeling and mental action in the struggle for existence and for social solidarity.

What has been the influence of religion in the development of social organization? Religion has always been connected with social order. In the control of families, tribes, groups, and even nations, religion has played an important part.

Religion has lent a powerful sanction to virtue and morality, for it has regulated the relationships of individuals in the home in the interest of order. Long before politics and civil law could be established, religion had made customs that preserved the equilibrium of the social group. It has always fostered a belief in immortality. Whether in its crude form as held by the primitive savage or in its perfected state, it has had more or less influence in the control of human society. In its early form it inspired fear and thus controlled social action, while in its later development the idea of immortality inspires hope and faith and courage, all very important elements in the development of society. It has strengthened patriotic feeling through its unique local character. The religion of the family developed family pride and glory, relating ancestors to gods. When the tribes expanded into a nation the god of the nation led the hosts in battle and preserved their lives and integrity. Thus religion became an inspiration to patriotic life. In upholding the central authority of the head of the family social order was developed. There was established on one side the governing class, on the other the governed. People learned to rule and to obey, to command and to serve, (Biblica, 1901).

The Anti-Social Results of Religion

On the other hand, religion has at times been a coercive weapon of reaction, and has opposed social developments which had for their aim the betterment of society. How often have religious institutions been found on the side of reaction in the struggle for freedom? Even in ancient Israel, as Cornill has remarked the outcome of the prophetic religion was to crush the free spirit of the common people and to bind upon them the rites and ideas of the religion of the narrow party of Jerusalem. It paved the way for the priestly domination of the following centuries, and had a share in preparing for the hateful spirit of the Pharisee. In early Christian times ecclesiasticism crushed the free spirit of the Montanist, drove into ecclesiastical exile that early forerunner of untrammeled thought, the Gnostic, under the leadership of such men as Cyprian and Calixtus narrowed the church to a sect, and bound it with the hard bonds of a party domination. It throttled free inquiry in the Middle Ages, making independent thinking a heresy, and laid the foundation of a revolt which has divided the world into hundreds of warring factions. It forced Galileo to recant his carefully established convictions that the earth moves around the sun, threw water upon the flaming aspirations of scholars and stifled the democratic longings of the common people. Clothed with the garments of ecclesiasticism in more recent times men have vilified such truth seekers as Darwin and belittled God's records written in the rocks and in the bodies of animals and men. Too often through its well-meaning representatives, religion has mocked the findings of careful and conscientious scholars, stood with the representatives of arrant wrong against those who in love of the truth have battled for the rights of the people. Nevertheless, such an attitude represents but one side of the work of religion, the conservative side. Even that side is needed in society, as a stabilizing force.

One must forget, moreover, that some of the mightiest revolutions have been inspired by religious innovations. The Hebrew prophets, Jesus and Paul, Mohammed and Buddha, who shall say of them and of the movements they inspired that they did not give the race a great impetus toward progressive development?

Why Has Religion Survived?

Science has superseded religion as an explanation of the nature of the universe. Its magical practices to control Nature have given place to applied science. Crowded out of its old place as a natural philosophy, and compelled to give up its early claims as a method of bringing the hostile forces of Nature and men under control, what is there left for religion?

As a scientific explanation of the universe religion has lost its old dominion. As a philosophy giving meaning to the universe and to the social relations it has only begun to come into its own. Its chief function always been, not explanation, but action. It has been a faith primarily, having only enough mythology attached to give an excuse to the rational faculty for the action. Therefore, it has survived, because it has provided us with a working hypothesis on which to adjust ourselves to the universe and the world of Nature to us. It is the expression of individual faith that there is a way whereby one can bring under personal control and for personal purposes the forces of nature. That faith has released for experiment the energy that was previously paralyzed by fear and doubt. Sometimes the means used were not adapted to individual purposes, but the drive of religious faith was still there to find another and better way. Through the ages from primitive to civilized man, religion – the belief that there is a power at once kindled the will to overcome difficulties and has survival value. Since the individual who believed survived, religion survived. Historically religion has produced what has come to be called "morale." It gave the fighting edge to life. Will religion continue to give an advantage in the struggle for existence? It all depends on whether present-day religion is as well adapted to make modern society adjust to the circumstances of this world as primitive religion was to the primitive man. Today's people may not need religion to enable them to be successful in raising crops or securing food supply, but some certainly seem to need a faith, which may be described as "assurance of things hoped for" and "a conviction of things not seen," to enable them to wax valiant in the fight against organized wrong entrenched in social institutions. Only such faith has made the world in which we live better than that in which our fathers lived. It alone can command the energy to bring about a social order wherein increasingly "dwells righteousness" (Biblica, 1901).

RELIGION IN PRACTICE

Religious behavior is varied. While no categories do justice to the diversity and richness of the human religious experience, it might be helpful to consider four forms of religious behavior: simple supernaturalism, animism, theism, and a system of abstract ideals (McGee, 1975).

Simple supernaturalism is prevalent in pre-industrial societies. It involves the notion of mana, a diffuse, impersonal, supernatural force that exists in nature for good or evil. With mana people do not entreat spirits or gods to intervene on their behalf. Rather, they compel a superhuman power to behave as they wish by manipulating it mechanically. For example, the act of carrying a rabbit's foot is thought to bring good luck, but the capacity to bring good luck is as much an attribute of the rabbit's foot as is its color or weight. One need not talk to the rabbit's foot or offer it gifts, but only carry it. Similarly, the act of uttering the words "open sesame" serves to manipulate impersonal supernatural power. Many athletes use good luck charms, elaborate routines, and superstitious rituals to ward off injury and bad luck in activities. Mana is usually employed to reach "here and now" goals such as control of the weather, assurance of a good crop, cure of an illness good performance on an exam, success in love, or victory in battle. It functions much like an old-fashioned book of recipes or a home medical manual.

Animists believe that spirits, whether helpful or harmful to people, may reside in humans, animals, plants, rivers, or winds. They are not gods to be worshipped but supernatural forces that can be manipulated to serve human ends. Rituals such as feasting, dancing, fasting, and cleansing are often performed to appease the spirits so that crops can be harvested, fish caught, illness cured, or danger averted. Animism is prevalent in sub-Saharan Africa.

Among indigenous peoples in the North and South America, a common type of animism is called *shamanism*, the belief that a spiritual leader can communicate with the spirits by acting as their mouthpiece or by letting the soul leave the leader's body and enter the spiritual world. The spirits, in effect, live in the shaman. By communicating with them, the shaman heals the sick, discovers lost animals, sees events in distant places, foresees those in the future, and forecasts prospects for farming, fishing, and hunting.

Another form of animism, popular among native peoples of Australia and some Pacific islands, is *totemism*, the belief that kinship exists between humans and an animal, or in some cases, a plant. The animal, called a totem, represents a human family, a clan, or a group of ancestors. It is thought of as a person with superhuman power and it must be treated with respect, awe, and fear. Killing, eating, touching, and even seeing the animal is often prohibited. The totem is relied on as a helper and protector, but it also punishes those who breach a taboo.

In *theism* religion is centered in a belief in gods who are thought to be powerful, to have an interest in human affairs, and to merit worship. Judaism, Christianity, and Islam are forms of *monotheism*, or belief in one god. They all have established religious organizations, religious leaders or priests, traditional rituals, and sacred writings. Ancient Greek religion and Hinduism are forms of *polytheism*, or belief in many gods with equal or relatively similar power. Hindu gods are often tribal, village, or caste deities associated with a particular place such as a building, field, mountain, or objects such as trees or animals.

Some religions focus on a set of abstract ideals. Rather than centering on the worship of a god, they are dedicated to achieving moral and spiritual excellence. Many of the religions of Asia are of this type, including Taoism, Confucianism, and Buddhism. Buddhism is directed toward reaching an elevated state of consciousness, a method of purification that provides a release from suffering, ignorance, and selfishness. In the Western world, humanism is based on ethical principles. Its adherents discard all theological beliefs about God, heaven, hell, and immortality, and substitute for God the pursuit of good in the here and now. Heaven is seen as the ideal society on earth and hell as a world in which war, disease, and ignorance flourish. The soul is the human personality, and immortality is deeds that live on after death for good or evil in the lives of other people.

RELIGIOUS ORGANIZATIONS

Norms, beliefs, and rituals provide the cultural fabric of religion. But there is more to the religious institution than its cultural heritage. As with other institutions, there is also the structural mosaic of social organization whereby people are bound together within networks or relatively stable relationships. We need to examine not only the religious customs of a people but the ways in which people organize their religious life. See Table 12.1 – Basic Tenets of World Religions – for detailed information about the variety of religious organizations.

Church and State

In 1978, when the whole world was shocked by the Jonestown tragedy, in which over 900 U.S. cult members committed suicide, President Jimmy Carter commented, “I don’t think we ought to have an overreaction because of the Jonestown tragedy by injecting government into trying to control people’s religious beliefs.” This is testimony to the unusually high degree of religious tolerance in the United States. Without this tolerance, the diversity of U.S. religions would not be possible. This diversity would have appalled some of the earliest settlers of this country. They came to the New World in order to establish a holy commonwealth, a community that would be ruled by church officials. In the Puritans’ republic, “theology was wedded to politics and politics to the progress of the kingdom of God” (Bercovitch, 1978: 47). Even after independence was won, some of the states had official religions. But the U.S. Constitution guarantees religious freedom by forbidding government interference in religious activities. Eventually the courts interpreted this guarantee to mean that church and state must be kept separate and the government, including state governments, must refrain from promoting religion.

TABLE 12.1 BASIC TENETS OF WORLD RELIGIONS

	Buddhism	Christianity	Hinduism	Judaism	Islam
Founded by	Siddhartha Gautama, called the Buddha, in the 4th or 5th century B.C. in India.	Jesus Christ, who was crucified around A.D. 33.	Hinduism has no founder. The oldest religion, it may date to prehistoric times.	The Hebrew leader Abraham founded Judaism around 2000 B.C. Moses gave the Jews the Torah around 1250 B.C.	Muhammad, who was born in A.D. 570 at Mecca, in Saudi Arabia.
Number of Gods	None, but there are enlightened beings (Buddhas)	One	Many (all gods and goddesses are considered different forms of one Supreme Being.)	One	One
Sacred Texts	The most important are the Tripitaka, the Mahayana Sutras, Tantra, and Zen texts.	The Bible is the sacred text of Christianity.	The most ancient are the four Vedas.	The most important are the Torah, or the first five books of Moses. Others include Judaism's oral tradition, the written form of which is known as the Talmud.	The Koran is the sacred book of Islam.
Basic Beliefs	The Four Noble Truths: (1) all beings suffer; (2) desire—for possessions, power, and so on—causes suffering; (3) desire can be overcome; and (4) the path that leads away from desire is the Eightfold Path (the Middle Way).	Jesus taught love of God and neighbor and a concern for justice.	Reincarnation states that all living things are caught in a cycle of death and rebirth. Life is ruled by the laws of karma, in which rebirth depends on moral behavior.	Jews believe in the laws of God and the words of the prophets. In Judaism, however, actions are more important than beliefs.	The Five Pillars, or main duties, are: profession of faith; prayer; charitable giving; fasting during the month of Ramadan; and pilgrimage to Mecca at least once.
Where	Buddhism is the main religion in many Asian countries.	Through its missionary activity Christianity has spread to most parts of the globe.	Hinduism is practiced by more than 80% of India's population.	Europe, Israel and the United States.	Islam is the main religion of the Middle East, Asia, and the north of Africa.

Source: Oxford Dictionary of World Religions (2012).

Thus, the United States has no official religion. But in practice, the separation of church and state is far from complete. In a sense, the U.S. government does support religion in general by exempting religious organizations from taxation. Historically, every day in public schools, students saluted the flag with the affirmation of "one nation, under God." Even at the opening of legislative sessions, presidential inaugurations, and other public ceremonial occasions, ministers, priests, and rabbis offer religious invocations or benedictions. The state occasionally even intervenes in religious affairs. Thus, church activities are investigated if a church is suspect of abusing its tax-exempt privileges or otherwise violating the law. The government has even acted on issues that some groups consider religious, such as prohibiting Mormons from practicing polygamy and forcing Christian Scientists to accept medical treatment.

There is, then, no strict separation between church and state in American society. Surveys show that most people do not object to the inclusion of religion in the public realm as long as the religion involved represents all faiths rather one particular faith. In times of national crisis, even public school officials are free to conduct prayer meetings, as they did soon after the terrorist attacks on September 11, 2001. The separation of church and state is more often fiction than reality (Goodstein, 2001).

Church and Sect

Christian organizations can be divided into two categories: *churches* and *sects*. Churches compromise with society; sects confront it. Many groups do not fit into either of these extreme categories, but mainline Protestant groups such as Episcopal and Presbyterian churches are examples of churches, while Pentecostals and Jehovah's Witnesses are often considered sects.

A *church* is a relatively large, well-established religious organization that is integrated into the society and does not make strict demands on its members. It has a formalized structure of belief, ritual, and authority. It is also an inclusive organization, welcoming members from a wide spectrum of social backgrounds. Thus, members often have little but their religion in common, and they may hardly know one another. Members tend to be born into the church, and the church sets up few if any requirements for membership. Its demands, on both its members and society, are far from exacting. Over the years, the church has learned to take a relatively tolerant attitude toward its members' failings. It has learned to reconcile itself to the institutions of society, coexisting in relative peace with society's secular values.

The church's compromises do not satisfy the *sect*, a relatively small religious group that sets itself apart from society and makes heavy demands on its members. It begins with a relatively small religious movement that has broken away from an established church. Time and again, groups have split off from Christian churches because some members believed the church had become too worldly. The sect that results holds itself separate from society, and it demands from its members a deep religious experience, strong loyalty to the group, and rejection of the larger society and its values. The sect is a tightly knit community offering close personal relations among its members.

Most pure sects do not last long. They either fail to maintain their membership and disappear, or they undergo change. Consider Methodism, which was founded in opposition to the Church of England. At first, it was a sect that sought to correct social injustices and to aid the poor. Then Irish immigrants brought it to the United States, where it was initially associated with the lower classes. But it has become a highly institutionalized religion today. It is successful, respectable, draws members from the middle class, and places less demands on those members than previously.

There appears to be a paradoxical relationship between *religiosity* and success. The more successful a religion is (in the sense of being more popular and more respectable in society, as well as having more members), the less religious its members tend to be (in the sense of spending less time reading the Bible, praying, or engaging in other spiritual activities). Established churches, such as the Episcopal, Methodist, and Catholic churches, are more successful than sects, such as the Amish and Jehovah's Witnesses. But members of sects tend to be more religious, devoting more of their time to such religious matters as reading the Bible, praying, and door-to-door evangelizing. They may show greater willingness to suffer or even die for their belief, as did their ancient counterparts such as Jesus, his disciples, and early Christians (O'Dea and Aviad, 1998).

RELIGIONS AND RELIGIOUS DIVERSITY

At the global level religion is one of the most significant dimensions of diverse cultures. In some nations, religion defines the political order and shapes many basic social institutions. Major religious movements such as the spread of Christianity and the growth of Islam, have defined major events in world history. Across different cultures many people share in the same faith but expressions of that faith differ from society to society.

The largest religion in the world, if measured in terms of numbers of followers is Christianity, with an estimated 2 billion adherents, followed by Islam with 1.1 billion adherents, then persons claiming no religion with 840 million, Hindus with 780 million adherents, and Buddhists with 323 million adherents. People of Jewish faith are a relatively small number with 14 million adherents, but are nonetheless one of the most significant religious groups (U.S. Census Bureau, 2010). See Table 12.2 for detailed information about Religious Bodies.

Buddhism

Buddhism is an extremely complicated religion. It does not follow a strict or singular theological god. Its origin is from Indian culture and it is most widely practiced in Asian societies.

The Buddha in Buddhism is Siddartha Gautama, born of the highest caste in India in the year 563 B.C. As a young man, he sought a path of enlightenment, based on travel and meditation. Buddhism thus encourages its followers to pursue spiritual transformation. Its focus on meditation has been adopted by many of the New Age spiritual groups in Western society. Buddhism involves a concept of birth and rebirth through reincarnation. Buddhists relieve themselves of their worldly suffering by seeking spiritual enlightenment (Bowker, 2012).

Christianity

Christianity developed in the Mediterranean region of Europe and rapidly spread between A.D. 40 and A.D. 350 to include some 56 percent of the population of the Roman Empire (Stark, 2008). It has spread throughout the world, largely as the result of European missionaries who colonized different parts of the world, proselytizing the Christian faith. Based on the teachings of Jesus, Christianity asserts faith in a Holy Trinity: God, the creator; Jesus, the son of God; and the Holy Spirit, the personal experience of the presence of God. Through the charisma of Jesus, Christians learned that they could be saved by following Christian beliefs and that there would be a life in Heaven. In the United States, Christianity is the dominant religion although there is great diversity in the different forms of Christianity.

TABLE 12.2 **RELIGIOUS BODIES - SELECTED DATA**

[Includes the self-reported membership of religious bodies with 60,000 or more as reported to the Yearbook of American & Canadian Churches. Groups may be excluded if they do not supply information. The data are not standardized so comparisons between groups are difficult. The definition of "church member" is determined by the religious body]

Religious body	Year reported	Churches reported	Membership	Number of Ordained Clergy Serving Parishes
African Methodist Episcopal Church	2009	4,100	2,500,000	6,000
The African Methodist Episcopal Zion Church	2008	3,393	1,400,000	3,867
The Alliance of Baptists	2006	127	65,000	320
The American Baptist Association	2009	1,600	100,000	(NA)
American Baptist Churches in the U.S.A.	2009	5,402	1,310,505	3,154
The Antiochian Orthodox Christian Archdiocese of North America	2007	256	430,000	480
Armenian Apostolic Church of America	2009	38	350,000	30
Armenian Apostolic Church, Diocese of America	2008	63	65,000	28
Assemblies of God	2009	12,371	2,914,669	19,421
Baptist Bible Fellowship International	2009	4,200	115,000	4,200
Baptist General Conference	2007	1,071	147,500	(NA)
Baptist Missionary Association of America	2008	1,287	126,056	824
The Catholic Church	2009	18,372	68,503,456	27,614
Christian Brethren (also known as Plymouth Brethren)	2006	1,145	86,000	(NA)
Christian Church (Disciples of Christ) in the United States and Canada	2009	3,691	658,869	3,931
Christian Churches and Churches of Christ	1988	5,579	1,071,616	5,525
The Christian Congregation, Inc.	2004	1,496	122,181	1,574
Christian Methodist Episcopal Church	2006	3,500	850,000	3,106
The Christian and Missionary Alliance	2009	2,021	432,471	(NA)
Christian Reformed Church in North America	2009	803	183,940	656
Church of the Brethren	2009	1,047	121,781	784
Church of God (Anderson, Indiana)	2009	2,192	250,202	4,273
The Church of God in Christ	1991	15,300	5,499,875	28,988
Church of God (Cleveland, Tennessee)	2009	6,654	1,076,254	4,877
Church of God of Prophecy	2007	1,860	89,674	4,340
The Church of Jesus Christ of Latter-day Saints	2009	13,474	6,058,907	40,422
Church of the Nazarene	2009	5,063	645,846	5,543
Churches of Christ	2006	13,000	1,639,495	(NA)
Community of Christ	2007	935	178,328	(NA)
Conservative Baptist Association of America (CBAmerica)	2006	1,200	200,000	1,800
Coptic Orthodox Church	2000	100	300,000	140
Cumberland Presbyterian Church	2009	643	65,591	(NA)
Episcopal Church	2009	6,895	2,006,343	4,868
The Evangelical Church Alliance	2009		295,001	2,435
The Evangelical Covenant Church	2006	783	114,283	1,486
The Evangelical Free Church of America	2008	1,475	356,000	1,503
Evangelical Lutheran Church in America	2009	10,348	4,542,868	8,654
Evangelical Presbyterian Church	2007	207	89,190	385
Free Methodist Church of North America	2009	1,053	75,586	(NA)
Full Gospel Fellowship of Churches and Ministers International	2007	1,273	432,632	2,631
General Association of Regular Baptist Churches	2007	1,321	132,700	(NA)
General Conference of Mennonite Brethren Churches	1996	368	82,130	590
Grace Gospel Fellowship	1992	128	60,000	160
Greek Orthodox Archdiocese of America	2006	560	1,500,000	553
IFCA International, Inc.	1998	659	61,655	(NA)
International Church of the Foursquare Gospel	2006	1,875	353,995	6,738
International Council of Community Churches	2009	137	69,276	548
International Pentecostal Holiness Church	2008	2,024	330,054	2,946
Jehovah's Witnesses	2009	13,021	1,162,686	(NA)

The Lutheran Church--Missouri Synod (LCMS)	2009	6,178	2,312,111	5,336
Mennonite Church USA	2009	920	104,684	1,503
National Association of Congregational Christian Churches	2001	432	65,392	507
National Association of Free Will Baptists	2007	2,369	185,798	(NA)
National Baptist Convention of America, Inc.	2000		3,500,000	(NA)
National Baptist Convention, U.S.A., Inc.	2004	9,000	5,000,000	(NA)
National Missionary Baptist Convention of America	1992		2,500,000	(NA)
National Primitive Baptist Convention, Inc.	2002	1,565	600,000	(NA)
Old Order Amish Church	2001	898	80,820	3,592
The Orthodox Church in America	2009	750	131,000	850
Pentecostal Assemblies of the World, Inc.	2006	1,750	1,500,000	4,500
Pentecostal Church of God	2008	1,134	98,579	1,134
Polish National Catholic Church of America	2008	126	60,000	103
Presbyterian Church in America	2009	1,719	341,210	3,645
Presbyterian Church (U.S.A.)	2009	10,657	2,770,730	7,142
Progressive National Baptist Convention, Inc.	2009	1,500	1,010,000	3,200
Reformed Church in America	2009	896	250,938	859
Religious Society of Friends (Conservative)	2004	1,200	104,000	(NA)
The Russian Orthodox Church Outside of Russia	2008	190	480,000	221
The Salvation Army	2009	1,241	400,055	2,282
Serbian Orthodox Church in the U.S.A. and Canada	2005	68	67,000	60
Seventh-day Adventist Church	2009	4,892	1,043,606	2,561
Southern Baptist Convention	2009	45,010	16,160,088	105,906
Unitarian Universalist Association of Congregations	2009	1,048	221,367	1,773
United Church of Christ	2009	5,287	1,080,199	3,884
The United Methodist Church	2009	33,855	7,774,931	23,944
United Pentecostal Church International	2006	4,358	646,304	9,224
The Wesleyan Church	2009	1,716	139,008	2,393
Wisconsin Evangelical Lutheran Synod	2009	1,279	389,545	1,296

SYMBOL:
NA Not available.
Source: National Council of Churches USA, New York, NY, 2011 Yearbook of American & Canadian Churches, annual (copyright).
For more information: http://www.ncccusa.org/ and http://www.electronicchurch.org

PROTESTANTS. Protestants form the largest religious group in the United States, although within this group there is much diversity. There are two main categories of Protestants: mainline Protestants and conservatives, also known as fundamentalists. Mainline Protestants include twenty-eight different denominations. They have a history of intergroup cooperation and social activism. Mainline Protestants tend to be less diligent about religious observance than either Roman Catholics or conservative Protestants. Many do not attend church regularly, but the majority claim to believe in the existence of God and the divinity of Christ (Chalfant, 1998).

Mainline Protestants have experienced declines in church membership and attendance in recent years. In 1962, Protestants were 67 percent of the population. That number continues to decline. There two principal reasons for the decline: the drop in religious affiliation and the growth in the number of conservative Protestants. Conservative Protestants include those groups variously labeled evangelical, fundamentalist and Pentecostal. These groups are more dogmatic among Protestants. The label "fundamentalist" is taken from the belief that the fundamental tenet of the Christian life is that the Bible is the literal word of God.

ROMAN CATHOLICS. Worldwide, with its emphasis on Church hierarchy, Roman Catholics identify the Pope as the source of religious authority. The Vatican in Rome acts as the system of religious governance,

with enormous power to influence the religious norms and beliefs of Catholic followers. The Catholic Church was once the ruling religious and political force in the Western world. It has members all over the world across all social and political boundaries.

The Catholic Church is typically perceived as having a strong hold on its members. Catholicism is a very hierarchical religious system, with religious values and codes of behavior mandated by the Pope and the Vatican. In recent years, however, the Catholic Church has embraced a number of liberal reforms. Mass is now typically celebrated in secular language after centuries of a Latin only policy. Laypeople have been granted larger roles in church rituals and church affairs. Many Catholics hold more liberal attitudes than the official church suggests.

In the United States, Catholicism has long been associated with immigrant groups who brought Catholicism with them, just as Protestantism in the United States was established by immigrants from other nations. Irish Americans, Italian Americans, and most recently, Latin American immigrants have tended to be of the Catholic faith. Recent immigration has actually increased the number of Catholics in the United States (Bowker, 2012).

Hinduism

Unlike Christianity, Islam and Judaism, Hindu religion is not linked to singular God. Hinduism rejects the idea that there is a single, powerful god. In this religion god is not a specific entity; rather people are called on to see a moral force in the world and to live in a way that contributes to moral and spiritual development. Karma is the principle in Hindu that sees all human action as having spiritual consequences, ultimately leading to a higher state of spiritual consciousness, perhaps found in the birth one experiences following death which is reincarnation.

Hinduism is deeply linked to the social system of India because the historical caste system in India is seen as stemming from people's commitment to Hindu principles. Those who live the most ideal forms of life are seen as part of the higher caste, with the lower caste as spiritually deficient. There are also several castes in between. The complexity of Hinduism can be seen in the fact that, at the same time it has been used to justify this caste system, one of the greatest world leaders, Gandhi, used Hindu principles of justice, honesty, and courage to guide one of the most important independence movements in the world. His teachings were also crucial in the development of the civil rights movement in the United States (Bowker, 2012).

Islam

Islam is most typically associated with Middle Eastern countries, in part because of the significance of Islamic faith in countries such as Iran, Iraq, and Saudi Arabia, which have been much the subject of world politics in recent years. Islamic people are also found in northern Africa, southeastern Asia, and increasingly in North America and Europe as the result of international migration.

Followers of Islamic religion are called Muslims. They believe that Islam is the word of God, revealed in the prophet Muhammed. The Koran is the holy book of Islam. The highly traditional or reactionary Islamic fundamentalists adhere strictly to the word of the Koran, believing that they are obligated to defend their faith and that death in doing so is a way of honoring God. Not all Muslims take such a fundamental view, although they are frequently stereotyped because of the prominence of Islamic fundamentalism in contemporary world conflicts. Muslims do have a highly patriarchal worldview, with women being denied the freedoms that men enjoy. As with other religions, the degree to which people adhere to this faith or interpret it conservatively varies in different social settings.

Judaism

Judaism has enormous world significance even though its adherents are relatively small in number. Its teachings are the source of both Christian belief systems and Islamic beliefs. More than 40 percent of the world's Jewish population now lives in the United States, making this the largest community of Jewish people in the world. The existence of the state of Israel, founded following the Holocaust of the second World War, has given Jewish people a high profile in international politics.

The Jewish faith is more than 4,000 years old. Under Egyptian rule in ancient history, Jewish people endured centuries of slavery. Led from Egypt by Moses in the thirteenth century B.C., Jewish people were liberated and now celebrate this freedom in the annual ritual of Passover. The Jews see themselves as "chosen people," meant to recognize their duty to obey God's laws as revealed in the Ten Commandments.

In the United States, Jewish Americans are a relatively small proportion of the population, and their number is declining as a result of a low birthrate and high rate of interfaith marriage. Jewish people nevertheless remain a significant religious minority. The periods of greatest Jewish immigration to the United States were in the mid-nineteenth century and between the 1880s and the first World War. Large numbers tried to immigrate to the United States in the 1930s when Nazi persecution of Jews in Europe intensified, but the United States turned away many of these refugees, forcing them to return to Europe where many were killed in the Holocaust (Sklare, 1971, 2011).

There are significant divisions of culture and religious practice within Judaism. Orthodox Jews, a small fraction of the total number of Jews in the United States, adhere strictly to a traditional conception of their religious faith. They observe the biblical dietary laws, honor traditional code of dress and behavior, and strictly observe the Sabbath, during which they may not travel, carry money, write, work, or do business. Reform Jews have a more secular orientation. Laypeople are typically excused from strict observation of religious rules. In Reform temples, where women and men are treated more equally, prayers are often in English, not Hebrew. In general, there is flexibility of religious practice among Reform Jews. Conservative Judaism falls between Orthodox and Reform in terms of strictness of observation (Bowker, 2012).

THE FUNCTIONALIST PERSPECTIVE ON RELIGION

Functionalist theorists look to the contributions religion makes to society's survival. They reason that if every known society seems to have something called religion, its presence cannot be dismissed as a social accident (Davis, 1951). If religion were not adaptive, societies would long since have evolved without it. Accordingly, they ask what functions are performed by religion in social life.

Durkheim: Religion as a Societal Glue

In *The Elementary Forms of Religious Life* (1912), the last of his major works, Emile Durkheim brought his concern with group forces to an analysis of the functions of religion. He selected for his study the Arunta, an

Australian aboriginal people. The Arunta practice totemism, a religious system in which a clan (a kin group) takes the name of, claims descent from, and attributes sacred properties to a plant or animal. Durkheim says that the totem plant or animal is not the source of totemism, but a stand-in for the real source, society itself. He contends that religion - the totem ancestor, God, or some other supernatural force is the symbolization of society. By means of religious rituals, the group in effect worships itself. Society harnesses the awesome force inherent in people's perception of the sacred for animating a sense of oneness and moral authority. The primary functions of religion are the creation, reinforcement, and maintenance of social solidarity and social control.

Durkheim observes that if we are left to ourselves, our individual consciousness - our inner mental states - are closed to one another. Our separate minds cannot come in contact and communicate except by "coming out of themselves." Consequently, social life dictates that the internal be made external and the intangible, tangible. Our inner consciousness is transformed into a collective consciousness through the symbolic device of religious rituals. By uttering the same cry, pronouncing the same word, or performing the same gesture, we inform one another that we are united in a shared state of mind. Simultaneously, we mentally fuse ourselves within a social whole. We generate a sort of electricity or collective euphoria that lifts us to an intense state of exaltation that overrides our individual beings. Religious rituals thus operate in two ways: First, they provide vehicles by which we reveal to one another that we share a common mental state; second, they create among us a shared consciousness that contributes to a social bonding.

Durkheim emphasizes the similarity in our attitudes toward society and toward God. Society inspires the sensation of divinity in the minds of its members because of its power over them. Moreover, society, like God, possesses moral authority and can inspire self-sacrifice and devotion. And finally, religion is capable of endowing individuals with exceptional powers and motivation. Accordingly, Durkheim says that the religious person is not the victim of an illusion. Behind the symbol-religion there is a real force and reality: society. Durkheim concludes that when religion is imperiled and not replaced by a satisfying substitute, society itself is jeopardized: Individuals pursue their private interests without regard for the dictates of the larger social enterprise. See Box 12.1 for additional information on Durkheim's sociological analysis of religion.

Additional Functions

Durkheim draws our attention to how religion functions as "social glue" that contributes to social cohesion and solidarity by integrating and unifying the members of a community. Moreover, when a society links its morality to religion, social control may be furthered. The enforcement of norms is greatly enhanced if recourse can be had to priests, the unknown, the divine, idealism, and supernatural agents.

Sociologists have shown that religion may perform other functions as well. For one thing, it helps people in dealing with life's "breaking points" (Ebaugh, Richman, and Chafetz, 2004). Much of the human experience is uncertain and insecure. Humankind is recurrently confronted with crises and haunting perplexities - floods, epidemics, droughts, famines, wars, accidents, sickness, social disorder, personal defeat, humiliation, injustice, the meaning of life, the mystery of death, and the enigma of the hereafter. Religion deals with these ultimate problems of life, provides "answers," and often offers the prospect of hope through magical control or spiritual intercession. Moreover, it assists people in the transitional stages of life. Most religions celebrate and explain the major events of the life cycle - birth, puberty, marriage, and death -through rites of passage (ceremonies marking the transition from one status to another).

BOX 12.1

FOCUS ON DURKHEIM

Durkheim's concern with social regulation focused on the more external forces of control, particularly legal regulations that can be studied, so he argued about the law books without regard to individuals. Later he began to consider forces of control that were internalized in individual consciousness. Being convinced that "society must be present within the individual," Durkheim, following the logic of his own theory, was led to the study of religion, one of the forces that created within individuals a sense of moral obligation to adhere to society's demands (norms), (Durkheim, 1903). Durkheim had yet another motive for studying the functions of religion - namely, concern with mechanisms that might serve to shore up a threatened social order. In this respect he was searchlng for functional equivalents for religion in a fundamentally a-religious age.

Durkheim was one of several French thinkers who pondered the problem of the loss of faith. Such questions intensified Durkheim's concern with the sociology of religion, adding to the intrinsic interest he had in terms of the internal logic of his system (functionalism). Basic to his theory is the stress on religious phenomena as communal rather than individual.

> "A religion is a unified system of beliefs and practices relative to sacred things, that is to say, things set apart and forbidden -- beliefs and practices which unite in one single moral community called a Church, all those who adhere to them" (Durkheim, 1903).

Durkheim was not concerned with the variety of religious experience of individuals but rather with the communal activity and the communal bonds to which participation in religious activities gives rise. Durkheim argued that religious phenomena emerge in any society when a separation is made between the sphere of the profane – the realm of everyday utilitarian activities - and the sphere of the sacred - the area that pertains to the transcendental and the extraordinary. An object is intrinsically neither sacred nor profane. It becomes one or the other depending on whether men (we) choose to consider the utilitarian value of the object or certain intrinsic attributes that have nothing to do with its instrumental value. The wine at mass has sacred ritual significance to the extent that it is considered by the believer to symbolize the blood of Christ; in this context it is plainly not a beverage. Sacred activities are valued by the community of believers not as means to ends, but because the religious community has bestowed their meaning on them as part of its worship. Distinctions between the spheres of the sacred and the profane are always made by groups who band together in a cult and who are united by their common symbols and objects of worship. Religion is "an eminently collective thing." It binds men (us) together, as the etymology of the word religion testifies (Durkheim, 1903).

But if religion, the great binding force, is on its deathbed, how then can the malady of modern society, its tendency to disintegrate, be upheld? Here Durkheim accomplished one of his most daring analytical leaps. Religion, he argued, is not only a social creation, but it is in fact society divinized. Durkheim stated that the deities which men (we) worship together are only projections of the power of society. Religion is eminently social: it occurs in a social context, and, more importantly, when men (we) celebrate sacred things, they (we) unwittingly celebrate the power of their society. This power so transcends their (our) own existence that they (we) have to give it sacred significance in order to visualize it. If religion in its essence is a transcendental representation of the powers of society, then, Durkheim argued, the disappearance of traditional religion need not herald the dissolution of society. All that is required is for modern men (us) now to realize directly that dependence on society which before they (we) had recognized only through the medium of religious representations. According to Durkheim, "We must discover the rational substitutes for these religious notions that for a long time have served as the vehicle for the most essential moral ideas," (Durkheim, 1903: 35). Society is the father of us all; therefore, it is to society we owe that profound debt of gratitude heretofore paid to the gods. The following passage, which in its rhetoric is rather uncharacteristic of Durkheim's usual analytical style, reveals some of his innermost feelings:

> "Society is not at all the illogical or a-logical, incoherent and fantastic being which has too often been considered. Quite on the contrary, the collective consciousness is the highest form of psychic life, since it is the consciousness of consciousness. Being placed outside of and above individual and local contingencies, it sees things only in their permanent and essential aspects, which it crystallizes into communicable ideas. At the same time that it sees from above, it sees farther; at every moment of time it embraces all known reality; that is why it alone can furnish the minds with the molds which are applicable to the totality of things and which make it possible to think of them" (Durkheim, 1903: 56).

Durkheim did not follow Comte in attempting to institute a new humanitarian cult. Yet, being eager as they were to give moral unity to a disintegrating society, he urged men (us) to unite in a civic morality based on the recognition that we are what we are because of society. Society acts within us to elevate us - not unlike the divine spark of old was said to transform ordinary men into creatures capable of transcending the limitations of their limited egos (Durkheim, 1903).

Durkheim's sociology of religion is not limited to these general considerations, which, in fact, are contained in only a few pages of his monumental work on *The Elementary Forms of Religious Life*. The bulk of the book is devoted to a close and careful analysis of primitive religion, more particularly of the data on primitive Australian forms of cults and beliefs. Durkheim's four major functions of religion may be classified as disciplinary, cohesive, vitalizing, and euphoric social forces. Religious rituals prepare men (us) for social life by imposing self-discipline and a certain measure of asceticism. Religious ceremonies bring people together and thus serve to reaffirm their common bonds and to reinforce social solidarity. Religious observance maintains and revitalizes the social heritage of the group and helps transmit its enduring values to future generations. Finally, religion has a euphoric function in that it serves to counteract feelings of frustration and loss of faith by reestablishing the believers' sense of well-being, their sense of the essential rightness of the moral world of which they are a part. By countering the sense of loss, which, as in the case of death, may be experienced on both the individual and the collective level, religion helps to reestablish the balance of private and public confidence. On the most general plane, religion as a social institution serves to give meaning to man's (our) existential predicaments by tying the individual to that supra-individual sphere of transcendent values which is ultimately rooted in his (our) society.

Religion may also be an impetus to social change. For instance, black churches have historically made a significant contribution to the mobilization of protest, as was evident in the civil rights movements of the 1950's and 1960's. The black ministers of Montgomery, Alabama, organized a bus boycott in 1955 and 1956 that was instrumental in bringing about the desegregation of the city's buses after Mrs. Rosa Parks was arrested for violating a local bus segregation ordinance. And the Southern Christian Leadership Conference (SCLC), led by the Reverend Martin Luther King, Jr., and other black ministers, was at the forefront of the black protest movement of the 1960's. In recent years Roman Catholic bishops in the United States have also been major proponents of social change.

THE CONFLICT PERSPECTIVE ON RELIGION

From the writings of functionalist theorists we gain a view of religion as a vital source for social integration and solidarity. We derive a quite different image from conflict theorists. Some of them depict religion as a weapon in the service of ruling elites who use it to hold in check the explosive tensions produced by social inequality and injustice. Others see religion as a source of social conflict and point to the religious wars of the Middle Ages and to present-day religious strife in the Middle East and elsewhere. Still others see religion as a source of social change.

Marx: Religion Is the Opium of the People

The stimulus for many of the contributions made by conflict theorists comes from the work of Karl Marx. Marx (1844) portrayed religion as a painkiller for the frustration, deprivation, and subjugation experienced by oppressed peoples. He said it soothes their distress, but any relief it may provide is illusory because religion is a social narcotic:

Religious suffering is at the same time an expression of real suffering and a protest against real suffering. Religion is the sigh of the oppressed creature, the sentiment of a heartless world, and the soul of soulless conditions. It is the opium of the people.

Marx saw religion as producing an other-worldly focus that diverts the oppressed from seeking social change in this world. It leads people to project their needs and desires into the realm of make-believe and obscures the real source of social misery and class conflict. More particularly, religion engenders a false consciousness among the working class that interferes with its attainment of true class consciousness. A Marxist reading of English history suggests that the development of Methodism in nineteenth-century England prevented revolution by redirecting workers' discontent and fervor into a religious movement (McGuire, 1981). And the Russian revolutionary Leon Trotsky was so aware of the similarity of revolutionary Marxism to religious sectarianism that in the late 1890s he successfully recruited the first working-class members of the South Russian Workers' Union among adherents of religious sects.

Marx viewed religion as an expression of human alienation. People shape social institutions with the expectation that they will serve their needs, but find instead that they themselves become the servants of the institutions they have created. The social institutions though, rather than providing for the wants and enriching the lives of the entire community, are taken over by the ruling class and used to oppress and victimize people. Thus people fashion gods, lose their knowledge that they have done so, and then find themselves having to live their lives at the behest of these same gods. As with the economic, family, and legal institutions, people no longer see themselves as the authors of their own products, but as part of an encompassing natural order that dominates and directs them. Hence, in much the manner that they are alienated from their labor, the members of the working class are alienated from the larger social environment: "The more powerful becomes the world of objects which they create, the poorer they become in their inner lives, and the less they belong to themselves. It is just the same as in religion. The more of themselves humankind attributes to God, the less they have in themselves" (Marx, 1844: 122).

A number of sociologists have agreed with Marx that there is an inherently conservative aspect to religion (Yinger, 1957; Glock, Ringer, and Babbie, 1967). The sense of the sacred links present experience with meanings derived from the group's traditional past. Religious beliefs and practices provide taken-for-granted truths that are powerful forces militating against new ways of thinking and behaving. Practices handed down from previous generations, including institutional inequalities and inequities, become defined as God-approved ways and highly resistant to change. For instance, American slavery was justified as part of God's "natural order." In 1863, the Presbyterian Church, South, met in General Synod and passed a resolution declaring slavery to be a divine institution, ordained by God. More recently segregation was justified on similar grounds. Said Louisiana State Senator W.M. Rainach in defending segregation in 1954: "Segregation is a natural order-created by God, in His wisdom, who made black men black and white men white," (Southern School News, 1954:3). Likewise, the Hindu religion threatens believers who fail to obey caste rules with reincarnation (rebirth) at a lower caste level or as an animal.

Religion may also legitimate changes favoring powerful and wealthy groups. Imperialism has often been supported by religious or quasi-religious motivations and beliefs. In the 1890's President William McKinley explained his decision to wage the expansionist war against Spain and seize Cuba and the Philippines as follows (quoted by McGuire, 1981:188):

> I am not ashamed to tell you, gentlemen, that I went down on my knees and prayed Almighty God for light and guidance more than one night. And one night late it came to me this way. . .There was nothing left for us to do but to take them all and to educate the Filipinos and uplift and civilize and Christianize them and by God's grace do the very best we could by them, as our fellow men for who Christ also died.

Religion, then, can be a potent force in the service of the established order. Religious organizations themselves are frequently motivated to legitimate the status quo because they also have vested interests to protect, including power, land, and wealth (Collins, 2008).

SUGGESTED READINGS

Hoffman, B., and Burke, K. Heaven's Gate: Cult Suicide in San Diego. (New York, NY: Harper, 1997).

Priest, R.J., Wilson, D., and Johnson, A. "U.S. Megachurches and New Patterns of Global Mission." International Bulletin of Missionary Research. (2010, Volume 34, pp. 97-104).

Tabor, J.D., and Gallagher, E.V. Why Waco? Cults and the Battle for Religious Freedom in America. (Berkeley, CA: University of California Press, 1995).

Terry, K., and Smith, M.L. The Nature and Scope of Sexual Abuse of Minors by Catholic Priests and Deacons in the United States: Supplementary Data Analysis. (Washington, DC: United States Conference of Catholic Bishops, 2006).

Warf, B., and Winsberg, M. "Geographies of Megachurches in the United States." Journal of Cultural Geography. (2010, Volume 27, pp. 33-51).

BIBLIOGRAPHY

Abercrombie, N., Hill, S., and Turner, B. *The Penguin Dictionary of Sociology* Third Edition (London: Penguin Books, 1994).

Adamczyk, A., and Pitt, C. "Shaping Attitudes About Homosexuality: The Role of Religion and Cultural Context." *Social Science Quarterly.* (Volume 38, pp. 338-351, 2009).

Barkan, S.E. "Religiosity and Premarital Sex During Adulthood." *Journal for the Scientific Study of Religion.* (Volume 45, pp. 407-417, 2006).

Berger, P. *The Sacred Canopy: Elements of a Sociological Theory of Religion.* (Garden City, NY: Doubleday, 1967).

Bowker, John. *The Oxford Dictionary of World Religions.* (New York, NY: Oxford University Press, 2012).

Chalfant, H., and Beckley, R. *Religion in Contemporary Society.* 2nd Ed. (Mountain View, CA: Mayfield, 1987).

Collins, R. *Sociology Since Mid-Century: Essays in Theory Cumulation.* (New York, NY: Academic Press, 2008).

Cornill, H. *The Prophets of Israel.* (Chicago, 1904).

Davis, K. *Religion Among Primitives.* (New York, NY: Free Press, 1951)

Durkheim, Emile. *The Elementary Forms of Religious Life.* (J. Swain Trans.) (Glencoe, IL: Free Press, 1947). (Original work published in 1915).

Emerson, M.O., Monahan, S.C., and Mirola, W.A. "Spirituality and Aging: Research and Implications." *Journal of Religion, Spirituality and Aging.* (Volume 20, pp. 95-134, 2001).

Finke, R., and Starke, R. *Patterns of Religious Commitment.* (Berkeley, CA: University of California Press, 1968).

Gaustad, E. S. and Schmidt, L.E. *The Religious History of America.* (San Francisco, CA: Harper, 2004).

Gundy-Volf, J. "Neither Biblical nor Just: Southern Baptists and the Subordination of Women." *Sojourners.* (pp. 12-13, 1998.)

Klassen, P. *Women and Religion.* (New York, NY: Routledge, 2009).

Lubbock, J. *Origin of Civilization.* (1874).

Marx, K. *Karl Marx: Selected Writings in Sociology and Social Philosophy.* (T.B. Bottomore Trans.) (New York, NY: McGraw Hill, 1964).

McGuire, M. *Religion: The Social Context.* (Belmont, CA: Wadsworth,1981, 1996).

Moberg, D.O. *Religion Matters: What Sociology Teaches Us About Religion in Our World.* (Upper Saddle River, NJ: Prentice Hall, 2011).

Morris, A. *The Origins of the Civil Rights Movement: Black Communities Organizing for Change.* (New York, NY: Free Press, 1984).

Noss, D. S. and Grangaard, B. R. *A History of the World's Religions.* 12th Ed. (Upper Saddle River, NJ: Prentice Hall, 2008).

Oguntoyinbo, L. "America's First Muslim College to Open This Fall." *Diverse Issues in Higher Education.* Retrieved from http://diverseeducation.com/article/13814/america-s-first-mulsim-college-t-open-this-fall.html.

Pew Forum on Religion and Public Life. *U.S. Religious Landscape Survey.* (Washington, DC: Pew Research Center, 2008.)

Regenerus, M.D. *Forbidden Fruit: Sex and Religion in the Lives of American Teenagers.* (New York, NY: Oxford University Press, 2007).

Southern School News. "Segregation." *Southern School News.* (1, November 3, 1954).

Stark, R., and Glock, C.Y. *The Churching of America: Winners and Losers in Our Religious Economy.* 2nd Ed. (New Brunswick, NJ: Rutgers University Press, 2008).

Uecker, J. "Religion, Pledging, and the Premarital Sexual Behavior of Married Young Adults." *Journal of Marriage and Family.* (Volume 70, pp. 728-744, 2002).

Weber, M. *The Protestant Ethic and the Spirit of Capitalism.* (T. Parsons Trans.) (New York, NY: Scribner, 1958). *Religion, Society, and the Individual.* (New York, NY: Macmillan, 1965).

Young, W.A. *The World's Religions: Worldviews and Contemporary Issues.* 3rd Ed. (Upper Saddle River, NJ: Prentice Hall, 2010).

GLOSSARY

Absolute score Please see **raw score**.

Achieved Adjectival form of the noun, achievement.

Achievement A process for allocating positions. One gets a position through achievement to the extent that one gets a position through one's own efforts.

Alienation This term is defined differently in the various sociological paradigms. In Marxian conflict theory, alienation refers to a subjective sense of a social actor whereby the social actor perceives her/himself as separated from her/himself, as separated from others, and as separated from the fruits of her/his labor. Marxist theory views alienation as resulting from the powerlessness of the proletariat.

Altruistic suicide In Durkheim's typology, if the solidary ties between an individual and the collectivity are extremely strong, the individual will sacrifice her or his own life for the collectivity. Durkheim terms this action altruistic suicide.

Anarchy Absence, or complete breakdown of, political rule or governance.

Anomic suicide One's level of frustration at not being able to satiate one's (economic, social, sexual, etc.) appetites can lead or drive one to suicide, which Durkheim terms anomic suicide.

Anomie Norms are in flux, guidelines for behavior no longer are clear.

Anonymity In research methods, the ethical guideline that the researcher is unable to identify a particular response with a particular person.

Anticipatory socialization Learning the roles and norms that attach to a position before we actually occupy the position.

Antithesis As a stage in the dialectical process, the clash of contradictions.

Artificial will Rational calculation, which is Ferdinand Toennies' term for a characteristic of human relationships in Gesellschaft. Human relationships in Gesellschaft are founded on rational calculation rather than on spontaneous attraction.

Ascribed Adjectival form of the noun, ascription.

Ascription A process for allocating positions. One gets a position through ascription to the extent that one gets a position through no efforts of one's own.

Association Reaching beyond primordial ties to establish common cause with others.

Association See correlation.

Attitude An orientation toward certain objects (including persons, whether oneself or others) or situations that is emotionally toned and relatively persistent.

Autarky A policy of self-reliance, whereby a country (or some other collectivity) avoids trade and instead produces everything (or the most vital things) by itself.

Authoritarian leaders These social actors coordinate the activities of the group to achieve the group goals, and they impose policies and activities on the group.

Authority Legitimate power.

Availability heuristic A cognitive rule of thumb that judges the likelihood of things in terms of their availability in memory: if instances of something come readily to mind, we presume it to be commonplace.

Axiom A logical proposition that most individuals would be willing to accept as valid.

Below replacement-level fertility A combination of fertility and mortality rates that leads to a negative population growth rate

Bigamy In a legal system where monogamy is the only legal form of marriage, if a person knowingly marries while still legally married to another person, the second marriage is bigamous; this condition is known as bigamy.

Bilateral descent Both the mother's and father's lines are used equally in determining who are one's relatives.

Blue-collar Occupations or jobs of lower prestige that involve manual labor.

Blue-collar workers This term is used to differentiate the manual worker from the white-collar worker. Blue-collar workers are manual laborers whose work is primarily physical rather than mental and deals with things rather than with ideas; this category encompasses skilled, semi-skilled, and unskilled workers, including farm workers, miners, and construction workers (Theodorson and Theodorson, 1969: 32).

Bourgeoisie In Marxian conflict theory, those who own the economic means of production.

Bureaucracy A type of social organization characterized by a hierarchy of offices with a rational-legal chain of command, promotion within which and recruitment into which occur on the basis of universalistic criteria (Weber).

Bureaucratic inertia The tendency of large organizations to continue with policies even when external conditions, including the needs of their clients, change.

Caste A type of group or collectivity defined by means of entrée and egress. One gets into a caste by being born into it and one gets out of it through death.

Causal reasoning Reasoning about cause and effect.

Cell In a statistical table, the place for each entry of data.

Census An official, usually periodic, enumeration of population.

Charismatic authority The right to command and the duty to obey that is legitimated on the basis of the exceptional qualities that are attributed to a leader by her or his followers.

Chicago school, the Sociological scholarship that emerged from the University of Chicago between World Wars I and II came to be known as "the Chicago School" because it had several distinctive characteristics. Sometimes the term "Chicago sociology" or "the Chicago school" refers quite generally to symbolic interactionism.

Class The various sociological paradigms and theories define this concept differently. In Weberian theory, people who have the same economic life chances; in Marxian theory, people who have the same objective relationship to the means of production are members of the same objective class.

Classical experimental design A research approach that uses an experimental group and a control group. All research subjects are measured on the dependent variable. Then, the research subjects are randomly assigned to either the experimental group or the control group. The researcher then manipulates the independent variable, after which all research subjects are post-tested on the dependent variable. The pre-test scores and post-test scores of the two groups are compared.

Cohabitation Living together in a sexual relationship without marriage.

Column In a statistical table, the vertical listing of data in a series of categories, all of which have a common classification.

Column caption In a statistical table, a title that describes the common classification of the data located in the columns.

Column heading Please see **column caption**.

Column marginals In a contingency table, the raw and percent frequency distributions found along the column edges or margins of the table.

Command economy, a Instead of allowing dispersed buyers and sellers to determine their own economic activities according to what economists call the laws of supply and demand, the state issues commands determining the overall direction of the economy according to a master plan. For the greater good, all economic decisions are centralized.

Common conscience Emile Durkheim's term for a characteristic of mechanical solidarity. What I believe, you believe, we all believe.

Comparison group In a quasi-experiment, the group to which the experimental group is compared. Members are not assigned to the experimental and comparison groups on the basis of random assignment.

Confidentiality In research methods, the ethical guideline that the researcher, while able to identify a particular response with a particular person, promises not to do so publicly.

Conflict theory Also known as social conflict theory. A sociological paradigm that focuses on the dialectics of social life.

Context of socialization A person, organization, or institution engaging in socialization. Also known as an agent of socialization.

Contingency table A bivariate statistical table. A type of statistical table. Sometimes called a 2 x 2 table (two-by-two table or a four-celled table or a cross-tabulation table or a cross-tab). A statistical table that presents a cross-classification of two variables. The table presents the number (and sometimes the percent as well) of cases falling in each combination of categories of the two variables. Please see **cross-tabulation table.**

Contraceptive prevalence rate The percent of women of reproductive age (15 - 49) who are married or in a union and are using, or whose sexual partner is using, a method of contraception.

Control group In an experiment, the group that is not exposed to the manipulation of the independent variable.

Control theory This theory predicts and explains how people define, and respond to, deviant behavior.

Co-opt To give someone the appearance rather than the substance of power.

Cooptation The appearance rather than the substance of power.

Core countries According to world-systems theory, the most advanced capitalist industrial countries to whom flow the lion's share of profits in the world economic system.

Corporate crime Crime committed by individuals in formal organizations for the benefit of the formal organization.

Correlation A relationship between two or more quantitative variables, such that an increase or decrease in the magnitude of one variable is associated with the magnitude of the other(s). When two variables are highly correlated, it is possible to predict the magnitude of one variable from knowledge of the magnitude of the other. Also known as a "relationship" or "association."

Cosmopolitan A person who adheres to the idea of cosmopolitanism; also known as a cosmopolite.

Cosmopolitanism Loyalty to the good of humanity as a whole even if it conflicts with loyalty to the interests of one's own nation (Robbins, 2012).

Cosmopolite A person who adheres to the idea of cosmopolitanism.

Counterculture A subculture that rejects key values and norms of the conventional society in which it is situated.

Coup d'état The seizure of political power by domestic military forces; a change of political power outside of the state's constitutional order.

Coverture The legal doctrine that upon marriage, the husband and wife become a single legal identity, that of the husband.

Creation myth A secular term for an explanation of how human beings came into being on planet earth.

Creative destruction According to Joseph A. Schumpeter, this is the essence of capitalism: the perennial cycle of destroying the old and less efficient product or service and replacing it with new, more efficient ones.

Crime From the point of view of consensus theory, crime is an unintentional act or omission of an act that violates the provisions of criminal statutory or case law, occurs without defense or justification, and is deemed by the state to be a felony or misdemeanor (Sue Reid).

Crimes against humanity Inhumane acts and persecutions against civilians on a vast scale in the pursuit of unjust ends (Goldstein and Pevehouse, 2010: 252).

Criminology The scientific study of law making, law, breaking and the enforcement of law (Edwin Sutherland).

Cross-tab Shortened expression for a **cross-tabulation table**.

Cross-tabulation table A method of ordering an displaying data, so that a cross-tabulation of two or more variables is presented; the table presents the raw number of cases and the percent of cases falling into each combination of categories of the two or more variables.

Crude birth rate The number of live births in a given year for every 1,000 people in the population

Crude death rate The number of deaths in a given year for every 1,000 people in the population.

Cultural capital The extent to which an individual, collectivity, or group is adept with regard to the cultural elements of the dominant culture. Sometimes referred to as social capital.

Cultural diffusion The transmission of cultural traits or social practices from one culture or subculture to another through such mechanisms as exploration, military conquest, social interaction, tourism, migration, immigration, the mass media, and so forth.

Cultural element Also called a cultural trait; a simple, identifiable, and significant unit of a culture.

Cultural lag A delay in cultural adjustments to changing social conditions; one part of culture changing at a more rapid rate than other, related parts.

Cultural pluralism A perspective and an approach to social relations that affirms that cultural heterogeneity is a goal that should be pursued and attained by society.

Cultural trait Please see cultural element, above.

Cultural universal A cultural element that is found in virtually all societies.

Culture Edward B. Tylor (1871:1) defines culture as "that complex whole which includes knowledge, belief, art, morals, law, custom, and any other capabilities and habits acquired" by humans as members of society.

Culture shock A disorientation which social actors may experience when they find themselves outside of their familiar culture and in a culture that they perceive as significantly different than their own.

Dark figure of crime Crime that occurs but that is not reported to the police.

Davies J-Curve, the An hypothesis about the relationship between need satisfaction and revolution, enunciated in 1962 by Sociologist James C. Davies. According to this hypothesis, revolutions are most likely to occur when a prolonged period of economic and social development is followed by a short period of sharp reversal. Expectations of improvement continue to increase, and the gap between what people want and what they get becomes intolerable and drives or produces the revolution.

Deduction In research methodology, a logical model in which specific hypotheses are developed on the basis of general principles. This is the traditional model of science.

Definition of the situation The process whereby one examines and evaluates a situation before arriving at a decision regarding the meaning and nature of a situation and before deciding which actions and behaviors are appropriate. If we define a situation as real, it is real in its consequences.

De-individuation A loss of evaluation apprehension and of self-consciousness.

Democratic leaders These social actors coordinate the activities of the group to achieve the group goals, and they solicit and welcome input from group members and use that information in formulating policies and decisions, which the group arrives at via consensus.

Demographic divide, the The clear demographic contrasts between less developed and more developed countries—in birth rates, death rates, rates of population growth, and population structure-- is known as the demographic divide.

Demographic transition theory A theory, first enunciated by Warren S. Thompson, that conceptualizes the long-term changes in fertility, mortality, and rate of population growth as experienced by the societies of the West as they industrialized or modernized—there is a transition from a situation of high birth rates and high death rates, with the associated low rates of population growth (First stage) to lowered death rates and high birth rates with the associated high rates of population growth (Second stage), to the low fertility and low mortality stage with its associated low rates of population growth (Third stage).

Demography The study of population structure; a sub-field of sociology.

Dependency theory A body of social-science theories predicated on the notion that scarce and widely-valued resources flow from a "periphery" of poor and underdeveloped states to a "core" of wealthy states, enriching the latter at the expense of the former.

Deviance Violation of a social norm whether folkway or more.

Dialectic A clash of contradictions.

Dialectical materialism The philosophical approach of Karl Marx and his followers to understanding social life. Karl Marx emphasizes material conditions, i.e., economic factors, as the basic causal forces that determine the history of humans.

Dialectics Clashes of contradictions.

Diaspora The mass movement of a people from one society to a variety of other places over a relatively short period of time.

Direct relationship As one variable increases in size or magnitude, so too does the other; or, as one variable decreases in size or magnitude, so too does the other. Also known as a positive relationship.

Divorce rate The number of divorces per 1,000 married women.

Domination The right-to-command-and-the-duty-to-obey relationships. The German word *Herrschaft* frequently is translated into English as "domination."

Doubling time The amount of time it takes a population of a given size to double in size

Dysfunction As used by structural functionalists, this term to refers to those instances wherein one or more "parts" of society operate in such a way as to disturb, hinder, or undermine the integration, adjustment, or stability of the system. For instance, incest is dysfunctional because it destroys the solidary order of the family. A synonym for negative function.

Economic means of production In Marxian conflict theory, the property necessary for economic production to occur..

Ego According to Freud, the part of the personality that is largely conscious and that mediates between the demands of the **id** and **superego**; Latin word for "I."

Egoistic suicide In Durkheim's typology, if the group is not sufficiently *integrated* (cohesive) to be able communally to mitigate the individual's sense of personal responsibility and guilt for perceived moral weakness and failure (sin), the individual's sense of personal responsibility and guilt may become overpowering, and the individual seeks refuge in suicide. Durkheim terms this type of suicide as egoistic suicide, which he sees as due to a strong value system, weak group integration, and to an overwhelming sense of personal responsibility.

Emigrants Persons, groups, or populations who are engaging in emigration.

Emigration The departure of individuals or groups from their home country or from a country to take up fairly permanent residence in another country.

Enclosure In England, in a series of acts of Parliament, the common land of villages was transferred to the private ownership of families, in a process known as enclosure.

Encomienda The encomienda was a legal system employed by the Spanish Crown during the Spanish colonization of the Americas, whereby the Spanish Crown owned the land but granted a conquistador, who became known as the encomendero, the labor of a specified number of Indians who lived on a vast tract of land.

Endogamy A norm of mate selection, wherein marriage should occur within (a) certain group or groups. Frequent bases of endogamy are class, race, ethnicity, religious affiliation, and noble status.

Epistemology The study or theory of knowledge, its origins, nature, limits an delimitations.

Ethic A principle of right or of good conduct.

Ethnic group A group that entertains a subjective belief in its common descent because of "similarities of physical type or of customs or both, or because of memories of colonization and migration" (Weber, 1968: 389).

Ethnocentrism A tendency to view the norms, values, and institutions of one's own culture or subculture as right and preferable to those of other cultures or subcultures.

Ethnography An empirically based analytical description of social life.

Exchange order The you-do-this-for-me-and-I-will-do-such-and-such-for-you behaviors and the social action related thereto.

Exogamy A norm of mate selection, wherein marriage should occur outside of (a) certain group or groups.

Experiment An investigation in which there is controlled manipulation of the independent variable by the investigator and precise observation and measurement both of the variables and of the results.

Experimental group In an experiment, the group that is exposed to the manipulation of the independent variable.

Experimental methods Social scientists refer to quasi-, pseudo-, semi-, and classical-experimental designs collectively as experimental methods.

Experimental realism The extent to which an experiment absorbs and involves the participants.

Extended family A family consisting of three or more generations.

External locus of control Perceiving oneself as lacking free will, agency, or choice and as buffeted about by forces over which one has no control.

Exuvial magic *Exuvia* is the plural form of a Latin noun that literally translates into English as the cast-off skins or coverings of various animals, including snakes. More generally, the term refers to any part of an animal—a cast-off scab, eyelash, strand of hair, piece of a hoof, or an entire organ—such as the heart, liver, brain, liver, etc. A belief in exuvial magic is found in many hunting and gathering societies. In exuvial magic, if a priest or shaman has even a part of a person (her or his *exuviae*), the shaman is believed to be able to control the entire person by performing certain rituals.

False consciousness In Marxian conflict theory, false consciousness is the lack of a subjective awareness of one's objective relationship to the economic means of production. If someone does not view things the way Marx does, that person is suffering from false consciousness. Thus, if a member of the proletariat were to vote for a candidate of a political party that supports the capitalist mode of economic production, Marx would say that such a person suffered from false consciousness.

Family A set of persons related by blood (consanguinity), marriage (affinal ties), the adult members of which are responsible for the rearing and socialization of any children they may have.

Family of orientation The family into which you are born.

Family of procreation The family that is formed when you bear or have children.

Fecundity The physiological ability or capacity or potential to bear children.

Female genital mutilation Also known as female genital cutting. Refers to all procedures involving the total or partial removal of the external female genitalia; includes such practices as female circumcision, clitoridectomy, and infibulation.

Fertility The actual rate of reproduction, as measured by the number of births, of a particular population.

Fictive kin The cultural practice of treating non-family members as if they were in fact members of the family.

Field research A way of knowing that examines people as they go about their everyday lives.

Fixation In Freudian theory, this is said to occur if a disproportionate amount of libidinal energy is invested in a particular bodily orifice, and personality is dominated by the traits associated with that level of development; as a result, psycho-social maturity is not attained.

Focal concerns Those concerns on which one expends one's attentional resources (Walter B. Miller).

Folk society An ideal type developed by Robert Redfield to characterize the type of society in which human beings have lived for most of their existence on this planet. Folk societies are small, isolated, non-literate, homogeneous, with a strong sense of solidarity; behavior is traditional, spontaneous, uncritical, and personal; kinship is the basic category of experience; the sacred prevails over the profane, and its members generally live at the subsistence-level of existence.

Folkway A Norm that has relatively mild rewards and punishments attached to it.

Foot binding The thwarting of the growth of a female's feet; a practice in China for a thousand years.

Formal leadership A social actor is the incumbent of a status to which authority is attached in a formal organization.

Formal organization A highly organized secondary group with explicitly stated goals, formally stated rules, and a system of specifically defined roles with clearly stated rights, duties, and obligations.

Fraternal polyandry A form of marriage in which a wife has two or more husbands simultaneously and those husbands are brothers.

Frequency The number of occurrences of a particular value or category of a variable in a data set.

Freuqency distribution A classification of data showing the raw or absolute number of occurrences of each subdivision, category, or value of a variable.

Function As used by structural functionalists, the "task" served by a part of society. Structural functionalists use this term to refer to those instances wherein one or more "parts" of society operate in such a way as to contribute to the survival or stability, or both, of society. For instance, one function of worshiping in common is to increase the solidarity of the community of worshipers.

Fundamental attribution error When we explain the actions of others, we commit this error when we overestimate the importance of personal dispositions (e.g., personality, temperament) and underestimate the importance of situational or social-structural factors.

G-8 Also known as the Group of 8, the G-8 is an annual forum at which the heads of state of the major industrial democracies, or their representatives, meet annually to deal with major economic and political issues facing their respective nations and the world as a whole.

GDP per capita at purchasing power parity (PPP) Gross domestic product (GDP) is the value of all final goods and services produced within a nation in a given year. A nation's GDP per capita is the value of all final goods and services produced in a nation in a given year divided by the population of the country as of July 1 of the same year. A nation's GDP at purchasing power parity (PPP) is the sum value of all goods and services produced in the country valued at prices prevailing in the United States in the year noted. Purchasing power parity takes into account the relative cost of living and the inflation rates of the countries, rather than just using the official exchange rates of their countries' currencies. A nation's GDP per capita (PPP) is the sum value of all goods and services produced in the country valued at prices prevailing in the United States in the year noted, divided by the population as of July 1 of the same year.

Gemeinschaft Ferdinand Toennies' term for a type of society in which social bonds are based on close personal ties of friendship and kinship. This pattern of relationships tends to be closely approximated in traditional rural-agricultural societies. In Gemeinschaft there is a predominance of intimate primary-group relationships and an emphasis on tradition, consensus, and kinship.

Gender roles Expectations of behavior (roles) attached to one's perceived sexual status as male or female.

General deterrence Deterrence is the belief that punishment can deter; in general deterrence, ego is punished so that law-abiding alters will not engage in crime.

Generalized other A term from the sociology of George Herbert Mead. The attitudes, expectations, and normative order of the larger social group.

Gesellschaft Ferdinand Toennies' term for modern urban industrial societies, in which secondary relations predominate, i.e., social relations tend to be formal, impersonal, contractual, specialized, and expedient.

Gesture In the symbolic interactionism of George Herbert Mead, any physical movement or vocalization that conveys meaning and that evokes a response in one or more persons.

Gini coefficient A commonly used measure of inequality, defined by Italian statistician and economist Corrado Gini; the range is from 0, where everyone receives the same income and there is no inequality, to 1, where one person receives all the income and everyone else gets none.

Globalization The, at least ideally, free flow of commodities and manufactures, capital, labor, knowledge, culture, and institutions around the world or "the globe.

Gong farmer A term that entered the English language in Tudor England (1485-1603) to describe someone who dug out and removed human excrement from privies (out houses) and cesspits. The word "gong" refers to the privies and cesspits as well as to their contents.

Great Leap Forward A policy adopted in China, 1958-1962, whose aim was for China to catch up with, and to surpass, Britain economically in less than fifteen years; the peasant masses were mobilized to transform (collectivize) both agriculture and industry simultaneously.

Gross domestic product (GDP) The value of all final goods and services produced within a nation in a given year.

Grounded theory Theory that is derived from empirical observation.

Group A collectivity of two or more persons that is characterized by sustained interaction, one or more shared goals, and a sense of solidarity.

Group polarization The tendency for group discussion to accentuate the members' pre-existing tendencies and attitudes.

Group-serving bias Also known as the ultimate attribution error; the tendency to perceive both the groups and social categories to which one belongs and which one uses as positive reference groups in favorable terms.

Hate crime Also known as bias crimes, hate crimes are offenses determined by law enforcement to have been driven by bias against race, religion, ethnicity, sexual orientation and, since 1994, disability.

Health transition Reduced mortality and hence in increased life expectancy. According to demographic transition theory, the health transition happens in Stage II of the demographic transition.

Honor killing Killing in order to restore the family honor; found as a familial obligation in some patriarchal societies and among migrants from such societies even today.

Hypothesis A tentative, testable statement about the relationship between two or more variables; the statement is intended to be tested empirically and either verified or rejected. A scientific hypothesis is derived from a theoretical system and from the results of prior research.

Id In Freudian theory, the part of the personality that is innate and that contains our sexual and aggressive drives; the part of our personality where the pleasure principle resides.

Ideal type A theoretical construct that contains all of the major elements of a recognized social phenomenon; an abstract model that describes the recurring characteristics of some phenomenon.

Identification One's sense of self (i.e., ego's answers to the question, "Who Am I?") that is rooted in group membership.

Ideology An idea or system of ideas that supports the status quo.

Immigrants Persons, groups, or populations who engage in immigration.

Immigration The entrance into a country of individuals, groups, or populations who have left their native country or another country to establish a new place of permanent residence.

Immiseration thesis According to Marxian economic theory, the nature of capitalist economic production logically requires both an ever greater reduction in real wages and a worsening of labor conditions for the proletariat.

Imperative order The various forms of power, authority, leadership, and coercion and the behaviors related thereto

Incest taboo This norm prohibits intimate sexual contact and marriage between people within prohibited degrees of kinship.

Income Wages and salaries earned from paid occupations plus unearned money from investmants.

Individualism A concept that gives priority and legitimacy to (a) placing one's own wants, needs, desires and goals over those of the collectivity; (b) defining the self in terms of personal attributes.

Induction In research methodology, a logical model of reasoning from specific instances to general principles.

Infant mortality rate The annual number of deaths of infants under 1 year of age per 1,000 live births.

Influence The ability to effect a voluntary change in a social actor's behavior, attitudes, or opinions via non-coercive means.

Informal leadership Social actors who are valued by a group because they conform to its norms and contribute to achieving the task or goal of the group.

Informal organization A system of personal reciprocal relationships that spontaneously develops as social actors interact within a formal organization.

Informational influence Conformity based on accepting as correct evidence provided about reality that is presented by other people.

In-group A group whose members have a sense of identification with and loyalty to the group and a sense of exclusivity toward non-members.

In-group bias The tendency for people who belong to an in-group to favor their own group

In-migrants Internal migrants are termed in-migrants when they arrive in the new area.

Institution A complex or bundle of norms. Also known as "social institution."

Interdependence Part of the sociological way of perceiving the world: the "parts" of society are viewed as interrelated, so that a change in one "part" has repercussions on at least one other part or parts and hence on society as a whole.

Intergenerational mobility This measure of social mobility compares the present position of individuals with those of their parents.

Internal locus of control Perceiving oneself as possessing free will, agency, or choice and as master of one's own life and fate; one believes that one's actions make a difference in one's life.

Internal migration A relatively permanent movement of a person, group, or a population within the borders of a country.

Internalization The process whereby norms, values, and statuses become internal to the individual, part of the individual's sense of self.

International Criminal Court (ICC) Located in The Hague, Netherlands, the ICC is a permanent tribunal for war crimes and crimes against humanity.

International migration A relatively permanent movement of a person, group, or a population across a national boundary to a new or host country.

Intragenerational mobility This measure of social mobility compares the position attained by a person at two different points in that person's life's work.

Inverse relationship As one variable increases in size or magnitude, the other variable decreases in size or magnitude. Also known as a negative relationship.

Kinship A relationship "based on family relatedness, as culturally defined. The culture determines which family relationships are considered significant, what the rights and obligations of specific types of related persons are, and what forms of organization exist among related persons." (Theodorson and Theodorson, 1969: 221)

Kuznets curve The hypothesis, named after Harvard economist Simon Kuznets, who first advanced the idea in 1955, that inequality increases during early industrialization, then decreases during later industrialization, eventually stabilizing at low levels.

Laissez-faire leaders These leaders are only minimally involved in the group's decision-making processes, and they intervene in these processes only when asked to do so.

Latent function In structural functionalism, Robert K. Merton's term for the unintended outcome or result of a social institution, behavior, event, and so forth.

lat-relationship A type of intimate relationship, quite popular in the Netherlands, where the couple lives apart together. "Lat" is an acronym for living apart together. In a lat-relationship, single people try to maintain a relationship without moving in with each other.

Leadership Coordinating group activities toward group goals.

Levirate The social practice whereby a widow is required to marry the brother of her deceased husband. The brother of the deceased husband takes his brother's widow as his own wife, takes care of her dependent children who become part of his family line and fathers children by his new wife if she is of child-bearing age, and these children become part of his family line.

Lex salica A system of compensation for the victims of crime or for the compensation of the family members of victims of crime during the early feudal period in some early German and Anglo Saxon societies; can be found in some societies today.

Libido In Freudian theory, the force of life. Libido's aim is the satisfaction of instinctual drives toward survival, pleasure, and the avoidance of pain.

Lineage A corporate kin group containing the descendants of a common ancestor who is considered to be the founder of the line or lineage.

Looking-glass self A term coined by Charles Horton Cooley to refer to the process whereby we develop a sense of self by internalizing our perceptions of the responses of others to us.

Lowest-low fertility A total fertility rate at or below 1.3 children per couple.

Loyalty Attraction to groups as groups.

Macro With regard to level of sociological analysis, large scale.

Manifest function In structural functionalism, Robert K. Merton's term for the anticipated or intended consequences or outcomes or results of a social institution, behavior, event, and so forth.

Marriage A socially and legally recognized relationship between two people, the unique trait of which is social recognition and approval of a couple's engaging in sexual intercourse, bearing, and rearing of offspring. When people marry, they become kin to one another.

Marriage rate The number of marriages per 1,000 unmarried females aged fifteen and older.

Material culture All tangibles that are transmitted from one generation to another.

Matrilineal descent (also known as uxorial descent or matrilineality) The cultural practice of tracing the lineage and one's relatives solely through the female line.

Matrilocal residence (also known as matrilocality) A rule of residence that states that upon marriage the ideal place for the newly married couple to live is with the family of the bride (usually with the family of wife's mother).

Measure of central tendency Central tendency refers to the grouping of data around the center or middle of a distribution or array of data and, hence, to what is "typical" or "average" in a data array. There are several measures of the average.

Measurement is a procedure for determining the value of a variable in a specific case.

Mechanical solidarity Emile Durkheim's term for a society held together by similarities, by the things the members have in common.

Menarche A female's first menstruation or menstrual period.

Meso With regard to level of sociological analysis, in between macro and micro.

Micro With regard to level of sociological analysis, small scale.

Migration A relatively permanent movement of a person, group, or a population across a political boundary to a new residential area or community.

Monogamy A form of marriage wherein each married partner has one spouse at any given time.

Moral entrepreneur A social actor who generates and enforces a definition of morality (Howard S. Becker). Individuals in the community who set the moral standards of proper behavior.

Morality A doctrine or system of right human conduct.

Morbidity Illness.

More Plural form of "mos." A norm that has strong rewards and punishments attached to it.

Mundane realism The extent to which an experiment is similar to everyday situations.

Natural will Spontaneous attraction, which is Ferdinand Toennies' term for a characteristic of human relationships in Gemeinschaft. Human relationships in Gemeinschaft are founded on spontaneous attraction.

Negative relationship As one variable increases in size or magnitude, the other variable decreases in size or magnitude; as one variable decreases in size or magnitude, the other variable decreases in size or magnitude. Also known as an inverse relationship.

Negative sanction A concept derived from behaviorist psychology, a stimulus that has the effect of reducing or eliminating the frequency or magnitude of a behavior to which it is applied. Also known as a punishment.

Neolocal residence (also known as neolocality) A rule of residence that states that upon marriage the ideal place to live is in an abode separate from that of the groom's family and separate from that of the bride's family.

Neonatal mortality Infant death that occurs within the first 27 days since birth.

Neonatal mortality rate The number of deaths under 28 days of age per 1,000 live births

Net emigration The amount by which the number of emigrants exceeds the number of immigrants.

Net-mortality country Demographic term for a country in which the death rate per 1,000 population is higher than the birth rate per 1,000 population.

Nonmaterial culture Sometimes called symbolic culture; all intangibles that are transmitted from one generation to another.

Nonprimordial group All groups that are not primordial.

Non-probability sample A sample in which it is not possible to determine the probability or chance that each case has of being included in the sample.

Norm A rule of behavior that is backed by positive and negative sanctions.

Normative influence Conformity based on a social actor's desire to be socially accepted by others.

Normative order The rules of behavior that are backed by rewards and punishments and the social action related thereto.

Nuclear family The simplest type of nuclear family consists of husband, wife (incipient nuclear family) and their dependent children (simple nuclear family).

Occupational Safety and Health Act The primary federal law, enacted in 1970, which governs occupational health and safety in both the private sector and federal government in the United States.

Old-age dependency ratio The population aged 65 and older as a percentage of the population aged 15 to 64

Oligarchy Rule of the many by the few.

Operationalization A process or procedure by which a variable is quantified. A set of precise, explicit, detailed instructions for how a researcher measures concepts and variables. This allows researchers to measure any changes that occur in the variable.

Organic solidarity Emile Durkheim's term for the type of solidarity that holds modern society together, in which unity is based on the interdependence of a very large number of specialized social roles.

Out-group All non-members of an in-group.

Out-migrants Internal migrants are termed out-migrants when they leave a specific area or region of a country to set up relatively permanent residence in a different area or region of that country.

Paradigm In sociology, a fundamental framework for understanding social life

Pariah group A group or collectivity that is highly stigmatized (Max Weber).

Participant observation A researcher is directly involved with the research subjects and reports on the findings.

Patriarchy Male supraordination.

Patrilineal descent (also known as *agnatic descent* or *patrilineality*) The cultural practice of tracing relatives and lineage solely through the male line.

Patrilocal residence (also known as patrilocality) A rule of residence that states that upon marriage the ideal place for the newly married couple to live is with the family of the groom (usually with the family of the husband's father).

Patrimonial rule In Weberian theory, arbitrary, capricious, erratic, idiosyncratic decisions of rulers.

Peasant An agricultural laborer tied to and dominated by an urban elite.

Percentile In statistics, one of one hundred points dividing a frequency distribution into one hundred equal parts.

Periphery countries According to world-systems theory, these countries provide the core with inexpensive labor, a large quantity of raw material, and a vast market for industrial and high-technology products; these countries are exploited by the core and semi-periphery but are too weak to exploit other counties of the global economy.

Pink-collar workers These laborers work in semi-skilled occupations that have a high concentration of females and low pay, such as day-care workers, wait-persons, cashiers, and check-out clerks.

Polyandry A form of marriage wherein a wife may have two or more husbands simultaneously.

Polygamy A form of marriage wherein a person has more than one spouse simultaneously.

Polygyny A form of marriage wherein a husband may have more than one wife simultaneously.

Population The total number of cases with a given characteristic or characteristics, or all members of a given class or set.

Population density The number of people per unit of an area—for instance, the number of people per square mile.

Population pyramid A technique of graphically portraying in the form of a pyramid the age and sex composition of a given population.

Positive checks Malthus used this term to refer to describe natural events—like famine, pestilence, and natural disasters—that serve to control, or lower, population growth by increasing the death rate.

Positive relationship As one variable increases in size or magnitude, so too does the other; or, as one variable decreases in size or magnitude, so too does the other. Also known as a direct relationship.

Positive sanction A concept derived from behaviorist psychology, a stimulus that has the effect of increasing the frequency or magnitude of a behavior to which it is applied. Also known as a reward.

Positivism The philosophical position that valid knowledge has as its source direct observations perceived by the senses (i.e., sight, smell, hearing, touch, taste).

Post-industrial society Societies in which the majority of the labor force is engaged in economic activity in the service sector of the economy.

Postneonatal mortality Death of an infant between 28 and 364 days of life.

Postneonatal mortality rate The number of deaths from age 28 days to under 1 year per 1,000 live births

Potlatch A custom in which a ceremonial feast is held at which people gain prestige by giving away or destroying wealth or property.

Power As defined by German sociologist Max Weber, the ability to get one's way in the face of opposition.

Pragmatism A philosophic view stressing that concepts and actions should be evaluated and analyzed in terms of their practical consequences.

Pre-industrial city Gideon Sjoberg's term for all cities existing within a non-industrial social order.

Preventive checks Malthus used this term to refer to or to describe those factors—like increasing the age at first marriage—that serve to control, or lower, population growth by reducing the fertility rate.

Primary group An intimate social group with common values or basic standards of behavior, and frequent, direct personal contact among its members.

Primary socialization Socialization that occurs within the first few years of our lives.

Primogeniture An inheritance system wherein the eldest child (usually the eldest son) inherits the entire estate upon the death of the father, with none of the inheritance going to the other children.

Primordial group A group that comes first in our experience. Examples include family, community, racial group, ethnicity, religious group, and so forth.

Probability sample A sample drawn in accordance with probability theory.

Progressive tax Any tax in which the rate increases as the amount subject to taxation increases.

Proletariat In Marxian conflict theory, those who sell their labor to those who own the economic means of production.

Prolocutor A spokesperson for a group or for an alleged common interest. Prolocutorship is a form of association, a form of solidarity.

Psycho-sexual development In Freudian theory, this concept indicates that the development of mind, personality, and sexuality are inextricably intertwined; one cannot understand the development of the mind and personality without understanding the simultaneous development of sexuality and vice versa.

Purdah The seclusion of women and girls from public observation. It is accomplished by females wearing concealing clothing from head to toe and by the use of high-walled enclosures, curtains, and screens within the home.

Qualitative analysis Please see **qualitative methodology**

Qualitative methodology Analysis or methodology that is not based on precise measurement and quantitative claims or statements.

Quantitative data Data in numerical form.

Quintile In statistics, one of four points dividing a frequency distribution into five equal parts

Random assignment In an experiment, research subjects are assigned randomly to one of two experimental conditions: to the experimental group, wherein they are exposed to the independent variable, or to the control group, where they are not exposed to the independent variable. Each research subject has the same chance of being assigned to one condition as to the other. Also known as randomization.

Random sample A type of probability sample. The simplest type of probability sample. A sample in which every case in the population has an equal probability of being included in the sample. Sometimes called simple random sample.

Rationalism The philosophical position that reason and logical thinking are the best basis of valid knowledge.

Rationalization In Weberian theory, the substitution of formal written rules and procedures for earlier spontaneous, arbitrary, capricious approaches. Weber viewed rationalization as a hallmark of the modern age.

Rational-legal authority The right to command and the duty to obey that is based on an organizational structure characterized by clearly defined rules and procedures, a hierarchy of authority, and impersonality.

Raw score In a cell in a statistical table, a score that reveals how much of the characteristic of interest is possessed by an individual or by an event, object, etc; any datum that provides an absolute, not relative, assessment of one's position on a quantitative variable. Also known as raw datum or as raw data.

Real income Income after controlling for inflation; it provides a fixed standard that we may use to make comparisons from year to year.

Redistributionist Someone who wants to take money from those who earn it and give it, or transfer it, to those who are less well off, financially speaking.

Relationship Please see **correlation**.

Relative deprivation Deprivation or disadvantage measured not by objective standards but by comparison with the relatively superior advantage of some other standard, such as our former selves, whom one desires to emulate. The term was used originally by Samuael A. Stauffer in *The American Soldier* (1950) (Theodorson and Theodorson, 1969).

Reliability refers to the extent to which the same or similar results are obtained when a researcher uses the same measurement instrument on the same or a similar sample or population of subjects

Replacement-level fertility The total fertility rate needed for a population to replace itself without either increasing or declining in size; in highly industrialized, high technology societies, this is a total fertility rate of 2.1 children.

Resocialization Socialization that represents a radical change in the person, that tears down one's old world view, beliefs, values, behaviors, and conceptions of self and thereby of others, and replaces them with new ones.

Resource curse The difficulties faced by resource-rich countries, including dependence on one or a few commodities, whose prices fluctuate; this dependence distorts their economies, because other industries are often neglected and wither.

Responsibility to protect (R2P)An emerging norm in international relations whereby governments worldwide must act to protect civilians from genocide or crimes against humanity perpetrated or allowed by their own governments.

Restorative justice In criminology, a movement that relies on nonpunitive strategies for crime control.

Ritual A "culturally standardized set of actions with symbolic significance performed on occasions" and by persons "prescribed by tradition" (Theodorson and Theodorson, 1969:351). Ritual is a basic part of social structure.

Role Expectations of behavior. The sociological view is that roles attach to statuses, i.e., to positions in a group.

Role playing Also known as role taking. Please see role taking, above.

Role taking Also known as "role playing." Taking the point of view, attitudes, or behaviors of another person by imaginatively constructing oneself *as* the other person, in order to be able to anticipate that *person's* real or likely behavior.

Routinization of charisma Max Weber's term for the transformation of charismatic authority into traditional or rational-legal authority or into a combination of rational-legal and traditional authority.

Row In a statistical table, the horizontal listing of data in a series of categories, of which have a common classification.

Row caption In a statistical table, a title that describes the common classification of the data located in the rows of the statistical table.

Row heading Please see **row caption**.

Row marginals In a contingency table, the raw and percent frequency distributions found along the row edges or margins of the table.

Rules of descent Normative structures that inform people regarding which of their biological relatives are to be considered as sociological relatives, what those relationships are, and what the reciprocal rights, duties, and obligations are of each of the relationships so specified.

Rules of residence Normative structures that inform people regarding where the ideal place to live is after they get married.

Sample Part of a population.

Science A way of knowing based on direct systematic observation derived from the senses, it attempts to develop general principles about a delimited range of phenomena and to state them in such a way that they can be tested by any competent person.

Scientific method Building a body of scientific knowledge through empirical observation, generalization, and verification. It consists of the following steps: (1) problem definition; (2) statement of the research problem in terms of a particular theoretical framework, and relating the research problem to findings of previous research;(3) statement of the research problem as an hypothesis or as hypotheses; (4) selecting an appropriate methodology or methodologies; (5) data collection; (6) data analysis; (7) conclusion regarding the research hypothesis, and relating the conclusion(s) to the original body of theory with which the study began.

Secondary group A non-primary group that involves only a segment of its members' lives. Relationships between members tend to be as means to an end outside of the relationship.

Secondary socialization Socialization that occurs after the first few years of our lives.

Self-help From the point of view of consensus theory, self-help is another term for vigilantism, "taking the law into your own hands," and other forms of violent retaliation by which people secure justice in the absence of state intervention.

Semi-periphery countries According to world-systems theory, semi-periphery countries are exploited by core countries; countries of the semi-periphery also exploit the countries of the periphery.

Sex ratio The number of males per 100 females in a population

Skewed sex ratio A sex ratio that departs significantly from 100

Social category A collectivity of re persons that does not form a group but that has at least one characteristic in common—e.g., eye color, occupation, height, etc.

Social conflict Conscious struggle between or among groups or collectivities over resources.

Social fact As defined by Emile Durkheim, a social phenomenon that is distinct from individual, biological, and psychological phenomena. Durkheim took the position that social facts should be explained only by other social facts.

Social institution See "institution," above.

Social mobility The upward, downward, or lateral movement of individuals, groups, or collectivities in a system of stratification.

Social structure Also known as social organization and social order, this concept refers to stable and recurring patterns of social relations.

Socialization The process whereby we learn roles and norms, develop a capacity to conform to them, and develop a sense of self.

Society A group of people with a common culture who share a sense of solidarity, occupy a particular territorial area, and who regard themselves as different than non-members.

Sociology The scientific study of society

Soft power The ability to affect others through the co-optive means of framing the agenda, persuading, and eliciting positive attraction; concept coined and defined by Joseph S. Nye, Jr., former Dean of the Kennedy School of Government at Harvard University (Nye, 2011: 21).

Solidary order The various types of solidarity and the social action related thereto.

Sororal polygyny A form of polygamy in which a man is married to two or more women at the same time and those wives are sisters.

Sovereignty. A state's right, at least in principle, to do whatever it wants within its own territory. According to the principle of sovereignty, states are separate, autonomous, and answer to no higher authority. The sovereignty principle means that states are not to interfere in the internal affairs of other states. (Goldstein and Pevehouse, 2010: 41).

Specific deterrence Deterrence is the belief that punishment can deter; in specific deterrence, ego is punished so that ego will not engage in crime again; also known as *special deterrence.*

State A territorial entity controlled by a government and inhabited by a population (Goldstein and Pevehouse, 2010: 10).

Status This concept has various meanings in sociology: (1) position in a group; (2) the esteem, honor, prestige, and deference from others that is attached to a position.

Stigma A stain or mark of disgrace, imposed by one social actor, whether individual or collectivity, on another.

Stratification The persistent and inheritable unequal access to scarce yet widely valued goods and services. Also known as social stratification, structured social inequality, and stratified inequality. Stratification is a characteristic of all known human societies, past and present.

Strong ties Relationships characterized by intimacy, emotional intensity, and sharing.

Structural functionalism Also known as social order theory, consensus theory, functionalism, structuralism. A sociological paradigm that focuses on the interrelations between the "parts" of society and the way that they assist the society as a whole to persist across time.

Structural view In sociology, perceiving social structures as consisting of "parts" and viewing those parts as interrelated, such that a change in one part effects the one or more other parts and hence the structure as a whole.

Subculture A culture within a culture; the more or less different folkways, mores, material and nonmaterial cultural elements developed by a group or collectivity within a society**.**

Sublimation In Freudian theory, turning our innate sexual and aggressive drives to ends no longer sexual and no longer aggressive.

Substructure In Marxian conflict theory, the economic foundation of society.

Superego According to Freud, the part of the personality that contains notions of right and wrong that we have internalized from our significant others who live within a particular historical period and a specific culture; our conscience.

Superstructure In Marxian conflict theory, all parts of society other than the economy.

Supportive social systems Parts of social structure--including the family, religion, work, school, and friendship systems—that provide individuals with social support.

Survey research A quantitative field-research method wherein a researcher systematically (1) gathers data about individuals or collectivities through the use of an interview or questionnaire administered to a population or a sample, (2) analyzes the resulting data through statistical analyses, and (3) interprets the results.

Symbol Something that stands for or represents something else.

Symbolic culture See nonmaterial culture, above.

Symbolic interactionism A sociological paradigm focusing on the process of interaction between human beings conducted at the symbolic level. This sociological way of knowing tends to focus in how human beings construct and attribute meanings to objects, events, and happenings in social life.

Synthesis As a stage in the dialectical process, the emergence of something new.

Techniques of neutralization Procedures that people use to place their conscience in abeyance so that they may beak norms; afterwards, people bring their conscience back "online" and resume living in the conventional moral order (Gresham Sykes and David Matza).

Technology A segment of culture that includes tools and knowledge, and that embraces all forms of productive technique used by humans and by some non-human primates to manipulate the physical environment in order to attain a desired practical result.

Theory A set of interrelated principles and definitions that conceptually organizes selected aspects of the empirical world in a systematic fashion.

Thesis As a stage in the dialectical process, the way things are.

Thomas theorem American sociologist and symbolic interactionist W. I. Thomas observed that if we define something as real, it is real in its consequences.

Total fertility rate The number of births per woman during her reproductive years, often measured as the number of births per female aged 15-45 years of age.

Total institution A place of confinement or partial confinement where persons of a specified type live, have limited contact with the rest of society, and follow a formalized life routine under the direction and control of a bureaucratic staff.

Total percents In a contingency table, the percentages in the marginals sometimes are called total percents because they are derived by dividing each frequency by the total sample size and multiplying the result by 100.

Totalitarianism A highly centralized political system that extensively regulates people's lives.

Traditional authority Power that is legitimated on the basis of custom.

Unobtrusive methods Research methods that do not intrude on the phenomena being studied.

Validity refers to the correspondence between what a measuring instrument is supposed to measure and what it actually measures. To the extent that a measuring instrument measures what it is supposed to measure, to that extent it has validity.

Value A nonmaterial cultural element; an abstract, generalized conception of what is desirable, to which members of a group feel a strong, positively-toned commitment and which serves as a standard for selecting and evaluating concrete means, goals, rules, and actions (Theodorson and Theodorson, 1969: 455-456).

Value inconsistency The conflict between two or more simultaneously held values.

Variable A characteristic that is common to a number of individuals, objects, groups, or events, and that has either different degrees of magnitude or different categories (for example, eye color: blue, brown, green, hazel, "other") so that individual cases differ in the extent to which they possess the characteristic (expressed in numerical values) or in the category of the characteristic into which they fall.

Variable, dependent A variable that changes in response to changes in another variable (the independent variable). This is the effect or Y variable.

Variable, independent A variable that is the cause of change in another variable. This is the independent or X variable.

Verstehen Max Weber's term for subjective understanding. For Weber, if we want to understand social life, we need to know how the social actors themselves perceive it. For Weber, subjective understanding is a legitimate part of understanding both social life and social issues.

Vertical mobility Movement up or down a hierarchy of positions in a system of social stratification. Vertical mobility is also known as vertical social mobility, upward mobility, or upward social mobility. Sociologists use these terms interchangeably and synonymously.

Voluntary association (1) Reaching beyond primordial ties to establish common cause with others, which is a non-primordial form of solidarity; (2) A formally organized, specialized, secondary group, in which membership is a matter of freely exercised choice and from which members are free to resign.

Vulcanization A process of making rubber stronger, more elastic, and more durable over time.

War crimes Violations of the law governing the conduct of warfare, such as unnecessarily targeting civilians or mistreating prisoners of war.

Weak ties Relationships characterized by low intensity and low intimacy.

Wealth The total value of money and other assets, minus outstanding debts.

Wergeld Please see lex salica, above

White-collar Jobs or occupations of higher prestige that involve mainly mental activity.

White-collar crime Activities of moral or administrative disrepute committed by respectable individuals of high social status during the course of their professions (Edwin Sutherland).

White-collar workers These workers engage in largely non-manual labor that is primarily mental in character; this term sometimes is used to refer to all workers whose labor is largely non-manual.

World-system theory A macro-level approach to understanding stratification, social change, and history that stresses that the world-system (and not nation states) should be the primary unit of social analysis.

Zero population growth (ZPG) A term coined in 1967 by American sociologist and demographer Kingsley Davis to refer to a condition of demographic balance where the number of people in a specified population neither grows nor declines; also known as replacement-level fertility.

INDEX

NOTE: Page references in italics refer to figures and tables.

A

B

C

F

G

H

I

J

K

L

Q

R

S

T

Y

Z